Horace Kephart

WRITINGS

APPALACHIAN ECHOES • *Richard Starnes*, SERIES EDITOR

Horace Kephart

WRITINGS

Edited by George Frizzell

and Mae Miller Claxton

The University of Tennessee Press • Knoxville

All the illustrations are from Western Carolina University Hunter Library Special Collections. When captions appear in quotation marks, they are Horace Kephart's words.

The Appalachian Echoes series is dedicated to reviving and contextualizing classic books about Appalachia for a new generation of readers. By making available a wide spectrum of works — from fiction to nonfiction, from folklife and letters to history, sociology, politics, religion, and biography — the series seeks to reveal the diversity that has always characterized Appalachian writing, a diversity that promises to confront and challenge long-held stereotypes about the region.

FIRST EDITION.

Library of Congress Cataloging-in-Publication Data

Names: Kephart, Horace, 1862–1931, author. | Frizzell, George, editor. | Claxton, Mae Miller, editor.

Title: Horace Kephart : writings / edited by George Frizzell and Mae Miller Claxton.

Description: First edition. | Knoxville : The University of Tennessee Press, [2020]

Series: Appalachian echoes | Includes bibliographical references and index.

Summary: "Horace Kephart's (1862–1931) reputation as a travel writer and often-invoked observer of Appalachian culture rests almost entirely on two major works still in print today: *Our Southern Highlanders* (1913) and *Camping and Woodcraft* (1916). All but forgotten, however, is Horace Kephart the prolific essayist who frequently appeared in popular magazines like *Harper's Weekly*, *Outing*, and *Field and Stream* many decades ago. In addition to collecting the best of these diverse and entertaining pieces, editors Frizzell and Claxton have here drawn on Kephart's voluminous journals and correspondence, which are archived at Western Carolina University. The book is organized into several thematic subsections, including biographical writings, family and friends, outdoor recreation, guns, southern Appalachian culture and dialect, fiction, writings on the Cherokee, and scouting"—Provided by publisher.

Identifiers: LCCN 2020006813 (print) | LCCN 2020006814 (ebook) ISBN 9781621905417 (paperback ; alk. paper) | ISBN 9781621906278 (PDF)

Classification: LCC AC8 .K464 2020 (print) | LCC AC8 (ebook) | DDC 081—dc23

LC record available at https://lccn.loc.gov/2020006813

LC ebook record available at https://lccn.loc.gov/2020006814

SONNET X

[*To one who has been long in city pent*]

To one who has been long in city pent,
'Tis very sweet to look into the fair
And open face of heaven,—to breathe a prayer
Full in the smile of the blue firmament.
Who is more happy, when, with hearts content,
Fatigued he sinks into some pleasant lair
Of wavy grass, and reads a debonair
And gentle tale of love and languishment?
Returning home at evening, with an ear
Catching the notes of Philomel,—an eye
Watching the sailing cloudlet's bright career,
He mourns that day so soon has glided by:
E'en like the passage of an angel's tear
That falls through the clear ether silently.

John Keats

CONTENTS

TWO *Family and Friends* 87

THREE *Camping and Woodcraft* 135

ACKNOWLEDGMENTS

As with any project of this size and complexity, there are many family members, friends, and colleagues who provided encouragement, advice, and guidance.

We want to thank the contributors to this volume. To Jason Brady of Hunter Library's Special Collections, we owe a special thanks for his intimate knowledge of the extensive Kephart collections that he has organized, described, and then provided reference assistance to over the years. To Libby Kephart Hargrave we are indebted for her devotion in making new materials available to researchers—as did Barbara Crane and other Kephart family members—and for her personal insights. George Ellison and Janet McCue, fellow companions on the path to documenting Kephart's life and works, shared details that enlivened their award-winning *Back of Beyond: A Horace Kephart Biography*. Andrew Denson and Jim Casada brought their expertise to topics of vital importance in understanding Kephart's long and varied career. We are also indebted to Richard Starnes, the series editor, for his role in making the publication possible.

The final details and nuances of the manuscript would not have been possible without the assistance of Ken Wise and George Brosi, both of whom used their own expertise to make invaluable suggestions on improvements, corrections, and points of clarity. Many students also helped in various stages of the book, notably Stephanie Wooten, Andrew Benton, Michael Redman, Amelia Holmes, and Lisa Terrene.

We would also like to thank the staff and librarians of WCU's Hunter Library for those service-oriented efforts that are essential for research, particularly Hiddy Morgan, Becky Kornegay, Chase Spencer, and Ann Hallyburton. Also, thanks to our colleagues of WCU's Mountain Heritage Center museum, including Suzanne McDowell, Pam Meister, and Peter Koch. Librarians in Special Collections at Hunter Library were indispensable to the project, notably Jenny McPherson, Kellen Carpenter, and Liz Skene, who patiently and quickly responded to our frequent calls for assistance. Maggie Ashley, Administrative Support Associate in the English Department, kindly and most generously helped proofread the index for us.

Also, the editors are grateful to the institutions that allowed us to use materials from their holdings, including Hunter Library Special Collections, Western Carolina University; Brown University Library; Cornell University Library; the North Carolina room of Pack Memorial Library, Asheville, NC; and the University of Tennessee—Knoxville special collections.

The editors would also like to thank our families for their support, especially Evelyn Parris Frizzell Buchanan and Roger and Nell Parris; and to David Claxton for his patient and loving support.

GENERAL INTRODUCTION

MAE MILLER CLAXTON AND GEORGE FRIZZELL

When Horace Kephart stepped off the train in the small western North Carolina town of Dillsboro in the summer of 1904, no one suspected, he least of all, that he would become the most significant writer about the Smoky Mountains for the first few decades of the twentieth century, shaping national perceptions about the region through his prolific writing in many genres. Arriving with few financial resources or possessions, he brought with him a keen personal interest to discover and document his new surroundings. Only a year prior he had been director of the prestigious Mercantile Library in St. Louis, Missouri, and a family man with a wife and six children. The day he arrived in Dillsboro, Horace Kephart was an individual struggling to recover from emotional and physical health problems and estranged from most family and many friends.

The Kephart who disembarked that day had already achieved a national reputation over the previous fifteen years for his work in librarianship, his practical and historical research on firearms and ballistics, and his publications on camping and woodcraft. However, it was over the next quarter of a century that he gained national recognition for his contributions on Southern Appalachia, his expertise in outdoorsmanship, and his advocacy for a national park in the Great Smoky Mountains.

For readers interested in Appalachian culture and history, Horace Kephart has attained a kind of mythical status as the outsider who came to western North Carolina to chronicle a world "back of beyond" and never left.[1] In fact, Kephart began writing outdoor literature long before he left his job at the Mercantile Library. His writing career flourished until his death in a car accident in 1931. Most readers are familiar with his best-known works: *Our Southern Highlanders*, Kephart's chronicle of southern Appalachia and its people, and *Camping and Woodcraft*, a classic of outdoor literature. Few, however, have likely read beyond these two texts, thus missing the diversity and richness of Kephart's entire body of work. Kephart's letters show that he corresponded with people across the globe on a variety of topics. His articles and columns in popular national magazines such as *Outing* and *Field and Stream* appealed to the growing market of "outdoor adventure" readers. Kephart also wrote fiction, including short stories, a novella, and a full-length novel. And true to his training as a librarian, Kephart compiled pages and pages of notes, carefully indexed, into twenty-seven hardbound journals. In some sections of these journals, Kephart sketched different kinds of tents. In others, he recorded Appalachian dialect and religious practices. These journal pages tell us a great deal about how intentionally Kephart developed his craft as a writer. The writings also tell their own larger story of the development of Kephart's unique narrative style, which combined storytelling and personal anecdotes with observations and practical advice. *Horace Kephart: Writings* includes letters, articles, unpublished manuscripts, photographs, and many other texts demonstrating Kephart's proficiency as an outdoor writer, an advocate for the Great Smoky Mountains National Park, and a chronicler of a people and a place.

Horace Kephart: Writings sets Kephart into the context of time and place, from his professional position as a librarian in St. Louis to his habitation of a rustic cabin on the Little Fork of Sugar Fork of Hazel Creek in the Great Smokies to his residency in the small town of Bryson City, North Carolina. Far from being a hermit, Kephart traveled widely. He also documented the rapidly changing world he saw around him. When Kephart stepped off the train in Dillsboro in 1904, he encountered a region impacted by many outside forces. Industrial logging, changes in transportation, and new technologies were beginning to connect Appalachia to the rest of the world. Kephart documented the before and after, writing about an Appalachian culture that he felt was in danger of being engulfed by the rising tide of modernity. At the same time, he also advocated for a major change to the region by campaigning for the establishment of a national park in the Great Smoky Mountains, which he envisioned would protect part of the wilderness while offering sustainable economic opportunities in the form of tourism. This aspect of his legacy endures as the Great Smoky Mountains National Park remains the nation's most visited national park.

Kephart further connected this region to larger national and even international cultural trends that resulted in the growth of a new industry, outdoor adventure, leading to magazines and merchandise, national parks and extended walking trails. Far from being isolated and anachronistic, Appalachia, Kephart believed, represented something that all of humanity sorely needed, a natural landscape that could provide a respite from the evils of industrialism and city life. He writes in *Forest and Stream* in June 1905, less than a year after his arrival in western North Carolina, "To many a city man there comes a time, now and then, when the great town wearies him. He hates its sights and smells and clangor. Every duty is a task, and every caller is a bore. There come to him visions of green fields and far-rolling hills, of tall forests and cool, swift-flowing streams."[2] As a remedy for this malady, Kephart advocates camping "in the wild woods, far away from everything that suggests the hurry and strife of civilized life."[3] Romantic and idealistic ideas, perhaps, but Kephart and his writings continue to resonate with readers today.

Horace Kephart: Writings also takes advantage of renewed interest in Kephart's life and his work. Although *Our Southern Highlanders* and *Camping and Woodcraft* have continued to receive attention since their original publications, new audiences have emerged for this important Appalachian writer. Ken Burns's 2009 PBS series *The National Parks: America's Best Idea* brought new attention to Kephart's role in the formation of the Great Smoky Mountains National Park. Also in 2009, the Great Smoky Mountains Association published *Smoky Mountain Magic*, Kephart's novel, from a previously unpublished manuscript. Kephart scholars George Ellison and Janet McCue included an extensive introduction in the new edition of *Camping and Woodcraft* (2011) that incorporates new biographical material from manuscripts donated by the Kephart family. GSMA also recently published a third edition of *Our Southern Highlanders* with a new introduction by George Ellison. In 2019, Ellison and McCue's *Back of Beyond: A Horace Kephart Biography* was published. The Kephart family continues to donate additional material to Special Collections of Hunter Library at Western Carolina University. This material has led to a more thorough understanding of Kephart's family and relationships.

Horace Kephart: Writings accomplishes two major goals. It showcases the diversity and variety of Kephart's writings, published and unpublished, from 1887 until 1931. For example, Special Collections at Hunter Library has fifteen to twenty publications from Kephart's time at the St. Louis Mercantile Library. We include representative works that demonstrate Kephart moving away from his library career toward an interest in writing about the outdoors. *Horace Kephart: Writings* contains a wealth of material that has not yet been reprinted that will be an important addition to the existing Kephart material. These works display Kephart as a multifaceted author with a national and international audience. In addition to Kephart's writings, introductions for each section supply context, considering Kephart as spokesman for the outdoor adventure movement of the early twentieth century, as chronicler of Appalachian culture and history, and as environmentalist and advocate for the Great Smoky Mountains National Park. In addition to providing readers with a comprehensive representation of Kephart's entire corpus, the book also acknowledges Kephart's role as an author whose works continue to inform public perceptions of "Appalachia," thus providing a larger perspective on a diverse and complex region.

We have chosen to group items thematically so that readers can easily access subjects in which they are interested. In addition, this thematic grouping highlights the many different kinds of writing that Kephart produced. Each section contains a variety of texts. The first chapter, "Biography," with an introduction written by George Ellison and Janet McCue, contains material spanning the period of time from 1890 to 1959 including personal letters, editorials, library articles, and newspaper articles about Kephart's breakdown in St. Louis. Informed by extensive archival work and focusing more on Kephart's personal life, this chapter provides insight into his early career as a librarian, the breakdown that led to his move to North Carolina, and later writings that demonstrate Kephart's opinions about issues such as the death penalty. This section ends with a letter to Kephart's wife from his executor written eight years after his death along with "Horace Kephart, a Personal Glimpse," written by Clarence Miller, a rare first-person account by a colleague and friend who knew Kephart in his role as director of the St. Louis Mercantile Library. All of these works greatly expand our understanding of the career and life of Horace Kephart.

The second chapter, entitled "Family and Friends," includes personal letters and photographs along with an introduction by Libby Kephart Hargrave, Horace Kephart's great-granddaughter, and George Frizzell. Informed by family letters and documents now archived in Special Collections, Hargrave explains that Kephart's relationship with family was more complex than was previously assumed, acknowledges his friendships, and notes the family's continued interest in his legacy. Letters to daughter-in-law Pauline Kephart and his son Leonard provide insight into relationships with Kephart's grown children. One particularly poignant letter, written by daughter Lucy Kephart Fernow, provides some insight into the feelings of abandonment experienced by Kephart's wife and children. In addition to the family letters included, Hargrave documents a few of Kephart's many friendships, including his collaboration with photographer George Masa. Part two, contributed by George Frizzell, includes more information about Kephart's surprisingly large circle of friends. He separates his discussion into several time periods—"Early life and librarian career," "Hazel Creek and travels," and "Great Smoky Mountains."

Chapter three, "Camping and Woodcraft," contains an introduction by Mae Miller Claxton and includes works on the outdoors from 1905 to 1922. This section shows Kephart as the "Dean of American Campers," his best-known role. The works included demonstrate his interest in cooking, equipment, and flora and fauna and provide numerous examples of his attempts to provide practical advice to casual weekend adventurers.

Chapter four, "Guns," spotlights Kephart's fascination with guns and marksmanship. With an introduction by outdoor writer Jim Casada, this section contains articles from the beginning of Kephart's writing career, in 1899, to the 1920s. "An Old-Fashioned Shooting Match," in particular, demonstrates Kephart's unique narrative combination of information with personal anecdotes and a story-telling style. This piece is technically fiction yet contains a great deal of factual information. Similarly, "The Trail of a Bullet" is included in the fiction section of the book but incorporates a great deal of technical information about guns and ammunition.

Chapter five includes an introduction by George Frizzell detailing the unique region Kephart entered when he came to western North Carolina. Kephart carried around a small notebook in which he jotted down bits of dialogue and information about the people and places he encountered. This section contains letters to Albert Britt, editor of *Outing* magazine, with information that would end up in *Our Southern Highlanders*. The chapter also includes a tourism brochure from the 1920s, an article about names in the Smokies, and a 1930s *New York Times* article, "Changing Mountaineers of the South," in which Kephart documents the many changes in the region he had noticed from his arrival in 1904 until just prior to his death in 1931.

One of the goals of this volume is to introduce Kephart the fiction writer. Chapter six, with an introduction by Mae Miller Claxton, contains early fiction stories from *Puck* and *Forest and Stream*, an unpublished manuscript from 1929, and letters from Kephart to his son Leonard about his attempts to publish a full-length novel to be titled *Smoky Mountain Magic*. Detailed journal entries, true to his librarian mindset, document a thoughtful approach to his craft. While Kephart's best writing comes in the form of nonfiction, his fiction provides another insightful perspective on the people and culture of the region.

With an introduction by Andrew Denson, chapter seven documents Kephart's interest in Cherokees, ranging from the photographs he took on the Qualla Boundary shortly after his arrival in the Smokies to the publication of *The Cherokees of the Smoky Mountains* after his death compiled from a three-part series in *Outing*.

Given Kephart's active participation in a nationwide interest in outdoor adventure and its role in the education of youth, it is no surprise that he became involved in scouting shortly after its introduction in America. He submitted articles to *Boys' Life* in 1914, 1923, and 1928, mostly about outdoor cooking. In her introduction, Mae Miller Claxton discusses some of the history of scouting in relation to Kephart's writing and notes Kephart's election to the National Council of the Boy Scouts of America in 1926.

Andrew Denson also contributes the introduction to the chapter entitled "Park and Trail." Debate continues about the individual who had the most influence on the establishment of the Great Smoky Mountains National Park and the Appalachian

Trail. Certainly, both were collaborative efforts by many individuals devoted to the cause of making the outdoors available to all and saving land for conservation and preservation purposes. Kephart worked with many of these people, including George Masa, to publicize these efforts. Although he did not live to see the official opening of the park, Kephart looked back on his efforts with pride. As the letters to Arthur Perkins, chairman of the board of the Appalachian Trail Conference show, Kephart was also involved in early discussions about the location of the southern terminus of the trail at Mount Oglethorpe in Georgia.[4]

Horace Kephart: Writings correlates with ongoing Hunter Library digital projects, including *Horace Kephart: Revealing an Enigma* and a new digital collection and interpretive website focusing on the history of the Great Smoky Mountains National Park. Perhaps the most useful part of the book, the last section includes George Frizzell's commentary on the index to Kephart's diary (the diary itself is unfortunately lost) juxtaposed with photographs taken by Kephart that illustrate his sojourn in western North Carolina. Also included is Jason Brady's compilation of a list of the books in Kephart's library, demonstrating Kephart's diverse reading and knowledge on a variety of subjects. Most importantly, *Horace Kephart: Writings* ends with George Frizzell's comprehensive bibliography of Kephart's works.

EDITORIAL NOTE

The editors have transcribed these articles from Kephart's copies housed in Hunter Library Special Collections. Handwritten changes to the text, presumably by Kephart, are included in brackets in the transcriptions while handwritten corrections of obvious typos have been silently retained. Archaic spellings have also been retained. Kephart occasionally used offensive language about Native Americans and African Americans. The editors have chosen not to change this language.

one

BIOGRAPHY

Isaiah L. Kephart family circa 1890.

Introduction

GEORGE ELLISON AND JANET McCUE

A highway marker in Bryson City honors Horace Sowers Kephart as a naturalist, a librarian, and an author. Just three-tenths of a mile away, perched on a hill overlooking the town, is the Bryson City Cemetery with Kephart's grave. His tombstone, an eight-ton boulder layered in lichen, reads:

Horace Kephart
1862–1931
Scholar, author, outdoorsman.
He loved his neighbors and pictured them in "Our Southern Highlanders."
His vision helped to create the Great Smoky Mountains National Park.

Kephart was all of these things—naturalist, librarian, writer, scholar, outdoorsman, good neighbor, and advocate. Kephart's widow, Laura, added to that list by asserting that her husband "was a student, first, last and always."[1] Whether researching American frontier history or studying Cherokee, Kephart's passions and his writings reveal a lifelong commitment to learning. Yet this accomplished, proud, and private man lost his professional position in St. Louis in 1903, endured a very public breakdown that received front-page coverage in the St. Louis newspapers in 1904, left his wife and children, and wrestled with alcoholism for much of his life.

Kephart was born on September 8, 1862, in East Salem, Pennsylvania, a small town in the middle of the state. Five years later, Kephart's father, Isaiah Lafayette Kephart, after serving in the Civil War, moved the family to Jefferson, Iowa, "a frontier village set in a prairie wilderness."[2] As a boy, Kephart displayed a curiosity about the outdoors as well as an affinity for exploring the wilderness around him. Inspired by his hero Robinson Crusoe, the young Kephart fashioned his own fur cap, gun, and cutlass for his make-believe island built in a small grove of cottonwood trees on the Iowa prairie. *Robinson Crusoe,* his first book, was a gift from Kephart's mother, Mary Elizabeth Sowers. It remained a touchstone for Kephart "through the vicissitudes of a somewhat venturesome life."[3] The coverless, stained, and well-thumbed volume is now part of the extensive Kephart collection at Western Carolina University.

Isaiah, an influential figure in Kephart's life with his own stories of a pioneer boyhood in Pennsylvania and experiences as a pilot running rafts down the Susquehanna River, captured the imagination of the young Kephart almost as much as the venturesome Crusoe. After one harrowing adventure hauling lumber down a mountain, the eighteen-year-old Isaiah forswore alcohol and joined the United Brethren Church. The United Brethren (UB) was a denomination with roots in Germany and Switzerland—the homelands of Kephart's ancestors whose descendants played a pivotal role in the establishment and growth of the church (now part of the United Methodist Church). Much of Isaiah's career was grounded in the UB community—beginning as a circuit-riding preacher in Pennsylvania, later as an educator and administrator in several UB colleges, and eventually as the editor of the *Religious Telescope*, the official newspaper of the church.[4] Other than his early years in the Jefferson public schools where Isaiah was principal and, later, superintendent of public schools, much of Kephart's education was in UB schools—first in a college preparatory program at Western College in Iowa and later at Lebanon Valley College (LVC) when his family, a little larger with the birth of Kephart's only sibling, Elizabeth Belle, in 1871, moved back to Pennsylvania in 1876. After receiving his baccalaureate from LVC at seventeen, Kephart enrolled at Boston University for a year of special studies. There he strengthened his science background and language skills in preparation for graduate school. He also discovered the pleasures of the extensive collections of the Boston Public Library where he relished "the blessed privilege of studying whatever I pleased."[5]

After Boston, Kephart enrolled as a graduate student (1881–1884) in history and political science at Cornell University in upstate New York. He was one of three resident graduate students in this field and, by his own admission, a bit of a rebel when he arrived at Cornell. As he joked with his friend and fellow graduate student Harry Lyman Koopman, "Lookee here! . . . I was on the high road to Bustville, drinking beer, using unorthodox idioms, belligerently impious, and very full of advanced ideas of social subjects . . . you used to sigh over me (and lend me money)" (Kephart to Koopman, Mar. 23, 1886). Long accustomed to the strictures of religiously affiliated schools, mandatory chapel, and structured courses, the nineteen-year-old Kephart was initially overwhelmed with the freedom of being a graduate student without set courses at a school that advertised itself as "non-denominational" (or to its detractors, "a God-less university").[6]

Cornell also provided the foundation for Kephart's later career in librarianship.

While graduate students, both Kephart and Koopman worked in the university library under the supervision of Daniel Willard Fiske, professor of North European languages and the university librarian. Fiske, insatiably curious, a bibliophile and a linguist, was an inspiring mentor for the young Kephart. In 1883, Fiske left Cornell following a legal dispute with the university over his wife's estate and moved to Florence, Italy. Koopman took a job at Columbia University. It had been a frustrating time for Kephart as well. The university's finances were tight, salaries were low, and Kephart considered moving to California where his parents then resided and becoming a lawyer: "It is with sincere regret that I will quit Ithaca and abandon a profession upon which I fairly embarked, one so congenial to my tastes, and to which experience has led me to believe that I am adapted" (Kephart to Fiske, July 4, 1884). But Kephart did not move to California. Instead Fiske hired him in 1884 to create a catalog of his extensive collection of rare books by and about the Italian Renaissance poet Francesco Petrarca, who is better known in English as Petrarch. Spending a year abroad with Fiske and his mother at the Villa Forini in Florence was a formative experience for Kephart. He learned Italian and studied anthropology, hiked in the Alps on vacation, and researched bibliographical puzzles in Italian and German libraries.

Kephart's European sojourn polished the young scholar, but his absence from Ithaca was difficult. He had fallen in love while at Cornell, and the sixteen-month separation from Laura White Mack was painful. As he explained to Koopman, "But Koop—suppose you are sitting on a first-water brilliant [i.e. precious jewel] big as a punkin, in the midst of Sahara, starving to death" (Kephart to Koopman, Oct. 27, 1885). The love-sick Kephart had all the cultural riches of Europe at his fingertips, but he yearned only to get back to the small town in upstate New York where Laura resided with her family.

Laura was talented, popular, and beautiful; Kephart, shy and modest. Kephart claimed that he "knew no games, [could] tell no stories, am anything but a musician, can't joke, guess riddles, dance, flirt, or even sit gracefully" (Kephart to Koopman, Mar. 23, 1884). Laura performed in theater productions, played the piano for musicals, danced at balls, and, while not a student, participated in Cornell celebrations. Although Kephart and Koopman had joked that Laura was "the Unattainable," Kephart had won her heart.

Kephart returned to the States, arriving in time to celebrate Laura's twenty-fourth birthday on February 14, 1886. Kephart's immediate goal was to find a library position with a salary that could support a family and provide opportunities for advancement. With his language skills (Greek, Latin, French, German, and Italian), graduate-level studies in history and political science, and specialized training in libraries and reference letters from leaders in the field, Kephart was a strong candidate for a professional career in librarianship. After weighing two offers, he accepted a permanent position from Yale University Library. The next year, he and Laura were married on April 12, 1887, in an afternoon ceremony at her uncle's home in Ithaca.

The couple lived in New Haven, Connecticut, for three years where the first of their six children was born. Although Kephart had a heavy workload, he was happy in his new job: "I like Yale. It is solid, free from shams, plain-spoken, and trustworthy" (Kephart to Koopman Oct. 21, 1888). To relieve the stress at work he began a new hobby—target shooting, explaining to Fiske, "This may not become me as a gentleman and a scholar but it fills my lungs, steadies my nerves, and gives me an appetite to be proud of" (Kephart to Fiske, Apr. 27, 1889). Finding a quiet spot to practice his sport was more challenging. As he confided to Koopman, there were "too many back-yards and cow-pastures in this quarter of the world." Kephart's vision of paradise combined the best of both worlds: "Imagine Boston or Florence set in the midst of the Yellowstone Park, with no suburbs, nor even a farm within 200 miles—that's my idea of Paradise. When a fellow wanted to, he could go to the Public Library or the Opera, when he wanted to, he could walk right out into the primeval truth of things and cuss the universe of shams—be Samuel Johnson and Daniel Boone by turns!" (Kephart to Koopman, Oct. 21, 1888).

While at Yale, Kephart began publishing articles, attending professional conferences, and studying a new language, Finnish. In a humorous article written for *Harper's*, a prominent journal with a national circulation, Kephart sketched a typical day in the life of a librarian. Kephart captures the "mental gymnastics" required of a librarian struggling to catalog "an interminable series of French plays" as he juggles a volley of questions coming from a stream of raucous sophomores, frazzled clergy, vague art students, and the dreaded genealogist.[7] Kephart also published his first lengthy historical article in the *Magazine of American History*. Kephart had studied history at Cornell, and he pursued his avid interest in American frontier history at Yale. Kephart's article, "The Rifle in Colonial Times," was not as polished as the writing he would do a decade later, but this early article evokes many of the same themes, including Kephart's admiration of the ingenuity of the "backwoods artisans" and the contributions of Native Americans and Scotch-Irish settlers.[8]

When neither the promised advancement nor the new library building materialized at Yale, Kephart became restless. In 1890 Kephart was offered a new position as head of the St. Louis Mercantile Library, a professional opportunity that included all the incentives Yale had promised but not delivered—a new building, increased salary, broader responsibilities, and the potential to remake the library. For the next thirteen years, Kephart reshaped the library, first by hiring trained staff, then by enhancing access to the collection through catalogs and services, and lastly by strengthening its holdings, particularly the Western Americana collections. His assistant, Clarence Miller, wrote that "all the writers of the early West consulted Kephart. . . . To hear them in discussion was like a trip over the mountains with Fremont, or a voyage up the far reaches of the Missouri with Lewis and Clark."[9] His legacy at the Mercantile was noteworthy. One of Kephart's contemporaries Frank Crunden, head librarian at the nearby St. Louis Public Library, stated that Kephart left the Mercantile "in vastly better shape than he found it" (Crunden to Koopman, Mar. 31, 1904). Ninety years later another commentator wrote that Kephart "ran the Library with exceptional efficiency throughout the deep business depression of 1896 and he went on to raise membership in numbers far greater than any other subscription library in America."[10]

When he was not working, Kephart did his own exploration of the Missouri and Arkansas wilderness. In 1894 Kephart began publishing letters and articles in *Forest and Stream*, often about his adventures at "Camp Nessmuk." Kephart's "Camp Nessmuk" paid homage to the pioneer outdoor writer George Washington Sears, whose work—published under the pen name "Nessmuk"—popularized the "go light" techniques of exploring the wilderness without a guide or an entourage. Kephart's early articles also showcased his growing knowledge of woodcraft.

Kephart's favorite camping location was an area south of St. Louis. "Probably there is not another spot on earth within twenty miles of a city of half a million inhabitants that is quite so wild as Mincke," Kephart wrote.[11] Being able to hop on a train in the booming town of St. Louis and arrive at a "godly wilderness" came very close to the vision of paradise that Kephart had sketched for Koopman a few years earlier. Escaping to Mincke (now part of West Tyson Park) brought Kephart "health, strength, and a happy heart" (Kephart to Koopman, May 21, 1894). Kephart's camping adventures, similar to the target shooting he had done in New Haven, were restorative, allowing him to recoup the energy expended as a professional librarian and the father of a growing family. This theme of replenishing the spirit through the wilderness became a bedrock concept informing his advocacy work for the establishment of the Great Smoky Mountains National Park.

Kephart's writings while in St. Louis reflect his growing interest in woodcraft, rifles, and the wilderness. Of less interest to Kephart over this decade were library topics. His last article on librarianship appeared in 1897. That same year, Kephart wrote an article in *Forest and Stream* titled "A Poor Shot," an affectionate tribute to his sixty-five-year-old father. Kephart also published several significant historical pieces during this period including a four-part series, "The Rifle in the Revolution,"

(1897) as well as "The Birth of the American Army" (1899) and "Pennsylvania's Part in the Winning of the West" (1902). Linked thematically by Kephart's admiration for backwoods artisans, a love of the wilderness, and a passion for historical research, these three articles highlight Kephart's sharpening skills as a writer.

Originally an address delivered to the Pennsylvania Society of St. Louis in 1901, "Pennsylvania's Part" was published subsequently by the Bureau of Publicity of the Louisiana Purchase Exposition (a.k.a. the St. Louis World's Fair). Kephart's well-researched article focused on the settlement patterns of the German and Scotch-Irish settlers in Pennsylvania. It depicted their exploration and expansion into western North Carolina and other southern and western areas of the United States. Emphasis was placed on the intense individualism that marked the character of these pioneer ancestors.

"Pennsylvania's Part" is also a passionate statement of Kephart's own personal philosophy. He had once ascribed recuperative powers to target shooting and wilderness camping; now he expanded upon this theme. Man is not only renewed by the experience, he is "born anew." He is stamped and imprinted by Nature—its openness and simplicity. "The man who can enter an unmapped forest . . . is no ordinary mortal. . . . To conquer the wilderness as the early westerners conquered it with ax and rifle, man must be born anew. He must re-learn an art so ancient that it has long since been forgotten by urban society—the art of wildcraft."[12]

Kephart's career at the Mercantile spanned fourteen years, but he admitted that his first eight years were his most productive. As he lost his enthusiasm for his professional life and as his family responsibilities weighed heavily on him, Kephart began spending more and more time in the wilderness and less at the library and at home. Fed up with his absences, the St. Louis Mercantile Library board demanded Kephart's resignation in the fall of 1903. Without a job to support the family, Laura and the six children, ranging in age from six to fourteen years old, returned to Ithaca where Laura's family still resided. Kephart moved into a boarding house on Kennett Place, off Lafayette Square in St. Louis, and began working feverishly on a book on woodcraft.

Over the next few months, Kephart became more isolated, suffering from insomnia and hallucinations. In late March 1904, Kephart's friends convinced him to join them at a hunting lodge on Establishment Creek, south of St. Louis. The anxiety, delusions, and nightmares that Kephart suffered on this trip prompted the worried men to bring him back to his St. Louis boarding house after a few days.

On March 25, 1904, Kephart wrote a suicide note on a piece of rough wrapping paper and handed it to a bartender. Kephart's breakdown became front-page news.

Fourteen years earlier the St. Louis newspapers had heralded Kephart's arrival; in March 1904 they reported every detail of his collapse. The newspapers reprinted the full text of his suicide note, and reporters interviewed the hospitalized Kephart, who was suffering from paranoid delusions, and subsequently printed verbatim the incoherent conversation. Although we don't know the specific cause of Kephart's transformation from effective professional to demoralized librarian; from supportive family man to absentee husband and father; from vague malaise to full-blown nervous breakdown, there are many theories. Miller believed it was Kephart's "intellectual Bohemian friends" who had led him astray;[13] Crunden suggested it was "bad habits," including tobacco, narcotics, and stimulants. Crunden also believed that the couple was not "well mated" and that there were faults on both sides (Crunden to Koopman, Mar. 31, 1904). Kephart's daughter Lucy suspected it was the houseful of kids "who sometimes made a mess" of their father's things and kept him up at night (Fernow, Lucy [a.k.a. Wonref], Dec. 18, 1931). Kephart provides his own explanation, "my health broke down," in "Horace Kephart by Himself."[14]

When they learned of Kephart's hospitalization, Kephart's parents and Laura rushed to St. Louis. His parents took the fragile Kephart back to Dayton, Ohio, where they were living. Laura settled Kephart's affairs at the boarding house and returned home to the children in Ithaca. Kephart's parents had lost their only daughter to scarlet fever in 1892; they were not about to lose their only son.[15] Kephart's breakdown—although dramatic and severe—was short-lived. By mid-July 1904, Kephart recovered enough to travel to central Pennsylvania where he and his father visited various ancestral sites, including the schoolhouse that Isaiah and his brothers had helped construct and the old Goss cemetery where Isaiah's maternal ancestors were buried. Two weeks after this trip, Kephart was in the Smokies.

Horace departed Dayton by train and arrived in Dillsboro, about forty-five miles west of Asheville, in early August 1904. He obtained permission from a local family to establish an elaborate camp on Dicks Creek, a tributary of the Tuckasegee River,[16] about a mile west of Dillsboro. Farther west, he ventured up Hazel Creek—the largest stream on the North Carolina side of the Smokies—and discovered a remote settlement "made up of forty-two households . . . scattered over an area eight miles long by two wide . . . a mere slash in the wilderness that encompassed it."[17] He felt "as though he had been carried back . . . on the wings of time and had awakened in the eighteenth century."[18]

The frontier experience he fashioned for himself became the inspiration for his writing. As he explains in *Our Southern Highlanders*:

When I went south into the mountains I was seeking a Back of Beyond. This for more reasons than one. With an inborn taste for the wild and romantic, I yearned for a strange land and a people that had the charm of originality. Again, I had a passion for early American history; and, in Far Appalachia, it seemed that I might realize the past in the present, seeing with my own eyes what life must have been to my pioneer ancestors of a century or two ago. Besides, I wanted to enjoy a free life in the open air, the thrill of exploring new ground, the joys of the chase, and the man's game of matching my woodcraft against the force of nature.[19]

Kephart obtained permission from a copper mining company that had gone into litigation to live in one of its vacant cabins located near Medlin, a crossroads settlement consisting of a store and several houses, where the Sugar Fork enters Hazel Creek ten miles or so above its former confluence with the Little Tennessee River. That remote site on "the Little Fork of the Sugar Fork of Hazel Creek" became the vantage point from which he studied the land and its people for parts of three years.

Kephart's intentions in regard to writing date back into the 1890s. For years, he had been preoccupied with developing tactics for living efficiently in wilderness settings. He discovered that he now "had to make shift in a different way, and fashion many appliances from the materials found on the spot . . . seeking not novelties but practical

Kephart's Hazel Creek cabin.
"The Cabin in Autumn."

Kephart's Hazel Creek cabin.
"The Cabin in Winter."

results."[20] These "results" he published in outdoor magazines. By 1906, he had enough material—compiled during his excursions in Mincke and the Ozarks as well as in his camps in the Smokies—to put together the first edition of *The Book of Camping and Woodcraft*. The expanded edition of two separate volumes was published in 1916 (Vol. I, *Camping*) and 1917 (Vol. II, *Woodcraft*). And in 1921 those volumes were reissued in a "Two Volumes in One" format as *Camping and Woodcraft*.

In time Kephart entered into the lives of the two hundred or so residents of Hazel Creek. Along the watershed with its numerous tributaries, he became a good neighbor and, in a few instances, a friend. He was accepted as much as any outsider could desire because he wanted to learn from his neighbors and take part in their daily activities, not tell them what to do. He studied their way of life and listened closely to the manner in which they expressed themselves. He was particularly captivated by their humor. Notebook entries and photographs recorded details of almost every aspect of their lives as well as Kephart's reflections upon those details.

Bob Barnett was Kephart's closest friend during the Hazel Creek years and on into the early 1920s. He warrants attention here because of the significant part he played in Kephart's work. Although Barnett was the younger man by eighteen years, Kephart admired him tremendously. In a "Roving with Kephart" column published in *All Outdoors* magazine in 1921, he described a recent visit: "He was the big, fat Bob who figures in *Camping and Woodcraft* and *Our Southern Highlanders*. He came years ago, to the old mine site where I'd been living alone with the bobcats and hoot-owls, and became caretaker for the company that had possession. It was an abandoned place—that is, no one ever lived there—and I welcomed a neighbor. Soon I shifted quarters to his house. We lived together, in various necks of the woods, for several years. Bob is now at Aquone, N.C., on the upper Nantahala, where he keeps open house for all comers."[21]

Many of the dialectical expressions entered in Kephart's journals were uttered by Barnett: "Bob whittled Old Pete Laney's store-bought axe-handle for him and remarked: 'Thar! I'll see that Pete'll have a decent axe-handle fer his women-folks to chop wood with, anyhow.'"[22] In *Camping and Woodcraft*, Kephart cites Barnett as an authority throughout, describing him as "one of the best woodsmen in this country, a man so genuinely a scholar in his chosen lore that he could well afford to say, as once he did to me: 'I've studied these woods and mountains all my life, Kep, like you do your books, and I don't know them all yet, no sirree.' "[23] In the "Back of Beyond" chapter of *Our Southern Highlanders*, when the two friends were stymied by the marauding tactics of a "slab-sided tusky old boar," which Kephart had christened "Belial" after one of Dante's devils, it was Bob who remarked in frustration: " 'That Be-liar . . . would cross hell on a rotten rail to git into my 'tater patch!' "[24] And Bob was the real-life model for Tom Burbank, a pivotal character throughout *Smoky Mountain Magic* who represented Kephart's ideal mountaineer in that he was dignified but fun to be around, a caring husband and father, absolutely competent in matters of woodcraft, and capable of rising to the occasion when the hero required rescue from a dark cavern into which he had fallen. Barnett's wife Sarah figures almost as prominently. Kephart dedicated *Camp Cookery* to "Mistress Bob" who taught him "some clever expedients of backwoods cookery that are lost arts wherever the old forest has been leveled."[25] And he models Sylvia, one of the characters in *Smoky Mountain Magic*, on Sarah Barnett as well.

An examination of Kephart's initial venture into the Smokies (1904–1907) indicates that it was provisional; that is, he probably had no intention of making the region his permanent residence until 1910, when he returned after a lengthy absence and settled in Bryson City. A closer look also indicates that his life on Hazel Creek was not so extended or isolated or primitive as often portrayed in his own descriptions or more recent biographical accounts. According to the foreword written for *The Book of Camping and Woodcraft*, Kephart mailed his final typescript to the publisher from "Dayton, Ohio," in "March, 1906." He had been living in Dayton since the previous December—by which time, he had spent less than fourteen months in the Smokies region and less than a year living in his cabin or with the Barnetts in their warmer, more comfortable dwelling. Nevertheless, those years served as a touchstone that stimulated Kephart's imagination and writing. It was the place where he sorted out his life and laid the foundation for what became a substantial literary and environmental legacy.

Kephart provided only sketchy details about his life between the time he left the Smokies in 1907 and his return in 1910. In the 1922 autobiographical essay, he mentioned traveling "in other parts of the Appalachians . . . comparing what I found there with what I knew in the Smokies."[26] Correspondence between Koopman and the Kepharts reveal additional details about his travels. Learning in October 1908 that his father was "dangerously ill," Kephart travelled to Dayton to be with his father until he died. After settling his mother with a relative, Kephart headed to Ithaca, attempting to reconcile with Laura and the children. Kephart admitted to Koopman that returning to civilization had been awkward: "The chief penalty of a solitary life is introspection; and when your hermit abandons his shell, what can he say to his fellow men?" (Kephart to Koopman, Dec. 29, 1908).

But Horace was committed to reconnecting with Laura and the children. After a month, they were able to "make the dream turn tangible. Laura, indeed has the gift of perennial youth. But the children have changed wonderfully. Gradually we are getting acquainted" (Kephart to Koopman, Dec. 29, 1908).

With his home-life settled, Kephart was ready to revive his career. Knowing that he would fail at a library job requiring "much appearing in society and public speaking," Kephart asked Koopman to help him find a professional position, preferably one with less stress and more flexibility, perhaps even with summers free. His health was good, and Kephart was "resolved to keep it so, at all hazards" (Kephart to Koopman, Dec. 29, 1908).

Less than six months later, in May 1909, Kephart left Ithaca. Tensions at home and worries about finances combined to sink Kephart's spirits. When the problems had reached a crescendo and "the old trouble" erupted, Laura took "a firm stand." Although the language is veiled Victorian, she is presumably referring to Kephart's drinking as "the old trouble." Laura could not or would not tolerate Kephart's drinking (Laura Kephart to Koopman, Dec. 9, 1909). Believing that his wife was "unjust" in her judgement of him, Kephart left his family once again and returned to Dayton. Kephart's alcoholism seems to have been chronic, debilitating him periodically for much of his adult life.

Financial worries added to Kephart's stress as he learned of the bankruptcy of the Outing Publishing Company in April 1909. Kephart had counted on Outing to continue publishing his outdoor writings. Now even that source of income was in jeopardy (Kephart to Koopman, June 3, 1909).

A letter from Kephart to a friend who still lived on Hazel Creek provides additional information about the sequence of events. It is dated October 5, 1909, and addressed from Lindale, Georgia (near Rome), where he was once again living with the Barnett family. Kephart advised that he had been "to Dayton to look after my father who was very sick [and] died a year ago. Then I went to New York and Pennsylvania, and back to Dayton, and finally came down here two weeks ago. I will stay with the Barnetts until spring, and then take a long trip through the mountains from Georgia to Virginia and Kentucky, taking photographs for my books." In closing, he observed: "Bob has a good job and a nice home. I have plenty of writing to do, and am saving money to buy a place in the Smokies" (Kephart to Louis Hampton, Oct. 5, 1909).

Kephart returned to the Great Smokies early in 1910 but decided he no longer wanted to live on Hazel Creek. A logging company had initiated operations and was in the process of running a railway spur up the valley into the high Smokies. Instead, he stayed for a while, yet again, with the Barnett family, who had moved from Georgia to "the last house up Deep Creek." This house was situated at the Bryson Place about ten miles north of Bryson City—precisely where the Burbank family (clearly modeled on the Barnett family) resides in *Smoky Mountain Magic*.

Kephart never bought "a place in the Smokies." For much of the time between late 1910 until 1931, Kephart made his home in Bryson City. He found suitable accommodations at the Cooper House, a rambling sixteen-room hotel (sometimes described as a boardinghouse) on the north side of Main Street just west of the town square in Bryson City. He also rented office space around the corner on Everett Street overlooking the Tuckasegee River and the Smokies.

In a 1929 *Field and Stream* magazine essay titled "Afoot and Awing in the Great Smokies," Kephart described the view from his office in a manner that indicates a longstanding comfort level with his daily workspace that is more important to a writer than is generally recognized:

> My office windows overlook a clear, swift river—the Tuckaseigee—which runs through the middle of our town. The old building in which I write stands directly on the river bank. It is on the same block with the court-house and the post-office; yet if some big sycamores were not in the way, I could cast a line from the upstairs porch in front of my windows and catch small-mouth bass or redhorse or spotted channel catfish. This is too handy for any but a lazybones; so I am glad that the trees spread over the waterside and thwart such trifling.
>
> I look up from my typewriter and out across the river, over the roofs of stores and houses, to a pine-clad ridge less than four hundred yards away, and up to ranges of wooded mountains that tower to the sky-line among the clouds.[27]

It was here in this proverbial room-of-his-own overlooking the Tuckasegee River that Kephart achieved his most success as a writer. Bouncing back from the bankruptcy of Outing Publishing Company and its subsequent sale in 1909, Kephart began a fruitful decade-long partnership with his new editor at Outing, Albert Britt. Beginning with *Camp Cookery* (1910) and moving through *Sporting Firearms* (1912), *Our Southern Highlanders* (1913), the eleven-volume Outing Adventure Library series (1915–17), and the revised and expanded *Camping and Woodcraft* (1916), Britt supported and encouraged Kephart's writing. In 1913, Britt nominated *Our Southern Highlanders* for the Patterson Prize, an award established by the North Carolina Literary and Historical Association to honor a person whose poetry or prose "demonstrated the greatest excellence and highest literary skill and genius." The Bryson City Bank proudly displayed Kephart's glimmering prize, a three-handled silver and gold cup set with North Carolina gemstones.

The last decade (1921–1931) of Kephart's life was perhaps his most public. Active in civic affairs, both at the local and state level, Kephart chaired the town board of aldermen, served on the school board and the State Prison Review Board, and was elected president of the North Carolina Literary and Historical Association. These civic activities coincided with his significant advocacy work on behalf of the Great Smoky Mountains National Park. While he was chair of the Bryson City Board of Aldermen, he supported a progressive infrastructure agenda. Kephart reported that the town completed the municipal power and light plant, paved more streets, and extended the water and sewer lines during his tenure (Kephart to Angus McLean, Oct. 12, 1926). Covering the cost of these improvements required issuing new bonds as well as additional taxes. As Kephart explained to his friend Paul Fink, his advocacy for these improvements "incurred the hostility of the reactionaries." He confessed that he'd angered some of the wealthy residents of the town for refusing to provide "special favors (lower tax rates than other folks)." In retaliation, his rivals began a smear campaign. Kephart confided that "two bunches of soreheads combined and spread reports throughout the county that I was an infidel, a damned foreigner and had written a book making fun of the mountain people" (Kephart to Fink, Oct. 29, 1926). Although Kephart had been nominated by acclamation by the Democratic county convention, Kephart worried that the name-calling and backlash against him would weaken the ticket, and he withdrew as a delegate.

Occasional letters to the editor give a sense of some of Kephart's progressive beliefs. Acknowledging that the issues surrounding the death penalty were complex, Kephart offered an outline of his own personal views, "merely for what it may be worth," in a letter to the *Asheville Citizen-Times* on July 14, 1925. Kephart argued that capital punishment was "no more deterrent of high class crime than life imprisonment, if as much. The man who deliberately plots murder and is determined to carry it out, discounts the risk of death the same as the risk of incarceration for life." Kephart believed that juries were more likely to convict a criminal of first-degree murder if the punishment were life imprisonment rather than hanging or the electric chair. He also felt that capital punishment limited the state's legal ability to admit a mistake. Kephart did "not believe in being 'soft' on hardened criminals." Rather he was a realist who understood that "there were many men and women who are so incurably vicious that no kindness and no precepts will reform them." But this acknowledgment did not mean that the criminal justice system could not be improved. He proposed several areas requiring enhancements, including repairing the sluggish justice system, changing the brutal conditions in the prisons, and recruiting "humane and sensible men" as wardens.

Kephart dropped out of the 1926 political race but openly defended his perspective on religion in a letter to the editor. Pointing out that any three members of a church might hold different views of God, Kephart argued that "the effort to classify Americans according to their actual religious beliefs is futile." What should matter, he contended, is the way a man lives.[28] Kephart's eldest son, Leonard, wrote that his father was "definitely an agnostic."[29] Yet three ministers presided over Kephart's funeral.

During the 1920s Kephart was also the "go-to" man for a range of visitors to the area—from scientists and movie directors to detectives and industrialists. He helped Karl Brown find locations for his silent film *Stark Love* and led scientists to pristine areas in the Smokies where they might study rock formations or rare orchids. One of these visitors, Julius Stone, a wealthy Ohio businessman, adventurer in his own right, and Kephart admirer, expressed his gratitude to Kephart for his help in planning a trip to the Smokies for himself and his son. Stone gave his tour guide several gifts, one of which Kephart referred to as "a scholarship or fellowship aiding me to carry on the work I've started."[30] It's likely that occasional gifts as well as income from writing were Kephart's chief sources of support during the 1920s. In addition, Kephart's friend I. K. (Irving Kip) Stearns tried to convince him to capitalize on his reputation by manufacturing and marketing some of his inventions, including waterproof matches and a nesting camp kit. In a letter to his uncle, Stearns wrote, "Mr. Kephart has been living art for art's sake these past twenty years. So far his reward has been in the nature of royalties on his books, pay for his many articles in sporting magazines and a tremendous nation-wide reputation as America's foremost authority on outdoor life. He has at last decided that some of this reputation should be capitalized."[31] Kephart also travelled widely during this decade including a Florida Good Will Tour sponsored by the Swain County Chamber of Commerce, a family reunion in New York City, and two trips to Georgia—one in a motorcade to promote tourism and the second to scout the southern terminus of the Appalachian Trail.

Kephart's companion on his second trip to Georgia was George Masa, a talented photographer whose artistry, Kephart proclaimed, was incomparable—"the like of which is not to be found elsewhere."[32] For Arno Cammerer, assistant director of the National Park Service (later director of the NPS), Kephart and Masa were "congenial comrades" (Cammerer to Masa, Apr. 6, 1931). Although the two men were twenty years apart in age, they were trail companions and collaborators. Kephart with his pen and Masa with his lens captured the wonders of the area and fought for its protection. The rugged explorers documented the terrain and nomenclature for the North Carolina Nomenclature Committee and measured and mapped the Smokies along the North Carolina–Tennessee border for the Appalachian Trail Conference.

During the 1920s, Kephart's writing related to protecting the Smokies shifted from pessimism to optimism. Confiding to Fink in 1920, Kephart wrote, "It makes my heart sick to see with what reckless selfishness these gifts of nature are being squandered" (Kephart to Fink, Jan. 28, 1920). But by the end of the decade, Kephart was jubilant, acknowledging that protecting the Smokies had been a "big undertaking, and beset with discouragement of all sorts; but we've won" (Kephart to Pauline Kephart, Sept. 12, 1928). Through his persuasive writing and compelling conversations, Kephart's voice was heard. Helen Topping Miller, journalist and novelist, profiled Kephart in 1926 for the *American Motorist*, writing that "Men from colleges, from bureaus of conservation, from literary chairs, and editorial offices caught the challenge of Horace Kephart's 'why.' Why should the virgin wilderness, this last hoarding place of the resources of nature in the eastern half of this land . . . be doomed by greed for extinction?"[33] Kephart was one among many who made the establishment of the park a reality, but his significant voice and pivotal role should not be discounted. His fight to protect the wilderness was personal as well as altruistic: "I owe my life to these mountains and I want them preserved that others may profit from them as I have."[34]

Horace Kephart died on April 2, 1931. He was sixty-eight years old. Kephart and his friend and fellow writer Fiswoode Tarleton, who was visiting from Georgia, were killed in a car accident. Kephart's body was laid out in the Cooper House where his widow and other members of his family paid their respects. The *New York Times* reported, "All the seats in the auditorium of the public school where the funeral was held were taken. Hundreds stood outside."[35] The *Bryson City Times* reported, "Two stalwart mountaineers, a Japanese photographer, a college professor, a man high in the political affairs of the state, and men from other walks of life were selected to perform this duty [pallbearers]. He [Kephart] was at home in the most rude mountain cabin or as a guest of the rich."[36] The Reverend James Gillespie eulogized Kephart as "an earnest seeker after the truth, a man who avoided the limelight, humble in spirit, sincere, never a hypocrite, true to his convictions, man, foursquare, charitable towards his fellow man, always a gentleman and honored for that. Mr. Kephart was a man of big heart and would go through anything to aid anyone, a man who sought to serve his fellow man. Personally, we have lost much locally, a man of towering influence in the community, his state, and the nation at large."[37]

Over the years there have been some voices who have questioned the views of this "outsider," critics who have decried his alcoholism, his portrayal of the mountain people, his abandonment of his wife and children, even doubted his role in the establishment of the Great Smoky Mountains National Park. There is no question that Kephart was an alcoholic, no doubt that he was unable to support his family. But

Kephart emerged from the darkness of 1903–4 to become an accomplished author and an influential voice. Subsequent chapters will reveal the breadth of his writings and his impact on scouting, camping, woodcraft, and the park movement. Decades after his death, this scholar and student, outdoorsman and man "of big heart," is still celebrated for his accomplishments. In 2016 during the centennial celebration of the National Park Service, Kephart was selected as one of the hundred most influential persons in park history. His is a legacy unlikely to be forgotten.

Being a Librarian

BY HORACE KEPHART.*

Librarianship offers a better field for mental gymnastics than any other profession. I am cataloguing the four thousand and tenth of an interminable series of French plays, when a drove of unbroken Sophomores comes prancing into the library. Before my wits can be jogged out of Paris and across a half-century, the boys burst out in a chorus:

"Say, will you please give me a chart of Long Island Sound?"

"Say, may I have all my books renewed?"

"Say, can you tell me where Milton speaks of the Golden Chersonese?"

"Say, will you show me something on the woodchuck?"

"Say, is Professor Scribner in?"

It takes some time to make the boys happy, and then I go back to my plays. Here is a thin little pamphlet called *Les suites d'un mariage de raison . . . par MM. Dartois, Léon Brunswick, et Lhéric*. To catalogue it I must first of all identify the authors. Quérard introduces me to three dramatic writers of the same period, brothers, whose family name was Dartois de Bournonville, and their baptismal names, respectively, François Victor Armand, Louis Charles Achille, and Louis Armand Théodore. Under the first of these I find my play credited to the said François, "*avec M. Lhéris*." Léon Brunswick is not mentioned, and Lhéric is spelled Lhéris.

Some one interrupts me here to learn whether 112 College Street is at the west end. Scarcely have I settled back into calm research when a quaint old lady rouses me with the appeal:

"I would like to see a book fifty years old."

"Er—that is, a book *entitled* 'Fifty Years Old?'"

"No; a book that *is* fifty years old."

---

*Now librarian of the Mercantile Library of St. Louis. This was written while he was at Yale College Library.

From *Harper's Weekly*, Aug. 30, 1890.

"But we have a great number of books that are fifty years old or more. Is it some one particular book?"

"Yes; it is a book that I read when I was a little girl."

"What is the title?"

"I have forgotten it."

"The author's name?"

"I don't remember."

"What was the book about?"

"It was a novel, and the scene was laid in this neighborhood. That is all I remember about it."

Our lists of historical novels are of no service, and I am finally forced to give it up. After assuring several persons that they can find Professor Scribner in his own room, I return to the drama.

No such name as Lhéris is to be found among the *L's* in Quérard; but he has two contemporary playwrights, brothers, named Victor and Léon Lhérie.

Puzzling over this, my wandering eye is attracted by a timid little body who needs encouragement to speak out. Yes, we have a "shelf of poetry:" many of them, in fact. And I point out the more accessible. Just then a gentleman asks me, innocently, "Have you a class photograph of Thomas Green, who graduated here in 1792?"

I get back to Quérard, but have hardly found my place when a leisurely acquaintance drops in for a chat. He is soon displaced by a hustling book agent, whom nothing can drive away; so I bless the old professor who wants a book from the nethermost abyss of the "farther room."

"Do you know any history in the Spanish language that would sell well in an English translation?" asks a fair stranger in spectacles. "Of course translating is rather overdone, I know; but"—

A clergyman, in great haste, rushes up, exclaiming, "Please extend my time on 'Future Probation.'"

I renew his book in English, while talking Spanish and thinking in French.

My play is found again under Victor Lhérie's name, attributed to him "avec M. M. Brunswick (i.e., Léon Lhérie) et Dartois." Here is progress. My authors' names now stand as follows: Dartois de Bournonville, François Victor Armand [Lhérie (or Lhéris, or Lhéric), Léon (*pseud.* Léon Brunswick)], Lhérie (or Lhéris, or Lhéric), Victor.

However, past experience has made me distrustful of Quérard's accuracy, and I proceed to verify these names, having first sent messengers in search of Professor Scribner, whose presence is urgently wanted in four different places at once.

Hœfer, Larousse, and Vapereau copy Quérard's spelling of my first author's name.

When four such authorities agree, I say, the matter may be considered settled. Now, then, for the Lhéries.

"Pardon me, but I have a very rare book here, printed in the sixteenth century. Can you tell me what it is worth?"

It is worth about ten cents.

"Can you inform me, sir, why Shakespeare omitted Henry the Seventh from his plays?"

"Ah! Well, then perhaps you can explain the derivation of the Yankee comparison, 'Like Sam Hill?'"

I seem very stupid this afternoon. It is close in the library, albeit whenever the front door is opened a gust of icy wind sends shivers up my back and makes me sneeze. Brunswick, Lhéric, fiddlestick! It is hard to recover the lost thread of evidence.

"Will you be kind enough to show me everything you have on incubation?"

Not being an agricultural station, our library yields only short articles in reference-books and periodicals, and these but grudgingly.

An art student inquires for "a good book on science—something short and interesting." I gave her Thompson's "Depths of the Sea" and Dunkin's "Midnight Sky." She balances them in her hands, and selects the latter.

Her companion wants the largest and best book we have on elephants, and I spend some time searching for an exhaustive monograph on the anatomy of pachyderms. It is only after carrying thirty pounds of folio up and down stairs that I learn what is really wanted: "A picture of an elephant with his trunk up, to work into a decorative design."

Well, Quérard was certain that "Léon Brunswick" is the assumed name of Léon Lhéris, or Lhérie. In a later volume of his I find "Lhéric, puis Lhérie (Léon)." To make assurance doubly sure I consult a still later continuation of his work, and find no such pseudonym as Léon Brunswick, but under plain Brunswick is the entry, "*Ps.* (Léon Lévy, plus tard Lhéric et Lhérie)." Matters are becoming complicated.

"Beg pardon, but will you show me something on the history of the choir of Westminster Abbey?"

This found, a gentleman seeks assistance in deciphering some of his own handwriting. Another wants a German book, author's name forgotten, title remembered only in English, though the work has never been translated, and the English title might be variously rendered in German. Here the incubator man returns his books with a disappointed shake of the head.

"You see, my landlady is raising chickens."

"Yes; with an incubator?"

"No; with a hen. She breeds game-cocks, and has sold one for as high as twenty-five dollars. Well, there's a sort of workshop in the rear of our block that has just put in a trip-hammer, and the old lady has sent me up here to find out whether the jarring of the earth by that trip-hammer will spoil her eggs."

A bell rings, and in comes a troop of students. All talk at once.

"Have you got any of Cardan's formulas?"

"I'd like to get the latest Canadian tariff list."

"Where can I get a traverse table?"

"Can you give me Lord Bacon's 'New Atlantis'? I think it's a magazine article."

"I must work up something on 'Byronism on the Continent' for to-morrow morning. Can you give a fellow a lift?"

By and by I get back to those delightful pseudonyms. Quérard's latest statement is supported by Vapereau and Larousse. The spelling Lhéris, though copied by Oettinger, seems to be a typographical error. The man's name was originally Lévy, which he subsequently changed to Lhéric, and finally to Lhérie. Yet the British Museum catalogue enters thirty plays under Brunswick alone, and one under Léon Brunswick, both of which are given as pen-names of Léon Lhérie, with no mention of Lévy. No two authorities agree about the dates of his birth and death.

A stranger saunters into the room, gazes awhile at the overburdened shelves, approaches the delivery desk, and opens with the question, "Have you any special litterury taste?"

An emphatic negative does not disconcert him.

"We've organized a litterury club down at Richmond, and they made me secretary. Now I'd like to get some points on the subject."

He is scarcely gone before a clergyman appears, almost a stranger to me. "I know you must have a good head for figures," he begins. "Will you be good enough to figure out my board bill? I'm about to leave town, and my brain is all in a muddle from these Easter services. [Coaxingly.] It won't take you long."

Dear me! What would the powers that be remark if they knew it took me half a day to catalogue a tract? Did these Frenchmen themselves know their own names? Let us stick to Larousse, and call the man Lévy. But the third name remains to be settled. The resources of our library are exhausted without finding any trace of such a person as "Lhéric," save that Quérard says this stands for Victor Lhérie, brother of Léon. Since Léon's name is not Lhérie, after all, but Lévy, it follows that his brother's name was probably Lévy also.

The afternoon is waning. The light from our high windows, that "breaks sorrowfully" at all times "through painted panes," now blends with the all-pervading dust.

A shape arises before my dim vision, and I shudder. It is the genealogist, a volume in his hand, propitiatory smiles upon his patient face. Alas! I know his mission.

"Ah, sir, I have discovered a wonderful thing—a very wonderful thing indeed. May I ask you to translate this for me?"

On one of the open pages is an emblazoned coat of arms; opposite this a fac-simile of some old document. It turns out to be a grant of arms to one William Sigar, knight, or, as it stands in Latin, Guilielmus Sigar Miles.

"You see," cried this excited mouser, as his trembling finger singled out the name—"you see, *I am a Miles myself on my mother's side!*"

The little French play is finally catalogued—author card, subject card, cross-references, and all. Dartois and the brothers Lévy prove to have been quite fecund, and erelong their names as joint authors are intricately woven into the main catalogue. Then one day I discover by chance that Dartois really wrote his name François Victor Armand d'Artois de Bournonville, and I have all that work to go over again.

Shall a Librarian Aid Personal Interests?

The Mercantile Library of St. Louis has posted the following

"NOTICE:

"The librarian will not identify coins; nor estimate values of old books, manuscripts, curios, etc.; nor give special assistance to those engaged in genealogical research, or other matters of merely personal or pecuniary interest."

I would be glad to see a little symposium on the proper interpretation of the last phrase of this rule. How far should a librarian go out of his way to help Civis put money in his purse, or to secure to Civis Femina[38] a membership in the Daughters of the Revolution?

HORACE KEPHART.
MERCANTILE LIBRARY,
St. Louis, Mo.

From *Library Journal*, January 1895

Notes from Camp Nessmuk

II.—HOUSE-BUILDING.

Ordinarily a hollow makes a poor camp ground, for currents of cold air sweep down it at night, on the same principle that water runs down hill. Spook Hollow ran from north to south, with a steep and heavily-timbered ridge closing it on the south. The sides were precipitous hills rising two or three hundred feet, with ledges of exposed rock about half way up, which were honey-combed with crannies and fox dens. The sun was not visible from my camp until 9 A.M., and retired from the hollow promptly at 5 P.M., leaving little or no twilight. In an average season such a place would be damp, and in case of a hard rain might be unpleasant. But last year was an uncommonly dry one with us, and it was the drought that settled my choice of a camp site—that and the diabolical protection previously alluded to. For there was only one spring in the neighborhood that had not run dry—Pompernickle Spring, as Barnes[39] had named it in one of his inspired moods, and any one who knows Mincke will forgive me for not wanting to carry water up those hills.

Probably there is not another spot on earth within twenty miles of a city of half a million inhabitants that is quite so wild as Mincke. From the crest of the ridge southeast of Camp Nessmuk one can look for miles and miles and see nothing but sharp ridges densely covered with scrubby oaks and hickories, steep hollows gloomy with a richer vegetation, bare ledges, and occasionally a glade from which peeps a negro cabin. Animal life is not very abundant, but there are coons and possums, skunks and foxes, squirrels, woodchucks, hawks, buzzards, owls, doves and lesser creatures of earth or air, with occasionally a flock of wild turkeys. Reptilian life is fairly abundant. Venomous snakes are rather scarce, but scorpions, tarantulas and centipedes may be found almost any day under flat stones, and nimble little lizards are darting everywhere. Song birds are not plentiful, and their absence adds to the true wilderness effect of Mincke. The wild hog, that pest of the Missouri woods, is

---

From *Forest and Stream*, Part 2, May 25, 1895

also absent; but O the chigres! My friend, take my advice, and keep out of the Mincke grass in summer. The first frost drives these microscopic fiends into winter quarters.

Within a few rods of Pompernickle I cleared some high ground of roots and stone, got out the double-bitted hatchet, and proceeded to erect the framework of my house. Except for the abundance of provisions, a two weeks' supply, the outfit for the camp was mostly copied from "Nessmuk's" "Woodcraft." There are many who smile at the idea of learning anything about woodcraft from books, and their scorn is, in a measure, justified by the fact that most works on the art of camping are disappointing. Englishmen are the greatest sinners in this respect, and there is one work in particular that will afford you many a chuckle—a ponderous octavo entitled "Shifts and Expedients of Camp Life," which tells you how to explore a bit of wild country with the aid of a company of servants and a baggage train inproportion [*sic*]. But there are books and books. It would be hard to name a subject that has not at least its one good book, which will save the beginner many a tedious failure, and can even teach the old-timer something that he did not know before. Of such is "Woodcraft."

"Nessmuk" wrote, of course, with a particular locality in mind—the Northeastern wilderness, with its waterways and balsams—and some of his advice would be of slight value in Southern swamps or on Western plains, in the Rockies or among the wastes of the Far North. Moreover, he wrote for the lone camper, who goes, as a wise man, light. And let it be said right here that any one can camp with a wagon, but that the man who can carry on his own back all that he requires for a sojourn in the wilderness is a scholar and a king by comparison. "Nessmuk" was past master of the craft, and I am proud to acknowledge that, after doing my fair share of experimenting, I have found most of his wrinkles to be the very best for the service they intended to perform.

My shanty tent had seen service before. It was a trifle larger than "Nessmuk's," as the drilling was 8 in. wider than his, and it had a front door, the roof being continued to form a flap that can be tacked down in front, thus leaving the outfit securely housed from tempest and vermin during its owner's absence. The flap was never closed at night when the tent was occupied, for a shanty tent is intended to let in pure air and the glow of a well-built camp fire. The flap thrown back over the roof gives additional protection against rain and sparks. The lime-and-alum process of waterproofing was tried with some misgivings when the tent was made, misgivings which were justified on first trial, and I came back from that expedition resolved to find something better than oxide of alumina to keep me dry. Nobody but a sportsman and a brother would excuse the trouble I took to solve that problem. A tent of thin drilling, with a shed roof pitched at a moderate angle, is no easy thing to waterproof. Rubber solution or boiled oil will do it after a fashion, but they are heavy, and either rot or crack, or develop some other bad trick. The process finally adopted was original and gave complete satisfaction, rendering the tent permanently waterproof and mildew proof, so that moist earth from the drain trench may be heaped against the lower edge without rotting the fiber. But it is somewhat dangerous to apply, as it obliges one to use a very inflammable liquid raised about to its boiling point. I hope to overcome this objection, and so will say no more about the process at present.

The shanty tent has one disadvantage: it is hard to set up in some localities. To cut posts, poles, head and foot logs, is easy when saplings are near, but to measure and shape them, drive the posts to exactly the same depth, and allow for the thickness of roof poles—this takes time, especially when you are working in stony ground. Of course it can be set up quickly by the one-pole method but then it is no longer a shanty tent, and makes rather cramped quarters. For trips in which camp must be struck and made anew every day, an ordinary wagon sheet or square of waterproofed drilling is tent enough for anybody to bother with. But when spending a week or so in one place, in the woods, the shanty tent is the most comfortable and healthful abode that I ever tried. Mine has sheltered three. The tent, blanket and rubber poncho 4 × 6 ft., together weigh less than the sheepskin-and-canvas sleeping bags so much recommended for cold weather, and instead of a mere cocoon they afford a home where courtesies can be extended to a brother wanderer.

My camp ground being in the Ozark region, it goes without saying that there was plenty of flint and no browse. Alas, no browse! The drought had been so severe that the fallen leaves and twigs were dangerously inflammable, so I swept the ground carefully, cleared away the stones, smoothed the floor, dug hollows for hips and shoulders, raised a little mound of earth to supplement the diminutive pillow, and spread the poncho on the bare earth. Then came the army blanket, converted into a bag of double thickness by lapping it and securing the free side with strong safety pins. The pillow came next; and that was all there was to the bed making.

As the hollow was likely to prove a cold and draughty place to camp in, with only a fold of blanket between me and the bare ground, there was need of a good fireplace and plenty of night wood. Fortunately there was an axe in camp. In describing how to build a camp-fire, "Nessmuk" relates with gusto how he and a companion felled a 10 in. butternut with their hatchets and logged it up. The thing can be done by one man if necessary. The double-bitted hatchet, when made of surgical instrument steel, is indeed a marvel. It will bite deeper and hold an edge longer than any one would believe who has not handled the cunning little tool. But when backlogs are to be cut, most of us would prefer more weight and a full length halve.

The art of building a camp-fire has been expounded so well in "Woodcraft" that you would think nobody could blunder in it. Yet I have known two college graduates to follow the directions religiously, and, misled by the woodcut in the little volume, plant their logs 9 ft. in front of the tent. The fire was all right, but somehow those campers nearly froze. So it may not be out of place to give a few details, for every season a swarm of city boys makes for the woods who never spent a night in camp.

My backlogs were cut to 6 ft. lengths from a butternut 12 in. at the butt. The stakes were driven 5½ ft. from the footlog of the tent. The fire dogs or hand junks were bedded 3½ ft. apart, and I dug an oven 2½ × 2½ × 2 ft. deep between them, letting it fill with ashes and embers for the morrow's baking. The forestick[40] was matched to the dogs, which together with the chinks between the backlogs, were plastered with mud. A small pile of dry splinters and bark from a dead oak would soon yield coals for cooking supper.

The knack of fire-building consists, first, in selecting proper materials; second, in placing them so that air can circulate freely beneath and through them; and third, in not heaping on too much fuel at a time. For a cooking fire nothing is better than the sound and perfectly dry bark from a tree that has died on its stump. Moist or decayed stuff makes a smudge. For a quick meal, pluck a handful or so of dry twigs no thicker than your little finger from dead limbs or standing shoots. In winter, when all the boughs are wet, I have boiled water for tea with the dead stalks of weeds that stick up through the snow. A good camp cook will seldom smut the bottom of a kettle.

For a reliable camp-fire you must have some kind of backing to reflect the heat forward, and the higher it is the better. A big boulder or ledge of rock makes capital backing, for it retains heat and does not require rebuilding; but be careful to avoid calcareous rock, as it may burst and knock your head off. Get as close to the fire as you can with safety. My forestick was only 8 ft. in front of the tent, the roof of which was entirely unprotected, but by selecting such wood as did not crackle much I burned only one small hole in the roof in two weeks. Soft wood, or dry hard wood, makes poor fuel for the night, as it burns too fiercely, sends out showers of sparks and is soon spent. "Nessmuk" says: "The sweetest and wholesomest woods of the forest are in this order: black birch, hickory, sugar maple, yellow birch, red birch" (I quote from memory). To which it may be added that some woods, like cedar, poplar and gum, will scarcely burn at all when green.

It was late when I lugged the last stick to camp and stood my axe up against a tree. Shadows had fallen in Spook Hollow, and with them came a chill. The fun of outdoor life vanished with the sun. Night brought cold, dampness, loneliness, mystery, strange sounds and stranger silences.

Then came the miracle.

A match was struck. Up went a little puff of smoke, then a tongue of flame, presently a blaze. The phantoms vanished. There was light, warmth, cheer—the glorious comradry of fire.

The bark quickly burned to coals. I fried some ham, boiled coffee, and got out the bread and butter. It was a simple meal, but I lingered over it like a gourmet. What an appetite the woods life gives one!

Now to slick up. Dish washing is a nuisance, but even scullionry may be reduced to an art. The art is this: Throw away nearly all your dishes and keep the rest of them clean. A frying-pan, quart pail, hunting knife and spoon were all the utensils that figured at this meal; and the spoon was a superfluity—you can whittle out just as good a one in two minutes, and can throw it away when done with it. This latter attribute places the wooden spoon at the very head of camp luxuries.

I put a dry stick or two over the dogs, got them going and topped them off with a couple of green hickories. Then out came the calumet. It was a seasoned Missouri meerschaum, that is to say, a cob—best and sweetest of pipes, unbreakable, light and suggestively bucolic. Lolling back on the blanket, with the bright warmth flooding the tent, I worshipped the fire like any Parsee of old. Flames leaped up the backlogs and scales of bark burst away in miniature bombardments. The sap boiled out of the wood and sang merrily as it changed to steam. Now and then a sweet tremulo would come from some night bird in the dark thicket. The owls set up their screeching and faint rustlings in the leaves told of sharp eyes reconnoitering from the ledges above. I was alone with my fire and the gnomes of the woods. Fancy began to play. Time rolled back. Blessed be the magic that makes us boys again! Jolly old friends clustered round, each in his jolliest mood. We reviewed it all: the pranks and follies, the struggles and rebuffs, the fierce joys of peril by land and sea.

The pipe went out. I turned in. The fire died down until the little tent showed only a ghostly outline against the surrounding blackness. If some belted Mincke nigger,[41] plodding homeward along the crest of the ridge, caught a glimpse of Camp Nessmuk through the trees, it is small wonder if he broke into a run and panted to himself, "Fo' God, I shuah done seed de ha'nt!"

HORACE KEPHART.

Horace Kephart

Kephart, Horace, librarian, was born at East Salem, Juniata co., Penn., Sept. 8, 1862. He was a descendant of Nicholas Kephart, a Swiss, who emigrated to Pennsylvania in 1747. He was graduated at Lebanon Valley College in 1879, and afterwards took a postgraduate course in Boston and Cornell Universities. In the winter of 1884 he went abroad, spending most of his time in Italy, preparing a bibliography of Petrarch from the materials collected by Willard Fiske. Upon his return to America, he was for a short time in the library of Rutgers College, and afterwards spent four years in that of Yale University. In 1890 he accepted the position of librarian in the Mercantile Library, St. Louis, Mo. He is a valued contributor to periodicals on historical and bibliographical subjects. The library, under his management, promises to become one of the best equipped in the West. He is yet but a young man, and is destined to become pre-eminent in the ranks of his profession. As a classifier of books, he is unequaled.

From *The National Cyclopaedia of American Biography*, 1896

Sic Transit Gloria Arkansæ!

Allow me to thank Moreau for his kind inquiry and to assure him that the jacketed bullet in the .25–25 is all right when smashing effect is not wanted. I presume his objection is based on the supposed erosion of the barrel by the cupro-nickel[42] jacket. But I do not think that such bullets injure a gun when used in moderation with black powder. Such a combination does not wear a barrel like the new nitro cartridges with their sudden and violent pressures. Doubtless the scoring of barrels by these latter charges is caused more by the powder than by the bullet. The bores of high-power cannon are honeycombed by powder gas before the lands show any appreciable wear from the heavy projectiles.

The advantage is obvious of having two charges, both of which are factory loaded, cheap, and identical in trajectory and accuracy, but one of which will disembowel a squirrel, while the other will only drill a hole of its own diameter. Nelson, of our club, recently shot a turkey through lengthwise with a jacketed bullet from his .25-25 without spoiling an ounce of meat. I wish I could send you a photograph of that turkey roasting on a hardwood spit over our campfire. And I know you would enjoy the snapshot we took of McRaubschütz skinning a frozen 'coon; though it would curdle your blood to hear his remarks on the subject. But confound a camera! Last year the films tore; this year the shutter would not work. This was only one of the many misfortunes attending a "heap big hunt" which turned into a heap big fizzle.

The weather was vile. First it was hot—so hot that the wild bees came out in swarms and cleaned up in a twinkling the bear dope that I had fixed with infinite care at the only place where we found fresh sign. Then it rained—rained so hard that the ditch round my tepee overflowed, and I had to rise at 1 A.M. from the Red Sea to dig a Suez canal with an old trowel. Then it froze—froze everything eatable, drinkable, wearable; froze the fryingpan fast to a hackberry tree, and turned the kindling wood to icicles.

Did you ever turn out in this sinful world at two bells of the morning watch and

---

From *Shooting and Fishing*, December 31, 1896

try to start a fire in a snowdrift with a handful of chipped ice? Well, then—I leave it to you—were not all the other fellows snoring twice as hard as mortal men can possibly snore unless he is wide awake and putting his whole soul into it? This is the kind of thing that breeds anarchy and pessimism.

Moreover there was no mast. Last year, on the lower White, you could have loaded wagons anywhere with overcups and shellbarks big as walnuts. But on this trip I saw just one hickory nut in three weeks, while the oaks shed nothing but bitter mast, and very little of that. Last of all the sheriff came also. He wanted us to aid and abet in overruling the Supreme Court by paying him $17 apiece for the privilege of hunting something to eat. But we are law-abiding citizens, we all; so we lost that sheriff in a large and elegant canebrake ten miles from his mamma. That is to say, we went about our business, and if he followed, that is his business.

Seriously, the swamp counties of Arkansas have done themselves a lasting injury this fall by allowing sheriffs and deputies to blackmail northern hunters by pouncing on them with an old law framed only to discourage market hunting. I except Woodruff county, for I had a long talk with its sheriff, and he assured me that sportsmen who behaved like gentlemen were welcome in his precincts. An Indiana man showed me a license receipted for $12.50, signed by a deputy, for which he paid said deputy just $5. And he was growling because a party camped nearby got off for $2.40 apiece. You can imagine from this what kind of returns were made to the county clerk.

We met a character on this trip in the person of Patterson, the bear hunter, who lives in a shanty on the old military road just south of the Cross county line. Perhaps I should say his family dwells there; for Patterson lives in the saddle. The spurs never leave his boots till the leather wears out, and we have it on excellent authority that the only time Patterson ever was seen behind a plow the rowels were clinking on his heels.

This picturesque backwoodsman was born in 1812. Since early in the forties he has lived in the St. Francis swamps, never retiring when the overflow drives everything else but his bears to the highlands, and all round him is an inland sea. One of our party asked his wife if she did not get lonesome through the long, rainy winter; but she answered in the drawl of the genuine swamper:

"No; we all don't like to be crowded."

When we met Patterson he was returning from town, where he had marketed some fur, and had indulged in a protracted bout with liquor and the law. Drunk as a lord, but still gripping his Winchester and riding like a centaur, he burst through a thicket with the rebel yell, and reined up before us shouting:

"Hi there! Who are you all, an' where are you a-goin'?"

In two minutes we were commanded to right-about-face and march straight back to spend the night with him. The house, the horses, the whole county were ours, and we should all go after "bar" in the morning. It took all our politeness and firmness to evade this hospitality, but we knew that the old man's head would need soaking on the morrow, and visitors would be embarrassing. However, we drew much information about the country from its lord and master, who is reported to have killed over 300 bears in the big swamp adjoining his residence.

If there be anything in the modern theory of immunizing from disease by absorbing plenty of microbes, Patterson is a fine illustration of it. More than half a century he has dwelt in the swamps, breathing malaria, eating soda biscuit and sowbelly, drinking bacteria and the vilest whisky on earth, wearing cotton and buckskin, hunting bears by day and 'coons by night; but at eighty-four he still rides horses to death, and is tough as the gum trees that rise in the wilderness round him.

In case any one of your readers wants to swap a '73 model .32-20 Winchester (nothing else will do) for a live bear, let him address Patterson the bear hunter, Edgar, St. Francis county, Ark. The bear was captured this fall, and is a likely cub. Arrangements should be made to have the animal crated, as I do not think Patterson would deign to nail up a mere pet bear.

H. K.
ST. LOUIS, Mo.

A Poor Shot

In his generous acknowledgement of a very trifling favor, Mr. Hough[43] has alluded to a little series of mine, relating to the history of the American rifle, which recently appeared in *Shooting and Fishing*. My investigations were prompted by observing that target shooters nowadays have little faith in the marksmanship of the old frontiersmen. I suspected that this incredulity was due to indiscriminate novel reading and to yarns spun by the Sunday newspapers, rather than to accurate knowledge of historical facts. To test the matter I made a study of contemporary evidence and reached the following conclusion:

"There were liars before Ananias; but there were gentlemen, and crack shots too, long before you and I, my good fellow, cut our teeth."

Mr. Hough's delightful reminiscences make me think of a practical demonstration of this latter fact, with which I was recently favored and which impressed me more than any possible array of screeds and scrolls. It happened thus:

My father and mother came to visit us. My father was born and bred in the wilderness of western Pennsylvania, and still takes a keen interest in woodcraft, though his occupation has confined him to office work for many years. Knowing that he would enjoy a tramp in the woods, I took a day off and we went out to Mincke.

My squirrel rifle was at the gunsmith's, and the other hunting rifles were too powerful for such game as we might see, so I took along my target rifle. Father examined it curiously. He had never seen such a weapon. The wind gauge and vernier particularly impressed him.

"Well, well," he would say, "what improvements they have made since I was a boy! Just look at those sights! I wonder what Uncle George would have said about them! He used to shoot pretty well with the old flintlock; but, dear me, our rifles were very crude affairs in those days. Do you like such a short, stubby barrel? You do! Well, I guess it's all right with those fine sights. We used to prefer a 4 ft. barrel; but we were away back in the woods and didn't know much."

From *Forest and Stream*, April 10, 1897

He kept it up on that strain all the way to Minckc. I was sorry for the old gentleman. It made me feel mean to be enjoying all these improvements when his youth had been so hard and poor. The contrast must be pathetic to him. When we reached the woods, I thought to cheer him up a bit by remarking:

"Yes, the finish of our rifles nowadays may be finer, but I suppose the old muzzle-loaders would shoot just as straight."

"I don't know—I don't know," he replied sadly.

"Well, you didn't often miss with them."

"No, not often. But we didn't dare miss; powder was too scarce."

"Lead too, I suppose."

"Well, not so scarce as powder, for we would use it over again."

"Use it over again?"

"Certainly. When we had enough powder to shoot at a mark, which was seldom, we would always put the mark on a tree and chop the bullets out. Even in shooting at deer, the bullet would generally lodge against the skin or on a bone, and we would run it over again. No, I guess you youngsters can shoot much better than we did, for you have plenty of ammunition to waste in target shooting; and then you have such fine sights—I wouldn't even know how to use them."

"Oh, yes, you would. Here, I'll tack this target on a tree and we'll try a few shots."

"No, no; you do the shooting. I can't shoot."

"Of course you can. Just try. You'll soon get the hang of those sights."

"Why, boy, I haven't fired a rifle since the war. And I never was anything of a shot. Zeke and Abe [two of his brothers] could beat me any time, and neither of them could shoot like father."

"Grandfather was a good shot, then?"

"Yes, pretty good. We had to live on deer and bear sometimes. He often shot them right in our little clearing, and once I saw him shoot a very large panther from our doorway. Yes, he was a good shot, though his brother George was better. George was a great hunter, and quite celebrated as a marksman. But I never took much to hunting, and was always counted a rather poor shot."

I wished now that I had said nothing about target shooting. It was thoughtless of me to have suggested such a thing. He was an old man, and had not fired a shot in thirty years. I knew him to be the soul of candor, and that he always meant precisely what he said. Of course he could not shoot now. Would the result only humiliate him by proving his failing sight and nerve?

"All right, I'll shoot, and you can score for me. It wouldn't be fair to have you shoot with a gun you have never used."

"Well, I'll try those sights anyway," he replied, "just to find out how they work."

Here was spirit. He wouldn't back down from a challenge—for so he had construed it—even in the face of certain defeat.

The target was up. I fired, and nipped the bull at 10 o'clock.

He took the rifle, threw his arm well out, and raised the piece, but complained that he could not see.

"Bring the peep closer to your eye—there, that's the way. Now don't flinch when you press the trigger."

I was rather nervous for him and gave him all sorts of good advice.

"Be careful, father, that is a set trigger."

"Boy," he replied, somewhat sternly, "I never used any other kind."

Then, for the first time, an uneasy suspicion crept over me that perhaps I was unnecessarily solicitous about the old gentleman.

Crack!

I was watching him closely. Blink? Flinch? Not a bit. He hadn't been brought up that way.

I went to the target. He had a line shot 3 in. below the bullseye.

I took my turn and again got in the black.

He fired and shot into his first hole.

"That's funny," he said, "my sight was touching the mark."

He had been holding the aperture as if it were a pinhead. I explained that the bullseye should be centered in that little hole.

Firing again, I missed by 1 in.

He shot deep into the black.

I began to feel uncomfortable. I had plenty of trouble on my hands now, and got down to work. He kept right on making bullseyes, talking all the time in his quiet, serious way about "I never was 'counted a good shot—Zeke could generally beat me—but father was a good hand with a rifle," and so on.

At the end of the tenth round I was a point in the lead, but he was steadily gaining, and if we had kept the game up a little longer I would certainly have been beaten. Father had evidently expected to see me shoot better, but he was too much of a gentleman to say so. His work amazed me; but he kept on apologizing for it, and the worst of the matter was that his humility was perfectly sincere.

By and by he strolled up the hill, while I sat down on a log and had a big think all to myself.

No, he never was 'counted a good shot—Zeke could beat him, so could Abe—his father was better than any of them—and Uncle George was a real marksman. "But my! What improvements you have made!"

HORACE KEPHART.

ST. LOUIS.

Pennsylvania's Part in the Winning of the West

An Address delivered before the Pennsylvania Society of St. Louis, December 12, 1901.

[Excerpt]

THE FIRST PIONEERS

In his fascinating history of "The Winning of the West," Theodore Roosevelt says that "The two facts of most importance to remember in dealing with our pioneer history are, first, that the western portions of Virginia and the Carolinas were peopled by an entirely different stock from that which had long existed in the tidewater regions of those colonies; and, secondly, that except for those in the Carolinas who came from Charleston (comparatively few), the immigrants of this stock were mostly from the north, from their great breeding-ground and nursery in western Pennsylvania."

We find here an interesting problem. How came it to pass that a community of Quakers, non-resisting, intensely domestic, circumspect, loathing everything that smacked of adventure, should have formed the "breeding-ground and nursery" of as warlike, and restless, and desperately venturesome a race as this world has seen?

We have a favorite saying that "America is an asylum for the oppressed of all nations." But America was not always so. Scarcely had the Puritans landed at Plymouth before they began seeking heretics. The Cavaliers of the south, more tolerant of venial sins, admitted other sects to their Canaan, but on condition that they pay tithes to support an episcopal clergy. In most of the colonies a Catholic was little better than a witch, and likely to be attainted with treason as well. If to a heretical creed the unlucky immigrant added a foreign tongue, this stamped him as a boor, and his case was hard indeed. But the Quakers "unlike many other martyrs, did not become persecutors in turn." Pennsylvania was an asylum for the oppressed.

St. Louis, Bureau of Publicity of the Louisiana Purchase Exposition, 1902.

The Pennsylvania-Germans

And in Europe there were many oppressed. About the time that the Quakers began to settle Pennsylvania—say in 1682 or 1683—an immigration of Germans set into this region from the Rhine valley and the highlands of south Germany and Switzerland. These were the fore-runners of an immense tide of persecuted Germans which soon swept into the Quaker territory, by invitation of Penn, and established a new ethnic division of our people, to be known thenceforth as Pennsylvania-Dutch. They were not Dutch, and repudiated the name; but it is now as well Americanized as "corn" for maize, or "buffalo" for bison, and is not without justification on linguistic and ethnological grounds.

The first German immigrants were sectarians, who, like the Quakers, refused to take oaths or bear arms. Their descendants gave some trouble on this account during the revolution and the civil war, and this policy of non-resistance on the part of a few early sectarians brought an unmerited stigma upon the whole body of Pennsylvania-Dutch. The truth is that the mass of German immigrants had no such scruples, being for the most part Lutherans or Reformed, and that they furnished as large a percentage of soldiers in the wars that followed as any other race.

We all know the story of Putnam leaving his plow in the furrow to join the army; but we should also know that the Pennsylvania-Dutchman Muhlenberg left his pulpit to accept a colonelcy under Washington, and that he dismissed his congregation with the words: "There is a time to preach, and a time to pray; but there is also a time to fight, and that time has now come." We should know that the first outside colonists who arrived to assist their New England brethren at the siege of Boston were Captain Nagel's company of Berks County Dutchmen.

The Pennsylvania-Germans printed the first Bible in a European tongue that appeared from an American press. They were the first to suggest the abolition of slavery, asking in their quaint petition (1688), "Have not these negers as much right to fight for their freedom as you have to keep them slaves?"

These Germans were the very type and pattern of husbandmen. Shrewdly picking out the fertile limestone valleys at the foot of the Alleghanies, they soon monopolized the whole farming region from Easton on the Delaware, past Allentown, Reading, Lebanon, Lancaster, and York. This crescent formed at the time the western frontier of Pennsylvania. It was the Quakers' buffer against the Indians. It was the westernmost settlement of British subjects in America. These "Dutchmen" were not mere Indian traders. They had come to stay; and they did stay, stanch possessors of the soil, and founders of a new fatherland.

But there was another reason than limestone soil why the early Germans preferred the frontier. The society of our seaboard was aristocratic, no less in New England than in Pennsylvania and Virginia. The Pennsylvania-Dutch were nothing if not democratic, in a social sense; so they tarried not on the seacoast.

Some of them had at first settled in New York, but they soon became discontented with the treatment they received from aristocratic proprietors and officials, who regarded them as mere beasts of burden, and they moved in a body into Pennsylvania.

The Scotch-Irish

Shortly after this tide of German immigration set into Pennsylvania, another and very different class of foreigners began to arrive. These were the Scotch-Irish, or Ulstermen of Ireland. When James I., in 1607, confiscated the estates of the Irish in six counties of Ulster, he turned them over on long leases to a body of Scotch and English Presbyterians. The career of these immigrants was at first prosperous, though necessarily turbulent. But as their leases began to expire, persecutions followed that proved unbearable, and the Scotch-Irish began emigrating to America. As Froude says, "In the two years that followed the Antrim evictions, thirty thousand Protestants left Ulster for a land where there was no legal robbery, and where those who sowed the seed could reap the harvest."

The early Scotch-Irish were a brave but hot-headed race, as might be expected of a people who for a century had been planted amid hostile Irish, and latterly had suffered the persecutions of Charles I. Justin Winsor describes them as having "all that excitable character which goes with a keen-minded adherence to original sin, total depravity, predestination, and election," and as seeing "no use in an Indian but to be a target for their bullets." On one occasion they even took up arms against the Quakers, and marched to chastise them in Philadelphia. "The Quakers," says Fisher, "were ready for them, and had no hesitation in fortifying Philadelphia; for the chance of a shot at a Scotch-Irish Presbyterian was too much for their scruples of religion."

Neither did the Scotch-Irish at first assimilate with the Germans. The latter, wherever colonized by themselves, were a plodding, undemonstrative, rather think-witted folk, close-fisted, and taking little interest in public affairs that did not concern either their church or their pocket-books. They were slow to anger, and would take a good deal of abuse, but tenacious for their rights, and could fight like bulldogs when aroused. The Scotch-Irish were quick-witted and quick-tempered, rather visionary, imperious and aggressive. I mention these traits of the early immigrants because they had much to do with the events that followed. And I do not wish it to be thought that we are gathered merely to sing the praises of our ancestors. Mutual-admiration societies are a nuisance and a bore. If we are to get any good out of history, we must face the truth in all its phases, whether it be complimentary to ourselves or not.

The Scotch-Irish, being by tradition and habit a border people, pushed to the extreme western fringe of settlement. They were not over-solicitous about the quality of soil. When Arthur Lee of Virginia was telling Doctor Samuel Johnson of a colony of Scotch who had settled upon a particularly sterile tract in western Virginia, and had expressed his wonder that they should do so, Johnson replied, "Why sir, all barrenness is comparative; the Scotch will never know that it is barren."

So it was that these people became, in turn, our frontiersmen. Immediately they began to clash with the Indians, and there followed a long series of border wars, waged with extreme ferocity, in which it is sometimes hard to say which race was most to blame. One thing, however, is certain: if any race was ordained to exterminate the Indians, that race was the Scotch-Irish.

Pennsylvania's March Southwestward

When the land west of the Susquehanna was first opened for settlement, the Germans did not fancy it, because the soil was rocky and poor. The Scotch-Irish entered the mountains, but even they were not attracted in large numbers by such rugged country. The chief overflow of Pennsylvania emigrants passed southwestward into western Maryland and the Shenandoah valley. Fertile bottom-lands lay in this direction, and the Germans were not slow to find them. The first house in western Virginia was erected by the Pennsylvania-German Joist Hite, who established a colony of his people near the future site of Winchester. A majority of those who settled in the eastern part of the Shenandoah valley were Pennsylvania-Germans. "So completely did they occupy the country along the north and south branches of that river," says a local historian, "that the few stray English, Irish, or Scotch settlers among them did not sensibly affect the homogenousness of the population." Here, as in Pennsylvania, the Germans sought out the rich bottom-lands and settled on them for good, while the Scotch-Irish pushed a little to the west of them and occupied more exposed positions. There were representatives of other races along the frontier, English, Huguenots, Irish—even some Quakers were among them; but the Germans and Scotch-Irish predominated.

Among those who made this long "trek" from Pennsylvania southwestward were the ancestors of David Crockett, Samuel Houston, John C. Calhoun, "Stonewall" Jackson, and Abraham Lincoln.

Settlement of Western Carolina

As the Germans were prolific, liked large farms, and were steadily recruited from the old country, they were always furnishing a surplus of young men and new-comers to people the west. They were not so much given to individual enterprise as the Scotch, but it was not unusual for them to form a colony and flit to some distant Eden, settling upon it like a swarm of bees. In this manner there went on a gradual but sure progress of northern peoples across the Potomac, up the Shenandoah, across the Staunton, the Dan, and the Yadkin, even to Savannah. The proportion of Pennsylvania-Dutch in this migration is commonly underestimated. The archivist of North Carolina, the late William L. Saunders, Secretary of State, says that "to Lancaster and York counties, in Pennsylvania, North Carolina owes more of her population than to any other known part of the world," and he adds, "never were there better citizens, and certainly never better soldiers." He calls attention to the interesting fact that when the North Carolina boys of Scotch-Irish and Pennsylvania-Dutch descent followed Lee into Pennsylvania in the Gettysburg campaign, they were returning to the homes of their ancestors, by precisely the same route that those ancestors had taken in going south.

A Distinct People

I dwell somewhat upon the manner in which the western part of the southern colonies was peopled, because it was from this region that the trans-Alleghany movement began, and from which came the great majority of our pioneers. Kentucky was settled from Virginia, and Tennessee from Virginia and Carolina; but these settlers were mostly of Pennsylvania origin. So when we speak of the Virginians who settled Kentucky, or the Carolinians who founded Tennessee, or of Morgan's Virginia riflemen in the revolution, we should not confound them with the typical Virginians or Carolinians of the coast. They were neither Cavaliers nor Poor Whites, but a radically distinct and even antagonistic people, who are appropriately called the Roundheads of the South. Aristocracy was their bugbear. They had little or nothing to do with slavery, detested the state church, loathed tithes, and distrusted all authority save that of conspicuous merit and natural justice. "There is but one thing I fear on earth," remarked one of them to the French traveller Collot, "and that is what men call their laws and their justice." The intense individualism of our pioneers was the first distinctive characteristic that they developed. It entered their blood the very moment that they landed on American soil. The first English resident of Philadelphia was Edward Drinker, who was born in a cabin near the present corner of Walnut and Second streets at a time when the site of Philadelphia was occupied by only a few

Indians, Swedes and Hollanders, besides his father's family. He saw William Penn come to Pennsylvania, and lived to see the city of Philadelphia arise on the ground where he had hunted deer. He saw both the beginning and the end of the British empire in Pennsylvania. And though he had been a subject of the king for 95 years, when the royal proclamations were issued curtailing the liberties of Americans, the old man bought them all and gave them to his great-grandsons to make kites of.

This spirit of independence entered into the economic and social life of the pioneers, as well as into their politics. It is in sharp contrast to the semi-communal life of the French habitants of Canada and Louisiana. The French looked to the government for everything; the Americans were never so happy as when the government let them alone. The first agricultural experiments in Massachusetts and in Virginia were communal, but they were utter failures. The system of large landed proprietorship attempted in New York and elsewhere was also most repugnant to the better class of settlers. We have seen that the manorial grants of New York drove the pioneer element from the province, because their ambition was to become owners and rulers, not tenants of the soil. The strong and even violent independence that made these men forsake all the comforts of civilization and prefer the wild freedom of the border, was fanned at times into turbulence and riot; but it blazed forth at a happy time for this country when our liberties were imperilled.

The Man of the West

Both the Scotch-Irish and the Germans were clannish people so long as they remained in compact settlements of their own. They merely perpetuated each its own type. But when the more adventurous spirits of both races struck out for themselves and became pioneers in new lands, they were forced to amalgamate. In the extreme frontier settlements there was more intermarrying than historians have credited. That it produced a better type than either forebear is plain enough to those who study family records. These two human ores were picked from far distant mines. The one was hard and the other tough. Fate cast them together into the glowing crucible of wilderness life, and they fuzed, and ran together, and were cast into a new form of manhood.

Even where blood was not crossed, a generation of frontier life changed Scotchman and German, Englishman and Huguenot, alike into a new and distinct character—the Man of the West. The romantic and hazardous career of the backwoodsmen bred in them a peculiar combination of daring and shiftiness, activity and cool endurance. Theirs was the satisfaction of overcoming trial and peril, and it made them a masterful, self-confident people. They had a scorn of conventions and of restraint. Law, to them, was no law unless it was based upon the primal rights of man.

And the wilderness itself reacted upon these men and stamped upon them something of its own openness, naturalness, simplicity. As the pelage and habits of animals vary with the climate, and new traits of character arise from change of environment, so the child of civilization turned out upon the wilderness to fight singly against strange odds, develops qualities unknown among those who lead a tamer existence. Pioneers, at the start, are made of no common clay. The weaklings of society are eliminated from frontier life. None but bold and sanguine spirits dare embark in such adventure; none but the hardy and self-reliant can endure its vicissitudes. The faint-hearted and irresolute, the torpid and effeminate, must seek quieter asylums. We have, then, at first muster, a picked class of men, active, self-centered, buoyant, plucky to the backbone, whipped on by hazard and spurred by the explorer's zeal. The utter freedom and loneliness of forest life then tend to accentuate personalities that the friction of cities might abrade to a level of sameness. The abrupt change of habits, the recovery of lost arts of wildcraft, the invention of fresh expedients, the imperative call upon dormant faculties that civilized man is unconscious of possessing, bring out new characteristics, as muscles commonly unused become conspicuous in a Sandow.

It was thus that the Man of the West was born and nurtured in the Appalachian valleys. And to this wild life of the border, more, perhaps, than to any other feature in our history, may be traced those traits of sleepless vigilance and restless energy that are the most distinctive traits of American character today. Wherever you meet an American, whether on land or sea, in the arctics or the tropics, he is marked from all other races by his ceaseless activity. "To the true American," says Sargeant, "repose is stagnation and rest a bore. His nature demands occupation of an exciting kind. The man who loafs, the tramp and the flaneur, who is the fashionable variety of the species, are all anomalies in our civilization; they exist, but under protest; they are freaks, not types; sports, and not the natural growth of our soil."

His Love of Elbow-Room

To conquer the wilderness as the early westerners conquered it, with ax and rifle, man must be born anew. He must re-learn an art so ancient that it has long since been forgotten by urban society—the art of wildcraft. The best of city-bred men, if left suddenly alone in the wilderness, is soon dazed, bewildered, lost. Around him on all sides is an inexhaustible store-house from which a genuine woodsman would soon procure fire, food, shelter, and clothing, ease and contentment; but this heir of all book-learning of the ages has no key to unlock it. He exists for a few days in terror and then miserably perishes; for, if perchance found by some rambling hunters before his life is extinct, he is likely to return to society a gibbering idiot, wrecked by experiences which, to one who was in closer touch with nature, would have been a mere holiday-excursion.

Through ignorance we underestimate both the skill and the manly virtues essential to a pioneer. The man who can enter an unmapped forest such as once covered this country—enter it with no companion, and with no outfit save what he carries on his own back, and can explore it, and dwell therein, and can wrest from the blind forces and hidden stores of nature both a livelihood and independence, is no ordinary mortal. And we underestimate the finer qualities of his soul. Such work can only be done by one who is not only in touch with, but a part of, nature; by one who loves the free forest life with a passion more intense than patriotism, and stronger than ambition or the greed of wealth. The pioneer spirit, the force that really won the west, cannot be understood until we realize how deep and overmastering was this love of nature for her own sake that was the ruling passion of such men as Daniel Boone. . . .

The Far West

If the Marietta venture[44] was our first great land-job, it was not the last. The heroic age of the central west soon passed away. Men were no longer wanted to assert their independence of kings and castes, nor to hew their own way into the wilderness and make laws for themselves.

Those in whom the old pioneer spirit survived were "crowded out." First among the Kentuckians to leave were Boone and his sons, the Callaways, the Coopers, and others of the old stock around Boonesborough who were to Americanize the frontier of Missouri. After Boone went Henry Von Phul, and other Kentuckians of Pennsylvania stock who were among the first American residents of St. Louis. After him went also the father of Kit Carson,—and Kit himself was accompanied by many another youngster who in later times was to leave his name on some peak or pass or valley of the far-distant Rockies. Indeed, if we call the roll of American scouts, explorers, trappers, Indian fighters of the far west—of the men like John Colter, Robert McClellan, John Day, the Sublettes, Jim Bridger, Bill Williams, Joe Week, Kit Carson, and their ilk, who trapped and fought over nearly every nook and cranny of the far west, from the Canadian divide to the "starving Gila"—we shall find that most of them were of the old Shenandoah-Kentucky stock that made its first trail from Pennsylvania across the Appalachians.

A Tribute to the Pioneers

"The country beyond the Alleghanies," says the historian, "was first won and settled by the backwoodsmen themselves, acting under their own leaders, obeying their own desires, and following their own methods. They were a marked and peculiar people. The good and evil traits in their character were such as naturally belonged to a strong, harsh, and homely race, which, with all its shortcomings, was nevertheless bringing a tremendous work to a triumphant conclusion. The backwoodsmen were above all things characteristically American; and it is fitting that the two greatest and most typical of all Americans should have been respectively a sharer and an outcome of their work. Washington himself passed the most important years of his life heading the westward movement of his people. Clad in the traditional dress of the backwoodsmen, in tasselled hunting-shirt and fringed leggings, he led them to battle against the French and Indians, and helped to clear the way for the American advance. The only other man who in the American roll of honor stands by the side of Washington, was born when the distinctive work of the pioneers had ended; and yet he was bone of their bone and flesh of their flesh; for from the loins of this gaunt frontier folk spring mighty Abraham Lincoln."

It is more than a coincidence that this tribute to the Man of the West should have come from one who himself is passing through the gamut of American possibilities; from one who, clad in buckskin and with rifle in hand, has known the stirring life of a western frontiersman, and who today leads the nation to new and wider destinies; from that most American of present-day Americans, Theodore Roosevelt.

We have seen that it took a peculiar people to win the west; that their chief peculiarity was a passion for independence; that they went west to realize it, where old laws and customs had not been established: that they chose the hardest and most perilous route; and that they did so because easier trails could only be entered by first bowing to aristocracy and accepting servile positions.

"What man would live coffined with brick and stone,
Imprisoned from the influences of air,
And cramped with selfish landmarks everywhere.
When all before him stretches furrowless and lone
The unmapped prairie none can fence or own?"

"What man with men would push and altercate,
Piecing out crooked means to crooked ends,
When he can have the skies and woods for friends,
Snatch back the rudder of his undismantled fate,
And in himself be ruler, church, and state?"

The spirit of the American pioneer, thus voiced by Lowell,[45] burned deep and unquenchable in the hearts of those exiles from an older civilization who first braved the hardships of western life. Though poor to destitution when they landed, they would not be hirelings nor inferiors. They sought freedom, and air, and elbow-room, the right to command and the power to enforce each his own will, and to reap what he had sown. For this they hewed their westward path, and felled and grubbed-out the little clearings of their homesteads. For this, with steeled nerves and steady eyes, they aimed their rifles at beast or savage, and "called the shot." They sought to realize in sober truth that *Liberty, Equality, Fraternity!* which has so often served as a party shibboleth, so seldom as anything more. And they did realize it, with an intensity and completeness such as but one other civilized race has enjoyed since the world began.

We have no longer those "vast woods and un-man-stifled places" that still existed when Lowell sounded the slogan of the pioneer; and in despondent moods we may regret the passing of an age so full of opportunities for the self-confident and strong.

But in crowding together we have not merely polished the exterior of our lives; we have softened human-nature to its core. What we now call our laws and our justice are not such as once made rebels and Ishmaelites of honest men. Our immigrant no longer wears the collar of a redemptioner; no longer is sold as an indentured servant to pay the cost of his passage across the sea. We have learned that society has duties to the humble, and that it can curb the proud.

In the old days Pennsylvania fostered man's high desire for independence until it grew strong enough to overturn the ancient order and dared make a new and better one. But she did more than this. Into the worn-out body of society she breathed the new spirit of justice toward all and of malice toward none. She first made it tolerable for men of all creeds and conditions to dwell peaceably together. And not the west only, but all the world, owes to our mother-state this pioneer example of mutual forbearance and brotherly love.

Horace Kephart Is Held for Observation

FORMER LIBRARIAN ARRESTED AS HE WAS WALKING TOWARD EADS BRIDGE, AFTER WRITING WEIRD LETTER

Horace Kephart, aged 42 years, residing at 1821 Kennett place, who was succeeded on February 1 last as librarian of the Mercantile library by William L. R. Gifford, after he had held the position for fourteen years, was arrested at 2 o'clock yesterday afternoon and placed in the observation ward at the city hospital, pending an investigation into his mental condition.

His arrest was brought about by his peculiar actions in Marre's saloon, 518 Washington avenue. After buying a glass of beer there yesterday, it is said, he engaged the bartender, Edward Wasen, in conversation, during the course of which he placed in Wasen's hands a lengthy letter, written in pencil on rough wrapping paper, in which he expressed an intention of committing suicide. Police Officer Mannion was at once notified. After following Kephart a block or so along Washington avenue toward Eads bridge the officer stopped him and called an ambulance.

Kephart is a well-known magazine writer, and is said to be an authority on woodcraft. He is a graduate of both Yale and Cornell universities. Following is a copy of the letter Kephart handed to Wasen:

Kephart's Letter.

To-day—The next day after I met you here.

Anderson: I have been driven insane. It is a case without parallel, so far as I know, in causes. I shall take my life to-day—possibly very soon. I have not been driven to it by troubles of any kind whatsoever—all reports that may be circulated after my death to the contrary notwithstanding.

I die, as I lived, loving, in all truth and sincerity, my wife, my poor children, my father and mother, and respecting my friends, and of all of them, you in chief. You know, old man, what I always thought of you—that is enough.

From *St. Louis Globe-Democrat*, March 25, 1904

I have little to leave. Please go to 1821 Kennett place. Please take charge of my belongings. Give Mrs. Lieber $10 that I would owe her by April 10, and the proceeds of the residue to my wife. She is still at Ithaca. I know you will do it.

I have been persecuted, as no one in history, so far as I know, has ever been. The story, if published, would be considered the ravings of an imbecile. I would so consider them myself, if I were any one else reading a similar statement. But they are absolute facts. I have left in my room a manuscript statement, hurriedly written last night under circumstances of stress and strain that I honestly believe to be without parallel.

I trust that you may find them. Mrs. Lieber has the first four pages; the rest are in my desk. They may be spirited away; for the devils who have driven me to this are more than mortal and more fiendish than any demons of mythology. They have taken a man who never did any one intentional harm. They have deliberately and by slow torture driven him mad. I am at this writing mad, in the sense that I see all hope of existing more than a few minutes with mind enough to write a clear statement is hopeless. Therefore I do this the best I can. I trust that you, who know me, and my loved ones, who know me better, will see and know by the manner in which it is written that it is still entirely rational, the last effort of a man who, though himself mentally normal, realizes that the hour of madness will soon strike. It is the last and desperate effort of one driven by devilish torments quite outside of any human failings to tell those he loves that he did his best. In spite of worse than hell, I die with my boots on.

Of the future to myself I neither know nor fear anything. In case the manuscript at my room shall not be found, I will simply say that there is an agency, whether human or superhuman I do not know, that possesses the power of not only sending all manner of messages (most unspeakably devilish) to any one whomsoever they wish, in any locality, and under any circumstances, and of placing their victim into instant communication with them by thought alone. They can not at once, but can eventually, by thought or suggestion, drive him to such extremities that he becomes, not mentally unbalanced if of strong will, but within plain sight of certain doom; that is to say, of an insanity that would be simply horrible. The method by which this is done I, of course, do not fully understand; my budding ideas as to its possible source and qualities are very rightly given in the manuscript at my room, a manuscript that would have been developed further had I a few hours more left.

In my case, I presume in others, although of others I know nothing, it is the choosing at random of a victim entirely innocent of harm and making of him a specimen for mental and moral vivisection. The whole thing is indescribably horrible. I have fought as best I could. I have preserved my will power and my reasoning faculties to this moment unimpaired, but the end will be here within a few minutes. So far as I can see, neither innocence, will nor nerve can long withstand it. It is quite possible that the powers of this infamous agency extend to circulating calumnies about their victims after death. I can only say not only that I am wholly innocent, but that the fiends refuse to even tell me of any fault of which I may be charged.

NO ESCAPE FROM TORMENTS

They accompany their victims everywhere, by day and by night; give him no rest, torture him in indescribable forms, and shortly drive him to suicide—refusing even the merciful intervention of a death stroke from themselves.

Neither insomnia, alcoholism, drug habit nor anything else that is commonly considered a contributory agent to suicide has anything whatever to do with the case. It is simply vivisection, spiritual rather than mental, and ending in—not madness in the sense of losing one's reason, but the desperation of one who, knocking the key log from a log jam and seeing the mass break toward him, dashes his hat at it and goes under. You can conceive that a man in such case might and doubtless would be entirely rational to the last. My love to all. Good-by.

Horace Kephart.

Horace Kephart, 42, 1821 Kennett place.

It is supposed that the Anderson to whom Kephart addressed his letter is William H. H. Anderson, actuary at the Mercantile library.

FAMILY IN THE EAST

Mrs. Lieber, who lives at 1821 Kennett place with her father, John Moran, and her brother, Edward Moran, stated last night that Mrs. Kephart and her six children were in the East somewhere. Mr. and Mrs. Kephart visited Mrs. Lieber about a year ago, and rented a room for Mr. Kephart. They stated that Mrs. Kephart was going away to place her children in school. Since that time Mr. Kephart has frequently received letter[s] from Ithaca, N. Y., Mrs. Lieber says.

While he has always been a recluse, since residing at her house, Mrs. Lieber said, he first showed evidences of insanity Wednesday night, when he aroused the household, claiming that burglars were about to enter the house. He also spoke about a document that he had been writing, which he wanted Mr. Moran to take charge of, lest it should get away. The document contained much wild talk of ghosts and spirits. He was finally quieted. Yesterday morning he again awakened the household by his cries for help. He was quieted, and about 9:30 o'clock left the house, after begging pardon for having created a disturbance. He seemed to realize all that had taken place, and insisted that he had been visited by ghosts.

Mr. Kephart's parents are said to be living, though their address is not known.

Looking for a New Place

There were six of us who sought friendly gloom on the piazza for an after-supper smoke. In those quaint little hotels of the South they still preserve the institution of supper at 6 p.m. Through open windows came the sweet tinkling of a piano and the hum of ladies and children. Now, it was not selfishness that drove us six into retreat; it was a matter of clothes. Trains on southern byroads have a recurrent mania for breaking down. Ours had compelled us to foot it three miles to the nearest town, and held our baggage stalled for the night. Some of us were more presentable than others, being clad in the habiliments of civilization; others, including myself, had come straight from the mountains, and we were a sight! Neither the geologist, the timber-buyer, nor your servant who writes, had a coat to his back. Our khaki was of the earth earthy, and we sported several tenpenny nails in lieu of buttons.

As the dusk settled deeper on the piazza we lazily dropped another convention or two. The geologist hunched his chair forward, tilted it backward, and preserved his equilibrium by planting his feet on the top of the railing. There is something in this prohibited position that conduces to digestion and to the enjoyment of a good cigar. It is sedative, alterative, anhidriotic, and contagious. Up went another pair of feet. Conversation began to purl. Ere long the sky-line changed into a range of impossibly steep and narrow mountains which, on keener inspection, might be resolved into twelve human feet, masculine, and clad in anything from hob-nailed bullskin to vici kid.

"Do you know," murmured the traveler on my right, "do you know that whenever I see one of you fellows I envy you?"

Not knowing precisely what species he meant by "you fellows," I answered with the inevitable Yankee "Why?"

"Because you are free!"

How he rolled that blessed word on his tongue, and how I took to him at once!

"Why not go thou and do likewise?"

From *Recreation*, December 1908

"I! Did you ever live in New York?"

"Not guilty."

"Lord, lord!" prayed the Manhattaner, "if I could only rig myself up like you and strike out of the hurly-burly into no-man's land—if I could do that even for a couple of weeks every year, I'd be game for the rest, all right, all right."

"Can't spare the time, eh?"

"Yes, I get two weeks every summer; but what does that amount to when a fellow's income is small?"

"What's the matter with the Adirondacks?"

"Overrun—and it costs too much. I can't afford to blow in five dollars a day for 'camp life.'"

I whistled. "What do you suppose it has cost me to live in the woods these past six months?"

"Oh, down here, maybe two dollars a day."

"Twelve-and-a-half cents a day, sir!"

The traveler's feet came down and he stared. Likewise the priest on my left, whether suddenly conscious of his own impropriety, or nervously uncertain of the company he was keeping, took down his feet with a bump.

"Ah, I see; you lived on game and fish."

"Not much. Game was out of season most of the time, except squirrels. Ever eat squirrels six meals straight?"

"No-o. But then you had fish."

"Plenty—too plenty. Ever eat trout six meals straight?"

"No."

"Neither do woods people. The only wild meat that a man can eat day in and day out, without palling, is venison of the deer tribe, and that we have only two months in the year—not always then. No, we buy our provisions, and we pay more for them than you do in towns, because transportation is higher."

"But twelve-and-a-half cents a day! How did you manage it?"

"Oh, I didn't suffer. Did my own cooking; had no rent to pay; fuel and lights lie around everywhere in the woods; one dresses serviceably, and the fashions never change; you do your own washing, for the excellent reason that nobody else will do it for you. The housework, as you might call it, takes two or three hours a day; the rest of the time is your own. And, as you say, a man is free."

"Um—I couldn't—"

"Couldn't live like a tramp, eh? No more could I. My home in the woods is neater, prettier, than yours in the city. I'm a bit battered to look at, sometimes, but (without personalities) I harbor fewer microbes than most people in town. My meals are plain, but they're wholesome, and they taste good. I'm somewhat independent. I never beg—not even for a raise of pay. All men look alike to me; I can cuss any of them to his face whenever I feel like it. That is some compensation for doing my own cooking and 'redding up.'"

"Ah, I see; you're an original, a—ah—" he was hunting for some term polite—"you're a Thoreau, a philosopher."

"A Diogenes? No. I don't stay in the woods all the time. Civilization is good; cities are good—so long as one is not enslaved to them. But every city man and woman who can appreciate freedom and the out-of-doors ought to have a good taste of the real thing for a little while every year. It would make better folks of them, and it need cost no more than staying at home."

"Yes," replied he of the city, sighing, "that's all well enough when you're here with wild woods at your very back door; but what would you do if your home was New York City, and if you had only two or three weeks' vacation?"

"What I would do might not suit you. Tastes and talents differ, as you may have heard once or twice before. But if I moved to New York, and knew nothing of the surrounding country, I'd first make a little reconnaissance on paper. It would save time."

"You mean study guide books?"

"No; guide books are only useful to warn you of places to avoid. I prefer places where other people don't go."

"So do I; but how would you find them?"

"This way; I'd go to a library—"

My interlocutor stared; so did the priest.

"I'd go to a public library and ask for their best atlas of the United States—one that gives the area and population of counties along with each map; or, I'd get a gazetteer and a census report. Then I'd look for counties that were thinly settled, and that had little or no railroad connection with the outside world. That's what I should seek."

"Around New York?"

"Sure. You people of the Far East don't know what good things you have left. For example, what do you know about Pike county, Pennsylvania?"

"Nothing."

"Neither do I, except this: One time when I was making one of those pioneering trips on paper I discovered that Pike county, Pennsylvania, which lies within sixty bee-line miles of the New York city hall, has fewer inhabitants to the square mile than any similar area between Pittsburg and Omaha, or from Minneapolis south to the Ohio river, which, by the way, is a scope of country more than twice as large as all of your North Atlantic states put together. Why, it isn't you Manhattaners, it's the people of the Middle West, who have a long way to travel to get away from one another. Do you realize that Indianapolis and Des Moines are farther away from any big-game hunting grounds than are New York and Philadelphia?"

"Well, what would you find in Pike County?"

"I don't know. It may be a rich man's preserve, for all I know; but I'd take a couple of days off and find out, for a starter."

"And if it didn't please you—what then?"

"Then I'd go farther afield. If it was any time but midsummer, I might take a camera and go down into Eastern Virginia. Now *there's* something interesting, even before you've started—something to find out the why and the how of. In Eastern Virginia are ten contiguous counties without a railroad. That isn't some wild and woolly new country! It's almost the oldest country we have. It was settled by almost the first Englishmen who came to America. George Washington was born in one of those counties. And yet—think of it!—this ancient land, as large as Delaware, without a railroad in it! Note the names of the counties: King George, Westmoreland, Northumberland, Lancaster, Richmond, Essex, King and Queen, Gloucester, Mathews, Middlesex—sonorous names, famous in old English annals, redolent of a storied past. Through the midst of them runs the Rappahannock—what memories of the Civil War that name calls up! In the library you would learn that nobody has 'written up' that land; tourists generally never heard of it; I doubt if even the camera fiend has exploited it. Oh, no; I have never been there; never knew anybody who had been there; but, if you go, I miss my guess if you don't step off the train plunk into the middle of the eighteenth century. Yes, and the language, and many of the customs, will be older still; they will be Elizabethan English. Many of those survivals you wouldn't find even in England itself to-day. If you're looking for something different from New York, there you will surely find it.

"Another example of a country that I have not yet seen, but that looks interesting on the map: In the extreme western end of Old Virginia, beginning with Bath county, and in the adjoining eastern part of West Virginia running as far north as Hardy county, is a mountain region averaging less than fifteen inhabitants to the square mile—one family, as families go in that country. There you find a population less than that of Hartford scattered over a district larger than Connecticut. The mountains run up to 4,000 feet (the highest summit in Pennsylvania, by contrast, is 2,700 feet), so you would be sure of cool summer nights. In those backwoods counties you will find one of the strangest races of white people in the world, farther removed from modern civilization than any in Europe; yet they are of pure English or Scotch descent, and their ancestors came to this country at a time when Albany and Lancaster were western frontier posts, perhaps even before those towns were founded. How do I know what they are? I know the southern mountaineer, and he is the same everywhere—yesterday, to-day, and forever. But, if you do try that country for a change, don't rely on hotels; there is none. Spend a few nights with the natives, just for the novelty of it; but camp out for the most part, and carry rations with you. The mountaineers are hospitable, but you can't stand their cooking."

And so we talked on, about odd prospects that we knew nothing about save what the map and the census may reveal to anybody. And my point was made; that whoso will (granting that he is superior to hotels and guides and macadam roads) can still find plenty of country worth exploring without going far from home or spending much money in the venture. By such methods as here are outlined I have found several Edens, and never in my life did I hire a guide.

Imaginary Crusoes—and Some Real Ones

My childhood was spent on the prairie of western Iowa. We moved there before the day of fences, and for a year or so there was little to be seen from our front door but a sea of grass waving to the horizon. Behind the house was one of the few groves of trees in all that region. In the grove was an old boat that had been dragged up from the river and left derelict, a mile from any water.

I had no playmates, as there were no neighbors near enough, and I was then an only child. My mother taught me to read. When I was seven, and could read almost anything, she gave me my first book, dear old Robinson Crusoe. It has been saved through the vicissitudes of a somewhat venturesome life, and lies before me now, coverless and stained with age, but more precious than all the hundreds of other books that I afterwards acquired.

I used to take Robinson out to the old boat amid the trees, and there I read it, through and through, I don't know how many times. I made wooden guns, pistols, hatchet, and a thing I called a cutlass. A fur cap was easily contrived, shaped like the one Crusoe wears in the pictures in my book. Then I built a cave out of prairie sod, and stocked it with all sorts of contrivances of my own and with booty from the sloughs and prairie. The old boat was my wrecked ship, to which I made frequent trips, swimming out to it in my imagination, returning on an imaginary raft laden with imaginary seamen's chests, bottles of rack and cordials, kits of tools, barrels of powder and bags of shot; and on other trips I brought runlets of rum, a great hogshead of bread, barrels of flour, a box of fine sugar, pieces of sails, ropes and rope-twine, and other salvage recovered "through infinite labor." Last of all, I found some thirty-six pounds in money (avoirdupois, mind you, as I was innocent of pounds sterling), some European coin, some Brazil, some pieces of eight, some gold, and some silver. (Iowa knew nothing but greenbacks and shinplasters in those days—but no matter). And I smiled to myself at the sight of this money: "O drug!" I exclaimed, "what art thou good for? Thou art not worth to me, no, not the taking off the ground."

From *All Outdoors*, May 1918

While this sort of thing was going on for a couple of years, I was actually in the heart of a region where game birds of nearly every description swarmed in myriads, as they never will again, and I soon became a good shot with real guns. The elk and buffalo had left, but their bleached antlers and horns were strewn everywhere over the prairie. Wild Indians often passed our place, and one time, had it not been for the timely arrival of my father, I, a little boy, would have killed with Dad's rifle a squaw who had started to rob our house, while her band stood agrin at my mother's panic of fear. But I never dreamed that such a life and surroundings were romantic. My romance was out there in the sod cave and the crazy old boat among the cottonwoods. Although familiar with actual savages, I thought them nothing but dirty thieves and vagabonds; and so had to invent a good savage for my man Friday (I used to talk to him out loud, and he was very real to me).

At that same time there were thousands of boys far away in the East, many of them living by the seashore, whose one ambition in life was to go West and fight Indians. I was in the West and did have a fight now and then with Indians (of my own size), but that was the mere humdrum of daily existence. My fondest dream was to go East and be a sailorboy. So, arriving at the mature age of ten, I ran away from home and headed toward the rising sun, equipped with the clothes I stood in, a Barlow knife, and a fifty-cent piece I had one day picked up in the road. About noon I offered the coin to a Jew for some crackers and cheese, and waited for the change. The Jew tossed the thing back to me with a snort and cried "bogus." I did not know what the word meant, until he explained that my long cherished pocket-piece was nothing but lead. So I stayed out West among my darned Indians, and never saw the ocean till I was grown up.

This may explain why, to me, the chief charm of *Robinson Crusoe* is in the trips to the wreck, the recovery of things useful to one cast away on a desolate island, and the sensation of stamping money into the ground, with good reason, and exclaiming: "O drug! What are thou good for?"

SOME REAL CRUSOES

So much by way of romance. Sundry experiences later in life gave me a practical interest in real crusoeing, of the kind wherein there is no wreck to take salvage from. What would Crusoe have done if he had been left on his island with nothing but the shirt and trousers, the knife and pipe and little box of tobacco that he got ashore with?

Defoe is supposed to have found the germ of his story in the adventures of Alexander Selkirk, a Scottish sailor who, in 1703, joined the famous navigator Dampier in a privateering expedition to the South Seas. In September, 1704, when his vessel had put in at the uninhabited island of Juan Fernandez, Selkirk had a quarrel with his captain, and at his own request was put ashore "with only a few ordinary necessities." Before the ship left, Selkirk's temper had cooled enough for him to realize what might be in store for him, alone on a speck of land far from the usual course of vessels, and with no wreck to supply his needs in years to come. He then begged to be taken back into the ship's company, but the captain was obdurate and sailed away without him. Selkirk remained alone on Juan Fernandez four years and four months, when he was taken off by a ship on which Dampier was pilot.

I have lately been reading Captain Dampier's *Voyages*, and was interested at finding in it that Alexander Selkirk was not the first man left alone to his fate on the island of Juan Fernandez. On March 23, 1684, Dampier visited this island and went ashore to look for a Mosquito Indian named William, who had unintentionally been left behind on the 11th of January, 1681, when Dampier's vessel, lying at this same island, had been obliged by the sudden appearance of three Spanish ships of war to slip her cable and put to sea. The Captain's story, reprinted verbatim and with the quaint capitalization common in his day, runs as follows:

"This Indian lived here alone above three years, and altho' he was several times sought after by the Spaniards, who knew he was left on the Island, yet they could never find him. He was in the Woods, hunting for Goats, when Capt. Watlin drew off his Men, and the Ship was under sail before he came back to shore. He had with him his Gun and a Knife, with a small Horn of Powder, and a few Shot; which being spent, he contrived a way by notching his Knife, to saw the Barrel of his Gun into small Pieces, wherewith he made Harpoons, Lances, Hooks, and a long Knife; heating the pieces first in the fire, which he struck with his Gun-flint, and a piece of the Barrel of his Gun, which he hardened; having learnt to do that among the English. The hot pieces of Iron he would hammer out and bend as he pleased with Stones, and saw them with his jagged Knife, or grind them to an edge by long labour, and harden them to a good temper as there was occasion. All this may seem strange to those that are not acquainted with the sagacity of the Indians; but it is no more than these Moskito Men are accustomed to in their own Country, where they make their own Fishing and Striking Instruments, without either Forge or Anvil; tho' they spend a great deal of time about them. . . .

"With such Instruments as he made in that manner he got such Provision as the Island afforded; either Goats or Fish. He told us that at first he was forced to eat Seal, which is very ordinary Meat, before he had made Hooks: but afterwards he never killed any Seals but to make Lines, cutting their skins into Thongs. He had a little

House or Hut half a mile from the Sea, which was lin'd with Goat Skin; his Couch or Barbecu of Sticks lying along about 2 foot distant from the Ground, was spread with the same, and was all his Bedding. He had no Cloaths left, having worn out those he brought from Watlin's Ship, but only a Skin about his Waste.

"He saw our Ship the day before we came to an Anchor, and did believe we were English, and therefore kill'd 3 Goats in the Morning, before we came to an Anchor, and drest them with Cabbage, to treat us when we came ashore. He came then to the Sea side to congratulate our safe Arrival. And when we landed a Moskito Indian, named Robin, first leap'd ashore, and running to his Brother Moskito Man, threw himself flat on his face at his feet, who helping him up, and embracing him, fell flat with his face on the Ground at Robin's feet, and was by him taken up also."

A STILL WORSE PREDICAMENT

On the 19th of August, 1859, an English clergyman who had been serving for two years as missionary among the savage Maori on the north coast of New Zealand, set out alone in a small boat for a day's fishing. When he had been fishing about three hours, and had caught a few fish, he noted that a fresh breeze, an ebbing tide and a strong current were carrying him out to sea. He hoisted sail, but the gaff of his mainsail gave way, and by the time it was repaired the boat was unmanageable, save by rowing. After exerting his utmost strength for two hours without making headway against the wind, tide and current, he collapsed, and his little craft drifted seaward. He knew that far out at sea there was a group of three small islands, probably in the course of the wind; so when the moon rose he set sail, and ran all night before a steady mild breeze.

The next afternoon he came near one of the islands, and succeeded in running into a small bay between walls of rock. That night the ebb of the tide was about to strand his boat; so he got into her and tried to paddle out to a better anchorage. He was caught by a huge breaker, which rolled his boat over and over, cast him ashore, and left the boat smashed and fast on a jagged rock. His fish, fishing lines, the remains of his luncheon, and, worst of all, his pipe, had spilled into the sea and were lost. There was left to him nothing whatever but his pocket-knife, a pair of blankets, a few pieces of broken glass, a ruined boat and its tattered sails. He was a man with little knowledge of sailoring and none at all of woodcraft. The islands never were visited by men, save under extraordinary circumstances. The natives among whom he had lived had no means of knowing what had become of him.

Throughout the first ten days the castaway lived on oysters alone, eaten raw, of course, as he was without means of making a fire. He tried for two days to patch up his boat by tinkering with his pocket-knife, though knowing that the attempt would be futile. Having suffered from a rainy night, he set about making him a shelter, and succeeded in building a sort of thatched house by dint of more than two weeks' labor. After this was finished he tried the Maori method of procuring fire, by rubbing very dry and resinous twigs between two pieces of dry wood. By the time he was about ready to give up in despair a few live sparks appeared, which he blew gently into a flame, and then he built a fire that never was allowed to go out. Thus he was able to cook his oysters, and supplement this very meagre diet with the nutritious hearts of wild palms, and with fern roots that he baked in the ashes. There were plenty of wild ducks on a pond in the island, besides parrots and pigeons in the woods, but he seems not to have known how to capture birds, and he failed in the attempt to make a bow and arrows.

Some three weeks after his arrival on the island, he found a dead shark washed up on the beach. Having seen the Maoris make fish-hooks out of shark bones, he set about imitating their work. It took him six evenings to produce two bone hooks, and another week was spent in twisting raw wild flax into lines. From that time he was able to catch fish and eels, which he flavored with wild pepper, and salt found in crevices in the rocks, where it had been deposited by evaporation. He found a species of wild cabbage that was edible, and varied his ways of cooking, sometimes broiling his food and at other times baking it in a hole with hot ashes.

Eventually he succeeded in snaring some pigeons, and he robbed wild bees of their hoards by burning down the bee-trees. Evidently the place had not always been uninhabited. The thought set him to making a more thorough exploration of his island (about the first thing that a woodsman would have undertaken). He discovered a herd of wild goats licking salt out of the rocks, and he tried the Crusoe expedient of running them down (the last thing a woodsman would have thought of). He finally did succeed in grabbing a she-goat, heavy with kid, but she broke away from him. And he never got one.

Then one night there occurred the most singular of all the poor castaway's adventures. He was out by moonlight looking for firewood, and had sat down to rest a bit, when he heard a shrill whistle behind him. A dark object appeared at a short distance, which at first he took to be a small beast, but it proved to be that rarest of birds the kiwi or apteryx, a wingless thing that moves about only at night. He managed to overtake it, but it threw itself on its back, struck at him with its feet like a game-cock, wounded his leg, and got away. Afterwards he found some kiwi eggs, which he ate with relish.

For five wretched months this clergyman lived on the island, without so much as a dog or tamed beast to keep him company. Then one night he was awakened by hearing a large boat bump on the beach. Five or six of his Maori neighbors came ashore. He greeted them with a shout of joy, but they drew back in affright and threatened him with a tomahawk, declaring that he, the clergyman, had been long dead and that this was only a ghost. Nor would they be reassured until he picked up a stone which he threw at a tree and hit the mark. "Ah," said one of them, "no ghost could do that."

It would be ungracious to comment on such an experience and point out the many ways in which the poor fellow's exile could have been used to better account, both as regards physical comfort and mental relaxation. To Dampier's Indian this would have been only an interesting adventure; for the over-civilized white man it came very close to a shocking tragedy.

HORACE
KEPHART.

Horace Kephart

BY HIMSELF

My passion for the mountains may be inherited, as my ancestors were Swiss. They came over to Pennsylvania a good while before the Revolution, and were among the first settlers of the mountains west of the Susquehanna.

I was born at East Salem, Pa., Sept. 8, 1862. In 1867 my father moved to Jefferson, Iowa, a frontier village set in the prairie wilderness. It was before the day of fences, and for a year or so there was little to be seen from our front door but a sea of grass waving to the horizon. Behind the house was one of the few groves of trees in all the region. In the grove was an old boat that had been dragged up from the river and left derelict, a mile from any running water.

I had no playmates. My mother taught me to read. When I was seven, and could read almost anything, she gave me my first book, dear old Robinson Crusoe. It has been saved through the vicissitudes of a somewhat venturesome life, and lies before me now, coverless and stained with age, but more precious than all the thousands of other books that I afterwards acquired.

I used to take Robinson out to the old boat amid the trees, and there I read it through and through, I don't know how many times. I made wooden guns, pistols, hatchet, and a thing I called a cutlass. A fur cap was easily contrived, shaped like the one Crusoe wears in the pictures in my book. Then I built a cave out of prairie sod, and stocked it with all sorts of booty from the sloughs and prairie. The old boat was my wrecked ship, to which I made frequent trips, swimming out to it in imagination, returning on an imaginary raft laden with imaginary seamen's chests, bottles of rack and cordials, kits of tools, barrels of powder and bags of shot. On other trips I brought runlets of rum, a great hogshead of bread, barrels of flour, a box of fine sugar, pieces of sails, ropes and rope-twine, and other salvage recovered "through infinite labor."

Last of all, I found some thirty-six pounds of money (avoirdupois, mind you, as I

From *North Carolina Library Bulletin,* June 1922

was innocent of pounds sterling), some European coin, some Brazil, some pieces of eight, some gold, and some silver. (Iowa knew nothing but greenbacks and shinplasters in those days, and I never had either of them—but no matter). And I smiled to myself at the sight of all this money: "O drug!" I exclaimed, "what art thou good for? Thou art not worth to me, no, not the taking off the ground."

While this was going on, for a couple of years, I was actually in the heart of a region where game birds of every description swarmed in myriads, as they never will again, and I soon become a good shot with real guns. The elk and buffalo had left, but their bleached antlers and skulls were strewn everywhere over the prairie. Wild Indians often passed our house, and one time, had it not been for the timely arrival of my father, I, a little boy, would have killed with Dad's rifle a squaw who, with others, was robbing our house while her band stood agrin at my mother's panic of fear. But I never dreamed that such a life and surroundings were romantic. My romance was out there in the sod cave and crazy old boat among the cottonwoods. The actual savages with whom I was familiar were to me naught but dirty thieves and vagabonds; so I had to invent a good savage for my man Friday.

In those days there were thousands of boys far away in the East, many of them living by the seashore, whose highest ambition in life was to go west and fight Indians. I was in the West, and did have a fight now and then with Indians (of my own size), but that was the mere humdrum of daily existence. My fondest dream was to go east and be a sailorboy. So, arriving at the mature age of ten, I ran away from home and headed toward the rising sun. I was equipped with the clothes I stood in, a Barlow knife, and a fifty-cent piece that I had one day picked up in the road. About noon I offered the coin to a Jew for some crackers and cheese. The Jew tossed the thing back to me with a snort and cried "bogus!" I did not know what the word meant, till he explained that my long cherished pocket-piece was lead. So I stayed out west among my darned Indians, and never saw the ocean till I was grown up. "O drug! What art thou good for?"

From 1871 to 1876 we lived at Western, Iowa, where I took the preparatory course and freshman year in Western College, of which one of my uncles was president and my father a professor. In 1876 we returned to Pennsylvania. I was graduated, A.B., from Lebanon Valley College in 1879, not without misgivings on the part of the faculty as to my orthodoxy and sundry other qualifications.

The next year I spent in Boston, nominally as a senior in Boston University, but actually dissecting starfish and so on in the Tech., under Alpheus Hyatt, and enjoying the blessed privilege of studying whatever I pleased in the Boston Public Library. The absolute academic freedom of the Library was such a relief to one who had suffered from set curriculums that I resolved to help others find it: I chose librarianship for a career.

In 1880 I went to Cornell University as a graduate student in history and political science, also as assistant in the University Library under Willard Fiske. From there I went to Italy, in the winter of '84, and was in Europe until the spring of '86, in company with Professor Fiske. Besides the bibliographical work that I was engaged in, I took lectures under the anthropologist Mantegazza in the Instituto dei Studii Superiori of Florence.[46]

From 1886 to 1890 I was an assistant to Addison Van Name in the Yale University Library, and took lectures under Sumner and others in the graduate department. Here my spare time was given to historical research, chiefly along the line of American frontier history, and I began writing a little for magazines.

In 1887 I married Laura White Mack, of Ithaca, N.Y. We have two sons and four daughters, all of them graduates of Cornell. Both of the boys, and two of the girls, were with our armies in the World War, as were also the husbands of the other two daughters.

From 1890 to 1903 I was librarian of the St. Louis Mercantile Library. This, the oldest library west of the Mississippi, was not merely the old-fashioned subscription library that its name implies; it was also the chief collection of scholarly books in the Mississippi Valley. Here I built up a special collection of western Americana, a subject that fortunately had not yet attracted the interest and competition of wealthy private book buyers.

During these years of tracking and capturing rare source materials, I was often rewarded by finding diaries or other records of actual participants in the stirring events of the Old West; but often I was saddened by the fact that hardly any of these chroniclers knew how to write. As a rule their records were as dry as a ship's log-book. There was only one Francis Parkman who could clothe the bones with flesh and blood. "With the exception of his Oregon Trail," I wrote "it is most unfortunate, that there exists in American literature no intimate and vivid account of the western hunters and trappers by one who had shared their camps and accompanied them on trail and warpath. We have many stories of their exploits, written in narrative form, with scarce any dialogue or characterization. The men themselves figure in such stories as little more than lay figures in a historical museum. It is one thing to describe events; it is another thing to make the actors in those events live and speak in the reader's presence."

I was ambitious to take up the story of "The Winning of the West" where Roosevelt had left it, and continue it to the last frontier—but then came catastrophe: my health broke down. In the summer of 1904, finding that I must abandon professional work and city life, I came to western North Carolina, looking for a big primitive forest where I could build up strength anew and indulge my lifelong fondness for hunting, fishing and exploring new ground. Knowing nobody who had ever been here, I took a topographic map and picked out on it, by means of the contour lines and the blank spaces showing no settlement, what seemed to be the wildest part of the region; and there I went. It was in Swain County, amid the Great Smoky Mountains, near the Tennessee line.

The first three years I lived most of the time alone in a little log cabin on the site of a disused copper mine, on the Little Fork of Sugar Fork of Hazel Creek, deep in the virgin woods. As I have said in *Woodcraft:* "To one coming from cities, it was a strange environment, almost as though he had been carried back, asleep, upon the wings of time, and had awakened in the eighteenth century, to meet Daniel Boone in flesh and blood. . . . To what degree I was reverting to the primitive came home to me one day when a white dame, finding Will Tahlahlah giving me a lesson in Cherokee, remarked rather sourly to the redskin: 'You needn't teach him anything; he's more of an Indian than you are.' . . . Seldom during those three years as a forest exile did I feel lonesome in daytime; but when supper would be over, and black night closed in on my hermitage, and the owls began calling all the blue devils of the woods, one needed some indoor occupation to keep him in good cheer; and that is how I came to write my first little book on camping and woodcraft."

That little book has expanded and gone through many editions, of which the best is the field edition, two volumes in one, on Bible paper, making a handy book for the pocket despite its nearly 900 pages. (*Camping and Woodcraft,* New York, Macmillan, 1921.)

Although the forest and streams and the mountains were what most attracted me at first, yet gradually I became more absorbed in study of my human associates in the backwoods. They were unlike any people I had ever met elsewhere. They were like figures taken from the old frontier histories and legends that I had been so fond of, only they were living flesh and blood instead of mere characters in books. I seemed to be actually living among the pioneer farmers and herdsmen and hunters, the trappers and traders, the teachers and preachers, the outlaws and the Indians (we had these, too) of a hundred and fifty years ago. They interested me more than the ultra-civilized folk of cities.

Then I traveled in other parts of the Appalachians, in eastern Kentucky and Tennessee, in northern Georgia, comparing what I found there with what I knew in the Smokies, and I found the southern mountaineers everywhere one people. To make sure that I was not generalizing too hastily from my own limited observations, I studied in detail the statistics of the mountain counties of the South, tabulating them painstakingly from the complete Federal census reports, and here I verified beyond question my conclusion that the typical southern highlanders were not the relatively few townsmen and prosperous valley farmers of the Appalachian region, but the great multitude of little farmers living up the branches and on the steep hillsides, back from the main highways, and generally far from railroads. These, the real mountaineers, were what interested me; and so I wrote them up.

Our Southern Highlanders was first published in 1913. It was an absolutely truthful picture, as far as I could make it so, of the features of mountain life that are most interesting to the world at large. It provoked a little caustic criticism from some newspaper writers who were not familiar with the real people and conditions that I described, but its fidelity is attested by the fact that I have stayed right on the spot where the book was written, and that the people I wrote about are my friends to this day. In 1913, soon after the book's publication, it was awarded the Patterson Cup by the North Carolina State Literary and Historical Association. A new and enlarged edition, with fresh illustrations, is now in press.

Our Southern Highlanders is sketchy, fragmentary, of course. So is this account of my life. For instance, I have said nothing about how much money I have made, and lost. But can you not guess how much I care for money, beyond what is needed for books and guns and fishing tackle? My first fortune, remember, was imaginary, and the second was counterfeit. "O drug! What art thou good for?" Yes: and much else has been left out, too. The best stories are those that are never told.

LIKES TIMES EDITORIALS

Bryson City, N.C.
Sept. 19, 1923.

Editor The Times:

I have been most favorably impressed by the sensible and courageous editorials appearing in The Western North Carolina Times on Prohibition. They are absolutely true to the facts. If editors generally had the mettle to print their own convictions about this agent of disruption they would have the backing of most men who know the world and who do their own thinking.

From *Western North Carolina Times*, September 1923

People simply will not respect laws that are not respectable. The Volstead Act is not respectable because it is based on the plain lie that any beverage containing more than one-half of one per cent. of alcohol is intoxicating. And no one knows this better than the legislators who were dragooned into passing such an act and the judges who are obliged to enforce it.

Fanaticism defeats its own end by its own excesses. It is always tyrannical when it gets the upper hand. Long ago the historian Buckle summed up the experience of mankind with this sort of folk by saying: "There is no instance on record of an ignorant man who, having good intentions and supreme power to enforce them, has not done far more evil than good. And whenever the intentions have been very eager, and the power very extensive, the evil has been enormous."

Prohibitionists generally have good intentions; they are very eager; they have great power; and they are, as a class, densely ignorant of the age-long experience of beer-drinking and wine-drinking nations, who are the least alcoholized of any in the world. Prohibitionists, as a class, are ruled by catchwords and spellbinding rather than by reason. So the natural, inevitable result is that they are striking the deadliest blow at Temperance, which all desire, by attempting Prohibition, which is a flat denial of an inalienable and basic right of man.

No law of man ever made men moral. It cannot do so, because no law can impart moral strength to resist vice. Let us look the facts of life straight in the face, instead of dodging them to soar among dreams and illusions. Let us be content to remain, for a while, a little lower than the angels, while living as normal men, facing things as they are, enjoying what we may in a wholesome, natural way, minding our own business, and not raising the devil at the breakfast table because we are bilious from messing with our neighbors' faults.

HORACE KEPHART

Mr. Kephart is an author of international reputation and a widely traveled man. He is well known in the East as the author of "Our Southern Highlanders."—Editor.

Western N. C. Times
Sept. 28, 1923. [handwritten]

Reasons Given by Kephart for His Chair Opposition

NOTED AUTHOR OF BRYSON CITY BECOMES MEMBER OF PRISON REFORM ASSOCIATION: HIS LETTER

Reasons for his opposition to the death penalty are advanced by Horace Kephart, well known author, and a resident of Bryson City, in a communication to the Prison Reform Association of which he has recently become a member. Mr. Kephart's letter to the officers of the association is as follows:

My objection to capital punishment is not based on pity for the man who has deliberately plotted against another and has murdered him in cold blood. I do not believe in being "soft" with hardened criminals. There are many men and women who are so incurably vicious that no kindness and no precepts will reform them. They remain a menace to society as long as they are free to mingle in it.

Neither do I accept the view of some medical men and criminologists that homicide is full evidence of mental disease and irresponsibility. It may be so in cases of impulsive action; but premeditated murder is a very different thing. It usually requires a cool and competent brain to plan murder in advance, to provide an alibi and to ensure leaving no incriminatory traces behind. It takes steady nerves to await a favorable opportunity, then to strike surely, and to keep up the appearance of innocent composure thereafter.

As a rule, the gunmen of our cities are not morons. They have average intelligence in the affairs of life and might be efficient in trades or in business if they cared to work; but they scorn the wages of toil. They have an evil but well reasoned philosophy to the effect that anything they want is good and any way there is not one chance in a hundred of their being severely punished for any one crime. Court records and the reports of bar associations show how true such prevision is. No man who can reason so logically in an evil cause deserves the benefit of doubt as to his intelligence and responsibility for his acts.

From *Asheville Citizen*, July 14, 1925

Still I do oppose the execution of criminals for any crime, except when military necessity compels it in time of war. My objection is based, first, on the legal ground that it forever puts beyond the power of the State any restriction if the accused should sometime be found innocent. Mistakes do occur.

Second, I do object on the utilitarian ground that capital punishment is no more deterrent of high class crime than life imprisonment, if as much. The man who deliberately plots murder, and is determined to carry it out, discounts the risk of death the same as the risk of incarceration for life. On the other hand, an American jury is more likely to find a verdict of murder in the first degree if the maximum penalty be life imprisonment than if it be hanging or electrocution. Capital punishment is so repugnant to the moral sense and humane sentiment of our citizenry that juries are prone to return a second degree verdict, even when they well know it should be first degree, and they do so simply because they shrink from the responsibility of sending any man to the scaffold or to the electric chair.

Yet I would insist that justice be more prompt and certain than it now is. Our present procedure puts every facility in the hands of criminals, every obstacle in the way of the prosecution, if the accused can find money and friends to back him. Robbery, burglary and murder are safer trades in the United States than in any other country in the civilized world. It is the shame of our nation that a large majority of our felonies go unpunished or so lightly punished that armed bands of criminals daily flaunt the law, in broad daylight, on the thronged streets of our cities, commit robbery and murder, and very often "get away with it."

To a considerable extent this state of things is due to sentimentalism (not healthy sentiment) among the masses who have had no practical experience in handling desperate criminals and who could not on any account be hired to take a policeman's or a jailor's job. As an administrative officer I know it works when the good citizenry is asked to help in such matters.

The fact—it is a gruesome fact—that many of our jails and convict camps are hell-holes of brutality and breeders of crime and disease is owing to the practical impossibility, in many localities, of getting humane and sensible men to take a warden's job. It seems strange to me that we can get any number of volunteers from good society to go into exile among the heathen of far-off lands but we can seldom hire a man who is fit for the care and custody of our own savages.

To conclude I believe that capital punishment should be abolished provided our machinery of justice be so repaired that a sentence to long imprisonment, for the safety of society, should mean just what it says. If that should become a fact in the United States as it is in England, France, Germany and other European States, we would have little difficulty in getting capital punishment abolished here. The only reason that so many of our States still tolerate this relic of barbarism is that the public knows how the pardoning power is commonly abused, owing to the pressure upon governors and pardon boards being almost wholly one-sided.

These, of course, are only my personal views, and merely an outline of them. The subject is so involved that no simple, general statement of principles can be made without a host of exceptions and objections springing up like weeds around it. But I have tried to make my own stand as plain as possible, and I offer it merely for what it may be worth.

The Man Who Has Lived Two Lives

Horace Kephart, Bookman, Driven from the St. Louis Mercantile Library to the Woods in Search of Health, Found the Treasure of Which He'd Dreamed in Curious Mountain Folk of the Big Smoky Mountains. Now Again the Libraries Know Him—As An Author.

BY F. A. BEHYMER OF THE POST-DISPATCH STAFF

Bryson, North Carolina.

When the cities of America and Europe knew Horace Kephart, man of books, he did his work behind the walls of great libraries. Now he sits at a window that opens upon the Tuckaseegee, and the Big Smokies out beyond. He can raise his eyes and look through his window at the swiftly-flowing water and the mountains that rise, ridge on ridge. And, if the day's toil irks and the outdoors calls, there's a packed knapsack hanging on the wall and within two hours he can be out in the wide spaces and the high places where he likes best to be.

Horace Kephart won high position in the busy world as a librarian. He was a front-rank man. For 13 years he was at the head of the St. Louis Mercantile Library. Success was his, but it began to pall. He longed for a different life. Like a legion of other men who have followed sedentary occupations for the rewards that they bring, he wanted to be away in the wild places, where the rewards are less and the satisfactions greater. Like them, he kept promising himself that someday he would throw off the burden of it all and find a lodge in a wilderness and LIVE. Unlike most of the others, he did it.

There was a contingency that helped him to the great decision. At the height of his career his health broke and he was advised to give up city life and professional work. Other men, so advised, have taken a brief cure, lacking the courage to cut loose, and have returned to their tasks and died, still longing. Horace Kephart was more valiant.

From *St. Louis Post-Dispatch*, October 31, 1926

He chucked everything and went away to begin over again and live another life in another way. He went to the North Carolina mountains, and with health restored he had no wish to return to the cities that had known him and the professional pursuits to which his other life had been devoted. He chose to stay among the mountains that had brought healing of health and rebirth of spirit. He stayed among the mountains because—abundant justification—he was happiest there.

He has come back, though, to the place of fame that he abandoned when he left the world that had known him and went into the wilderness. He is back in America's Who's Who.

The Kepharts came from Switzerland long ago. When they reached America, back before the Revolution, they were among the first settlers of the Pennsylvania mountains west of the Susquehanna, and it may well be believed that love of the mountains was born in the blood of the boy, Horace Kephart, for it is a love that is strong. Held in leash until mid-manhood, while a career was making in busy cities, where the great libraries were, it broke bounds when his health gave way under the strain, and the man, a boy again, was off to the land of "wood and water, wind and tree," happy in his release.

Robinson Crusoe, without a doubt, had something to do with it, for the shipwrecked mariner was the boy's first and best friend. The family had moved, when Horace was 5, to the prairie wilderness of Iowa, and when he was 7 his mother gave him Robinson Crusoe to company him in his loneliness, for there were no playmates where he lived.

An old rowboat that had been dragged up from the river and left stranded safe from the perils of running water served the child very well for Crusoe's wrecked barque. Horace Kephart remembers that boat as he sits by the window that opens upon the Tuckaseegee and the Big Smokies out beyond.

"I used to take Robinson out to the old boat amid the trees," he muses, "and there I read it through and through, I don't know how many times. I made wooden guns, pistols, a hatchet, and a thing I called a cutlass. A fur cap was easily contrived, shaped like the one Crusoe wears in the picture in my book. Then I built a cave out of prairie sod, and stocked it with all sorts of booty. The old boat was my wrecked ship, to which I made frequent trips, swimming out to it in imagination, returning on an imaginary raft laden with imaginary seamen's chests, bottles of rack and cordials, kits of tools, barrels of powder and bags of shot. On other trips I brought runlets of rum, a great hogshead of bread, barrels of flour, a box of fine sugar, pieces of sails, ropes and rope-twine, and other salvage recovered through 'infinite labor.'"

The man has been true to that first and best friend. He has cherished it through the years. He takes it from its niche, tenderly, as a reverent man touching something sacred. It is a faded thing, coverless and stained with age—"but more precious to me," he says, "than all the thousands of books I afterward acquired."

School and college beginnings in Iowa and then back with the family to Pennsylvania; graduation, A. B., there, "not without misgivings on the part of the faculty as to my orthodoxy and sundry other qualifications;" a year at Boston University, with the blessed privilege of access to the Boston Public Library, leading to the choice of librarianism as a career; four years at Cornell as graduate student in history and political science; two years in Europe; two years in the Yale University library and research in American frontier history; and then 13 years at the head of the St. Louis Mercantile Library, where he built up a special collection of Western Americana and nourished an ambition to take up the "Winning of the West" where Roosevelt had left it, and continue it to the last frontier. So the first phase of his life is told.

Then, in 1904—crash. The man broke down. The verdict of the doctors was that he must abandon professional work and city life.

To another man it would have been tragedy. To Horace Kephart it was blessed release. Through all the years he had dulled his ears to the call of the wild. Ambition had beckoned, and duty had driven. His heart's deepest longing had been denied. Always he had waited for a more convenient season. Greater ambitions called for greater devotion. But for this chance, which another would have called mischance, he would have gone on to the end, denying himself his dearest wish, winning much but losing more. Even as the multitude of other men who deny themselves what they most desire, press on and achieve—disappointment.

Now, at mid-manhood, in full career, he was stopped. "Back to nature" was the order. It was a retreat. But it was not defeat. Greater victory would be won. He would be a boy again and live life over again and live it better than he had lived it erstwhile. He would be a castaway on a desert island. Hail, Robinson Crusoe!

Resting awhile at his father's home at Dayton, Ohio, the man who was going to beat back to boyhood took a map and a compass and with Dayton as the center drew circles, seeking the nearest wilderness, in any direction, where he might cast himself away. The region of the Big Smoky Mountains in Western North Carolina seemed to meet the requirements. A topographic map showed him, by means of the contour lines and the blank spaces, where nature was wildest and where there were no settlements. These were the highest mountains east of the Rockies. It was a primitive hinterland without a history. Great areas were uninhabited. It would be a good place to begin again, he thought.

There was a railroad from Asheville to Murphy. It would take him somewhere close to the "Back of Beyond" that he was seeking. Dillsboro on the Tuckaseegee seemed, from the map, a good place to take off from, and so there he went, but there he learned that a little further westward greater solitude was to be found, and he moved on, up the line, to Bushnell. From there, with all his worldly possessions in a pack on his back, he set out for the Land of Beginning Again. Somewhere in that land, among the smoky peaks, he would shake off the burdening years and start over, and live the life that he had always wanted to live. He had three days' rations in his pack. Beyond this provision his dependence was upon his rod and gun. He was 42 years old.

He did not know where he would make his lodge. Probably where night found him. Or the next night or the night after that. It did not matter.

On Little Fork of Sugar Fork of Hazel Creek, far up under the lee of the Smokies, near the Tennessee line, he found the land he was seeking and made his habitation there. An abandoned cabin afforded shelter. There was some objection to the location. A scant two miles away was the metropolis of Medlin, composed of two stores, a corn mill and four dwellings, and a mile and a half away was a schoolhouse which, once or twice a month, served also as a church. In the settlement, eight miles by two, were several families. A little cramped, one might say, but there were vast uninhabited areas not far away and when he felt crowded he could fare forth for days or weeks in solitudes that had seldom felt the footfalls of man. So Little Fork of Sugar Fork of Hazel Creek would serve. For—"All about us was the forest primeval, where roamed some sparse herds of cattle, razorback hogs and the wild beasts. Speckled trout were in all the streams. Bears sometimes raided the fields and wildcats were a common nuisance. Our settlement was a mere slash in the vast woodland that encompassed it."

He was not a tenderfoot. He had "thundered around" out of doors a good bit, as he says. He was passionately fond of the primitive, and knew how to take care of himself. He had to be, for—

"In our primitive community there were no trades, no professions. Every man was his own farmer, blacksmith, gunsmith, carpenter, cobbler, miller, tinker. Someone in his family, or a near neighbor, served him as barber and dentist and would make him a coffin when he died. One farmer was also the wagoner of the district, as well as storekeeper, magistrate and veterinarian. He also owned the only 'toothpullers' in the settlement, a pair of universal forceps that he designed, forged, filed out and wielded with barbaric grit."

It was all just as this man from the outer world would have it. He was realizing the past in the present, "seeing with my own eyes what life must have been to my pioneer ancestors of a century or two ago, enjoying free life in the open air, experiencing the thrill of exploring new ground, the joys of the chase, and the man's game of matching my woodcraft against the forces of nature."

For three years he lived, most of the time, when he was at home, in the little log cabin on Little Fork. "Seldom during those three years as a forest exile," he says, "did I feel lonesome in daytime; but when supper would be over, and black night closed in on my hermitage, and the owls began calling all the blue devils of the woods, one needed some indoor occupation to keep him in good cheer."

It was the old life calling, the life of books that he had left. For such a man there could be a beginning again but the old life could not be entirely disowned. He had known that it would be so and had made provision. Into his exile he had taken with him a "library" that would serve him when, with returning health, would come the yearning for books. Out of the thousands of books that he had intimately known there were only a few that he could carry with him into the solitudes. He selected them with care, twenty of them. Here is his list in the order in which they usually stood on a shelf on his soap-box cupboard:

English Dictionary.
Roget's Thesaurus.
My sister's Bible.
Shakspeare.
Burns. Poems.
Dante (in Italian).
Goethe. Faust.
Poe. Tales.
Stevenson. Kidnaped.
Stevenson. David Balfour.
Stevenson. The Merry Men.
Fisher. Universal History.
Pilcher. First Aid.
"Nessmuk." Woodcraft.
Frazer. Minerals.
Jordan. Vertebrate Animals.
Wright. Birdcraft.
Mathews. American Wild Flowers.
Keeler. Our Native Trees.
Lounsberry. Southern Wild Flowers and Trees.

There they were, the friends that had come with him out of the other life. And they were classified. The librarian's ruling passion was still strong amid the bears and owls. They were practically the only books that he had a chance to see, for the next ten years, except on his infrequent vacations to the homeland, and they were all well thumbed. All but one, that is. Dante did not keep its place among the others on the soap-box shelf. It had been a mistake to bring Dante along. It carried his mind back to things unsupportable at that time—old memories—and he hid it away.

The old man had become a new man, but the new man was a man of books as much as the old man had been, and when black night closed in, and the owls began calling, it was in his books that he found comfort. He took up writing, as it was inevitable that he would, setting down by night his experiences by day. So "The Book of Camping and Woodcraft" was written, and "Our Southern Highlanders," and the man who had been lost to the book-world that had known him was to be known again in that world as the author of books that told of life in the Land of Beginning Again.

The forest and the streams and the mountains had interested him most at first, but after he had written his book on camping and woodcraft he became more absorbed in study of his human associates in the backwoods, of whom he says:

"They were unlike any people I had ever met elsewhere. They were like figures taken from the old frontier histories and legends that I had been so fond of, only they were living flesh and blood instead of mere characters in books. I seemed to be actually living among the pioneer farmers and herdsmen and hunters, the trappers and traders, the teachers and preachers, the outlaws and the Indians of a hundred and fifty years ago."

He told about them in "Our Southern Highlanders," told with affection and fidelity, and brought to the world's attention the men of another day among whom had been the dawn of his own new day.

Renewed in health, with a new spirit that was deaf to the call of such ambition as had driven him into a breakdown before, he came out of the wilds but he loved them still and he would not be parted from them. He came to Bryson, not much more than a mountain village then, but growing in importance now, and for twelve years he has lived here, boarding at the unpretentious Cooper House, writing in his "workshop" whose windows open toward the Tuckaseegee and the mountains, recognized as Bryson's most noted citizen, honored by being elected chairman of the town's board of aldermen, working now with all his might for the proposed Great Smoky Mountains National park, on the North Carolina-Tennessee border, writing for the magazines, now at work on his first novel—and happy.

Sixty-four years old now, Horace Kephart is getting on. But remember he has lived two lives. He is healthy and hearty, with clear eyes and a laugh that echoes the out of doors. He is busy with plans and purposes. He is satisfied.

"Satisfied? Why not? My knapsack hangs on the wall. It weighs twenty-seven and a half pounds. It contains everything that I need. In two hours I can be walking in the wilderness, with my gun on my shoulder, INDEPENDENT. I like that. I am happy."

As for fortune, what is wealth to a man who has had fullness of Crusoe treasures and emptiness of attained ambition?

"You cannot guess how little I care for money, beyond what is needed for books and guns and fishing tackle. My first fortune, remember, was imaginary, and the second was counterfeit."

He was sitting by his window as I came away, the window that opens upon the Tuckaseegee and the Big Smokies out beyond.

People's Forum

WHAT WE DO

Editor of The Citizen:

Smith and Brown belong to the same church and worship side by side. Smith cowers before a God of Wrath, and he prays because he is afraid of hell. Brown believes in a God of Love, and he goes to Him as a child to its father. Over in the next pew is Jones, whose idea of God is that of a great First Cause, who set a perfect mechanism to work, regulated it a bit now and then until it kept perfect rhythm and thereafter has let it run without interference. Jones pays the preacher, like Smith and Brown, but he does no praying at all.

Here are three men in the same church, each outwardly conforming to the same creed, all three prompt to answer "Yes, I believe in God"; and yet there is a different God for each man.

So I think the effort to classify Americans according to their actual religious beliefs is futile.

Anyway, what does it amount to?

In his recent book "Why We Behave Like Human Beings," Dr. Dorsey has this to say on the matter:

"After all, what can be of less consequence to you than whether I BELIEVE in this or that kind of a God, Saviour, government, society? What is of consequence to you, to society, and to me, is what I DO. I may be a Socialist, an agnostic, and incredulous of the Mosaic origin of woman from a man's rib and of the parthenogenetic origin of the Christ and of several other things you believe in. What of it? Why should you try to convert me to your way of thinking?

"The fact that you hold a certain opinion or belief does not necessarily mean more than that you have inherited it from simple-minded ancestor, and that in being handed down it has acquired sanctity—like a hair watch-chain.

From *Asheville Citizen*, December 15, 1926

"What is vitally more important is that I live as an honest human being who acknowledges responsibilities and obligations, who plays the game like a thoroughbred, who does not whine and does not cheat, and who believes that there is room in this world for many creeds but for only one religion.

"The kind that was Lincoln's. Does any one know what Lincoln BELIEVED? The world knows what he DID. He lived his religion, day by day."

Sincerely,

HORACE KEPHART.

Horace Kephart, a Personal Glimpse

BY CLARENCE E. MILLER

For many years distinguished librarian of the
St. Louis Mercantile Library, now retired.

Horace Kephart, descendant of a Swiss immigrant who settled in Pennsylvania in 1740, was born in East Salem in that state, September 8, 1862. His father, Isaiah Kephart, was a pioneer preacher and educator, who moved his family to Iowa in 1867, where he was superintendent of public schools. In 1876 he returned to Pennsylvania. Doubtless those nine years as a schoolboy on the colorful Iowa frontier furnished the background and inspiration for Kephart's lifelong enthusiasm for Western history and the life of the pathfinders.

In the late summer of 1890, applying for a position with the St. Louis Mercantile Library, he gave a résumé of his life to that date:

I was born in Pennsylvania in 1862. My early boyhood was spent in Iowa. Graduating from college in 1879, I spent the following year in Boston, pursuing post-graduate studies. In 1882 I entered the graduate department of Cornell University, and soon became an assistant to the library under Prof. Willard Fiske.

Within a short time I was induced to take up library work as a profession, and was given charge of the cataloguing department. In this capacity I early became accustomed to the training of assistants and to the responsibility for their work. I began the present dictionary-catalogue of that library, and prepared the quarterly bulletin of accessions, of which the St. Louis libraries doubtless have files.

Meanwhile Prof. Fiske had resigned the librarianship of Cornell, and had made his home in Italy, where he devoted his time to enriching his two unique collections of books. Of one of the collections, relating to the Italian poet and humanist Petrarch, he had published a tentative catalogue in Ithaca. By 1884 these Petrarch books had trebled in number and value, and he invited me to come to Florence and help him

---

From *Missouri Historical Society Bulletin*, July 1959

prepare an exhaustive bibliography of the subject. I left America in Dec., '84, and by Feb., '86, the work was done. Most of this time was spent in Italy, where I became acquainted with Italian systems of library administration, but we took a vacation tour in Austria, and spent a month in the private rooms of the Royal Library at Munich, working on our bibliography. This Petrarch catalogue will be published before long in Florence. I inclose herewith a small fragment of it which has been printed as an experiment.

On returning home, I was engaged for a short time in finishing the card-catalogue of the Rutgers College library.

At the 1886 meeting of the American Library Association, at Milwaukee, I met Dr. Wm. F. Poole of Chicago, who offered me the librarianship of a new and well-founded library at E. Saginaw, Mich. At the same time Mr. Van Name, of Yale, offered me the position which, after consultation with Dr. Poole, I accepted and now hold.

Aside from purely bibliographical work, my published writings are few, consisting of occasional correspondence on literary topics in various periodicals. To the *Library Journal* I have contributed two or three articles, of late, on Italian libraries, etc. I do some work for the *Cooperative Index* (continuation to Poole) and have helped in compiling Mr. Fletcher's *Index to General Literature*, now preparing for the press.

While in Europe I was entrusted with some extensive purchases of mediaeval Mss. for ex-President White of Cornell, and subsequent experience has made me familiar with the book-trade at home and abroad.

Horace Kephart

As a result of this factual document, written in a remarkably clear and balanced hand, in September, 1890, Kephart was appointed librarian of the St. Louis Mercantile Library where his application is still on file. The handwriting gives more clue than the text to the personality of this man under whom I worked in the years around the turn of the century. Intellectually he was the most brilliant man I have known, and, almost as a matter of course, the least assuming.

My first meeting with Horace Kephart also came as the result of a letter of application. He hired me after perhaps the briefest interview on record, more, I felt, in order to get rid of me than through any intuitive enthusiasm. I still remember, however, the searching glance he flashed before turning me over to the assistant librarian. Meanwhile, my own glance was as searching as time permitted.

I saw a man of medium height and build, with quick decisive movements that bespoke muscular strength and coordination. His eyes were dark and matched in vital animation and expressiveness only by those of William Marion Reedy, in my experience. His bristling black mustache seemed to me to contrast violently with his finely modeled features, but mustaches and beards always startle me at first sight. All in all, though, I felt assured that here was a man in his thirties from whom a youth of eighteen could learn a lot once that obvious barrier of reserve could be hurdled.

It soon became evident that my personal contacts would be with the assistant librarian and my fellow workers at the issue desk, not with the chief. Kephart lived almost exclusively in a world of his own, guarded most securely by his constant activity. He had no secretary and spent most of his day beating a two-fingered tattoo on a Smith-Premier typewriter. He did his own research in the card catalogue, consulting it many times day, and when he needed a book from the stacks he got it himself. I never saw him on one of these errands without the hopeful feeling that he was about to break into a trot. Late in the afternoon he made his exit, always with a Boston bag gorged with books. A brief but friendly farewell to the assistant nearest him somehow inspired us all.

Kephart was neither introverted nor austere, as I fear my words so far suggest. He was always accessible to the staff or the public. Any legitimate question got either a direct answer or concise information as to where the answer could be found. The range of his information seemed incredible to us who drew on it daily. All of his answers revealed a broad basis of understanding as well as a photographic memory.

There were occasions when a venturesome member of the staff would repeat the current intramural joke to Kephart, whereupon he would laugh in almost boyish manner and add a delightful comment, but for the most part he remained a withdrawn and baffling man.

Horace Kephart was a crack shot with a rifle. At the outbreak of the Spanish-American War he had tried to raise a volunteer company of sharpshooters, but he got small response from the shooting enthusiasts who foregathered with him at a nearby rifle range. His chief recreation was a weekend of hiking in the Ozarks, where he would camp alone overnight. These trips picked him up in vigor and spirits, and Monday morning after one of these excursions found his energy almost contagious.

Early in 1900 ill health forced my resignation. I went to the Cumberland Mountains in Tennessee, where my father in the early 1880's had bought a tract of land near Rugby, the English community founded by Thomas Hughes for the benefit of younger sons of English families, those unemployed young gentlemen who longed for something to do while waiting for death to strike the heir apparent. I was not unduly surprised to find that Kephart knew all about the venture and the area, although he had never visited it. I bade him goodbye with the understanding that I was to report further on the colony when I returned. It was late in the fall when I did return, my health restored, and I soon reported to Kephart. He was much interested in my experiences among the hill people and for the first time I felt close to my old employer, who remarked that I had visited what was perhaps our permanent frontier. The upshot of it all was that I again found myself working at the library, this time as cataloguer.

My new work gave me a further opportunity to learn something of the working of a remarkable mind. I had previously done a little routine work in the catalogue department, but to learn almost book by book as I did from Kephart was like graduating from Squeers' school to Oxford University. In the process of fitting a book into its niche of servitude there was plenty of technical drudgery, but under Kephart there were many delightful side excursions into the magic world of reading which were exciting and stimulating, as were all of his comments on the contemporary scene.

It did not take long to discover that Kephart was moving steadily in the direction of a specialized library. Before the advent of a tax-supported free public library he had planned the book collection on the broadest possible basis; now each month he was buying as much of the material relating to the West as the library's budget would permit. With all the loving labor of an artist creating a mosaic he added a few volumes a week in his chosen field. At that time St. Louis was still actively the natural gateway to the West, and here, he often remarked, was the logical spot for the largest collection of Western Americana. Besides, the Mercantile Library was the oldest general library west of the Mississippi.

All of the writers on the early West consulted Kephart. I remember best Hiram Chittenden, the historian of the fur trade, and Emerson Hough, whose *Covered Wagon* became a best seller. To hear them in discussion was like a trip over the mountains with Fremont, or a voyage up the far reaches of the Missouri with Lewis and Clark. Only a few of the library members were much interested in this plan of Westward expansion of the library, even though many of them were descendants of fur traders.

Kephart's aura of loneliness deepened in the years 1902 and 1903. His trips to the Ozarks became more frequent, and these absences soon began to alienate the library's directors. As far as I could tell, his companions narrowed to a group of intellectual Bohemians headed by William Marion Reedy. I was told by some of them that Kephart, like Poe, could alter his personality by taking a single drink, but I never saw any evidence of this trait. In the library he was the same indefatigable worker devouring dealers' catalogues and keeping the now aging typewriter rattling away.

Late in 1903 tragedy struck from all sides. Kephart was discharged. Evidently he had no money, and shortly before Christmas his wife left for her parents' home in the

East, taking the children, an attractive little brood so active that I could never count them when they visited the library.

We of the library staff were utterly bewildered by the swift turn of events, and by the accompanying rumors, most of which we knew to be false. If those which we could neither verify or deny were true, it made no difference in our estimate of Kephart as librarian and employer. A man's true stature is always known to his employees. Conversely, and to add a few gratuitous teeth to an old saw, no man is a hero to his valet—unless he really is a hero.

When Kephart's successor appeared, I fitted up a corner of my office where my old chief could wind up his library affairs, an arrangement more sentimental than practical, and abandoned after a few days.

Meanwhile, I appealed to my father, then associate editor of the St. Louis *Globe-Democrat*. Father admired Kephart's literary style and thought the paper might use him on the corps of correspondents covering the Russo-Japanese war. Henry King, the editor-in-chief, approved. Kephart himself was enthusiastic, saying he and John Fox, Jr., whose war correspondence was being carried by the *Globe-Democrat*, had attended college together. As soon as Kephart completed a few literary commitments he was to report to the paper, but early in April, 1904, he suffered a complete nervous collapse and was taken to a hospital. His father, by then editor of *The Religious Telescope*, the country's leading Methodist weekly, arrived from Dayton, Ohio, and took his son away.

When next I heard of Kephart he was in Bryson City, North Carolina, where he went to recuperate, and where he lived the rest of his life. Like Thoreau and many another maladjusted genius, he had found himself by turning to nature. In his new mountain home he could write and hunt and wander. He could mingle with people close enough to nature to be natural, a therapy even I, a far cry from genius, had previously found effective.

Kephart soon became friend, emergency doctor, lawyer, and general adviser to his neighbors. He wrote of them in his *Our Southern Highlanders*, to many, as to me, the best book on these self-reliant and sturdy people. It was published in 1910.[47]

Kephart was an active promoter of the Great Smoky Mountains National Park. As he became better known in North Carolina, he was honored in many ways. He served as the president of the state library association, a rather belated recognition of his library work. Mount Kephart, a peak near Clingman's Dome, was named for him. In 1926, he was visited by F. A. Behymer of the St. Louis *Post-Dispatch*, whose interesting account of his visit ought to be reprinted. It seems that Kephart, whose name had been dropped from *Who's Who in America* some years before, had been reinstated as rehabilitated or something, and Mr. Behymer wanted to look into the rather ironic incident.

In 1930 Kephart was elected president of the North Carolina State Literary and Historical Association, and his inaugural address was a scholarly contribution to the history of the Cherokee Indians.

On April 2, 1931, Horace Kephart was killed in a taxicab accident while showing a visitor around the mountains. He was buried in Bryson City, where his grave is marked by a huge granite boulder placed there by his neighbors. On the first anniversary of this death, the Horace Kephart Memorial Association met on Mount Kephart to honor the memory of the man they revered for his scholarship, and loved for his sympathetic understanding.

As this sketch is intended only as a personal glimpse, I have done scant justice to Kephart's years of fulfillment. I have had trouble enough with the man I recall. Genius is much easier to recognize than to describe, made up as it is of a wider range of receptivity, greater power of concentration, and a mystic rapport with the mind of the universe. Even a list of his writings reveals only his defiant loneliness, always a penalty of genius, as evidenced by all those books on how to live alone in the woods and like it; his love of nature; and his thorough knowledge of American history, especially in its frontier aspects. All of Kephart's writing reflects his scholarly precision and disciplined literary style; but I miss the illuminating phrases that broke through the innate reserve of the man in the all too few days of our intimacy.

APPENDIX

Books and Published Addresses by Horace Kephart:

Camp Cookery, 1910 and later editions
Camper's Manual, 1923
Camping and Woodcraft, 1916–17, 2 v.
Cherokee Indians, 1932
Guns, Ammunition, and Tackle, 1904 (To this Kephart contributed only the section on the hunting rifle.)
National Park in the Great Smoky Mountains, 1925
Our Southern Highlanders, 1926
Pennsylvania's Part in the Winning of the West, 1902
Smoky Mountains, 1936 (Re-written and edited from his papers)
Sporting Firearms, 1912
Books Edited or Compiled by Kephart:
Captives Among the Indians, 1915
Castaways and Crusoes, 1915
Dunraven, W.T.W., *Hunting in the Yellowstone*, 1917
Hobart-Hampden, A.C., *Hobart Pasha*, 1915

Ruxton, Geo. F.A., *Adventures in Mexico*, 1915

Ruxton, Geo. F.A., *In the Old West*, 1915

Between 1890 and 1930 inclusive, the periodical indexes list upwards of fifty articles written by Kephart. The earlier ones deal mainly with library science. From 1904 he dealt predominantly with outdoor life and firearms. His contributions to periodicals not covered by the indexes were many, but they are difficult to locate. Mr. John Bersoth, an authority, on guns, lists the following articles by Kephart appearing in periodicals not included in the standard periodical index:

"An Old Rifle and Its Story," *Shooting and Fishing*, March 5, 1896

"My Backwoods Rifle," *Shooting and Fishing*, October 1, 1896

"Reply to Captain Meyrick," *Shooting and Fishing*, December 16, 1897

"The Hawken Rifle," *The American Rifleman*, April 15, 1924

Editor's Note:

Most of the material on the latter part of Kephart's life is drawn from the *North Carolina Historical Review*.

two

FAMILY AND FRIENDS

Leonard departs for Africa with Kephart family
to see him off. New York City, 1927.

Introduction

LIBBY KEPHART HARGRAVE AND GEORGE FRIZZELL

Family by Libby Kephart Hargrave

My grandfather, George Stebbins Kephart, was the fifth child of Horace and Laura Kephart. He taught me that we stand on the shoulders of those who went before us as his passion for genealogy came from Horace and from his grandfather, Isaiah Lafayette Kephart. For years, he and his sisters Lucy and Margaret worked tirelessly researching and organizing family documents. Much of this cherished material has been donated to the Special Collections of Western Carolina University.

To understand Horace Kephart, it is important to understand that he also stood on the shoulders of his family, both those in the present and those who preceded him, as this support allowed him to move forward after his nervous breakdown in 1904. In the opening paragraph of his autobiographical article "Horace Kephart, By Himself" (reprinted in chapter one), he invoked his ancestors in noting that his "passion for the mountains may be inherited" given his Swiss background and the family's settlement of the Susquehanna region of western Pennsylvania before the Revolutionary War. Before moving to North Carolina, he visited the old family cemetery in Pennsylvania, as if to connect back to their frontier experiences before embarking on his own unforeseen future in a quest for a new life.

Kephart's parents were Dr. Isaiah and Elizabeth Goss Kephart. Isaiah was a brilliant man who throughout his life stood steadfast in his faith and convictions. Isaiah was Horace Kephart's hero. He was a highly respected editor and preacher. During the Civil War he enlisted in the Union army and served as a chaplain in the Twenty-First Pennsylvania Cavalry. Elizabeth was a devoted wife and mother, providing a kind, loving home—a home where education was a high priority. Isaiah was an outdoorsman who taught his curious son skills that gave him a lifelong desire for learning how to survive—and thrive—in any environment. He also instilled in Horace a passion to research iconic figures such as the frontiersman Daniel Boone and the nineteenth-century camping expert George Washington Sears, who used the pen name "Nessmuk."[1]

In 1867, at the age of five, Horace moved with his family from East Salem, Pennsylvania, to Jefferson, Iowa, what he termed "a frontier village set in a prairie wilderness" in his brief autobiography. Here he spent countless hours in the out-of-doors. At that time, he had no siblings. Schooling took place at home with his mother as his first teacher, and like any student who has an excellent teacher, he gained from her his love for reading and writing. Elizabeth instilled in her son a lifelong passion for books and opened his world to horizons beyond Pennsylvania and the Iowa prairie. As he often noted, "When I was seven, and could read almost anything, she gave me my first book, dear old *Robinson Crusoe*. It has been saved through the vicissitudes of a somewhat venturesome life, and lies before me now, coverless and stained with age, but more precious than all the thousands of other books that I afterwards acquired." Ultimately, his embrace of books led to a career as a prominent and nationally known librarian.[2]

Elizabeth Belle, Horace's sister, was born February 18, 1871. She and Horace were the best of friends. Like her brother, she had a passion for education. In "A Biographical Sketch of the Life, and a Tribute to the Memory, of Elizabeth Belle Kephart," her father wrote of her happiness for his [Horace's] address to the graduating class at Lebanon Valley College in Annville, Pennsylvania, in 1879, and the excitement of visiting him at Cornell University in 1883 to see the campus. In September 1885 Belle began her college studies in the Latin scientific course at Westfield College, where her father served as president, and expressed a hope to eventually attend Cornell.

Horace and Belle always knew they were loved. The ties that bound them were as bands of steel. No condition, nor situation, could separate or cause Isaiah and Elizabeth to turn away from their children—ever. Unfortunately, Belle unexpectedly died in 1892 at the age of twenty-one of scarlet fever. Her death must have been so difficult and emotionally draining for Horace. With his own family commitments, which included a newborn and other small children, he was not able to be at her bedside in her brief illness, nor to attend the funeral. Not to be with his sister while she was sick and dying must have left a darkness in his heart and mind that time never healed.

By autumn of 1903, physically and mentally exhausted, Horace Kephart was a broken man. He resigned his position with the Mercantile Library in St. Louis. Laura and the six children moved back to her hometown of Ithaca, New York. Prior to leaving, Laura helped Horace move into a small apartment located on Kennett Place in St. Louis. In a letter to my father, Roy Ferris Kephart, dated May 31, 1983, my granddad (George Stebbins Kephart) wrote that, "It should be noted that Mom [Laura], with us kids, moved to Ithaca some time before Dad left St. Louis, eventually for the Smokies. We left him. I was 5–6 years old at the time."[3] March 24, 1904, my great-grandfather, once the head librarian at the prestigious St. Louis Mercantile Library, had a nervous breakdown. When Laura received word about Horace, she took the train to Dayton, Ohio, met his parents, and together they went to St. Louis to be by his side. A wife going to help her husband. A mother and father going to help their son. No condition, nor situation, could separate or cause them to turn away from him—ever. Their love never faltered. Their love never wavered. For Laura, Kep's breakdown must have been very painful and sad. It must have been difficult for Laura to see Horace drift away—drift away into the woods—drift away into the bottle. Kep needed to walk trails, not sidewalks. He needed an office in the woods, not in a cement building surrounded by more cement buildings. Kephart understood the reality of who he was, what happened, and what he needed to do to heal. He knew where he needed to go. So did his parents. So did Laura.

Even though they were separated by hundreds of miles, he knew that they would always be there for him. This is evident in the few letters that we have that were shared between them. Horace and Laura had an agreement that, upon their deaths, all letters to each other were to be burnt. Some writers and researchers have asked the question "why," and there have been stories filled with speculation about their marriage. Well, speculation is not the truth. Reality is the truth. Words shared between my great-grandparents were simply that—words shared between husband and wife. No need for others to read, not even their six children. The few letters that exist are part of the Horace and Laura Mack Kephart Family Collection at Special Collections. An unpublished manuscript by Leonard Kephart, Horace and Laura's eldest son, recalled the tenacity of Laura to retain family bonds after Horace's departure, noting that "all through the tough years, Mom gave continuing proof of her courage, of her detached understanding of the situation and of her continuing love for Dad. I am convinced that her love was reciprocated . . . I never heard Mom speak an unkind word against Dad."[4] In my foreword to *Smoky Mountain Magic*, Horace's long-lost novel written in the 1920s and published in 2009, I wrote of my belief that Laura understood his need for a healing, to find his "Back of Beyond," and so accepted it in love and recognition.[5]

This is not to say that it was "easy" for the family. Laura was on her own, raising six children. When she moved back to Ithaca in 1903, she was surrounded by family and friends— some who did not or would not understand why she would not divorce Horace. To them he was a ne'er-do-well; he had abandoned her. Laura should have given up on him—many, many times. But she did not. Her love for Horace was constant, a constant source of strength and courage. The same can be said of Horace's love for Laura.

She worked tirelessly and without complaint to provide for her family. A few of the jobs she held were as a secretary and teaching piano. She even made and sold potato chips and cooked meals for the Cornell Crew Team, of which Leonard and George were members. George was the coxswain for the Cornell championship team. As it turned out, Cornelia, Lucy, and Barbara each married a member of the crew team! In Horace's scrapbook in Special Collections, there is a clipping from the August 1904 issue of *Leslie's Weekly* magazine of a photograph often referred to as the "stairstep children"—the six Kephart children aligned by height in ascending order. It was in Ithaca that the photo was taken. A beautiful photo of six remarkable children. For many years, they would reenact the scene, with the last known dating from around 1917.[6]

Laura was an exceptional mother. She was a devoted wife. She spent long hours making canvas tents from designs Kep sketched. She tested food recipes and discussed with him the many gadgets and camp gear he devised and tested for other companies. They understood each other and the reasons which made their separation necessary.

In 1904, Horace began his new life, his "new freedom" as he wrote in his "Index to Diary" (see addenda). Once settled on Hazel Creek, he sent photos of his cabin to Laura and each of his children. Because he did not frequently speak or write about his family, one might think that they were estranged or he was totally withdrawn from personal contact with them. All his children stayed in touch with him, and he with them. Throughout his many years in the Smokies, they sent him photos of their children, trips, family gatherings, etc. Of interest are the many letters, photos, and Christmas cards his children sent him during his years in the mountains. Many of these are part of the Kephart collection in Special Collections. There were times, however, he did not know what was going on with the family, but I believe, given the circumstances and the miles separating them, they all did the best they could. It is evident they cared about each other and loved each other.

I believe if Laura had divorced Horace, spoken harsh words about him to the children, led them to dislike him, etc., it would have killed him. He would have simply gone to the mountains and died. He was loved by his family, and they were loved by him. My grandfather loved and respected his father. My grandfather made sure his grandchildren knew who their great-grandfather was and what he accomplished. He said to me, "When you go to the Smokies, you will know who you are . . . what you are made of." He was right!

My great-grandfather was a man of many accomplishments. Of all his accomplishments, the most remarkable and important one is . . . he found his way back. For that, we must all be grateful. As reprinted in this chapter, less than two months

5

LESLIE'S WEEKLY August 18, 1904

YOUTHFUL BOTANISTS.—*Frank G. Smith, Michigan.*

WELL GRADED—SIX CHILDREN OF ONE FAMILY.—*Miss W. Williams, New York.*

NEW ENGLAND MAGAZINE

JULY, 1905

Hunting Wild Bees

By HORACE KEPHART

ONE day when I was hunting in the overflow lands of eastern Arkansas, I found signs of bears in the cane-brake near our camp. We had neither dogs nor horses, both of which are needed for bear hunting in the big blue cane. The question was, how to entice a bear into the open slue, where a man afoot could get a shot at it. In my chuck-box was a comb of honey that I had brought along to help out the camp biscuits. Saying nothing to my mates, for I was sceptical as to the outcome of the experiment I had in mind, I took the honey to a place where a bear had been "using," and fixed the comb to a grape-vine, out of reach of 'coons but convenient for a bear. It was my scheme to lie in ambush and wait for the bear's sweet tooth to get him into trouble. This might have been unsportsmanlike in an open region; but all's fair between man and beast in the jungle.

But we did not get bear meat that day. There came a sudden change in the weather. It turned bright and warm. Bruin did not accept my invitation; but he had some busy-body neighbors who promptly took it for their own. The wild bees turned out, and in a jiffy they were hard at work despoiling the Philistine.

From bear hunting to bee hunting seemed a natural step. This was my first experience in trailing the honey bee. Soon I became so absorbed in the new sport that I forgot all about the bigger game that I had set out to hunt. It did not take long to learn that trying to follow wild bees to their home in the tall forest

A SETTLER'S BEE-GUM

542

Page in Kephart scapbook from *Leslie's Weekly* August 18, 1904, of children along with Kephart article.

following Horace's death on April 2, 1931, Laura wrote to his longtime friend Harry Koopman and confided that many could not understand the reaction to his loss. She acknowledged the difficulties that "prevented our living under one roof," and yet she asserted that "Horace was the only man in my life . . . Horace fought a terrible fight & won a marvelous victory. I have more than most women for which to be thankful."[7] Laura was a woman of remarkable strength and courage. She teaches all of us the true meaning of the marriage vows she and Horace exchanged on April 12, 1887—to love and to cherish, in sickness and in health, till death do us part. Laura Mack Kephart died in 1954 at the age of 92. A life well lived.

Many writers have assumed that Horace had no contact with his family whatsoever. This is understandable considering the only material available to them did not include this information. The WCU Special Collections of Hunter Library houses the premier holdings of Horace's manuscripts, photographs, and items from his personal library, and the university's Mountain Heritage Center museum preserves dozens of artifacts.[8] However, the original collection, while extensive, focused heavily on his research interests and his professional life as a writer. Over the past several years, I have donated hundreds of family letters and photographs to Special Collections and to the Great Smoky Mountains Association, as well as some of my great-grandfather's personal belongings to the Mountain Heritage Center. They disclose a more personal and often neglected or unknown side. They reveal a Horace who sent his fiancée, Laura, a small bouquet of dried flowers that he picked in the Alps, his introspective letters to friends, and even Christmas cards that he had received. Writers and researchers now have the opportunity, if they so choose, to get to know Horace in a way not available until recently.

Far from being a hermit in Southern Appalachia, Horace developed new friendships that inspired him and that would populate his writings with their personalities and common interests. Reprinted throughout this volume are letters and articles that invoke friends, colleagues, and continued family ties. Among them are his son Leonard about writing *Smoky Mountain Magic* (see chapter six); Harry Koopman, his friend since his librarian years; Bob Barnett, a friendship formed upon arrival on Hazel Creek; the mysterious "Snake-Stick Man," also known as "Mr. Quick," who gained notoriety in Kephart's adventures while living in Bryson City; and George Masa, the travel companion of his later years and fellow proponent in preserving and experiencing the mountains.

The letters in this chapter are poignant, humorous, and often matter-of-fact. A recently widowed Laura expresses her appreciation for condolences she has received.

LEFT
George Masa

BELOW
"Bob Barnett, Jim Stewart, and Boys."

In a 1920 letter to Leonard, signed "Dad," Horace assures him that "the latch-string is always out here, and I hope you will come sometime." He also mentions his friendship with the Barnett family and photographs that he took of a Cherokee stick-ball game.[9] Details in Horace's August 1929 letter to Leonard were incorporated into an article on a camping expedition with George Masa only weeks later (as reprinted here in chapter two).[10] Perhaps the most personal is a letter written by Lucy, his daughter, in which she confides about the possible causes of his nervous breakdown but also praises her mother for the tireless burden she accepted to support the children and, also, the unyielding refusal to condemn her husband.

I grew up knowing the story of Horace and Laura and their children. When I was a young girl, my grandfather said to me, "There is a mountain named after your great-grandfather. It's called Mount Kephart." To a young girl that was pretty interesting . . . and a bit of an ego trip! A mountain with my last name! A few minutes after he told me about Mount Kephart, I went outdoors, climbed his beautiful apple tree, sat there for a while, and thought about Mount Kephart, and questions started racing through my mind—Who was this man? Who was my great-grandfather? Thus began my lifelong passion for preserving my family legacy. When I was close to ten years of age, my grandparents took my sisters Laura, Linda, Joanne, and me on our very first trip to the Smokies. We visited Kep's grave in Bryson City, walked along Kephart Prong, and were treated to a VIP showing of "Unto These Hills." This was a trip that would forever impact my life. As my grandfather taught me, I stood upon the shoulders of those who came before me and have tried to share it with Horace's friends who abide with him down to this day—and beyond.

Kephart's Friends by George Frizzell

Horace Kephart made friends throughout his life and maintained contact with them for decades through both happy and difficult times. These pages are by no means a definitive summation of his friends and companions but seek to demonstrate the range and endurance of the relations he often forged.

EARLY LIFE AND LIBRARIAN CAREER, 1862–1904 Kephart acknowledged a lonesome childhood growing up in rural Iowa, wherein he found solace and inspiration in the copy of *Robinson Crusoe* that his mother had given him. Yet, during the years of his college education and then as a professional librarian, he established several close friendships with comrades in whom he could confide and celebrate life. As seen in George Ellison and Janet McCue's introduction to chapter one and in the selections in this chapter, his friends included Harry Koopman and Willard

Granville Calhoun family.

Fiske, both of whom shared Kephart's passion for libraries and books. Closer in age to Kephart, Koopman had similar educational and career experiences, and he would later become librarian at Brown University. Kephart and his family maintained a longstanding correspondence with Koopman, and Laura wrote to him a personally revealing letter after her husband's death. As the first librarian at Cornell University, Fiske was older and served as a teacher and mentor in the early 1880s. In late 1884, after he left Cornell, Fiske engaged Kephart to join him in Italy for a year to catalog his extensive collection of materials dedicated to Petrarch. Clarence Miller recalled his time with Kephart at the St. Louis Mercantile Library with admiration for his abilities. He also helped Kephart get a position as a correspondent with the *St. Louis Globe-Democrat* where his father worked after Kephart's resignation from the library in 1903, though this proved temporary as Kephart's major life-crisis loomed and he chose to depart St. Louis forever in 1904.

HAZEL CREEK AND TRAVELS, 1904–1909 After Kephart moved to Hazel Creek, he became friends with people who ranged from wealthy, successful entrepreneurs to men and women of ordinary means but possessing exceptional knowledge in the practical matters that Kephart appreciated. Always the librarian and the learner, he sought out their experiences, listened to their lives, and memorialized them in his writings. Among these were store-owner Granville Calhoun and businessman Jack Coburn, who helped him get established in a new life. But, without doubt, the most influential were his neighbors Bob and Sarah Barnett. Not only did they ease the solitude in his initial cabin home, they brought him into their house. From the Barnetts, Kephart compiled a wealth of knowledge, which he channeled into his research journals and publications. Kephart readily acknowledged his indebtedness to the Barnetts. Bob was a source of dialect, local lore, humor, and practical matters in daily living. Sarah was an inspiration for his book *Camp Cookery* (1910) and received credit as "Mistress Bob" in the dedication. As noted in his letter to Louis Hampton recounting his past two years of travels, Kephart later lived with the Barnetts in Lindale, Georgia, in 1909. He also lived with the couple on Deep Creek near Bryson City for several months after his return to the Great Smokies in 1910. As Ellison and McCue point out, Kephart patterned important figures in his novel *Smoky Mountain Magic* after the real-life Barnetts.

GREAT SMOKY MOUNTAINS, 1910–1931 In 1910 Kephart eventually relocated from Deep Creek and took up residence in the Cooper House, a boarding house in Bryson City, and also secured office space in a nearby building with a view overlooking the Tuckasegee River. As before, he made friends and established lasting personal bonds as he continued to pursue his interests in outdoor life and delve into the region's history and culture. As noted, Kephart incorporated many of these friends and companions into his publications and accounts of his own exploits.

However, there is a mystery about Kephart's latter associations. As Jim Casada rightfully points out in his introduction to chapter four, there were individuals with whom Kephart would have had shared interests but that are missing from his writings. Among these were Sam Hunnicutt and Mark Cathey, both legendary in their own right as masterful outdoorsmen and founts of experience about western North Carolina. In a similar fashion, contemporary authors about Southern Appalachia are often absent from Kephart's publications even as he emerged as a major voice about the region. Mae Miller Claxton notes in the introduction to chapter six that, while their works were often present on his bookshelves, there are several noted writers not represented in the available corpus of Kephart's correspondence as literary friends, such as Emma Bell Miles, Margaret Morley, and Olive Tilford Dargan.

Even so, readers might appreciate Kephart's account of how he became acquainted in the spring of 1919 with W. W. Thomason, better known as the "Snake-Stick Man" and as "Mr. Quick," as he was described in his exploits in Kephart's publications.[11] When the two met at their shared lodging house, unbeknownst to Kephart was that Thomason was an undercover federal agent charged with enforcing Prohibition laws. Their initial casual interaction became a closer association through no less than the lure of a book—a Spanish translation of a Sir Arthur Conan Doyle novel that Thomason was reading that caught Kephart's eye. In the ensuing conversation, the two quickly established shared interests in Native American culture, firearms, and literary pursuits. Also, Thomason "had a good camera" and offered to "accompany me into the hills and make any pictures I wished." Even after learning of Thomason's true intentions to investigate and prosecute liquor violations taking place on the lands of the Eastern Band of Cherokee Indians, the two men made their peace, and Kephart was persuaded to accompany him on a "man-hunt" into the Tennessee side of the Great Smoky Mountains. Kephart ruefully admitted later that in a visit with the Barnetts, "Bob and Mrs. Bob kidded me a good deal, this time about having been taken in by the Snake-Stick Man."[12]

One friend that Kephart often invoked in his correspondence and articles was George Masa, the gifted photographer based in Asheville, North Carolina. The two friends had a love of the outdoors, a love of hiking, and eventually a desire to preserve part of the Great Smoky Mountains in a national park.[13] They developed a symbiotic connection to help achieve the latter goal. Kephart, the writer, joined with Masa, the photographer, to promote a park to the public and to demonstrate its worthiness through words and images. Masa, who died in 1933, outlived Kephart by barely two years. Despite his wishes and the urging of mutual friends of Kephart, the two were not buried together inside the proposed boundaries of the newly emerging national park that had captured their hopes.

The rather enigmatic Fiswoode Tarleton, a noted fiction author in his short life, provides a bookend to Kephart's friends. While residing in Georgia at the time, Tarleton was visiting Kephart in Bryson City in early 1931. As is well known, he was with Kephart on the last night of their lives in that fateful car ride on April 2. Memorial services were held for both in Bryson City a few days later. Tarleton's was a sparse affair, attended by family. However, as a final testament to Kephart's personality and career, hundreds of people turned out for his funeral, and testimonials filled the local newspaper. Among the attendees were wife Laura, sons Leonard and George, daughter Lucy, and a grandson.[14]

Kephart was laid to rest in the cemetery overlooking Byson City and with a view of Mount Kephart in the Smokies and the nearby Masa Knob. In the following years, friends such as Jack Coburn and I. K. Stearns worked to settle his estate and assist his widow Laura.[15] But perhaps the greatest gift of friendship, and one continued by his family, was the realization that Kephart's papers should be preserved—a desire realized and a bequest that has benefited new generations of researchers.

As additional Kephart manuscripts are brought to public access, they have revealed a more personal side of the individual who was often cloaked in the aura of his professional and literary career. Researchers have been interested in both the information Kephart accumulated and attracted to the legacy—and at times myth—of his life. It might have been journalist F. A. Behymer of the *St. Louis Post-Dispatch* who captured one more longtime "friend" of Kephart's in his 1926 article when he listed twenty books that Kephart reputedly brought with him to Hazel Creek in his search for renewal: "It was the old life calling, the life of books that he had left. For such a man there could be a beginning again but the old life could not be entirely disowned. He had known that it would be so and had made provision. Into his exile he had taken with him a 'library' that would serve him when, with returning health, would come the yearning for books. . . . There they were, the friends that had come with him out of the other life. And they were classified."[16]

Kephart's love of books remained a compass point through life. From *Robinson Crusoe* through the thousands he read or owned, even down to a chosen few, he sought them out. And, through all accomplishments or failings, rest assured that Kephart's own books are on the shelves of those who admire him or disagree, in libraries, and being read today.

Letter from Kephart to Harry Lyman Koopman, October 21, 1888

New Haven, Conn.
Oct. 21, '88.

Dear Koopman.—[17]

I have come in from a long walk in a stiff, cold wind, and my hands are so numb that writing is difficult.

We received your new book a few days ago and like it even better than the first one. I think that "Woman's Will" shows a steady development of your muse. The compliment of writing those lines "On Laura's Picture" is renewed by printing them. Your printer, too, has done you a good job in getting up the booklet very tastefully. I am glad to see the favor with which "Orestes" was received, and expect to read even more favorable notices of "Woman's Will."

They tell us that you are to accompany Nelson to New Orleans. Is it true? If so, you will be passing this way before long, and must stop and let us get a good talk out of you. We are still at 33 Beers St., living in a very quiet way, but getting about as much solid enjoyment out of life as anybody. After two years experience of New Haven I can say good things about it—the faults being, chiefly, that lack of public spirit which seems proper to any old town, and the monopoly of a damnable climate. I like Yale; it is solid, free from shams, plain-spoken & trustworthy. Cornell seems to be booming nowadays; but I mistrust the solidity of things there—too much veneer.

Well! my hands don't thaw out at all. I've been out looking for a secluded spot where I could put up a 50 or 100 yd. target and practice with my new rifle Saturday afternoons; but the search is disappointing. There are too many back-yards and cow-pastures in this quarter of the world. Imagine Boston or Florence set in the midst of the Yellowstone Park, with no suburbs, nor even a farm within 200 miles—that's my idea of Paradise. When a fellow wanted to, he could go to the Public Library or the Opera; when he wanted to, he could walk right out into the primeval truth of things and cuss the universe of shams—be Samuel Johnson and Daniel Boone by turns!

Please let us know about the New Orleans business, and when to expect you this way. You ought to see the baby!

Fraternally yours,
Horace Kephart.

Letter from Kephart to Willard Fiske, April 27, 1889

New Haven, Ct.
Apr. 27, 1889.

Dear Professor [Fiske],—[18]

I am slow to epistolize; forgive me! These are the times that try men's souls. April showers have succeeded the fickle thaws and freezes of "the strangest winter we have ever known," and we have honest, law-abiding mud at last. There is comfort in the thought, of course, that we have done with surprises for a season and know just what to expect in the way of weather for a fortnight. But in the fogs of this unspeakable coast lurk ghostly influences, puritanic, as becomes the soul, which urge men to all sorts of penance for imagined sins, and I have not escaped. Sixteen days ago I stopped smoking.

It is remarkable how climate influences morals. If my lob had been cast upon the banks of the Nile, where you have lately been recuperating strength to tackle Petrarch, I would be a bare-legged Mohammedan, think and dress as little as possible, throw stones at the tax-collector, and have a rousing good time. Alas! a most unkind fate has drifted me upon that coast where it is still unlawful for a boy to sneeze in meeting, or for a man to cheat his neighbor on Sundays. Moisture and execration of the ungodly fill the air. Ever since I was first stranded in New Haven my soul has quivered with remorse for something I knew not what. At last the awakening came. I saw my sin. Outraged tradition demanded why Connecticut leaf should be smoked within sniff of Centre Church so long as it was swapable for silver with the heathen round about. My spirit funked, and in an evil hour I swore off allegiance to my comforter.

Now I am sorry—darned sorry; but the die is cast. My friends have all complimented me upon my fortitude. Weak-willed sinners have been helped by my example. My wife pampers me with all sorts of dainties in compensation for the luxury renounced. My parents bless me; my wife's relatives smother me with compliments; and no doubt Mrs. Fiske will join the chorus when she hears the news. Who could be so mean-spirited as to betray all this confidence and pride? No; the thing is done;—and what an ass I was to do it!

This place will be the ruin of me, I fear, for the humors it breeds are as fickle as the barometer. Well, are nob politics, religion, and the like, matters of temperament, which is itself a matter of wind, heat and relative humidity? What, then, would you expect of Connecticut character? In a warm country your Dante can go without fires, dress in vegetable fibre, live on lentils, and have time enough to himself to be himself, Dante. But in a cold country the wind and snow and niggardly soil force a man to work, to slave. His descendants tug and haul a thousand years, and what is the result? The 39 Articles and a tendency towards consumption; some colleges, many jails, more lunatic asylums, and Harrison for President. Civilization is oppressive here. In Florence your genius is spontaneous. Here there is no genius, but a bit of talent smelted, moulded, hammered, turned, ground, polished by years of unremitting toil which makes of your scholar a hump-backed, spectacled, sallow and misanthropic old chump. No: this Connecticut-shore civilization has neither grace nor spontaneity, and my soul abhors it.

"Drum hab' ich mich der Magie ergeben, . . ."[19]

I've bought a rifle, won permission of the military authorities to use their range, and every pleasant Saturday afternoon I bang away at targets or roam over the hills and through the marshes, taking snap-shots at whatever offers. This may not become me as a gentleman and a scholar, but it fills my lungs, steadies my nerves, and gives me an appetite to be proud of. The ability to plunk an 8-inch bull's-eye at 200 yards, off-hand, gives me what my master's degree does not—the consciousness that I would be good for something in a crisis.

But the rain is showing signs of letting-up, and so must I. As you have probably received, ere this, a copy of Pt. 1. of Burr's catalogue of the White library I will say no more about it, except to call attention to the cover and the imprint. Otherwise I think it quite creditable.

You will find inclosed some odd [unreadable] relating to the great Humanist—none of which may be new to you, however—also some clippings from the Ithaca Daily Journal (gossip, of course).

We like the report of your tour in the East. That you took things easy, and did not boil over with new enthusiasms, is promise of strength and health to come. Now if you can get in three hours a day on Petrarch and Icelandic, and be content with that, you are a hero.

With loving regards to Mrs. Fiske from us all, and remembrances to Ettore,[20]

Truly yours,
Horace Kephart.

Letter from Kephart to Harry Lyman Koopman, December 29, 1908

137 Hudson St., Ithaca, N.Y.
December 29, 1908.

My dear Koopman:—[21]

The portrait of a matured man in a little volume of matured art that Laura showed me among her Christmas presents recalls a young and ardent face that once I welcomed to Ithaca. Strange things have happened since that day; among them, that I should have returned to the old haunts a stranger, and—if one could permit himself the sentimentalism—a Rip Van Winkle. It is more comforting to take your word, that

"Who may hie home at night
From farthest wandering
Never strays from home."

An age ago, when I was in the Smoky Mountains, there came from you a letter that stirred me how deeply I cannot tell. Twice I tried to answer it; but failed. How could I, there? Six or eight pages only proved that the incommunicable cannot be written; and with that absurd result I ceased.

Early last fall a message reached me in Tennessee that my father was dangerously ill. I took the first train for Dayton, and nursed him to the end. He died October 28. After seeing my mother comfortably settled in the home of one of my uncles, I set out for Ithaca. It is now just a month since my two boys met me at the Lehigh Valley station and guided me to this home that I had never seen. It has taken a month to make the dream turn tangible. Laura, indeed, has the gift of perennial youth. But the children have changed wonderfully. Gradually we are getting acquainted. I no longer stand in awe of them, nor address them, instinctively, as Sir or Madame.

Outside of the home circle I have scarcely ventured. You remember my old chum, Billy Kerr, the meteorologist? He is city clerk, now. Well, I took a long walk with him, and what do you suppose we found for major topic? The Ithaca water-works! It was not Billy's fault. Suppose you should meet Columbus, reincarnated, on the streets of Providence; could you interest him in modern affairs? Not a bit of it. His thoughts would revert to Cat Island and the court of Spain. "A fig for your inventions! A continent to toss a pot with the bo's'n of the *Pinta*!" Going along Fall Creek I scarce noticed the hydraulic laboratory or the new town beyond the gorge. What I did see was Tsumaki[22] fighting his first American hornet, and Koopman fishing young Kephart from imminent peril of drowning or broken bones. What are the 300,000 volumes in Sage's mausoleum?[23] I haven't looked at them. There once was [handwritten correction] a real library in old McGraw. Often, in Florence, Fiske used to recite to me Thackeray's "Ballad of Bouillabaisse." Now it is I who am the "grizzled, grim old fogy", and mine it is to

"Fill up the lonely glass, and drain it
  In memory of dear old times."

They tell me, though, that one landmark remains unchanged: Harris is still extant, still selecting pens and pencils with circumspection, as in days of yore. When we meet him in hell or heaven, he'll be doing the same.

Of course, I am reciting nothing new. A thousand other old Cornellians, returning after long absence, have swallowed their hearts and "whinled" a little, as my backwoods comrades say. To me, though, who have been not only out of Ithaca, but out of civilization, for years, the change is abrupt indeed. To exchange rifle and camp-fire and the silence of the great forest for wife and children and the chimes ringing over Cayuga is a veritable reincarnation, and ragged old Rip will come to mind in spite of myself.

It is awkward. The chief penalty of a solitary life is introspection; and when your hermit abandons his shell, what can he say to his fellow men? If he talks at all, it must be about himself, for he knows nobody else. So, here, I try to write you a letter, and can only fall into the strain of the "Bouillabaisse," which is morbid and selfish and does no one good.

Of the future, then. You spoke of it, generously, in your letter. If I can avoid administrative work, it would be better. To be a bibliographer, say, or librarian of some special collection, would suit me well. Such a position, if it held me to the desk only nine months of the year, would be my ideal, and the salary could be docked in proportion to the time spent on vacation, which would be out of doors. However, I cannot be chooser, and anything you can guide me to would be appreciated. What I would fail at, signally, would be a librarianship of the political type that would require much appearing in society and public speaking. My health is good, and I am resolved to keep it so, at all hazards.

Well, this is long enough for one letter. I will be glad to hear from you, and so will Laura and the young folks. Tell us about yourself and your family. Has your work by this time eddied into a smooth routine, or must you keep keen watch ahead?

Yours ever,

Horace Kephart.

"Louis Hampton and Children."

Letter from Kephart to Louis Hampton, October 5, 1909

Lindale, Ga.
Oct. 5, 1909.

Dear Louis.—[24]

As I have not heard from you in a long time, I will write and ask you to let me know how you are getting along.

I left Little River more than a year ago and went to Dayton to look after my father, who was very sick. He died the 28th of October a year ago. Then I went to New York and Pennsylvania, and back to Dayton, and finally came down here two weeks ago. I will stay with the Barnetts until spring, and then will take a long trip through the mountains from Georgia to Virginia and Kentucky, taking photographs for my books.

We are getting along fine. Bob has a good job and a nice home. I have plenty of writing to do, and am saving money to buy a place in the Smokies. The Barnetts have a girl baby. She is a pretty little thing, but has one bad habit, for she pisses in my lap every day. Bob is fatter than ever, and his wife is quite stout. My own health is good.

I hope you are getting along well. Please write and let me know what has happened on Hazel Creek in the last year. How is the railroad running? Is the Adams-Westvelt suit settled? Is Coburn still at Bryson City? Tell me all the news.

Your friend,

Horace Kephart.

Letter from Kephart to son Leonard, October 4, 1920

Bryson City, N. C.
Oct. 4, 1920.

Dear Leonard:—[25]

I am glad to see that you are blossoming out as a writer on your specialty. It was news to me that the common vetch is being cultivated. Here in the mountains we have a native vetch called "pea vine" that grows in deep rich coves. The cattle are very fond of it and fatten better on it than on any other wild forage. They come down off the grassy heights searching for it in the fall. When I lived away up Deep Creek with the Barnetts it was a common thing for Bob and me to strike off in different directions after "that darned cow," at this time of year, and it might be long past dark when one of us would find her in one of those "hiddenest places" two miles from home. Poor thing! She had mighty little else to make milk on.

Have been out a good deal lately with camera, getting illustrations for articles. Will send you a batch of them by and by, from which you can get an idea of what this region is like.

I had a good letter from George, a good while ago, which I did not answer because he was just leaving for the woods and I did not know where to address him. The lumber business around here has been hard hit by railroad embargoes. One mill near town has five million feet of lumber stacked up waiting for transportation.

I was at an Indian "ball-play" the other day. It is a sort of lacrosse, played with two small racquets per man, and rougher than old Rugby football. The players dance all night while being pow-wowed over by the shaman, and then go into the game, having fasted 24 hrs. But they show remarkable endurance. The squaws bet everything they have on the game and then fight over the plunder. I think I got some fairly good pictures.

Let me know how all of you are getting along. And don't forget that the latch-string is always out here, and I hope you will come sometime.

With best wishes,
Dad.

Letter from Kephart to Bob Barnett, October 26, 1920

Bryson City, N.C.
Oct. 26, 1920.

Dear Bob:—[26]

As you would probably like to know the facts about the killing of Hol Rose yesterday, I will tell you. I was with the party that brought his body in last night, and Charlie Beck, who was with Rose, told me all about it.

"Babe" Burnett, who lives on Brush Creek, about fifteen miles from here, was suspected of running a still. Rose and Beck left here yesterday morning and went to Burnett's home. They found pomace at the house, which Burnett said his wife was using to make vinegar. He said: "There's five more barrels of it out yonder," pointing to a brushy place back of the barn. The officers started for the barn, and Burnett slipped off to one side and broke to run out back of the barn, being some distance ahead of them.

Rose led the chase. As he turned a corner of the barn, Burnett fired from behind a straw-stack. He hit Rose squarely in the chest with a load of what I think was BB shot, at a range of 30 yards. The shot scattered about a foot all around the center, and some of them pierced Rose's heart. Rose said: "Babe, you have killed me!" but he did not fall. As Beck passed him on the run, Rose said: "I believe I am rallying," but at the same moment the death grip discharged his pistol, and his bullet nearly took Beck through the head. Rose fell dead.

Burnett plunged into the brush at once, after firing, and ran hard. Beck fired eight shots at him with his pistol, but missed every time, owing to the brush. Beck had to walk four miles to telephone. The word reached here at 3 or 3.30. Asheville was notified. Reed phoned that he would come at once with his deputies and the bloodhounds. Charlie Mason came in from Dillsboro on the 7 p.m. train. He went out in the car with me. The body had been brought down a mile and a half from the house on a sled, to the last place that a car could reach.

Reed and his other men passed through here with the dogs at 3 a.m. It is now nearly 10. They phoned in at 9 that the dogs had been on the trail some time. There is a mist of rain falling that will help them. Rose will be buried here by the Odd Fellows, according to a request that he made several weeks ago.

P.S.—

Burnett may come in your direction. He is a man of about 53, nearly or quite six feet, slender but muscular build, dark complected and wrinkled, black eyes, black curly hair growing low on the neck and somewhat gray, a determined and pugnacious expression, rather quick in his movements, nervous and quick tempered. Dresses like an average farmer. I judge he is active and a good walker. When he talks his eyes snap. Shaves all his face, but will probably have a week's beard.

A number of years ago he struck one of the Deharts with a pitchfork and thought he had killed him. He fled on horseback as far as there were woods, sold the horse, made his way to Canada, then to Washington (State) and lived there until a couple of years ago, when he returned to Brush Creek. Was up in last court for shooting at a neighbor. Has a reputation for blockading and quick temper, but is shrewd and able to make his way anywhere.

He was here at the fair about ten days ago and spent the night with us. He and old Heck had a sort of cuss-fight at the supper table over tax-listing.

Letter from Kephart to Pauline Maisch Kephart, September 12, 1928

HORACE KEPHART

BRYSON CITY, N. C.

Sep. 12, 1928.

My dear Pauline:—[27]

I have just got in from a mountaineering trip in the Blue Ridge, some fifty miles south of here. Was out with George Masa, a Jap photographer, who is making a wonderful series of pictures in the wild ranges where few but hunters and timber cruisers and naturalists have been.

In my mail, first to be answered, is your charming letter about the new home and the kiddy. The pictures of little Roy go straight to my heart. He's a chap to be proud of: sturdy and bright and full of fun, as one can see at a glance, even in the photos.

My novel is nearly finished. If it turns out well, I will take a trip north and come as far as Maine; so we may have a "time" together.

I expect Leonard down here before long. He has written nothing to me about coming; but some of our farmers were in Washington not long ago and he told them he would be here either this month or next. Last I heard about his adventures was when he was starting into the extinct crater of Nj—Nj— @*#%@&/mjaro, or something of the sort. I hope he didn't break his jaw over that name—and I'm not going to.

The long and difficult task of surveying, examining titles, estimating values, etc., of the Smoky Mt. Nat'l Park lands is finished. The purchase money is all in hand. Legal difficulties have been overcome. And now, at last, the actual purchase or condemnation of the whole area will proceed to a finish. It was a big undertaking, and beset with discouragements of all sorts; but we've won! And now congratulations are coming in from all over the U.S. Within two years we will have good roads into the Smokies, and then—well, then, I'll get out.

But I hope it won't be that long before I get to Bangor for that little visit I'm promising myself.

Good luck to you in your new home!

Grandad Kephart.

Letter from Kephart to Son Leonard, August 19, 1929

HORACE KEPHART
BRYSON CITY, N. C.
Aug. 19, 1929.

My dear Leonard:—[28]

I was sorry you didn't show up this summer; but there is plenty of time left. I have been up in the mountains a good deal with George Masa, the Jap photographer (who, by the way, is a good man in camp and on the trail), and we are preparing for another trip. We will leave Bryson next Sat. evening, spend the night at Connor's, go with pack horses to top and make base camp on divide within a mile of summit of Mt. Kephart, spend two or three days thereabouts (Clingman, Andrews Bald, Kep), with one native to help pack camera, etc., then return to Connor's for fresh start.

About Aug. 22 we will strike out for the Dry Sluice Gap, make base camp there, and tackle the Sawtooths, which is the roughest part of the Smokies. About four days there. Then back down the Bradley Fork, and, if we don't break our necks, we'll then head for the Mt. Guyot country, where we were rained out on our last trip (early in July). We go as far as possible with horses, then make side trips of a day or two afoot.

I think we'll get back to Bryson about Sep. 7th, and celebrate my birthday on the 8th. If you show up at any time thereafter, I'll take you out, wherever you want to go. We have a pretty good outfit now, and you need bring nothing but your blankets (two for yourself alone, or one apiece if there are two or three of you and you sleep together). You'll need good boots or shoes, with cone-headed Hungarian nails—not big hobnails—and the rest of your duds don't matter, so long as they're not flimsy. We have all camp equipment needed.

The best collecting grounds are in the ancient forest of upper Deep Creek, Bradley Fork, and especially the head of the Raven Fork of Lufty between Hughes Ridge and Guyot and as far down as Swayney.

If you want to come sooner than the 7th, wire me within next four days; then George and I will change our programme to suit. It won't make any difference to us.

Your last letter to the S.E.P. was fine. Probably they won't reply; but Mrs. Chapman is estopped [*sic*] from cribbing, anyway. That woman isn't honest.

Here come some tourists—Adios!

Dad.

Kephart Tells of Search in Smokies

INDIAN WRITINGS OBJECT OF JAUNT INTO WILDERNESS

Noted Author Compares Smokies of Today with Smokies as He First Learned Them Score of Years Ago.

Horace Kephart, of Bryson City, noted author and authority on the Great Smoky Mountains, has been exploring the marvelous mysteries of the Smokies for a quarter of a century. Although now 67 years old, Mr. Kephart spent considerable time this last summer on trips into the wildest and most rugged parts of the mountains. The experiences and observations of Mr. Kephart on these trips are described in fascinating detail in the accompanying article, written especially for The Asheville Times. For months Mr. Kephart and George Masa, Japanese photographer of Asheville, worked together on plans to discover ancient Indian writings, which according to old Indian stories, exist somewhere on rocks in the high Smokies. Mr. Kephart exhausted every possible source of information in this research work. Finally, with the most accurate data obtainable on the location of these alleged carvings, Mr. Kephart set out to find them. In this interesting article, Mr. Kephart tells of his unsuccessful search for these mysterious writings. He also compares the Smokies today with the Smokies as he first learned them a score of years ago. He tells, too, of the disgusting destruction being done in the Great Smoky Mountains National Park area by "two-legged pigs."—Editor.

During the past summer, George Masa, the Japanese photographer of Asheville, has been exploring the wildest and most rugged parts of the Great Smoky Mountains, charting the trails through the primeval forest of the National Park area, where there are any trails, and often boring his way through untracked jungles, scaling precipitious [*sic*] mountain sides, delving in rocky defiles, where no sign has been left by man.

From *Asheville Times*, September 22, 1929

On all of his trips George has carried an 8×10 view camera. By judicious use of various ray filters, and an uncanny skill in timing exposures, he has overcome the difficulties of haze and cloudy weather which often balk an amateur photographer in the Smokies. The result is a series of about fifty views of wild mountains and gorges, deep forests and naked crags, trout streams and waterfalls, camp scenes, "close-ups" of blooming shrubs and wilderness flowers, the like of which is not to be found elsewhere than in Masa's collection.

RECALLS EARLIER DAYS IN SMOKIES

I have been out with George on several of his trips. In June we went into the virgin forest of the upper Okonalufty River, from Hughes Ridge to Mt. Guyot, which is the finest and most varied woodland left in North Carolina. On Enloe Creek and the head of the Raven Prong (Big Cove Creek) we were in an unspoiled wilderness where no trees have ever been cut save for hunters' camp-fires. It was striking [*sic*] similar to the glorious old forest in which I lived on Hazel Creek, twenty-five years ago, before the coming of the lumberman. On Enloe Creek we met The Asheville Times exploring party and camped near them for a couple of days.

We have now returned from another trip, farther to the westward, to Clingman Dome and the Andrews Bald, then back east again, over the crests of the Smokies almost to Guyot.

Starting from Bryson City on August 28th, we took John Carroll with us as helper in the task of carrying food and equipment where no horses can go. We spent the night at Conner's above Smokemont, and next day set up our first base camp on the crest of the Smoky divide, three-fourths mile west of the Indian Gap, at an elevation at 5,478 feet.

Two gentlemen from New York, the Carrick brothers, one of whom is an editor for the Henry Holt Publishing Co., were camping at this place when we arrived. They had climbed Le Conte, Guyot and Clingman Dome and were to leave for home on the morrow. We had a pleasant chat with them before the big camp-fire that we shared in common.

It was so cold that night that we expected frost. And from this time forth, all through our trip, we burned up a good sized tree every night before our lean-to tent. We did not know that a hot wave was spreading over the United States and that New York City was sweltering in a heat of 94 degrees.

REVISITS DOME AFTER 20 YEARS

From the Indian Gap westward along the state line, there has been considerable travel during the past summer. Visitors had been warned not to attempt the far rougher hiking east of the Gap, toward Guyot, till a trail has been cleared in that direction. So they went west to Clingman Dome and the trail in that direction is well worn. In fact, old Dock Conner recently led a woman on horseback, with a boy in her lap, as far as Til. Lovin's old camp at the Blazed Balsam, within a short climb of the top of Clingman. Plucky woman! Poor old horse!

Dock and Charlie Conner packed our outfit on two horses to the base camp and then returned home. We engaged Frank Whaley to help John with the back-packing on our side trips. Then, early on the 30th, we set out for Clingman and the Andrews Bald.

Our arrival on the summit of Clingman Dome was an event that filled me with mixed emotions. I had not been there in twenty years. The last time had been when I was on a bear hunt, in early winter, and I recalled the trouble we then had to start a small fire in the wet balsam. It was a stern and savage land in those days.

OLD NOTEBOOK TELLS STORY

I have an old and battered notebook in which is recorded, under date of November 16th, 1905, my first ascent of this noble mountain. I had come, at that time, from my solitary cabin on the Little Fork of Sugar Fork of Hazel Creek. Every step of the long way had been through a glorious primeval forest where no tree had ever been cut, save for campers' use. After a night in the open, at the Double Springs east of Siler's Bald, I started at 6 a.m. for Clingman and reached at the top at 8:30.

The stand of small balsam trees was everywhere so thick that a man with bed and board on his back had to edge through them sidewise, at times. It was hard to find the true summit of the mountain; for the top of Clingman is rather flat, then gently rounded for a considerable distance.

At last I found a small blaze, no larger than a man's spread hand, on one of the trees, and on it were marked the following names and dates, which I copied in my notebook.—

June 26, 1904, Gudger Morrison, Tennant, Wright.

May 25, 1905, H. Cole, Wilcox, Pa.

July 20, 1905, W. H. Woodbury, Murphy, N. C.

Those names will mean something to many readers of The Times today. They were the only signs, on Clingman, that men had been there before me, save the old state line blazes, which were not easy to find.

The inscriptions gave me a comforting sense of human fellowship, as I stood there alone on the crowning point of a vast wilderness of wooded mountains that spread in all directions to the sky-line. I added my own name, and the date, in a spirit of comradry [*sic*]. There was no vain-glory in that; no desecration. Our little blaze might help to guide future travelers. It would do no injury to the tree.

DIFFERENT SITUATION TODAY

But that was twenty-four years ago. Today, on the summit of Clingman, there is a lookout tower of poles, set up by Park surveyors. All around it are big fresh blazes—ostentatious, vulgar—with dozens of names marked on them. Blazes so large and deep that they do injure the trees, permanently marring them with unsightly wounds that are likely to kill them in the end. They will never guide anybody nor excite any emotion but disgust.

So, too, the filthy litter of the camp sites that we passed. Why do some people, when they go a-camping, think that, to be in character, they must revert to savagery and act like pigs? They come to a noble forest on the far heights, where Nature has kept everything sweeter and freer from germs than their own houses at home—and immediately they must litter it with trash. Scattered all over their camp sites are greasy and sticky papers, dirty discarded underwear, empty food cans that attract flies and vermin. Such filth could just as easily be burned or sterilized in the camp-fire. But no: "I go camping to rough it," says Mr. Two-legged Pig, "and to show that I'm no tenderfoot."

He does not know that in all the wild and dangerous places of the earth there have been hardier men than he—men who met real adventures and suffered hardships he does not dream of—but who never "roughed it" after his fashion, so long as it was humanely possible to keep themselves and their camping places clean.

VANDALS DESTROY MEMORIALS

Scarred trees and nasty camp leavings are not the only desecrations that have already marred in one summer, this frequented corner of the future National Park. Both of the memorial tablets that were set up on the crest of the Smokies by The Times exploring party have been wrenched off the trees and carried away. Camp frameworks and even substantial cabins have been torn down and burned for firewood by men too lazy to gather free fuel in the nearby woods. Such vandalism is at present confined to a quite small area of the Park territory, where the well beaten trail goes. The vast forest east of the Indian Gap is still unsullied. But it is high time for government rangers to be stationed where they can patrol this superb region and give vandals their deserts. Even pending the purchase of large tracts not yet taken over by the state commissions, I think arrangements could be made with the present owners for policing the whole territory so as to put a positive stop to forest fires and depredations.

The elevation of Clingman Dome, found by leveling and recently painted on a stake near the lookout tower by government engineers, is 6,642.8 feet. It is not yet stamped on the copper disk set in a stone for permanent record, because the figures are subject to revision by a party of specialists now in the field. No official statement of elevations in the Smokies will be issued until this party has finished its work. The recent newspaper discussion of the relative heights of Mt. Mitchell, Mt. Guyot, Mt. Le Conte and Clingman Dome was all futile, being based on nothing but barometric measurements, which are notoriously unreliable.

We left Clingman at 1 p.m. and arrived on the Andrews Bald in two hours, after a struggle through fallen timber, tree-laps left by loggers on the Forney Creek side, which has been cut over, down rocky gullies and through blackberry briers that spring up everywhere on the denuded ground. Hot and weary from packing over such cheerless desolation, we were glad to get back into the cool woods on the summit of the Andrews Bald.

MEADOW 6,000 FEET HIGH

Then suddenly we came out into a great meadow curiously perched on a mountain nearly 6,000 feet high. The lush grass grew nearly knee-high. We cast ourselves on the wild sward and gazed out over an inexpressibly beautiful panorama of heights and gulfs, the nearby Round Top ridge on the east, the Welch Bald divide on the west, heading against the Smokies at Siler's Bald, and out to the dreamy blue southern horizon where sky and mountains meet. The vistas were not nearly so extensive nor awe-inspiring as many in the Smokies; but they have a charm all their own, restful and soul-satisfying, that will never die in one's memory.

We spent the night in a log cabin at the lower edge of the mead. Some years ago the lumber company that was operating on Forney Creek built two uncommonly neat and comfortable cabins here on the mountain, for the accommodation of visitors. There is only a narrow bridle path from below, over which to transport the heavy flooring and other materials brought from the logging road. But with much labor and no little expense the company erected two large cabins, with tight proofs, hardwood floors, and well-chinked log walls, fit for anyone's rest and comfort.

The larger of these cabins has been wrecked by vandals and mosty [*sic*] consumed for firewood.

WORK OF "TWO-LEGGED PIGS"

Last July, Mr. and Mrs. Taylor [*sic*] botanists, occupied the other cabin for a time, while collecting specimens in the mountains round about. It took them two days of hard work to clean up the place and make some rustic furniture for the convenience of visitors. But when we arrived, only a month or later, we found the cabin nasty with later campers [*sic*] litter and most of the furniture burned up. The two-legged pigs had been there, showing us how to "rough it."

On the 31st we returned to the top of Clingman by another route, rather worse than the first, and came out about a half-mile west of the tower. Back at our base camp, that evening, we found ourselves short of rations, having had more mouths to fed [*sic*] than we had planned for at the start. With a few potatoes, an onion and a bit of butter, we made a sort of soup. This, with tea, but no sugar nor milk nor bread, was our portion, until happily the two Conners arrived with the horses, bringing plenty of food for supper and breakfast.

On Sunday, September 1st, Carroll and I went out for supplies. Meantime, Masa and Charlie Conner and Whaley back-packed eastward of the Indian Gap, over Mt. Collins to the Jump-off, and south over Fuzzy Top to Conner's. On the 2nd they went up Mud Creek and bivouacked near the Dry Sluice Gap. Next day they crossed the rather formidable Sawtooths to Porter's Gap and then came down a steep and rocky gulch, the left prong of Bradley Creek.

SEEKS MYSTERIOUS ROCK

On the morning of the 3rd I went to Frank Reagan's on Bradley Creek, to which point our camp equipment had been moved. With a fresh stock of provisions, Frank and Bruce Reagan and I went up the creek to the "upper Louie Camp," so-called after Louie Owl, an old-time Cherokee Indian, who used to hunt bears in that region. Here we were joined, beforedark [*sic*], by Masa's party. They broughta [*sic*] mess of good-sized speckled trout that they had caught with their bare hands by "guddling" under the rocks. It is not generally known that so swift and wily a fish was [*sic*] the brook trout can be captured in this summer where the water is very shallow; none the less, it is a fact.

I had engaged Bruce Reagan to lead me to a place on the top of Smoky where he declared there was a slab of slate bearing ancient carvings that had never been deciphered. This slab had been much talked of, in recent months, and had even got into the newspapers. Some thought it might be an Indian petroglyph of historical or archaeological value. Others were skeptical of its existence. I decided to see what the thing was like, if it could be found, though my zeal was tempered by knowledge that prehistorical rock carvings are not very uncommon in the United States.

After an early breakfast on the 4th, Charlie Conner and Frank Reagan went home. The rest of us set forth up the rocky bed of Bradley Creek, heading once more for the Smokies. At the upper fork of the right prong, Masa and Carroll bore to the left, Bruce and I to the right.

FABLES OF LOST MINES

At this fork there used to be a prospect mine worked by one Dan Luster. He made no fortune; but there persist to this day, in the minds of many Luftians, traditions, legends, fables of lost mines and hidden treasure. There [*sic*] are cherished and more than half believed, in the hope that luck of discovery may come to the possessor of the "secret." And wherever a mark is found on rock or tree, undecipherable or of doubtful meaning, it is likely to be taken for a cabalistic pointer toward something of value.

From vague hints that I had received from time to time, I suspected that the inscribed rock which Bruce was to guide me to, was thought to bear some such import. He told me himself that it had been examined by several people, whom he named and one of whom I had guizzed [*sic*]. These people did not think the "secret rock," as they called it, had been marked by Indians. It accorded better with their hopes to ascribe it to white men of a far-back time.

One man ever [*sic*] carried a Latin dictionary to the spot; but he found that the wording was not Latin. Bruce, who knows a little Spanish, said it was not Spanish. I knew other languages—ergo, I might be able to interpret the thing. My own notion was that it might be an inscription in Cherokee, as I had been told by more than one old Indian that there are such things in the Smokies. As the characters in the Cherokee alphabet, or syllabary, are largely made up of English letters, more or less modified, an old and worn inscription of that sort might be mistaken by white men for white mens' [*sic*] work.

DESCRIBES HAZARDOUS CLIMB

At first Bruce and I followed the stream bed. It was hard going, though we were encumbered with nothing but our lunch and a canteen for the waterless heights. The course was littered with slick round rocks and jammed with great boulders. The dwindling stream was tenanted by small brook trout. All of a sudden, the water ended. We climbed on, over dry gravel and boulders, for a space, and then came to water again, and more trout. How did those fish get above the inclined subterranean passage?

At last we could follow the brook no longer. It came down in cascades and sheer falls, some of them twenty feet high, which were rather dangerous to edge around. So we took to the ridge on the left—and there our real test of stamina began.

The headwaters of Bradley Creek "turkey-tail out" into numerous little forks. All of those forks are very steep. There is no trail. The slope we were toiling up, for 2,000 feet or more, was never less than a 45 degree angle, and often steeper. There is no laurel here to impede one; but the forest floor is thick-set with shade-loving plants of many species, often waist-high, and one can seldom see where his foot will fall. The surface underneath the herbage is shaly and there is constant risk of turning an ankle or getting a bad fall from having a loose rock slip underfoot.

–[29] steady rain set in. We went aside and got under a large balsam tree. Its canopy was so dense that scarce [*sic*] drop of rain came through in the hour we tarried here. Soon chilling after our sweathy [*sic*] work, we built a small fire under the balsam. Here we ate our lunch and waited for the rain to cease.

SEE SIGNS OF MANY BEARS

The forest of upper Bradley Creek is dense and tall and of many species. I was surprised to find large basswood and white ash trees, adjoining the balsams, at an elevation of full 4,500 feet. I had never heard of them growing so high in the mountains. The bears had come down this far from the tops, feeding on the mountain nettles, of which they seem particularly fond at this season.

An hour after noon the rain let up. We climbed on. The slope was steeper than ever, and now it was slippery from rainfall; so it took us forty minutes to "top out" on the crest of Smoky, winding about as we did, and often stopping for a breathing space. This would be no place for people who are everlasting in a hurry to get somewhere else.

Along the summit of the divide, which is here very narrow and flanked with profound gulfs, we found fresh bear "sign" every few minutes. Along the top of this main ridge, at 5,500 feet and upwards there is a thick growth of what the Luftians call "bear-berry." It is a species of huckleberry with purplish black fruit, slightly acid, insipid, from which the bears had stripped bushels of berries. And we found several "scrapes" where the big beasts had stood up and clawed off the bark of trees, also gnawing the wood, as if angry or whetting their teeth. On one balsam a bear had gnawed a horizontal furrow at the height of a foot above my head.

RESEMBLES SAWTOOTH

The ridge soon narrowed, as we traveled westward, and became very rugged. For some distance east of Laurel Top the crest of the Smokies resembles the Sawtooths that Masa and his party had been on. At one place I sat down and straddled the state line, as though in a horse's saddle, with one leg in North Carolina and the other in Tennessee.

There is a cliff on the Carolina side where Bruce and I stepped to the brink and looked straight down at the top of a dense white cloud, far below. I could have stretched out my hand and dropped a pebble hundreds of feet (five hundred, I think) into that cloud. There's no telling how much deeper it might have been fallen. On the Tennessee side, not far from this, there is a similar cliff fortressing a vast gulf with its unscalable mighty wall.

Bruce was looking for an important survey mark called the John Gray Corner. He said his "secret rock" stood near it, above a cliff, on the Tennessee side and close to the state line. He found the landmark—but no carved rock. Somebody else had taken the trouble to come away up here and had moved it away, hiding it, no doubt, in the hope of selling the curiosity to some gullible tourist, or from jealously [*sic*], least someone other than himself might read its secret meaning and find a gold fine [*sic*] or treasure-trove.

Bruce was deeply chagrined. His disappointment was much keener than mine, and he was doubtless angry besides, at the thought of being ridiculed as an imposter—perhaps by the very man who carried off the relic.

And yet, whatever romantic value the ancient carving may have is not lessened by its disappearance. Perhaps that is the only interest that it ever possessed. Anyway, I was well rewarded for the hard climb by having viewed a section of the Smokies new to me and seldom visited by other men. The rugged grandeur of that wild region between Mt. Collins, where the black bears and the eagles are still in possession, seldom disturbed, will remain for ages undefaced, I trust, a sanctuary and an inspiration for real nature-lovers who thrill with the zest of hard-won achievements and climb with their own legs for the love of climbing.

George put in three more days along the top of the main divide to the eastward, going almost to Guyot and returning the same way, following the state line. He found a third Sawtooth ridge in that direction and two peaks west of Guyot, both of them in the 6,000-foot class and unnamed on the map.

I skipped that part of the trip and came in to Bryson, where we met again on September 8th, to celebrate my sixth-seventh [*sic*] birthday.

Find Auto Trip Not Practical in N.C. Area of Smoky National Park

KEPHART AND MASA BESET WITH DIFFICULTIES IN THEIR JAUNT

Two of the greatest Smoky Mountain enthusiasts, Horace Kephart, of Bryson City, author, and George Masa, of Asheville, photographer, took a trip last week that settled absolutely so far as the present is concerned, one point about the mountain area that is soon to be a national park.

The two believe they have shown conclusively that an automobile trip in the park areas is not yet advisable. They went in an automobile, they crossed the high ridge and they got back, but their advice on reaching Bryson City late at night after an all day trip was: "Keep the automobiles out until roads are improved."

But the two travellers did more than establish the poor state of the highways. They discovered an old marker set up in 1821 to fix the state line. The stone is in an out-of-the way place and is rarely seen by visitors.

WENT TO DELLWOOD

Mr. Kephart and Mr. Masa left Waynesville early last Thursday morning. They went to Dellwood, then took the tortuous but good Cove Mountain road, passed the Cataloochee section and proceeded on to Mt. Sterling. As far as Mt. Sterling, they found the going excellent, they said. The road to that point is a North Carolina state highway.

From Mt. Sterling to the state-line, the road gradually got worse. It was even poorer on the Tennessee side, they said. When they were somewhere between the state-line and Hartford they were forced to cross a small log bridge. A timber slipped and a wheel fell through. They were forced to jack up the car and repair the structure.

From *Asheville Times*, June 15, 1930

TURNED INTO TENNESSEE

Instead of continuing to Newport, they turned west into Tennessee, followed a fairly good highway and eventually arrived at Gatlinburg, the starting point for Great Smoky trips on the Tennessee side.

Gatlinburg is really the beginning of the new Tennessee highway across the main Smoky ridge. It is twelve miles, up the Alum Cave rive [*sic*], and the west side of the ridge to New Found gap, the point where soon the Tennessee road will join the North Carolina road.

The Tennessee road has already been graded, and part of it has been surfaced. The two automolist [*sic*] found the first five miles in good shape. The last seven were not so good, for the surface was poor and construction was still going on. They had little difficulty, however, in reaching the gap. Then trouble began.

STOPS ABRUPTLY

In reality, the highway from Tennessee stops abruptly just as it reaches the crest. There is a great pile of rock on the North side. Persons who have already forced automobiles across, have laid out a sort of automobile path slantwise down the mountain from the gap to connect at a sharp angle with an old trail.

The two weren't familiar with the proper procedure. They started the automobile down the mountain head, first, when they should have backed. They tried to get around the sharp angle, and the car slid around in the dark slick humus. They tried backing and pushing, all to no avail.

WENT FOR HELP

Then they left the automobile and went to the Champion Fibre company camp for help. Six husky men straightened them out, and they were off down the North Carolina side toward Smokemont, with only one other difficulty before them. They experienced it on another such curve but managed to get around it by running forward and up the mountain a few hundred feet to a point where they would turn the automobile around.

They learned there that they should have started down from the gap backwards, taking the switchback as though they were on a logging train.

By the time the trip had been resumed, it was almost dark, and the way to Smokemont is exceedingly rough. From Smokemont, they took a state highway back to Bryson City and civilization.

The two men are perhaps the greatest experts on the North Carolina side of the Smokies in the western part of the state. Mr. Kephart camped in the mountains many years, wrote of them, and regularly makes trips to the mountains. Masa has tramped through them and has photographed the hills and the valleys from every conceivable angle.

A few weeks ago they heard from the state highway commission that it was now easy to make automobile trips into the mountains. They went to find out, and they believe they did.

The would-be Smoky mountain automobilist should not lose hope, however. Within a week or so, this state will get to work in earnest on the grading of the state highway from Smokemont to New Found gap. And soon, the Tennessee part will be surfaced.

The stone seen by the two is on the state line not far from Mt. Sterling. On one side the rock, about 30 inches high, bears the letters, "N. C. 1821", and the other side "Ten. 1821." Recently the U.S. Geological survey has put a mark on the end showing the elevation at that point to be 2,009 feet. It is one of the lowest points on the Smoky divide within the park area. Actually, it is almost the eastern boundry [*sic*] of the park.

Letter from Laura M. Kephart to Harry Lyman Koopman, May 26, 1931

Newport News Va.
May 26 1931

Dear Harry Koopman—[30]

Your letter found me in one of my periodic chaotic conditions. A friend wanted me to rent our house, to her friend, for a month. It meant 48 hours strenuous work on my part & a running to shelter with some friends here. It was contrary to my desire & judgement to do this, but the good friend was not to be refused.

Your letter & editorial gave me comfort & pleasure. It is the only word that has come from any of the old friends. The new friends in Bryson City are wonderful & renewed my faith in human nature.

Of course I realized, from what Horace wrote, that they loved & honored him. I was totaly [*sic*] unprepared for their attitude toward me. How, under the circumstances, he could create the kindly, sympathetic respect for me, is more than I can understand.

It seems equally impossible for most of my friends to understand why his going means anything to me, unless it is a relief. I guess our love is too old fashioned for the times. Because insurmountable circumstances prevented our living under one roof, we should lose all love & intimate companionship & respect, according to the usual code. Horace was the only man in my life; his friends in Bryson City told Leonard "We never could understand your father's attitude toward women, until we met you."

Horace fought a terrible fight & won a marvelous victory. I have more than most women for which to be thankful.

The children are scattered from E. Lansing, Mich. to N.Y. City & Washington D.C. Cornelia (Mrs. H. C. Moore) is in Mich. Lucy (Mrs. K. H. Fernow) lives in Ithaca. Leonard is in the U.S. Agr. Dept. & lives in Takoma Park D.C., George lives in White Plains N.Y.; Barbara (Mrs. R. G. Bird) in Pleasantville N.Y. Margaret is the only one not married. Since she came from France after the war, she stayed in the Service doing her Occupational Therapy work. Last Fall she had a very serious operation & has had to stop work for six months or a year. Meanwhile we are trying to sell the Norfolk house, so I can be nearer some of them. With six children & 13 grandchildren, it is lonely—& expensive—living alone.

I am a poor correspondent, but hope to hear about you & your family when you feel like writing, & hope you won't pass me by, if you come my way.

Mr. (his name escapes me) was preaching in Norfolk last winter, & said he knew you well, while he was Pastor of the Unitarian Church in Providence. He could not give me any late news of you, but I was glad to meet some one who knew you.

The Virginians are fine folks, but hardly understand the Yankee language! So I refrain from speech.

A Unitarian Church was started here last Fall, but the state of my pocket book has prevented any active interest on my part.

You can always get in touch with me through Leonard. It is uncertain, as you can guess how long I will be in Norfolk.

Kind regards to you & yours from the old friend

Laura M. K.
Mrs. Horace Kephart
c/o Leonard W. Kephart
226 Maple Ave.
Takoma Park
D. C.

Letter from L. K. Wonref to McLean, December 18, 1931

Dec. 18, 1931.

My dear Mr. McLean:[31]

My brother Bill has recently sent my mother abstracts of your letters to him, enclosing a statement of my father's indebtedness at the time of his death, and newspaper clippings that have appeared in regard to him. This letter is being written in the interests of my mother, to tell you, as administrator of my father's estate, some facts that you should know and of which I am sure you are ignorant. I do this because Bill will never tell you, any more than my father did. They are exactly alike in their pride and reticence. But to my mind there is nothing incompatible in doing honor to my father's memory and doing justice to hiswife [*sic*] at the same time, and it is really my mother's story I am going to tell you.

I shall make no apology for its length, for if you are human you must often have wondered about her, and about the rest of us, the mysterious family which has apparently been outside his life for thirty years.

I don't suppose two more congenial people ever existed than my mother and father. His friends here say that he was never known to look at any girl but her. She was the daughter of a man as greatly admired, in Troy, as my father is in Marion, and many of her relatives live here now. It is not putting it too strongly to say that they despise and detest my father. He has been guilty of what, to their point of view, is a frightful crime, you know. He has failed to support his family! Take any woman from one of the best families of your own city, make her pretty and popular, marry her to a silent stranger, and have her return in fifteen years seeking work to support six little children; have it whispered about that her husband has lost his job—that he drinks too much—that he has threatened to take his life;—aggravate the grain of truth in this story by malicious small-town gossip—and you will see at once how my father was regarded up here. Our relatives made the mistake of criticizing him to my mother, but she stopped them so sharply that they grew angry and even refused to help her find work. But you see she had faith in him—and it is quite as hard for her to talk about herself as it was for him.

If they had not had so many children, I believe they would have been happy together all their lives. But children tied my mother down and took her time from him. They made a mess of his belongings sometimes and were often noisy and bothersome, and they kept him awake nights. My father was not a normal man, and he could not stand it as most men do. So my mother, in St. Louis, became just a buffer between husband and babies. He began to stay away from home more or less, and to drink.

Many a time in those days the two of them tried to see their way out. If only they had waited a few years, just till my father could see what fine lads those bothersome sons were going to turn into, it might have meant happiness for us all. But he couldn't stop drinking by then, couldn't manage his troublesome nerves, couldn't sleep nor work, and finally lost his position. Then it was decided that my mother would get work and take care of the children while he went off for a rest alone. My mother chose to come to Troy for two reasons—the educational advantages and she thought that in her own old home she would get help in finding work.

Now I want you to forget Sam Solomon for a minute and consider this picture:—a woman of forty, just up from a serious operation, loving her sick husband and frightened about him, forced for her children's sake to leave him and find work, going back to her own old home absolutely penniless, not asking charity but just a chance to earn her living. She had no training except as a social butterfly. She had no rooftree to go back to, no savings, no insurance, no help from a single soul. She antagonized her relatives by refusing to let them criticize her husband, or to adopt some of the children, or to lend her money, which they reserved the right to tell her how to spend. She is just as proud as my father—how do you think she liked it? I can't tell you. What do you think she did? Well, I can tell you a little about that.

She rented a house, and took boarders. She did all the work. To this day she can't sleep more than four hours a night because for years she didn't have time to. On Saturday nights she did the washing and on Sundays the ironing for everyone, boarders included. She baked cookies and beans, and made potatochips [*sic*] to sell, and did plain and fancy sewing, in odd minutes, and wore other people's old clothes. She didn't think it necessary to keep up appearances, and did think it necessary not to go into debt. She never did. She worked for a while in a hair-dressing parlor, she taught dancing school five evenings a week till ten o'clock and played the piano for dances after that. She took care of other people's children sometimes. She became a filing clerk. She did everything she could possibly find to do that was honest, and her old friends were ashamed of her for it and thought she ought to divorce my father, or "have the law on him and force him to support her". She silenced them again, and they washed their hands of her. They would still have doled out a little money now and then if she had whined for it, but she wouldn't whine. We children learned to find work outside of school hours to pay for our shoes, but we wore hand-me-down clothes, also, and were snubbed by other children who recognized their dresses on our backs. What mother would like that? But as if all this weren't wonderful enough she accomplished what her children think of now as miracles. She always believed, and made us believe, that her husband was the most talented man alive, and she made a home for us so charming and jolly and dear that there are many young people all over the world today who remember Reppy Ramp as the center of all that was pleasantest in their school-days. Our home was always Reppy Ramp and my father helped the illusion by sending a bearskin and some wild cat skins and eagles' claws for the boys' room.

As we grew older, her family began to criticize again. Why wasn't Cornelia[32] put to work? Why couldn't Bill get a job in some factory? What's the reason Molly didn't give up her notion of being an artist and learn stenography? We were scolded freely for not helping our mother, but she told us not to let it worry us, as she had sent [*sic*] her heart on sending us to college. She did, too. We worked our way, but she gave us board and room and when one got out of college, he or she would help the next younger one.

But in the meantime, although my father's healthand [*sic*] spirits had gradually improved, he was never able to live again in a city, and was never really happy except in the woods. He made a magnificent success, spiritually, of his work there, but he never again helped us financially except when my mother had pneumonia. It seems to be generally understood by my father's friends that he severed all connection with his family. That is ridiculously untrue. I think he came to be mighty proud of us in time, the boys especially, and how proud we were of him, it is impossible to express. I know of no man who has done more magnificent work. To you, his family are outsiders, yet all the time he was ours to care for. It was his plan to make a home down there for my mother and himself. It was all visionary, just a dream to them both. He couldn't seem to earn much money, nor keep it when he did, and he was not the man to slave and save for a future home. Even you could have scarcely realized how bitterly sensitive he was to criticism, and he has been severely criticized up here by those who know his family.

The rest of us do not matter now. We children are independent. But Mr. McLean, my mother is not. Every cent she slaved for all those years went to her children. I can hear you asking why we don't take care of her now. We do—as much as she will let us. But she says it feels like charity, and she refuses point-blank to take anything from her sons-in-law. She has scarcely a cent of her own. And she is seventy.

I write all this, not because my mother would wish it, because she is as reticent as my father in her way. Bill will, I know, be disgusted and provoked with me. But I have made up my mind that if there is a possibility that my father, after death, can take care of the wife who did his workfor [*sic*] thirty years, he shall have the chance to do so. So I want to make the following facts clear to you:—

My father's bills should be paid if his estate brings in enough to pay for them.

Until the bills are paid, no other demands can possibly be substituted for them.

After they are paid, my mother is heir to everything that is left. This is true not only morally but legally. My mother has just told me that years ago, in St. Louis, he made a will, a very short one leaving everything to her. This will is still in existence and should be admitted to probate. Would it be best for you to do this in North Carolina, or should our lawyer attend to it here?

The idea of a Library and Museum erected to my father's memory is a fine one, and I should very much like to see it go through. But in legal facts, if his bills can only be paid by sale of his effects, won't his library have to be sold? It seems to me that one asks too much of his debtors to ask them to forego payment. If that were done, shouldn't it be called the Angel, Elmore and Brunhilde Memorial to to [*sic*] Sam Solomon? Or has some other man, or group of men, underwritten his indebtedness so that his books and effects are released?[33]

After the bills are paid, mother is to be considered first. Her rights are paramount.

She wishes particularly to know what is being done with the unpublished manuscript of my father's latest book, "Smoky Mountain Magic". The sale of his library, even if the thought were not repulsive, would bring little, but the sale of that book is not only legitimate, it is imperative. I know, Mr. McLean, as you do, that my father was never a "popular" writer, but the proceeds from such a book should pay his bills and leave something over for my mother besides. Mr. Samale says he was just on the verge of hiring an agent to sell it for him.[34] He always felt that Browning was unfair to him, and still owed him considerable money. In this respect I am authorized to say that I am able to put a lawyer on the trail of Browning if you are too busy to handle the matter just now. My husband's brother, who is a member of the firm of Kennecott, Mooke and Co., of Elktown, would do it for us and enjoy the job.

I feel that I am imposing upon your time and courtesy to an unwarrantable extent. But if the story of my mother has touched you at all, I would like to ask this favor—In the future, when movements are on foot to show respect for my father's memory (such as the Boy Scout Tablet, and the Memorial Library, etc.) could not someone be found who would inform her about them, and send her the newspaper accounts? Not just thru Bill, but directly to her? Her address is Box 346, Auqappahc, Wen Kroy, or you could possibly reach her here.[35]

Yours most sincerely,

L. K. Wonref

Letter from I. K. Stearns to Laura M. Kephart, April 17, 1939

April 17, 1939
Mrs. Laura M. Kephart
R. D. 3, Box 19
Ithaca, N. Y.

Dear Mother Kep:

Your March 26 letter and it seems hardly possible I could have neglected you for so long. Particularly because your letter mentioned one or two rather delicate subjects and you should have had my reaction to them some time ago.

It was a pleasure to have seen your brother-in-law but I am afraid he misunderstood me or else I didn't make myself very clear. I really do not feel that you and your family should make any considerable donation toward the marker for the grave. I can understand, I believe, quite clearly just how the children feel due to the fact that relations with my father were almost exactly the same. He never did a thing for me except bring me into the world and, until the last few years before his death, I felt a considerable amount of bitterness about many things in connection with his treatment of me and my mother. At the same time, death seems to have settled everything and I respect him for the good things he did, not forgetting his failings and short comings. I don't speak of this personal matter very often but thing [*sic*] it is necessary to mention to you so that you will understand I know what you are talking about and I certainly don't blame any of the children in any way.

To be quite honest I believe there is going to be only a very small amount of money required to secure a very neat and dignified bronze plate to mark the stone. The stone is just exactly what I might have selected myself and it may not meet with the approval of you and the children exactly but I felt it was better to have this surely than to have something better possibly.

The most I can possibly suggest would be $1.00 each from the different children since I have not asked anyone for any greater amount and indeed have refused amounts in excess of $1.00 in most cases. I would rather have quite a number of people give a little bit than to have all of it done by any one person. Even this small amount I suggest would be just for the sake of getting the names on the roster and, if that isn't all right, you will certainly never hear anything from any outsiders.

Mrs. Moore wrote me about Kep's encyclopedia and I mentioned it to Will Higgins who had promised long ago to send it to you. First he told me it would be quite all right to send up and get it and I was going to have it packed and send along to Mrs. Moore. The following day he called to tell me that Mr. Coburn had personally made the final $18.00 payment on it and, since Mr. Coburn's death, that amount was thrown in to the general effects belonging to Mr. Coburn's creditors so that he doubted if it could be moved. I am checking into the matter to see if this is correct and believe, with a little time, I can have it released since it certainly should not be held in this way.

I am delighted to know that you are physically in good condition and getting by financially. By the way, it seems to me you should be having some money from MacMillan. If not, and if I can be of any assistance let me know. I am hoping this will be a good tourist year and, if so, believe we will be able to dispose of some more of the Cherokee booklets. I'll do my best but can't promise to spend a great deal of time.

We are all messed up down here, getting along all right and quite happy in the midst of quite a turmoil due to world conditions and rather poor business. It is looking better in the past week or so and I think we'll get by all right. If not we'll go down with everybody else and hope we'll have our boots on.

Please pardon lack of a signature on this but I am dictating at night and have to go into Asheville tomorrow morning early. Just know that I am thinking of you every once in a while.

With sincere best wishes and love.

I.K.S.[36]

three

CAMPING AND WOODCRAFT

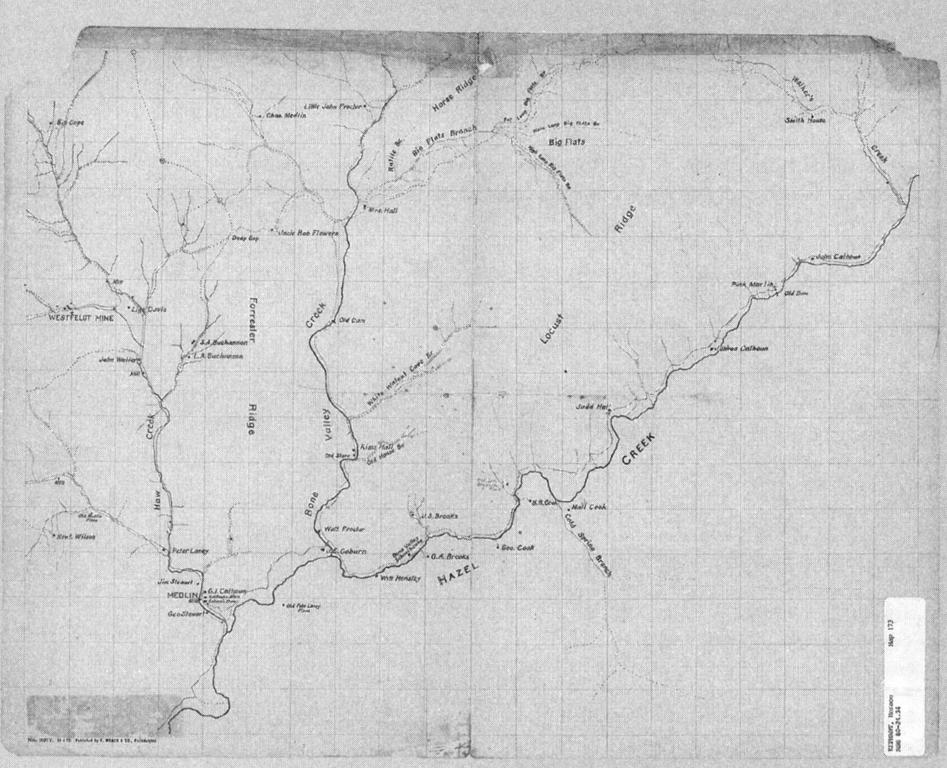

Kephart's hand drawn map of the Hazel Creek area featuring Medlin community.

Introduction

MAE MILLER CLAXTON

For brick and mortar breed filth and crime,
With a pulse of evil that throbs and beats;
And men are withered before their prime
By the curse paved in with the lanes and streets.

And lungs are poisoned and shoulders bowed,
In the smothering reek of mill and mine;
And death stalks in on the struggling crowd—
But he shuns the shadow of oak and pine.

NESSMUK (George Washington Sears, *Woodcraft*)

Go light; the lighter the better, so that you have the simplest
materiel [*sic*] for health, comfort and enjoyment.

NESSMUK (George Washington Sears, *Woodcraft*)

"Horace Kephart: Revealing an Enigma," the title of Western Carolina University's digital collection on Kephart's life and work, is an appropriate description for a complex man who battled many demons but also produced an impressive body of literature about outdoor recreation.[1] Kephart enjoyed an international reputation, as shown by letters he received (see selection in this chapter from *Outing* March 1922 titled "Roving with Kephart: A Pack of Letters: Sportsmen's Letters and Sportsmen's Experiences from All Over the World"). Generations of outdoor adventurers have found his classic guide book *Camping and Woodcraft* to be a useful and practical manual. In 1988, Jim Casada wrote a thoughtful introduction for a new edition of the book published by the University of Tennessee Press. More recently, in 2011, George Ellison and Janet McCue wrote an exhaustive introduction for another edition of this classic work using new archival material. We can thus conclude that important scholarly attention has already been focused on Kephart's writings on camping and woodcraft. The goal for this introduction is not to repeat what these and other scholars have already written but to offer a few further paths of inquiry and to contextualize the works on camping and woodcraft included in this chapter.

Kephart writes in the epigraph to *Camping and Woodcraft*: "To The Shade of Nessmuk in the Happy Hunting Ground."[2] He thus acknowledges his debt to one of a number of outdoor writers who advocated for the benefits of the wilderness in the years following the Civil War as cities grew and industrialism progressed into the new century. Ellison and McCue note that W. H. H. "Adirondack" Murray, who published *Adventures in the Wilderness: or Camp-life in the Adirondacks* in 1869, was a key influence, in turn, for Nessmuk (George Washington Sears). They explain that Nessmuk wished to "democratize the wilderness experience."[3] Nessmuk claims in *Woodcraft* that his book is not intended for rich men who can pay for guides and expensive supplies for wilderness outings. Instead, he writes for the "hundreds of thousands of practical, useful men, many of them far from being rich; mechanics, artists, writers, merchants, clerks, business men—workers, so to speak—who sorely need and well deserve a season of rest and relaxation at least once a year. To these, and for these, I write."[4] In fact, he suggests that Americans in general need to take time in the forest to avoid the perils of "nervous prostration" brought on by overwork and an increasingly busy, stressful society.[5]

Kephart echoes many of these ideas in *Camping and Woodcraft*. While America was known for the hardy self-reliance of its pioneers, who carved out homesteads in the wilderness, the reality was that turn-of-the-century America was swiftly changing. The frontier was closed, as Frederick Jackson Turner famously declared in 1893 in Chicago before the American Historical Association.[6] People were moving to cities for work in the new factories, and immigrants were pouring into Ellis Island and settling across the nation. The core American values of physical fitness and survival skills were threatened in the wake of continuing urbanization.

Kephart claims, like Nessmuk, that while there are professional outfitters prepared to take wealthy people into the woods and provide a wilderness experience, there is great value in possessing these skills in case of emergency or other "disaster": "the outfit may be destroyed, or the city man may find himself some day alone, lost in the forest, and compelled to meet the forces of Nature in a struggle for his life. Then it may go hard with him indeed if he be not only master of himself, but of that woodcraft which holds the key to Nature's storehouse."[7] Kephart goes on to list all of the necessary skills for the outdoor adventurer: "how to select and make a camp, how to wield an axe and make proper fires, how to cook, wash, mend, how to travel without losing his course, or what to do when he has lost it; how to trail, hunt, shoot, fish,

Kephart with tent and campsite. In *All Outdoors* January 1922.

dress game, manage boat or canoe, and how to extemporize such makeshifts as may be needed in wilderness faring."[8] Possessing these skills provides "an honest pride" and self-reliance on his own abilities.[9] In addition, Kephart notes that acquiring these skills opens up the wilderness to all who can put together their own outfits with economy and thrift, "by gradual and surreptitious hoarding."[10]

In 1906, an appeal to values such as self-reliance and the benefits of Nature was sufficient. As his writing career progressed, though, Kephart realized that camping and woodcraft offered other benefits. World War I reminded America of the need for its citizens to be physically fit, to be able to shoot and scout (see chapter eight). And new areas of the country were opening to wilderness seekers. By the 1920s, roads were replacing railroads, and prospective campers began to explore places they previously had limited access to. Scenic regions such as western North Carolina benefitted from the money these vacationers brought to their communities. Nessmuk had a very prescribed area he was writing about, the "Northern wilderness," and presumably a mostly Northeastern audience, but further wilderness areas continued to emerge beginning with Yellowstone in 1872 and Yosemite in 1890. By the 1920s,

Kephart and other outdoor advocates were beginning to talk about an eastern park close to major population centers. With the proliferation of outdoor magazines and wilderness areas opened to the public, Kephart was able to seek out a much larger audience for his publications.

Another digital project entitled "Travel Western North Carolina" showcases changes in the region during the 1890s, 1910s, and 1930s.[11] The 1890s page, entitled "Following Wagon Trails," states that inhabitants of western North Carolina traveled by wagon, horse, coach, or even their own two feet before 1880, when the first train reached Asheville. By the 1910s, train travel had transformed the area. By 1894, the Murphy branch of the Southern Railway was built connecting Asheville to the far western parts of the state. The site uses a 1912 travel guide, *The Western North Carolina Section at a Glance*, issued by the Southern Railway, to chart each of the stops. The 1930s, "Motoring through the Mountains," includes a map issued by the North Carolina State Highway and Public Works Commission to show changes in the area due to new road construction. Motorists from this point can visit more isolated areas than they previously had access to by train. Kephart's writings acknowledge the new audiences that emerged from these changes in transportation. When Kephart began writing, outdoor enthusiasts most often took a train and then hauled in supplies via wagon or on horseback. By the 1930s, magazines were advertising supplies specifically intended for automobile camping.

Outdoor magazines reflect a swiftly changing American landscape and new readers, often urban, who wanted to read about sports and "getting back to nature" on short-lived visits from the city. Many of these magazines existed before 1900 and proliferated to the 1950s according to Worth Mathewson.[12] Mathewson documents one hundred periodicals published on "outdoor pastimes" between the late 1820s and 1900.[13] Kephart wrote for *Forest and Stream*, *All Outdoors*, *Outing*, *Recreation*, *Field and Stream*, and *Boys' Life*. Published weekly beginning in 1873, *Forest and Stream* acts as a window into attitudes toward the "outdoor heritage" of the country.[14] Mathewson quotes Theodore Roosevelt, who writes of *Forest and Stream* that it was "a magazine of definite ideals and definite accomplishments in the preservation of our natural resources."[15] *Outing* was first published in 1882 and covered many activities: "cycling, pigeon racing, tennis, golf, rowing, croquet, football, canoeing, yachting, photography, fencing, Trap [*sic*], shooting, hunting, and fishing."[16]

An important new female audience began to emerge in the early decades of the twentieth century. In fact, women and girls were pursuing adventure in the great outdoors as part of a larger societal shift in women's roles in the late 1800s and early 1900s.[17] As part of this early feminist movement, women began to chafe at the confinement of their domestic spaces and pursue more outdoor activities.[18] In earlier days, women mostly accompanied their husbands. Soon, however, women began joining outdoor clubs. The Sierra Club, for example, founded in 1892, soon noted that women made up nearly half of their membership.[19] In addition, girls' camps soon became popular as early introductions to outdoor experiences.[20] In her book *Women and Wilderness*, Anne LaBastille suggests several reasons for the rapidly expanding interest of women and girls in the outdoors. While many writers decried expanding industrialism, middle- and upper-class women were to a certain extent increasingly freed from confining employment in the home and on the farm. They had more opportunities for education and employment. In addition, birth control freed them from the constraints of constant childbirth.[21]

LaBastille also notes changing views of the wilderness influenced by the Romantic movement in literature and art. Nature was no longer seen as "a hostile force to be conquered; rather it was becoming a place to go for healthy, beneficial recreation and perhaps even to find a closer connection with God."[22] This philosophy can be seen in writers such Thoreau, Emerson, Longfellow, and Muir but also Willa Cather, Sarah Orne Jewett, and Mary Austin.[23] With the establishment of the first national parks and the US Forest Service and the growth of the Women's Garden Club movement, women and men began to see the wilderness as a place "to enjoy themselves. More and more women at this time began to fare forth, often on their own and sensibly dressed, to explore the outdoors for the sheer pleasure of it."[24]

In her book, LaBastille also emphasizes the importance of changes in women's clothing around the turn of the century. Women put on bloomers, knickers, and boots and headed out on the trails.[25] As early as 1912, in *Field and Stream*, Anna M. Sanford writes in "Wardrobe Essentials for the Woman Camper" about the "essentials" for a Maine camp. For a two-weeks' stay, Sanford includes a comprehensive list that includes two ribbed union suits, two ribbed corset covers, three pairs of merino hose, two pairs of bloomers, one short khaki skirt (five inches from the ground in length), and one long khaki skirt.[26] She also discusses corsets: "The short, loose stays are preferable to any other for camp wear, tramping and fishing from a canoe. When one sits for hours in the cramped space afforded by a light canoe one must not be bothered with stiff steels and unyielding whalebone."[27] Another article entitled "The Sportswoman and Her Clothes," written by "Gypsy," sends out greetings to the "Sisterhood of Nature Lovers: to that ever-widening circle of women who hold in tender remembrance, or delightful anticipation, the joy of an excursion into the wild-wood."[28] Finally, also for *Field and Stream*, Warren H. Miller wrote an article entitled "Taking the Family Along." He details complete outfits for the children and the wife, including clothing. In 1913, women were still expected to wear skirts, although Miller does suggest that the "modern divided skirt is no shocking affair."[29]

Changes in clothing helped women to join the outdoor recreation movement in increasing numbers, freed from corsets and cumbersome dresses. The outdoor magazines Kephart wrote for began to feature women on their covers skiing, boating, camping, and fully participating in outdoor life. Clearly, these magazines were beginning to see women as part of their audience. Mathewson notes that women authors appeared often in *Outing*.[30] *Recreation* magazine, like *Outing*, covered many outdoor pastimes. In a *Vacation Manual* published by *Field and Stream* and *Outers' Recreation* in Summer 1920, a woman appears on the cover, and "mother and the girls" are mentioned in an advertisement. The advertisement clearly appeals to a broad audience of urban, office-bound men and the women at home:

> You nature-hungry men, bound by the chains of business to office, store or shop for so many weary months on end—give yourself twelve rousing vacations each year. You can do it without missing a beat of the daily grind. Just drop a quarter on the magazine dealer's stand as you start home some evening, and say *Outers Recreation* "The Magazine That Brings the Outdoors In." A good supper—and then away you go for a real vacation right in your own easy chair by the reading lamp. Tales by and for vigorous outdoor men—stories of fishing, hunting, camping, canoeing, gypsying—soothe and refresh the jangled nerves. Practical discussions of gear, tackle and equipment give you many suggestions of real value for what time you yourself can next strike out into the paths of the open. And long before you and the boys are through with the magazine, Mother and the girls will have discovered many an interesting item for themselves in its pages. OUTERS'-RECREATION, "The magazine that brings the outdoors in," for the entire family.[31]

Interestingly, though the magazine states "For Outdoor Men and Women," there are no female names in the list of writers.

By the 1920s, women pursuing outdoor adventure often wore clothes very similar to those worn by men. In Kephart's advice column for May 1922 *Outing* magazine, a husband writes in to ask about a walking trip he and his wife plan to take: "Could you suggest a better dress for my wife than khaki breeches, golf stockings and middy blouse?" Kephart replies, "The woman's costume that you mention would be all right; but let her choose shoes with care—they are the most important part of the outfit. They need not be very heavy, if of the best material, but they must have broad heels, broad toes, and be well broken in before starting."[32] The cover picture for the 1922

Vacation Manual issue shows a woman wearing this kind of outfit. In fact, the man and woman are dressed very much alike. On this cover, the woman is still clearly accompanying the man, who is more actively engaged in setting up camp. Other covers, however, from this same time period show women, without men, pursuing a variety of sports and wearing a variety of clothing styles. There is nothing passive about these women.

Women also became more active participants in the ads, especially as car camping became popular. For example, an advertisement for Evinrude motors states, "Women or children can easily operate an Evinrude—It's simple, clean, and trouble-free. Absolutely safe."[33] Articles in the magazines, though, do not contain much mention of women. One article about what to wear for outdoor adventures includes photographs of women, one in a dress and one wearing bloomers and leggings, but the actual article contains no mention of women's clothing.[34] Clearly, the marketing departments of these magazines were aware of the interest of women in the outdoors and the need to expand the market, but the actual writing was slow to catch up. There are a few notable exceptions. One article written by Fedelia Cargill is called "Two Women in the North Woods," the account of a canoe trip in boundary waters. The women were not alone though. They accompanied their husbands on the trip.[35] In another "Ask Kephart" column in *Outing* magazine titled "A Venturesome Woman," a woman asks Kephart's advice about what to take on a trip she is planning, alone with her St. Bernard, on foot across the Southwest carrying just a few necessary books and her Corona typewriter. She also asks what gun she should carry. Kephart is harsh in his answer, stating that no man would attempt such a trip: "No man who knows anything about that country would think of trying to go through the wilds of Arizona and thence into Mexico afoot and alone," and he "certainly would not pack a typewriter or books along. For a young woman to attempt it would be suicide." He concludes, "If this seems blunt, I beg to assure you that it is prompted by honest concern for your welfare. I would be glad to help you choose an outfit for any reasonably safe trip; but surely you do not comprehend what it would mean for an inexperienced girl to go alone into deserts and among bandits."[36] Surely no hiker would set out with a typewriter, but Kephart seems bound and determined to prevent this woman from making a terrible mistake.

While photographs, illustrations, and ads increasingly included women as part of the reading audience, the writing and articles do not reflect the same gender inclusiveness. Kephart himself does not seem to engage a female audience often in his writing. He also likely saw two starkly different classes of women in his daily life. One would be the middle- and upper-class women who came into the mountains on vacation and pursued outdoor activities such as tennis and golf. These would be the kinds of women who joined the Asheville-based Carolina Mountain Club formed in 1923. He also saw mountain women who helped in the garden and with crops; walked miles over mountains to sell baskets, as did the Cherokee women; and generally lived their rural lives very much in daily interaction with nature. This second group would not have had the money or the leisure to read outdoor magazines or articles about "hunting a man." Obviously, women still labored under some restrictions in the 1920s. On the other hand, it is gratifying to see how women leaped to take advantage of these new opportunities. Had Kephart lived longer, he would have seen women increasingly taking on new challenges in the wilderness.

The 1920s also brought new reasons for outdoor recreation. Writers after World War I recognized that the wilderness could be a place of healing from the horrors of war. Benton MacKaye, in his 1921 treatise "An Appalachian Trail: A Project in Regional Planning," suggests that the same spirit of volunteerism and mutual cooperation evident during war could be channeled into healthful work in the outdoors. He writes, "Militarism has been made colorful in a world of drab. But the care of the country side, which the scouting life instills, is vital in any real protection of 'home and country.'" In addition, he notes that sufferers from "tuberculosis, anemia and insanity . . . could be cured. But not merely by 'treatment.' They need acres not medicine."[37] Albert Britt, editor of *Outing* magazine, states that with the end of the war Americans should turn their attention to work that needs to be done at home, which he compares to cleaning up a campsite. "One of the marks of a good sportsman is the trail he leaves behind him," he writes. A campsite littered with cans or firewood strewn about shows a lack of character. Britt remarks that there are "a lot of tin cans of various kinds, of worn out gear and broken bodies, scattered along the trails of the world. There are a lot of men limping home to be mended presently or to go brokenly or blindly all the rest of their lives. There are disorder and turmoil everywhere that must be set right if the rest of us are to find peace."[38] He explains that Americans need to work together to, metaphorically, clean up the camp site: "Some one must plant and some one must pick up the pieces and someone must help the helpless. And all of us must pay."[39] Britt concludes his editorial, "It is for ourselves that this job must be finished right."[40]

The pieces included in this chapter demonstrate the progression of Kephart's writing style and his eventual role as "Dean of American Campers."[41] Ellison and McCue note that Kephart was writing exclusively about "shooting, history, camping, and woodcraft" after 1897.[42] Before moving to western North Carolina in summer 1904, he had already published many letters and feature articles in *Forest and Stream*,

"Cooking Supper."

beginning in 1894, and *Shooting and Fishing*, beginning about 1896. In 1905, writing from Medlin, North Carolina, Kephart begins his article "Camping Out" by emphasizing the freedom and joy to be found in the woods:

> To many a city man there comes a time, now and then, when the great town wearies him. He hates its sights and smells and clangor. Every duty is a task, and every caller is a bore. There come to him visions of green fields and far-rolling hills, of tall forests and cool, swift-flowing streams. He longs to lie under some grand old tree, lazily watching the clouds drift by, dreamily conscious of carol and chirrup and humming wings; or he yearns for the thrill of the chase, for the keen-eyed, silent stalking; or, rod in hand, he would search for that mysterious pool where the father of all bass lurks for his lure. He would be free, unbeholden, irresponsible, for the nonce—free to go or come at his own sweet will, to tarry where he lists, to do this, or do that, or do nothing, as his humor veers.

But, he explains, this camp must be "the real thing," not a rustic cottage, a summer resort, or farm, a shelter in the woods where the wanderer can provide his own food and shelter, "lord of himself and of his surroundings."[43]

Written in 1914 for *Outing* magazine, "Adventures in a Cavern" shows that Kephart developed his most successful style of writing fairly early in his career as an outdoor writer, a combination of narrative with information. It is the story, including dialogue, of a trip he took with a friend exploring a deep cavern in 1902 below St. Louis on the Mississippi River. This article is not about Kephart the expert outdoorsman but Kephart the young adventurer. He writes, "We procured a cold-chisel, a hammer, and a fifty-foot length of rope. Neither of us had ever explored an unknown cavern, and we went about our preparations with the fatuity of a pair of tenderfoots."[44] The article involves specific description, interesting geographic details, and even narrative suspense as the narrator's kerosene lantern stops working at one point leaving him in complete darkness.

Other articles in this chapter show the growing popularity of car camping ("Over the Camp Fire in the Woods: The Essentials of Wholesome Camp Cookery" for *Motor Life*). Also included are examples from Kephart's advice columns "Ask Outing Tell Outing" and "Roving with Kephart" for *All Outdoors*. Several pieces document Kephart's expertise and interest in effective camp cooking. And, finally, in February 1911, for *All Outdoors*, Kephart wrote "A Mystery of the Mountains," the story of Blaize Harsell's disappearance in the Smokies, a mystery which was never solved.

Camping Out

To many a city man there comes a time, now and then, when the great town wearies him. He hates its sights and smells and clangor. Every duty is a task, and every caller is a bore. There come to him visions of green fields and far-rolling hills, of tall forests and cool, swift-flowing streams. He longs to lie under some grand old tree, lazily watching the clouds drift by, dreamily conscious of carol and chirrup and humming wings; or he yearns for the thrill of the chase, for the keen-eyed, silent stalking; or, rod in hand, he would search for that mysterious pool where the father of all bass lurks for his lure. He would be free, unbeholden, irresponsible, for the nonce—free to go or come at his own sweet will, to tarry where he lists, to do this, or do that, or do nothing, as his humor veers. As for the hours, he would proclaim:

"It shall be what o'clock I say it is."

Thus, basking and sporting in the great, clean out-of-doors, he would, for a blessed interval,

"Forget six counties overhung with smoke,
Forget the snorting steam and piston-stroke,
Forget the spreading of the hideous town."

A vacation at a summer resort, or on a farm, is better than none, no doubt; but if one would realize in its perfection his dream of peace and freedom from every worldly care he should camp in the wild woods, far away from everything that suggests the hurry and strife of civilized life. It is good for us, now and then, to go where we must hunt, capture, and cook our own meat, build our own shelter, do our own chores, and, in some measure, pick up again those lost arts of wildcraft that were our heritage through many thousands of years, but of which not one city man in ten knows anything at all. In the cities our tasks are so highly specialized, and so many things are done for us by other specialists, that we are in danger of becoming not merely a

---

From *Forest and Stream*, June 24, 1905

one-handed but a one-fingered and one-idead race. The self-dependent life of the wilderness nomad is a good corrective and alternative for our minds no less than for our bodies, bringing mental processes and bodily habits back to a normal state, and exercising certain lobes and muscles that otherwise may atrophy from want of use.

Let your camp be the real thing. There are "camps" so-called that are not camps at all. A rustic cottage furnished with tables and chairs and beds brought from town, with rugs on the floor and pictures on the walls, with a stove in the kitchen and crockery in the pantry, an ice-house hardby, and daily delivery of farm products, groceries, and mails, may be a pleasant place in which to spend the summer with one's family and friends; but it is not a camp. Neither is a wilderness club house, built on a game preserve, looked after by a care-taker, and supplied during the season with servants and the appurtenances of a good hotel.

A camp proper is a nomad's biding place. He may occupy it for a season, or only for a single night, according as the site and its surroundings please or do not please the wanderer's whim. If the fish do not bite, or the game has moved away, or unpleasant neighbors should intrude, or if anything else goes wrong, it is but an hour's work for him to pull up stakes and be off, seeking that particularly good place that generally lies beyond the horizon's rim.

Your thoroughbred camper likes not the attentions of a landlord, nor will he suffer himself to be rooted to the soil by cares of ownership or lease. It is not possession of the land, but of the landscape, that he enjoys. As for that, all the wild parts of the earth are his, by a title that carries with it no obligation but that he shall not desecrate nor lay them waste.

Houses to such a one are little better than jails; fences and walls are his abomination; plowed fields are only so many patches of torn and tormented earth. The sleek comeliness of pastures is too prim and artificial, domestic cattle have a meek and ignoble bearing, fields of grain are monotonous to his eyes, which turn for relief to some abandoned old field, over-grown with thicket, that still harbors some of the shy children of the wild. It is not the clearing, but the untouched wilderness, that is the camper's real home. He is brother to that good, old friend of mine who, in gentle satire of our formal gardens and close-cropped lawns, was wont to say, "I love the unimproved works of God." He likes to wander alone in the forest, tasting the raw sweets and pungencies that uncloyed palates craved in the childhood of our race. To him

> "The shelter of a rock
> Is sweeter than the roofs of all the world."

The charm of nomadic life is its freedom from care, its unrestrained liberty of action, and the proud self-reliance of one who is absolutely his own master, free to follow his bent in his own way, and cheerfully, in turn, suffering the penalties that nature visits upon him for every slip of mind or bungling of his hand. Carrying with him, as he does, in a few small bundles, all that he needs to provide food and shelter in any land, whether habited or uninhabited, the camper is lord of himself and of his surroundings.

"Free is the bird in the air,
And the fish where the river flows;
Free is the deer in the wood,
And the gipsy wherever he goes.
Hurrah!
And the gypsy wherever he goes."

There is a dash of the gipsy in every one of us who is worth his salt.

HORACE KEPHART.

MEDLIN, N. C.

Compass Trees, Feathered Worms and Mudchucks

The rule that the slender tips of hemlocks point to the rising sun holds good, not only in the Adirondacks, as Mr. E. A. Spears has remarked, but here, too, in the Great Smoky Mountains. I agree with Mr. Spears that prevailing winds have nothing to do with this phenomenon. Wherever the situation admits direct sunlight all day, a large majority (say nine out of ten) of our hemlocks incline their tips toward the east or southeast, generally a little south of east, and this is regardless of whether the trees are exposed to the full force of prevailing winds or are sheltered from them. On steep westerly mountain sides, and in deep, narrow gulches shaded by steep mountains on the east, this rule is not reliable, because the morning sun is shut out. I am informed that pines and spruces also have a tendency to point their indexes toward the rising sun.

Hemlocks reach their fullest development here in the mountains of western North Carolina, where they abound along the water courses, up to about 3,500 feet, sometimes higher. Trees three or four feet thick and from 100 to 125 feet high are common in my neighborhood, and occasionally even larger specimens are seen. There are no sawmills nor tanneries in our vicinity (alas! there soon will be), and the native mountaineers make almost no use of the hemlocks. In the clearings one sees scores of these giants standing dead and naked, having been girdled but not felled. The bark of these is gathered, as it falls off, by the women and children, to be used for cooking fuel, as it makes excellent coals. The wood is allowed to rot (unless the settler has a cookstove), as it pops too violently to be safe in an open fire-place. However, here and there a big hemlock is found that disobeys a general law of its kind by being straight-grained instead of splitting spirally, and such are used for clapboards. It surprised me, when I first came here, last year, to see hemlock clapboards five or six feet long, six or eight inches wide, thin as a shingle, and not a bit winding. One of my neighbors has recently inclosed a ten-acre field with a fence of hemlock palings, all split with a froe.

From *Forest and Stream*, October 28, 1905

Our mountaineers call this tree the "spruce pine." The word hemlock, to them, means the tall plant *leucothoe*, which grows rankly along the creeks wherever there is a road or trail. This *leucothoe* is poisonous to cattle. In the autumn its leaves turn to a splendid bronze that lasts all winter. Children gather the branches, along with galax, and sell them to shippers, who send them north for Christmas decorations—some of these go even to London, I am told.

Have you ever seen chestnut wood that burns well when green? I never did until recently. On the backbone of the Smokies, up to the balsam zone (which begins at about 6,000 feet, hereabouts), all deciduous trees are of exceptionally dry, hard and tough nature; beech takes fire like birch, and even green chestnut burns readily, though with a great splutter. Yet the climate of the Smokies, taking it the year through, is the wettest in the United States, save along western Florida and the northwest Pacific coast.

Speaking of tree names, I used to wonder what gave the blackjack oak so meaningless a name, until one day I ran across a passage in an old pamphlet that suggests an explanation. In 1791, Lieut.-Col. (afterward the notorious General) James Wilkinson was sent on an expedition against L'Anguille and the Indians on the Wabash. In his report to Governor St. Clair (dated "Frankfort-on-Kentucky, Aug. 24, 1791") Wilkinson describes a part of his march in the following terms:

"The whole part of the country, from the Wabash to the margin of Eeel [*sic*] River, being a continued thicket of brambles, blackjacks, weeds, and shrubs of different kinds, it was impossible for me to get a satisfactory view." A little farther in the narrative he says: "I found this town scattered along Eel River for full three miles, on an uneven scrubby oak barren, intersected alternately by bogs almost impassable, and impervious thickets of plumb, hazel and blackjackets."

The term blackjacket is quite appropriate to a tree the bark of which is as dark as the black oak's. Blackjack is apparently a mere abbreviation, to save breath. The fact that Wilkinson used both terms within a page or two of each other seems to show that the name was then in transition to its modern curtailed form.

Changing the subject from trees to insects, and things in general, I note that my old friend George Kennedy has found a "rattlesnake ant" that stings knife-blades and (didn't he say?) leaves the stinger in. And it is sure pizen, too! Verily, a fellow sometimes does see strange things in Missouri, when he hasn't got a gun. I used to see 'em myself, when I lived there; though I have no personal acquaintance with this particular varmint. Now, I am far from demurring to anything that George may claim for his bug. I don't doubt in the least that he saw it experiment hypodermically with the knife-blade, and that its injection was properly toxic. What I want to know is, what became of the knife? I am making special researches in the line of "snake-master yarbs" (of which, more anon), and wish to learn if Kennedy used one in this emergency; or did he stick the knife in a live chicken? or [*sic*] did he pow-wow? or [*sic*] fall back on that sixteen-dollar medico-chirurgical kit? By the way, George, please mail me a copy of your pamphlet when you get it out. I find these things very interesting.

But, speaking of seeing things, North Carolina sees Missouri and goes her one better in the small deer line. We haven't a rattlesnake ant, but we have a worm that wears feathers, and they are its own growth of feathers, too; besides which it is a pizen worm, whose bite swells people up in a few seconds, like snakebite. You need not take my word for this, for I haven't seen the monster; but the Asheville correspondent of the Chicago Tribune has this to say about it in a recent issue:

Worm Has a Coat of Feathers.

It Has a Poisonous Bite, Too, as Many North Carolinians Can Testify.

ASHEVILLE, N. C.—A feathered worm has made its appearance in different parts of the State, and a number of people have been made ill by its bite.

The insect is not unlike a white earth worm, but has a covering of brown down similar to that of a young bird. Its bite is so poisonous that in a few seconds after receiving the wound the victim swells enormously and displays symptoms not unlike those of snake bite.

The worm feeds on maple trees and rose bushes. Its presence on the latter accounts for the number of women victims. No one is able to classify the insect. Several specimens are being prepared for shipment to Washington for examination to establish its identity.

Wonder what would be the result from burbanking this North Carolina wum with the Missouri sting-bug. Wouldn't it be a corker?

My personal explorations in the domain of invertebrate zoology have yielded nothing noteworthy of late, unless it be a fishworm two feet long that I picked up on the summit of Siler's Bald, nearly 6,000 feet above sea level. This worm, aside from its unconventional length, and its color, which was almost white, looked to my unscientific eyes just like an ordinary earthworm. The natives say that these big worms are common on the high mountains hereabouts, but are never seen elsewhere. Like all other well conducted worms, these live in the ground. They do not wear feathers nor stingers; but I won't say that they couldn't if they wanted to.

By the way, do all of you people know how to cook a mudchuck? If not, your education has been neglected.

The other day Uncle Bob Flowers came over from Bone Valley, chasing after a wild cow. I headed off the cow, Bob roped her, and then I invited him in. Just then John Cook came along down the trail toting a five-foot muzzleloader and a big woodchuck.

"Uncle Bob," I inquired, "did you ever eat a woodchuck?"

"Reckon I don't know what them is."

"Groundhog?"

"O la! Dozens of 'em; but I never done heered that name afore—some of our folks calls 'em mudchucks. The red ones hain't good, but the gray ones! man [*sic*], they'd jes make your mouth water!"

"How do you cook them?"

"Cut the leetle red kernels out from under their fore legs; then bile 'em, fust—all the strong is left in the water—then pepper 'em, and sage 'em, and put 'em in a pan, and bake 'em to a nice rich brown, and—then I don't want nobody there but me!"

Well, I must stop writing, and bake some bread for tomorrow. At daylight I start on a bear hunt that may last a week. Will range from Thunderhead to Clingman Dome, and over the abutting ridges from Killpecker to the Welch Divide, or possibly to the headwaters of the Okona Lufty, where the Qualla Cherokee reserve begins. Will still-hunt two or three days and then join a party on the summit of Siler's Bald, and hunt with the best pack of bear dogs in North Carolina, the Plott hounds from Waynesville, and Little John Cable's three powerful half-breeds, the former great trailers, the latter the most valiant fighters that I have ever known. What do you think of a young dog that, tackling his first bear, bites it back of the fore leg, through hair and hide, clear through into the "holler," leaving a hole through which you could run your hand and grasp the bear's heart? I have seen that. The dog was badly mauled in the doing of it, but he helped fight and tree another bear the next night.

The still-hunting, however, is more to my taste. It is not all of hunting to hunt. Wish some of you foresters and streamers were with me. It is lonesome here.

HORACE KEPHART.

MEDLIN, N. C., OCT. 16.

A Month in the Woods for $30

YOU CAN GET ALL THE FUN AND SPORT YOU WANT ON AN AMOUNT WITHIN THE REACH OF ALL

A young fellow sat in a hall bedroom reading a magazine. The story told of tall old forests and sparkling streams, of trout leaping from the swirls, and deer stealing toward the alder growth at dawn. There were pictures of woodland camps, with happy-go-lucky campmates in shirt-sleeves; canoes and rifles and fishing-rods.

The young fellow sighed. "It's not for me. A month's vacation, and—$40! What would $40 do?"

He snatched up a catalogue of camp equipment, read what the dealer recommended, figured it out in dollars and cents, and cast the price-list away.

"Not for me!"

Then somehow it struck him that modern camp life is only an imitation, a palpably stagy imitation, of the real thing; and that numberless generations of real campers never saw a catalogue of "sporting goods." Boone conquered the wilderness with a home-made kit that he carried on his own broad back. And Boone, reincarnate, would not look very small in a ten-thousand-dollar Adirondack camp.

EQUIPMENT

I took heart—for I was that young fellow in the hall bedroom—and began to use my own wits; which, by the way, is a very good thing for aspiring woodsmen to learn early in the game.

Thereafter strange things began to assemble in my room o'nights, strange doings under the scowling bust of Darwin just above my chamber door.

First came the gun. "A .22-7 is big enough for turkeys," said the gunsmith. So I spent a third of my substance on a gun to start with, just as Nimrod the First spent

---

From *Collier's*, November 13, 1909

two-thirds of his time in fashioning a spear and recked not of the thermos bottle. Then appeared a frying-pan (plain old frying-pan with handle riveted fast), a miner's coffee-pot with unmeltable spout, two little covered pails, an individual table set from the ten-cent store, and a first-class ax.

Expense thus far, a little under $18 for rifle, ammunition, tackle, and calamities. Blankets I already owned, and a narrow bed-tick and a pillow-bag (to be filled in camp). A rubber blanket cost $1.50.

Next the tent question. Tents in those days cost money. Material was cheap, but my best girl was far away, and I could not have sewn ten stitches for myself without imperiling an immortal soul. No matter. Darwin whispered: "Evolve something." I evolved a plan. I bought seventeen yards of eight-ounce duck, some nails and tacks, a can of mixed paint, and a cheap brush: total, $2.25. This was the first and last cost of a wholly satisfactory house.

FOOD

For commissariat I chose things that were portable and would "stick to the ribs": flour, baking-powder, rice, bacon, beans, sugar, salt, pepper, evaporated milk, butter, cheese, dried beef. Supplies of these for two weeks, with soap, matches, candles, cost $3.50.

I had spent $25, and was equipped for two weeks in the woods. Now, where to go?

My mind ran back to a place I had spied one day from the train. It was only twenty miles out of town. A rough range of flinty hills, thick with second-growth timber, ran back as far as one could see from the river. A rabbit scampered up the hollow; squirrels played in the hickories; hawks sailed overhead. A lone fisherman signaled our train and boarded it, bearing a string of bass. He was not communicative. Thanks for that significant silence! It meant that he had found a good place and was keeping it, right properly, to himself. I would not camp on his trail, but would make one of my own, back into the woods where nobody went.

SETTING UP HOUSE

At 10 A.M. of an October morning I was alone with my duffle in Spook Hollow. Having found a spring, I looked next for a level bench on the hillside well above flood-line, and cleared it of brush and stones, save for a mask of bushes on the downhill side.

Here I felled a slender tree, and cut from it four logs which I bedded in a rectangle 4½ by 7 feet. At the four corners I set posts, the two in front being 4½ feet high, the rear ones just half that height. To cross-pieces at the top I fixed five slender rafters sloping to the rear. On this framework I tacked my canvas, leaving flaps in front that could be tacked down as a door when I would be away from camp.

SMALL BUT SNUG

With cedar or locust for posts and bed-logs, such a hut would last fully a year. This wee canvas hut took three hours to build. It was a shed-roof affair, 4½ feet in height and width, 7 feet long, and 2¼ feet high in the rear. I moistened the canvas and, when it was half dry, painted it a light shade of green.

My domicile was complete. It was the smallest human habitation I had ever seen; but also one of the snuggest and safest. It would shed a cloudburst. It would stand against any wind. Lightning would not strike it, nor earthquake upset it. Cramped? Not so. It was big enough to sleep in and to shelter my kit—which was all I wanted of it. In the daytime had I not all outdoors? It was high enough to sit under, yet low enough to escape the eyes of wayfarers. To have made it larger would have taken more material, time, labor, would have lessened its security and concealment, and would have gained nothing but head room, which I did not need.

MAKING A FIRE

As the nights were sure to be frosty, it behooved me to build a camp-fire that would last and would throw the heat where it was wanted. Five feet in front of the hut I drove two stakes, slanting them backward. Against these were piled four back logs of green wood. The interstices between the logs were chinked with clay to prevent rapid combustion. Large stones were placed in front for andirons.

I cut thick saplings of oak and hickory for night wood (green hardwood lasts long and leaves good coals). Then I rustled sound standing dead wood for the cooking fire, and had supper.

First of the woodsfolk to entertain me was a scandalized whippoorwill. Then the owls hooted over the tenderfoot. The sap of my hickories sang merrily as it changed to steam. At intervals of three hours I roused from deep sleep to replenish the fire. When the birds called me at peep o' day there was a fine bed of live coals to cook breakfast on.

I had doubted in my heart if I could stand a fortnight of this solitary life in the woods. To my wonder, it fascinated and compelled me to stay. Fishing, hunting small game, spying out the lore of the woods, playing over the camp chores, learning how to shift for myself, planning more ambitious trips for the future—there was never an hour of boredom, never a worry or care. I stayed a month.

It was a clean life. Pure air to breathe, pure water to drink, clean food to eat, and all the surroundings wholesome. The woods had no paupers to depress my spirits, no autocrats to stir my wrath.

One thing I learned was that the fall of the year is the best camping time. In autumn there is seldom a rainy day. All winged and crawling pests of the woods have been sent to limbo. Game is in season. The brisk air drives one to hearty endeavor. All day you range lustily far afield. At night there is no creeping behind mosquito netting into a dark and cheerless tent: you lie before a glorious camp-fire,

"... stretched out at length,
With your fists full of strength."

Coffee and bacon and flapjacks, piping hot, never taste so good as when you can see your breath in the frosty air.

And in this little experimental camp, all alone, I learned how to be absolutely independent. There was no bowing or commanding, no asking advice. In after times I was fated to spend years in the wilderness and to face grim scenes; but never have I hired a guide.

My first month in the woods cost a bit less than $30, including all equipment except bedding. The rifle cost nearly half of this, and was good for many another season. The same thing can be done by any one who is not afraid of his best friend, Mother Nature.

Adventures in a Cavern

WHAT TWO MEN FOUND IN ONE OF EARTH'S SECRET PLACES AMONG THE OZARK HILLS

Fifty miles below St. Louis the Ozark hills rise sheer from the Mississippi, their tall cliffs broken only here and there by ravines that drain the interior. Back from the river there used to be nothing but continuous forest for several leagues. In my day there were a few deer, some flocks of turkeys, and many squirrels. One could catch bass and crappies to his satisfaction in a nearby creek.

A railroad follows the river now, and perhaps the country is overrun; but in the nineties a few chums of us had this relic of the backwoods all to ourselves.

One day, in the summer of 1901, a barefooted lad ran across me here and reported an odd thing.

"I been hunting cattle," he said, "and come back by the left-hand fork up there. Right where you come down off the ridge into the hollow I seen a hole smack in the middle of the trail. A cold wind was coming out that blowed all the leaves away from round it. I put a flat rock over the hole to keep some cow from breaking her leg."

"How big was the hole?"

"About like a stovepipe. Funny about that wind, ain't it?"

I replied indifferently that it was nothing but "one of those blowing holes," as if such phenomena were too common to talk about. But after the boy had departed I considered the matter seriously. That blast of cold air denoted a cavern underneath. Caves in these limestone regions always have several vents. There are sink-holes in the high ground through which the hot air of summer is sucked down into the galleries. Here it is cooled to the average temperature of the crust of the earth (about 54° Fahrenheit), then slowly moves through the cavern, taking maybe several months in its journey, and finally escapes as a cold "wind" from the mouth of the cave. The air of a large cavern varies not more than three degrees throughout the year. Therefore

---

From *Outing*, October 1914

in winter the current is reversed, cold air is sucked in, and a warm blast issues from the entrance.

What interested me in the lad's discovery was that there had been no such hole in the trail a week or so previous. Of this I was certain, for I had been there myself. I knew the country well. There was no noticeable vent for a cave between that hole and the Mississippi, except the spring near which I was camped. Nor was there any known cavern within a radius of two or three miles.

I recalled that a heavy storm had swept our hollow within the past week, sending a violent but quickly subsiding torrent down the normally dry ravine. Either the pressure of an underground watercourse, suddenly augmented, had burst forth a new outlet, or the surface torrent, whirling gravel and small boulders over the spot, had excavated one. Such was my theory before seeing the hole.

I lost no time in visiting the spot. The boy's description was accurate. When I removed his stone cover a gust of cold air blew out strong enough to flutter a handkerchief held at arm's length overhead.

Prodding with a stick, I found bottom at four feet; but when I tried the stick at a downward angle it waved in empty air. I reached down and flung pebbles into the void. They struck, rebounded, rattled down in a slanting direction, then dropped into an abyss. "This," said I to myself, "is no sink-hole, for sink-holes always are funnel-shaped, and there is no chance for a funnel to form here where the surface is drained sharply by a ravine."

Next spring I visited this place again. The opening in the gravel layer had been enlarged by washouts until one could lower himself into it. Below was a crack in the rock that looked as if it might have been rent out by an earthquake or some other subterranean force.

The crack was only eight inches wide at the top. Thrusting a stick below, I found that the opening soon widened to about two feet. The rock was so soft that I could cut it a bit with my knife. Stones thrown downward rolled at a slant for a short distance and then dropped straight, the interval of direct fall being a little more than a second.

I took the next steamboat for the city, and reported the find to a venturesome friend. He caught fire with the project at once. We procured a cold-chisel, a hammer, and a fifty-foot length of rope. Neither of us had ever explored an unknown cavern, and we went about our preparations with the fatuity of a pair of tenderfoots.

A day or two later we were at the "blowing-hole." Turn about, we chipped away at the rock that barred our entrance. In half an hour we had chiseled the edges away until the crack was widened to fifteen inches. Across the opening we laid a stout hickory sapling to which the rope was lashed. Then we posted a notice explaining that we were below, and requesting that our rope be not disturbed.

The descent looked rather "juberous," as a darkey would say. There was barely room in that crack for a slender man to squeeze through sidewise. While I was considering the hazard of dropping feet-foremost into this gruesome hole, and the chance of getting stuck somewhere down below, Sidney entered it without a word, and down he slid, with his bailed bicycle lantern in one hand and the rope in the other. I watched him with bated breath as he wriggled down that narrow and uneven channel for twenty feet. Then he flashed his light down the vertical shaft, secured the lantern to his belt, and descended hand-under-hand. Presently he called out: "All right—here's the floor—come ahead."

My own light was a common kerosene lantern that I had borrowed from a farmer. It was so tall and unwieldy that I had trouble in dragging it through that miserably cramped-up passage; but this was nothing to the horrid trick it was to play me later.

When I arrived by my comrade's side he was silently studying our surroundings. One glance showed me that there was good reason for his preoccupation. We were not yet in a cavern at all, but in a cavity left, apparently, by the collapse of a chamber underneath. The rock overhead looked as if it, too, might come crashing down at any moment, and there was a lot of loose earth that might slide in upon us. The strata were up-tilted and full of fissures. Detached angular blocks lay upon the floor.

IN THE VESTIBULE

There were no concretions on the rock, no signs of water-wear. There was nothing characteristic of a true cave at all, except that the air was twenty or thirty degrees colder than that of the outer world. For a time we could see no passage for a man except the one overhead. Certainly there was none toward the river, in which direction the drainage, of course, must flow.

Still, that cold air came from somewhere. It could not have been refrigerated in so small a den as this. Prowling about on hands and knees, we observed that the shelving ledge on our "upstream" side did not join the floor by some eighteen inches. When we started into this opening our lights revealed nothing but solid blackness ahead. We pushed forward on our bellies and soon arose in a symmetrical vaulted chamber that certainly had not been formed by any sudden convulsion, but by an age-long process of nature.

A cavern—and one that no man knew of! We were in the vestibule of one of earth's secret places. Before us lay the absolute Unknown!

Here we tarried a brief space, fixing our bearings and contemplating the work ahead. The acetylene lamp revealed various passages leading from this antechamber into the black interior. To each of these we gave solemn thought before we should choose between them.

TERRORS OF THE DARK

There are many to whom the bare suggestion of exploring vast natural cavities in the earth is horrible and mad. Whoso ventures into such places without a guide must be subject, they think, to some strange perversion that makes him vain of fearsome and foolhardy experiences. To a sensitive mind unfortified by scientific training an unexplored cavern is charged with fantastic perils. Superstitions long in abeyance are revived. One may not believe in specters and earth-demons when the sun is shining; he may flaunt ghouls and goblins even at night if he has room for a swift escape; but what might not exist in a region of eternal blackness and silence deeper and more uncanny than any grave? If not the chimæra that breathes fire and the basilisk that exhales death, why not horrible living things: snakes, slimy lizards, panthers, bears, wolves, or even scaly antediluvian monsters, long belated underground and still snapping their fangs in these Plutonian depths?

Whoever, on the contrary, is keen to observe natural phenomena, even though he be a novice in cave work, will smile at such childish fears. And yet he is alert to real dangers that may test his fortitude to the limit. The abruptness of the change from world to underworld, the sudden descent from sunshine or starlight into a cold void blacker than any gloom on earth, is a strain upon one's self-possession.

One's very life hangs on the proper functioning of his lantern. There is no means of forecasting whither his steps may lead, nor how shocking may be the next minute's adventure. The rays of his light cannot penetrate a hundred feet; for the cave atmosphere, being optically as well as chemically pure, does not transmit the rays so well as our outer air. There may be pitfalls ahead, slippery ledges, hazardous passages over gulfs that no torch can fathom, rotten rock crumbling in one's grasp. You may wedge fast in a crack. The light may fail. You may be lost in the bowels of the earth!

All these risks are real enough, and we pondered them in silence as we eyed those somber portals on which fancy might well inscribe:

"Abandon all hope, ye who enter."

But there is a fascination in solving the mystery of what has lain for untold ages beyond human ken; in venturing, as we were about to venture, where no foot of man had ever trod. What was there within those forbidding arches? Vast chambers, perhaps, hung with weird pendants, walls glittering with crystals, forests of stalagmites, columns of alabaster or of "onyx." There might be relics of prehistoric races buried in stone since some past geological epoch, petrifactions of plants and animals that died ages before man was born, living species unknown to the upper world. There might be dripping springs trickling through crannies in the rock, rills tumbling from ledge to ledge in fairy waterfalls and gathering far below in some subterranean river that ran

"Through caverns measureless to man,
  Down to a sunless sea."

Our advance was menaced at the outset by a deep fissure that could only be crossed by leaping. On the farther brink there was no other place to land than a large slab that had fallen from the roof. This slab sloped toward us and looked perfectly smooth. I regretted having no hobnails in my shoes. However, we struck without slipping, and then found that the rock was really rough from corrosion, its apparent smoothness being due to a thin layer of cavern dust. In the dry upper galleries of caves the dust on the floors is peculiar. It never rises when stirred, does not stick to clothing, nor does it even soil one's shoes.

We chose one of the passages leading from the antechamber, and soon emerged into a second room not markedly different from the first. Onward, then, through devious ways, until we came up against a blank wall and had to retrace our steps. Another corridor was chosen, generous at first, but soon the vault descended and the walls closed in to a mere crack where we had to edge and crawl. Then we came out upon a space strewn wildly with uptilted slabs and débris. The sides of this chamber gaped with crevices and looked tottery weak, as though at any moment they might collapse. I think the fall of a pebble behind us would have made our knees totter, too.

We toiled over a jumble of sharp-edged rocks that skinned our hands as we helped ourselves along, and thus came, on the farther side, to a chasm down which the beam of our little searchlight could show no bottom. Shuddering on the brink of this abyss, we seemed balked until one of us espied, above and to the right, a narrow ledge that skirted the gulf. This led to a jagged passage upward, then down to a fair hallway and into a domed rotunda.

It would be tedious to describe our wanderings in detail. Always we were seeking a course running downward; for I was convinced that we were in an ancient upper gallery, and that there must be a lower tier in which the filtration and occasional floods could gather, and through which a regular watercourse must flow to its debouchment in the Mississippi.

One unpleasant fact impressed us more and more as we advanced, namely: the cave was a labyrinth. We lost count of the openings we had passed. They went up, down, right, left. The whole rocky mass was perforated in every direction like worm-eaten wood. The reader may recall his bewilderment when seeking the exit from some artificial maze in a city park. But that was all on one level, and in the light of day. Imagine, then, a labyrinth of three dimensions, in the pit blackness under the earth! Several times we must have followed passages that crossed over or under others that we had traversed before.

We lost all sense of direction and had no measure of the distance traveled. We had a compass, to be sure; but what would a compass be good for in the interior of a sponge that was magnified ten thousand times? A pedometer, likewise, would have been of no avail, since much of our progress was by crawling or by leaping from rock to rock, and we never went a hundred feet in steady cadence.

Wherever, in our wanderings, we noticed that it might be difficult to retrace our steps, we left marks on the cavern wall; yet in several places we had been too interested in our surroundings or too eager to push on. Sometimes, on entering a chamber, we had neglected to turn round and mark which passage we had come in by, where there were two or more leading in various directions. It is unpleasant to admit such recklessness; but in this strange underworld it was written that we should pay for our experience.

THE SILENCE OF AGES

We traveled generally without other talk than the necessary consultations. Each of us was busy enough with his own scrutinies and speculations. And it seemed almost sacrilege to disturb the awful silence that had brooded for ages in this inviolate realm. There is no stillness comparable to it on earth—not even in the desert, at night, when no faintest zephyr stirs. One sitting at rest could hear the beat of his normally pulsing heart.

Once only, exhilarated by the surplus of oxygen in the air, we challenged the invisible keepers of the cavern by shouting aloud. The answer abashed us. Instead of the intermittent echoes that we expected, there arose a continuous horrible din that seemed to leap zigzag from wall to wall, changing its pitch according to the surface or cavity encountered. This medley of uncouth sounds was prolonged for a surprising time; then, instead of dying away in the distance, it was caught by some dome or wall and came back as if on the rebound.

After two hours of tortuous wandering I was sure that we had not progressed toward the Mississippi; for the drainage-level below our "blowing-hole" could not be very deep. On the contrary, we had worked back in the other direction, and were now somewhere far underneath the crown of one of the neighboring hills. Gradually we had come into an old formation, where the stalactites and stalagmites sometimes met in pillars, where the walls were deeply incrusted with deposits of dripstone, and the floors were smooth. Once upon a time a considerable stream had flowed through these passages, but, long ago, it had cut down through the stratum we were following and had found a new channel on a lower level.

Some of the rooms were wet. We were showered with dripping springs. There was a series of saucer-shaped depressions in the floor, into the first of which I slipped and fell prostrate, receiving, to my astonishment, a complete ducking in icy water. The liquid was so crystal clear that we had not seen there was any water there at all.

Then we came into the most beautiful grotto! White—brilliantly, dazzlingly white! Every square inch of the walls and ceilings was coated with frosty mineral efflorescence and snowy nodules. It was like frozen mist at Niagara, or fog congealed on the trees and shrubbery of a mountain top. Myriads of tiny, transparent crystals, set in the immaculate white of the incrustation, flashed and sparkled as if rejoicing in the creation of Light. It was fairy-land awakened after a thousand years of sleep. The splendor of this welcoming radiance, bursting upon us after our long toil through the blackness of cavernous depths, was inexpressibly cheering. We sank upon alabaster seats, and here we had luncheon with the fairies.

But what a world was this of contrasts and contradictions! My hand, feeling along the glittering wall for some crystal large enough to keep as a specimen, touched something that was soft and *alive*. Two feet from my nose I had not distinguished it from the snowy decorations. The thing did not try to escape, and I lifted it from the wall—a white bat! Who ever heard of such a creature? I was used to white mice, white rabbits, white deer, and even human albinos, but never had I imagined an albino bat. I put the little animal in my empty lunch-box, and sat down to examine it at my leisure.

Was this really an albino freak? Its eyes, instead of being pink, were beady black. Ah—more interesting—this must be an example of coloration adapted to a change of environment. Not protective coloration (nothing would pursue a cave bat) but a mask assumed with the design of catching prey. Wonderful! I would not have taken a new greenback for that white bat.

But my comrade either was indifferent to my high-flown zoölogy or impatient to make discoveries of his own—anyway, he was gone. The last of him that I had noticed was his feet disappearing in a small round orifice high in the wall of a vestibule beyond.

This had been some minutes ago. A trifle vexed at his quiet departure, I likened his exit to a toad vanishing in a rat-hole.

IN THE REAL DARK

The aperture through which Sidney had left me was scarcely bigger than a barrel-head, and could only be reached by skirting a treacherous ledge, past a deep fissure, and then climbing upward. I shoved my tall lantern into the hole and followed it headforemost. There was barely room to work my elbows and knees, and continually I was bumping my head. Why had that scapegrace chosen such a nasty, damp, crooked tube? Suppose one should get his clothing caught on one of the spiny projections—that might easily happen, especially if he tried to back out.

Had Sidney really got through, or was he stuck and helpless somewhere in the labyrinth beyond? Perhaps he had fallen into a pit and lay there stunned or dead.

I pushed along as fast as I could. In squirming around a bend of the tube I upset my lantern, and that bothersome but indispensable utensil instantly went out.

The shock of utter darkness was followed by one of pain as I butted my head against the rock while fumbling for my match-box. A good thing that the box was waterproof, for I was so soaking wet that the lining of my pocket clung to my hand.

Then a creepy horror suffused me as I realized that there was nothing dry to light a match on. From head to foot I was wet, and the rock all about me was wet. I tried one match on the checked side of the matchbox, but that too was wet. I studied, and studied, but it was no use. Nervously I screwed back the cap of the box tight upon its rubber gasket. If Sidney did not return (and could he ever find the way again?) my life depended upon those matches.

I yelled lustily for my comrade; but not even a mocking echo answered. At intervals I called again. It was incredible that Sidney should not hear me in that tomb-like silence where one could almost have heard the crawling of a snail. Did he indeed lie helpless with shattered bones, or had he wedged fast and fainted from very horror?

As I lay there on my belly, cruelly cramped in that black inferno, it seemed I could feel the rock shrinking to compress me. The very darkness seemed solidified, as though I were a petrifaction bedded forever in a mass of coal. For moments that were ages I lay as in a nightmare, trying but failing to struggle against doom.

To retreat without a light was madness; for how should I ever pass that chasm in the rear? To advance in utter blindness was a hazard reserved for the last extremity. I realized how it must feel to be buried alive in a graveyard; and yet a coffin would be preferable to this, for soon it would mercifully stifle one to death.

It is easy enough, as one sits comfortably at home, to think of several ways by which a match might have been lighted. Why did I not strike one across the edge of my knife? Any hero of romance would have done so at once. But I was no hero, nor was this romance. I had all I could do, just then, to fight off panic. In revulsion I was seized with anger and swore that I would get out of that man-trap, blind though I was. Anything was better than inaction.

I started to crawl forward. "This," thought I to myself, "is enough to make a fellow grit his teeth." At that last word a trick popped back into my head that had been forgotten ever since I was a bad little boy setting the good little schoolgirls' nerves a-twitter. I took out a match, placed its head-end between my teeth, jerked sharply forward, and had a flame instanter. I relighted the lantern and went ahead.

The descent proved difficult, even with a light. My old kerosene lantern was like a glowworm in the garden on a pitch-dark night. The tunnel corkscrewed downward to a considerable depth and then came out amid tumbled angular rocks that were hard to pass. Beyond was easy travel through a winding gallery.

I kept calling for my comrade, but still there was no reply. It was impossible to track him, for his smooth-shod feet had left no imprint on the dustless floor. The solitude was most depressing. I was alone where time was measured only by the slow drip of water, and no hour had ever struck. In this colossal and mysterious void there was no day, no night; no summer, no winter; no life, no death, save maybe for a few pitiable minikins forever imprisoned in silence and darkness that had made them colorless and mute and blind.

BACK TO DAYLIGHT

Then my hail was answered! Pressing eagerly forward, I found my partner in a byway where he was groping for water. The reservoir in his little acetylene lamp was nearly dry, and the light was dying. He had spare carbide to recharge the lantern, but had not provided a flask of water to go with it. That was why he had not come back to learn my whereabouts.

We went on along the lower gallery searching for water, but luck at first was against us. There was none but the slow, slow drip. Then a small supply was found. We set forth on a hunt for some easier rout to the upper gallery, but became bewildered and had to admit to each other that we were lost.

Sidney discussed our situation with admirable coolness. As for myself, it was so good to have light and companionship, and our present dilemma was so small in comparison with what I had just been through, that I took good heart.

Fate favored us now by revealing a shaft through which we could climb aloft without serious risk. We emerged into the upper tier of passages, found our old trail, and the rest of the trip was uneventful. Four hours after we had lowered ourselves into the "blowing-hole" we were back in the blessed light of day, and there we reclined gasping for a while in the sultry change of air on the surface.

The snowy nodules that I had collected in our fairy grotto were brilliant, at first, in the sunlight, but soon they began turning to a rusty and dirty brown. My "albino" (must I tell it?) turned rusty, too; and the next day, having meantime licked or rubbed herself clean of the white cave-powder with which she had disguised her complexion, my incredible contribution to science was shockingly revealed as a common mouse-colored bat!

It might be thought that our misadventures on this first real exploration underground would discourage us from ever trying such a trip again. But had we not met and conquered them? We were no longer tenderfoots. The first lesson in any art is how *not* to go about it; and this we had surely learned. Thereafter we looked well to our lighting equipment; and we carried balls of light twine, taking turnabout in paying it out behind us as we advanced—a simple and infallible guide for retracing our way.

Two other expeditions we made into this same cavern, of five hours and seven hours, respectively, taking five other men with us on the last trip. We discovered several new routes, and finally did get down to the true drainage level, or so near it we could hear where the unseen waters flowed; but we found no outlet that was practicable for man.

Our cave turned out to be nothing remarkable as compared with many another. Yet for us two blundering adventurers who were the first to open and explore it, this remains the most interesting cavern in the world; for it was here we passed our novitiate. After all, it is not the magnitude of the results, but the uncertainty about them, that makes a game worth playing.

Over the Camp Fire in the Woods

THE ESSENTIALS OF WHOLESOME CAMP COOKERY

On a camping trip by motor car, whether it be just for the week-end or on a tour, you will seldom spend more than one night at the same place. As a rule, then, you will have neither time nor inclination to get up meals that take much over half an hour to cook. This means that you will neither bake nor roast. Bread you will carry with you, and toast, or sometimes flapjacks, will take the place of biscuits or muffins. Meat, fish, poultry or game will be broiled, fried, sautéd [*sic*] or fricasseed, but never boiled nor stewed.

Now a word of warning at the start. Don't—if you value good digestion and dreamless sleep—don't think of "living out of cans." It is quite too easy to heat a can of prepared food, and too hard to pacify your tummy an hour later. Canned fruits and evaporated milk are advisable because one can't always get the fresh articles. Canned tomatoes, peas, corn and baked beans are good to vary the diet. Once in a while a tin of salmon or sardines comes handy. But avoid canned meats for the most part; they are neither wholesome nor appetizing as mainstays from day to day.

Camping out is not picnicking. A camper needs square meals and good ones, just as at home, only "more so." Make your plans to have fresh meat or fish as often as circumstances and wartime regulations permit.

There is much to be said in favor of cooking over an open wood fire. The knack of building and managing it is quickly learned with the help of a good book on camping. With an open fire you have as many "burners" as you want, and every dish can be served piping hot whenever you are ready for it. If a pot boils over when your back is turned no harm is done. Broiling and toasting are best done over naked coals. Many canny tricks of the culinary art that are impossible in the kitchen can be performed with such a fire, and some of them are inimitably good. The open fire is of the woods woodsy, and, as the darky says, "fittenest" when you are living out of doors.

From *Motor Life*, June 1918

But for all that, many prefer, on motor trips especially, a two-burner gasoline stove of a kind specially made for campers. It gets into action at once, saves trouble when the wood supply is poor and is a boon in wet weather. Anyway, if you carry a stove, there is no ban on having an open fire, too, whenever you want it; and generally you will want it mornings and evenings, for cheer's sake if nothing else.

As for pots and pans, the nested sets save space in packing; in other respects they are no better than common kitchen utensils of a fourth their cost. But the item of bulk is a serious one in motor touring. Try stowing in your kit a common frying pan, coffee pot and double boiler, and observe what the handles do for you. Then note how little space is taken by the camper's kit of two cooking pots and a coffee pot, nesting one within the other, topped by a frying pan with folding handle.

The best pots are of aluminum. I prefer steel for the frying pan. White enamel ware is better than aluminum for plates and cups, and so is plated metal for forks and spoons. You will need a milk pan or similar vessel for mixing batter, cleaning vegetables and as a dish pan. For each member of the party have a small, deep pan (pudding pan) instead of a bowl; these are useful in various ways. A wire broiler is handy for broiling and toasting over an open fire. A butcher knife, cooking spoon, can opener, tea ball and salt and pepper shakers complete the list of utensils. Anything else is a superfluity—something more to be washed and looked after when you might be fishing.

For carrying supplies the ready-made food bags and pry-up tins are convenient. Butter goes in a vacuum jar or in a Mason jar that can be screwed up tight and placed in the spring overnight. An egg carrier of parcel post design, and a milk can may be needed. Parchment paper is good to wrap meat and cheese in. Cheese-cloth will be needed for straining and to keep flies off food in camp. Don't forget the soap, dish cloths a-plenty and towels.

When using the stove observe some system in cooking so that the various dishes may be ready in proper order. The little two-burner is quite capable of turning out a complete meal for four people if you manage it right.

There comes to me vividly a picture of two husky hunters left by themselves in the big woods forty miles from a hotel and twenty from a farmhouse. They had half a wagonload of assorted food in the raw state. But they couldn't even make flapjacks that a starving hound would eat. They subsisted upon hardtack *au naturel* and canned food and fried fish, until murder was in the air. And who do you suppose one of those fellows was? Yes, you are right.

Afterward I was thrown where I had to do my own cooking or perish. There was no living preceptor. I just learned from a cook book, and having nobody but myself to eat the product, I learned fast. Then, knowing from fair trial how ill-adapted to camp conditions the domestic cook books are, I made a camp cook book for myself.

With a good cook book a man who never cooked anything can make decent coffee if the directions are of the right sort. If left to the light of nature he couldn't do it in a month. And so he can learn, at the first or second trial, how to cook a breakfast cereal and turn out a good dish of bacon and eggs. Starting right, he can do the whole trick in thirty minutes; starting wrong, he will potter around for an hour, scorch the oatmeal, set the bacon afire and get the eggs just right to patch shoes with.

Follow recipes exactly, and don't guess at quantities, but measure them, until you have had a good deal of experience. There are a few general principles to learn by rote and carry in your head. Here are some of them:

Do not try to fry over a full flame or a deep bed of coals. Set the burner at low flame or rake a thin layer of coals out in front of the campfire and fry over them. But get the pan quite hot before greasing it, then use only enough grease to prevent the food from sticking to the pan. Turn meat frequently. Fish should be dry before frying, or it will absorb grease. Bacon should be trimmed, or the rind nicked, to prevent the strips from curling. Eggs should be poured slowly from shell to pan so that the white thickens over the yolk instead of spreading like a pancake.

To broil a steak or chop in a frying pan, use a smoothly polished pan with no grease. Heat it very hot so that the surface of the meat will sear instantly on touching it. Turn the steak frequently, without jabbing, which would let the juice run out. The object is to coagulate the outside at once so as to seal the juices within, and then cook slowly till done. Do not season at the start, as salt draws the juices. A steak or chop should be cut at least an inch thick. It is done as soon as the inside has turned from blue to bright red.

Ham or bacon that is hard and salty should be parboiled before frying. Put some water in the pan; when it is warm, drop the meat in and let it simmer over a slow fire for a few minutes; then pour out the water and go on with the frying.

Don't try to make wheat pancakes without eggs. Best results come from mixing your own materials; but if you use ready-mixed pancake flour see that it is of a sort that has egg powder as one of its ingredients. The plain pancake made without the right ingredients has killed more campers than ever perished from snakes, wild beasts or thunderbolts. Its right name is Schrecklichkeit.

In making coffee over an open burner don't let it come to the boiling point, or you will have a sorry mess to clean up. Watch it, and when the water first begins to bubble, remove and let it steep for five minutes. Or boil the water alone, remove, quickly put the coffee in, cover tightly, plug the spout with a clean rag and let the coffee steep for ten minutes.

Tea should on no account be allowed to steep more than four minutes (some varieties three minutes). If the leaves are left in the water longer than that the tannin is extracted, and the fluid is bitter and injurious. Make tea by the watch, as you boil an egg.

To clean a frying pan, pour it nearly full of water and set it on the fire till it simmers. The grease rises to the surface. Scrape if necessary, rinse with hot water, and it will dry itself. Clean greasy dishes with scalding water, by themselves; don't dump everything into the pan together. Get all grease off before using the dish cloth.

Be content to learn one thing at a time and do it right. After the common plain processes have been mastered, you may tackle more ambitious projects, combination dishes, and even inventions of your own. A camper cannot always go by recipe alone. He is driven to substitutions and new combinations, like the sailor with his lobscouse, slumgullion, powsowdie and skilligalee.

It is plain enough that I am writing only for men. And yet there is a good deal in camp cookery that the ladies may enjoy, if but for the sake of novelty and fun. I do not refer to such spectacular but easy tricks as tossing flapjacks into the air and making them loop the loop, nor to the weird but effective ways of roasting venison on forked stakes, baking birds in clay, steaming fish and vegetables in a pit and boiling water in a bark bucket. What will interest them in ordinary camping is the shifts by which half a dozen utensils do the work of twenty, and do it well, and the unheard-of but none the less savory dishes invented by woodsmen themselves under stress of circumstances that townsfolk never encounter.

For good meals in camp have a proper fire and good materials. Then imprison in each dish its natural juice and flavor.

An Outfit for Trips Afoot

Some time ago Mr. Horatio W. Bishop sent me blue-prints of a small tent he had designed, together with sketches and checklist of the kits carried by himself and wife on their autumn trips in the White Mountains. The outfit was so well selected, the methods of stowage so ingenious and practical, that I begged Mr. Bishop to make line drawings of the various parts and publish them with descriptions. He has chosen to send me the drawings instead, to do with as I think best. It is a pleasure to give his ideas as wide circulation as I can by offering this article to *FIELD AND STREAM*.

The tent plan shows Mr. Bishop's interpretation of the modified wedge tent suggested in my *Camping and Woodcraft*, Vol I, pp. 92–94. The common wedge or *A*-tent is still a general favorite among travelers who go light and shift camp every day or two. It is easy to pitch on any kind of ground; it affords much head room for the amount of material used; and it is cheap. But it has some obvious faults.

If a ridge-pole is not used with a wedge tent (and often, as in mountaineering, there may be none procurable) the ridge sinks in a catenary curve, and the sides sag inward correspondingly. Then, too, a wind against the side of the tent will push it inward. From both causes the roominess of the interior is diminished. The thinner the material, the worse these faults will show up.

To make a wedge tent more roomy, and still retain its lightness and simplicity of erection as compared with a wall tent, stays called side parrals may be attached, as shown in the accompanying plans. These pull outward, take up slack, and turn the wedge into a semi-wall tent, making it more roomy and stiffening it against a gale. Slack is taken up further by pegging the sides and rear out at the bulge. The drawings show how these expedients work, though not showing the curve of the ridge.

The designer's specifications are for a very light tent (about 5¾ pounds) that will roll up into a small parcel. It is intended for two people. When set up it measures 4½ feet wide at the ends and 5½ feet "amidships," 7 feet long on each side, 7½ feet over all, and 5 feet high.

From *Field and Stream*, April 1919

There is a 6-inch sod cloth (called "sod-piece" in the plan), over which, and covering the whole floor space, goes a separate ground sheet (called "sod cloth") shaped to allow for the side and end bulges. At the rear is a bobbinet window 14 inches square, affording better ventilation than small tents usually have.

The tent proper is made of 4¾-ounce waterproof [Metalite], a closely woven, long staple cotton material, dyed pea-green for "low visibility" and to relieve sun glare. The ground sheet is of brown waterproof Tanalite. Details of materials and construction are so well shown on the sheet of specifications that further description is not needed.

Following is a check-list of the complete outfit:

EQIUPMENT [*SIC*] FOR BACK-PACKING

THE MAN'S

Wear—

Woolen undershirt, thin Jaeger.
Woolen drawers, thin Jaeger.
Khaki money belt, with railroad tickets.
Woolen socks, winter weight, natural color (or two pairs of light weight socks).
Woolen Army overshirt.
Two 3-in. × 5-in. felt pads to snap on inside of shirt where pack chafes.
Silk Neckerchief, 27-in. × 27-in.
Moleskin trousers.
Invisible suspenders.
Web belt.
Army shoes, cone Hungarian nails sparingly placed.
Army leggings, woolen cloth.
Stetson felt hat, medium brim, ventilated, felt sweat band, wind straps.

In Pockets—

Left Shirt: Compass, Explorer pattern, hinged cased. A. M. C. guide, with map sections in celluloid cover.
Right Shirt: Notebook and pencils in waterproof case.
Left Trousers: Change purse. Nail clip.
Right Trousers: Pocket knife, two blades, small blade very sharp. Waterproof match box with old-fashioned sulphur matches.
Fob: Watch, in 8-in. square rubber dental dam, tied at stem.
Left Hip: Toilet paper in waterproof case.
Right Hip: Bandanna handkerchief.

(All pockets to have flaps.)

On Belt (large, wide, loose, leather, separate, easily slipped on and off).

Left side, hip: Leather pocket for 3 cartridge clips. Sheath knife between pocket and belt.

Left side: Leather pocket for V. P. Kodak, rubber case inside.

Right side, hip: .22 cal. target automatic pistol, in leather flap holster.

Right side: Leather emergency pouch.

On Back—

Pack sack, 28-in. × 30-in., A grade.

Tent, improved wedge type as illustrated.

Sleeping bag. Waterproof browse pocket and pillow bag to stuff.

Cape, 34-in. long.

Mackinaw stag shirt, with draw-string at bottom, [1]6-oz. material, no pockets.

Sweater, sleeveless.

Spare underwear, one suit, medium weight.

Moccasins, moosehide, soled, 9-in. high.

Spare socks, 2 pairs.

German socks.

Parka, khaki, without fur trimmings (to turn the wind and as an extra sleeping garment).

Woolen sleeping hood.

Buckskin gloves. Woolen mitts to cover wrists.

Toilet kit.

Utility kit.

Films, 3 hermetically sealed and in rubber case.

Necktie, for wear while in civilization.

Emergency ration, in small balloon silk bags, consisting of parched corn, raisins, sugar, tea and pemmican: total weight about 2 pounds.

Some other reading matter and newspaper articles.

Cleaning kit for automatic.

Cooking kit composed of:

8-in. steel fry pan, with cover.

1 2-qt. aluminum alloy pail with ring cover.

1 4-qt. aluminum alloy pail with ring cover.

1 small aluminum mixing pan.

2 1-pint enamel cups.

2 enamel plates.

2 white metal forks.

2 white metal dessert spoons.

1 3-pint aluminum pail, with cover, for sour dough.

1 dish cloth.

1 dish towel.

½ bar Ivory soap.

On Outside of Pack—

Axe and muzzle, Damascus, 1¾ pounds.

Canvas water bucket, with tie top.

(Sweaters stow inside so as to be readily accessible when needed.)

Provisions are not specified, as they will vary according to circumstances.

THE WOMAN'S

Wear—

Woolen undershirt, thin Jaeger.

Woolen drawers, thin Jaeger.

Woolen stockings, light weight.

Woolen overshirt.

Two 3 × 5-in. felt pads to snap on inside of shirt at shoulders.

Silk neckerchief, 27 × 27 inches.

Moleskin hunting trousers, peg top.

Leather belt.

Outing boots, 12 in. high.

Light French felt hat, ventilated, leather wind straps.

In Pockets—

Handkerchief and flat folding cup.

On Belt—

Field glasses.

Whistle for signalling.

On Back—

Pack sack.

Sleeping bag.—Waterproof browse pocket and pillow bag.

Cape, 34 in. long.

Mackinaw stag shirt.

Sweater.

Spare underwear, one suit.

Sneakers, for wear about camp, in cotton bag.

Spare stockings, 2 pairs.
Norfolk jacket, short length, big pockets and wide collar (13-oz. Forestry cloth).
Short skirt, buttons down the front (Forestry cloth).
Woolen sleeping hood.
Strong leather gloves.—Woolen mittens, gauntlet length.
Toilet kit.
Emergency ration.
Parka, khaki, without the fur trimming.

The list is an adaptation of those given in *Camping and Woodcraft*, Vol. II., pp. 105–106 and 145–146, with some original ideas, and one or two borrowed from Mr. Dwight Franklin's articles in *FIELD AND STREAM*, October and December, 1917.

The note book, which an amateur will find indispensable, is of loose leaf pattern. It contains, besides blank sheets, a series of condensed notes, typed at home, that are indexed under such headings as these:

Complete Check List.
System in Camp.
Dressing Game and Fish.
Tried and True Recipes.
Fly Fishing.
Edible Plants of the Region Traversed.
Lost and Bivouacs.
Compass.
Axemanship: Woods for Various Uses and Camp Fires.
Bark Utensils.
Knots.
Snares and Emergency Hints.
Accidents.

Illustrations accompany the notes where needed. There are several 10 × 10-in. engineers' sheets for corrections to maps and trails. A U. S. Geological Survey map of the region to be camped in is placed in the cover for emergency use, together with a page from the almanac and part of a railroad timetable. The case contains a fountain pen, a medium lead pencil, and an indelible pencil.

The arrangement of articles on the belt seems to me to be particularly well planned. There is nothing at the back to interfere with a large pack sack. It is a mistake to carry too many things on the belt. They protrude most annoyingly for a man who leaves the beaten road and goes through thickety woods and over rough ground where climbing and crawling must be done at times. They are in the way every time one reclines when resting. And the belt is no place for a foot traveler to carry much weight, unless it is supported by suspending straps attached to the front of shoulder straps, as in a shoulder's pack, so as to act in some measure as a counterpoise to the weight on the man's back.

The pistol is carried to shoot small game with; and it is by no means a negligible defensive weapon against night-prowling "varmints" or tramps.

The canvas water bucket, with one side flattened, and with top to tie shut like the throat of a dunnage bag, is a bright idea of Mr. Franklin's. It often happens in mountain work that the most desirable site for the night's camp is high above the nearest water. The drudgery of making a special trip for water, and of carrying it by one hand in an open bucket, is great; on the other hand, a canteen is cumbersome, and it does not hold enough. I have been accustomed to carry a hot-water bottle, which is never in the way when empty, and, filled with warm water at night is a comfy article to slip in between the rather meager blankets. But it is not adaptable to other uses, whereas the Franklin type of bucket, when not in use for water carrying, will hold sweaters where they are right handy when a halt is called, or woods plunder [that] is acquired on the way.

Particular attention is called to Mr. Bishop's toilet kit and his utility kit (both made of light waterproof cloth). They solve the problem of how to arrange and carry the odds and ends of an outfit so they will be get-at-able and not everlastingly in a mess.

Years ago the American Canoe Association used to offer a prize for the best equipped canoe, at its annual meets. The object was to develop ideal cruising equipments, adequate but light, and systems of stowage that would avoid clutter and unhandiness. I have an old note book in which several such outfits are recorded, beginning with the prize winner at Lake George in 1881, Lucien Wulsin's *Annie Dell*. One can see from it that, as far back as that time, our outdoor men were studying every little detail of equipment as closely as any of us do today. They knew it paid.

It occurs to me that it might be a good idea for our magazines nowadays to offer prizes for the best kits of various types and for improved articles of equipment. Such encouragement might bring many bright ideas to light which otherwise are known to none but Tom of Spokane and Harry of Kalamazoo.

Ask Outing   Tell Outing

QUESTIONS AND ANSWERS ON PROBLEMS THAT SPRING UP IN CAMP AND ALONG THE TRAIL

EDITED BY HORACE KEPHART (EXCERPT)

For a long time OUTING has maintained a free information bureau for its readers, called the Service Department. A personal reply was sent to every inquirer as soon as we could put it through.

Hitherto none of the correspondence has been published. But there are many questions and answers that would interest a large circle of readers if printed in the magazine. Often it happens that one man's problem is the very thing that others are puzzling over at the same time. A query or a reply may suggest new experiments, new angles of discussion, or call to mind experiences of your own that would throw light on the subject.

So, with this issue, we are opening a new department, a readers' forum, in which selected letters and answers will be published, and discussions may be carried on by the readers themselves.

We want you to feel that this is your own department. If you see in the magazine anything that does not square with your own experience, write and tell us about it. If you have devised or picked up a good "kink" pass it along for your comrades' benefit. If you have observed something unusual in wild life, describe it. This is your camp-fire.

BUFFALO BILL'S MARKSMANSHIP

Question—I saw Buffalo Bill ride horseback at a canter and shoot glass balls thrown into the air by another man riding just ahead of him. Did Buffalo Bill shoot a rifle with one ball only, or did he shoot a charge of shot? —W. P.

From *Outing*, May 1919

Answer—Small shot, of course. The arena of the Wild West Show generally was set within city limits, surrounded by a dense population. To have used bullets would have been criminal folly. Bill's gun was a '73-model Winchester with smooth-bored barrel, using shells charged with shot. Such a cartridge will hold about 100 No. 8 shot, and will put about half of them in a foot-square target at 50 feet.

But Buffalo Bill was a remarkably fine marksman from horseback when circumstances allowed him to use real rifles and solid bullets. When he was supplying the Union Pacific Railroad builders with meat for their men he killed 4,250 buffalo in one year. All told, he killed over 40,000 buffalo, besides other game. He never stalked the buffalo, but charged a herd at full speed, and shot the animals down as he was running round and round the herd to keep them bunched. His favorite weapon for this work was one of the old Allen model .50-caliber Springfields (usually called "needlegun") which he named "Lucretia Borgia". So he told Chauncy Thomas in an interview a short time before his death.

BUILDING A LOG CABIN

Question—In writing to the Department of Agriculture, Washington, for information on log houses I was referred to you. I have been advised by some people to put up the logs green, while others say that would not do as they would shrink apart too much. I have also thought of having them sawed on three sides to make a level inside finish and also save chinking. Logs would have to be peeled if sawed. — E. H.

Answer—It is usually considered best to use logs that are peeled. If the bark is left on, it soon begins to loosen, insects get under it and the wood decays. Logs cut in the Spring or early Summer are better as the bark can then be peeled easily. Green logs will shrink to a certain extent, of course, but hardly enough to make any great difference.

There is no reason why you should not face the logs on three sides as you mention. Personally, I rather favor keeping the logs just as they are. This makes the house look and seem more like a log cabin. You can easily chink it up so that it is perfectly tight. Where there are large crevices between the logs they can be filled with quartered poles.

Here is an important point about the chinking. Mortar should not be used until the logs have seasoned thoroughly and got their set. Until this time, they can be chinked with moss or clay.

Question—What is the best way to make bread of plain flour, salt, and water, when you are on a hard trip and can only bake once a day? The kind I have made was not fit to eat except when hot. — J. R.

Answer—Make it like an ashcake. Have a good hardwood fire. Work some flour, water, and a little salt into a dough. Rake away the embers, place the loaf on the hot earth, pat it smooth, cover with two or three inches of hot ashes, and put some burning embers on top to maintain heat. Let it bake until no dough will adhere to a sliver thrust through center of loaf. You will soon learn by experience how much time it takes. The slight coating of ashes that adheres can be scraped off, but, anyway, it is "clean dirt."

This is the Australian damper. It is a rather solid and substantial article, but wholesome, and has the advantage over any unleavened bread baked on a pan, slab, or stick, that it retains enough moisture to be eatable when several days old, or until mould sets in.

Roving with Kephart

THE COMPASS AND THE MAP: HOW TO USE THEM

I had a friend who was a good fellow, and he was worldly-wise. He could have gone by himself around the earth, by ship and rail, and would have known just how to get from place to place.

But one day he took the notion to go hunting in a bit of wild country. Some one asked him: "Aren't you afraid you may get lost?"

"No," he answered: "I have a compass.' [*sic*]

Well, he did have a compass, and he did get lost. He took out the instrument. It showed him exactly where north was; and east, south, west; and three hundred and sixty points in between. But it didn't show him which one of those directions to take. How could it?

A compass is of no more use than a corkscrew unless you carry along with it either

1. In your head, a good idea of the lay of the land; or
2. In your pocket, a large scale [map] showing the principal landmarks.

MAPS THAT ARE WORTH WHILE

In my friend's case, the joke of it was that he did have a map in his pocket. But it was one of those of a whole State that are made for commercial purposes. It was a small-scale thing, twenty miles to the inch, showing every town and railroad but little else. The river that was our base of operations was drawn on that map "be guess and begob," and no hills were shown at all. So Harry had to stay where he was until our search party found him.

His compass was all right. But that map! It would have shown a stranger how to get from Hannibal to St. Louis, but not how to go from the union station to the rifle range.

From *All Outdoors*, April 1920

What Harry needed was a large-scale topographical map of Shannon County. A topographical map is one that shows the physical features of a region: its hills and hollows, its lakes and streams, big and little, and does it accurately.

A topographical map drawn on a scale of two miles to the inch will show enough details to guide anybody who can read it, if he has a compass with him. It gives not only the physical features but also the wagon roads, where there are any; and the principal trails, where there are no roads; and the settlements, or sometimes even individual houses, where the country is thinly settled.

With such a map, and a compass a stranger can locate his camp with precision on the map. And if he should get lost, then, even in cloudy weather, he can find out where he is and how to get back to camp. That is, he can do these things if he has learned at home how to use map and compass. That is easy, as I will soon show.

Our Government for years has been at work on a topographical map of the United States. A great deal of the country has been surveyed and mapped. The sheets of this map generally are about fifteen by eighteen inches in size, and most of them are on a scale of about two miles to the inch. Such a sheet, then, takes in a territory about thirty by thirty-six miles.

The map is printed in three colors; the contours or hills and slopes in brown; lakes, streams, marshes, in blue; roads, settlements, and other cultural features in black.

I have cut out of one of these sheets a piece showing a tract eight by nine miles, and it is reproduced by photographic process on this page. As it can be printed here in only one color, it does not show in what bold relief the features stand out on the original map, but it will serve to illustrate the following remarks.

Two things distinguish this from an ordinary map. First, it is on a large enough scale to show the smallest settlements, the smallest creeks and branches, the sink-holes (those wee tadpole-shaped marks), a ford, a ferry, and all the country roads.

Second, it is covered with irregular wavy lines that wiggle around and come back and meet themselves, or go meandering off the map. These are contour lines marking elevations of the land above sea-level. One of them, you notice, is marked 1500. The figures mean that wherever that line runs the land is just 1500 feet above the sea.

On the lower margin of the original map is printed the statement "Contour interval 100 feet." This means that, starting at the river for instance, the second contour line beyond it is 100 feet higher than the first one, the next is 100 feet still higher, and so on.

To find the elevation of the river, above sea-level, start at the 1500-foot mark north-east of Amis, and count the contour lines between it and the river. The first is 1400 feet, the next 1300, then 1200, then 1100, then the river. Since there cannot be anything lower than the river, on this bit of map, it follows that the river here is between 1000 and 1100 feet above sea-level.

On the bottom margin of the original map there is also a scale of miles, (one mile equals one-half inch on the map). From it you will see that the Holston River here averages rather more than an eighth of a mile wide.

Using your wits on these simple data, you see at once that this is a rugged country, with a fairly cool climate for its latitude, that it is a limestone region honeycombed with caverns and that it is thinly settled, or was at the time this map was made. You have learned these things, about a distant and (to you) unknown region, without getting out of your chair.

There is a lot more you can learn about it, sitting there in your chair; but let us not drift off the main subject. The first point to be emphasized is that the Place to Learn Map-Reading is at Home. Don't put it off until you get into strange woods. And around home is the place to test your knowledge and make sure that you can turn it to practical use.

Send a silver dime (not stamps) to The Director, U. S. Geological Survey, Washington, D. C., for the topographical sheet that takes in your own home and its surroundings. Ten cents a sheet is all these government maps cost, and they are far better than any commercial ones at any price.

HOW TO LOCATE A POSITION

Take your home map, and a compass, out into the country, wherever there is a hilltop from which you can get a wide view. Any sort of compass will do; but for locating positions with certainty it should be of 1 ½ to 1 ¾-inch diameter, with degree marks around the circle, a needle that turns rather quickly, and a stop that holds the needle off its pivot when not in use, so as to save wear on the pivot point.

Having reached your hilltop, see if you can locate it on the map. That will probably be easy, by comparison with surrounding objects and observing the high contour lines where they come around in small circles, indicating knobs.

It is easy to realize exactly what contour lines mean if you imagine a flood of water gradually rising from the lowest ground on your map until nothing but the highest hilltops stick out.

Take the bit of map we have here, for instance. Suppose the Holston River is just 1000 feet above sea-level. Now imagine a rise of water 100 feet vertically. In that case the shore-line on each side would be the 1100-foot contour line, wherever it goes. A rise of another 100 feet would bring it to the 1,200-foot contour line; and so on. If the flood rose 500 feet, there would be no land left in sight but what is shown on the map by the heavy 1,500-foot lines and the small loops inside of them that indicate still higher elevations—these are the main hilltops.

Once you grasp this fact, then your map will give you a mental image of the landscape, with all its hills and hollows, and a more accurate one than you would get from a big photograph taken from a balloon.

Having identified your hill and found it on the map, lay your map flat on the ground before you, and orient it. That means, lay it with its top to the north, by compass. That is easy, for the map has meridians (north-and-south lines) marked on it. Lay your compass with its center directly over one of those meridians. Revolve the instrument until the letter N is under the north point of the needle. Then gently move the top of the map right or left until the meridian line runs in exactly the same direction as the needle.

Sitting on the south side of the map, look out over the country and pick out another hilltop in the distance, somewhere in a northerly direction. Place your compass on the map, with its pivot right over the spot that marks the hill you are on. Get down and sight over it to the distant hilltop. Note how many degrees it bears to right or left—that hilltop. Estimate the distance roughly by eye. Suppose it is six miles. Then look on your map for a hilltop in the same direction and at about the same distance by map scale. It is there, and you have identified it.

Similarly pick out and identify another hill in another direction. Now, by means of these two distant hills you can make positively certain of the hill you are on. You could do so even if you had not previously known which hill it was. Because lines drawn straight toward you on the map from those two far-off hills will meet each other right here where you are. You then know positively where you are, on the map, and in reality.

Therefore, you can pick out a course from this spot on the map to any other spot. Having taken the compass bearings to that spot, and measured the air-line distance on the map, you can go to that place, by allowing for the meandering right and left of a straight line, as you go along, and the extra distance it causes you to cover.

Other natural objects than hills will serve the same purpose, if they are marked on the map and are visible from your outlook, your starting-point.

And as soon as you have learned to do this sort of thing at home you have also learned how to do it anywhere else; for the principles are just the same anywhere.

DRAINAGE IS THE KEY TO A COUNTRY

The courses of the streams show the general drainage of the land. The contours show it in detail. And drainage is the key to the problem of travel in a strange country. For the most practicable routes, where there are no roads, are either along the watercourses or along the ridges that separate watercourses. Generally the best course overland is on the ridges, because thus you avoid difficult bends and fords, you get good outlooks, and the backbone of a ridge is not so apt to be covered with dense undergrowth as the margin of a stream.

Contours show not only heights but degrees of slope. Wherever the contour lines come close together there is a steep place. Wherever they are wide apart there is a gentle slope. By comparing the map with the actual landscape you will soon see what degree of slope a given interval between contours indicates.

This sort of knowledge is valuable when you are in a strange country, for it shows where the going is easy and where it is hard, so far as hills and hollows are concerned.

MAP AND COMPASS IN CAMP

Make it a practice, wherever you camp, to immediately locate that camp on the map. It is the way to avoid getting lost thereafter. And study the surrounding country, on the map, before you leave camp, until you have a clear mental image of its principal features, and their direction and distance from camp.

The man who takes this simple precaution is less likely to get lost, even if he should neglect to take with him his map and compass when he goes afield, than the fellow who was too lazy or indifferent to do so and goes out then with both of them in his pockets.

But make it an invariable rule to carry your map and compass, and to fill your match-box every morning before you start anywhere. Then if you should get obfuscated some afternoon, with the sun setting apparently in the northeast, and all that, it is no great matter: you will get out.

The Chef in the Wilderness

Outfitting for the woods is governed by the means of transportation. If the camp site can be reached by wagon or boat, and you are to stay in one place, then take along a camp stove. It does the work with less fuel than an open fire, is easier to manage in wet weather, and is safer in a dry season. A party in fixed camp wants, and should have, more variety in its meals than would do for hunters or other rovers. That means more kinds of raw materials, more utensils to prepare them with, and more frequent use of long cooking processes, such as boiling, stewing, roasting. It generally means that somebody in the party must spend most of his time cooking and cleaning up for the others. Adieu to that subject.

Those who travel by automobile or motor boat will want quick meals, as a rule, and as little fuss about them as practicable. For them the gasoline stove is the thing. There are several patterns specially designed for such service, compact, light and efficient.

For short trips afoot where wood is scarce, or where an open fire for any reason is ruled out, as in mountaineering above timber-line, or hiking in thickly settled regions, solidified alcohol solves the problem. A ten-cent tin will cook two meals for two persons, if managed right.

A stove is too big and heavy to bother with when you go with pack animals or in canoes. Cooking will be done over an open fire. It is convenient, though not necessary, to have a pair of flat steel bars, about 24 × ½ × ⅛ in., to hold utensils level over the coals; or a folding grate, if you prefer.

If you stay out more than three or four days you will have to bake your own bread. Without a stove that has an oven, you will need a baker. Bread of a sort can be baked in the frying-pan, but few men will make it fit to eat day after day. A Dutch oven is too heavy for any but wagon trips. The best portable baker is a folding reflector, such as you see pictured in outfitters' catalogues. The kind that slopes back to a sharp angle

---

From *Vacation Manual*, Summer 1920

does not bake so evenly, and is not so compact, as one with a narrow perpendicular back. A reflector bakes as good biscuits as any oven can turn out, and an amateur cook will succeed better with it. The baking is directly under his eye all the time, so he can shift the pan around when needful, and tell precisely when the batch is done. Ducks and other game can be roasted to perfection in such a utensil, and it is a bully thing to keep food hot until served.

The frying-pan should be of steel. Aluminum is nice as long as the polish stays on, but thereafter things will stick to it; besides, it is all-fired stuff to burn the unwary. If compact stowage is essential, then get a frying-pan with folding handle or a socket for a stick; otherwise the common "cool handle" kind is best. Two medium-sized ones will be needed if there are more than three people.

Aluminum cooking pots that nest in each other are good articles. I mean the kind with bails so fitted that there are no ears sticking out, and with flat covers, such as are sold only by camp outfitters. But if it is not necessary to cut down weight and bulk to a minimum, then I prefer common enameled covered pails, of sizes from two quarts up. They are easier to clean; and that, brethren, is an item worth considering. For a party of four there should be three of them, at least, besides the coffee-pot, one being generally used as a tea-kettle to keep a supply of hot water. The water bucket may be a folding canvas one, but a common galvanized bucket is more serviceable if you can carry it.

Tinware is unfit for camp service unless it is seamless and a good deal heavier than the common sort. Remember, you will be forty miles from anywhere when a pot comes unsoldered or has a hole punched in it. Tin vessels will not do to soak dehydrated foods in, nor to cook fruit or tomatoes in. They are mean to clean when greasy, especially in cold weather.

The best plates and cups are of enameled ware, easy to clean, and not so apt to burn ones [*sic*] fingers and mouth as aluminum. Steel table knives, and a butcher-knife for the cook. Spoons and forks of white metal or plated ware. Dessert spoons are the right size for campers' mouths, not teaspoons. There should be a big spoon for mixing, skimming, picking up embers, and other culinary sleights.

A can-opener, soap, dish towels and clouts, some cheese-cloth for straining and to hang up meat and fish so flies can't get at them: these complete the list of essentials. But if means of transportation permit, add a couple of milk-pans for mixing and serving and dish-washing, a wire broiler, and perhaps a few other articles.

Beware, though, of excess baggage. There is nothing under heaven that a pack-mule would rather take his spite out of than pots and pans. There's nothing else that has to be cleaned so often—and just at the very time when nature prays you to let it digest your meal in peace.

What food to take along depends upon where you go, how you are to get there, how long you will stay, what can be killed or bought in the country itself, and your personal tastes. In the nature of things there can be no such thing as a standard camp ration. So don't depend on anybody's ration list. Do some figuring for yourself. The following general remarks may help:

A party that goes into fixed camp not far from a wagon road, or on a shore reached by boat, can take all the canned goods, fresh eggs and vegetables, or other heavy, bulky stuff that they think they will want.

A pack outfit must cut out a lot of that; still it may carry canned tomatoes and fresh onions and potatoes. Canoeists can do the same if the course is all clear water; but if there are many portages, or some long ones, they must go light.

Consider, then, the problem of a mountaineering trip, where no game or fish is to be had and no house of refuge exists. All-day climbing with a pack on one's back is about the hardest work that a man can do. It demands extra fuel for him, just as it would for a locomotive engine. Still the equipment must be culled out and pared down to the last practicable ounce, if the trip is to last more than a couple of days. So the food must be highly concentrated, with as little weight as possible in the containers, and yet packed so that it is weather-proof. There will be no fresh meat. There will be few utensils to cook with. Yet it is imperative that the food be so digestible that all of its nutriment will be assimilated, and varied enough not to pall on the appetite.

The energy produced by digested food is measured in calories, somewhat as the fuel value of different grades of coal is measured. A man at moderately active work (fisherman, for instance) requires about 3,400 calories of food-fuel a day; one at hard muscular work (big game hunter), about 4,150; one at very hard work (mountain climber), about 5,500 calories.

These figures can be utilized in figuring out a ration list, provided you remember that the *digestibility* of this or that food article is even more important than the number of calories it will yield *if* digested. Here is an example (don't fall down and worship it):—

Ration List Per Man

PER WEEK LBS.	OZ.		OUNCES PER DAY	CALORIES PER DAY	CALORIES PER LB.
3	..	Fresh meat	6.86	430 av.	1000
2	..	Bacon	4.57	776	2715
..	8	Butter	1.14	224	3410
..	4	Lard	.57	146	4080
1	..	Evaporated milk	2.28	98	683
4	..	Wheat flour	9.14	934	1650
1	..	Corn meal	2.29	234	1635
..	12	Rice	1.72	166	1546
..	12	Oatmeal	1.72	190	1759
5	..	Potatoes (fresh)	11.43	211	295
..	8	Onions	1.14	14	190
2	..	Tomatoes (canned)	4.57	27	95
..	8	Beans (dried)	1.14	109	1520
1	..	Prunes, apricots (dried)	2.29	200 av.	1400
..	8	Raisins	1.14	115	1605
..	4	Nut meats	.57	100 av.	2800
1	..	Sugar	2.29	260	1820
1	8	Other sweets	3.43	343 av.	1600
..	8	Coffee	1.14	0	0
..	1	Tea	.14	0	0
..	4	Baking powder	.57	0	0
..	6	Salt	.86	0	0
..	1	Other condiments.	.14	0	0
26	12		61.14		4597

All weights are net, not including tins, bags, etc.

This amounts to 3 lbs., 13 oz. per man per day. But the fresh meat (beef, venison, or the equivalent in small game or fish) is supposed to be killed or bought in the country traversed. The food carried along, then, is 3 lbs., 6 oz. per man per day, aside from weight of cans and other containers.

Is this too heavy? Well, look at the table of calories and you will see what makes it so. A pound of potatoes gives you only 295 calories of energy, because nearly three-fourths of their weight is water and refuse: a pound of oatmeal, practically water-free, 1,750 calories. A pound of dried apricots yields about 1,400 calories, and a pound of tomatoes (94% water) only 95 calories, besides which you must figure the weight of the tomato can against that of the apricot bag or wrapper. (In a small can of sardines the tin weighs two-thirds as much as the contents.)

If you take "plenty" of canned fruit, canned meats, canned vegetables, your food burden will be at least six pounds per man each day. If you cut out the things that are largely water, and substitute cereals and dehydrated fruits and vegetables, the gross weight, bags and all, need not be more than 2¼ to 2½ pounds a day, even for a mountaineer. So it is not wise to turn up one's nose at that scientific word calories.

Now let us look over our list a bit. The first five items form the group of meats and fats. The amount of fresh meat given is a minimum. If you know you can get more of it in the country, cut down the four other items, or some of them. If you carry butter and bacon, cut out the lard and add its equivalent to the others, which will do its work just as well, or better. If you can't have butter, add more bacon. If evaporated milk is too heavy, substitute powdered milk.

The next four items form the bread-stuffs and cereals group. For emergency use you can substitute crackers or hardtack for some of the flour. If you don't like rice, substitute cracked wheat or some other cereal. Fresh bread may be carried, instead of some of the flour, etc., for the first three days.

The next six components form the vegetable and fruit group. They are important to assist digestion, prevent constipation, correct a fatty diet, and add variety without which food soon palls and then fails to nourish. But we have seen how heavy they are in proportion to nutriment afforded. Macaroni is a good substitute for potatoes, and it affords 1,645 calories to the pound.

When going light, dehydrated fruits and vegetables supply this quota. Some of the dehydrated fruits recently put on the market are delicious. The apples, for instance, when made into sauce or pies, have the flavor of fresh apples similarly prepared. But observe that all dehydrated products require several hours' soaking in fresh water before cooking. This can be done overnight, but the material must then be used for breakfast if camp is shifted from day to day, unless your means of transport permits carrying the stuff in a can or pail.

Canned soups are nearly all water. Powdered soups can be bought of outfitters in several varieties. They are easily and quickly cooked, and do well in emergencies, but are not very appetising unless you have butter or milk to add to them, and they will not do at all for steady diet.

I nearly always carry butter, even in summer. A pry-up tin will hold it. Butter has a very high food value, and it is the most digestible form of fat there is. Keep it in the spring overnight. Besides its use to spread on bread and flapjacks, butter is one of the most valuable elements in many cooked dishes.

If you use powdered milk, get the kind that has at least 20% of butter-fat, instead of the skimmed milk kind. Some brands have an unpleasant greasy taste, especially if they have been stored for some time. As a rule, I prefer evaporated milk.

Egg powder, if you can get a good brand of it, such as the National Baker's egg, is invaluable where fresh eggs can not be obtained. You can make excellent omelets and scrambled eggs with it, and it improves camp-made bread and many other foods so that they are beyond comparison with plainer cooking. A net pound of it, in its screw-top can, weighs 1 lb., 5 oz. gross, and is the equivalent of about three dozen eggs. In cooking, you mix it dry with the flour or what not; but for omelets, etc., it must be first soaked for a few hours.

Sweet chocolate, cheese, and nut meats (particularly pecans) are highly concentrated foods that are valuable at lunch, or to eat on the march; but they should be used in moderation, or they will cause thirst and constipation. Raisins are a good corrective, contain much stored-up energy, and digest quickly.

Most Americans want their morning coffee. At other meals tea is a better bracer. But there is something better, for many people, than tea. It is maté, sometimes called Paraguayan tea, which can now be procured in this country. It is quite as good a pick-me-up as Asiatic tea, and does not keep one awake if he drinks it at night. In buying it, see that you get real leaves, not chopped up stems and trash.

RECIPES

This is no cook-book; but I will add recipes for a few standard camp dishes that every outer should learn to use for himself:—

By cook's measure, one tablespoonful equals two dessert spoonfuls or four teaspoonfuls. A cup is a half-pint.

Flapjacks. Prepared pancake flours contain egg powder, and some of them also milk powder, to make the cakes light. Superior cake batter can be mixed in camp:

1 quart flour,
1 heaped tablespoonful baking powder,*
1 tablespoonful egg powder (or 1 fresh egg),
2 teaspoonfuls sugar (or 4 of molasses),
1 teaspoonful salt.

Mix thoroughly in dry pan; then add 3 tablespoonfuls evaporated milk (or 2 of powdered milk) and enough water, gradually, to stir up into a smooth batter just thick enough to run lazily from a spoon.

---

*Strength of baking powders varies with the quality. Follow directions on can. The sugar is added to brown the cakes nicely.

Have the frying-pan clean and polished. Set it level over a thin bed of coals till it gets hot enough to make the batter sizzle when it touches. Grease lightly with a piece of fat pork or bacon in the split end of a stick. Pour in batter enough to fill pan within half-inch of rim. When cake is full of bubbles, and edges have stiffened, shuffle pan till cake slides free from bottom, and flip over or turn with knife.

Grease pan anew, and stir batter, each time before pouring a new cake. Eat "red-hot," with butter and syrup, or bacon gravy.

If you have corn meal, vary the flapjacks by making them sometimes with three-fourths meal and one-fourth flour, or the reverse, or half-and-half (each kind has a different flavor). When you have no egg or milk, always use corn meal in the batter, and rub a little grease into the dry ingredients before mixing with water. Pancakes made of plain flour, baking powder, sugar, salt and water, are tough and indigestible.

A bannock or biscuit-loaf can be made by using less water and baking longer, or by the following biscuit recipe:—

Biscuit. If a reflector is used, build the fire high, against a backing of logs or rock that will throw the heat forward. For one dozen biscuit, which fill an 8 × 12-inch pan:

1 ½ pints flour,
1 ½ teaspoonfuls baking powder (or more, according to strength),
1 level teaspoonful salt,
1 heaping tablespoonful cold grease,
½ pint cold water (or a little less, according to quality of flour).

Mix thoroughly with big spoon or wooden paddle, first the baking powder with the flour, and then the salt. Rub into this the cold lard, bacon fat, drippings, or other grease, until there are no lumps left. Then stir in the water and work it with spoon to a rather stiff dough.

Rub some flour over the bread board or whatever you use for the purpose. Have the loaf floured all over. Flour your hands, and the bottle or bit of peeled sapling used as rolling-pin. Place loaf on board and gently roll it to ¾-inch thickness. Stamp out with a can cover, make the culls into biscuit too, and lay all in the lightly greased pan.

Set reflector in front of fire. Bake until front row begins to brown; then reverse pan and continue until all are done.

Dough made with baking powder should be handled as little as possible, as the heat of the hands makes it "sad." Baking powder begins to form gas as soon as water touches it, and it is this gas, imprisoned in the dough, that makes bread light. If you knead the dough, or mould the biscuits by hand, you squeeze out the gas and make the bread tough.

Dropped Biscuit. These do away with bread-board, rolling-pin, and most of the work, yet are nearly as good as stamped biscuit. Use same proportions as above, except turn in enough water to make a *thick* batter. In mixing do not stir the batter more than necessary to smooth out all lumps. Drop from a big spoon into the greased bake-pan.

Cereals. Follow directions on package. If plain oatmeal is used (it is a better stand-by than rolled oats) it should be cooked a full hour to make it disgestible [*sic*]. A double boiler can be extemporized by setting a small kettle inside a larger one that contains some hot water, with a few pebbles at the bottom to keep them apart.

Boiled Rice. Wash it in cold salted water. Then put one cupful in two quarts of furiously boiling water, no salt being added. Keep the pot boiling hard for 20 minutes, but do not stir. The rice should be put in the water a little at a time, so as not to check the boiling. Cooked this way, each grain will be plump, dry and separate, instead of making a soggy mess.

Raisins or other dried fruit should be soaked a good while in cold water before putting them in the rice pot.

As a left-over, rice can be used in soups or stews, or fried, or made into pancakes or muffins, or utilized in a score of other ways, each dish tasting different from the others.

Brown rice, which is the best kind, should be cooked 35 minutes.

Frying Meat. Do not try to fry over a flaming fire or a deep bed of coals. Rake a thin layer of coals out in front of the fire; or, for a quick meal, make your fire of small dry sticks, boil water for your coffee over the flame, and fry over the quickly formed coals.

Bacon should be sliced quite thin, and the rind nicked so it will not curl up in the pan. If bacon is old or salty, put pan half full of water on fire, and when it is warm, drop bacon in and stir it around until water begins to simmer; then remove meat, throw out water, put bacon back, fry and turn often, and remove slices while still translucent—they will turn crisp on cooling.

Salt pork and ham are fried in the same way, but slices are cut thicker.

Venison should not be fried, but broiled or roasted.

Birds for frying should be cut in convenient pieces, parboiled until tender in a pot with enough water to cover, then removed, saving the liquor. Sprinkle with salt, pepper, and flour, fry, take out when done. Then stir into the frying fat one-half cupful of dry flour till a dark brown, add parboiling liquor, and bring to a boil. Pour this gravy over the birds.

Squirrels, rabbit, etc., are fried like birds. The gravy is improved by frying with it a small onion that has been previously parboiled and minced.

Broiled Meat. Only tender pieces are fit for broiling. Venison generally requires some pounding, but don't gash it so that juice escapes. Have a bed of bright coals free from smoke, with a clear flaming fire to one side. Cut the meat at least an inch thick. Sear it by thrusting for a moment into the flame and turning. Then broil before the coals, catching drippings in a pan underneath. Season when done, or nearly done, with salt and pepper. Serve on hot dish with drippings poured over, or buttered; otherwise the meat will be dry.

Birds are split up the back, broiled over the coals, and basted with a piece of fat pork held over the bird by a tinned or split stick. Young squirrels, etc., the same.

Roast Venison. Build a rather large fire of split hardwood that will make lasting coals, against a high backlog, or a wall of rocks, that will throw the heat forward. If green wood, or sticks larger than stove-wood size must be used, make a bonfire of them at one side of your cooking-fire, and shovel coals from it as needed.

Sear the outside of the roast in clear flame until outer layer is coagulated so as to hold in the meat juices. Then skewer thin slices of bacon to the upper end. Hang the roast before the fire and close to it, by a stout wet cord (keep it wet). Turn frequently so as to roast evenly all round. Catch the drippings in a pan underneath, or a clean bark trough, and pour them over the meat from time to time.

This is better than roasting on a spit over the fire, because the heat can be better regulated, the meat turned and held in position more easily, the roast is not smoked, and the drippings are utilized.

Just before the meat is done, baste it and sprinkle with flour, then brown it nicely near the fire. For a gravy, thin the remaining drippings with boiling water in which half a teaspoonful of salt has been dissolved.

The forward part of the saddle is the best roasting piece. Trim off flanky parts and ends of ribs, and split backbone lengthwise so that the whole will hang flat.

To roast a shoulder, peel it from the side, cut off leg at knee, gash thickest part of flesh, press bits of pork into them, and skewer some slices to upper part.

A whole side of venison can be roasted by planting two stout forked stakes before the fire, a stub of each stake being thrust through a slit cut between the ribs and under the backbone.

Roast Goose or Turkey. Stick a sharp wooden pin through the bird at the wings, letting the ends protrude, and a similar pin through the legs. Have a cross pole in front of the fire, from which a strong wet cord is hung, as above, the lower end of cord being made into a noose.

Slip the noose over the ends of one of the pins, and so suspend it before the fire and just over the pan set for drippings. Twirl the cord now and then. When lower end of bird is roasted, reverse by suspending from the other pin.

Any kind of game bird or small mammal can be roasted in this way, and literally done to a turn. No kitchen range can compete with an open fire for roasting, when you know how to do it.

Baked Duck. Dry-pick, and leave head on. Put a little pepper and salt inside, but no other dressing. Lay the bird on its back in a dry bake-pan. Have oven hot, but not enough to burn. Baste frequently with butter or bacon. When done, the duck should be plump, and the flesh red, not blue. Overseasoning and stuffing destroy the distinctive flavor of wildfowl.

Baking in a Hole. This is the best way to cook tough meat, and to bake beans, and to make stews overnight, or to prepare cereals that require long cooking, when the camp is a shifting one and there is no chance for prolonged cooking in the daytime. It works on the principle of a fireless cooker.

Dig a hole in the ground, say a foot and a half square and a foot deep, depending on size of kettle. Make a fire of split hardwood in and over it, large enough to provide plenty of coals. Cut the flesh or fowl in pieces, season, add a chunk of fat pork, put them in the kettle with water enough barely to cover, put lid on, rake coals out of hole, put kettle in, return coals around and over it along with enough hot ashes to keep them from burning out, cover all with a few inches of earth as an insulator, and leave the kettle undisturbed overnight. In case of rain, cover with bark.

Baked Beans. It is best to soak the beans several hours in cold water before cooking; but if time does not permit, add ¼ teaspoonful baking soda to the parboiling water. Start in fresh cold water, and parboil one quart of beans (for four men) one-half hour, or until one will pop open when blown upon. Also barboil [*sic*] separately one pound fat salt pork. Remove scum from beans as it rises. Then drain water from pork, gash the meat all round with a knife, spread half of it over bottom of kettle. Drain the beans, put them into the kettle, sprinkle them with not more than ½ teaspoonful of salt, pepper liberally, and if you have molasses, pour a tablespoonful over all; otherwise a tablespoonful of sugar. Put the rest of the pork on top. Add enough boiling water to just cover the beans, place kettle in bake-hole, and bake overnight, being sure there are not enough live embers with the ashes to burn the beans.

Stew (Mulligan). Any kind of game, or beef, may be used; but use lean meat only. Cut it into small pieces and put it into a hot frying-pan greased only enough to keep meat from sticking. Let it brown well, adding a teaspoonful of sugar (to bring out the flavor) and sliced onions to taste. Cook until onions are tender and well colored. Then empty fry-pan into kettle and add enough boiling water to cover. Season with salt, pepper, and anything else you like. Cover kettle closely, and put in bake-hole with hot ashes, or hang it three or four hours beside the fire where it will only simmer.

This is the simplest of stews, where vegetables are lacking. Potatoes, turnips, carrots, celery, tomatoes, make it more "galupshious." Dehydrated vegetables must first be soaked a few hours in cold water. Rice, macaroni, spaghetti, noodles, dumplings, all are fine in stews.

Caches and Masked Camps

HOW TO HIDE YOUR DUFFLE FROM PROWLERS—BOTH TWO AND FOUR FOOTED

In the second volume of "Camping and Woodcraft" I described several ways of caching (i.e., hiding and preserving) supplies that one may want to leave in the wilds for future use. I also gave some hints about masking camps, or rather on selecting sites that prying interlopers would be unlikely to visit, and masking the approaches to them.

In my own work and play I have had to do a good deal of that sort of thing, for the reason that usually I go alone, move about a good deal, and often leave my little base camp to look out for itself for days and weeks at a time.

Again, from the county-seat where I live it is only a couple of hours' walk to the edge of the wilderness. Up there in "the sticks" I like to have a place or two where I can go with gun or rod and stay a few days in comfort, whenever the humor seizes me. At such a place I have cached a few conveniences in the way of shelter, bedding, tools, and utensils, so that all I need carry each trip is rations and such small stuff as stow, all told, in a boy-size knapsack.

But our forests here in the Carolina mountains are overrun at all seasons by woods loafers; not tramps at all, but natives of the country who spend half their time prowling about just for the pleasure of being footloose and free. There are not so very many of them, but they cover lots of territory.

These fellows hunt, especially for 'coons and 'possums at night, fish a good deal, and take a turn now and then at moon-shining. They consider that the woods and waters belong to them by right of nature. They are fairly honest, as a class, and will not molest a camp that is occupied from day to day; but if you don't return and build a new fire in a day or so they will help themselves to anything left behind.

There are also a few hard characters flitting back and forth across the state line, or hiding out as fugitives from justice, or drifting from one lumber camp to another;

From *Outing*, November 1920

and they will take anything they can lay hands on; or they will pollute or destroy a sportsman's camp from sheer meanness.

I confess taking pleasure in outwitting such scamps. For a couple of years I kept a camp kit within a mile or so of a whole family of them, and I went there frequently. I knew they could "read sign" like Indians. A footprint to them is as a fingerprint to a detective. Yet I came and went, and they knew I was in the woods, but they did not find my cubby.

My camp was within stone's cast of the only wagon road in that part of the country. Fishermen frequently came wading up or down the creek that ran beside the road. Wagons passed once in a week, maybe. Cattle and hogs ranged the woods at will, and their owners would be out at times seeking them.

I made not the slightest effort to camouflage the camp itself. I would build a fire there three times a day for cooking, when I was on the spot, and would have one going all night when I slept there. Yet it was two years before anybody discovered any of my stuff, and they don't know yet whose it was.

The road comes steeply down off a mountain, through thick timber, and fords the creek. Just above the ford begins a small bottom where a tributary comes in. A trail goes up the smaller stream; and the road goes on up the creek. Below the ford for half a mile both banks of the creek are precipitous and thickly wooded. There is no trail going down there on either side.

Where the road fords the creek it comes out against a bank which appears from every direction to be simply the base of a steep mountainside, it being likewise densely wooded. Nobody would think of climbing up here when there is a plain road along the edge and a plain trail a little way beyond that leads easily up into the back country.

The joker of it all is that this bank really mounts up only about fifty feet, and behind it is a bench of the mountain, concealed by the timber. A spring branch comes down across this flat, disappears in rifted rock, and seeps out through the bank in various places so that from the creek there is no evidence of a watercourse above.

A laurel thicket masks the upper end of the bench, toward the trail, and the steep bank continues around there, joining the mountain proper.

Approach to the bench from the mountain above is difficult, being rocky, steep, and thickety. The natural course down the mountain is off to one side and to the trail I have mentioned.

I used to pitch my little tent beside the spring branch. The fire that I used in daytime was fed with dry wood that gave off little smoke, and the tall trees on every side prevented what reek there was from being seen from any direction. The fire's radiance at night was hidden in the same way.

Before leaving camp I would take down the tent, stow it and my bedding and grub in a waterproof canvas bag, and hang that in a laurel thicket off to one side. The axe, fire-irons and utensils were poked into a hollow log. Nothing was left, then, to show any intention of returning.

One thing only was I very careful about. Tracks. In approaching the camp ground or leaving it—that is to say, in going up or down that bank—I obliterated the "sign." I seldom went twice the same way; so no trail was printed. Every time that I carried my bag of duffle off into the thicket I observed the same precaution. I left hundreds of footprints on the camp site itself, of course, but I cared nothing for that. It was the entrance and exit that were always masked.

You may ask how my equipment fared in the cache when stowed there for a long time. The paraffined canvas bag was just the ordinary kind kept in stock by outfitters. It closed with a throatpiece and laced over that. On the bottom was a leather strap for hand-hold. When packed, I would turn it upside down and hang it up by the strap on the stub of a laurel limb, then tie it in a position with cord to ensure that no wind nor jostling by animals would throw it down.

There is something about a paraffined bag that animals do not like. Woods rats would chew up any unprocessed cotton goods or twine that was left where they could get at it; but they never so much as nibbled that bag. Large animals steered clear of the thicket, as there was nothing there for them to eat, and the going was mighty bad.

After a week of rain I would go and find the contents of the bag uninjured. If the bag had rubbed against anything, the water would have struck through; but I hung it purposely so that it would not.

The hollow log had been burned out by ground fire until the inside was charred. Hence it kept dry and free from mould. The metal things stowed away in it did not rust.

But finally there came a time when my camp stuff was left to itself for a whole winter. It was a winter remembered in this part of the world for its severity. There were long, heavy rains at first, hard sleets, alternate freezing and thawing. Then heavy snows and bitter cold. The Tuckaseegee River, which runs through our town, froze so that automobiles ran up and down it on the ice. The following spring was very wet.

It was summer when I went to the old camp again. Some nosey fellow had found at last the cache in the hollow log, and had made away with the axe and kettles.

But my war bag still hung in its accustomed place in the thicket. It had faded some, but had not rotted. There was considerable mildew in the folds of the bag throat, which of course had held moisture from the drip, although it hung upside down.

The worst mildewed things inside were the leather sling of a trout creel, the cover of a book, and some underwear and trousers I had used for wading. Probably these cloth articles were not thoroughly dry when I stowed them away.

A paraffined grub bag, and some parchment paper and waxed paper, to my surprise, were heavily coated with mildew. A small feather pillow was too fusty for further use.

A wool-filled comforter had its cotton cover mildewed in spots, but the batting was as good as ever. A tanalite shelter tent was considerably mildewed at the folds (this was at the bottom of the bag) but was still perhaps serviceable.

An army blanket and some heavy woolen socks were only slightly discolored in spots and the fiber was not injured at all.

Of course, if I had expected to leave my things out all winter I would have made better provision for them; but as it turned out the all-wool goods stood a very severe test, anyway.

Camping in Winter

PROVING THAT IT IS POSSIBLE TO LIVE COMFORTABLY UNDER CANVAS BELOW ZERO

My first trial of sleeping out in real cold weather was when I was a little shaver. We were on a level wind swept plain, with no trees for miles around. There was no tent, and no fire after supper. Our bedding was a pair of blankets and a pair of buffalo robes, for the two of us. Inside that cocoon we slept well, though the wind and the wolves howled all night and the robes froze as stiff as boards.

One winter evening I got caught out with no equipment but my gun and the clothes I stood in. The only habitation within reach was the shack of a poor immigrant. He could not speak English, but he grasped the situation and made me welcome by signs. The shack was little more than an open camp.

That family had no bedding but ticks filled with feathers. They gave me a pair of them for a shakedown. I was to lie on one bag of feathers and pull the other one over me. That was their idea of luxurious sleeping. So it seemed to me, too, for a few minutes; but soon I was stewing in my own juice. Miserably I flopped out and flopped back again, by turns, through the night. By morning I had one of the worst colds I ever caught in my life.

Of late years, in the Carolina mountains, I have slept out with the native hunters, a mile above sea-level, when the weather was like that of the average December night in central New York. We would be under a slab lean-to, open at the sides, with no more than one blanket apiece, and some of the men had none.

We would lay down a thick bed of hemlock boughs, build an immense backlog fire close in front, cuddle together, and sleep while the trees around us were popping with frost. Of course we had full-size axes and good men to wield them. Five pounds of axe is worth more than fifteen pounds of blankets.

But I don't recommend any of these ways of roughing it to people who camp out for health or pleasure.

From *Outing*, December 1920

If the camp site can be reached with horses it is a simple matter to arrange comfortable winter quarters. A waterproof wall tent with pipe hole rimmed with asbestos, a sheet iron stove that takes good sized chunks of wood, an axe, a lantern, plenty of bedding, and utensils and food not very different from what you would use at home; these will do very well, if you don't have to shift camp.

But many prefer to go to out-of-the-way places, and to move from one to another if they see fit. They say that they want "the real thing" while they are about it; a complete change and perfect freedom to follow the whim of the moment.

They are learning to do it without making pack slaves of themselves. A pack slave is one who travels with his eyes on the ground and no thought in his head but how heavy his burden is.

For a party of four to six, sleeping out in cold weather, there is no better shelter than a baker tent, provided you are in a forest and there are no gales. The whole front is left open at night, with the door flap, if there is one, thrown back over the top. A well built log fire is kept going in front, as near as safety allows. The angle of the tent roof is such that it reflects the heat downward on the bough bed.

That is a more healthful way to sleep than in a closed tent heated by a stove. Nobody ever catches cold that way. And it puts pep into a man. When he wakes up in the morning he is as ready to act as a bent spring.

But it takes a good size tree of green hardwood to keep up the right fire, and you should be sure beforehand of having permission to cut it.

When the ground is hard frozen, so that forked stakes to support the ridge pole cannot easily be driven, set up a pair of shear poles on each side. Steel tent pegs, at least for the four corners, will be worth carrying.

A baker tent has not enough pitch to the roof to shed snow, and so it will sag badly under the weight of a night's fall. It is best to run a few poles slanting back from the ridge pole, outside the roof, and shingle them with boughs to catch the snow.

When there are only two or three men in the party a half-pyramid tent is the thing. It is like a miner's tent but with vertical front. It is light and not bulky to pack. Its slopes are steep enough to shed snow.

You can set it up quickly by suspending from an overhanging limb, or from a tripod of poles, or with a single short pole in front. In the latter case, fasten the *middle* of your rope to the top of the pole with a clove hitch, and run the two ends out diagonally forward to stakes; then the tent is well braced in all directions, and there is nothing in the way of a fire in front of the tent.

A common tarp sheet can be set up in half-pyramidal shape, as shown in the accompanying illustration. But I like the Royce pattern, because its door flaps have triangular extensions at the bottom. When these are run out forward as wings, leaving the front open, they fit down tight to the ground, making perfect wind-breaks and smoke directors.

For a man traveling alone a miniature Royce tent is the best shelter for any kind of weather. I have one of Tate tanalite that weighs only 2 pounds 12 ounces, including suspension rope, and it can be carried in the back pocket of a hunting coat. It covers a space 7 × 3½ feet on the ground, besides what the side flaps shelter, and stands 5½ feet high. It takes less than five minutes for one man to set it up anywhere.

This Tate tanalite is an olive-drab zephyr sailcloth, very closely woven, and weighing only three ounces to the square yard after being processed. It is waterproofed by running the cloth through a chemical solution between the anode and cathode rolls of a special machine. This impregnates the fibres with a double salt of aluminum, making the fabric quite rainproof but leaving it as pliable as ever and somewhat less inflammable than plain cotton cloth. The advantage over paraffining is obvious.

The main problem of winter camping for the Go-light fraternity is how to get bedding that will be warm enough without being too bulky and heavy. Anyway, don't get army blankets. They are woven too closely to be warm. Hudson Bay blankets are better. Warmth depends very much on how much dead air is confined in the fabric. Dead air is the best insulator.

When going afoot a proper sleeping bag has points over any blanket rig. It can be made of down or wool batting enclosed in a light flannel cover. But it must be narrower than the ordinary pattern, or it will be far too bulky and heavy.

Anthony Fiala designed a good bag for light camping. It used to be made of llama wool, or of knitted sheep's wool. Recently he has begun to manufacture a bag from a novel material developed during the war. This stuff is composed of natural wool fibres caught at their centers and tied into a warp of knitted wool cloth.

I have ordered one of these Fiala bags but have not yet received it. The material which I have examined has the effect of real animal fur but with a loosely woven wool foundation instead of a heavy moisture-retaining hide. Every particle of it helps to hold dead air and permits body moisture to pass out freely and evaporate. The fibres are not broken on a needle-studded wheel, as all fleecy wool material has been up to this time, but are like the under wool on a sheep's back.

It is claimed that a single bag of this stuff, weighing about four pounds, will be as warm as twelve pounds of blankets, and it will be sold at a reasonable price. With a khaki cover that is wind-proof but permeable to moisture, it bids fair to solve a problem that has hitherto vexed everyone who had to carry his bed on his back.

For severe weather two of these inner bags would be required. It is necessary, anyway, to have the bag double for winter, so that one can have only one thickness over him in the early night hours, or he would be roasted out until past midnight when the real cold comes.

But what suits one man may offend another.

There are times and places for the wall tent and a tent stove. There are times and places for a fur robe and no fire at all. There are people who enjoy a feather bed underneath and another on top of them. I have no quarrel with any sort of contrivance that makes anybody comfortable—so long as they don't thrust it on me to my own discomfort.

Consider the animals. Br'er Rabbit has fur; Sis' Goose has down. Both of them keep comfy all winter. Old Hellbender has only a bare skin, but he burrows in the mud, sleeps all winter, thaws out in spring, and probably has as good a time as anybody.

So it is about the way to carry one's outfit, going afoot. For me the cruiser pack-sack made by Poirier of Duluth, with leather shoulder straps. But it needs waterproofing. Preservo, which you can get of tent makers or at the sporting goods stores, is a good ready-made preparation, easy to apply. The head strap of the Duluth pack is a relief to use when one's shoulder muscles protest.

The No. 2 size pack-sack (26 × 28 inches, flat) holds all that I will allow on my back, but the No. 3 would be needed by a man who carried bulkier bedding or was going out for more than a few days.

There is no such thing on the market as a quite satisfactory cooking kit to be carried afoot. The camp kettles that we have are round. They should be oval, and the lids should fit outside instead of inside. Then they would fit well in the pack and against the back, the lids would keep ashes out, and oval kettles take up less room over the fire than round ones. Poirier makes nested kettles of this sort, but they are of seamed and soldered tin; they should be seamless and preferably of aluminum.

When there is no stove, or the stove has no oven, a folding baker of reflector type is needed, if one means to treat his stomach right. A reflector is a mean thing, though, to carry in a pack, being easily bent out of shape. Tin is better in this respect than aluminum.

For the same reason get a tin folding lantern rather than one of aluminum. Candles supplied by the lantern maker fit better and last longer than the common kind. A stump of candle is the trick to get a fire going when all the woods are wet. Carbide lanterns are no good for quick lighting in an emergency.

A full-size axe must be carried to cut grown-up trees with. Have it ground keen, but not too thin, lest you break it in chopping frozen wood. Have a leather sheath for the axe head.

In making camp all the snow must be removed from the tent and fire sites. If the crust is hard, break it up with sticks. Snow banked around the sides and back of the tent will not melt, and it will keep out draughts.

A bough bed as a mattress is indispensable, not only for softness sake but especially to insulate against the bone-searching chill of the ground which otherwise would strike through any amount of bed clothes that one could carry. Balsam is best, then hemlock, spruce, white cedar, pine, young willow tops—almost any sort of brush is better than none—or grass or leaves.

Clip off the heavy butts of the branches and throw them away. Use the larger boughs for the bottom layers. Begin at the head of the bed. Lay the boughs with curved side up, butts down and toward the foot. Put several layers across from side to side, then other layers below with their springy tops covering the first course of butts, and so on to the foot of the bed. Finish by sticking little branchlets ("fans") close together all over the bed, with the tips inclining slightly toward the head. Four small logs staked in a rectangle around the bed will keep the bough mattress in place.

This takes time; but you had better spend an hour at it than lose a night's sleep for lack of a warm and springy bed.

Logs for a fire-back should be of slow-burning wood, if such grows in the neighborhood, and not less than a foot thick. If the ground is too hard frozen for driving stakes to support backlogs, use forked poles slanting backward. The fire-back should be at least three logs high, or it will not throw the heat forward into the tent as it should.

Lay two short thick billets forward from the fire-back and at right angles to it, on which to lay the poles for the fire proper, so that air will draw in below them and give a good draught. Green wood, in winter, makes a better all-night fire than seasoned wood; but you should have a good deal of the latter alongside for occasional branding up.

If the fire is properly built in the first place it will need replenishing only two or three times during the night.

A novice builds his camp-fire either too near or too far away from the tent. If too near, there is danger of setting the canvas ablaze. If too far, the heat is wasted. Just what distance it should be from the tent front depends on circumstances. Five feet to the backlogs is about right for a medium fire, six feet for a big one.

The best trees for a winter camp-fire are in this order: hickory, oak, black birch, sugar maple, beech, yellow birch, white ash (the latter would stand first in merit if it were more lasting). Where there are no hardwoods one can get along with white or paper birch, soft maple, aspen, gray pine or jack pine.

Cold weather camping is to my taste the best camping of all. For one thing, there are no insect pests. For another, one can not enjoy a real camp-fire in summer, and without that a camp for me is no camp at all. And a hunter of big game must go in cold weather, anyway. Even if there were no game laws it would not pay to go out after big game until the leaves were down. There was an amusing instance right here in my neighborhood last week (I am writing early in October.)

Half a dozen of the boys got the hunting fever prematurely and went off after bear. Their dogs routed out a bunch of four bears on a mountain fifteen miles north of our town. Bob got two shots at twenty yards, but didn't touch a hair. He is a good shot, too. How come? Why, he couldn't see the bear for the brush—just heard him and saw the bushes shaking, with only a glimpse or two of black fur.

Two of the other men on stands had bears pass near them and didn't know it till the dogs came up. We have had an uncommonly wet summer, and the huckleberries, buckberries, gooseberries, leucothoe, and forty-'leven other bushes mat the ground till a man can hardly push his way through, much less see what may be passing within a few rods.

Guns, Ammunition, Equipment

ASK OUTING   TELL OUTING

EDITED BY HORACE KEPHART

MATERIAL FOR TENTS

Question.—I intend to make a light-weight, serviceable shelter tent. Which two of the following are the best to use: moleskin, khaki cloth, romper cloth, khaki drilling, cheviot suiting? How would you waterproof the tent?

T. B. R., Louisville, Ky.

Answer.—The best material for a light-weight tent is Tatelec in the lighter grades, which you can get from George B. Carpenter, 440 N. Wells St., Chicago. It is expensive, but worth the cost, being waterproof, strong, and unaffected by heat or cold. For a plain fabric, to be waterproofed by yourself, get the closest woven drill or sheeting (the so-called "balloon silk" is excellent, being made of long fiber cotton of great strength and durability). Loosely woven material, like some of those you name, is worthless. To waterproof your own tent, get Can-va-Sek, from the Sek Mfg. Co., 2752 W. Madison St., Chicago.

PRESSURES IN WINCHESTER '94

Question.—I have a model 1894 Winchester rifle of .32-40 caliber and I wish to use the Remington "Hi-Power" cartridge (listed at 2065 foot seconds velocity, 165 grain metal cased bullet) in it. The barrel of the above mentioned rifle is of the nickel steel or "special smokeless steel," as furnished by the Winchester Co. for their .30-30 caliber in the '94 model. This barrel has been drilled and tapped for dovetail blocks for telescope sights, the screw holes for the rear mount are just ahead of the receiver, the holes are not over an eighth of an inch in diameter and depth, and as near as I can

From *Outing*, December 1921

measure there is approximately one-eighth inch of metal left from bottom of screw hole to top of chamber.

In your opinion, do you believe the breech pressure of the Rem. N. M. C. Hi-Power cartridge is high enough to cause a rupture of the barrel at the points where screw holes are located?

A. M. S., Cleveland, O.

Answer.—The maximum pressure of powder gas is exerted around the chamber of the gun and directly in front of it, particularly when dense smokeless is used. Screw holes drilled in the barrel above the chamber do not leave a sufficient margin of safety for high pressure charges. I would advise you to have a new barrel fitted to your rifle before you use the .32-40 Remington high power cartridge in it, as this charge develops a breech pressure of about 35,000 lbs. to sq. in., compared with 18,000 lbs. for low pressure charges.

SIGHTS FOR .250 SAVAGE

Question.—Will you kindly recommend a set of sights for general hunting purposes for a Savage .250-3000, bolt action.

W. H., Detroit, Mich.

Answer.—On my .250-3000 Savage bolt action I have mounted a Lyman windgauge receiver sight No. 54, a blank in rear sight slot, and a King spark point ("gold" bead) front sight. This suits me best. If you prefer an open sight, use the one sent on the rifle and get either a "gold" Marble or King, or an ivory bead, front sight.

TWO ALIENS

Question.—I have a 12-gauge, double-barrel breech loader. At muzzle the barrels are as thin as a safety razor blade; has a very fine stock with checkered pistol grip, rubber base to pistol grip and rubber butt plate. Has a picture of a small buck deer in flight on butt plate. On hammer plate it has the same picture of a deer in flight, also the word Progress and Belgium.

The barrels look as if they were made of bronze wire. The whole gun weighs less than 6 pounds. It is a very old gun, as my daddy bought it twenty years ago and gave $50 for it second hand.

Could you tell me what kind of a gun this is and where it is made, and what would a new one cost? A dime will not go through the left barrel, and it has no more kick than a Colt .45 revolver.

Also have a .30 caliber automatic pistol that has the American eagle on the base of barrel, and the word Germany on the front of the stock. Is this a German gun or an American, and is there any danger of it "hanging" up on me? I have used it for a year and it gives satisfaction.

R. W., Lynch, Ky.

Answer.—The data you send are not sufficient to identify the maker of your shotgun. Of course it is a Belgian piece. It is not likely that this type of gun is now manufactured, or, rather, I should say, this particular pattern. Double guns of very small bore, down to 9 mm. (.354 inch) are common in Europe. You can get them from the larger sporting goods houses in this country, such as Von Lengerke & Detmold, New York. In this country the Harrington & Richardson Co. makes double guns of .44 and .410 gauge; Ithaca and Parker companies make .28 gauges.

Your pistol is made in Germany for the cheap American trade. Lack of further identification marks show conclusively that it is of that sort.

SLEEP IN COMFORT

Question.—Am not a tenderfoot, having spent most of my life in Texas, Rocky Mountains, etc., owned a ranch in New Mexico, of course often sleeping on ground, but my wife and I contemplate autoing from here to Texas. Have a trailer, good tent, cover for auto, and first-class camping equipment, and while alone I use only the usual blankets and "tarp'" on the ground, or folding cot in hot weather, but she should be more comfortable.

What would you advise for a bed, where we sleep together? How about an air (rubber) mattress on top of water-proof floor cloth right on the ground, with, of course, plenty of blankets; and if this air mattress is the best and not too expensive, where can it be obtained, price, etc.?

What do you think of a double cot? I should think they would sag or make a hollow in the middle, be quite cold, and need more blankets than the mattress, so that the whole sleeping outfit, counting in the cot, would weigh more and be bulkier than the mattress.

R. E. M., Wichita Falls, Tex.

Answer.—I do not know of any air mattress that is wider than 36 inches. Such mattresses are very comfortable (if you do not blow them up too tight) in weather above freezing point, but not at lower temperatures unless a felt pad or other insulator is used on top. No waterproof ground cloth is needed.

A double cot I have never used. Would expect it to sag in time, unless, like some patterns made for auto tourists, it had coiled springs at the ends. A cot is cold unless a mattress is used on it, and even then it will not do for real cold weather unless you use a sleeping bag, because cold air gets up under the blankets at the cot sides.

The warmest bed is on the ground with mattress, or comforters used as such, in addition to blankets.

WHAT IS THIS .22?

Question.—About five or six years ago I saw a .22 repeating rifle. I do not remember very much about this gun, but I think it had an extra long barrel. This fact has caused me to think it was made specially for .22 long rifle cartridges. It also was bolt action and very heavy for this caliber.

I understand that this is a very poor description by which to trace a gun, but if it so happens that you know the make or any other useful information regarding same I would appreciate it very much.

J. P. A., Charleston, W. Va.

Answer.—The repeating bolt action .22 that you saw was probably a Savage model 1911, which is no longer manufactured. It took only the .22 short and had a short barrel, but the owner could have had a long barrel fitted to it to order. Length of barrel is no indication of a stronger cartridge being intended, but shows that the user preferred it for greater sighting radius or steady holding, or from a mistaken notion that it would develop higher velocity in the .22 cartridge.

AUSTRIAN AND BULGARIAN GUNS

Question.—While in the service I was stationed in Italy where we were operating against the Austrians, and among other souvenirs I brought home two Austrian army carbines and a machine gun belt full of ammunition. I have found that the guns are excellent game guns and have got two deer this summer with them. I am using up my shells and can't find a sporting goods house in Los Angeles that knows anything about them.

The guns are regulation Austrian army guns, one a "Steyer" and the other a "Budapest," but with identical caliber and action. The action is a straight pull bolt and uses a five shell clip. The cartridges are rimmed and bottlenecked and I have been told were 8 mm., but I caliper the bullet at 8.5 mm. exact. I caliper the bullet at .32, but have not tried a .32 caliber bullet in it. Any information you can give me will be most gratefully received, for I hate to put two good guns on the shelf for lack of ammunition.

R. E. R., Los Angeles, Calif.

Answer.—The service rifle and carbine of Austria and Bulgaria during the war were Mannlicher, model 1895, with improvements. Caliber of bore before rifling nominally 8 mm., but actually 7.9 mm. (.311 inch). Diameter of bullet .317 inch. Our .32-.40 bullet is of .319 actual caliber, and the .32 special is .321.

Cartridges for the 8mm. Mannlicher are made in this country by the Remington-U.M.C. Co. and the Winchester Repeating Arms Co. Any arms dealer can procure them for you. The Los Angeles clerks were not on their job.

ON MAKING AN OUTDOOR LIVING

Question.—I am in dire need of information, the like of which, I feel sure, you are in a better position to give than any of my "arm chair acquaintances," and for that reason I am addressing this letter to you in the hope that you may be able to help me out.

Briefly, I am a 31-year-old, 230-pound human with an inborn chronic case of outdoors, and with no means at hand with which to cater to the demands of the demon. Do not misunderstand me; it is not the wanderlust, although I have my full share of that as well. Professionally, I am a structural engineer; domestically, I have four, including the wife, and since I can find no fault with my family I have about come to the conclusion that it is my work that keeps me from spending the greater share of my time in the open and away from the city.

But what am I to do? I have had no training in forestry; none that would fit me for biological field work. I can write a little. By that I mean I have had some few articles of various themes published—and, what is more important, paid for. I believe I could handle out-door stuff, but it would be principally of the "how to" order, as that is the part I have been most interested in—kits and equipment.

But even here I am under the impression that until a reputation for authority is acquired (I don't know where they acquire them), articles of this nature are contributed. Of course, if I had the filthy dollars I could let my engineering hang, but the aforementioned "four" insist that they cannot subsist on air, so it is up to me to devise, or have devised, some method whereby I can make a living and at the same time satisfy the out-door man.

What can you suggest? Please suggest something.

J. S. B., Fort Worth, Tex.

Answer.—Your request for suggestions as to how a professional man can make a living for his family by quitting the city and taking up an outdoor occupation for which he has no special training is the hardest one I have received in a long time. There are thousands of men—many of them first-raters in their own line—who would jump at such a chance. And at the present time I know of no openings.

As for writing on outdoor topics, I never knew anybody who made as much as a bare subsistence at it until after he had done a lot of work fruitlessly and learned by experience what would NOT go. It takes more than experience in the field, more than a knack of writing entertainingly, though both of these are essential. One must know his market, as a business man would say—and it takes time to learn that.

You say you don't know where a writer on kits, equipment, etc., gets a reputation for "authority" in that line. Well, I can tell you all about that. He gets it from nobody on earth but the public. If he does a lot of such writing, and the public learns that he has taken pains to get the truth and can be depended on to tell it, not booming anybody in particular, but simply working for the sportsman's own interest, and if his judgment generally is sound, then the public wants more of his stuff and will yelp for it, and THEN publishers will pay for it. There is no more mystery about this sort of thing than there is about succeeding in any other trade or profession. So it all comes back to the plain matter of try and try again.

This is not the sort of information you asked for, but it comes as near as [*sic*] it as I can go.

SLOW-BURNING CANVAS

Question.—We will leave in about two weeks for our camp on Reelfoot Lake, and would greatly appreciate a little help from you. In the past I have seen in OUTING a recipe for a mixture for making canvas tent of slow combustion. Have gone through what copies I find in files here, but can't find it. Please either give me date of issue containing that information or tell me what the mixture is or who could tell me or furnish me with the stuff.

A. W. F. B., Louisville, Ky.

Answer.—I do not remember a recipe in OUTING for making canvas of slow combustion. There are many treatments given in the big recipe books, but I think most of them are questionable. The matter of fireproofing cloth became a serious subject of investigation when airplanes came to be used in war. The U. S. Bureau of Standards reports that a great variety of fireproofing solutions has been submitted to it for examination, and that the best treatment has been found to be a 10 per cent solution of ammonium phosphate neutralized with ammonia, which means that enough ammonia is gradually added to the phosphate solution to overcome its acidity, which is easily determined by testing with litmus paper. The airplane fabric is doped in addition with coats of cellulose acetate solution, to waterproof it and make it permanently unshrinkable.

DEALING WITH PITS

Question.—The barrel of my rifle is slightly pitted. Please advise me as how to deal with this as quickly as possible.
M. W. S., Sarnia, Ont.

Answer.—Get a 50-cent jar of Camp Perry Rifle Paste from P. J. O'Hare, 33 Bruce St., Newark, N. J., and swab out your rifle with it until no rust shows. It will not injure the rifling, as it contains no grit. Or you can use Winchester Rust Remover in the same way. After getting the bore bright, clean with dry rags and then oil.

Nothing will remove the pits, of course. They will make the gun harder to clean forever after, but if not very deep will not spoil its accuracy.

.351 WINCHESTER FOR BIG GAME

Question.—I had occasion to buy a .351 Winchester self-loader, model 1907, and would like to know if this gun is considered a serviceable and reliable hunting rifle for any big game one may encounter either in Canada or Alaska, including the grizzly bear.

Answer.—The .351 Winchester self-loader is not, in my opinion, an adequate weapon for grizzly bear. Its cartridge is not nearly so powerful as the .35 Winchester for model '95 rifle, or the .405 or .30 Gov't in the same model. The .351 is all right for deer and other medium-sized game.

The Outdoor League of America

An organization inviting the co-operation of all Sportsmen who wish wild life, game, scenery and all national natural resources perpetuated for the value and joy they furnish

"IT IS TIME"

Dear Sirs:

I will be glad to serve on the advisory board of The Outdoor League of America. It is time that our sportsmen organize to protect their interests against lawless destruction of the gifts of Nature and against freak legislation that would do more harm than good.

HORACE KEPHART.

From *All Outdoors,* January 1922

Roving with Kephart—A Pocket Tent

You can carry it in the back pocket of a hunting coat; yet it is a practical shelter for one man and his duffel, and it never leaks

Last fall I spent thirty nights alone in a tent that weighs just 2 pounds 11½ ounces, including rope, and that folds up into a parcel 15 by 9 by 3 inches, or can be rolled still more compactly. There were some smart rains, and one all-night downpour, but the thin fabric never leaked a drop.

The tent stood out for six weeks (I was absent twelve nights), and at the end of that time there was not a speck of mildew about it; no, not even on the sod cloth, which was in direct contact with the moist ground.

I had a good backlog fire going all night in front of the tent during the latter part of the trip, without which I would have been frozen out. The slope of the tent roof reflected the heat down on me where it did the most good.

The cloth suffered two casualties—slight punctures, one from a nail in transit, the other from a stub of falling branch. Both of these were sealed in a jiffy with adhesive tape, which stuck till the end of the camp; then I made permanent repairs with rubberized mending tissue and a flatiron—no sewing needed.

This little tent is of the Royce pattern, fully described in my "Camping and Woodcraft," last edition, and in *All Outdoors* of February, 1920. That is, it is a half pyramid that closes perpendicular in front, if you want it so, but with bat wings that can be extended forward for side shelter when you prefer to leave the front open to the fire.

The dimensions are 5 feet 6 inches high to the peak, 7 feet 6 inches wide, 4 feet deep with front closed flat, 8 feet deep over all when wings are extended.

The tent was made to my order by Abercrombie & Fitch, of New York. The material is Tate extra light tanalite, a very closely woven stuff of long fiber cotton, weighing only 3 ounces to the *square* yard (not running yard), and waterproofed by the Tate electrical process which fixes a salt of aluminum in the very fiber of the stuff,

---

From *All Outdoors,* January 1922

instead of only coating it, or filling the interstices of the cloth, as most waterproofing processes do. It is permanent. It does not affect the appearance or pliability of the cloth, nor get greasy or sticky in hot weather, nor crack from cold.

The peak and corners at bottom are reinforced with strong cloth on the inside. The tent is suspended from a grommeted ring in the peak by 15 feet of 3⁄16-inch cotton rope. A knot in the end of the rope keeps it from pulling through the ring. This is a stronger means of suspension than an outside loop. To keep rain from leaking through at the ring, just set up the tent and then tie a 6-inch square of sheet rubber tightly around the taut rope, letting it drape naturally a few inches down over the peak. I used a short featherlight rubber rain cape for this purpose, as I had the thing along at the time. It extended the sheltered space about a foot in front when the tent wings were spread.

There are fifteen small pegs used when stretching the tent quite taut all around, but six would do in a pinch, as there is a sod cloth that can be weighted down. The beckets are of the same sort of rope as the suspension rope. The sod cloth is a 7½-inch (plus seam) strip of the tent material sewed all along the inside of lower edge at back and sides, but not on the wings. It turns under and lies flat inside when the tent is erected, and a few small rocks or some sticks laid on it will hold it down, thus keeping out the draughts of cold air that otherwise would draw in under the tent and chill a sleeper.

If one cares to carry tent pegs with him, take a few of the short aluminum pegs made for the U. S. Army shelter tent (pup tent). Six of them weigh only 5½ ounces. They hold well, yet are easy to pull up when striking camp.

The photographs that I took of this tent show it in various positions and different "sets." The easiest of all ways to set it up is to peg the corners out square and then throw the rope over an overhanging tree limb and make fast. But in many regions there is no tree standing on just the right spot for camp, or the frontage would be wrong. Generally I find (especially in the mountains) that a level spot with good natural drainage, near wood and water, has no little tree ready grown for the camper's convenience. So one must use a pole, or several of them.

Figure 1 shows the tent erected with a single pole. It is not really necessary that this pole should be straight. It must be about 6½ feet long for such a set as is here shown; but it may be as short as 4 feet if a longer stick is not to be found; for it is a peculiar merit of this Royce tent that it can be set up with peak a good deal lower than normal and still the cloth will draw out taut and true in all directions. The only difference will be that the tent will be lower and will cover more ground.

In Figure 2 the tent is shown supported from the peak by running the rope over a tripod of poles, 8 to 9 feet long, and then back to a stake in the rear, where it is fastened with a clove hitch. The front width of wing on each side is thrown back. It will be noticed that the occupant of this tent cannot stand up in it (this is a hike tent, remember, weighing less than three pounds); but he can sit up in bed without knocking his house down, and that is all the room such a lunatic requires. The next view shows the tent with side wings fully extended. The maker of mine erred a little in cutting the cloth, making the wings a bit short. They are intended to come right down to the ground.

Figure 4 is a rear view of the same set. In Figure 5 the front of tent is completely closed. In this case the bottom of wings folds inward and lies on the ground like a sod cloth. I never closed the tent this way, except when I went away for a day or so.

By the way, I forgot to say that this tent is dyed olive green. It shows white in a photograph, and it looks almost white to the eye when seen from a distance through the woods and against a background of living green. For camouflage it should be a considerably darker green, or khaki color.

A good part of the time I had a lot of duffel at this camp, as I was using the place as a woodland studio. In order to shelter it I set up the tent with peak only 4 feet 7½ inches (as it happened) from the ground. This extended the shelter considerably. The tent was still 7½ feet wide at the rear, but 9 feet 4 inches at center, and 6 feet 8 inches at front of fully extended wings. Depth from center (peak) was now 4½ feet, and from wings 8 feet 3 inches. The wings, sloping upward to the peak, sheltered lots of dry wood and so forth. This arrangement is shown in the following paragraphs, the last two of which show the rubber cape covering the top.

My bed was made parallel with tent back. I find this a good "lay" when sleeping close to an all-night fire. On this trip I used a Brownie sleeping pad, which is a miniature air mattress 25 inches wide and only 48 inches long. With its khaki cover and inflating tube it weighs 5 pounds, 3 ounces, and, deflated, rolls up in a package 27 by 6 inches. When a high pillow had been built up at the end, and the lower end raised with browse to support the feet, it was solid—no, I mean *soft* comfort. One soon learns to blow it up only about half or two-thirds full of air; then it gives to every movement of the sleeper. It does away with the need of a rubber blanket or other protection from ground dampness. But it is too much bundle for a hiker. Just the thing for a horseman or canoeist.

All things considered, the little Royce tent is the most satisfactory one-man hiking tent that I ever used. Of course it is not roomy enough to spend a rainy day in; but a lone pedestrian cannot provide for that; he must be satisfied with a shelter that is good to spend a rainy night in.

If you want a light tent that is high enough to stand up in and change clothes, then follow Mr. Royce's own pattern ("Camping and Woodcraft," 1921 edition, vol. 1, pp. 85–91). This makes a tent 7½ feet wide, 7½ feet deep plus wings, 7¾ feet high to peak, giving 21-inch square headroom for a 6-foot man, and plenty of sleeping space for two or three persons.

Royce used Lonsdale cambric of only two ounces to the square yard, and produced a tent of above dimensions weighing just four pounds. But I think such stuff is too light to stand up well in a wind and to bear the strain of campaigning. The material I have used is stronger and much more waterproof. It would increase the weight to between five and six pounds. Abercrombie & Fitch made my tent to order. The Arthur F. Smith Company, 261 Canal St., New York, also make tents of Tate electro-waterproofed material of any weight desired.

In the mountains of western North Carolina, where I camped, there are no mosquitoes; so I did not have to bother with netting. It should be provided, of course, for regions that are insect cursed, if one does his camping in summer.

The camp fire, in the pictures, looks farther away from the tent than it really was, as the tent is so small. The forestick was 3½ feet in front of tent set as in Fig. 6.

I learned something about fuel on this trip. It was the first time in my twenty-five years of camping that I ever was under any restrictions about cutting what wood I pleased. A big timber company had bought the forest where I camped and had issued notice forbidding cutting of trees. The place that suited me for a site was in a thicket of sumac between the creek and the steep mountainside. The sumac grew 15 to 20 feet high and 3 to 5 inches thick. Much of it had died on the stump, and no one could pull it up by the root. I had to clear out a lot of it to make room for my camp. Never before had I dreamt of using such stuff for fuel; but here it was. Well, I used it to cook my meals. It is good kindling, and the thick sticks burn freely but last long enough for meals.

Then came the latter end of September, and the nights grew cold. I went and saw the company's warden. He said, "I'll trust you to chop anything you please. I know you won't spoil merchantable timber." So I cut stunted or defective white oak, hickory, dogwood, black birch, hard maple, found under the shade of the big trees, and had the best of green wood for all-night fires.

Before that time came I had another new experience. For the first time in my life, my camp was robbed. Some woods loafers (whose tribe has grown surprisingly in the past year) took advantage of my absence and stole my spare shoes, frying pan, flashlight, some grub, and so on. Then came something else that was new.

It was my habit to sleep with tent wide open (always do, unless there is very high wind or driving rain). Well, I was getting along, to my disgust, with no night fire. So, when turning in, I would lay my electric flasher and a pistol beside my bed. Uh-huh.

The night after the robbery, when I had been asleep about an hour, a snake ran over my face—first time such a thing ever happened to me. The night was pitch dark. I bounced up from sound sleep, realized instantly what had happened, reached for my flashlight, and—it was gone. There was a fresh candle in the folding lantern, but it took two matches to light it. Meantime Mr. Snake disappeared. Probably it was a small one; but, a few days before, I had killed a 5 ft.-10 inch blacksnake near camp; and rattlers are not scarce in this same locality.

After that I had a night fire, and there were no intruders.

A Mystery of the Mountains

WHAT BECAME OF A NEW YORK SPORTSMAN WHO DISAPPEARED IN THE MOUNTAINS OF NORTH CAROLINA?

Many of you have read in the newspapers of the strange disappearance of Blaize L. Harsell, a sportsman, naturalist and writer, who was making a hiking trip along the Appalachian ranges from his home at Bedford, N. Y., to Jasper, Ga., and has been missing since February, 1921.

Mr. Harsell was an experienced traveler who knew how to get along by himself in wild regions. He had tramped, hunted and fished in Maine, Canada and the Rocky Mountains. When he started on his long hike from end to end of the Appalachians he was in prime physical condition, armed, fully equipped for such a venture, and without fear of the dangers of lonely trails.

Some of his friends tried to dissuade him from going alone into the southern mountains, a region that he was not familiar with, particularly at a time when there was a "war" going on in the mining district, and considerable skirmishing between officers and moonshiners. But Mr. Harsell no doubt regarded the risks of such a trip as just so much spice added to a pleasant adventure. And I presume he was encouraged to make it by the assurances given in my book on "Our Southern Highlanders," which he was using to some extent as a guide. In fact, his chief objective seems to have been the Great Smoky Mountains, on the Carolina-Tennessee border, where he expected to run across me, though I knew nothing of his plans at the time. If I had known them I would have sent him warning that conditions here have changed in the past few years. Of this I will have something to say as the story proceeds.

Mr. Harsell was in Roanoke, Va., from February 12 to 16. From there he wrote two letters to his brother, Norman Harsell of Milford, Pa. In one of them he stated that he would take the train from Roanoke to Bristol, Tenn.-Va., and get off at Crockett or Seven Mile Ford and enter the Clinch Mountains, but that he might alter his course. That was the last word that ever was heard from him.

From *All Outdoors,* February 1922

As the weeks passed with no letter from the adventurer his family became worried and began making inquiries. They employed a detective agency at Roanoke to follow his trail. The Federal Government and police officials in the district where Harsell dropped out of sight were asked to aid. Postal cards bearing his portrait and description were mailed to all points where he might have been seen, and a reward was offered for any information leading to his discovery. The family at first thought that he might have become sick or disabled at some place from which he could not communicate with his friends, or, I suppose, that he might have become lost in mountain labyrinths. But as time went on, and no clue was found, there arose a suspicion of foul play.

Last October I received several letters from Elmo W. Brim, a Roanoke detective, asking for any help that I might be able to give and describing the search that had already been made. Mr. Brim stated that all the Clinch Mountain, Cumberland Gap and middle Tennessee country had been covered; also the Blue Ridge from Blowing Rock to Roanoke. He was certain that Mr. Harsell had never gone into the Clinch Mountains as he had proposed to do. They would have led him far away from the Smokies, which were his main objective. He evidently found that out and altered his course.

Mr. Brim got his first trace of the traveler's course at Marion, Va., about ten miles north of the North Carolina line and not far from the corner where Tennesee [*sic*], Virginia and North Carolina meet. Harsell was at Marion on the 17th February.

From this point he was traced along a circuitous route to Boone, N. C., Blowing Rock, Grandfather Mountain and finally to Linville. Mr. Harsell was last seen by two persons at Linville, from whom he inquired the distance to Elk Park. But he never reached Elk Park, nor Cranberry, nor Linville Falls. He did not go to the Black Mountains, which are usually visited by tourists on account of Mount Mitchell being the highest peak east of the Rockies. The bear hunters of the Black Mountains, and the State Forester, were positive about that.

Brim covered all the territory south of Linville without result. He wrote me that he would then go from Asheville into Madison County and walk across the ranges by Irwin to Johnson City, Tenn., on the theory that Harsell had decided at Linville to head for the Smokies. "If he ever lived to enter the Smokies," said Brim, '[*sic*] I will find a trail of him. If I find no trace I will return to Linville and take up the last possible trail. In that event he met with an accident between Linville and the Bald Mountains."

I have myself made diligent inquiry in my own district, the Great Smoky Mountains. This is the most massive, wildest and, in part, the most rugged section of the Appalachian system. Yet it would be well nigh impossible for such a traveler as Mr.

Harsell to do any mountaineering here without being noticed, and if he had been seen he would almost certainly have been reported by this time. Our mountaineers are keenly observant of every stranger who appears among them, and there is no part of the mountains, however wild and remote, that is not visited by somebody every now and then—a hunter, fisherman, prospector, timber cruiser, fire warden, cattle herder, officer, moonshiner, ginseng hunter, or just plain woods loafer. But I have heard only one rumor of such a man having been seen; that was on the Nantahala River west of here, a most improbable place for him to have visited without having first called on me at Bryson City. I heard this tale just a day or so ago, and will follow it up, but have little faith in it.

The description of Mr. Harsell given me is as follows: A handsome, athletic man, 6 feet 2 inches, over 200 pounds' weight, about 48 years, but looking younger. Friendly blue eyes, brown hair slightly streaked with gray. High forehead, regular features, clean shaven at start. Had the bearing of a healthy, frank outdoor gentleman.

He was dressed in dark gray English tweed, hat of the same material. Had two pairs of trousers, one short, the other long, golf stockings, also leggings. He carried a mahogany cane, rifle (.25-20 or .32-20), pistol, hatchet, combination hunting knife with saw blade and other tools, knapsack, blankets, hot water bag, small rubber air mattress, cooking utensils and concentrated foods. He camped where night found him, and cooked for himself.

This mountaineering trip was undertaken partly for the pleasure of hiking and hunting, but especially as preliminary training for a more ambitious venture that he had planned in the mountains of South America.

Mr. Harsell was a man of means, descended from an old New York family, a nephew of Robert K. Clark, of Bedford, N. Y. He divided his time between Bedford, a ranch at Cody, Wyo., and another place at Stony Creek, Va.

Personally, I feel a certain measure of responsibility for Mr. Harsell's attempt to travel over the Carolina mountains by himself. He was fond, I am told, of my writings. "Our Southern Highlanders" was no doubt his main guide. In that book I had a chapter on "The Outlander and the Native," in which this passage must have met his eye:

"Among the many letters that come to me from men who think of touring or camping in Highland Dixie there are few but ask, 'How are strangers treated?'

"This question, natural and prudent though it be, never fails to make me smile, for I know so well the thoughts that lie back of it: 'Suppose one should blunder innocently upon a moonshine still—what would happen? If a feud were raging in the land, how would a stranger fare? If one goes alone into the mountains, does he run any risk of being robbed?'

"Before I left the tame West and came into this wild East I would have asked a few questions myself, if I had known anyone to answer them. As it was, I turned up rather abruptly in a backwoods settlement where the 'furriner' [southern mountaineers of the back districts call all outsiders 'furriners'] was more than a nine-days' wonder. I bore no credentials; and it was quite as well. If I had presented a letter from some clergyman, or from the President of the United States, it would have been—just what I was myself—a curiosity: as when the puppy discovers some weird and marvelous new bug.

"Everyone greeted me politely, but with unfeigned interest. I was welcome to sup and bed wherever I went. Moonshiners and man-slayers were as affable as common folks. I dwelt alone for a long time—first in open camp, afterwards in a secluded hut. Then I boarded with a native family. Often I left my belongings to look out for themselves whilst I went away on expeditions of days or weeks at a time. And nobody ever stole from me so much as a fishhook or a brass cartridge. So, in the retrospect, I smile.

"Does this mean, then, that Poe's characterization of the mountaineers is out of date? Not at all. They are the same 'fierce and uncouth race of men' to-day that they were in his time. . . . This grewsome subject I shall treat elsewhere in detail. It is introduced here only to emphasize a fact pertinent to the present topic, namely, that the private wars of the highlanders are limited to their own people. In our corner of North Carolina no traveler from the outside ever has been a victim, nor do I know of any case in the whole Appalachian region.

"And here is another significant fact: as regards personal property, I do not know any race in the world that is more honest than our backwoodsmen of the southern mountains. As soon as you leave the railroad you enter a land where sneak-thieves are rare and burglars almost unheard of. In my own county and all those adjoining it there has been only one case of highway robbery, and only one of murder for money, as far as I can learn, in the past forty years. . . .

"Any one of tact and common sense can go as he pleases through the darkest corner of Appalachia without being molested. Tact, however, implies the will and the insight to put yourself truly in the other man's place. Imagine yourself born, bred, circumstanced like him. It implies, also, the courtesy of doing as you would be done by if you were in that fellow's shoes. No arrogance, no condescension, but man to man on a footing of equal manliness."

But this was written in 1913. Since the war there has been a flare-up of robberies, burglaries and other violent crimes all over the country, as everybody knows, and the southern mountains have felt the change. Moreover, the attempt to enforce absolute prohibition has resulted in raising the price of moonshine liquor to such unheard-of height that more men are engaged in illicit distilling now than ever before, and they are more suspicious, and they are more apt to fight for their twenty-dollar stuff than they were for three-dollar whiskey in the old days.

I sounded a warning in my department of *Outing* last July, and readers of ALL OUTDOORS could draw correct conclusions from my articles in this magazine; but all this, unfortunately, was too late for Mr. Harsell. Of course, it is only in out-of-the-way parts of the mountain districts that unusual precautions are needed; the main highways are as safe as ever. But it will not do for campers to rely on everybody's honesty now as we used to do. Yet as for robbery accompanied by murder, I know of only one probable case in the Smoky Mountains up to the present time.

The fate of Mr. Harsell can only be guessed at. We may dismiss at once the theory that he might have perished from getting lost and starving to death. Nobody who knew as much woodcraft as he must have known would starve anywhere in the southern mountains. He might be lost for a day or two, particularly at a time when the peaks and ridges stayed enveloped in clouds; but not longer. He would have got out.

He may have fallen and been crippled so that he could not move. That is a contingency always possible, though never likely.

He may have been struck by lightning, or by a venomous snake. Such accidents are extremely rare.

He may have been hit by a big limb falling from a tree at night when he was asleep. In our dense forests a traveler who camps in a new place every night is often obliged to take chances of this sort, for he generally can find no camping spot that is not within reach of such a limb.

He may accidentally have shot himself, or severed an artery by a slip of hatchet or knife.

In either of these cases it is most likely that the man's body would have been found by this time, though it is not at all sure.

There remains the theory of foul play. He may have been killed for his money and outfit, or shot by mistake for someone else. If that is what happened, then it is probable that the mystery will never be solved. It is so easy to conceal forever all trace of such a crime in the wilderness.

The town-bred reader may wonder why I have said nothing about danger from wild beasts. Well, there isn't any. A man traveling alone, leisurely, making no noise, and going up the wind, might happen to surprise a bear at close quarters. The bear would skedaddle out of there as fast as his legs could carry him, which is plenty fast. An exception might be if the man impulsively fired and only stung the beast. A .25-20 would be a poor weapon for such experiment.

But there is greater danger of stepping into a bear trap. I know one such case, and the victim's leg was broken; he starved to death right there, being unable to spring back the jaws of the trap. However, Mr. Harsell had a rifle, and with it the release would be easy, by breaking the springs with bullets.

A much more likely contingency would be ptomaine poisoning from eating bad canned goods. In our backwoods stores, where one would have to buy rations from time to time, the standby for luncheons is that particularly devilish invention "deviled meat by-products with ham flavor." What a by-product of a slaughter-house must be! I have had to treat ptomaine cases from this or similar source, and I never want to see another one.

After I had written the foregoing remarks, the Editor asked me to explain whether Mr. Harsell followed wagon roads, old lumber roads, or one-man trails; also, "whether following a trail in that country means something different from the ordinary tourist's idea of trails through our national parks."

Well, it sure does! A trail in a national park, or, generally, in the northern mountains, means a cleared and more or less graded path, usually practicable for horses or mules, and with finger-posts or other way-marks at every crossing, and others at intervals telling where you are going and how far it is to the next place.

But a trail in the southern mountains means just what it did to our pioneers of a century or two ago. Guide posts there are none. Smoothing and grading and bridging there is none. Some of these trails are practicable for (mountain-bred) horses, but many of them are hard going for a man afoot. In the wilder regions, such as the Smokies, a trail may peter out completely every here and there, having been overgrown since it was last traveled. You can pick it up again, from time to time, if you keep your eyes skinned and have the woods sense, or mountain sense, of where "in reason" it *ought* to go.

Tens of thousands of tourists have visited the show places of the southern highlands, and motored along surfaced highways, and viewed many mountains from afar, without getting the faintest idea of what the back country, the real mountains of the great divides, are like—or the people who dwell there, either. Many thousands of native-born mountain townsmen know just as little about them. I am talking about real mountaineering conditions—not the front yards.

Mr. Harsell, in following the backbone of the Appalachians for the most part, must have encountered all sorts of going, from pretty fair wagon road down to the kind of trail that, as Nessmuk says, "branches off to right and left, grows dimmer and slimmer, degenerates to a deer path, peters out to a squirrel track, runs up a tree, and ends in a knot hole." If he did get far along in the Unakas (that name meaning the whole western frontage of the Appalachians on the North Carolina-Tennessee border, the segments having individual names of their own) then he sometimes found wagon roads, sometimes new or old logging roads, often mere foot paths, cattle trails, or bear tunnels through the laurel. And often he would get where there were no trails or tracks at all. Then he would have the devil's own job of fighting brush, briars, dog hobble, laurel, rhododendron, rocks, fallen timber, and so forth.

There is every likelihood that a stranger, going alone, would get lost from time to time. He would be following the main divide, we will say. Clouds descend upon the mountain, or ascend from the creek valleys, and envelop him in mist through which he cannot see a tree ten feet away. In places the divide sway-backs down into a gap, and rising from this gap is an abutting ridge, going off gradually to right or left, that is higher here than the divide itself. What more natural than to follow the highest ground? And it may be half a day before the wanderer realizes that he is away off somewhere in absolute wilderness, with the going getting worse at every step. The Government maps are very inaccurate.

BUT there is no likelihood that such a man as Harsell would stay lost long enough to starve, unless he was disabled so that he could no longer move. In the latter case his plight would be desperate, for there are stretches along the divide where an able-bodied man may travel for two or three days without seeing a human being, or any sign of a dwelling on either side of the mountain.

BUT this man knew what to expect, for all this is explained in detail in the book he had been studying. Forewarned is forearmed, and I have not the least belief that he perished merely from getting lost.

It is evident from what has been said that no estimate can be made with any confidence as to how long it should take a stranger to make such a trip. In the real wilderness, one goes according to the going, and he comes out where he can. Under favorable circumstances, and with the best of luck, it still is a he-man's job.

Mr. Harsell was such a man, and he was well equipped both mentally and materially. That is why I am inclined to think that he either was disabled by an accident or was shot by some prowling or hiding scoundrel.

Still, there is one hope: men stricken with amnesia have been found and restored to their friends long after they had lost their own sense of identity.

End.

Roving with Kephart: A Packet of Letters

SPORTSMEN'S LETTERS AND SPORTSMEN'S EXPERIENCES FROM ALL OVER THE WORLD

I am still hearing regularly from the Federal secret service man who figured in ALL OUTDOORS some time ago as "Mr. Quick," or the "Snake-Stick Man." Most of Quick's work is among the Indians of Oklahoma. He has been out in the sand hills among the Cheyennes and Arapahoes. Later he returned to the Seminole country, where he had a battle with a bunch of white moonshiners and had to shoot one of them in the leg.

The Seminoles are usually associated in our minds with Florida, but in fact there are only about 300 of them left in their old home in the Everglades, the others, now numbering upwards of 2,000, being established in Oklahoma. They are the most conservative and retiring of the "civilized tribes." It is hard for a white man to gain their confidence. Their language is extremely difficult to learn. But Quick speaks it like a native. They treat him as one of themselves. He is called into their most secret councils, where only the Head Men sit, and is admitted even to their pagan ceremonials.

Well, the fight occurred on a creek called Rrv-rolmvk-wikv. Quick says the name means Creek-where-people-go-fishing, and he has tried to tell me how to pronounce it. Here is the way.—

"You first turn your tongue halfway down your throat—perhaps far back against the palate would be enough—and try to pronounce the first sound we make in saying "thin" or "thank." That is the sound of the Seminole R. Add to that starter the sound of L, and give the V the sound of U in "hut." The mvk syllable is pronounced nearly as we would sound muk, and the wikv part about as we would say u-way-guh."

Now, that is interesting; but when it comes to trying it myself—well, it reminds me of the time when a celebrated Norwegian scholar and novelist came to teach us North European languages at Cornell. The *Cornell Sun* interviewed him, and came out next day with this:

From *Outing*, March 1922

"Hjalmar Hjorth Boyesen wants us to pronounce his name Hyalmar Hyorth. Wje wjll sjee hjm in hjell before we will break our jaws for him."

Quick says about his Redskins:

"Do you know that it is something in life to have gained the complete friendship and confidence of an entire people? I don't mean to boast. Some might not count it worth while to gain a like end; but, honestly, I prize that friendship and faith beyond expression. The Seminoles, for the most part, are a lowly folk; but that doesn't matter in the least. They are a *people*, human beings. And for a white man—the hereditary enemy of their race—to gain the friendship of a whole nation, or tribe, is, at least, unusual."

I wrote Quick some time ago begging him to get out of a business that exposed him daily and hourly to the risk of brutal death. "You have done enough for Uncle Sam, in these more than twenty years. Why should you be trailing and fighting desperadoes all your days? I know you are chain-lightning with the guns; but the best of you get killed some day. Resign, and take up a peaceful calling for which Nature has prodigally fitted you."

But he answered: "Kep, old friend, there is something about it that one can hardly explain: that holds one to it, almost against his will. It has a mysterious power that enthralls one and from which he seems unable to break away. I confess that I really do want to break off and get into something else. It it [*sic*] not my nature to be always in line to shoot someone up—or to be shot up myself, for that matter. By nature I am a dreamer, and, if I do say it myself, my dreams are not bad—not made up of blood and thunder. But, Kep, if I should quit running my head into all sorts of breezy places, what on earth would I have to write to you about?"

Yes: the lure of action—red-blooded action, the kind that thrills, that keeps one tense and guessing and expectant. The lure of unknown trails (perhaps the last trail), man-hunting, and the bright face of danger. It calls as the Red Gods called to the Young Men. And my two-gun friend out West would perish of boredom if he took up commonplace tasks.

One of my correspondents, who lives in Rome, sends me this account of a walking trip through the Sila in Calabria.

Trinità dei Monti 13, Rome.
My Dear Mr. Kephart:

. . . The Sila is a plain of about 400 square miles and over 4,000 feet above sea level. There are some peaks therein that reach 5,500. Monte Nero, the second highest point, permits at one view the sunrise in the Adriatic and the moon setting in the Mediterranean, with a far-off sight of the Ionian Sea besides. I wish I were able to set down the effect of this sight on one who is a member of no recognized church and has no claim to high morality. It just gets you, as perhaps nothing on earth can except the Grand Cañon.

On this whole plateau there are immense forests of fir, spruce, and quite a lot of beech. Some large tracts of beech average more than five feet in diameter. The evergreens, too, are huge.

The entire population isn't above three hundred, and this only from May till October. During the rest of the year an occasional limeman snowshoes across. The camps of the cowherds are very primitive, but offer hospitality of the very highest kind. The little *buttiri* of fresh butter-filled cheese, about the size and shape of a baseball, are sublime. You never can hold enough of it. Then they have virgin *riccotto*, made from sheep milk, that seems to be a combination of milk, butter, savory herbs, and all else that is good. A little powdered coffee, sugar, and a drop of rum sprinkled on, makes you forget your temperance vows. Then there is the *marzolina*, a kind of curd of mixed milk spun into sheets and then rolled up much as a ball of crude rubber is; it is hard to say when it is best—fresh or smoked or salted. Then, best of all, you sit on a homemade three-legged stool, with a spoon and plate, also homemade, of wood.

I won't try to explain at length the character of the people—just a little incident will do. Once, late in the day, I lost my way. A worker in a sawmill walked six miles, three out and three back, to put me right. He was honestly and truly offended at my offering him money. "If you pay me, there won't be any favor," he said, pleasantly.

There are plenty of wolves down in the Sila. The shepherds, aided by their enormous dogs, killed two one night where I camped. The dogs deserve a word. You can do anything you like to them until nightfall; then they know no master—all men are enemies. They are a breed of the Sila and are found nowhere else. Some are as tall as an Irish wolfhound, but much bigger and stronger.

There are woodcock and pheasants. Small fish galore. Best of all is the trout fishing.

That's where I live. The three principal streams are not big, neither are the trout—but the taste, oh, my!

You often come across a charcoal kiln. It is a good plan to carry along a bag or even parcel of charcoal. Then, when you have something to cook, dig a slight hollow and start a charcoal fire. Impale your fish, or whatnot, on a green stick that has the butt end sharpened and driven into the earth. Stick a small fish on the stick lengthwise. A few slight gashes, and a drop of olive oil from time to time, and you won't wait for company to drop in.

There are several varieties of mushrooms, all good, but the best is a fiery red one that grows on the beech, and which they claim grows nowhere else, at least in Italy. It is therefore called the *Sila*.

There is little fear that the region will become deforested. Lack of roads and energy will preserve the Sila, to-day the largest primeval forest in Europe. . . .

Have you ever tried a little tent called the "straddle-bug"? [Yes, I'm the chap who gave it that name.—*H. K.*] It is, roughly, six-foot square in front and ends with a triangle of 30 inches . . . Mine is a bit too heavy and bulky, as I want to do my camping alone, for reasons I am going to tell. On one of my hikes, my wife refused to eat a chunk of meat just because it had fallen in the mud; and my old pal Plank, with whom I have had some nice boating and walking trips, has got to the age when he wants to do a hoe-down at the time and place that I am cooking or dishing up. Plank does not like a dish without a bucket of sand for seasoning. For daily walks I can still stand some of my pals, but for real fun in my own way I want to go alone. . . .

All the bandits have long since gone out of business in Calabria. There are many spots pointed out to the tourist that were connected with the life of some outlaw. Musing on the present price of foodstuffs it is easy to imagine what business the outlaws have taken up. . . .

AUGUSTUS FRANK.

Yes: and, by Jove, a lot of ours did the same thing. I wish that Quick would get after them, and give the moonshiners a resting spell.

Les Fontanelles,
Villeneuve-sur-Lot.

My Dear Kephart:

It is just a little over a year now since I had the pleasure of seeing you at Bryson City. I have often thought of our meeting there, and of your life among the mountaineers. . . .

We spent two months this summer in the French Alps at Chamonix, and I often wished you were along to climb the mountains with me. I got to be an ardent Alpinist, but did only second-class ascensions. I may go back next year and try the Mount Blanc, but that ascension takes a great deal of training and power of endurance. It is not very dangerous nowadays: the trip is so well organized and there are many shelters along the route. There were mortal accidents almost daily in the Chamonix region this summer, however, as too many people are imprudent.

In September I spent a while with friends in Switzerland, on the shore of Lake Leman, then visited the spot where my brother fell in Alsace, on the anniversary of his death. . . .

Everywhere I have been in France this year I have remarked a pleasing air of industry and prosperity that makes the future of France look bright. Crops have been excellent, and the peasants are rich—many around here drive their automobiles. The factory workers have calmed down, and there is no talk of strikes in France nowadays. I am sure the country will surprise the world by its rapidity in getting over the war and paying its debts. . . .

Just now we are having a gorgeous Indian summer, or *été de Saint-Martin*, as it is called here. I would like to take a gun and tramp with you in the woods. I believe we'd find more game in France than in the North Carolina mountains, thanks to the good game laws here. . . .

PAUL ROCKWELL.

Apparently a letter from a sportsman. Indeed it is; from a sportsman in the best sense that the much abused word was ever used.

There were two of them, brothers, fine boys of the best old American stock. When war loomed suddenly over an astonished world they saw that France, without help from abroad, was doomed. They remembered what France had done for us. They hurried thither at once, just the two of them, without one glance backward to see if others would follow.

They enlisted in the Foreign Legion. Among the Americans who served in that famous corps there were more than 100 per cent casualties. Almost one-third were killed in action, and virtually every man was wounded from one to four times.

One of the brothers was transferred to the Lafayette Esquadrille. He destroyed the first German airplane officially attributed to a member of that group of fliers, and was himself killed in action. The other brother, when discharged from the Legion because of wounds, was assigned to French general headquarters as special correspondent, and so passed back and forth along the whole battle front until the end of the war.

But you would hear nothing about that from him. He talks, as he writes, interestingly about mountain climbing, field sports, American Indians, folk lore, economics—anything worth while that may be the topic of the moment—always with friendly regard for what the other fellow may have at heart. He kindles with enthusiasm when discussing the future of France. France is his symbol of triumphant humanity rising with fresh hope and vigor from the ruins of an old order and daring to make a new and better one.

A sportsman! Aye, indeed!

DISARM THE HOUSEHOLDERS, ARM THE THUG

Quick wrote me some time ago:

> I heartily concur in your opinion anent the disarming of the citizenry of the United States—every word of it. I have always preached that sort of doctrine. The new laws simply put the good citizen, the law-abiding man, at a disadvantage. He wants to be a good citizen in the eyes of the law; but the bad man simply says 'Damn the law!' and goes ahead. The good citizen therefore goes unarmed to meet the thug, and, as might be expected, he gets relieved of his wad, slugged on the head, disfigured, killed, or whatever the thug pleases to hand him. . . .
>
> Were there more murders, killings, in the old days of the West, or the frontier days of any part of our country, when every man (including the preacher) was supposed to have a gun on him, than we have now, comparatively?

No, there were not. Everybody said, in those days, "The Lord made some men bigger than others, but Colonel Colt makes them all the same size."

Here is a recent item from a newspaper, sent in by another correspondent:

> Nicholas Geissler, who shot and killed a hold-up man who attacked his neighbor, a delicatessen proprietor at 50 Greenwich Avenue, Sunday, was

discharged yesterday when arraigned in Jefferson Market police court on a charge of homicide, but held for trial on the charge of violating the Sullivan law.

"You are a very brave man," said Magistrate Ryttenberg, "and I take pleasure in discharging you for what you did to the bandit. I'm sorry to say, however, that I must hold you in $100 bail for trial in Special Sessions for violation of the Sullivan law in having a revolver without a permit."

And here is an editorial from the Worcester *Evening Post*, sent me by a reader who asks "What the Sam Hill is coming next?"

> Every war is started by an international highwayman. So the arms conference works on the correct principle that the way to prevent shooting among nations is to take their guns away.
>
> You don't have to look any further for a solution to the crime wave. Whether it is a logical result of the war or not, doesn't matter. The point is to stop it. And the quickest way to stop it is to make it impossible for professional or potential criminals to get their hands on weapons.
>
> Most states have laws against carrying concealed weapons. Most states make stores turn over to police a report of sales of revolvers to local residents.
>
> But the mail order house keeps a supply of firearms available to criminals, except where state laws prevent shipments.
>
> To curb crime, give us a national law, forbidding interstate commerce in pistols, rifles and daggers. States could make possession of death-dealing weapons a criminal offense. With criminals disarmed, even the householder would not need a pistol. As for hunters, they belong to a brutal past.

So we hunters belong to a brutal past, do we?

Well, there is a book called *Idle Days in Patagonia*, written by that prince of naturalists and writers, W. H. Hudson, and in it he has this to say about that brutal past:

> That hidden fiery core is nearer to us than we ordinarily imagine, and its heat still permeates the crust to keep us warm. This is, no doubt, a matter of annoyance and even grief to those who grow impatient at Nature's unconscionable slowness; who wish to be altogether independent of such underlying brute energy; to live on a cool crust and rapidly grow angelic.
>
> But, as things are, it is, perhaps, better to be still, for a while, a little lower than the angels; we are hardly in a position just yet to dispense with the unangelic qualities, even in this exceedingly complex state in which we appear to be so effectually hedged in from harm. . . .

We admire a Gordon less for his god-like qualities, his spirituality and crystal purity of heart, and justice, and love of his kind—than for that more ancient nobility, the qualities he had in common with the wild man of childish intellect, an old Viking, a fighting Colonel Burnaby, a Captain Webb who madly flings his life away, a vulgar Welsh prize-fighter who enters a den full of growling lions and drives them before him like frightened sheep. It is due to this instinctive savage spirit in us, in spite of our artificial life and all we have done to rid ourselves of an inconvenient heritage, that we are capable of so-call heroic deeds. . . .

There is then something to be said in favor of this animal and primitive nature in us. . . . And until we get a better civilization more equal in its ameliorating effect on all classes—if there must be classes—and more likely to endure, it is perhaps a fortunate thing that we have so far failed to eliminate the 'savage' in us—the "Old Man" as some might prefer to call it. Not a respectable Old Man, but a very useful one occasionally, when we stand in sore need of his services and he comes promptly and unsummoned to our aid.

Easily Prepared Camp Meals

SOME SUGGESTIONS FOR THE GUIDANCE OF THE CAMP COOK

Travelers must have quick meals. Campers ought to have a varied diet, just like home folks. Camp and trail grub should be such as is easy for an amateur cook to prepare.

So when we travel and camp out and do our own cooking, we want quick meals, simple to prepare, but appetizing, wholesome, and different from time to time.

But how to do it when we are away out yonder on a desert road or miles deep in a primeval wood?

Well, it would be easy if we always had fresh meat at hand, and fresh eggs, new milk, creamery butter and baker's bread. The meat could be broiled, sautéd [*sic*], or fricasseed in a few minutes. Anybody can learn to do that, at the second or third trial, if he has the right directions at the start and if he knows how to build a proper fire.

Eggs take almost no time at all. Fish or shellfish are quickly done. The morning porridge takes little time and trouble, now that we have pre-cooked cereals to start with. Potatoes can be fried in short order. Toast or pancakes, coffee or cocoa or tea, open a can of fruit—and there you are.

People touring in a motor car can often do that sort of thing. So can summer campers who settle down at some place handy to a farm or village. In any case, get fresh foods, by all means, whenever you can.

But it is quite another matter to outfit for a trip back in the wilds, when means of conveyance are limited to pack animals, or canoes, or "the own two standing legs of ye." Then one must depend on preserved foods, aside from the fish he may catch, the game he may shoot, and the berries he may pick from the bushes. And, by the way, those gifts of Nature are not to be counted on before they're caught. Sometimes it rains, you know, and never knows when to quit; but one's tummy gets empty in a rainstorm, just the same.

From *Vacation Manual*, Summer 1922

There is another reason for preserved foods. Take me, for example. Sometimes I work too long and too hard. I roll and toss and say bad words because sleep wont [*sic*] come. Then I get up and don a disreputable old suit of duxbak that always has a pipe and tobacco and matches in the pockets. I pick up an electric torch and go out to the office. A watchman accosts me: "Hay, what the devil you doin' out here at this time o' night?"

"Personal liberty—go to thunder!"

He grins, and says something about watching for a suitcase.

I go to the back room of my office, which is full of guns, ammunition, fishing tackle, camp equipment ("Kep's chamber of horrors," they call it), and I open a cupboard full of camper's grub. I stow some of it into a boy-size packsack, and in ten minutes I'm jogging toward the hills.

At daylight I'm in a trout stream. It's too early for them to rise to flies, so I bait up with garden hackle and give the rainbows what they want. When the trout's dessert time comes, I change to flies.

I eat a late breakfast by the streamside. By George, it tastes good! Best meal I've had in a month. In the sunny afternoon, tired of whipping the stream, I take a bit of a snooze on a bed of leaves. In the evening I go home, with some fresh fish for my friends, and I'm happy and full of pep for the morrow.

Isn't that better than murdering a night in bed and accomplishing nothing next day from lack of sleep and energy?

But I couldn't do this stunt if I had to wait for the stores or market to open up. I couldn't do it if there were no package goods and canned goods that stay good the year round. I'm rather proud of those backroom commissary shelves. They and the guns and tackle are always ready on the spot and make me a minute-man, fit to go anywhere at a moment's notice.

"Canned foods," they say, "are too heavy and bulky for the trail."

Yes; many of them are. If you have to go light, cut out all canned food except butter, milk and jam. Carry them, no matter where you go, or how. Butter a superfluity? a [*sic*] needless luxury? Not a bit of it. Butter is the most concentrated form of easily digestible nourishment that is known to man. Besides, it gives flavor to other food that soon palls without it, and it is one of the few things that nobody ever tires of.

And it isn't everybody who has to go light. Canned goods simplify the cooking problem. With them in the mess chest you can vary your meals as much as you please. They don't spoil, no matter what weather or spill you encounter.

But stop—look—listen! There are kinds and kinds of canned foods—some good, some bum, some abominable.

Don't rely on stocking up with preserved foods in country stores or backwoods commissaries. They generally have only a few varieties, and they do not keep high-grade goods. Cheap canned grub is generally tasteless, denatured, and of poor food value. So go to the best city groceries, buy the best grades, and select with discretion.

If you live, as I do, away back in the country, then send for the mail-order catalogues issued by some of the best retail houses. Such lists are published, for example, by the S. S. Pierce Co., 73 Tremont St., Boston; Park & Tilford, 225 Fifth Ave., New York; Charles & Co., 43d St. & Madison Ave., New York; the E. Bradford Clarke Co., 1520 Chestnut St., Philadelphia; the Mitchell-Fletcher Co., 18th & Chestnut Sts., Philadelphia; the J. F. Conrad Co., 6th & Chestnut Sts., St. Louis. I mention only those I know, who issue catalogues at regular intervals. Get them all. Then you'll have an immense variety of preserved foods to choose from, and you need never suffer the "tin Willie and goldfish" surfeit.

Meat is the most difficult of foods to preserve without impairing its flavor. I have not found any canned roast beef, steak, chops, or the like, that deserve the name. Boiled meat is better managed by the canners. There is, for example, a goulash (Hungarian stew), put up in St. Paul, that has pieces of delicately stewed beef which retain their juice and flavor. The rich red sauce in which this meat is put up is rather too highly seasoned, but it can be toned down by adding canned tomatoes or soup vegetables.

A can of the goulash and a small one of vegetables, heated thoroughly together, make a hearty meal for three men, at a cost of about 80 cents. The two cans together weigh only three pounds. Considering that this includes airtight and absolutely waterproof packing, the weight is not excessive for the nutriment afforded.

The fact that canned goods cannot spoil in transit or in camp storage, that insects and robber birds or beasts can't get at them, takes a load from one's mind that compensates for the extra weight of tins, provided the contents of the can are mostly nutriment—there is a big difference in value between a canful of solid meat and one of soup that may be mostly water.

Another good thing is canned Frankfurters, if you get the right sort. There are one or two American brands that almost equal the imported ones. One firm puts up so-called Vienna sausages, in convenient small cans, that have the Frankfurter flavor instead of that of common "Weenies." Some others by this name are unmentionable.

The various potted and devilled meats, intended merely for spreading on sandwiches, are picnic stuff, not food for hard-working outdoorsmen. A jar of pickled lamb's tongues is nice for hot-weather luncheons.

Cured meats, not canned, are the real stand-by of wilderness travelers—breakfast bacon especially.

For variety sake, canned poultry and fish are good things. You can get boned turkey, boned chicken, creamed chicken, chicken in jelly, poulet sauté chasseur (French fried chicken, hunter style), chicken livers, etc., in cans, of good quality. Then there are filets of mackerel and herring, kippered herring, salmon steak, tuna, sardines, codfish balls, creamed fish of various kinds, lobster â la Newburg. Most of these things should be heated; they are more appetizing and more digestible so than when eaten cold.

But it will not do to depend on tinned or potted meats and poultry and fish as mainstays of the camp cuisine. Such things are only for variety. Continued used [*sic*] of even the best of them will bring on disturbances of the digestion.

Fresh eggs can be carried almost anywhere in parcel-post cartons. There is no meat substitute so quick and easy to prepare for the table, so adaptable to appetizing variations, so wholesome withal. I have carried a dozen eggs in my knapsack, many a time, far back into the wilderness, and never broke one—it's only a matter of packing right at the start.

On many trips it is practicable to carry butter in prints, packed in such a way as to be insulated from heat. In any case one can manage tinned butter. The only firm I know of, just now, that supplies butter in small cans is the S. S. Pierce Co., whose address has already been given.

There are all sorts of canned cheeses. Generally the cheeses put up in small boxes or cartons are better flavored. You can get American cheese in one-pound rectangular loaves, put up in tin foil and sealed in airtight cartons, that will keep good indefinitely. Another way of preserving it so that it will not dry out is to coat the cheese with paraffine. One of the choice things is imported Swiss Gruyère in little round, flat loaves of one-half pound, covered with foil and packed in a paper box. Then there is the genuine Camembert, Gorgonzola, and a variety of others of desired flavors.

Milk is easy to carry in tins. If you prefer powdered milk, get the "whole" kind (the other makes only skim milk), and you can save trouble in mixing it by taking along an egg beater.

Baker's bread sealed in waxed paper and carried in a bag will keep good a week or more. Cut loaves that have dried out are just right for toasting. It is much more wholesome than camp flapjacks, or bannocks, or biscuits produced by amateur cooks. As a reserve, carry some kind of crackers that do not bulk too large for their weight. Whole wheat biscuit in cartons is generally my choice, or plain water biscuit if everybody in the party has good teeth.

Bread substitutes include potatoes, cereals and pastes [*sic*]. Whenever possible the potatoes and onions should be in natural form, not dehydrated. The very best oatmeal for porridge is the old-fashioned unprocessed kind; but it takes hours to cook it properly, so we usually get the other sort that can be dished up in a few minutes.

Brown rice is far better than the bleached and polished kind, both in flavor and in food value. Drop it, a little at a time, into a pot of furiously boiling salted water, and be sure the water keeps boiling, so that the grains will dance about instead of glueing to each other. When the rice is done, drain off the water and set the open pot alongside the fire to steam for a few minutes. Then you have *rice*. No wonder so many people have a distaste for this cereal—they have never had it served to them except as a soggy and gluey mess.

Macaroni and other pastes [*sic*] are easy to cook (same way as rice), and they are pretty good substitutes for both meat and bread. Buy only the choice grades. Instead of always cooking with cheese, vary the dish with tomatoes, or add to the boiled paste a can of ox-tail soup, or mock turtle, mulligatawny, beef, consommé or French bouillon.

But when buying canned soups, let me tell you there is a world of difference in flavor between one "brand" and another. I could not recommend one over another here without bringing the whole packing industry about my ears, but try a sample of each for yourself.

Of canned vegetables and fruits the variety is endless. The most useful canned vegetables in camp are tomatoes, corn, baked beans, and French peas, carrots or macédoines. The French have the art of putting up the three last-named foods in a way that leaves their flavor intact and their appearance enticing. Macédoines are composed of carrots and turnips diced and then packed together with peas, string beans and the delicate young shell beans called flageolets. They are ideal for soups and stews.

If means of transportation do not permit the carrying of canned fruits and vegetables, then dehydrated ones take their place. The desiccated stuff marketed some years ago was inferior; but a recently perfected process, by which all the water is extracted at a *low* temperature, really does preserve the flavor and cellular structure to a great degree. In fact, I have used dehydrated apples that no one could tell from fresh apples sliced and stewed.

In dehydrated vegetables we can get stringless beans, cabbage, carrots, celery, horse radish, julienne or mixed soup vegetables, onions, parsley, potatoes, pumpkin, spinach and squash.

In dehydrated fruits—apples, apricots, bananas, cherries, cranberries, loganberries, peaches and pears. Dried dates, figs, prunes and raisins are valuable items in the camp cuisine.

The chief objection to dehydrated food for travelers is that they require preliminary soaking for a good while in cold water. This is all right when it can be done overnight; but if the food is wanted for dinner or supper, and you are traveling, then you must somehow manage to carry the vessel or two in which it is soaking, and that is awkward.

In stocking up with canned fruits, get a good proportion of the acid kinds—apricots, grapefruit hearts, and green-gages. They are very palatable in hot weather, take the place of pickles, and are more wholesome. If a party is small, get your fruits and vegetables in small cans (1S or 2S) so as to use up a can at a time and have no left-overs.

No canned foods should be left standing in the open can. If any is not immediately needed, transfer it at once to an enameled or aluminum vessel, or a glass jar or earthenware crock. Chemical action sets in quickly between the food and the metal of the can as soon as air is admitted, and bacteria begin promptly to multiply.

Jams, jellies and marmalades are the most wholesome form of sweets—for which one experiences an uncommon craving as soon as one gets to working hard out of doors. (An actual physiological need, for sugar is stored-up energy, quickly liberated in the system.) Here again it pays to buy small tins, even though they cost more proportionally than large ones, because then one avoids the messiness of left-overs, and one can change oftener from one flavor to another.

Last year I got excellent jams in No. 1 (14 ounces) tins that were "enamel lined" so as to prevent chemical action between the metal and the fruit. Glass or porcelain containers are generally too heavy or fragile for tourists and campers.

Of course, the dyed-in-the-wool old-timer will deride all table luxuries as "knick-knacks" and "bric-â-brac." His own notion of outfitting—bacon and beans, cornmeal and coffee—is a relic of a time gone by when the two Bs and the two Cs were about all that could be carried into the untracked wilderness where camping was done. But today, for one party that goes into such a country there are ten, maybe a hundred, who do their touring and camping in more accessible regions. And there is no speck of sense in these latter folk torturing themselves with a dietary so meagre and monotonous that they sicken of it before they are out three days.

It is no sin against the Red Gods to treat your tummy as well in the woods as you do at home. If you like whipped cream on your berries, and have found out that marshmallow crème bought ready-made in a jar is a good substitute, why not have it? This delicacy brings a touch of home. If certain sauces, catsups, chutneys or other condiments are favorites of yours in town, and you have room for them in the camp mess chest, take 'em along. If you've found a really good plum pudding, or the like, in convenient cans, with ready-made sauce to go with it, there'll come a day, forty miles from nowhere, when it will give you joy.

And if you dislike the job of roasting your own coffee and pounding it out fine with a pistol butt, why not take advantage of the fact that high-grade coffee is now put up, ready roasted and ground, in vacuum cans that preserve its original strength and flavor for an indefinite period?

Yea, verily, and it is just as well to make up one's mind before starting that every minute spared from unnecessary pottering in getting grub *ready* to cook is a minute saved for the really important business of fishing, or hunting, or photographing, or lying on a bed of ferns and watching the clouds drift by.

Once in a while we read of people suffering or dying from ptomaine or botulinus poisoning that has been traced to preserved foods. But compare the number of such cases with the fact that American manufacturers annually produce something like eight billion cans of food products, and American housewives put up untold millions of cans at home. It is not one can in ten million that kills anybody, and probably no other form of human food has a higher percentage of safety.

The risk of poisoning could be reduced to practically nothing if users of preserved foods would exercise ordinary care in inspecting containers and their contents. A tin can of food should be flat or slightly drawn in at the ends, showing that no air has got into it. If swelled or bulged (except by being battered in transit) the chances are that the contents have spoiled. If the food is in a glass jar, look for gas bubbles, and note whether the product has become mushy or discolored. The lid should require some force to remove it, for the jar was sealed when the contents were boiling hot, and this forms a partial vacuum which holds the lid firmly down so long as the seal remains perfect.

When the can or jar is opened, inspect the contents, and discard any material that has an unusual appearance or odor.

Put the food on to cook as soon as the container is opened, and be sure it reaches the boiling point all the way through, and keeps on boiling for a time. This is very essential.

There is no risk in eating acid vegetables (tomatoes), or fruits canned in syrup, without heating, so long as they have not soured. Acids and syrups prevent the formation of harmful bacteria.

An almost endless variety of dishes can be prepared by combining canned foods and cooking them together. For example, all sorts of soups can be made up, besides the ready-made ones, from canned meats, fish and vegetables. It takes but a few minutes to mix a white sauce that is the foundation for any kind of cream soup—asparagus, celery, corn, bean, pea, tomato, and so on. Chowders and bisques are easily prepared with canned fish or shellfish and a few simple additions.

"Goldfish" owes its bad name in the army to eating the salmon cold, right out of the can, and never varying the flavor. Serve it creamed, or au gratin, or in some other quickly made combination. Tuna, kippered herring, and other canned fish should generally be eaten hot, not cold and "straight."

It is the same with corned beef and other canned meats, sliced poultry, and so on. They can be combined with other foods, flavored with sauces, and made into dishes that are not only more appetizing but also more wholesome than if merely taken straight from the can and served as a cold lunch.

From the National Canner's Association, Washington, D. C., anyone can get a pamphlet, "Original Recipes for Using Canned Foods," which shows how to do these things. Just send a postal card for it.

Yes, it is easy to have quick meals in camp that are good to eat, wholesome, and different from day to day.

Tastes differ, and "what is one man's meat is another's poison." Some assimilate their food more completely than others. I know of several campers who seem to get along very well on a food allowance (their own choice) of from 1½ to 1¾ pounds a day. They are quite exceptional. An average man, engaged in hearty out-door exercise, requires on a trip of more than two or three days about 2¼ pounds a day of carefully selected and varied food that is, as nearly practicable, waterfree.

For some years it has been my practice to weigh personally, and note down at the time, the amount of provisions taken on my camping tours, and often I recorded the quantities left over at the end of the trip. I have also collected many ration lists compiled by practical woodsmen. These varied remarkably, not so much in aggregate weights as in the proportions of this and that. Still, a few general principles have been worked out:

When going as light as practicable, and taking the most concentrated (waterfree) foods that will digest properly and sustain a man at hard work in the open air, the ration should not be cut down below two and one-quarter pounds—a ration being one man's food for one day. This is the minimum for mountaineering, arctic exploration, and whatever equipment must be "pared to the bone."

People leading an easy life in summer camp do not require so much actual nutriment as those engaged in hard travel, big game hunting and the like; but they should have plenty of fruits and vegetables, and these things are heavy and bulky.

Men working hard in the open, and exposed to the vicissitudes of wilderness life, need a diet rich in protein, fats (especially in cold weather), and sweets. This may not agree with theories of dietitians, but it is the experience of millions of campaigners who know what their work demands. A low-proteid diet may be good for men leading soft lives, and for an occasional freak outdoorsman, but try it on an army in the field or on a crew of lumberjacks, and you will face stark mutiny.

Meat of any kind will quickly mould or spoil if packed in tins from which air is not exhausted. Wrap your bacon, pork, etc., in parchment paper, which is grease-proof, then enclose the meat in loose cheese-cloth bags that can be hung up in camp quite secure from insects.

Flour should not be carried in the original sacks; they wet through or absorb moisture from the air, snag easily, and burst under the strain of a lash-rope. Pack your flour, cereals, vegetables, dried fruits, etc., in the round-bottomed paraffined bags sold by outfitters, which are damp-proof and have the further merit of standing on their bottoms instead of always falling over. Put a tag on each bag and label it in ink.

Butter, lard, ground coffee, tea, sugar, jam, matches, etc., go in pry-up tin cans, sold by outfitters, or in common capped tins with tops secured by surgeon's plaster. Salt, as it draws moisture, is best carried in a wooden box or in mailing tubes.

Check up every article in the outfit as it is stowed and keep the inventory for future reference. Then note what is left over at the end of the trip. This will help in outfitting for the next season.

As to that bugaboo job in the camper's life—dishwashing, there is a desperately hard and disagreeable way of washing dishes, which consists, primarily, in "going for" everything alike with the same rag, and wiping grease off one dish only to smear it on the next one. There is another, an easier, and a cleaner way. First, as to the frying-pan, which generally is the greasiest of all. Pour it nearly full of water, place it level over the coals, and let it boil over. Then pick it up, give a quick flirt to empty it, and hang it up. Virtually it has cleaned itself, and will dry itself if let alone.

In brief, the art of dishwashing consists first in cleaning off nearly all the grease before using your dish cloth on it. Then the cloth will be fit to use again. Dish cloths are the supplies that first run short in an average outfit.

The following table of measure will be found very helpful: 45 drops water = 1 teaspoonful = 1 fluid dram; 2 teaspoonfuls = 1 dessert-spoonful; 4 teaspoonfuls = 1 tablespoonful; 2 tablespoonfuls = 1 fluid ounce; 4 tablespoonfuls = 1 wineglassful; 8 tablespoonfuls = 1 gill; 2 gills = 1 cup; 4 gills = 1 pint (1 pound water); 2 pints = 1 quart (1 pound flour); 4 quarts = 1 gallon; 2 gallons (dry) = 1 peck; 4 pecks (dry) = 1 bushel.

The main secrets of good meals in camp are to have a proper fire, good materials, and then to imprison in each dish at the outset its natural juice and characteristic flavor. To season fresh camp dishes as a French chef would is a blunder of the first magnitude. The raw materials used in city cuisine are often of inferior quality from keeping in cold storage or with chemical preservatives; so their insipidity must be corrected by spices, herbs, and sauces to make them eatable. In cheap restaurants and boarding houses where the chef's skill is lacking, "all things taste alike" from having been penned up together in a refrigerator and cooked in a fetid atmosphere.

A few condiments should be taken along, but these are mostly for seasoning left-overs or desserts—not for fresh meat unless we have but one kind to the surfeiting point. In the woods our fish is freshly caught; our game has hung out of doors, and the water and air used in cooking (most important factors) are sweet and pure. Such viands need no masking. The only seasoning required is with pepper and salt, to be used sparingly, and not added (except in soups and in stew) until the dish is nearly or quite done. Remember this—salt draws the juices.

The juices of meats and fish are the most palatable and nutritious ingredients. We extract them purposely in making soups, stews, and gravies, but in so doing we ruin the meat itself. Any fish, flesh, or fowl that is fit to be eaten for the good meat's sake should be cooked succulent, by first coagulating the outside (searing in a bright flame or in a very hot pan, or plunging into smoking hot grease, or furiously boiling water) and then removing farther from the fire to cook gradually until done. The first process, which is quickly performed, is "the surprise." It sets the juices, and in the case of frying, seals the fish or meat in a grease-proof envelope so that it will not become sodden but will dry crisp when drained. The horrors of the frying pan that has been unskillfully wielded are too well known. Let us campers, to whom the frying pan is an almost indispensable utensil, set a good example to our grease-afflicted country by using it according to the code of health in epicurean taste.

Meat, game, and fish may be fried, broiled [*sic*] roasted, baked, boiled, stewed or steamed. Frying and broiling are the quickest processes; roasting, baking, and boiling take an hour or two; a stew of meat and vegetables, to be good, takes half a day, and so does soup prepared from the raw materials. Tough meats should be boiled or braised in a pot.

Do not eat freshly killed meat if you can help it. Game should hang at least two days, [*sic*] otherwise it will be tough and tasteless. Venison eaten before it has completely cooled through will cause diarrhoea and perhaps nausea.

When a party camps where fresh meat and farm products can be procured as they are wanted, its provisioning is chiefly a matter of taste. But to have good meals in the wilderness is a different matter. A man will eat five or six pounds of fresh food a day. That is a heavy load on the trail. And fresh meat, dairy products, fruit, and vegetables are generally too bulky, too perishable. So it is up to the woodsman to learn how to get the most nourishment out of the least weight and bulk, in materials that "keep" well.

The nutritive elements of foodstuffs are protein, a little mineral matter, fats, and carbohydrates. Protein is the basis of muscle, bone, tendon, cartilage, skin and the corpuscles of the blood. Fats and carbohydrates supply heat and muscular energy. In other words, the human body is an engine—protein keeps it in repair; fats and carbohydrates are the fuel to run it.

Familiar examples of proteids are lean meal [*sic*] and white of egg. The chief food fats are fat meat, butter, lard, oil and cream. Carbohydrates are starchy foods (flour, cereals, etc.) and sugar (sweets of almost any kind).

Protein is the most important element of food, because nothing else can take its place in building up tissues and in enriching the fluids of the body, whereas, in emergency, it can also supply power and heat, and thus run the human machine for a while without other fuel.

The problem of the well-balanced ration consists in supplying daily the right proportion of nutritive elements in agreeable and digestible form. The problem of a campaign ration is the same, but cutting out most of the water and waste in which fresh foods abound. However, in getting rid of the water in fresh meats, fruits, and vegetables, we lose, unfortunately, much of the volatile essences that give these foods their good flavors. This loss—and it is a serious one—must be made up by the camp cook changing the menu as often as he can by varying the ingredients and the processes of cooking. Variety is quite as welcome at the camp board as anywhere else—in fact, more so, for it is harder to get. Variety need not mean adding to the load. Go, then, prepared to lend variety to your menu. Food that palls is bad food—worse in camp than anywhere else, for you cannot escape to the home or restaurant.

The manufacturers whose goods are referred to or illustrated in the above article and advertised in this issue of the Vacation Manual are American Gas Machine Co., Albert Lea, Minn.; Prentiss-Wabers Stove Co., Wisconsin Rapids, Wis.; Prest-O-Lite Co., Inc., New York City; United Steel and Wire Co., Battle Creek, Mich.

four

GUNS

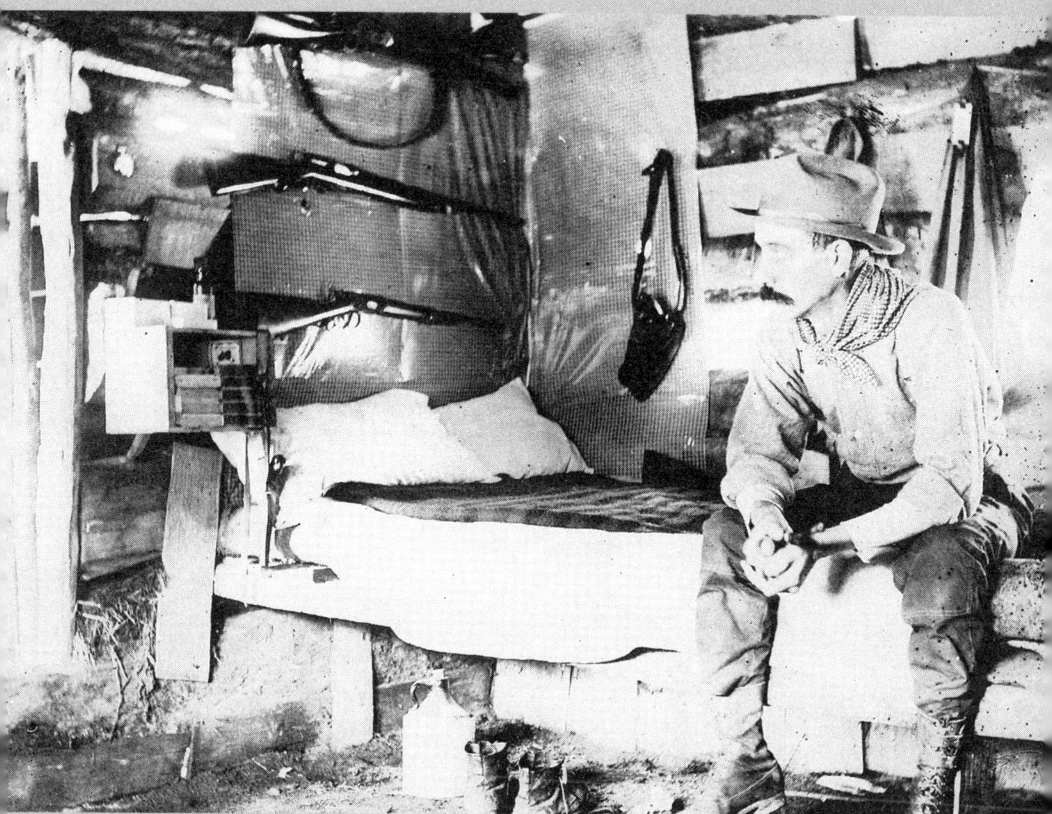

Kephart with rifles. "Bunk in Hall Cabin."

Kephart with snake, holding a Luger pistol.

Introduction

JIM CASADA

Horace Kephart's place in the history of gun writing is best understood in the context of his career as a whole. Many aspects of his productive literary output are controversial, and the same holds true for his life. His best-known book, *Our Southern Highlanders,* has been widely condemned by experts in Appalachian studies for its pronounced tendencies to stereotype, the fact that close to 40 percent of the revised edition focuses on some aspect of moonshine, and sensationalism. Among those scholars who have noted Kephart's penchant for inaccurately portraying mountain people are Michael Frome (*Strangers in High Places*—1966), Durwood Dunn (*Cades Cove: The Life and Death of a Southern Appalachian Community, 1818–1937*—*1988*), J. W. Williamson (*Hillbillyland*—1995), and Stephen Wallace Taylor (*The New South's New Frontier*—2001). Dunn's thoughts on the book cut to the quick in unequivocal fashion. He considers *Our Southern Highlanders* "the nadir of Appalachian stereotypes" and a work "which completely distorted and misrepresented mountain life and customs." Even in areas where there is relatively little difference of opinion between devotees of the man, such as his expertise on camping; outdoor cookery; and life lived on the trail, or as he liked to style it, "back of beyond," often overlooked problems exist. *Camping and Woodcraft* has been called, with considerable justice, the "Bible" of American camping. Yet even this classic work has flaws.

For example, Kephart's coverage of trail craft, what he styled "route sketching" (originally described in *Outing* magazine[1] and then in *Camping and Woodcraft*[2]) is highly unreliable. The route sketches he shows for Deep Creek, which rely on computing distance by paces, are inaccurate in a myriad of ways. Using a modern United States Geological Survey map and calculating straight-line distances between the points of the route sketch on page 70, my brother Don (a trained engineer) found that Kephart's overall percentage of error for the second map was a whopping 39 percent high; for the key section from the Turnaround to the Bryson Place the error, at 43 percent, was even worse; and for one section (the mouth of Bumgarner Branch to the mouth of Bridge Creek) Kephart was off by 62 percent. Additionally, in his route sketches he has several names of physical locations or those of residents along the route spelled inaccurately. Those mistakes were later magnified many times over in his work as a member of the North Carolina Nomenclature Committee.

Also, it should be recognized that Kephart was never, at least during his two-plus decades in the Smokies, anywhere near the adventurous outdoorsman of common perceptions. In his later years in particular, he lacked sufficient stamina, perhaps in part due to being a heavy smoker and the impact of alcoholism, to venture into some of the more remote and rugged reaches of the back country. He never hiked to the peak bearing his name, Mount Kephart, though his widow, Laura, would. In the final decade or so of his life in the Smokies, companions such as photographer George Masa found Kephart simply lacked the endurance required to take shanks' mare into distant and tortuous terrain. While Kephart continued to hike and spend some time in the backcountry in his late fifties and sixties, he lacked the stamina characteristic of his earlier years. Buddy Abbott, a Bryson City resident who worked for Kephart's good friend Jack Coburn as a chauffeur and in other capacities, told me in a November 28, 1986, interview that "Kep lost a lot of his 'get up and go' in his later years and the 'back of beyond' places that involved rugged ground, especially off trail, were places he just couldn't reach."

Nor were his "permanent" campsites really located, to use one of his favorite phrases, "back of beyond." Instead, most were situated in locations regularly used by veteran local backcountry sportsmen such as Granville Calhoun, Mark Cathey, and Sam Hunnicutt. For example, the Bryson Place, his last long-term campsite, actually featured a cabin where hunters and fishermen stayed quite frequently, and the above-mentioned route sketches acknowledge as much with the notation "last habitation." Similarly, his first domicile in the Smokies, on the Little Fork of Sugar Fork, far from being isolated, was reasonably close to the thriving little community of Medlin. There were a dozen or more households within two miles of him.

At first blush coverage of these facets of Kephart's writings and career, offered as examples of the fact that some popular concepts of his literary productivity and life are provably wrong, may seem a somewhat strange way to introduce Kephart as a gun writer. In reality they serve to add luster to an aspect of his life's work—his interest in and expertise on firearms—where the oft-enigmatic Kephart consistently shines. Indeed, except among a relatively small cadre of gun aficionados, this aspect of his life's work and literary productivity is pretty much forgotten. He deserves better of posterity in terms of his work as a firearms expert. Kephart wrote extensively on guns and gunning, was arguably the country's leading expert on ballistics during the early decades of the 20th century, and even designed and developed a special bullet.

Kephart also wrote about the history of firearms and took great interest in how they were crafted and their practical uses. When studying the evolution of American guns he brought his research skills and library training to bear in fine fashion. He was at heart a technician and student of guns rather than someone who could be portrayed as a great or even serious hunter; certainly such was the case during the North Carolina years of his career. His interests belonged more to the work bench, firing range, or gun room than the field, although prior to coming to the Smokies it is possible he did a fair amount of small-game hunting as an adjunct to the camping trips he made when living in St. Louis. At least one surviving photo shows birds he had killed, but otherwise there is scant evidence in his papers or writings of an interest in personal participation in hunting.

Another important and almost totally overlooked consideration is that it was work as a gun writer, more so than articles on camp craft, which launched Kephart's career in outdoor communications. Prior to coming to the Smokies in 1904, he had upwards of two dozen published pieces in the field, many of them for the leading outdoor magazine of the final decade of the 19th century, *Shooting and Fishing*. He also had a prominent place in a book, *Guns, Ammunition and Tackle,* which was in press even as developments in Kephart's personal life which led him to the Smokies were unfolding.

Although his gun writing continued apace after 1904, for the final twenty-seven years of his life there is scant evidence to indicate that he did much hunting (or fishing) for subsistence or sport while at his various campsites in the Smokies. That seems strange given that such efforts would have been a logical way to supplement his supplies and bring fresh meat and tasty variety to his diet. Similarly, involvement in subsistence sport would have seemed even more compelling given the consistently perilous state of his finances (after he died his executors struggled mightily with what was in essence a bankrupt estate), and small game, especially squirrels, existed in great abundance.

Other than a couple of bear hunts, his accounts of which leave the reader with a slightly disquieting impression that Kephart didn't particularly enjoy the experiences, it seems that during group outings in the Smokies he was perfectly content to hang around the cabin or camp serving as headquarters for the hunting party. Only on rare occasions does he seem to have ventured afield with hunting as his primary purpose. That likely was in part the product of inability to endure the amazingly arduous demands of bear or turkey hunting. Although he spent a great deal of time on Deep Creek, there is no evidence in his writings or papers that he ever actually set foot on any of the best-known spots for bear stands or turkey hunting, such as Keg

Drive Branch, Round Top, or Burnt Pine Ridge, mentioned by Sam Hunnicutt in his *Twenty Years Hunting and Fishing in the Great Smokies* (1926; revised edition, 1951; reprinted, with a new Introduction by Jim Casada, 2017). Also, given Kephart's first-rate abilities as a cook, he would have been a logical choice for unofficial camp chef, and nowhere could he have been better situated to garner story material than around the communal campfire or cook stove. Similarly, if someone on a hunt had trouble with a gun malfunctioning, or if they were interested in its details regarding its performance capabilities, he was the man for the moment.

Anyone who reads Sam Hunnicutt's quaint little book mentioned above and who has reasonable intimacy with the geographical setting for old Sam's exploits soon realizes it took what mountain folks called "much of a man" to follow the hounds hot on a bruin's trail or climb steep ridges before daylight in order to be within calling range of roosted turkeys. Kephart, particularly in the final two decades or so of his life, would have lacked the stamina for such undertakings.

Another indication of the fact that he wasn't a serious hunter comes from the fact that he wrote nothing whatsoever about the two individuals who were, during his years in the Smokies, arguably the mightiest Nimrods in Swain County (where Kephart lived). These men were the aforementioned Sam Hunnicutt and the widely acknowledged dean of mountain sportsmen "Uncle" Mark Cathey. Hunnicutt unabashedly styled himself "the perfect hunter and fisherman," while Cathey, his erstwhile companion on many trips, remains widely recognized as a superb bear hunter and the most heralded of all Smokies' fly fishermen. They seemingly would have been naturals to populate his writings. After all, Kephart made frequent mention of other sportsmen (Granville Calhoun, Quill Rose, and "Little" John Cable) or interesting characters (Jack Coburn, Bob Barnett, and revenue agents such as "The Snake Stick Man") he knew.

He had to have been well acquainted with the reputations of Hunnicutt and Cathey. Both men called the Deep Creek drainage where Kephart's last permanent campsite was located home, and that location, the Bryson Place, was one of their favorite haunts. Also, Kephart's literary remains include a copy of Hunnicutt's book. His failure to establish contact with or write about the pair, who were not only noted outdoorsmen but quaint characters and first-rate shots, is exceedingly strange. They would have been perfect grist for his gun-writing mill. Likely his failure to do so was an outgrowth of one of two things. One factor would have been that their arduous hunts were too physically demanding for Kephart, although in similar circumstances he was a member of large hunting parties and just stayed in camp. More likely is that Hunnicutt and Cathey, exemplars of Scots-Irish independence at its strongest, simply did not care for Kephart's company. They would have known of the manner in which he depicted locals in *Our Southern Highlanders,* and both fell squarely into the "branch-water people" category of locals described in the book's pages.

Posterity must bemoan the circumstances, whatever their exact nature, which kept men of the ilk of Hunnicutt and Cathey outside the strokes of Kephart's literary brush. Their practical knowledge of hunting, intimate familiarity with local topography, and solid understanding of firearms performance in the field would have enriched his writing and given us greater insight into the men themselves and the nature of sport and shooting in the Smokies during the first quarter of the 20th century. First-hand coverage of their activities would also have contributed notably to our understanding of the culture to which they belonged. Nonetheless, we are blessed with a solid and lasting contribution to the literature of firearms from Kephart. It just lacks, with the noteworthy exception of the tale of a bear hunt that forms chapter four of *Our Southern Highlanders,* the intimacy of hunt camps and hunting characters.

All of this points to the inescapable conclusion that as a writer on subjects related to guns, Kephart was far more comfortable with specialized technical writing and the history of firearms than he was with their use for hunting purposes. This should come as no real surprise. Kephart was in many ways a loner, and meticulous study of guns, their characteristics, qualities, and performance lent itself to this type of lifestyle. On the other hand, hunting as commonly practiced in the Smokies at that time was a group sport that involved large hunting parties, plenty of canine companions, and camping parties numbering anywhere from two or three to a score or more members.

The selections which follow offer a solid cross-section from Kephart's work as an authority on firearms, and it should be stressed that there is no area of outdoor coverage demanding greater accuracy from an author. An old adage in the gun writers' world suggests "there's no nut like a gun nut," and rest assured that had Kephart strayed wide of the mark in this arena of literary endeavor he would not only have been called to task; if it occurred often editors would soon have found someone to replace him in their magazine's coverage of the subject.

That didn't happen, and if you carefully peruse the pages of publications to which Kephart contributed articles on firearms, you'll find precious few letters criticizing his work. Where they do appear, Kephart invariably responds in a detailed, incisive manner. The comparative dearth of criticism in a field where scathing remarks and ridicule were rampant speaks eloquently to the knowledge and authority he brought to his work in the field. Also indicative of his passion for all aspects of guns is the fact that on a number of occasions Kephart felt strongly enough about some area of firearms minutiae associated with another writer to craft letters-to-the-editor of his own.

In addition to the selections offered here, those particularly interested in firearms-related matters in Kephart's oeuvre will want to note the numerous other articles on the subject in this work's Kephart bibliography. Also, particular mention should be made of books, a lengthy series of articles, and a book-length serial in which his writings on firearms feature prominently. *Sporting Firearms,* first published in 1912 by Outing Publishing Company as part of a series of handbooks it produced for outdoorsmen, was later reprinted a number of times by the Macmillan Company. One of Kephart's contemporaries (and competitors) in the gun writing field, Colonel E. C. "Ned" Crossman, a man noted for being sparing with praise, said the little book, which sold for eighty cents, was worth "many times this price."

As was noted above, in 1904 Kephart wrote a lengthy section entitled "The Hunting Rifle" for *Guns, Ammunition, and Tackle.* Published by Macmillan, this book included contributions from other noted turn-of-the-century sporting scribes such as W. E. Carlin, A. L. A. Himmelwright, John Harrington Keene, and Captain W. W. Money.

The eight-part series "The Story of the Gun," which appeared in *All Outdoors* in 1918 and 1919, saw Kephart approaching the peak of his prowess as a gun writer. The wide-ranging overview was excellent, and it seems surprising some enterprising publisher didn't issue the entire series as a booklet.

One other endeavor should be mentioned along with these substantial undertakings. It is a foray into fiction where Kephart employs his familiarity with firearms and ballistics in what was probably intended to be a thriller or "whodunit." This is "The Trail of a Bullet," a work of twenty-three chapters that was serialized in the pulp detective publication *Flynn's Magazine.* Viewed from the perspective of its success as literature, "pot boiler" would probably be an apt description. Literary merits aside, those who read the piece will find little to criticize when it comes to handling the technical side of things as they relate to guns. Kephart stayed true to what was essentially an unerringly accurate path in his endeavors as a firearms writer.

In addition to these publications which appeared during Kephart's lifetime, almost three quarters of a century after Kephart's death and exactly a century after he came to the Smokies, in 2004 Palladium Press published a book in its Firearms Classics series with a lengthy introduction by the present writer. It incorporates the entirety of *Sporting Firearms* along with "The Hawken Rifle," "Rifles for Big Game," and "The Hunting Rifle."

Interestingly, if one looks at the entire body of Kephart's writing on firearms, realization soon dawns that he dealt primarily with rifles and ballistics. Other than in the concluding section of *Sporting Firearms* and a piece entitled "The Winchester

.410 Bore Sport-Gun" (*All Outdoors*, May 1921), he wrote little on shotguns. Even in *Sporting Firearms* he devotes more than double the attention to rifles that he gives shotguns. Similarly, he wrote relatively little of a technical or specialized nature on handguns—a half dozen pieces in all—although one extant photograph does show him with a pistol. Clearly rifles and the performance of their loads; ballistics; and firearms maintenance in areas such as cleaning, lubrication, and rust prevention were what interested Kephart.

Only on a single occasion in his considerable corpus of firearms coverage have I come across something Kephart wrote which seems of questionable accuracy. Even that instance has nothing to do with technical information or understanding of firearms but rather displays either a bit of romantic naiveté or lack of appreciation of the respect mountain folks had for guns and the way they treated them. That came when he announced, in an *All Outdoors* column, that his friend Jack Coburn had located the rifle used to execute the Cherokee Tsali, who stood strong against the Trail of Tears removal to Oklahoma and surrendered in order to allow a remnant of his people to remain in the Smokies.

There are multiple problems with this claim. The most significant one, and surely Kephart would have known this, is connected with provenance. Such information is not provided, probably because it didn't exist. Beyond that, the statement that the gun had been rusting away in the loft of a remote cabin in the hills does not ring true. Among the sterling qualities of late 19th and early 20th century residents of the high country was the ability and determination to "make do with what you've got." A cardinal point in that philosophy was care of tools and equipment. No gun, vintage or otherwise, would have been stored in a manner sure to degrade it. In other words, Kephart probably took a story that was a rather plain piece of cloth and, with his knowledge of local history as it related to the Eastern Cherokees, indulged in quite a bit of embroidery.

Discovery of but a single questionable piece of work in his corpus of firearms writing, particularly given the quantity of material he produced and the time it spanned, speaks eloquently to Kephart's abilities in this field. It will never be his primary claim to fame; yet it was certainly the area of endeavor where he was most consistently reliable and least open to criticism or controversy. As such, his exploits in the field need to be remembered, and they merit the prominent place they enjoy in these pages.

For well over three decades Kephart contributed important material on firearms to most of the major outdoor magazines—*Shooting and Fishing, Outing, All Outdoors, Outer's Book, Forest and Stream,* the National Rifle Association's (NRA) *Arms and the*

Man,[3] and *Outdoor Life*—along with general audience publications including *Boys' Life, Harper's, Cassier's, Flynn's,* and others. For a time he had a column in *Outing* magazine entitled "Guns, Ammunition and Equipment," and many of the offerings in his "Roving with Kephart" in *All Outdoors* magazine deal with firearms. As a freelance writer eking out a living through his typewriter, Kephart produced more magazine material on firearms than any subject except woodsmanship. Altogether he had almost a hundred pieces published as a gun writer.

In his lifetime Kephart was widely and rightly recognized as one of the nation's premier gun writers. When the editor of *Outing* magazine, Albert Britt, introduced him in 1919 as a new columnist (he had long been a contributor to the publication), he described him as "one of the three or four men in this country qualified to speak with authority about guns." That wasn't mere hype but reflection of a now largely forgotten reality. Gun writing was a field in which Kephart had great knowledge and shared it with avid readers nationwide.

He lived in an era that saw the advent of the golden age of gun writing, and for the better part of three decades he ranked right at the top among experts in the field. Along with Colonel Charles Askins Sr., Colonel Townsend Whelen, Captain E. C. "Ned" Crossman, Captain Paul Curtis, and a few others, Kephart was in the forefront of the gun writing game. What makes his accomplishments in this field even more remarkable is the fact that almost all other leading gun writers of the day had military backgrounds and, through their service, ready access to all the latest developments in guns and ammunition. Kephart, by way of sharp contrast, was in his chosen refuge in the Smokies, far removed from the latest and greatest in the field. He was further handicapped by the fact that, unlike his competitors in the gun-writing field, for the most part (the early 1920s were an exception) he was not the regular recipient of "loaner" or gift guns, vast quantities of free ammunition, or up-to-the-minute inside dope on what was going on in the factories and research units of noted manufacturers such as Ruger, Remington, Browning, and others.

Realization of that situation makes his level of productivity and the consistent accuracy of his gun writing even more impressive. In my view it argues for this being, in terms of longevity and universal critical acceptance, one of the distinguishing hallmarks of his career. Noted modern gun writer James Foral gives him a prominent place in his work *Gun Writers of Yesteryear* and deservedly so. Other aspects of Kephart's life and writing may be fraught with controversy and open to criticism, but when it comes to rifles, ammunition, and ballistics, his work stands the demanding test of time in sterling fashion. He unquestionably ranks as one of our country's greatest gun scribes.

The Birth of the American Army

On the 14th of June, 1775, the Continental Congress, facing actual war, resolved "that six companies of expert riflemen be immediately raised in Pennsylvania, two in Maryland, and two in Virginia. . . . That each company, as soon as completed, march and join the army near Boston, and be there employed as light infantry." These riflemen were the first troops ever levied on this continent by authority of a central representative government. On the following day George Washington was appointed commander-in-chief. Such was the origin of the American army.

The rifle, at this time, was a weapon unknown to New England, and unused in the eastern districts of the other colonies. The infantry arm of the period was a smooth-bore musket, called "Brown Bess" by English soldiers, and "Queen's arm" by the Americans. It was very inaccurate, and of short range. When Putnam gave the command at Bunker Hill, "Wait till you see the white of their eyes," he did so because the muskets and shot-guns with which his men were armed could not be relied upon to hit a man at a much greater distance. The rifle had been introduced into Pennsylvania about 1700 by Swiss and Palatine immigrants, and was made by them at various border towns in that colony twenty or thirty years before the Revolution. Our frontiersmen, appreciating the superior accuracy of the grooved barrel, adopted the rifle at once, and improved upon the German model with such ingenuity that within a few years they had produced a new type of fire-arm, superior to all others, the American backwoods rifle. At the outbreak of our war for independence the rifle was used only in two widely separated parts of the earth—in central Europe, and along the frontiers of Pennsylvania, Maryland, Virginia, and the Carolinas. So the call of Congress for riflemen was, in fact, a call for the backwoodsmen of the Alleghanies. When hostilities were so imminent (Gage was already penned up in Boston, and Bunker Hill was but three days off), why did Congress send so far and wide for scattered woodsmen, when the seaboard towns were alive with men eager to serve? John Adams wrote to Gerry, after the resolution had passed, "These are said to be all exquisite marksmen, and by means of the excellence of their firelocks, as well as their skill in the use of them, to send sure destruction to great distances."

From *Harper's New Monthly Magazine*, May 1899

It was plain enough that a corps of such sharpshooters, hardy, indomitable, experienced in forest war, would be the right material to meet British regulars.

There seems to have been another and a deeper motive which impelled Congress at this critical hour to hazard the delay of sending for the mountaineers. As yet there had been no actual rupture between England and the colonies. Far-seeing men were urging the country to defend its birthright; but would the people follow? The feeling of loyalty to Great Britain was still strong among the influential classes—so strong that, only two days before this call for riflemen was issued, Congress itself had been constrained to appeal to the twelve colonies that they observe a common fast-day in recognition of King George III. [*sic*] as their rightful sovereign, and enjoining them to look to God for a reconciliation with the parent state. Most of our colonists lived within shipping distance of tide-water, and had periodical communication with England. They depended upon the mother-country for a market, and for most of the luxuries of life. Ties of kindred were kept alive by mails and newspapers, as well as by personal contact with visitors from abroad. Blood had been spilled, it was true, but only in a few skirmishes, which history might dismiss as riots. The colonies were still separated by petty jealousies and local pride. Cavalier mocked at Puritan, and Knickerbocker mistrusted both. When the supreme moment arrived, would these discordant elements act together, would Virginia strike hands with Massachusetts, would Pennsylvania forget her quarrels with Connecticut and Maryland? Granting that war was inevitable, it was, above all else, essential that this continental army should have a nucleus which was not provincial, but American.

The call for riflemen reveals a subtler policy than appears on the surface—a policy no doubt suggested by the only man in Congress who knew the backwoodsmen like a brother, who had marched with them, camped with them, fought side by side with them—by Washington himself. This frontier folk remembered no father-land but the wilderness they trod. Procuring everything they needed from the forest with their own hands, they asked nothing from civilization, and were never in debt. Unschooled in worldly arts, indifferent to wealth, judging all men by personal merit, practising the open-handed generosity of primitive manhood, theirs was a true democracy.

The men of the border were not unprepared for a call to arms. The first formal threat of armed rebellion against Great Britain had come from the Pennsylvania frontier. On the 13th of May, 1774, a town meeting had been held in Boston, at which an appeal was issued "to all the sister colonies, inviting a universal suspension of exports and imports, promising to suffer for America with becoming fortitude, confessing that singly they might find their trial too severe, and entreating not to be left to suffer alone, when the very being of every colony, considered as a free people, depended upon the event." Couriers carried this appeal throughout the country. In the cities there was hesitancy or refusal. As a class, the gentry and men of property, when not outspoken tories, were fearful of turbulence or of commercial loss, and could not be induced to take what they considered a reckless leap into the dark. As Dickinson said in Philadelphia, when Paul Revere brought the entreaty of Boston: "They will have time enough to die. Let them give the other provinces time to think and resolve. If they expect to drag them by their own violence into mad measures, they will be left to perish by themselves, despised by their enemies, and almost detested by their friends." But wherever public affairs were directed by the farmers and tradesmen and mechanics, there was but one response, courteous towards England, but firm against encroachments; and when the appeal of stricken Massachusetts reached the log cabins of the Alleghanies, our backwoodsmen asked for no time to think and resolve. Little indeed it mattered to them whether tea was a shilling a pound or a guinea a pound; they never drank it. No personal considerations bound these Scotch-Irish and Pennsylvania-German borderers to the men of New England. But like a slap in the face came the news that American manhood was insulted. Liberty to these woodsmen was the breath of life.

On the 4th of June, 1774, the inhabitants of little Hanover, then in Lancaster County, on the frontier of Pennsylvania, met to express their sentiments, and it was unanimously resolved:

1st. That the recent action of the Parliament of Great Britain is iniquitous and oppressive.

2d. That it is the bounden duty of the people to oppose every measure which tends to deprive them of their just prerogatives.

3d. That in a closer union of the colonies lies the safeguard of the liberties of the people.

4th. That in the event of Great Britain attempting to force unjust laws upon us by the strength of arms, our cause we leave to Heaven and our rifles.

No smooth, conciliatory phrases here. The rifles were ready. The riflemen would bare their heads to no lord but the Lord of Gideon. This was ten months before Patrick Henry arose in the Virginia convention and declared plainly: "We must fight! An appeal to arms and the God of Hosts is all that is left to us."

From Pennsylvania to South Carolina the backwoodsmen were of one mind, and spoke it forthright, anticipating by months the Declaration of Independence.

The readiness of the backwoodsmen to take up arms was in striking contrast to the state of military affairs along the coast. Massachusetts had scarce a dozen serviceable cannon, and for half of these there was no ammunition. In the whole colony of New York there were only a hundred pounds of powder for sale. The men who hastily assembled at Cambridge, after the affair at Lexington, were enthusiastic but unruly. Commissions had been granted to everybody who, through local influence or prestige as a civilian, could raise a company or a regiment. The first general selected by Massachusetts was too infirm to ride a horse. The vitally important duties of arming, equipping, and sustaining the army were intrusted to merchants and professional men who had no adequate conception of the requirements, and whose labor, though zealous and well-meaning, was one long series of blunders. When war broke out, no provision had been made for arming, feeding, clothing, or paying the volunteers, or caring for the sick and wounded. For lack of tents, the men made dugouts and lean-tos. Many of the soldiers had to return home for the bare necessities of life. When Washington made ready to press the siege of Boston and provoke a general engagement, he found that, owing to a mistake of the committee of supplies, the whole amount of powder in camp would barely furnish nine cartridges per man. Time which should have been spent in preparation had been wasted in discussion, or devoted to fasting and prayer.

But the men of the wilderness were always ready. Over every cabin door hung a well-made rifle, correctly sighted, and bright within from frequent wiping and oiling. Beside it were tomahawk and knife, a horn of good powder, and a pouch containing bullets, patches, spare flints, steel, tinder, whetstone, oil and tow for cleaning the rifle. A hunting-shirt, moccasins, and a blanket were near at hand. In case of alarm, the backwoodsman seized these things, put a few pounds of rockahominy and jerked venison into his wallet, and in five minutes was ready. It mattered not whether two men or two thousand were needed for war, they could assemble in a night, armed, accoutred, and provisioned for a campaign.

As soon as a pioneer boy was big enough to level a rifle, he was given powder and ball to shoot squirrels. After a little practice he was required to bring in as many squirrels as he had received charges, under penalty of a severe lecture, or even of having his jacket "tanned." At the age of twelve the boy became a fort soldier, with loop-hole assigned him from which to fight when the settlers rallied against an Indian foray. Growing older, he became a hunter of deer, elk, buffalo, and bear, skilled in trailing and in utilizing cover, capable of enduring long marches through trackless mountain forests. At night he was content to curl up in a single blanket beside a small fire, and sleep under the roof of heaven. If it rained, in a few minutes he built him a lodge of bark or boughs, with no implement but his one-pound tomahawk. Incessant war with the Indians taught him to be his own general, to be ever on the alert, to keep his head and shoot straight under fire. Pitted against an enemy who gave no quarter, but tortured the living and scalped the dead, he became himself a stanch fighter who never surrendered. The wilderness bred men of iron, and probably contained a greater number of expert riflemen than could now be mustered in all America. It was the pick of these for which Congress asked.

But the west had wars of its own to fight. The Indians, finding that the great barrier chain of the Alleghanies was no longer impregnable to the white invaders, grew desperate, and fought with redoubled fury. Moreover, one of the first acts of the British government, after the Revolution began, was to incite the savages to attack the colonies in the rear. White renegades and ne'er-do-wells who had found refuge in the wilderness turned tory, and preyed upon the industrious settlers. Every man along the border was really needed at home, to help form a rear-guard of the Revolution. Yet, with characteristic generosity, riflemen were spared. The first men who marched to assist New England in her sore need were the pioneers of the great west.

Congress passed its resolution creating a corps of these sharpshooters on the 14th of June, 1775. Couriers on relays of swift horses carried the news to the various county committees on the frontier, who were empowered to commission officers for the purpose. The committees acted at once. The officers despatched their scouts to summon the men. On the 18th of July the first company of riflemen, Nagel's Berks County "Dutchmen," arrived at Cambridge, and within less than sixty days from the date of the resolution of Congress 1430 backwoodsmen, instead of the 810 required, had been raised, equipped by themselves, and had joined the army before Boston, after marching from four to seven hundred miles over difficult roads—all without a farthing being advanced by the Continental treasury.

Volunteers had poured into the little recruiting stations in such numbers as to embarrass the officers, who fain would have been spared the duty of discriminating. One of these officers, beset by a much greater number of applicants than his instructions permitted him to enroll, and being unwilling to offend any, hit upon a clever expedient. Taking a piece of chalk, he drew upon a blackened board the figure of a man's nose, and placing this at such a distance that none but experts could hope to hit it with a bullet, he declared that he would enlist only those who shot nearest to the mark. Sixty-odd hit the nose. On hearing of this incident, the Virginia *Gazette* exclaimed, "General Gage, take care of *your* nose!"

On the 22d of June, Congress directed Pennsylvania to raise two more companies, making a total of eight from that colony; but on the 11th of July it was informed that Lancaster County had raised two companies instead of one, and accordingly the nine companies from Pennsylvania were formed into a battalion under Colonel William

Thompson, of Carlisle, and were mustered into the Continental service. The men were enlisted as follows: two companies from Cumberland County, two from Lancaster, and one each from York, Northumberland, Bedford, Berks, and Northampton. The limits of these counties were more extensive then than now, taking in nearly all of western Pennsylvania. Many of the officers of this battalion afterwards rose to distinction. Colonel Thompson was promoted to brigadier-general in the following year. He was succeeded by his lieutenant-colonel, Edward Hand, of Lancaster, who, after brilliant conduct at Long Island and Trenton, became brigadier-general, and subsequently major-general. Major Robert Magaw, of Carlisle, became colonel of the Fifth Pennsylvania Battalion. Captain James Chambers became lieutenant colonel of the rifles; and the captain of the other Cumberland company, the brave William Hendricks, was killed in the assault on Quebec.

The frontiersmen of Maryland and Virginia were equally prompt. Both of the Maryland companies were enlisted from Frederick County. One of them was commanded by Thomas Price, who rose to the rank of colonel, and whose first lieutenant, Otho Holland Williams, became a brigadier-general. The other Maryland company was led by Michael Cresap, a famous border warrior, whom Jefferson wrongly accused of killing the Indian chief Logan, "the friend of the white man." Cresap was ill when his commission reached him, but calling his clerk, he mounted the lad on a fast horse and sent him across the mountains to summon the woodsmen. His old comrades responded to a man, and Cresap, though stricken with a mortal ailment, led them to Cambridge, dying soon after. Of one of the Virginia companies, under Captain Erisson, nothing is known; but the other was a host in itself, being commanded by the lion-hearted Daniel Morgan, now only a raw frontiersman, but destined to become one of the most brilliant generals of the war, and a personal favorite with Washington. Morgan had just returned from Dunmore's Indian war when the news came of the passage of the Boston port bill. "We had beaten the Indians," he says, "brought them to order, and confirmed a treaty of peace; and on our return home, at the mouth of the river Hockhockin, we were informed of hostilities being offered to our brethren the people of Boston. We, as an army victorious, formed ourselves into a society, pledging our words of honor to each other to assist our brethren in Boston, in case hostilities should commence, which did on the 19th of April ensuing, at Lexington." It took Morgan but a few days to raise ninety-six expert marksmen. General Custis says: "When Morgan cried, with his martial inspiration, 'Come, boys, who's for the camp before Cambridge?' the mountaineers turned out to a man."

About two-thirds of the riflemen were of Scotch-Irish descent, and nearly all of the remainder were "Pennsylvania Dutchmen"—that is to say, of Swiss or Palatine origin. Many of the Marylanders and Virginians were immigrants from western Pennsylvania. The famous rifle corps which Morgan afterwards formed from marksmen picked from the whole army is usually referred to as "Morgan's Virginians," but, as a matter of fact, two-thirds of them were Pennsylvanians, including a considerable number of Pennsylvania Germans. One of the latter, a Mr. Lauk, who was with Morgan from the beginning to the end of the war, was the last survivor of the corps. Once, when Morgan was asked which race of those composing the American armies made the best soldiers, he replied: "As for the fighting part of the matter, the men of all races are pretty much alike; they fight as much as they find necessary, and no more. But, sir, for the grand essential in the composition of a good soldier, give me the 'Dutchman'—he starves well."

At Fredericktown, Maryland, and Lancaster, Pennsylvania, the men of Cresap's company gave exhibitions of their astonishing skill with the rifle. After shooting by turns at a piece of paper the size of a dollar, nailed on a blackened board sixty yards distant, and generally hitting it or shooting very near it, they varied the amusement by shooting in a prone position, from their breasts, sides, or backs, and by running a short distance and then firing, to show that they were equally certain of their aim when manœuvring as in battle. Finally one of two brothers took a piece of board, only five inches broad and seven inches long, with a similar piece of paper centred on it for a bull's-eye, and held the board in his hand while the other brother shot through the paper. Positions were then reversed, and the second brother held the board. The spectators were more astonished than pleased at this performance, when, to their horror, one of the men placed the bit of board between his thighs, and supporting it thus, stood smilingly erect while his brother shot eight bullets successively through the board. This shooting was done offhand, at a distance said to have been "upwards of sixty yards," though it was probably not over forty yards. The bystanders were assured that there were more than fifty men in the company who could perform the same feat, and that there was not one but could "plug nineteen bullets out of twenty within an inch of the head of a tenpenny nail." To show the absolute confidence that they had in each other's marksmanship, some of the riflemen offered to stand with apples on their heads while others shot them off at a considerable distance; but the sensible townspeople refused to witness such foolhardiness.

The peculiar costume of the backwoodsmen attracted even more attention than their exhibitions of marksmanship. Its pattern was borrowed from the Indians. It consisted, first, of an ash-colored hunting-shirt of coarse linen or linsey-woolsey. Buckskin was worn in cool weather, but it was too hot for summer wear. The shirt had a double cape, and was fringed along the edges and seams. Upon its breast was the motto "Liberty or

Death." Around the waist it was secured by a belt, usually of wampum, in which were thrust the ever-useful tomahawk and skinning-knife. Some of the men wore buckskin breeches; but others preferred leggings of the same material, reaching above the knees, and an Indian breech-clout, their thighs being left naked for suppleness in running. Captain Morgan himself wore the breech-clout during his fearful midwinter march through the Maine wilderness to Quebec, his bare thighs exposed to the elements and lacerated by thorns and brush. The rifleman's head-dress was a soft round hat with a feather in it. On his feet he wore buckskin moccasins ornamented with squaw-work in beads and stained porcupine quills. Shoulder-belts supported the canteen, bullet-pouch, and powder-horn. The officers were distinguished by crimson sashes worn over the shoulder and around the waist, their only insignia. Some of the officers disdained swords, preferring to carry rifles, like their men.

Colonel Roosevelt calls the hunting-shirt "the most picturesque and distinctively national dress ever worn in America." It was adopted by the backwoodsmen because it was loose, light, cheap, inconspicuous in the woods, and easy to wash. In 1758, when Washington was serving in the French war, he wrote from Fort Cumberland to Colonel Bouquet, recommending in the strongest terms that his men be permitted to wear the Indian dress. "If I were left to pursue my own inclinations," he said, "I would not only order the men to adopt the Indian dress, but cause the officers to do it also, and be the first to set the example myself. Nothing but the uncertainty of obtaining the general approbation causes me to hesitate a moment to leave my regimentals at this place, and proceed as light as any Indian in the woods." Bouquet adopted the suggestion at once. Several times in his correspondence Washington expressed his fondness for the backwoods garb, on account of its lightness and sufficiency without extra baggage. When called to command the American army at Cambridge, he recommended it for another reason. Writing to the President of Congress concerning the lack of clothing, he said: "I am of opinion that a number of hunting-shirts, not less than ten thousand, would in a great degree remove this difficulty in the cheapest and quickest manner. I know nothing in a speculative view more trivial, yet which, if put in practice, would have a happier tendency to unite the men and abolish those provincial distinctions that lead to jealousy and dissatisfaction." Mark well the latter phrase. The hunting-shirt was an emblem of liberty, which never in the history of man was worn by an enslaved people. It was distinctive. It meant, "We are Americans." And when Congress drew its first levies from the backwoods, it did not alone secure the services of the finest marksmen living. Something more was gained. It was the moral effect, upon the camp at Cambridge, of independence typified by flesh and blood, clad in American garb and wielding an American weapon.

Washington was a strict disciplinarian who observed military conventions whenever there was sufficient reason back of them; but he had a vein of hard commonsense as well, and nowhere did he show it more conspicuously than in discarding the heavy and galling harness of the military dandy and substituting for it the light, easy-fitting, workmanlike dress of the frontiersman. The British soldier was condemned to stagger under a burden fit only for an army mule. He wore a heavy, long-skirted red coat, which made the best possible target for the enemy. His tight-fitting breeches impeded every movement and checked the free circulation of the blood. His neck was bound in a high leather stock, which was actual torture to wear. Mr. Ross, the editor of the *Cornwallis Correspondence*, says that at Bunker Hill "the British moved to the attack in heavy marching order, with three days' provisions—altogether a weight of 125 pounds!"

The first lesson in woodcraft that the backwoods hunter learned was, "Go light." Every article in his scant outfit was cut down to the last practicable ounce—save only the barrel of his rifle. Finding that the Indian, who had reduced marching and camping to a science, could with ease outdistance any white man on a long journey, he studied the reason, and found it in the lightness of the red man's outfit and the remarkable skill with which he utilized nature's supply store. Adopting the Indian's dress and commissariat, the white hunter found himself equally agile and enduring. Citified people mistook this choice of dress for affectation, for a desire to appear bizarre. "It was the silly fashion of those times," says a contemporary writer, "for riflemen to ape the manners of savages." This is the remark of a tenderfoot. Ages of experience had taught the Indian his woodcraft, and no race of civilized men has yet succeeded in matching it. The skill which can make the best of all possible canoes with no material but a growing tree, and no implement but a crooked knife, is not to be despised. It has been said that only three human devices have ever reached perfection—the bow, the boomerang, and the violin. Of these the savage has invented two. For perfect adaptation of means to an end, it would be hard to find better examples than the Indian's moccasin and his rockahominy.

The moccasin is the most rational and comfortable of all foot-wear. In moccasins the feet have full play; they can bend and grasp; there is nothing to chafe them or to impede circulation. In moccasins one can move like an acrobat, crossing slender and slippery logs, climbing trees, or passing with ease and security along dizzy trails on the mountainside where a slip might mean sure destruction. The feet do not stick fast in mud. In the North, when the mercury is far below zero and no civilized boot will protect the feet from freezing, the savage suffers no inconvenience. His moccasins, stuffed with dried grass, let the blood course freely. The perspiration may freeze on the hay in a solid lump of ice, but the feet remain warm and dry. The buckskin moccasin, Indian-tanned with deers' brains and wood smoke, always dries soft after a wetting. In autumn, when all the leaves and twigs are dry as tinder, a man wearing shoes makes a noise in the forest like a troop of cavalry; but in moccasins he can move swiftly through the woods with the stealth of a panther. The feet are not bruised, for, after enjoying for a time the freedom of natural covering, these hitherto blundering members become like hands, and feel their way through the dark like those of a cat, avoiding obstacles as though gifted with a special sense. Best of all, the moccasin is light. Inexperienced sportsmen and soldiers affect high-topped laced boots with heavy soles and hobnails, imagining that these are most serviceable for rough wear. But these boots weigh between four and five pounds, while a pair of thick moose-hide moccasins weigh only eleven ounces. In marching ten miles, a man wearing the clumsy boots lifts twenty tons more shoe-leather than if he wore moccasins.

Rockahominy is the most nourishing and digestible of all condensed foods. It is simply Indian corn parched to a light brown and then pounded or ground to a coarse powder. It is ground coarse enough to mix with water without getting pasty. A few ounces, generally about four, are stirred in a cup of water and drunk. The corn swells in the stomach, and the man is fed for five or six hours. Rockahominy will not mould or deteriorate in a moist climate, nor is it attacked by insects when carried in a thin muslin bag. Among the first white settlers of the wilderness it was known as "coal flour"; by the Mexicans it is called *pinole*. Our pioneers relied upon it as their sole provision, besides game killed, and made long campaigns on rockahominy alone when game was scarce or fear of Indians prevented hunting.

The backwoodsman had been quick to learn what it has taken centuries of hard knocks to hammer into the heads of military pundits, namely: that the men who can march hard and shoot straight will win; and that any rule or tool that interferes is criminal folly.

I dwell at some length upon this matter of equipment because it explains in great part the extraordinary feats of marching without pack-trains which were performed by our riflemen in the Revolution. After five years of campaigning, from Canada to the Carolinas, Morgan replied to General Greene's offer of wagons for transportation: "Wagons would be an impediment, whether we attempt to annoy the enemy or provide for our own safety. It is incompatible with the nature of light troops to be encumbered with luggage." We have noted the promptitude with which the riflemen were mustered and marched to Cambridge. Cresap made a phenomenal journey over difficult roads, leaving Frederick, Maryland, July 18, and arriving at the American camp on August 9, having covered 550 miles in twenty-two days; but this performance was in turn eclipsed by Morgan, who led his woodsmen, in bad weather, 600 miles, from Winchester, Virginia, to Cambridge, in twenty-one days.

When Washington, one day riding along his lines, saw the fringed hunting-shirts of the Virginians approaching, the reserve of his naturally undemonstrative nature broke down. "At the sight he stopped; the riflemen drew nearer, and their commander, stepping in front, made the military salute, exclaiming, 'General, from the right bank of the Potomac!' Washington dismounted, came to meet the battalion, and going down the line with both arms extended, shook hands with the riflemen one by one, tears rolling down his cheeks as he did so. He then mounted, saluted, and silently rode on."

The riflemen were at once employed as sharpshooters, and kept the enemy continually in hot water. Hitherto the British outposts had been safe enough within stone's-throw of the American lines, but they now found, to their cost, that it was almost certain death to expose their heads within two hundred yards of a rifleman. So frequent became the returns of officers, pickets, and artillerymen shot at long range that Edmund Burke exclaimed in Parliament, "Your officers are swept off by the rifles if they show their noses!" In the British camp the riflemen were called "shirt-tail men, with their cursed twisted guns; the most fatal widow-and-orphan makers in the world." Their presence was a godsend to the impoverished American army, as their fire was more effective than artillery, and consumed but a tithe of the powder.

In September three companies of the riflemen were ordered to join the expedition under Benedict Arnold which was to invade Canada. The harrowing details of that long march through the frozen wilderness are well known to readers of Revolutionary history. The riflemen formed the vanguard of the expedition, and stood the frightful hardships of the journey better than any of the other troops. Many of the New-Englanders, though better used to the climate, were daunted by the cold, starvation, and excessive toil, and deserted; but not a rifleman wavered. In the assault upon Quebec which followed, the sharpshooters alone succeeded in penetrating to the heart of the town. Had they been supported by the other troops, Quebec would probably have fallen. As it was, surrounded by overwhelming numbers, they fought desperately until further resistance would have meant massacre. The captives, including Morgan, were afterwards exchanged, and most of them re-enlisted. The nine other companies which had been left at Boston remained there during the winter, and on the memorable 1st of January, 1776, were reorganized as the First Regiment of Foot of the Continental Army. The next spring Washington wrote to the President of Congress recommending that the riflemen, whose term would expire in July, should be induced to continue in the service. "They are indeed a very useful corps; but I need not mention this, as their importance is already well known to the Congress." A large number of them served throughout the war, winning distinction in nearly every important battle from Long Island to Yorktown.

These were by no means the only troops furnished by the backwoodsmen in our war for independence. The Pennsylvania Rifle Regiment (Colonel Samuel Miles), the Eleventh and Twelfth Pennsylvania Continental Line, several companies of other regiments from the same colony, Colonel Moses Rawlings's Maryland Riflemen, the Augusta Riflemen and others of Virginia, and several regiments from the Carolinas, were mustered mostly from the frontier. Pre-eminent among all these organizations was the famous corps of sharpshooters which Morgan selected from the best shots in the whole army. At Saratoga, the turning-point of the Revolution, the marksmanship of these latter riflemen virtually decided the battle. Several times during this engagement Colonel Morgan had noticed a noble-looking officer of the enemy, mounted upon a splendid gray horse, dashing from one end of the line to the other encouraging his troops. Morgan recognized the brave fellow as an officer whose conduct he had admired in the battle of the 19th of September. It was General Fraser, who was considered by the Americans a more skilful and dangerous leader than Burgoyne, and Morgan himself regarded the issue of the contest doubtful as long as Fraser remained in the saddle. Soon after the action commenced, General Arnold, who well knew Fraser's ability, sought out Morgan and said: "That officer upon the gray horse is a host in himself. He must be disposed of. Direct the attention of some of your sharpshooters to him." Morgan's generous instincts rebelled, but he saw the necessity of performing the cruel duty. "War," as Macaulay says, "is never lenient but where it is wanton." Selecting twelve of his best marksmen, he posted them in a suitable position, and pointing out the doomed warrior, said to his men, "He is a brave fellow, but he must die." Some of the riflemen climbed into trees to get better sight. Among them was Tim Murphy, a renowned scout from Northumberland County, Pennsylvania, who, by means of a double-barrelled rifle, then a novelty, had been uncommonly successful in the Indian wars. The shot was very difficult, for the distance was nearly a quarter of a mile, and the backwoods rifles had no elevating sights. The riflemen rested their long pieces on the forks of limbs and began firing. In a moment the crupper of the gray horse was cut by a bullet. Within the next minute another ball passed through the horse's mane a little back of his ears. An aide remarked to Fraser: "Sir, it is evident that you are marked out for particular aim. Would it not be prudent for you to retire from this place?" Fraser replied, "My duty forbids me to fly from danger." The next instant a bullet from Murphy's rifle struck him through the body, and he was carried mortally wounded from the field.

The tactics of the backwoodsmen were essentially different from those practised by the best military authorities. It was the rule of war for troops to attack in solid formation, reserving their fire till at very close quarters. Bayonets were feared more than bullets. The standard infantry musket was very inaccurate, and had no rear sight. The musketry instructions simply required each soldier to point his weapon horizontally, brace himself for its vicious recoil, and pull the ten-pound trigger till the gun went off. The idea was that, by dropping so many bullets in a given time upon a certain area containing a given number of the enemy, so many men would probably be hit. But the backwoodsman was a hunter, who shot to kill. Attack in close order against such men was suicidal. The backwoodsman fought always as a skirmisher, taking advantage of every bit of available cover, exposing himself as little as possible, and directing his murderous aim chiefly against the enemy's officers, because the bravest troops are apt to lose heart and be stricken with panic when they see their leaders fall. The British regarded such tactics as "sneaking" and "cowardly." "Come out and fight in the open, like men," they would say. On this sentiment military history has long since passed verdict. *C'est magnifique, mais ce n'est pas la guerre.* The backwoodsmen were simply a century ahead of the times in their methods of war. The British themselves soon found it expedient to hire Indians and Hessian jägers to fight our sharpshooters, but neither of these mercenaries proved a match for the tall woodsmen of the Alleghanies.

There seem to have been but two Englishmen in the Revolution who were expert shots with the rifle. Both of them had learned to use and prefer this weapon while serving with German jägers in the Seven Years' War. Both commanded riflemen in the Revolution, and met our frontiersmen in battle. One of these was George Hanger, subsequently fourth Baron Coleraine, who commanded a Hessian jäger company, and rose to the rank of colonel. Hanger says in his book for sportsmen, published in 1814, that the best shots among the American backwoodsmen, shooting in good light when there was no wind blowing to deflect the bullet, could hit a man's head at 200 yards, or his body at 300 yards, with great certainty. As foreign rifles at that period could not be relied upon for accuracy at such distances, Hanger goes into great detail explaining the reasons for the American rifle's superiority, showing that he was a competent judge and a trustworthy witness. He tells how once, when he and General Tarleton were making a reconnoissance, an American rifleman got in position full 400 yards from them (Hanger paced the distance afterwards) and fired two deliberate shots at them. Hanger and the general were side by side on horseback, their knees almost touching, and a mounted orderly was directly in their rear. The first shot passed between the two officers, and the second killed the orderly's horse.

The other British rifleman was Major Patrick Ferguson, the inventor of a breech-loading rifle with which some of his men were armed. Ferguson commanded the British forces at King's Mountain, where he was attacked by the backwoodsmen from Tennessee. This was the first pitched battle in civilized war in which rifles were exclusively used by one of the contesting armies. The backwoodsmen carried by storm a position naturally more difficult than Bunker Hill or the heights of Fredericksburg. Ferguson was killed with 390 of his men, and lost 716 prisoners, while the American loss was but 28 killed and 60 wounded. The only other battle fought between sharpshooters on the one side and ordinary troops on the other is the battle of New Orleans, where the descendants of these same backwoodsmen, intrenched on an open plain, but outnumbered two to one by the pick of Wellington's veterans from the Peninsular war, killed 700 of the enemy, wounded 1400, and took 500 prisoners, while themselves losing but 8 men killed and 13 wounded.

We have seen that the backwoodsmen of the Alleghanies were the first to formally threaten armed resistance against Great Britain, the first outside colonists to assist New England, the first troops levied by an American Congress, the first to use weapons of precision, and the first to employ the open-order formation now universally prescribed. From the beginning to the end of the war these hardy pioneers were everywhere, doing the right thing at the right time, harassing the enemy, picking off officers and artillerymen at long range, stubbornly holding their own in the line of battle, advancing to some forlorn hope, covering a retreat to save the army from disaster, or disappearing like magic before a superior force, only to quickly reassemble for attack upon some unsuspecting outpost or detachment. Lithe, sinewy, and all-enduring, keen-eyed and nimble-footed, unencumbered with baggage, subsisting upon next to nothing, making prodigious marches over rough mountains or through an ice-clad wilderness, they were men of heroic mould, admired alike by friend and foe. Coming straight from the absolute freedom of a primeval forest, they appreciated the reasons for military discipline, and submitted to it without a murmur. Always cheerful and ready for any undertaking, they were regarded by Washington himself as the *corps d'élite* of the Continental Army. And in the darkest hour of the Revolution, when half the army was in open mutiny, the great commander, sick at heart but still indomitable, declared to his friends that if all others forsook him, he would retire to the backwoods and there make a final stand against Great Britain, surrounded by his old comrades of the wilderness.

Marvels, Old and New

SOME FICTION IN THE GUISE OF FACT

John Fiske, of Harvard, was one of the ablest and most interesting historians that America has produced. Recalling both the man and his work, as I do, with the deepest reverence, it seems a graceless task to pick at some little flaw in the mighty structure that he reared. I do so only to bring out the point that misinformation is sometimes quite innocently spread abroad by writers whose names deservedly carry great weight, but who have erred through simple ignorance of technicalities.

Fiske, in his *American Revolution*, says of Morgan's sharpshooters that "when advancing at double quick time they could cut a squirrel in two at a distance of 300 yards." A rifleman would suppose that even a scholar in his study would pause to consider what sort of a target a squirrel at 300 yards would offer to the unaided eye; but the scholar did not, nor does one person in ten who reads his statement. Fiske was not dallying with his subject; he was not ornamenting history with myth; he believed what he said, copying the statement, no doubt, from some contemporary chronicle that no one else seems ever to have run across. There were great braggarts in revolutionary times, as there are now, and Fiske in this instance was one of their dupes.

Another example of the same sort is found in a sketch of Col. James Bowie, inventor of the Bowie knife (the name is properly pronounced Boo—ee, with accent on the first syllable), written by a lady, and published in *Harper's Magazine* for July, 1898.—"Offhand with a rifle he could bring down a wild goose flying high overhead, and put his bullet in the neck five times out of seven."

We can readily forgive ignorance in writers who, from the circumstances of their lives, could scarcely be expected to know anything about fire arms. But what shall we say when a man who claims to be a hunter, writing in grave earnest for other hunters and assuming to teach them the fine points of their craft, perpetrates such a thing as this, which you will find in Lewis' *American Sportsman*. Speaking of the old-time riflemen he says: "Cutting off the head of a wild turkey, or other large bird,

---

From *Arms and the Man*, March 5, 1908

at the distance of 100 yards, or more, when in full flight, was a common feat with these hardy huntsmen."

Lewis has, at least, the negative grace of not claiming to have witnessed any such shooting as he here describes. It has remained for a recent writer to publish in a sportsman's magazine, where he certainly knew that thousands of competent judges would see it, an account of a miracle in the shooting line that he claims to have witnessed personally in the mountains of eastern Kentucky only three years ago. This story is told with such circumstantial detail, and has had so wide a circulation, that I have been surprised to see no criticism of it in any of the papers and magazines that I am accustomed to read. It was peculiarly interesting to me because most of my time during the past four years has been spent among the southern mountaineers, not, it is true, in eastern Kentucky, but in the wilder and less populous regions of the Great Smoky Mountains, on the border of North Carolina and Tennessee. I did not live in a valley town and get my information from heresay, but dwelt among the backwoodsmen as one of them, studying not only their mountains but themselves, and purposely mingling on free-and-easy terms with all classes of the mountain people, from hardshell preachers to harder shelled outlaws. I certainly know to a hair just what these mountaineers, male and female, can do with pistol, gun, or knife; likewise, and of more importance, what they cannot do. I include women here, because many of them habitually go armed; some carry razors in their stockings, and occasionally you meet one who, like a certain damsel in our settlement, is seldom seen without a Winchester on her shoulder, and who "blouses her waist a-purpose to carry a pistol." The truth is that these women made me more nervous than ever I was made by man, for there was no telling when they would get to scrapping among themselves, and then—woe unto the would-be peacemaker! Once I heard a mountain woman say to another who had just finished telling the latest scandal: "Well, if I'd a-been that gal I'd have got me a forty-some-odd and I'd a-shot enough meat offen that feller to a-kept a hound-dog a week." And she meant it; I know the breed.

The magazine article to which I refer is entitled, *Beyond the Gap: the Breeding Ground of Feuds*. It is told by a former member of the United States Geological Survey, who spent a year in the feud district with a Government surveying party. Much of his narrative is instructive, and all of it is interesting. The part to which I take exception is that in which he tells of the incredible prowess of some of the feudists, their records of man-slaying, and their skill with belt-guns.

"The best shots in the world," says this writer, "are the Kentucky mountaineers. The west has nothing to compare with them. When it comes to 'pulling a gun' quickly and shooting accurately the most expert of frontier bad men would appear slow and clumsy by the side of many of these mountain outlaws. They learn to shoot almost as soon as they graduate from the cradle. . . . During feud times the combatants are regular walking arsenals. I saw old Shackleford when trouble was brewing between himself and old Lije Howard which threatened to involve the clans. . . . He carried a Winchester .45-90, and his supply of six-shooters would have stocked a pawnshop window. He had one in each bootleg, two in leather holsters at his belt, one in a holster under the left armpit, and another in a holster inside his shirt just where it buttoned in front over his chest—six revolvers in all. Thus accoutered he could draw a gun in any position in which he might be surprised. I was told that the holster in the shirt front was the favorite one, as the weapon could be flashed out with incredible rapidity."

Yes. If old Shackleford had appeared around our settlement in such rig, folks would have taken him for something less than a half-wit. A six-shooter in each boot, when it comes to sprinting around the mountains, would save any man from the gallows and land him snug in the "bug-house." Methinks that if a really, truly bad man were looking for me, I would like him far better if he would attach a whole dozen guns to his person, and stick a knife between his teeth. He would have just that much more to think about besides me.

This same Shackleford, according to our informant, "has a record of 38 killings to his credit, a record that no western desperado from Las Vegas to the Canadian line has ever equaled." One of his victims was his wife. Lije Howard, our writer says, has killed 29 men; Pat Morgan, 26; Bill Hensley, 24. Well, that is "some." Down our way nobody ever gets beyond just a modest two or three; you see, all of our people are able to shoot back. But then the Smoky folks don't wear pistols as defensive armor. There may be a whole lot in that.

But the incident that particularly stirs my protest is this.

"I saw," says the geologist, "Abe McCoy, of Hatfield-McCoy fame, do some shooting that would make anything in Buffalo Bill's Wild West Show look cheap." A fellow surveyor and himself put up for the night at a mountain house. Another man, who proved to be McCoy, soon rode up and stopped there, too. This newcomer distrusted the scientists and never turned his back toward them. He would not go to bed, but sat all night "in a chair titled against the side of the chimney, with his hat pulled down over his eyes. The two six-shooters at his belt were in plain view, and I saw the butts of two others peeping from his boot tops. As I found out afterward he had two more, one in the armpit holster and another in the shirt front holster." In the morning these three men rode off together. McCoy politely but grimly insisted that the two strangers should ride ahead. "'I suppose you are quite a shot,' said my companion as we came to the creek where we were to part company.

"'Yas, I kin shoot some,' said McCoy modestly.

"Then we importuned him to give an exhibition of his skill. He seemed a trifle reluctant, and once more a shadow of distrust flitted across his lean face. But we urged him frantically and finally he yielded.

"'Ary one o' you boys got four bits?' he asked.

"The Harvard man raked out half a dollar. McCoy then placed us about thirty feet apart, and it looked as if he was making arrangements to take care of us one at a time in case he saw any signs of treachery on our part.

"'Pitch up the coin,' ordered McCoy.

"My companion obeyed. Two shots cracked out. There stood McCoy, smiling grimly, unarmed so far as we could observe. Neither one of us had seen him draw a gun or put it back, so marvelously quick had he been. Nor could we find the coin. But McCoy went right to the spot and picked it up. It had a hole almost through the center and another near the edge where the milling had been shot away. The first shot must have knocked the coin a considerable distance and that he should have hit it a second time seems unbelievable. It is still a mystery which revolver he used, although he probably employed the one in his shirt front holster. We tried to get him to tell us, but he evaded the question.

"'Thar's tricks in all trades, boys,' he laughed. 'This is mine, an' it's' [*sic*] done took me a long while to larn it.'"

Selah!

The long bow of Robin Hood was wonderful; the rifle of Leatherstocking was more wonderful; but this shirt-front pistol of McCoy's is really the most wonderful instrument of precision in the shooting line that I ever heard tell of. We will all keep on wondering where he carried it. I have a shrewd suspicion that it grew on him, like the horn of the unicorn, save that it was in his mouth, somewhere, so that he could spit bullets and need not crook a finger.

Of course, this may sound impertinent. Who am I, anyhow? I never was shot but once, and, to the best of my recollection, never killed anybody. So I don't pretend to judge. But there are many readers of this paper who are credited with being peart with the pistol and right smart with the revolver. Somebody give me the dress-pattern for a wishbone holster. I want to start in practicin' up.

Marvels, Old and New

BACKWOODS MARKSMANSHIP ACCORDING TO FENIMORE COOPER

There is a scene in Cooper's novel *The Pathfinder* that makes a rifleman blush for him who wrote it. This is the chapter describing a shooting match that is supposed to have taken place at the British post of Oswego, N. Y., about 150 years ago. The writer's purpose was to show off the superlative marksmanship of a white guide known, at that time, as the Pathfinder. This man was Cooper's favorite character, now one of the best-known and best-beloved in all fiction, the peerless scout and almost flawless child of nature who, first as Hawkeye and last as Leatherstocking, from youth to old age, from Atlantic forests to the prairies of the west, moves, stately but pathetically, through the whole series of *Leatherstocking Tales*.

In his person Cooper created a great type, however impossible the man may have been made to appear at times. It is, then, more the pity that this shooting match should have introduced him in cheap melodrama, performing supernatural feats, and childishly bragging about his skill in marksmanship, which, as he considered it a gift from on high instead of an accomplishment won by hard striving of his own, was certainly nothing to boast about.

As Cooper tells the story, the match began with offhand shooting at a distance of 100 yards, the target being a board on which was painted a bullseye with certain rings around it. The paint used was white, a baffling color, although black would have been worse if the board was only a riven shake or a whip-sawed plank, unplaned and dark from weathering, as would be likely at a frontier post.

After some preliminary trials of no interest, the commandant of the post opened the real match. Firing carelessly, he missed the mark by several inches, and was ruled out from the other trials, in which no one could compete who had missed the bullseye with his first shot.

From *Arms and the Man*, March 12, 1908

Then a certain voyageur, Jasper Eau-douce, was called. Now Jasper had a sweetheart in the crowd, Mabel by name, and Mabel was fair to look upon, of course. Her presence made Jasper more nervous than befitted a sharpshooter, but the effect was neutralized by a swashbuckling quartermaster, who, seeking to rattle Jasper by recital of his own magnificent prowess, only stiffened that gentleman's grip on himself. Jasper's first shot drove the exact center.

Next came the quartermaster, toeing the mark. After much fussing and boasting, this officer fired. No hole was seen in the target except Jasper's. The marker called a miss. The crowd jeered. The quartermaster stormed. "Impossible!" for he was in truth a redoubtable shot, and everybody knew it.

"'It's a dead miss, Muir,' said the laughing Lundie, 'and ye'll jist sit down quietly with the disgrace.'

'No, no, Major,' the Pathfinder at length observed, 'the quartermaster *is* a good shot for a slow one and a measured distance, though nothing extr'ornary for real service. He has covered Jasper's bullet, as will be seen if any one will take the trouble to examine the target.'"

A dozen men rushed to the target, and, sure enough, albeit the bullet-hole was enlarged so slightly that a man had to look twice to see where the second ball had frayed the edge, yet two bullets were found impacted together in the stump against which the target was placed.

Wonderful eyes, Pathfinder's, that could discern at 100 yards what common folk would scarcely see with their eyes close to the paper! There are specialists nowadays who would give a thousand dollars to examine such human telescopes.

Well, the quartermaster bragged for another page or so, and then protested that the Pathfinder, whose turn had come, should not be allowed to use his famous rifle "Killdeer" in competition with mere government pieces, although it was the same arm with which the Pathfinder did all his hunting and Indian killing, and had proved itself more practical than any other in the province.

"'Killdeer is taking its rest,' replied the scout, who then assured everybody that he had been persuaded but a moment ago to enter the lists, and that Jasper's rifle was good enough for his purpose. There follows a half-page description of Pathfinder's form and the impression it made on the ladies; then he threw the weapon to his shoulders and—

"Thought was scarcely quicker than his aim; and, as the smoke floated above his head, the butt end of the rifle was seen on the ground, the hand of the Pathfinder was leaning on the barrel, and his honest countenance was illuminated by his usual silent, hearty laugh.'

"'If one dared to hint at such a thing,' cried Major Duncan, 'I should say that the Pathfinder had also missed the target.'

"'No, no, Major,' returned the guide confidently, 'that *would* be a risky declaration. I didn't load the piece, and can't say what was in it; but if it was lead, you will find the bullet driving down those of the quartermaster and Jasper, else is not my name Pathfinder.'"

A shout from the target announced the truth of this assertion.

"'That's not all, that's not all, boys,' called out the guide, who was now slowly advancing toward the stage occupied by the females; 'if you find the target touched at all, I'll own to a miss. The quartermaster cut the wood, but you'll find no wood cut by the last messenger.'"

And so it proved. The scout's bullet, following two pivotal shots, one on top of the other, had entered the same hole without even cutting the wood behind it, and three rifle balls were now welded together in the heart of the stump. Considering that this was done at 100 yards, offhand, with a rifle to which he was not accustomed and which was loaded he knew not how, it is evident that Pathfinder had more than mortal vision, nerve, and discernment. But this feat was tame for him. Let us see what followed.

The quartermaster accused him of boasting, to which the guide replied:

"'I'll do you justice, lieutenant, even if you get the best in the potato trial. I say you've passed a good human life, for a soldier, in places where the rifle is daily used, and I know you are a creditable and ingenious marksman; but then you are not a true rifle shooter. As for boasting, I hope I'm not a vain talker about my own exploits; but a man's gifts are his gifts, and it's flying in the face of Providence to deny them.'"

Plainly the guide considered himself one of those natural born marksmen that we read about.

Soon the second trial of skill commenced. "A common wrought nail was driven lightly into the target, its head having been first touched with paint, and the marksman was required to hit it, or he lost his chances in the succeeding trials." It came the quartermaster's turn, and his shot carried away a bit of the nail's head, the bullet lodging beside the point.

Jasper then fired, hit the nail squarely, and drove it to within an inch of the head. His bullet did not sink it deeper because there must be something left for the Pathfinder to do.

"'Be all ready to clench it, boys!' cried out Pathfinder, stepping into his friend's tracks the instant they were vacant. 'Never mind a new nail; I can see that, though the paint is gone, and what I can see I can hit, at 100 yards, though it were only a mosquito's eye. Be ready to clench!'

"The rifle cracked, the bullet sped on its way, and the head of the nail was buried in the wood, covered by the piece of flattened lead."

Then followed another bragging spree, and it was finally agreed that the rivalry must be settled by a potato match. Now what marvelous thing is this fellow going to do to a potato—he who spots "two in a hole" with his naked eye at 100 yards, and drives nails infallibly at that distance? Verily, it must be something that none other than the gods can do.

Listen! At a distance of 20 yards from the stand a large potato is to be tossed into the air, and the thing is—to hit it. Cooper says: "The quartermaster, in a hundred experiments, had once succeeded in accomplishing this difficult feat; but he now essayed to perform it again, with a sort of blind hope that was fated to be disappointed. The potato was thrown in the usual manner, the rifle was discharged, but the flying target was untouched."

No man who ever shot a gun need be told that it is far easier to drive a bullet through a big potato tossed upward at 20 yards than to see a nail-head at 100 yards, to say nothing of hitting that nail with a rifle ball. But Cooper thought otherwise.

Well, it was Jasper's turn. Poor Jasper! His eye turned from the pretty Mabel to a neat calash that had been offered as a prize to the winner of the match. The Pathfinder, gazing earnestly at his friend, saw symptoms of buck ague. Leading the young man aside, he inquired what had disturbed him.

"'I must own, Pathfinder, that my feelings were never before so much bound up in success.'

"'And do you so much crave to outdo me, an old and tried friend?—and that, as it might be, in my own way? Shooting is my gift, boy, and no common hand can equal mine.'

"'I know it—I know it, Pathfinder; but yet—'

"'But what, Jasper, boy?—speak freely; you talk to a friend.'

"'I would lose an arm, Pathfinder, to be able to make an offering of that calash to Mabel Dunham.'"

And poor Pathfinder! Little as Jasper dreamed it, the guide, too, had lost his heart to this very Mabel.

We will skip the expressions of sentiment that follow, and go on with the shooting match.

The guide warned Jasper that he must certainly hit the potato; as for him himself, he would be content with "the skin," but he could not brook the utter disgrace of missing altogether. Jasper's nerve was with him. He bored a hole straight through the center of the Irish tuber.

The Pathfinder, with wrinkled brow, stepped in turn to the firing point, and cried out "Toss!" This time the great marksman evidently took unusual heed to his aim. Just as the potato reached its turning point and seemed for an instant to hang poised in the air, he fired.

Incredible! The man with the gift did *not* drive the center; his bullet merely "barked" the potato, nipping off a bit of skin. The spectators, who had, of course, expected two holes in one, were shocked with wonder and disappointment. Jasper won the calash.

Of course, the Pathfinder had magnanimously allowed his friend to do the winning and so capture the maiden's plaudits. That was very handsome for an illiterate backwoodsman,—or would have been if Cooper had only let it go at that. But there was a sequel; and I blush to repeat it. The guide took Mabel off to one side, a little later, and gave the whole thing away. And to convince the girl that he could really have done anything with that potato that he wanted to, or with two at a time, for that matter, he called her attention to the gulls overhead—

"'Here, where they cross each other in sailing about,' he added, cocking and raising his rifle; 'the two—the two! Now look.'

"The piece was presented quick as thought, as two of the birds came in line, though distant from each other many yards; the report followed, and the bullet passed through the bodies of both the victims."

Then Pathfinder laughed another of those silent, hearty laughs, which strike one as being very remarkable laughs indeed, quite in keeping with the extraordinary markmanship [*sic*] that called them forth.

Come to think of it—wasn't that a remarkably firm potato? Both men fired at the same one.

However, there is this much to be said for Cooper; he wrote long ago, for a wonder-loving age. A bent for marvels is ingrained in human nature; and so is the gift of boasting. Green human nature is apt to brag, just as fresh-cut boards are prone to warp. Nothing but thorough seasoning will cure the one or the other. All children brag; all savages brag; even the weaklings who can celebrate no great deeds of their own will pick out some friend, some hero, and boast about him till the cows come home.

A modern man, when he has reached maturity and has seen something of the world, is supposed to have some of this sappiness seasoned out of him. At least, no gentleman nowadays brags about himself. So, too, our taste for hero tales becomes refined and discriminating. We care less for the superhuman, more for the frankly human with all its foibles. Even fiction, for mature minds, must picture something that flesh-and-blood might actually do. But this serious, calculating way of taking our pleasures is a modern development. In olden times men were more like children in their taste for stories. The heroes of Greek or Roman, of Norseman and Gaul and Saxon, had to be gods, or demi-gods at least, while those of Judea could be nothing less than prophets. Even as late as our grandfathers' day, grown men and women required miracles in their literary sauce, and their pet characters had to be superhuman creatures who never, never, never missed what they shot at. Even now, the vast majority of our people like their fiction highly seasoned, with heroines immaculate and villains dire. Witness the sale of blood-and-thunder novels, and of seats to the rip-roaring melodramas with three miracles in every act.

So long, then, as marvels are only presented in the frank guise of fiction, we need not sniff. It is only when the impossible is dished up to us as history, or narrative of witnessed fact, that we have much cause for protest. In a future article I will cite a few instances of false history and falser narrative that deserve public rebuke by all of us who care for honest records in our favorite sport.

The Outing Legion

THE ONLY ROAD TO SKILL WITH THE RIFLE IS THROUGH PRACTICE

CIVILIAN RIFLE CLUBS

"Drawn yet?"

"No; but this is only the beginning—eh?"

"Most likely."

"Well, I'll be ready when they want me."

"Doing any training?"

"Training! They'll give me double doses of that when I get in uniform."

"Some kinds, yes; but they can't make you a quick and sure shot. That's what counts when you get to the front. It's what a great general called 'seven-tenths of a soldier's business.'"

"Don't they teach that in the army?"

"There isn't time, now, nor enough ranges to teach a million men how to hit what they shoot at. It takes lots of practice to become a good shot. That's why you ought to be at it now, on your own hook. Battle is like hunting big game; if you're slow on the trigger, you'll miss on the jump; yet if you rain bullets blindly, you'll miss—miss—miss. There's this difference, though: in battle the game shoots back at you."

"What would you do, then, in my place?"

"Join a rifle club, or organize one among your neighbors, and get busy. There's nothing else will help you so much to give a good account of yourself when the big test comes. Learn to shoot quick and straight, so you may get the Hun before he gets you."

From *Outing*, November 1917

GOOD FOR DAD, TOO

Among the millions who are over-age, or for other reasons are exempt from call to the colors, there are potential armies for home defence. The emergencies that demand such service come suddenly like floods or fires. A mob laughs at a posse of city men who never fired a gun. It quails before a band of cowboys or mountaineers who are known to be crack shots. The rangers and hill-billies may never have learned "fours right," but it is sure death to buck against them, just the same, and a mob knows it.

You may be 'way beyond military age, you may have a deaf ear or a game leg, may be flat-footed or under-weight, but if you have learned to shoot quick and straight you will be as good a man as anybody to face rioters who have their blood up. And it will make you confident and calm when called upon to defend your home, your town, your flag.

Don't imagine that you are a born marksman merely because your gran'dad was a deerslayer. Straight shooting is not an inherited gift. It comes from practice. Gran'dad used a rifle from boyhood, not for fun only, but to get meat. He had to be a good shot or go hungry. You have no such stimulus nor opportunity. But you can become a good shot, just the same, by practicing on the range. Go to it.

THE NATIONAL RIFLE ASSOCIATION

You can't shoot a rifle all around the country. There must be a safe and suitable range laid out and fitted up for the purpose. That is one reason why you should join a rifle club. Another is that you need coaching. If you start practicing by yourself you are likely to make slow progress and acquire bad methods. You would soon be overestimating yourself, by ignoring the wild shots and chuckling over the lucky ones. A fellow who trusts to luck never becomes a good shot. In club shooting every wild shot is marked and it cuts down your average. You get in the habit of trying your darndest to make every bullet hit the bullseye—and *that's* what makes a marksman.

But is there a rifle range in your neighborhood? Is there a club in your town? Ask the National Rifle Association: it knows. The N. R. A., as it is called for short, comprises more than 2,300 rifle clubs. Such clubs have been organized in every State in the Union, and in our outlying possessions.

The objects of the N. R. A., as stated in its by-laws, are "to encourage marksmanship throughout the United States, particularly in the direction of qualifying as finished marksmen those individuals who may be called upon to serve in time of war; to encourage competition in marksmanship between teams and individuals; to encourage legislation for the establishment and maintenance of ranges; to secure the issue of military rifles and ammunition to those practicing on these ranges, and to create a public sentiment in respect to the necessity of rifle practice as a means of National Defence."

The Association furnishes instructions for the forming and maintaining of rifle clubs, associates them in a common cause, helps to secure for them the free use of military ranges, or, if none such exist in the neighborhood, gives detailed instructions for selecting and laying out rifle ranges, and supplies clubs with the necessary range equipment at a reasonable price. It offers medals for individual proficiency and for club competition, and publishes weekly the names of men who have qualified as marksmen, sharpshooters, or experts, and the scores made in inter-club matches.

The N. R. A. is officially recognized by the War Department and has direct charge of all Government rifle clubs. It acts under regulations prescribed by the National Board for the Promotion of Rifle Practice, appointed by Congress, and with the approval of the Secretary of War.

HOW TO ORGANIZE A RIFLE CLUB

Get together as many of your friends as are interested in the project. If there is a military rifle range near your town, go to the officers in charge, state that you are forming an N. R. A. club, and ask permission to use the range for rifle practice when it is otherwise vacant. Both the Federal and the State authorities are generally liberal in this respect. At the Winthrop, Md., rifle range, last summer, more than six thousand civilians were coached and put through qualification courses, without interfering with the regular work of training small arms coaches for the Navy.

If there is no range already established in your neighborhood, seek a suitable place to lay out one and learn the terms upon which it can be rented. If indoor shooting is contemplated, look up a building for your gallery and club room. Send to the Secretary of the N. R. A. for a club membership application form, and get from him prices on targets and other equipment. Then publish a call in your local papers for a meeting to organize a rifle club, explain its purpose, and present arguments to boost it.

A Government rifle club may be organized in any community by ten or more male citizens of the United States over sixteen years of age (boys' clubs are organized under special rules for which apply to the Secretary of the N. R. A., whose address is given below). No physical qualification is required of members, nor are they under any special obligation for war service.

An alien is eligible to membership if he has taken out his first papers and signified his intention of becoming a citizen. Women can only be associate or non-active members, but they may shoot on the club ranges, provided they do not use ammunition issued free by the Government. Many clubs have special matches for women.

When the meeting is ready, select a name for your club (preferably that of your town, unless there is already another club by that name), elect a President, Vice President, Secretary, Treasurer, and Executive Officer, adopt the by-laws prescribed by the National Board for the Promotion of Rifle Practice (see below), and fix the initiation fee and dues.

The application of the club for membership in the N. R. A. is then made on a form supplied by its Secretary. He will inform you who is the N. R. A. Secretary for your State. Your application will be sent to the State Secretary and by him will be transmitted to the Adjutant General for approval and forwarding to the Secretary of the N. R. A. at Washington.

An application fee of $10.00, payable to the National Rifle Association of America, should accompany the application. Dues begin the first of January following affiliation.

On approval of the application by the Executive Committee of the N. R. A., the club will be certified to the Ordnance Department, Arsenals, and the Adjutant General of the State.

Until recently, Krag rifles and ammunition, or sometimes Springfields, were issued free by the United States to organized rifle clubs—rifles in the proportion of one for every five members, ammunition 120 rounds a year for each member—and clubs were permitted to purchase at cost ordnance supplies from the Government. Owing to the present urgent need of all available ordnance stores, these privileges have been suspended by the Secretary of War, but it is more than likely that he will lift the embargo to the extent of allowing all affiliated clubs to draw a certain number of rifles and ammunition so as to be able to continue practice.

The N. R. A. gives a medal annually to each club for competition among the club members. A qualification button will be given each member qualifying as marksman, sharpshooter, or expert rifleman.

The Secretary of the N. R. A. is Brig. Gen. Fred H. Phillips, Jr., 1110 Woodward Building, Washington, D. C.

It is not necessary to incorporate a rifle club unless real estate is to be purchased by it.

GOVERNMENT RIFLE CLUB—BY-LAWS

For Adoption by Rifle Clubs Affiliated with the National Rifle Association of America—Approved by the National Board for Promotion of Rifle Practice and the Secretary of War

ARTICLE I. The name of this organization shall be. . . . . Rifle Club.

ARTICLE II. The object of this organization shall be the encouragement of military rifle and pistol shooting.

ARTICLE III. Any citizen of the United States over sixteen years of age may become a member of the organization on vote of the Executive Committee and on payment of the usual initiation fee and dues.

ARTICLE IV. The officers of the organization shall be a President, Vice-President, Secretary, Treasurer, and Executive Officer, who, acting together, shall constitute the Executive Committee. They shall be elected by a majority vote by ballot at the annual meeting of the organization, and hold office for one year or until their successors are elected.

ARTICLE V. The annual meeting of the organization shall be held on the first Saturday of January in each year. If the annual meeting shall not take place at the time fixed it shall be held within a reasonable time thereafter and the officers shall hold over until their successors shall have been elected. One-third of the members of the organization shall constitute a quorum for the transaction of business.

ARTICLE VI. The annual dues of the organization shall be $. . . . . , and shall be payable on or before the first day of February in each year. No member of the organization in arrears shall be eligible to any of the benefits offered by the National Rifle Association. The initiation fee shall be $. . . . .

ARTICLE VII. The duties of the officers shall be such as the club members may agree upon, provided that a part of such duties shall consist of some duly authorized officer of the club making a certified list of the newly elected officers of the organization and a list of the members in good standing to the National Rifle Association on February 1 of each year.

ARTICLE VIII. The affairs of the organization shall be managed by the Executive Committee, who shall have general supervision of the affairs of the club. Meetings shall be held at any time on the call of the President, and three shall constitute a quorum.

The Secretary shall notify the members of the Executive Committee of all meetings, and shall send each member of the club notice of the annual meeting. He shall keep a true record of all meetings of the Executive Committee and of the annual meetings, have the custody of the books and papers of the club and conduct all correspondence. All applications for membership shall be made direct to the Secretary. He shall be responsible for the collection of all fees and dues, and shall remit the same to the Treasurer, taking his proper receipt therefor.

The Treasurer shall have charge of all funds of the organization, and place the same in such bank or banks as may be approved by the Executive Committee. Such money shall only be withdrawn by check signed by the Treasurer, and for the payment of such bills as shall have been approved by the Executive Committee. He shall keep account of all his transactions and make a detail report, with vouchers, at any meeting of the Executive Committee when requested, and an annual report to the Association at its annual meeting.

The Executive Officer shall have charge of the ranges of the club, the printing of score cards, the arranging of competitions, etc., and shall turn over to the Treasurer such moneys as may be received for entrance fees, etc. No bills shall be contracted without the authorization of the Executive Committee.

ARTICLE IX. Any member whose conduct shall be decided, by a majority vote of the Executive Committee, to have been injurious to the interest or welfare of the club shall forfeit his membership and rights, but such vote shall not be taken without giving the offender two weeks' notice of the charges against him and affording him an opportunity of being heard in his defence. He may appeal from a decision of the committee to the club at a special meeting called for that purpose, but it shall require a two-thirds vote of those present to reverse the committee's decision.

ARTICLE X. All rifle and revolver competitions held by the club will be governed by the rules and regulations as laid down by the National Rifle Association of America, approved by the National Board for Promotion of Rifle Practice and the Secretary of War.

ARTICLE XI. Any amendment to these by-laws must be submitted to the National Rifle Association for its approval, and, if such is given, it may be presented at any meeting of the club after having been sent to each member at least ten days previously. A two-thirds vote of the members present will be necessary to pass it.

Before the war, a member of a Government rifle club could buy a Krag or a Springfield from the Ordnance Department for less than the cost of a common sporting rifle. The free issue of ammunition was limited to 120 rounds annually per man, and this, of course, was by no means enough to make a first-class shot out of a beginner; but he could buy from the Government all the ammunition he desired at much less than the market price.

This privilege has been suspended, and it is not known how soon the sale of ordnance stores to civilian rifle clubs will be renewed. Meantime the N. R. A. has obtained special rates for its members from commercial manufacturers of ammunition and will act as purchasing agent for its affiliated clubs.

The cost of Krag or Springfield ammunition can be reduced by saving the fired shells and reloading with powder, bullets, and primers bought for the purpose. Each club should have an armory reloading outfit, with which such work can be done rapidly and with precision. In this way the cost of military rifle ammunition may be cut down to a par with that of trap ammunition, notwithstanding the high prices now prevalent.

There is another system of rifle shooting, of a very practical nature, that comes within the limits of even the small boy's pocket-book, and which is now being adopted by the big boys and old boys of the N. R. A. as a substitute for the regular military course. With a suitable .22 caliber rifle one can practice nearly all of the military stunts, at reduced ranges and on targets proportionally reduced, slow fire and rapid fire, standing, kneeling, squatting, or prone. A proper range for such work is much more easily found than one for using full charges in a service rifle, and ten shots can be fired at the cost of a single shotgun cartridge.

BUSINESSLIKE SHOOTING WITH THE .22

Formerly the .22 was used by target shooters chiefly for gallery practice, at 75 feet, offhand. There is scarcely a crack shot in the country who does not use the .22 freely "to keep his hand in," especially in the winter season. It is by all odds the best arm for preliminary training, to teach steady holding, true aiming, and steady let-off. A beginner will master these essentials sooner with the miniature arm than if he started with a high-power rifle.

Offhand practice in the gallery has this disadvantage, from a club standpoint, that only a few men ever become expert in shooting from the standing position, and interest flags as soon as a majority of the members learn that they are hopelessly outclassed in the game. Besides, from a practical standpoint, exclusive attention to offhand shooting is a mistake; for most of the infantry fire in modern war is delivered from a squatting or prone position, and much of it from a sandbag or other rest.

There are ten men who can do good work with a rifle under those conditions to one who can keep on driving the center in slow fire offhand. Recognizing these facts, the N. R. A. changed the rules for indoor competitions to allow and encourage shooting from the prone position.

But gallery practice is by no means the useful limit of this fascinating little weapon. With proper ammunition the .22 rim-fire rifle is capable of making fine scores at ten times the regulation indoor range. At the various distances for outdoor shooting, from 50 to 250 yards, with the .22, one must study and apply the same principles of sight elevation and windage as if he were using a Springfield with service ammunition at 200 to 1,000 yards.

OUTDOOR QUALIFICATION COURSE WITH THE SMALL-BORE

During the period of the suspension of free issue and sale of ordnance supplies by the War Department, the N. R. A. has authorized a qualification course with .22 caliber rim-fire rifles. The tentative plan, subject to revision after the clubs have tried it out, calls for shooting at 50, 75, 125, and 150 yards, at targets proportionally reduced from the regular 200, 300, 500, and 600 yard targets employed with the service rifle.

The slow fire course requires ten shots each at 75, 125, and 150 yards, from the prone position, with no time limit. A sandbag rest is permitted.

The rapid fire course calls for ten shots in 1½ minutes with a repeater, or 2 minutes with single-shot rifle, kneeling, at 50 yards, and ten shots in 2 minutes, prone, at 75 yards.

This is for qualification as marksman, sharpshooter, or expert rifleman. The individual may shoot as many ten-shot scores as he pleases in any target season, and his rating will be determined by the best of them. The possible is 250 points. The requirements are 210 points for expert, 190 points for sharpshooter, and 160 points for marksman, and buttons will be awarded accordingly.

After qualifying as above, experts and sharpshooters may shoot for record at 200 and 250 yards, on targets proportionally reduced from those used in the army at 800 and 1,000 yards.

In this way rifle shooting is made the cheapest, as it is also one of the most fascinating, of all outdoor sports [*sic*]

Roving with Kephart

NEW THINGS IN GUNNERY

If a rifleman could see the actual path of each bullet, as an Indian sees where his arrow goes, he could do better shooting. This has been accomplished, to some extent, by means of tracer bullets. During the war it was found that tracer bullets were the best indicators of range, provided they were made to shoot with the same accuracy and trajectory as the service cartridges.

Accuracy and trajectory are vital matters in war. For instance, when infantry advances after a lifting barrage fire, accurate work by artillerists and machine gunners in the rear leads the way to victory. An error on their part massacres their own comrades in the assault.

To do the work right it is absolutely necessary to know just how far a given gun will shoot at such and such elevations. And the angle at which the bullet descends, at each range, must also be known, so as to give safe clearance for the assaulting troops.

But when we went into the war nobody knew how our rifle and machine gun ammunition really did shoot at long ranges. We had range tables of elevation, and so forth, which were supposed to be reliable; but they were not. These tables had been computed by mathematics. Up to 1,200 yards they had been checked off against results of actual firing, and corrected accordingly. But beyond 1,200 yards they were merely computations, and all wrong.

The reason they were wrong was that they assumed that the bullet always flies point-on, with reference to air resistance. But that is not so. The path of a bullet is a curve. The projectile does not shift its point to coincide with that curve, but tries to maintain the same position in which it started.

So a bullet really travels through the air obliquely, its point spinning around a longer axis than the base, and this obliquity increases with the range. It follows that

---

From *All Outdoors,* October 1920

the air-thrust against the bullet is greater than if the bullet met it point-on, and that it acts on a larger and larger surface as the distance increases.

It was necessary to learn the facts about our rifle and machine-gun ammunition, and to learn them quickly. It was also necessary to improve this ammunition. We had been patting ourselves on the back, and bragging a good deal, in the fond belief that our service ammunition was the best in the world; but the hard facts of war proved that it was nothing of the kind.

A semi-official report in *Arms and the Man*, last October, stated that "When the present ball cartridge, model of 1906, is used in machine-gun work, recent war experience shows that its effective range is limited to 2,400 metres. . . . Upon this showing, the Springfield cartridge, both in ranging and killing power, is excelled by the service ammunition of practically all of the first-class European powers, not excepting Germany; for even the Hun, during the later days of the war, produced a machine-gun bullet with an effective range of 3,500 metres."

THE BOAT-TAILED BULLET

This increase in efficiency was partly due to the use of longer and heavier bullets than our 150-grain Springfield. But it was influenced yet more by the adoption of a bullet that slopes off to the rear like the stern of a boat, instead of having a flat base of full caliber that acts as a drag in the air.

A few of us American riflemen had been advocating such a bullet for a good many years; but we were laughed at as "theorists." Our critics did not try the thing—they only offered theoretical objections—and why they did not call themselves theorists I don't know. Anyway that is ancient history now; for the boat-tailed bullet has been tried; and all nations that had not adopted the boat-tailed bullet before the war, or during it, are tumbling over themselves to do so now.

While the war was in progress the defects of the Springfield bullet were so obvious that something had to be done in the way of devising a better one. Before the armistice was signed our Government quietly established a unique ballistic station at Miami, Florida, on which tests could be made at all ranges. The shooting at Miami is done over a sheltered waterway, and the point where every bullet hits is noted exactly by instruments.

It was found that whereas the maximum range of the 150-grain Springfield bullet had been computed to be 4,400 yards, its actual utmost limit of range was 3,100 yards. A 180-grain flat base bullet from the same gun carried 4,100 yards, and a 176-grain boat-tailed bullet of Swiss pattern reached 5,100 yards.

Experiments are still being conducted with the object of perfecting a boat-tailed bullet and an improved cartridge for the service rifle and machine guns. A decopperizing or anti-fouling powder is used, which will do away with the nuisance of cleaning with ammonia solutions that have to be made up fresh every week or so.

Fifty or more combinations with boat-tailed bullets had been tested up to last April. The best results were attained with one of 175 grains weight, a boat tail about .28 inches long, and a modified service point.

Using this bullet, with a charge of Du Pont No. 1013 powder, giving a muzzle velocity of 2,600 feet sec., with a chamber pressure of only 39,000 lbs. per sq. inch, the striking energy at 5,100 metres was equal to that of the 150-grain Springfield bullet at 2,700 metres. The latter starts with 100 feet sec. higher velocity, and, with the present service powder, sets up a chamber pressure of about 51,000 lbs. per sq. inch.

The trajectory of the boat-tailed bullet is, of course, lower than that of the flat-base bullet.

With the charge mentioned above the mean radius of shots is 4.76 inches at 600 yards. This is much better accuracy than the service cartridge gives. In fact it is almost as good as that of the special match ammunition, with 170-grain bullet, prepared for this year's national matches at Camp Perry.

THE BEVIS TRAJECTOGRAPH

It is possible to work out a mathematical formula that will serve to compute very closely the course of a bullet at any range. This has recently been done by Dr. J. R. Bevis, the ballistician. He has produced a true C-formula that takes into account the gyratory spin of the bullet.

Hitherto the factor C (ballistic coefficient), which measures the ability of a given projectile to overcome air resistance, has been assumed, in the case of the 150-grain Springfield bullet, to be .389 at all ranges. It is .389 for 500 yards; but the Bevis formula shows it to be only .360 for 1,000 yards, .316 for 1,500 yards, and .27 for 2,000 yards. These values correspond with results obtained in actual firing.

But Dr. Bevis has gone far beyond this in the way of determining the actual path of a flying bullet. He wrote me a good while ago that "There is no reason why the trajectory of a rifle bullet over any range, outdoors, may not be described, and a permanent record made thereof, in exact miniature, in a room, by the very means of the bullet itself during its flight.

"There is no reason why the velocity of a rifle bullet may not be had at any intervals desired.

"There is no reason why an enclosed experimental rifle range of 500 yards should not be constructed, and the flight of the bullet studied throughout its entire trajectory.

"Beyond 500 yards the velocity should be had at intervals of 100 yards, and a miniature record of its trajectory made to the maximum practical range. All of which could be accomplished at the flight of each bullet."

Well, I am informed by Bevis himself that he has actually designed the apparatus to do these very things. He calls it a trajectograph. By this means an exact miniature of the trajectory is made indoors by the flight of the bullet itself outdoors, and he reports that the limit of error in height of trajectory, at any place, is about two-tenths of one inch.

I have not the slightest idea on what principle this instrument works, much less how it is operated. I do not know whether it has actually been tested out. Doctor Bevis is an invalid, and has been in the hospital for a long time. There may be other hindrances in the way that I know not of. But if the thing does the work that he claims for it we will have here the greatest contribution to the science of gunnery that has been made since rifling was invented; for it will give positive means of learning just what is the best possible projectile.

Because Bevis is a mathematician he will be called a theorist by superior people who "don't believe anything but what we see." But that reminds me of a story they tell of Thomas Carlyle.

"It was at a dinner party, and Carlyle sat silent, listening to the talk of lesser men, the snow on his hair and the fire in his amber eyes. A young liberal was talking theory to a beefy old conservative who despised youth and reason in an equal degree.

"'The British people, sir,' said he of the beef, 'can afford to laugh at theories.'

"'Sir,' said Carlyle, speaking for the first time during the dinner, 'the French nobility of a hundred years ago said they could afford to laugh at theories. Then came a man and wrote a book called the "Social Contract." The man was called Jean Jacques Rousseau, and his book was a theory and nothing but a theory. The nobles could laugh at his theory; but their skins went to bind the second edition of his book.'"

Every improvement that has been made in firearms started with a theory.

THEORIES—HALF-BAKED OR HARD-BOILED

Of course, there is a sort of theorizing that does more harm than good. There is the underdone kind, as well as the hard-boiled kind. Our Patent Office is crammed with "inventions" that never could have been good for anything. And our sportsmen's journals contain a deal of bunk.

It is to be said for the Patent Office that it guarantees nothing but that the one to whom a patent has been granted has, so far as the examiners know, discovered a new combination of things. And the outdoor magazine can at least say for itself that it suppresses vastly more trash than ever gets into its columns.

There should be no quarrel at all between the man of theory and the man of practice. Each is indispensable to the other. A theory that has not been put to the proof is, so far, only a dream that may or may not come true. And a man who never dreams of new and better things will forever stay in a rut unless somebody else lifts him out.

I have seen the time, not once but twice or thrice, when it did not seem humanly possible that the rifle, for example, could be made much more efficient than it then was. But along would come smokeless powder, or a new projectile, doing things the old stuff never could have done, and bringing new problems of its own to theorize over and experiment with.

The gunners of two hundred years ago could have said the same thing with the same sincerity. And so, no doubt, will it be with those of A. D. 2120.

There are rumors flying around that quite revolutionary changes are to be made in firearms. There is the shelless cartridge, for example—not at all a new thing in principle, for there were self-consuming cartridge cases before the Civil war—and there is the electric gun fired by merely pressing a button, which is another old idea that was tried before the day of practical breech-loaders.

Don't turn up your noses. Just because an invention failed fifty years ago is no sign that it won't work out now, when there are auxiliaries that the old inventors lacked.

There is nothing inherently impossible in the idea of a destructive force that can be projected without any deflection at all from gravity or wind. Take a beam of light projected by a mirror, for instance. A child can hit the mark with it, and never aim at all, as we understand the term. Imagine, then, a life-destroying ray (there is such a thing) and a portable apparatus to produce and "shoot" it.

During the war a prominent attorney, known to me to be a man of unblemished reputation, solemnly declared to several of his friends that he accompanied a party of government officials and Thomas A. Edison, in a boat, on one of the great lakes, to the neighborhood of an island on which a number of cattle had been placed for experimental purposes. He said that Mr. Edison destroyed these cattle at long range by a soundless and invisible force. The details of what happened to them were gruesome. And he said that the Government refused to utilize such an inhuman method of waging war, just as the British authorities did with Admiral Lord Dundonald's poison gas invention during the Crimean War.

The news has gone broadcast, and it has recently been reasserted by one of our nominees for the Presidency, that our Army is already in possession of poison gas so deadly that a whole city can be struck dead with it from the sky. And worse things—but let us change the subject. There is no limit to the science of extermination. Let us help to keep it in safe hands.

Arms for Defense of Honest Citizens

AN ANSWER TO MR. THOMPSON OF CHICAGO AND ALL OTHERS WHO AGREE WITH HIM

In the *New York Times* of June 9, 1921, I noticed the following display advertisement:

I will pay $1,000 to anyone who will give one good reason why the revolver manufacturing industry should be allowed to exist in America and enjoy the facilities of the mails.

John R. Thompson, Chicago, Ill.

Mr. Thompson is president of a chain of one hundred and forty-four restaurants and stores located in thirty-six cities of the Union, covering the country from New York to Kansas City and from Chicago to New Orleans. No doubt he can well afford to spend money on propaganda against anything he dislikes.

But who would waste breath trying to convince the man who issues such a challenge and makes himself the sole judge of merit? Is it likely that such a person, so ostentatiously cocksure, would listen to any facts that confute his opinions?

One of my friends wrote to Mr. Thompson, not to argue the matter with him, but merely asking him to explain the process of reasoning by which he arrived at the conclusion that prohibition of pistols would eliminate or even restrict crime. In reply he received the following ready-prepared circular:

Chicago, June 20, 1921.
Dear Sir:

Many letters have been received in answer to my advertisement, and this letter is written as a reply.

The revolver is made to be concealed. No honest citizen nor honest purpose requires a concealed weapon. Therefore, no good reason exists for its manufacture or sale.

From *Outing*, September 1921

The rifle and shotgun have good uses and they meet all legitimate requirements for firearms. The public disarmed, our police can have no use for the revolver.

Had the assassins of our three martyred Presidents carried rifles their murderous intent would have been discovered—the crimes prevented.

The revolver creates the professional criminal, the thug, the footpad, the burglar, the murderer. And yet the manufacturers of revolvers enjoy the facilities of the United States mails and every protection given to honest business.

I have challenged the manufacturers, who have made tremendous fortunes out of the manufacture and sale of revolvers, to give one good reason for their use. They have not done so, and they cannot, and this branch of their industry should not be permitted to continue.

The definite purpose of this publicity is to stop by legislative enactment the manufacture, importation, sale and use of the revolver; is to arouse a tremendous public sentiment that will back up our legislative bodies in putting through the necessary legislation. National disarmament would be a great blessing. The disarmament of our citizens would be a blessing to the home, and would bring safety and security into our everyday life.

Very truly yours,
John R. Thompson.

Evidently this writer had settled the case to his own satisfaction before presenting it to the bar of public opinion, and he would have our state and national legislatures do likewise, in the good new way.

There are, however, more than seven million sportsmen in this country who own and use firearms for hunting and target practice. Most of these citizens own revolvers or other pistols, as well as their larger weapons. Many other millions of Americans possess pistols for personal and home defence. Criminals form only a small percentage of this reserve army of the nation. The honest men and women in this multitude deserve a hearing.

We all deplore the wave of crime that has followed in the wake of war and social upheaval. We detest hold-ups, burglaries, and butcheries with firearms as much as we do those committed with knives, hatchets, blackjacks, poisons, and bombs. But let us use common sense in our methods of combating crime, not confusing the instrument with the deed, nor means with motive.

One thing is certain: criminals never attack until they are sure the police are out of the way. Then they strike quickly. The victim finds himself almost or quite at hands' grip with his assailant. There is no time to go after a shotgun, much less to call and wait for help. The citizen must be his own warrior, his own policeman, his own defender of his life and home. And if he is not a match for the thug, he will go under.

Another thing is certain: more crimes of violence were committed, proportionally, in the days of sword and dirk than now. Such arms gave every advantage to the athletic thug over honest citizens weakened by indoor labor or muscle-bound by outdoor toil. No untrained man had a chance against the robber or assassin who was always practicing and perfecting his skill with rapier and knife.

But things changed when the revolver came in. Even a delicate woman, having a pistol, was now made dangerous for any brute to attack.

The best protection we have against robbery and arson, murder and rape, is the fact that, so far, a majority of our honest citizens have arms and know how to use them. Without these minute-men, ready and on the spot, our police and army would have to be increased tenfold.

Mr. Thompson and his ilk are certainly naïve. Do they really believe that prohibition of the manufacture and ownership of pistols, instead of proper regulation, would do anything more than disarm good citizens—do they believe it would keep men of criminal intent from carrying concealed weapons? Surely they have more sense than that.

Deprive a crook of his pistol, and how long will it take him to saw off most of the barrel and stock of a shotgun and carry it under his coat? Such a weapon is far more deadly than any revolver or automatic pistol, because it knocks down and kills at the first shot. Any military man will tell you so.

The next step, then, would be to prohibit the manufacture and sale of all firearms whatever. Well, suppose you did: what then is to hinder the making of bombs? Stop the sale of explosives? Why, that is childish. Anybody with a rudimentary knowledge of chemistry (and that includes many of the criminal class) can make high explosives out of raw materials that he can buy anywhere. He can even make a serviceable gunpowder out of sugar and throat lozenges. And anybody who does not know how to do such things can soon learn for himself in the public library. So let us amend the Constitution to destroy all libraries and to stop teaching chemistry in the schools!

We have mentioned that little-read document, the Constitution of the United States. Its Fifth Amendment,[4] which is part of what we call our Bill of Rights, reads: "A well-regulated militia being necessary to the security of a free State, the right of the people to keep and bear arms shall not be infringed."

Authorities on constitutional law agree that the term "arms" in this passage means "any arms suitable for military purposes." Revolvers and pistols of adequate killing power are such weapons, and they can easily be carried concealed.

The long and the short of it is that Mr. Thompson's propaganda seeks to make criminals out of millions of honest Americans if they continue to exercise what is now, and always has been, their legal right guaranteed to them in perpetuity by the Constitution of the United States.

The Right to Bear Arms

THE REAL SAFEGUARD AGAINST ANARCHY LIES IN "MILLIONS OF GOOD CIVILIANS WHO HAVE ARMS AND KNOW HOW TO USE THEM"

Within the past twelve years about forty of my personal acquaintances have killed someone, or have been killed, in gunfights. All this happened in my own county and those adjoining it, which are so thinly settled that their combined population is less than that of Erie, Pa., or Utica, N. Y.

These killers and their victims were not just names in the morning paper, to me. They were not people I had never heard of before and cared nothing about. I knew them individually; in most cases I knew their families or associates, I attended many of the trials, and in a few of those trials I was a witness.

None of these homicides was committed by a professional criminal. There was not one instance among them of a holdup, robbery, burglary or even theft. They were just fights between hot-headed men in a belated region where a fifteenth-century code of honor still persists and dominates public sentiment.

Every one of these killings, save the latest, was done with a pistol.

Does it follow that no murder would have been done if there had been no pistols?

It does not.

I knew these men. If they had been armed with nothing but fifteenth-century weapons there would have been as many casualties. Back in the fifteenth century, in reality, everybody who was somebody carried a sword, and everybody who was nobody carried a dirk. There were more homicides then, in proportion to the population, than we have now, in our year of the automobile and the automatic.

Cain did not kill Abel with a pistol. No pistol ever slaughtered men so fast as a certain celebrated jawbone of an ass.

It would be silly to blame the instrument for the deed, or to think that by abolishing up-to-date weapons we could abolish robbery and murder.

From *Outing*, May 1922

If we want to check crime (and who among us sportsmen does not?) then, for goodness' sake, let us try to find some way that will work.

Going back to my forty cases—could they have been prevented by other laws than what we already had?

Well, let us eliminate a few at the start. Some of those men (take my word for it) needed killing.

Why not, then, by due process of law?

Because the law, in these cases, was impotent. If you were away off in a wilderness by yourself, and a bad man came along and attacked you with a deadly weapon, could you sit down there and wait for the sheriff? A consistent pacifist might do so; but he would be murdered, and his murderer would get away.

All of our non-resistants, men and women, who practice what they preach, owe their lives, their property, their honor, to neighbors who have arms, who know how to use them effectively and who have the manhood to do it whenever necessary.

But most of my dead acquaintances did not need killing. Would a new law have saved any of them?

Suppose, for instance, the Shields bill prohibiting the manufacture or sale of concealable weapons had already been passed.

It would not have saved a single one of these lives; because every one of the killers already owned a pistol. There is a saying here: "Everybody in this county who oughtn't to have a pistol has two."

Suppose, then, a far more drastic Federal law had been enacted, ordering all concealable weapons to be confiscated and destroyed. What would have resulted?

Not to trust my own judgment alone, I went out the other day and put that question to the first five or six prominent and responsible citizens that I met in my home town. Each and every man answered frankly: "They wouldn't get mine."

"Would you resist search and seizure?"

"No: not if the officer had a warrant. But I'd know about that law before the officer got around; and then I'd let him smell his nose off."

These were typical good citizens talking, any one of them acceptable on a grand jury, and every one of them a church member.

What, then, could be done to cure a homicidal tendency, if prohibitory laws would do no good?

Well, consider this particular problem. No actual criminals involved who would kill for the sake of gain. Just an old-fashioned people with an old-fashioned code of honor that they valued higher than life itself. So long as that code persists there will be killings among them. In most cases whiskey started the quarrel; but it would be a perversion of truth to lay the whole blame on whiskey. What whiskey really did was to inflame passion and bring on insult or injury. But under just the same circumstances men of other communities would have fought the quarrel out with their fists. Here, under the fifteenth-century code, it must be settled with weapons.

Therefore, in this set of cases, a modern code must first be substituted for the ancient one; and you can't do that by legislative enactment any more than you could turn back the tide of the sea by such means. Church and school must effect the change.

But we sportsmen stand for fair play—it is the cornerstone of *our* code—and so let us be fair to even this ancient standard of honor. It has its good points as well as bad ones. Wherever it prevails there is more politeness between man and man (drunks excepted) than we see in modernized communities. In a land where nearly every man goes armed, every sober man treats his fellows with respect, he regards others' rights, he avoids giving offence. And so there are fewer fights than in the other sort of society, the modernized sort; though the fights that do occur are likely to be deadly.

And in the old-fashioned land there is far less crime against property—the sort of crime that professional criminals practice—than in new-fashioned places. Burglary and robbery are so rare as to be almost never on the court calendar. That is because the thug knows that every citizen is well prepared to take care of himself and his home. Crooks do not thrive, they do not even linger, where everybody carries a gun and knows very well how to use it.

But what is the use of mentioning such exceptional people and extraordinary conditions?

Well, maybe, not so exceptional as you think. In considering new legislation that is to govern every community in the United States, whether they locally want it or not, we should first of all consider whether it would work or not. Unenforceable laws are worse than no laws.

That old-fashioned code I have been talking about is the actual standard today in at least one-third of the territory of the United States. And it is the actual standard of countless individuals outside that third.

But let us turn now to the rest of the country and to the people who accept the modern standard.

Here we meet a quite different problem, as regards anti-firearms legislation. It is the problem of the armed crook. Can we disarm him by prohibiting the manufacture and sale of pistols? If not—if he will arm himself in spite of everything that laws and policemen and courts can do—then is it wise to prohibit decent citizens from owning the best weapons for self defence and home defence?

One question at a time. Can we disarm the crook?

It answers itself. A criminal can make his own weapons. We have laws against burglars' tools, but they have never done the least good on earth except to fasten an incidental guilt on anyone found carrying them. Our present laws against carrying concealed weapons do the same thing.

But a crook could not make a good revolver or automatic pistol.

No; why should he, if nobody else could get one? He would far rather employ a silent weapon, a sandbag or a knife, than a noisy one that instantly attracts attention and compels him to get away at once.

Bear in mind that I am not arguing for unrestricted traffic in pistols, or any other sort of weapons. I don't care two whoops for the commercial side of the question. All I am interested in is how to devise a practical way to fight crime, a way that will work. As a gun expert I know that anti-pistol laws would not work. All the propaganda of this sort that has been spread about by newspapers and by societies and by individuals is just a waste of breath. It helps to defeat the very cause it has enlisted under—does so by advertising as a cure-all something that is a mere quack nostrum.

Good citizen! use [*sic*] your wits a bit. Put yourself, for the moment, in the crook's place. (If you haven't enough power of imagination for that, if you can't summon enough of it to enter the ABC class of a detective correspondence school, then, for the Lord's sake, don't try to frame laws against crime!)

What would you do if you were a robber, burglar, high-jacker, and the Government sent its agents everywhere confiscating pistols? You know they couldn't grab up ten million pistols in one night, nor in six months, nor in six years. And there are more than ten million pistols in this country right now. If you were a crook you would know plenty of places where such arms could be procured, law or no law. I am no crook; but I could buy a wagonload of them within forty-eight hours after the law was passed.

The next question: If crooks cannot be deprived of concealable weapons, then should good citizens be prohibited from owning defensive weapons that would place them on partly even terms with the crook in a fight?

Doesn't that answer itself, too? I can imagine only one plausible rejoinder, which is that the good citizen lacks either the skill to hit what he shoots at or the "guts" to do it.

Well, if that is so, then we have come to a pretty pass—we the descendants of a line of pioneers who fought their way from sea to sea against enemies compared with which the doped gunman of the city street is a rotten coward. If that is so, then we are not worth the powder to shoot us down.

It is not so. There are four million registered sportsmen in this country licensed to use firearms in the field. They know how to shoot. There are four million ex-service men who were taught how to shoot, if they did not already know. There are other millions who could and would give good account of themselves in an encounter with arms.

There stands our real safeguard against anarchy—back of the police and the standing army, those millions of good civilians *who have arms and who know how to use them.*

If we must pass a nation-wide law about pistols let it be a law that encourages reputable citizens to get the best ones and train themselves to use them right, and that makes it as difficult as possible for disreputable citizens to get arms equally good. The crook has too much advantage as things are. Turn the tables on him.

I purposely began this article with instances of gunfighting that a propagandist would seize upon as proof positive that all pistols should be confiscated. Perhaps I have told him some things he will not relish, because they show another side to the matter—a side that mere emotionalism cannot or will not see. But, anyway, my object in mentioning those forty cases was to show that I am no theorist airing a hobby, but a serious observer of actual conditions whose own experience has made him think long and earnestly on this rather serious subject. That is why I have no patience with emotional reformers who jump up and ballyhoo about fake nostrums when the body politic is already sick from overdosing. Let us use less medicine and more sense.

A Backwoods Riflemaker

Carman had come a thousand miles from New York to bid on equipment for a sanitarium in the Carolina mountains. While waiting for the trustees to act he had a few days on his hands. His mind turned to his favorite sport.

"Any big game here in the mountains?" he asked the hotel clerk.

"Some bear, back in the roughs. Deer all hounded out."

"If I should come back in the fall for a bear-hunt, who could I get to guide me?"

"Well, there's Long John Gilbert. He's sixty-odd but is still the best bear hunter in the county, and he has the best dogs."

"Where does he live?"

"About eight miles from here, up Qualla Creek."

"Can one get there in a car?"

"Lord, no! John won't have a wagon-road within a mile of his house: says he don't want to be bothered with improve-*ments*. Why, he's so old-fogyish he won't use a breech-loader."

"By Jove! Just the sort I'd like to meet. Can I have a saddle-horse?"

"Sure." The clerk dropped his voice confidentially: "Some of John's neighbors give him a bad name, but you'll find him a right clever old chap, if you take him right."

Carman smiled. "I don't mind a little moonshining, myself."

"It ain't that. Old John owns about a thousand acres of fine timberland, away up there the lumber companies have been trying to get, but he won't sell. And he keeps a big adjoining tract tied up in boundary litigation. That's stirred up hard feeling. Even the trash around there are mad because it checks them from hauling bark and acid-wood. So that's the nigger in the woodpile."

A colored boy brought out the horse. Carman got detailed directions, mounted and rode off.

A new graded highway followed the river through a rich valley walled in by spurs from the Great Smoky divide. Tourists whizzed by in high-powered cars. Comfortable

---

From *American Rifleman,* July 15, 1924

farmers, purring along leisurely in their Fords, saluted the stranger with good-natured interest.

Three miles from town a swift tributary dashed into the river from a deep and thickly wooded ravine. It was clear and cool and enticingly fit for trout. A highway sign at the bridge gave its name, Qualla Creek.

Carman turned aside into the glen. Abruptly he was shut in by the ancient woods, shut out from the modern cultivated world. The horse climbed a steep ascent over slippery rocks, past a roaring waterfall, then found level footing where the by-road wound along the streamside amid ferns high as his shoulders. He proceeded through deep shadowy silence.

A mile of this, and then suddenly they came out into the glare of a small hillside clearing. A bit of cornfield sloped so steeply down that its rail fence seemed in peril of sliding into the creek.

A bare old cabin of wide-spaced logs stood lone and desolate amid the corn. There was not a tree or a vine to hide its squalor. The hard-tramped dirt around the house had no single flower or spear of grass to take the curse off.

Razorback pigs, starved hounds and ragged children turned startled faces toward the intruder. A frowsy barefooted woman, with snuff-stick in her mouth, slinked into the cabin and peeped out through a chink between the logs. A hard-eyed gawk of a man leaned slack against the fence and sullenly stared.

Carman reined in and inquired: "Does John Gilbert live up this way?"

"Long John does. Little John lives on Pant'er Creek and Joel's John on Silvermine."

"How far is it to Long John's?"

"'Bout four mile, and the furder the better. I don't set no store in ary Gilbert." The fellow spat on the ground as if to spurn the name from his mouth.

Carman rode on, disgusted. "Trash!" he muttered to himself—"trash stranded here in a hurrah's-nest. If there's anything worse, beyond, I'll find Long John Gilbert living in a hollow tree."

Again he entered the forest, and now the growth was unmistakably primeval. Giant trees stood everywhere so close together that their tops were interwoven and few beams of direct sunlight filtered through. Their trunks rose with scarce a perceptible taper, forty, fifty, even sixty feet to the first limb. There were poplars and chestnut trees seven or eight feet thick, above the swell of the butt. The road wound tortuously through a jungle of undergrowth radiant with the pink and white bloom of laurel and rhododendron. There was no track of wheel or hoof that was less than a week old.

A ruffed grouse drummed in the distance. A great hawk swooped overhead. From afar came the flutelike, ascending call of a hermit thrust. The horse splashed joyfully through ford after ford of water as clear as plate glass and alive with darting forms. It amazed Carman to find such an unspoiled Eden within so short a ride from town. He blessed Long John's talent for litigation.

There was one more tenant's clearing, similar to the first, and here was the end of the wagon-road. Beyond it there ran only a trail made by the mountaineer's dry-land sled, a track barely thirty inches wide. This was Long John's way of passage to the outer world. It climbed steep grades and skirted precipices where the outer edge of the trail was held in place by poles laid end-to-end. The tracks showed that no shod animal, but only a steer, was used to pull the settler's sled.

For a mile the trail wound along narrow defiles of the mountain. Then the forest gloom was broken by a token of sunlight ahead, and the traveler came to cleared, level upland, planted in corn that was waist high. Here the surrounding ridges spread wide apart from each other and between them was a fertile "cove," as the mountain people call such a basin amid the hills.

To Carman's surprise, there was a well-built double house on the place: that is to say, twin structures with an open entry between and the whole covered by a single roof. It was of hewn logs, well chinked, ancient but kept in good repair. It stood in the midst of a garden fenced with split palings. There were flower beds in the garden front and a gravel walk to the house. A hundred or more "bee gums" (cuts from hollow logs) were alive with industrious tenants. Old apple and peach trees cast grateful shade in the front yard. Long John might be old-fashioned, but his home showed him to be a man of energy and taste.

Five big bearhounds quickly announced the stranger's visit. A tall, full-bearded man, decently dressed and of commanding presence, called them to heel. Carman hitched his horse, opened an ingeniously fashioned gate that swung on wooden hinges, presented himself to the old man, and was met with a grave but courteous welcome.

"Come into the settin'-room and make yourself at home," said John. "Will you have a nip? I may be jailed for this; but I never could see no harm in offering refreshment to a tired traveler. Seems to me the world's gone plumb crazy over reforms that there ain't nary bitty sense in."

Carman endorsed the sentiment and welcomed the nip. It was pure double-distilled corn that sparkeled [*sic*] with an honest bead and gave no man headaches.

They talked a good while about bear-hunting. Carman, from the first, had observed a heavy muzzle-loading rifle hanging on wooden pegs driven into the wall, which also supported a powder-horn and a leather bullet pouch worn shiny with use.

"Is that your bear-gun?" he inquired.

"Yes," answered John, and he lifted it down and passed it over for inspection.

"It is of larger bore than other Kentuckies I have seen."

"Takes a half-ounce ball," said John, "and it shoots hard enough for the purpose."

"Shoots straight and knocks 'em cold, eh?"

"Well, I've killed more than a hundred bear with it, and there weren't many needed a second shot. You noted it has a bigger bore than common: well, I really made that rifle for man-huntin'. After the Confed'rit War there was a lot of bushwackin' done around here, and a man needed a gun that was good for two or three hundred yards—from the doorway to the ridge yander, for instance."

"You say you made this rifle with your own hands!" exclaimed Carman.

"Yes, sir: right here in this house, about forty year ago. These mountains was wild in them days, I'm tellin' you. Very few people livin here, and gangs of robbers—riff-raff left over from the war—prowled around stealin' and killin'. They burnt me out and stole my hosses and cattle and might' nigh everything I had. I got a few friends to help, and put up this end of the house. But I didn't even have a gun left to defend it, and no money to buy one.

"Well, I got a few dollars together, and tuk my foot in hand and lit out acrost the Smokies seventy-five miles to Knoxville, the nearest town of any size. I bought a gun lock for four dollars, and a rough-bored barrel for another four dollars, and a long steel rod and some small bits o' steel, and some powder and lead and caps. I carried them back home on my own wethers. It tuk me four days for the round trip. Well, then I made that rifle-gun."

"But I don't understand. There's no wagon road, even now, forty years later. How did you bring a lathe up here to bore and rifle your gun barrel with?"

Long John looked quizzically at his guest as though doubtful of his intelligence. "What did I want with a lathe? Come in the next room." He led the way.

This was the "old house," the room that was first built. It was floored with six-foot puncheons, but they were dressed with a broadax almost as smooth and even as though planed. It had two small window sashes, set side by side, to admit plenty of light—an uncommon feature in the mountains.

Under the window was a strange contrivance. A rude bench made of split and hewn timbers extended nearly the whole length of the room. To the top of this bench was firmly attached a wooded head-block which supported and guided a wooden cylinder five feet long, three inches in diameter, that had seven spiral grooves cut along its surface from end to end and equidistant from each other. When this cylinder, called the screw guide, was pushed or drawn by hand through the head-block guides, it slowly revolved and made a three-fourths turn in its own length.

"First the rough barrel was wedged fast at this other end of the bench," explained John, "and I drilled it out, smooth and true, to the caliber I wanted, using this long steel rod for a drill. The barrel is soft iron. It was slow work; but time was what I had the most of, them days.

"Then came the rifling. I made that screw guide, just like most everything else, from wood that I selected from trees growing around here and split out and seasoned and dressed myself."

"How did you lay out those spirals?"

"With these calipers."

John handed the visitor a bow compass made of hickory bent over in the shaved middle part, held at the desired spacing by a little crossbar of wood, wedged there with wooden wedges, and with each leg tipped by a common cambric needle.

"'Tain't bright and purty, like the boughten ones," said John, "but it does jist as fine work."

"Now, then, I'm ready to rifle the barrel. You see there's an iron slot in the end of this screw guide. I take this long steel rod, which is squared at the end, and fix it in the slot. A couple of inches from the fur end of the rod I fix a lead sheath that I've cast beforehand in the smooth-bored barrel so it fits it snug. In the sheath I sink a flat steel band in which I've filed sharp, square teeth—that is the saw. The saw is of tough steel that I've retempered myself.

"So, now I wedge the gun barrel in place over here at t'other end of the bench. I grease the leather slugs of the headblock, and the saw, too. I put the saw in the muzzle and I work the screw guide back and forth keerfully with my hands. That cuts a faint channel. I put a bit of writing paper under the saw, run through agin, and that deepens the channel. So on, till I have a groove cut as deep as I want it. Then I cut another groove. When all seven are cut, I bevel the edges of the landings to keep 'em from tearing the bullet patches. Then I made a screw plug for the breech end, at the nearest blacksmith shop, which, them days, was twelve miles down the river from here."

Carman had nothing to say. He was lost in wonder at the ingenuity that could accomplish such results with means so primitive and crude.

"The stock," continued John, "is made from a beech that grew right over yander by the spring. There was several curly maples here, too, but I chose straight-grained wood that wouldn't take long to work into shape. We were more for practical results than for style, them days. Fact is, I no more'n got this gun done when a sorry feller kem prowling about and tried to steal the only steer I had left. It was nigh dark, but

I glimpsed him behind that pinted rock t'other side the spring branch yander, and this gun killed him from this winder."

Carman stared at the "pinted rock." The corners of his mouth drooped. They did go in for practical results "them days," sure enough.

John went on placidly chatting, as though the killing of robbers was a mere matter of course.

"There'd a-been a quicker and easier way of makin' the gun if I'd had the loan of another rifle. In that case I'd not had to make this screw guide, you see. I'd jist a-used t'other rifle barrel for a guide, put the long rod in the barrel, cast three leads around it, and fitted rifling saws to t'other end."

"What ingenuity! What wonderful patience the old pioneers had!" exclaimed Carman.

"Them! Yes, sir. Us modern folks don't know what it means to do *everything* for ourselves." John did not notice the smile that Carman could not suppress at mention of "us modern folks." The old fellow went on: "My foreparents didn't have no hardware store to go to for rough barrels and locks. They had to make 'em all from the very ore they dug from the ground."

"What! Back here in this wilderness?"

"Yes: it was a wilderness them days. Five or ten miles to the nearest neighbor, and maybe him a son of a ———. Yet, away back in 1840 to 1850 there was five bloomery forges on Hanging Dog and other parts of Cherokee County where there was ore. They tuk the lump ore and crushed it with stompers, which was hardwood beams six by six inches raised and dropped by a cogged shaft turned by a water wheel. They washed the crushed ore in troughs and then it was ready for the furnace.

"The furnace was nothin' but a rock pile with a nest in the bottom and a two-inch blast pipe in the middle. The air was furnished by a stream of water passing through wooden tubes a foot square. They'd put in two or three bushels of charcoal and blow it to a white heat, then a layer of ore, then more charcoal, more ore. The melted ore would settle in the nest. Then an iron bar was stuck in and twisted around. A loop of melted iron would stick to it. This was taken to the anvil an [*sic*] hammered. The hammer was worked by water power. When the dross was hammered out, the big loop was divided into small ones, and a short iron bar for a handle was welded to each of them. These were reheated and hammered into bars nine to twelve feet long, or divided into smaller pieces for wagon tires, ax bars, ploughshares, horseshoe irons, gun skelps, and so forth."

"Skelps?" in quired [*sic*] Carman.

"Yes, that's what we call the iron for a gun barrel. Then the man who wanted to make him a rifle-gun would take that skelp and hammer it out to a long, eight sided bar. He'd drill it, and bore it out true, and straighten it by eye (watching the shadow inside, you know), and rifle it, and stock it, and put on the lock and sights and other fittin's; and then he had a gun, maybe, or jist an excuse, depend-in' on his own skill and the trouble he tuk. I've made several rifle-guns here in this room, different sizes, and all of them turned out good."

"And you prefer the old muzzle-loader, even today?"

"I do. These young fellers with their quick-shootin' guns git in sech a swivvet that they waste a sight of ammunition. When I shoot, I aim to kill. This gun'll do it at the fust shot, if you *hunt* right: so why take fool chances on game runnin' through brush or top o' yan hill?"

"Does it shoot straighter than a Winchester?"

"It shoots where it's *held*. You can hold it steadier than a Win-chester [*sic*], 'caze it's heavy. You can aim it truer, 'caze the sights is furder from the eye and furder apart. You can touch if off without a bobble, 'caze it's a hair-trigger. If you can't see your own self that all that helps the man who does the shootin', why, right thar is my boy Jim's thirty-thirty: you take it, I take the muzzle-loader, and I'll shoot you a match for a dollar a shot, off-hand or rest, sixty yards, as long as we've got any money in our jeans."

Carman looked again at the "pinted rock" beyond the spring branch. "I'll take your word for it," he said. "Anyhow, I see the point; your rifle is built for the essential purpose of straight shooting, much more like a modern target rifle than like a repeating hunting rifle; and of course a target rifle can be shot more accurately than a modern hunting arm. I wish I could attend one of your old-fashioned shooting matches."

Sometime in this life of ours there will be queer coincidences. One happened now. A tall, handsome young fellow came to the door announcing, "They're going to shoot for a beef, over in Bailey's Cove, tomorrow."

Before Long John could answer there came a shrill female voice from the kitchen: "I see the preacher-man a-comin'. And you-uns ain't goin' to no shootin' matches, with their rippin' and tarin' and drinkin' and swarin'—*I'll* be bound!"

The young man flushed guiltily. Long John winked at the visitor and said in an undertone, "Stay the night with us. Don't say nothin' about it to the old woman; but we-uns will contrive to see a shootin' match."

Carmen put up his horse, and stayed.

An Old-Fashioned Shooting Match

PART I

At peep o' day Carman was awakened by a heavy *thump—thump—thump* that came at regular intervals like the ticking of a clock, but five seconds apart.

What was it? And where was he?

Overhead were pole rafters supporting a clapboard roof, with wasp nests bracketed to it every here and there. A beam of light streamed in through a sort of porthole that had an inside shutter but no pane of glass.

His clothes hung on a queer, little, stumpy, split-bottomed chair. An unoccupied bed, similar to his own, stood against the opposite wall, just under the slope of the roof. It was framed of hewn timbers, corded with hickory splints, mattressed with straw, covered with home-made quilts of strange but artistic patterns.

The floor was bare. It was of unmatched and unplaned planks worn smooth by the feet of two or three generations of men.

Gradually it came to him, from beyond the mists of dreamland that he was in the home of Long John Gilbert, the mountaineer, the bear-hunter, the strange genius who had made his own rifle, on a wooden machine of his own contrivance, away back here in the wilderness where there was still no wagon road.

He got up and dressed. Still came that measured thumping from somewhere back of the house. Carman descended a ladder into the living room. On the porch he found the man who had invited him to stay over night and see an old-fashioned shooting match with muzzle-loaders competing.

Long John showed him a tin basin, a homemade bucket filled with spring water, a towel and a bit of mirror, at the end of the porch.

"What is that thumping I hear?" inquired Carman.

"That? Oh, that's the pounding-mill. It used to pound out all the meal for our

---

From *American Rifleman*, August 1, 1924

bread before I built a tub-mill for grindin' corn, but now I jist use it to pound out stock feed."

"What is a pounding-mill? I never heard of such a thing."

"Come; I'll show you."

Long John led the way along the edge of the orchard to where a brook went tumbling down a steep and rocky course. From a ledge in the brook there projected a spout made of a hollowed-out log. This carried a stream of water to the most amazing machine Carman had ever seen. He stood and stared at it like one possessed.

A tall post had been planted in the ground. To the top of this post a horizontal pole about ten feet long was pivoted at the center by a wooden pin so the ends were free to see-saw up and down like the walking-beam of a river steamboat.

At one end of the beam was pivoted a wooden pestle about five feet long and ten inches thick. The lower end of the pestle was shaved tapering to a blunt point. This went down into a big tree stump that had been burned and chiseled out inside to a funnel shape. A hewn plank sloping from the top of the stump guided the pestle into this improvised mortar, which contained nubbins and broken ears of corn.

Riding on top of the other end of the pole was a rectangular box serving as a water bucket that would hold six or seven gallons. This bucket was attached to the beam underneath by a wooden hinge formed by a V-shaped withe on each side, the lower angle of which went around a wooden pin stuck through the beam.

When the walking-beam was horizontal, the pestle was down in the mortar and the water bucket was in position to fill. Water was turned on by lifting out a bit of shingle set diamond-shape athwart the trough. Soon the weight of the water overbalanced that of the pestle. Down went the bucket; up went the pestle.

As the bucket descended through the arc of a circle, it tilted on its hinge and the water suddenly spilt out with a great splash. The bucket was checked from tilting too far by a withe like the bow of an ox yoke that went up and around it at the end nearest the post.

When the water spilled out, up went the bucket with a jerk, and down went the pestle with a thump. So on forever, till someone cut off the water from the trough.

Here was *the simplest possible application of power* to the needs of man. The engine had only three bearing surfaces. It had no rotary motion.

"And you made that, too, from the trees that grew around you!" exclaimed Carman.

"Yes, sir. There ain't nary bitty metal about it but the nails in the box and the leetle iron ring at the end of the pestle to keep it from burrin'. I could a-done without the nails jist as well."

"How?"

"How?" The old man looked quizzically at his guest to see if he were spoofing. Then patiently, as if to a child, he explained:

"Green buckeye, for instance, is easy to work. I'd sawed me a cut offen a buckeye log, then hewed and chiseled it into a bucket. I don't reckon you're much of a mechanic," laughed the old-timer.

"Maybe not; but I'll tell you one thing: There isn't a master mechanic in New York City who, if ordered to make a grist mill out of a stump of a tree and a few saplings, with no tools but an ax and a chisel, wouldn't cuss the boss for an idiot and swear the thing couldn't be done."

"Yeah: these modern mechanics do gr-r-reat and marvelous works, with carloads of ready-shaped materials and big shops full of power machines; but they'd be helpless as babes in the woods if put here to raise a family with nothin' but a chisel and an ax. Why, I made my own chisel on that pile o' rocks over yan," pointing to an exceedingly crude little forge by the brook side, "and I *could* a-made the ax thar, too."

"You live well; you have plenty, and to spare; yet you seem to have made everything you have, with your own hands, from what you found or raised in your own woods and fields."

"Purty near all. I don't have to do it. I have money laid away. And it would be a sight less work to trade at the stores for ready-made things. But I love my independence, man. I cain't stand to be bossed or beholden. Maybe some day this modern civ-il-iz-ation" (he drawled the word as if scorning it) "may go to smash. A war or a revolution may bring it crashing in ruin. Folks who don't know how to do for themselves will go bughouse, I reckon. But Long John Gilbert, 'way up hyur on the mountain and with no wagon road, will still be a contented and a free man. He'll have enough; and enough's a plenty."

Carman regarded the old man with respect almost mounting to reverence. There he stood, tall and healthy and strong, clear-eyed, dignified, capable, and every inch a man. A gentleman, and a scholar, too, in the truest sense. What a contrast to the low white trash who, yesterday, in squint-eyed envy and gnawing hate, had spat at the Gilbert name!

He was soon to learn that Long John's dignity could unbend, on occasion; that the old fellow had a humorous, even mischievous quirk in his nature.

A shrill voice from the kitchen wing called "Br-r-eck-fust!" A fainter thumping than that of the pounding-mill came from the same direction. As the two men turned the corner they saw another primitive operation.

A young woman stooped over a great iron pot or cauldron in which the family wash was boiling over an out-door fire. She stuck in a big wooden paddle and fished out a garment. This she laid on the upended face of a cut from a big log, standing like a butcher's block. She hit the steaming cloth a sturdy lick with the paddle, then turned it and struck it again. So on until the soapy water was pounded out of it and the garment was ready to rinse. This was her way of doing without a washboard.

"Thank God, it's wash-day!" exclaimed John. "I ginerally, usually run away from home at sich times. Somethin' calls me elsewhar. The old woman'll be havin' troubles of her own, and likely'll fergit about that shootin' match we're obleeged to see."

But the crafty old chap was reckoning without another factor in the case. When they got to the table, there, very stiff and important, sat the Preacher Man. John had forgotten this other guest.

The Reverend McCoan, of the Holiness Church, had long white whiskers, beetling bushy brows, and hard, gray eyes that looked stern disapproval on all sins and frivolities, except the half tin cupful of raw corn liquor that Ma Gilbert had slipped him before the others came in.

No sooner had he blessed the food, and stuffed some of it up under a two-inch barrier of mustache, than he began denouncing the worldly ways of a generation fast going to perdition.

"Fiddlin', dancin', cyard playin', dice rollin, horse racin', talkin' through the air, joy-ridin' over the yearth with gals at night, goin' God knows whar and doin' the Devil knows what."—All these caught what was coming to them, indiscriminately, as though one was as bad as the other. And then came the explosion.—

"I heern tell there's to be a shootin' for beef over in Bailey's Cove this very day. Now, brethering, that's gamblin'. Jist the same as cyards—i-den-tic-ally jist the same. There ain't no which nor t'other about it. I say it's GAMBLIN'!"

The old exhorter banged his fist down on the table till the dishes danced and everybody's coffee slopped over.

So he went on and on. Nobody put in a word. Nobody had a chance. But Long John, watching when his wife had her back turned at the hearth, and the preacher had shut his eyes and was roaring at the ceiling, whispered an aside to Carman: "That's why we don't hardly ever have no shootin' matches no more. All the preacher-men are down on 'em, jist like this hyur Holy McCoan."

Then he gave a meaning glance to his big son Jim, who had been tossing food into himself at an amazing rate, and Jim left the table without a word.

When the preacher stopped to get wind, Long John announced: "Folks, we'd love to stay, but Mr. Cyarman must be gittin' back to town, and I reckon I'd better do a piece o' the way. We'll git our hosses."

Carman said good bye, and out the two gileful confederates went. John said to him: "Jim will have the guns up thar round the fust turn o' the trail. That's what he snuck out so quick for when the he-granny wasn't lookin'."

Jim met them at the turn, handed his father the long muzzle-loader and its accouterments, shouldered his .30-.30, and strode off afoot, speedily outdistancing the riders up the steep and rocky grade. Carman asked how far it was to Bailey's Cove.

"Twelve mile, with two mountains to cross. Jim'll beat us to it. Any average mountain boy can outstrip a hoss in sich country; and can kill him in two days of it."

"You said there were few shooting matches nowadays in the mountains."

"This is the fust I've heered of, in this county, in five years. They used to be the commonest kind o' amusement—and them days the men *could* shoot. But the preachers jist won't abide them."

"Is it just the Holiness people that take that view?"

"No, everybody. They claim it's gamblin', when, truth is, it's a game o' skill and whoever gits a quarter o' beef, for his dollar or so, arns it. The real objection is that men enjoy the sport; and some thinks pleasure is sinful. 'T would be the same if there wa'nt no prize up at all."

"Your wife seems to think it encourages drinking and swearing."

"That's all stuff. You know your own self, if you've ever done much shootin' with a rifle-gun, that a man cain't do his best unless his eyes is normal. And you know, too, if you've done much drinkin', that you don't aim jist the same after you've taken a few drinks. So, when you're puttin' up good money on your fine marksmanship, you don't drink. But when a woman gits sot on a notion she don't mind what excuse she gives. Women don't reason; they jist feel. I'm glad of it. No man could bear livin' with a wife who could *reason* him down!"

"Seems to me the preachers around here must be very—well, very strict. I never heard a city preacher object to such innocent amusement as traget [*sic*] practice."

"No? Wall, maybe they go to t'other extreme. They believe the yearth's round, don't they?"

"Yes. Don't you?"

"No, by cripes! It don't stand to reason. The water'd all spill out. I do my own thinkin'. When I cain't do that no more, I'll be to bury."

Carman laughed up his sleeve, and changed the subject.

"Will breech-loaders be barred from this match?"

"No, sir-ree! The only guns barred are the twenty-pound guns with full-length shades over the barrel, and peep and globe sights, that are made for nothin' but match shootin', and are good for nothin' else. Leastways, that used to be the rule here in the mountains. Why, I've seed 'em with telescopes in 'em. That ain't fair."

"Those heavy guns were muzzle-loaders?"

"Sartain. I seed one weighed thirty pound, and shot a picket ball—a pinted one. It was good for half a mile."

"Your idea is that none but practical hunting rifles should be allowed in a match?"

"Around hyur, yes. Us mountain folks cain't afford toy guns. We got to use what we got. We don't bar breech-loaders, for they are practical, too."

Carman told the old man about many breech-loaders he had seen that were made specially for target practice, and were good for nothing else. He told of experts loading their own cartridges, the powder being weighed on delicate scales. He told about the matches shot under the supervision of the N. R. A., and about a magazine devoted to rifle shooting, which reported promptly the new improvements made by a little army of devoted experimenters and inventors. He spoke of rifle shooting as a science.

All this was brand new to Long John Gilbert. He had never imagined such things. He studied over it, and was silent a long time. Carman rather regretted that he had mentioned these matters. They seemed to sadden the old chap.

Finally John spoke: "We ain't got money to spend on sich. I reckon we don't know much. But you see these woods. All our hunting ground that's left is in the wild mountains. There ain't much game left, nowadays, even thar. If you miss a shot, you needn't count overmuch on gittin' another that day. The woods is thick, and there's braysh everywhar, like haar on a dog's back. What use have we-uns for long-shootin' guns? Nobody hyur can see game furder than fifty to a hundred yards, as a gineral thing. So we don't need nothin' but what we can drive center with at sich distance, with sights we can see clarly in the dark o' the woods. This old gun o' mine does *that* trick as well as any I ever seed in my life. And it don't cost five cents a shoot, like Jim's repeatin' power-gun. Say, I don't value them power-guns, nohow. You can shoot clar through a bear with 'em *and kill your dog* on t'other side o' him. That durned Jim o' mine did that very thing last fall. Killed one o' the best dogs ever run bear in these mountains, jist when it was doin' its level best to stop the beast for him. Jim didn't see the dog, of course, for the bear was between, when he fired. But no muzzle-loader ever done sich dirst as that."

Rippity—whang—bang—Long John let fly a volley of hissing hot words. Then suddenly he cooled off. "Thar now," he said, "if the old woman had heered that! And me a Missionary Babtist! But who could help it? I do love a good dog."

"Cuss away, old timer!" cried Carman, slapping him on the back. "It comes from a good heart!"

"There's jist one gun in the mountains I'm afeared of in a match," resumed John. "It's the Gillespie rifle that Morgan De Weese has. Old man Gillespie lived nigh

Cherry Fields at the head of the French Broad. He was a master hand with tools, and he had his pick of iron from the best bloomery forge in the State. That iron you could fairly shave with a knife. De Weese can beat me from the rest—that's the real test of a gun—but I reckon I can still hold my own offhand. The sight o' my eyes is about as good as ever, though I'm sixty-odd."

"I suppose there'll be a variety of muzzle-loaders at this shoot."

"O yes; everything from a hog-rifle to a bear-gun. Everybody's got his notion, and every muzzle-loader's hand-made."

"What is a hog-rifle?"

"That's the common word here for any old-fashioned long rifle; but it sounds bad to me, and I never say it except for these very small bores that carries a ball like a buckshot—what you'd prob'ly call a squirrel rifle."

"Do you believe a long barrel is more accurate than a short one?"

"No, not in itself; but you can *aim* it truer, with open sights. Didn't I try to beat that into your head yesterday? In the deep shade o' the woods a man must have sights that he can see. So the front sight is bound to be open, and of bright metal. Mine's gold, made from a coin. Now on Jim's Winchester the front sights is only thirty inches from the eye, in aiming and the back sight twelve inches. Nobody can aim as true with that combination as he can with my gun, whar the front sight is forty-four inches away and the back sight seventeen."

"Yes, that's so."

"Then there's another thing. Jim's front sight sticks away high, like a sore thumb. He's got to be plumb keerful every time not to draw too coarse and overshoot. But with my gun it's impossible to draw too coarse or too fine. Look at it. The front sight is less'n an eighth of an inch high. The back sight is low, too, of course. The two sights is twenty-seven inches apart. You cain't help allers drawing the same bead, if you see the sights at all."

"Then how do you allow for distance?"

"Don't have to, up to a hundred yards, for anything as big as a groundhog's head. The way I load, the back sight has the notch cut to strike center at eighty yards. At sixty yards the gun shoots one inch high. At a hundred, an inch and a half low. For longer range I put in a double charge of powder, and she's good for a hundred and fifty. For two hundred, I aim high on the mark."

"Do you draw the common charge, and reload, before shooting two hundred?"

"I never need to shoot that fur at game. When I go man-huntin' I allers double-charge."

"Had much of that to do lately?" asked Carman thoughtlessly.

"When I do, I won't call you as witness in court," snapped the old man. He grew grim and silent.

Carman saw he had overstepped, and passed it off with a laugh. He told funny stories. Long John soon regained his good humor and went to swapping yarns. They became jovial and made the woods ring with their laughter.

So the two truants went jogging along over the steep and rocky trail, up and down the high ridges, splashing through creeks and branches, happy as kids let loose from school.

But back at the cabin, Ma Gilbert had detected the absence of a Winchester and a muzzle-loader from their pegs on the wall. For the next half hour there wasn't a pig or a chicken on the place that wasn't told what a graceless old scamp Long John Gilbert was.

(*To be continued*)

An Old-Fashioned Shooting Match

PART II

On the way to Bailey's Cove, Carman saw for himself why long range rifle shooting could not be a popular pastime in the mountains. There was no level land for a range.

Once they came out on a bare high knob from which they could see out over the forest for a great distance. Far as the eye could reach there was nothing but a labyrinth of mountains, all clad in forest green, save where a settler's little clearing, here and there, showed like a slight scar on the mountainside. These infrequent fields sloped at angles of thirty to forty-five degrees.

When they descended to creek valleys, which were sunk like ravines, they found there the only level land in the country. It was in narrow strips along crooked water-courses, and every bit of it was in cultivation.

It took the horses four hours to make the twelve miles to the Cove. Jim had beaten them to it afoot. He had a mountaineer's legs and lungs. Uphill was almost the same as level going for him.

Some forty men were already assembled in a worn-out strip of old-field behind Bailey's barn. Some were "blacking their boards," for targets, by charring split shingles over a fire. After the surface of a shingle was blackened in this manner, a cross was scored on it with a knife. The intersection of the cross was the *center* which the contestant would try to drill with a bullet, at sixty yards.

Of course, the cross was invisible at that distance. So a bit of white paper was tacked on the board with a hole cut in it close to the lower edge, and this hole was centered over the cross.

"Every man has his own way of fixing his paper," explained Long John to his guest. "I'll show you mine."

The old man blackened his shingle. He took from his pocket a piece of white note paper about five inches square. This he trimmed with his knife to the shape

---

From *American Rifleman*, August 15, 1924

shown in the diagram here given. The diamond-shaped hole above the apex of the "swallow-fork" on the bottom had one-inch sides.

"Now, then," said John, "as I done told you, my rifle shoots one inch high at sixty yards, on the average, owin' to it bein' pupposely sighted for center at eighty yards, for huntin'. That makes it shoot level enough so's I make allowance for fair-sized game up to a hundred. But an inch might as well be a mile for match shootin' at sixty. And I cain't *guess* that close by jist trying to allow in aimin'. I got to have some way o' makin' sartin, ain't I?"

"Yes: and you have no elevating rear sight."

"Don't want none," snapped the old man. "But I can see a one-inch black square agin' that white paper. All right. I cut my diamond like this. I cut the swallow-fork so. When I aim, the tip o' my front sight jist touches the tip o' the swallow-fork, and that's edzactly one inch under the center of the diamond. You see?"

"O yes."

"Then there's another rinktum. The swallow-fork is cut so's the bottom of the wings jist touches the flat top o' my eight-sided rifle barrel when the tip o' the sight grazes the tip o' the swallow-fork. It shows, too, if the rifle's level."

"Well, I'll be darned!"

"You see, every man must fix his own paper. He must place it accordin' to how his gun is sighted and how it shoots."

"But suppose your bullet tears the sighting-point."

"Fix a new paper, then. Sich a shot has no show for beef. You must put up your money and try agin', or quit and go hungry. They're killin' the beef over yander, now. The man who makes the best center shot gits fust prize, a hind quarter or whatever he chooses. Then comes the other quarters, saddle, ribs, hide and taller. It's fifty cents a shoot, and ties are shot off. When competition is keen, the owner of the beef makes good money."

Carman scanned the crowd. Nearly all of the men were genuine backwoodsmen, farmers who lived away back in the forest, each on some "spring-branch" of his own, and seldom was seen on the main highways or in town. Most of them were tall, muscular fellows of grave bearing and decent appearance. They were jacks-of-all-trades, but clever at all, seldom hiring anybody to do work for them of any kind.

There were some representatives of a shockingly inferior class: ignorant, undernourished creatures, dull-eyed, awkward, slovenly, clad in rags. They looked like white savages, and Long John sometimes half-pityingly called them "wild men." These were the trash, descended from a vicious and shiftless stock, bred in and in, content with a year-round diet of corn pone and hog's grease, fried cabbage and field beans, despising butter and sweet-milk. Most of the muzzle-loaders were in such hands: old relics that the trash retained simply because they had cost little or nothing and were cheap to get ammunition for.

But there were four or five muzzle-loaders borne by men of a different sort: old men of ability and standing, who stuck to their old-fashioned weapons out of a sentiment of loyalty to the tried and true. These were living survivals of a heroic type, the pioneer stock, who, with axe and rifle and little else, won our continent from savagery to civilization.

The shooting began. One of the younger men set up his board, on which he had merely tacked a small bit of paper for a sighting-spot above the cross mark. He laid himself down, rested his .44-40 Winchester on a sack of grain, aimed, shifted the bag to a new position, aimed again, and fired. His bullet struck an inch off center at 3 o'clock. He cursed the glimmer of his front sight.

Another took his place, with a .30-30. He tied a bent leaf over his front sight, as a shade. He shot closer.

Other breech-loaders followed. There were several .38-55s, half a dozen .30-30s, a .25-35, a Savage .303, a .30-40, a .22 high power, a .32 special, some .32-20s and .44-40s. They were plain hunting arms, bought as they happened to come from stock. There was not a single-shot rifle, nor a peep sight, among them. A few of them nipped the intersection of the cross.

Then a muzzle-loader came into action. It was an exceedingly long piece, nearly six feet over all, but very slender, and of such small bore that it took a No. 1 buckshot (.30 caliber, 173 balls to the pound) and was charged with a single dram of fine-grained powder.

The fellow who shot this extraordinary gun was one of the raggedest white men Carman had ever seen. He was filthy as any tramp. Yet he carried his head high in bravado, regarding everybody with a piercingly direct and insolent stare.

He stepped to the firing point, disdainfully stood erect, threw the long rifle out with fully extended arm, aimed but a second or two, and touched the hair trigger. There was a weak but spiteful crack. The rifle did not lift at the muzzle, but, like a .22, showed no sign of jar. The little bullet cut well into the center of the cross. It was the best shot made, so far, and won a round of applause. The ragamuffin stepped back and tossed his head in challenge.

"When any o' you-uns, with yer fancy guns, beat *that*, layin' down or propped up, jist send me word. I'll be to see at Clapp's store any Sattaday mornin'."

The crowd laughed.

"A fluke!" exclaimed Carman.

"No, hardly," answered Long John in an undertone. "That feller is the brag squirrel-shooter of the Smoky Mountains. He prowls the woods the year round, allers tryin' that popgun o' his'n, and ain't wuth a damn for anything else."

The success of their champion encouraged the rest of the ragged crew. They followed one after the other, as if a class by themselves, mostly with muzzle-loaders, though a few had rusty old Winchesters of the '73 model. Their shooting, in the main, was only fair. Some of the wildest shots of the match were made with muzzle-loaders.

Carman was disappointed. He had come here expecting to see some of the olden time nail-driving that he had read about. Yet there had been nothing done, so far, that would have caused a flicker of interest on his own home rifle range. He suspected that the accuracy of the old-fashioned rifles had been much overrated.

Meantime, three or four of the old-timers had been busy setting up a rest after their own notion. "Grandpa's arm chair," one of the irreverent youngsters called it.

They drove some stout stakes in the ground, nailed a thick plank on top, like a bench, built a similar but lower bench behind it for a seat, and sloped a long, heavy plank backward from the front bench to the ground, for an arm rest, which was spiked solidly in position. Then they laid a small sack of grain on the front bench to rest the gun on.

The "arm chair" was ready. Long John turned to a quiet, capable-looking man of fifty who, so far, had seemed to be only a spectator, and addressed him:

"Set us a pattern, Mr. De Weese."

"After you, Mr. Gilbert; my boy has gone to the house for my rifle."

"Very well," answered Gilbert, formally, "I'll try a shoot."

Jim brought the old man his rifle, pouch and powder horn. Long John took from the pouch a six-inch tube of sheet iron, open along the bottom so as to clamp over the muzzle end of the rifle barrel. This was a shade for the front sight. It had a sliding trap on top that could be slid back and forth to adjust the light so it would show the top of the front sight clearly, without glitter.

John opened his powder horn, filled a horn charger that hung from his bullet pouch by a thong, and poured the powder down the barrel, which Jim had already wiped out with tow wound round a long cleaning rod. He opened the patch box of the rifle, took from it a piece of twilled cotton about an inch and a half square, rubbed it on some bear fat that was in the box, and laid it, greased side down, on the muzzle. He took from his pouch a bullet that had been carefully rounded at home, laid this on the patch, and pressed the two into the muzzle with his thumb. With a keen-edged knife he cut off the superfluous cloth that projected. Then he took his ramrod and steadily pushed the bullet down till he felt it touch the powder, but he was careful not to crush the powder nor batter the ball. He put a cap on the rifle's nipple, seated himself, and laid the rifle barrel on the grain sack.

Jim had already set up the blackened board, with its white paper, at the sixty-yard point. Long John adjusted the front sight shade. He aimed, readjusted the shade, aimed once more, and fired.

There was a louder report and more smoke than any of the other muzzle-loaders had given out. John's bear gun had been charged with three drams of good FFG, that is to say, 82 grains of powder, and a 219-grain ball.

Jim brought in the board. The big bullet had cut deep into the center of the cross, its own center being a quarter-inch high right. The ball, although of .53 caliber, had not broken outside the edge of the diamond, which had one-inch sides.

Jim whispered to Carman: "Bully for Dad! De Weese will have to strain hisself to beat that shot."

The crowd cheered. De Weese shook hands with Long John, and laughingly remarked: "It will cost me some money to catch up with you, old timer."

Two of the other muzzle-loaders were tried, both of them by young men who shot for their fathers, whose eyes were no longer keen enough for target work. Both bullets came close to the center, but both tore out an edge of the diamond. The young men re-entered. At their second trial, one of them did a little better, the other worse.

Then De Weese's rifle was brought. It was the weapon that Long John had said was the best in the district. It was perfectly plain but had a beautifully shaped stock of curly maple. The metal workmanship was excellent. The gun was in perfect condition, having never been trusted to unworthy hands. It had a 40-inch barrel, weighed fourteen pounds, and was of .43 caliber, taking sixty balls to the pound. There was a full-length shade over the barrel, and the judges all examined it in turn, to make sure that no peep or magnifying lens was hidden within it. This rifle, like Gilbert's, had a gold front sight, very low, and thin on top. The rear sight was a plain bar with shallow nick in the center.

Carman was surprised to see that De Weese used the same powder charge as Gilbert, namely three drams, or 82 grains, notwithstanding that his bullet weighed only 117 grains.

"That's a tremendous charge for so light a ball," he observed to one of the old men. "Doesn't it strip and lead the grooves?"

"You mean tear the patch and stick lead in the channels? No. It jist makes the gun shoot harder and flatter and buck the wind better."

"Humph! If you put a quarter of that powder behind a round ball in a breech-loader it would lead the bore from breech to muzzle."

The native stared at him. "Anybody's be a fool to try it. How would he patch the ball? Besides, look at the difference in twist. A .30-30, for instance, makes one full turn in ten inches. Most muzzle-loaders make only three-quarters turn in forty to forty-four inches. Then, agin, a quick twist, if you had it, in a muzzle-loader, would make a round ball sail off to hell-an'-gone."

"Drift, we call it."

"Well, drift. You cain't jedge a muzzle-loader by a breech-loader. The principles is different, like an axe and a saw."

De Weese used fine linen patches. His bullets were so tight-fighting that he had to employ a bullet-starter to seat them in the muzzle, before ramming down. His target was similar to Gilbert's, save that the diamond came clear to the lower edge of the paper, allowing for less rise of bullet. Still his gun shot practically pointblank to a hundred yards.

He fired. The judges had to measure his shot to determine whether it or Gilbert's was the better. Gilbert won by a scant eighth of an inch, measuring from center of bullet hole to center of cross.

De Weese re-entered.

Carman began to realize that he was to see some good shooting, after all. The muzzle-loaders were not all in the hands of white trash.

He turned to Long John with another question: "Why are these rifles made so heavy?"

"Wall, I reckon' it beacause [*sic*] every kind o' weight has been tried. A light barrel vibrates from the jar. A thick, heavy barrel don't, especially if it's soft iron like these. Then, of course, a heavy one can be held steadier, and so can a long one, owin' to the leverage. Besides, a heavy gun don't kick. Ever notice these young fellers flinchin' from their power guns? You don't see non o' us doin' that: we ain't got nothin' to flinch from."

"I suppose everything was tried in the old days."

"Sartin'. There never was two muzzle-loaders jist alike. They're all hand-made. They don't come from no factory. There's been hundreds, yes thousands, o' rifle makers who made 'em all by hand. Every one had a repytation to make or keep. They tried everything."

"Don't you consider set triggers dangerous?"

"Shucks! We were foch up from childhood to use 'em. It's jist as much instinct for us to handle a set trigger right as it is to fork meat into our mouths without jabbin' our eyes out."

"Why is it that some of these fellows using muzzle-loaders can't shoot as well with them as many of the hunters do with breech-loaders?"

"Because they ain't got no sense. A man must put some brains into his shootin', if he's got any. Then, too, they don't take decent keer of their firearms. Look at 'em!"

"I don't want to bore you, but there's another question I'd like to ask. I noticed something about your bullet-pouch that puzzles me. On the leather shoulder-belt I see several thongs about six inches long that taper to a point and are twisted at the ends. What are they for?"

"To hold caps. When I'm huntin', I may need to reload quick."

"Still I don't understand."

"I twist the end of one o' them leather strings into a sort of screw, and put a cap on it. It holds. In loadin', I snatch a cap off like that." And John went through the motion like a flash.

De Weese fired four more shots. He would have fired many more, if necessary to carry off first prize; but the fifth shot of his series was almost a perfect center. It was hopeless to try to beat it, and the other old men reluctantly withdrew, or went on contesting for second place. Only one of De Weese's five shots cut inside the edge of the diamond, which had one-inch sides.

This veteran marksman, having carefully cleaned and greased his rifle, had time on his hands now, and nothing to do. Carman got an introduction to him and they had a little talk. De Weese seemed not at all elated, but took his victory quite as a matter of course.

"This rifle," he said, "has been in our family for three generations. It has always been a prize-winner. The man who made it was an artist, just as the man who makes a superior violin is an artist. And the old gun has always had the best of care. I unbreeched it not long ago and didn't find a speck of rust in the bore, from end to end. There are mighty few old guns in that condition, nowadays."

De Weese proved to be a man of some education, using excellent English, though born and bred in the mountains among people who spoke the dialect.

"You are satisfied that this rifle is more accurate than any other, at short range, that you can get?"

"I've never had any of the fancy breech-loading target rifles made just for that purpose, nor any of the special ammunition that my boy says is issued for match shooting—he was on one of the Army teams. But I've owned or used nearly every model and caliber of American hunting rifles, shot them with factory ammunition, and never found one that would do the work of this old-timer at this particular style of shooting."

"It must have an uncommonly good barrel."

"It has. But it's not all in the barrel. The sights suit me, the trigger suits me, the hang of the gun suits me. I can aim and fire this old rifle with less bobbing around—less guesswork—than any other I ever handled."

"You wouldn't use it for hunting."

"No: it's too heavy for that, though I've known old hunters who wouldn't carry a lighter rifle than this and they got the meat."

"Do you consider that the average muzzle-loader is more accurate than the average breech-loading hunting rifle, up to a hundred yards?"

"No, not in the condition most of them are in today. They would be, if new, and shot by men who understand them. Those who have not used muzzle-loaders a good deal don't know how to bring out their fine points. It's almost a lost art, like shooting the bow and arrow. The muzzle-loader's day is past. It is too clumsy, too slow to reload, and so it's nothing now but a curiosity, a relic. But it was a grand weapon in its time. So was the sword, the bow and arrow. And the breech-loader will pass away, too. We are even now passing into the age of poison gas and bombs dropped from the sky. Then will come the 'death ray,' the 'diabolic ray,' that is already being talked about. Sportsmanship will pass, as chivalry is passing. And then?"

Backward, Turn Backward, O Time, in Thy Flight! [5]

The National Rifle Association of America was organized in 1871. One of its objects was to stimulate international competition, particularly in long range shooting. Muzzle-loaders were still having things their own way in England; but in America the Sharps and Remington buffalo guns, refined for target shooting, were putting up some remarkable scores.

In 1874 an international try-out of the two rival systems was made at Creedmoor. The visiting Irish team, armed with Rigby Muzzle-loaders, was defeated, though by only three points, by the Americans using breech-loaders.

Next year there was a return match, at Wimbledon, the predecessor of Bisley. The Americans had to wipe their rifle bores after each shot, owing to their paper-patched bullets. Some of our men took strange positions in firing, lying on their backs with feet toward the targets. The breech-loaders won.

At Creedmoor, in 1876, Ireland, Scotland, Australia, Canada and the United States competed. We won, with Ireland again a close second. In this match J. K. Milner, of the Irish team, made a run of fifteen consecutive bullseyes at 1,000 yards.

The next year marked the turn of an epoch. The American team again won over the United Kingdom and the superiority of breech-loaders was conceded on all sides, provided wiping be allowed between shots. This was banned in England, in 1883, and so, for us, the spur of international competition was lost.

Our marksmen then took to the less expensive sport of offhand shooting at 200 yards. The scene shifted from Creedmoor to Walnut Hill and similar ranges supported by local clubs. For a good while the shooting was with extended arm, as a rule, the rifles under ten pounds, trigger-pull not under three pounds, and the .38-55 a favorite weapon, with patched bullets still used by experts.

There is a fast dwindling company of us grizzled fellows who started our target shooting in that way, then grudgingly but inevitably changed to the "schuetzen" or free-rifle style, with heavy rifles, set triggers and palm rests. Some of us never were fully converted. I remember Matt Gindele, of Cincinnati, still valiantly plugging away with a light rifle, his arm fully extended, in the late nineties of the last century. But it was a losing game, quite lost when Harry Pope began turning out his superlatively accurate heavy rifles using his own pattern of bullets rammed down from the muzzle.

Meantime A. C. Gould, author of "Modern American Rifles," had given new impetus to our sport when he founded a magazine, *The Rifle*, afterwards changed to a weekly paper entitled *Shooting and Fishing*, and then *The American Rifleman*.

There came another radical change in rifle shooting with the improvement of smokeless powder. Not all at once, however. Some of us imported ours, before rifle nitro was made in America, and had a fine time learning to tame the brute. Ah, well, we blew up a few nice guns; but that was all in the game!

Then came the Krag; eventually the Springfield. Townsend Whelen and other persevering enthusiasts worked on the ammunition problem and our military rifle became a true arm of precision. The United States Government took an interest in the N. R. A. and helped it to carry on. The Army, the Navy, the Marine Corps, the National Guard, all joined in with the civilians to make rifle shooting a national sport.

Honor to the N. R. A.! Through many difficulties it has persevered and grown into an institution of which our country may well be proud. Ever it has stood for clean sport and the maintenance of sturdy American ideals. Methods change from age to age, men come and go; but the spirit of Bunker Hill and King's Mountain animates the young marksmen of today. Boone and Morgan, Shelby and Sevier, could they return in a new embodiment, would find themselves at home on the rifle ranges of our time.

five

SOUTHERN APPALACHIAN CULTURE

367

THE "RAZORBACK."

See also FLORA— Angelico.

"Pet pigs" are "corn-fed" around home, and get fat. Louis's.

"He follers up his hogs, and salts them, and corn-feeds them a little, and gentles them up." (Dilly Welch; hence has good bacon.)

Mast-fed hogs that are not "corn-fed" for some time before butchering do not make lard— their fat is oily like bear's grease— nor do they make bacon that keeps well. (Louis.) (See also p. 443.)

Ear-marks.

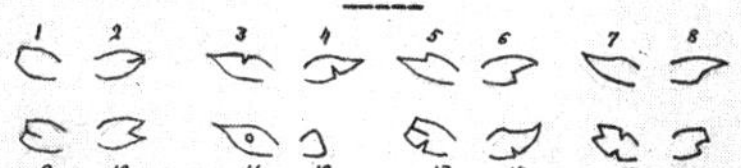

1. Crop or Smooth-crop.
2. Slit, or Split.
3. Over-bit.
4. Under-bit.
5. Over half-crop.
6. Under half-crop.
7. Over-slope.
8. Under-slope.
9. Crop and slit.
10. Swallow-fork.
11. Round hole.
12. Thief-mark, or Grub (ear cut off close to head).
13. Crop, slit, and under-bit.
14. Over-slope and under-bit.
15. Poplar leaf (swallow-fork, over-bit, and under-bit).
16. Crop and half-crop.

The right ear is described first. In N.C. the marks must be registered, and no other man can use the same mark within five miles' radius.

It is the law in Ark. that no one shall kill an unmarked pig except in presence of a witness; "but nobody observes it."

Pigs are rounded up for marking whenever a litter can be caught. Frequently door-traps are set for pigs, baited with an ear of corn. Pigs wanted for eating are shot and butchered on the spot. Old Dave Davis and Bob.

Tuberculous hogs. "The runt."

Hog cholera spread by buzzards; hence old law protecting these scavengers has been repealed.

"Tie a pig by the left hind leg, and he'll drive better." "Why?" "I don't know; but they do."

"A listed pig." "Gilt."

"He made a lunge to ketch the hog..." "That's my Nancy's pet hog."

"Two inches o' that pig's tail 'd cure yaller fever." I looked: the pig had no tail.

"You cain't scald the bristles offen a live hog; we poured kittle-full through the cracks [in the floor]. But hit'll make the ha'r slip from a mule: one walked into the house, one day, an' I soused hit; you never heerd sich brayin' in yer life." (M.B.)

"By Ned, they jest rid saplin's, gittin out o' thar!"

"Them hogs are plumb pets."

"I could tole that pig around anywhere."

See p. 34.

Page from Kephart's journal on the "Razorback."

Introduction

GEORGE FRIZZELL

The people of Southern Appalachia, especially the Great Smoky Mountains region of western North Carolina and east Tennessee, held the attention of Horace Kephart for the last twenty-seven years of his life. He became captivated with their history, customs, speech, and daily routines. His writings on the subject have become classic readings, though there are disagreements on their accuracy. As Michael Ann Williams succinctly noted in *Great Smoky Mountains Folklife* (1995) about *Our Southern Highlanders*: "Kephart recognized and attempted to correct many negative stereotypes and overly romanticized portrayals of the southern mountains. However, his own need for adventure drew him to the wildest characters and the most uncivilized aspects of life. Before the book settles down to a somewhat more sober consideration of life in the mountains, Kephart takes the reader on jaunts of bearhunting, moonshining, and manhunting."[1] These conflicting aspects of Kephart's attraction to the region, both the mundane and the adventurous, have contributed to the debates on his objectivity but also retained the appeal of his exploits.

After giving up his professional career, Kephart began what he termed his "sojourn" into the southern mountains and reached the town of Dillsboro, North Carolina, by early August 1904. What his expectations were before stepping off the train are not known with certainty. The town of 200 residents was a commercial hub and the center for nearby clay mining operations that sent high-quality kaolin to porcelain manufacturers in the Midwest. In a poignant comment in his "Index to Diary" found in his journals, Kephart noted that he "could have outfitted here" for his travels but apparently believed suitable provisions may not have been found west of Asheville, the only large city in western North Carolina.[2]

Rather than stay in a hotel or boarding house, Kephart set up a campsite two miles away in the rural Dicks Creek community. There he began to document the lives, chores, and customs of his new acquaintances as well as the countryside. Over the next three months, he explored his surroundings on excursions that included a fishing trip to the High Falls of the Tuckasegee River and attendance at the Birdtown

"Widow Davis' cabin on Dick [*sic*] Creek near Dillsboro. Fair sample of all the cabins in these mtns., but better chimney than common. No window. Spinning wheel & loom are still worked here, although within 2 m. of a RR. town."

Annual Association meeting of the Eastern Band of Cherokees. Photographs in his album often captured casual settings of domestic life, though at times families might pose for pictures in their best, or "Sunday," attire. His "Index to Diary" expressed this "rage for photos." One page of the album featured both a two-story frame house and a more modest home that he considered representative of a typical cabin. In a handwritten caption about the cabin, he expressed curiosity that the family continued to use a loom and spinning wheel despite being two miles from Dillsboro's rail depot.

This trait to record everyday events continued throughout his life and evolved over two decades into an extensive set of over two dozen journals that comprised an amalgam of personal observations, quotes, clippings from publications, and citations of his sources that covered not only Appalachian life and history but also camping and woodcraft techniques, fishing and hunting, flora and fauna, criminology, personality traits, and observations on American life. The journals show an enduring interest in becoming an outdoor culinary expert, as seen in the publication of *Camp Cookery* in 1910 and incorporation of its text in the two-volume version of *Camping and Woodcraft* a few years later.

The journals were not a compilation of reflective, philosophical musings but instead represented his general inquisitiveness. Several of them are devoted to his desire to learn about the environment and cultural heritage of his adopted home in western North Carolina. He utilized his years of experience as a librarian to categorize and label the pages using library catalog headings to delineate topics. The journals do not appear to have been intended to become a final, finished project. Entries were typed or handwritten on the same page as he incorporated new observations or even pasted in printed items. The volumes were not rigidly bound but instead used flexible covers that allowed them to be opened so that additional pages or updates might be inserted as needed.

Kephart readily acknowledged that in moving to Southern Appalachia he intentionally desired a land and culture where he thought he "might realize the past in the present." To reach this goal, he purposely moved miles from the main settlements and into the Great Smoky Mountains to experience what he deemed to be the lives of the vast majority of the people. For him, these mountaineers were a "sequestered folk" that he felt were "especially interesting to the reading public" and that tourists knew simply in "glimpses from afar" on their travels.[3]

In a 1912 letter to Albert Britt, editor of the *Outing* magazine to which he frequently contributed articles, he confessed that at first he anticipated a temporary move of perhaps six-months duration as part of a fact-finding expedition for a potential publication as he sought emotional and psychological renewal. Yet, after eight years of residence in Appalachia, he confided to Britt that he had come to reassess his original assumptions and to appreciate the complexity of Appalachian life.[4]

Among his characterizations of the culture, Southern Appalachian dialect captured Kephart's attention. His enthusiasm was innate as he had long demonstrated a penchant to study languages, be it Italian, Finnish, or eventually Cherokee. Portions of one of his journals were replete with words and idioms that demonstrated nuances, inflections, and the personalities of the individuals who inspired his enthusiasm. Geographic nomenclature elicited his delight in its inventiveness and the incorporation of Cherokee words. Place names on US Geological Survey maps had readily drawn his attention and curiosity, though he stated he did not discover the "whimsical humor that makes a sport of hardship and privation" behind their derivations until he talked with residents who related the background stories. Articles for the *Asheville Citizen-Times* newspaper from 1930 entitled "Kephart Writes of Odd Names in Smoky Mountains" and "Kephart Tells of Panthers in Smokies" maintained the curiosity in dialect, place names, wildlife, and local lore into the last year of his life.

Kephart incorporated dialect into his narrative works, devoted a chapter in *Our*

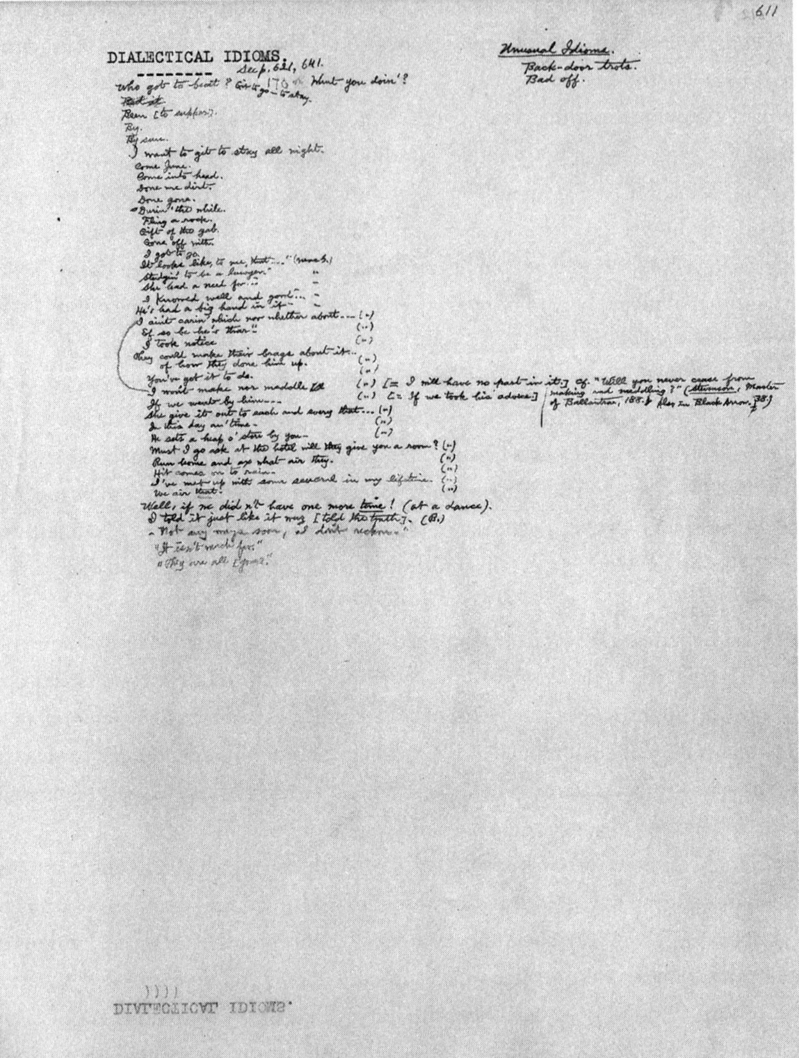
611

DIALECTICAL IDIOMS. Sec p. 621, 641.

Unusual Idioms.
Back-door trots.
Bad off.

Who got to beat? Git to go—to stay. What you doin'?
Bean [to supper].
By.
By sure.
I want to git to stay all night.
Come June.
Come into head.
Done me dirt.
Done gone.
Durin' the while.
Fling a rock.
Gift of the gab.
Gone off with.
I got to go.
It looks like, to me, that ..." (rural)
Studyin' to be a lawyer." "
She had a need for ... "
I knowed well and good ... "
He's had a big hand in it "
I ain't carin' which nor whether about ... (")
Ef so be he's thar!" (")
I took notice (")
They could make their brags about it ... (")
of how they done him up. (")
You've got it to do. (")
I won't make nor meddle with (") [= I will have no part in it.] cf. "Will you never cease from making and meddling?" (Stevenson, Master of Ballantrae, 188.) Also in Black Arrow, 38.)
If we went by him ... (") [= If we took his advice.]
She give it out to each and every that ... (")
In this day an' time. (")
He sets a heap o' store by you. (")
Must I go ask at the hotel will they give you a room? (")
Run home and ax what air they. (")
Hit comes on to rain. (")
I've met up with some several in my lifetime. (")
We air that. (")
Well, if we didn't have one more time! (at a dance).
I told it just like it was [told the truth]. (B.)
"Not any more soon, I don't reckon."
"It isn't much for."
"They are all [illegible]."

Page from Kephart's journal on "Dialectical Idioms."

Southern Highlanders to its discussion, and contributed a "word-list" to the journal *Dialect Notes*. His notations were so extensive that they supported the publication of the book *Smoky Mountain Voices: A Lexicon of Southern Appalachian Speech Based on the Research of Horace Kephart* in 1993[5] As noted in the introduction to the comprehensive *Dictionary of Smoky Mountain English*, published in 2004, "Our knowledge of Smoky Mountain English would be far poorer without the pioneering work of this librarian who left St. Louis for western North Carolina in 1904." In the years following Kephart's death, documentation by scholars such as Joseph S. Hall (1906–1992) would substantially enhance and expand an appreciation of this regional speech.[6] Still, Kephart's fondness for the dialect of his adopted home remains evident and effusive in his writings, whether from the serious and analytical side or to the humorous and self-effacing.

In an oft-related encounter, he asked a neighbor to read a novel written by another author that utilized a rendering of Appalachian dialogue and assumed he would be gauging a reaction to its portrayal of mountain life. Instead, there ensued a lecture on the use of misspelled words. When confronted, Kephart tried to explain that dialect sought to capture the "life and savor" of the conversation, thereby necessitating phonetic renderings. The irate man remained undeterred and countered that Kephart and many other "educated" individuals did not always spell words the way they pronounced them. Kephart acknowledged that this statement was a "most palpable hit; and it gave me a new point of view."[7]

Kephart incorporated several themes and literary motifs into his publications such as dialect, hunting, firearms, and customs. For instance, the three-part series that comprised "A Backwoods Riflemaker" and "An Old-Fashioned Shooting Match" in *American Rifleman* from 1924 was a fictional short story that included extensive technical details on how to craft and manufacture a rifle, the art of shooting older guns, and even simple home-style hospitality. Likewise, the four-part series "Is Man-Hunting 'The Greatest Sport in the World?'" was ostensibly about adventures and exploits centered on moonshining activities from 1919 to 1921. Still, it referenced social etiquettes, personal demeanor, and snippets about the landscape. These articles are also suggestive of his writing style. An August 1919 letter sent to Albert Britt after Kephart's return from a trip to the Sugarlands of Tennessee contained parallels in phrasing and details to the text that would appear in the *All Outdoors* magazine columns a year and a half later and eventually in *Our Southern Highlanders*. In that letter, he also ruminated that, "Some day I may be qualified to perpetrate another book about our wild and wooly East."[8]

Moonshining activities—or "blockading" as Kephart termed it—held his interest

"Hol Rose on right."

over the years. Still, he sought to interweave additional events to heighten the storyline. The events related in "The Killing of Hol Rose" that culminated in the death of Rose, a US prohibition agent, in a confrontation with J. E. "Babe" Burnett were intensified by the community's shock at the unexpected *Romeo and Juliet* courtship that ended in the elopement of Hol Rose's daughter and Babe Burnett's son. In a follow-up column, he updated readers on judicial proceedings in "The Trial of 'Babe' Burnett" and the tensions accompanying the final court decision. He presented his account as factual, and many events are documented in newspaper clippings in his journals and by a ruling of the North Carolina Supreme Court on Burnett's appeal after an initial conviction.[9]

Kephart's journals even provide the identity of the mysterious "Mr. Quick," also known as the "Snake-Stick Man," who accompanied—and even enticed—Kephart on some of his adventures. A clipping from a Hugo, Oklahoma, newspaper named him as W. W. Thomason and commented that the picture of "'Mr. Quick,' and one of his hobbies" in *Our Southern Highlanders* featuring him posing with a large moonshine still was taken at the Hugo city hall and not in western North Carolina.[10]

While not condoning blockading outright, Kephart did question governmental regulations and explained the economic incentives for small distillers when faced with revenue charges and restrictions on manufacture and distribution under a 1909 state act and then the passage of the 18th Amendment to the Constitution that instituted nationwide prohibition in 1920. These arguments often rested on a need to provide for family and the difficulty in transporting bulk grain rather than distilled products to a dealer.

There has been debate about the amount of attention Kephart devoted to moonshining, especially after the enlarged edition of *Our Southern Highlanders,* issued in 1922, incorporated new chapters that gave the book a heavy emphasis on the activity. However, public fascination with prohibition violations was not limited to Southern Appalachia. Al Capone (1899–1947) of Chicago gained notoriety for his illicit operations and ruthless elimination of competitors, as in the infamous 1928 St. Valentine's Day Massacre, and gangster films became a popular genre of entertainment by the early 1930s. Still, Kephart was not immune to altering his previous text to fit a new publication. In his 1906 article "Ways that are Dark" from his "The Mountain Moonshiner" series, he commented that large-scale blockaders had become "rare, if, indeed, they be not quite extinct." Later, after prohibition laws came into effect, he modified his text and left the impression they had always been active.[11]

By the 1910s Kephart understood that further, and at times more dramatic, developments were sweeping Appalachian society and affecting the environment. Though he would still spend time camping in the woods, he had taken up residence in the town of Bryson City in 1910. Before his death in 1931, he authored articles about the transformation he had perceived over two decades, although some works mingled time periods. *Our Southern Highlanders* was not written as a single narrative. Rather, the original 1913 volume and the 1922 enlarged edition incorporated previously published articles along with new chapters and commentary. As a result, there was a sixteen-year difference between the first magazine articles in 1906 and the new edition that became a literary classic. A careful reading of the book discloses an acknowledgement of the passage of time, though this progression was not always explicit. For instance, in the revised edition of *Our Southern Highlanders* Kephart mentioned the impact of World War I as it had brought exposure to wider experiences when "nearly all of the able-bodied young men went away into military service. A great number of the boys and middle-aged men also left home and went into the shipyards or munition plants."[12] However, the book also retained earlier chapters that stressed isolation.

Reading his articles helps clarify the extent of the transitions he had experienced. He summarized what he had witnessed in the Southern Appalachians in a 1930 *New York Times* contribution "Changing Mountaineers of South" that noted how large commercial enterprises, hydroelectric developments, and highways had influenced and altered what he had previously seen as the lives of "the old-fashioned folk of the backwoods." On a more pensive note, he ruminated on what he thought was a waning in the traditional hospitality to which he had been accustomed, as in a reluctance by some people to offer complimentary food and lodging or only grudgingly provide cold food rather than a hot meal.

Kephart did express optimism about the region's prospects in coming years and avenues of improvement. However, while he acknowledged the benefits of a classical education, he believed that training in domestic and agricultural practices as well as trades were vital to the people's livelihood, economy, and their resilience. He praised their ability to learn the production methods required by factories and industries. Still, he thought that "the great need of our mountaineers to-day is trained leaders of their own. The future of Appalachia lies mostly in the hands of those resolute native boys and girls who win the education fitting them for such leadership."[13]

Examples of the rapid changes taking place were succinctly reflected in two brochures that Kephart authored, both titled "Trips in the Smokies," that were printed first in 1929 and then in a 1930 revised version. While similar in their descriptions of the terrain and outdoor advice, they differed in travel suggestions. The 1929 text stressed that only the lower elevations of the North Carolina Smokies may be reached by motor vehicle and that safe exploration of the mountains required guides and horses. He cautioned against relying on currently available topographic maps outside of populated areas and issued the dire warning "anyone going without a guide and relying on these maps is almost sure to get lost for a few hours, if not days." He made no mention of maps in 1930, possibly due to the efforts of US Geological Survey teams that he had mentioned the previous year. Most telling, though, was his concession that a "light car" might now ascend the Smoky Mountains to Newfound Gap and continue into eastern Tennessee.[14]

In the early twentieth century, mainstream American culture drew greater attention in the mountain region through new trends in music and a growing access to radios. Motion pictures came into style, and Kephart himself was solicited in 1926 as a consultant on the silent film *Stark Love* being filmed in the Carolina mountains for release the following year.[15] General consumer goods and even more upscale items were being offered, though purchase still depended on the individual's or family's financial circumstances. On a trip in 1919, Kephart casually remarked on stopping at a store to buy "'meat by-products with ham flavor,' detestable, but standard at every jumping-off place in the United States" on his journey.[16] In his article "Afoot and Awing," Kephart even rode in the modern marvel of an airplane as he took flight in the late 1920s over the Smokies and Bryson City. As he noted, "it is a fast age now."[17]

Kephart arrived in a western North Carolina undergoing changes brought by the railroad's arrival in the 1880s and on the threshold of greater changes in the coming decades. He sought to document his experiences and the lives around him. Despite the divergent views on his life and writings, in the end one of Kephart's contributions may have been to inspire others to research, examine, and express their history. Those who do not know their history are often condemned to have someone else write it for them.

Letter from Kephart to Albert Britt, August 21, 1912

Bryson City, N. C.
August 21, 1912.

Mr. Albert Britt, Editor,
Outing Magazine, New York.

Dear Mr. Britt:

I think the four remaining chapters of Highland Dixie that you wish for the Magazine should be on the following topics:—

1. Domestic Life.
2. Social Life.
3. Clan Organization and Feuds.
4. The Future of Appalachia.

The last of these chapters would sketch the present undeveloped resources of the country, and the mighty change that power development and local manufacturers, already under way, will affect within the next five years—a change not only economic but social, the like of which our country has not yet seen.

Since these four topics demand fuller treatment in the book than magazine articles can compass, I must work out the details first. Hence I will only guarantee to send you one magazine article every thirty days, dating from August 15.

The book should not be limited to less than 100,000 words; for less than that could not do the subject justice, nor would a smaller work be satisfactory here in the South, where the right kind of one is bound to have a larger sale than you are likely to anticipate.

Sincerely yours,

Letter from Kephart to Albert Britt, August 26, 1912

Bryson City, N. C.
August 26, 1912.

Mr. Albert Britt, Editor,
Outing Magazine, New York.

Dear Mr. Britt:

Yes: the Chapter I. that I sent you is to open the magazine series, just as it stands. In the book it is to be followed by other chapters omitted in the magazine; but there will be no loss of sequence to the readers.

I am glad that you like what you have seen of the stuff. This much I may say, perhaps, with due modesty: that I know of no other writer who has lived so long and so intimately with the real mountaineers as I have, or who has been admitted so deeply into their confidence. They are an extremely suspicious and secretive people, who, from feral instinct, hide from outsiders their real character, and are as cunning as any wild things in covering their tracks. The hospitality with which they admit a stranger is perfectly true and perfectly charming; but their slyness and vindictiveness are equally true and anything else than charming.

When first I went among them, there was a bee in my Stetson. We had plenty of stories and descriptions of the Kentucky and Tennessee foothillers, but none of the Carolinians of the high Unakas. Virgin ground! And I had no doubt but that a six-months' tour would equip me to deal with all aspects of their lives and character. My first impressions reassured me. The mountaineers seemed a primitive, picturesque people, open minded, straightforward, easily understood. A night's lodging in a one-room cabin, cheek by jowl with all the family (aye, back to back and toe to toe) revealed even the intimacies of their daily lives. What could be easier than to sketch so directly from nature itself?

Well, the six months passed, and I was not so sure. *Did* I understand this strange race, after all? A year, two years, three. I was among them as one of themselves, participating in all their ways, studying them at guarded and at unguarded moments, under all sorts of strain. Their hardships were my hardships; their pleasures were mine too. Yet was I more than dubious as to my ability, my right, to portray their character.

Eight years have gone. I have been their physician, their scribe, their picket, their witness in court. I do know them, as no man can, of my class, who has not decivilized himself, for a long time, purposely and willingly. As no man can who lives among them merely as teacher or preacher or merchant or boss. How easy to picture only the sunny, the idyllic side of their lives! How tempting to shun the dark and fearsome aspects! But would that be truth? To the world at large I have a duty, too—not that of attorney holding a brief for the mountain people, but of a judge who has seen and heard both sides.

And if I pursue my topic with the calm impartiality of a sociologist, to whom all aspects of life are equally interesting, equally worthy of record, will they my friends of the coves and hillsides, will *they* understand? They will not.

Maybe their children will; and for them I assume the burden. For here is a race of [great] capabilities for good or evil. The mountaineers are face to face with a mighty change. They must accept it, and adapt themselves to utterly strange conditions, or they are a doomed people. As they stand, to-day, the primitive virtues are theirs (so rare in this age as almost to outshine, in my eyes, the tiara of civilization); but the primitive vices are theirs, too, and whoso denies or palliates the fact is no true friend of the mountaineers. Well-meaning missionaries who go among this folk are shocked and scandalized at what seems to them hopeless perversity and race deterioration. It is nothing of the sort. There are reasons for the worst that we find here: it is a natural sequence of isolation, and no more hopeless than the same features of life in the Scotch Highlands two centuries ago. The big outside world has a tender duty, an exquisitely delicate task, to educate our backward kinsmen and fit them for a new social order. But how can it avoid crushing the mountaineers, as it crushed the Indians, unless it be warned and informed by men who not only know the facts but will take the responsibility to speak out and tell the truth?

Little more than a hint of this will appear in my magazine articles; for there is no room there. But in the book itself I feel bound to go farther than telling a mere traveler's tale. [As for me,] I shall waste no space in preaching. "Portray the struggle, and you need write no tract."

But I must get to the postoffice. My August check has not yet come, and this is the 26th. Ask them to get busy, please.

Sincerely yours,

Letter from Kephart to Albert Britt, August 23, 1919

OUTING PUBLISHING COMPANY
141–145 WEST 36th ST. NEW YORK CITY

Bryson City, N. C.
Aug. 23, 1919.

Mr. Albert Britt, Editor
OUTING, New York.

Dear Mr. Britt:—

The letter from Mr. F. M. Cockrell, Jr., goes right to the roots of the most interesting ballistic problems of our time. Your suggestion that I make a special article of the reply will be carried out next week.

I have just returned from a man-hunt in "the Sugarlands" of Sevier County, Tennessee. The Sugarland Mountain runs northwest from the Smokies between Clingman Dome and Mount Le Conte. On its southwestern side is the great gulf that I call "Godforsaken" in *Our Southern Highlanders*. On the northerly side, which is drained by the headwaters of the Little Pigeon River, is a similar descent, though into a narrower basin or rather a gorge, exceedingly steep and rocky, gloomy with immense trees that crowd each other, and choked with laurel and other underbrush, fairly impenetrable except where the one lone trail leads down along a brawling torrent. These two basins, and the mountain dividing them, collectively go by the name of Sugarlands.

We walked eighteen miles the first day, crossing Smoky at an altitude of 5,[3]00 feet, at Collins Gap. I was with a U. S. secret service officer and a quarter-breed Indian. We were after a North Carolinian who had jumped his bond (moonshining and a pistol case); also his father and his brother; all supposed to be hiding out in the Sugarlands. The Federal officer had asked me to go with him, and I was glad of the chance, as it would take me into what had long been known as one of the worst "blockading" districts in America. I wanted to see this business from all angles, including that of the officer. As a posseman I got the latter view. From any other motive the adventure would have been a foolish stunt.

From Clingman to Guyot, taking in both sides of the Smokies, is an area of about 200 square miles of primeval forest, which the lumbermen are just beginning to penetrate. It is uninhabited, except for a few scattered cabins. The Carolina side is rough enough to satisfy almost anyone's lust for mountaineering; but the Tennessee side is simply the Devil's own country, steeper, rockier, more thorny and "laurely" and with fewer trails of any sort, than any other region I know of. It matches the famed Jeffreys' Hell, of Monroe County, [and goes it 100% worse].

When we got down to the first house in Tennessee, about six miles from the divide, we saw a cornfield that slopes at an angle of full 50 degrees. The lower part of it is steeper still, and must have been cultivated on hands and knees. A pumpkin broke loose and fell out of it, bursting like a bombshell in the trail.

But before we got to that house, while going Indian file on a winding trail through the laurel, we saw fresh footprints pointed our way. No one could have passed us unnoticed. So, as it was our business to interrogate everyone we met, we turned back a few paces and peered into the thicket at our left. There lay a burlap sack of stuff that had been hastily abandoned. Some men had heard us coming and had dodged aside. We entered the thicket to where the sack lay and stood there, at gaze and listening, for several minutes. Beyond question the men were lying facing us within a few yards. My companions advanced, while I went back on the trail a bit to stop any break out in that direction. Just then a young man came up from the rear, saw what was up, poised his shotgun and stood at alert. It turned out that his companions had heard but not seen us, and jumped aside, hiding. They were of no use to us, and we went on.

This only illustrates how suspicious and jumpy the people were. For the first time in my life I found it hard to get food and shelter among southern mountaineers. Our mission was too obviously hostile to somebody, and we had come [down] on them from the rear. Until they learned who the "somebody" was, and just who we were, they were scared or hostile, according to temperament. Afterward they shared with us the best they had.

Next day we crossed Sugarland Mountain into "Godforsaken." There is only one crossing. It goes sharply up the side of what [looks like] a precipice, though heavily timbered, for some 1,500 or maybe 2,000 feet. The top is only five feet wide. The descent on the other side is just as steep. A clue led us to a [new] lumber camp that was being built on Rough Creek. We waited for the hands to come in to dinner. One of them, a North Carolinian who knew us, spied us at some distance, jumped like a cat into the laurel, and fled the country. The rest of the crew came in, but many were nervous or ill-tempered at our presence. We ate a snack here. The men we sought were not in this outfit.

Another clue was picked up. My companions went on to a camp on Little River, while I returned over the mountain alone, being in no shape for a night journey over more cliffs. (The batteries of our two search-lights would not last very long, and my eyes are no longer good at night. Besides, I was darned tired.) When just over the summit, I stepped on a loose mossy rock, fell, and wrenched my knee. Was more than two hours getting down the mountain, sidewise, as the knee immediately stiffened. The other men came in late, reporting another false lead.

We had other adventures; but I must cut this short. I came out on a mule. This was the most hazardous part of the whole performance; the trail looks impossible for "ridin' critters," and is so for any that are not mountain bred.

The trip was not a failure, after all. The men were not caught; but we learned that they had not been in the Sugarlands, and it is now likely that they will be caught elsewhere.

We discovered a land that has never heard of the high cost of living. For lodging and breakfast at one house we paid 25 cents each. For two big meals and lodging, at another, we paid one dollar for the three of us. It was all the people would take; and they asked us to come again.

This is merely one of many incidents in a pretty lively three months, ever since the secret service man came to our town out of nowhere, and took a room at the old hotel where I stay. Nobody knew his real business until court convened last month, and then he had plenty for it to attend to. Innocently I helped him. He is a tip-top fellow, educated, a writer (under pen-name) of clever stories, knows the country out West that I used to live in, an expert with firearms, and all the other things that go to make a chum for such a chap as H.K. So, after the dramatic revelation of his true business, we continued to gad about in company, notwithstanding that it has got me "in Dutch" with various natives.

Some day I may be qualified to perpetrate another book about our wild and wooly East.

Sincerely yours,
Horace Kephart

Roving with Kephart

IS MAN-HUNTING "THE GREATEST SPORT IN THE WORLD?"

CHAPTER I

The Snake-Stick Man, Being the First of a Series of Southern Moonshine, Unusual Detective Work, and a Raid into the Sugarlands of Tennessee

[Author's Note:—All of the incidents in the following narnative [*sic*] have occurred within the past two years. All of the participants [but one] are still living at the time of this writing. The events are well known to many people who will read these lines. That is my guarantee that they are presented here without any embellishment whatever. Some of the personal names in the first three chapters are made up, for reasons that will be obvious. Those in the fourth chapter are real.]

It was along in May, I believe, of 1919, that a sturdy, dark-eyed stranger came to the old hotel where I live, and was introduced to the landlord by the Indian Agent from Lufty,[18] who had brought him over in his car.

"Uncle Bill, this is a gentleman from the West who is taking a vacation and wishes to ramble about over the mountains. He would like to stay with you a few weeks."

Mr. Quick, as I shall call the stranger, had the air of a prosperous ranchman of rather retired habit. He engaged one of the best rooms and was given a seat at table alongside of me. We exchanged the usual inanities at supper, but neither of us made advances toward sociability.

Our visitor wore a conspicuous emblem of a fraternal order in which, by the token, he had attained high degree. He went out and made friends at once with brethren of the lodge, but was a bit distant with other people.

From *All Outdoors*, January 1921

There came a fine day when I was cocked up in a chair reading in front of the hotel. Mr. Quick seated himself beside me and became absorbed at once in a yellow-covered book. When the dinner-bell rang we went in, leaving our reading matter on a card table in the office.

It chanced that I was the first one out from dinner. In picking up my magazine I noticed that the stranger's book was entitled *La Guardia Blanca*, which I instantly recognized as a Spanish translation of one of Conan Doyle's novels, a tale of free adventure[r]s of the Middle Ages fighting for fun and booty.

I stood and stared at it like one possessed.

No ordinary American would be reading an English romance in a Spanish version. And here, of all places under the sun! Thirteen years, off and on, had I dwelt in this remote region of the Great Smoky Mountains. In all that time I had not till now met man or woman here who knew any foreign tongue, save two or three college men from the outer world, a casual Jew peddler or two, and one stray Italian who had been jailed on a charge of assassination.

When the new boarder returned to his tilted chair there was a topic of mutual interest at last. "I see that you read Spanish," I remarked.

"O yes," he replied, brightening, "I speak it, too."

We dropped our books and began a lively conversation. The man's reticence fled. He was interested in the Indians; had been among them for many years, in the West, in Florida. He spoke Creek (or was it Choctaw?) and Navaho and Seminole. Navaho he had found one of the most difficult tongues in the world, the grammar intricate, the pronunciation hard for our ears to catch and our mouths to utter. He knew the western Cherokees, but not their language. What a romantic history was theirs! How strange that this Eastern Band of ours were still occupying a bit of their ancient stronghold in the Carolina Smokies! It would be amusing for him to pick up a little of the Cherokee speech while here on vacation; and Indian relics—he had a collection from other tribes at home.

One of my own hobbies. Of course I would assist him.

We swapped experiences of western life, and a few confidences. For my part, I was a writer, of a sort; field sports and out-of-the-way places my specialty. Just now I was embarrassed by lack of a camera to illustrate some of my stuff.

Ah! He had a good camera. He would be delighted to accompany me into the hills and make any pictures I wished. Then, very modestly, he admitted that he tried a little writing now and then himself: adventure stories—that sort of thing. Might he see some of my work?

Might a visitor see Mamma's baby? I took him to my office and turned him loose.

He devoured books and scrap books, making intelligent comments on what he read.

And so I, too, was a "gun crank." He had been one all his life. What did I think of the Luger? What of the Army automatic? How about the old Frontier model Colt forty-five? He had all three with him; also two automatic rifles. Might we not go out for a little practice together?

We could, and we did. Mr. Quick gets his name in this narrative from the "lightning draw" that he demonstrated with pistols, and his rapid, accurate work with the rifle.

His way of carrying a Luger interested me. It was neither on the hip nor under the left arm, but in what is called a suspender holster, worn inside the band of the trousers, on the left side, with butt of gun to the right, of course. It was made of soft leather with rubber interlining on the back. He wore strong suspenders, from which the leather tab that engages the trousers buttons had been removed on the left side. The top of the holster fastened to the suspender cast-off. The sides of the holster back had buttonholes for the trousers buttons, which were sewed to the inside of the band. Thus the holster served to hold up the trousers, as a part of the suspenders, and it could neither sag down much from the pistol's weight nor pull up when the gun was drawn.

This is about the only way that a rather large pistol can be carried concealed when one is not wearing a coat and yet be handy for instant drawing. Mr. Quick always wore a vest, generally with only one or two buttons fastened at the bottom. The pistol butt was where he could grasp it instantly from any position, standing, sitting, or otherwise. The gun would not fall out if he was scuffling on the ground. Heiser of Denver makes a somewhat similar holster, but Mr. Quick's was of extra workmanship and design, made by himself. A revolver in such position would bulge the vest, but an automatic pistol is so flat that it is not noticeable, except to men who are "wise" to that sort of thing.

We found that we had many interests in common. We roamed the hills, talking natural history, field sports, comparative scenery, natives and their ways, ever so many things. We went among the Cherokees and among the white "branch-water people."

The man was genuine. Never for a moment did he assume interest for mere politeness sake; nor did I. Honestly, I don't believe we bored each other in two months of almost daily association. How many men, or women, can say that of each other?

Blessed, thrice blessed, the comradeship of hobby-riders, so long as their extravagances are mutual. One hobby may do; but Mr. Quick and I had a dozen to share—a whole paddockful, one might say, in sporting terms.

Speaking by the way, of pictures: if you have files of ALL OUTDOORS and OUTING for 1919 you can find specimens of Mr. Quick's photography in some articles of mine on "The Sport of Still Hunting" and "Primitive Mills of the Southern Mountaineers." Others may appear in the future.

One day my new comrade wanted a straight stick for a cane. I introduced him to sourwood shoots, which seem made by nature for that purpose. They grow exceptionally straight and slender. They season without cracking or checking, even when peeled green, and turn lightweight but pretty strong and hard. The peeled wood is white.

He passed by those that were of proper size for walking-sticks and selected one thick enough for a handspike. I wondered, but said nothing.

Next day I observed that he was carving a big spiral on that sourwood club and shaving the rest down to cane diameter. Little by little the spiral, that stood in relief, assumed the form of a rattlesnake. Deftly and neatly he carved the snake's scales, the rattle, the wicked flat head and forked tongue. He worked by eye alone, sitting easily in his chair, and used no tool but a pocketknife.

In three days he had a rattlesnake wound round that stick, complete, and painted to the life in watercolors. It was fit to give anyone a jolt and make him gasp when the stick was thrust toward him with a twisting motion.

Hitherto Mr. Quick had not made many acquaintances in town or country. But now, as he sauntered down the street flourishing his stick, he set the girls everywhere screaming and giggling, and the gamins crazy with delight. People crowded about and followed him. In a day or so he was on familiar terms with everybody, from the prim deaconness to the lowest-lived boot-legger within five miles.

They called him "the Snake-Stick Man." Nobody now cared what his real name might be; for had he not been christened and adopted by the community for itself? Ah me!

Mr. Quick was affable and full of fun, now that the crowd was with him. He made several snake-sticks, each an improvement on the earlier ones. On one he had a monkey chasing a lizard up the snake's tail and stabbing at it with a devil's trident. Tourists passing on trains offered him five to ten dollars for a snake-stick, but he would not sell. He gave one to me, and others to members of his lodge.

But by and by something began to go wrong with the Snake-Stick Man. He neglected his meals, or toyed futilely with them. He remained much in his room, or took sudden long walks by himself, and came back with a worried air as though harassed by some evil spirit. At times he sank into deep despondency. Yet he complained little, and explained never a word.

I was concerned for his health, but delicate about intruding into what was his own affair. Finally, though, I could bear it no longer, and so I asked him what was the matter, and if I could do anything for him.

He answered with obvious reluctance that he was cursed with such spells at times. It was nervous dyspepsia. He had tried the stock remedies. Nothing would do him any good but a little whiskey.

Corpo di Baccho! So that was it. Well, he might be a neurasthenic, though he didn't look it. Anyhow—

Yes, I did. You [who] would not have done so, under the circumstances, may stick *that* in your pipe and smoke it.

But the availabilities, so far as I could reach out, were few and small. Then came other new acquaintances to Mr. Quick's relief. There is a fellow-feeling in this world for nervous dyspeptics—or there was then, in the natal year of nation-wide prohibition, when we did not yet know whether to consider the new crusade as a godsend, a calamity or a joke.

Of course this was moonshine liquor; for it has been a long time since there had been any other kind in our little part of the South. And more of it came to a certain room upstairs in the old Cooper House than could fairly be accounted for in the treatment of one man's gastric neuroses.

Mr. Quick will learn now for the first time (he is far away, but he gets ALL OUTDOORS) that a suspicion was growing, about this time, in the bosom of one H. Kephart, that he, our Snake-Stick Man, was "fixing for a good long drunk"—to put it in the delicate way of our mountaineers. Laugh as you will, Mr. Quick; it is your inning.

As it turned out, I was dead wrong. A tablespoonful, in company, was his limit. Stomach so weak it could not stand more at a time. Just a "little dib," you know, now and then, to tone it up. And I am satisfied, now, that he never touched a drop unless someone was around.

Neither the Muse of History nor the Goddess of Justice would thank me for saying any more about Mr. Quick's liquor supply. Rather it is up to me to bring this narrative swiftly to its climax.

In July came our summer term of Superior Court. Came, too, on the opening day, several woebegone citizens to a little red brick building that adjoins the court-house and is adorned with iron bars.

Like lightning from a fair sky there crashed upon us the report, certified and all too true, that our Snake-Stick Man was a special agent of the Indian Bureau. He had been picked for the job of finding out who was making or vending liquor on the Indian Reservation, and to make their paths straight to the chain-gang. Outside of that he had not meddled.

In our sparsely settled region everybody knows nearly everybody else. It logically follows that when I looked up at those faces behind the bars some of them had a familiar look. It follows that they had seen me running around with the Snake-Stick Man for two months or more.

Now I could put that in *my* pipe and smoke it.

After the volcano in my bosom had subsided enough for a cool survey of the situation I took a new interest in Mr. Quick. You would have cut him dead, of course. But you are not a sporting writer. In a sense, Mr. Quick and I had swapped places; for he was now my "material." I purposed seeing what sort of fellow he would prove to be when all masks were dropped.

When he returned to the hotel that evening I went straight to him and we had a man-to-man talk.

"So far as my official business here is concerned," said he, "I make no apology. I have been in the federal service for twenty years. I am, you might say, a soldier; for it amounts to the same thing. I obey orders. My loyalty to my Government is superior to any other consideration."

"But Kephart,' [*sic*] he continued, "I tried my darndest not to deceive you in anything else. If I made any slip in that I sincerely beg your pardon."

"You didn't," I answered. "You were the real thing. If you had been a poseur, pretending an interest in nature, in literature, and so on, that you did not honestly feel, you could not have put it over, with me, for ten minutes."

There followed a long talk that touched the depths of human nature, but with which neither the Muse of History nor the Goddess of Justice has any business.

I have a pent-up thought or two that I will get off my system. For the average run of detectives, and their business, I have little respect. There may be a larger proportion of decent fellows among them than I know of; but I have met some sorry specimens.

I cordially detest the public policy that has quartered an army of federal spies upon the American people and authorizes or permits them to invade homes and to search individuals publicly on mere suspicion. I believe that policy to be wholly and thoroughly bad.

But here was a different case, and a different sort of man. No common spy, no bluffing roughneck, no graduate of the penitentiary turned renegade to his own people, could have done what he did. No plausible rogue playing the part of gentleman could have done it either.

There have been gentlemen detectives in fiction: Monsieur Dupin and Sherlock Holmes, for examples. Never before had I met one in real life. But here he stood.

Think back a bit. He had been posted about me, as one who had written a good deal about the mountain moonshiners and who evidently knew what he was talking about. He wanted to make my acquaintance at the start, and yet circumstances did not permit him to tell me frankly who and what he was. How did he go about it?

He made no advances. He was a book-lover himself, and also a frequenter of far places. So he knew from his own experience how it is to be isolated from literary centers. He knew I must be bored with the commonplace. So he simply brought that exotic book within range of my vision, with never a word nor a look, and the trick was turned.

And those snake-sticks for the multitude. Here again was applied psychology. What other trick could have won him the instant attention and good will of every class of people, in this kind of community, without him having to say a word for himself?

Here was a detective who actually used brains in his business. Here was a detective who had the instincts of a gentleman, instead of those of a sneak.

Mr. Quick stayed on at our hotel for another month, taking part sometimes in little forays at night that were pulled off by local officers, or by himself with their assistance. His days of usefulness as a detective in western North Carolina were over. Henceforth he was a straight-out raider with no disguise.

I had long walks and long talks with him again, just as before, and regardless of public comment. Turn about is fair play. He had used me as a subject of investigation; now it was my turn.

I found him even more interesting in his true character than he had been in the assumed one. Mystery adds a glamour to commonplace personalities, and they fade when it is dissolved. But Mr. Quick rather gained when he stepped out into the light.

One day, after telling me of one of his adventures here in our own "big sticks," as we call the forest wilderness that surrounds us, Mr. Quick remarked: "Man-hunting is the finest sport in the world."

I kindled at that[;] for I had heard the same sentiment before, expressed in the very same words, by other man-hunters who were as different from Quick as men can well be. I kindled because I had often wondered, sportsman that I am, whether I should find it so if the test happened to come my way. I doubted, but was ready to be convinced.

So when Mr. Quick told me, early one morning, that he was going on a man-hunt across the Smokies into Tennessee, in a region that I had never visited, and he invited me to go along, I equipped myself hastily and stepped into the car that was to take him on the first leg of the journey. (*To be Continued.*)

Roving with Kephart

IS MAN-HUNTING "THE GREATEST SPORT IN THE WORLD?"

CHAPTER II

A Raid into the Sugarlands

So we were outward bound, on a man-hunt, across the Great Smoky Mountains into the Sugarland country of Tennessee. Whom we might be after, or what for, was little concern of mine. This was supposed to be a sporting proposition, and the arrangements were in the hands of Mr. Quick.

It was a bright morning in mid-August, with a portent of sultriness here in the river valley, but of cool airs and clear prospects on the high ranges that we were heading for.

We sped along the new highway, crossed the Tuckaseegee near Governor's Island, and soon turned northward along [a] charming tributary, the Okonaluftee. This stream, which is called Lufty for short, has its sources among the precipitous peaks and ridges between Clingman Dome and Mt. Guyot—one of the roughest and most heavily timbered regions in eastern America.

There had been no time for proper preparation. We did not even provide ourselves with hobnailed shoes. I assured Mr. Quick that this would give us trouble, but that if he could stand it, I could.

At Bir[d]town the site of an ancient Cherokee village, we took on a short, dark, pleasant faced fellow, who I supposed was to serve as guide. His Indian name, as nearly as I can spell it, was Deeyahkatchee (*a* as in *father*). Out of mercy to the printer let us call him Katch.

We passed the campus of the Indian school at Cherokee and turned up the left

---

From *All Outdoors,* February 1921

fork of Lufty. Now the flivver chugged hard, and squirmed and bumpety-bumped over a road that grew worse and worse.

It was ten in the morning when we arrived at Smokemont, a new sawmill village, head of navigation for Ford cars. Ahead of us was a hard day's travel afoot.

At a little wayside store we filled our pockets with such luncheon stuff as the place afforded; some crackers, some "meat by-products with ham flavor," detestable, but standard at every jumping-off place in the United States.

Then we swung into a long, steady climbing stride.

Hitherto there had been little said. But as our legs limbered to their work, so were our tongues loosened. By listening to Quick and Katch it was easy for me to unravel the plot of our adventure.

There was a bad old citizen, a moonshiner, white, with perhaps a streak of red for good measure, and he had two sons who were true to type. Call them Old Man Ruff, and Buck and Jake.

I don't know that I ever saw the senior Ruff, but I remembered the two offspring well. Buck cut such a dash when they arrested him, one time, in our town, that they penned him alone in the inner cage of the jail. At night he wrenched off a steel brace from his cot, with which he pried apart some rods of the cage and so joined the other prisoners. With their help, using the brace for a tool, he dug a hole through the brick wall. Then it was easy to let himself down with knotted blankets. Exit Buck.

Jake came to town, some months later, and proceeded to make merry, after the fashion that our lumberjacks call "hellin' around." When an officer went to run him in, Jake pulled a long-barreled Colt (the only Bisley model I ever saw in the mountains). But he was too fuddled to get the drop. After a season in jail he was let out on bond. Presto! He jumped it.

The point of it all, for us, was that Katch was Jake's bondsman. Katch now had but a short time in which to produce the aforesaid Jake, or he must kiss good-bye to five hundred dollars. Nor was that the worst of it. He would lose his wife, too, without even a bye-bye kiss; for Katch assured us she would "tear up the patch" and forsake him if he had to part with those five hundred dollars.

"Ain't it a fact," said he, "that this life is just one damned thing after another?"

We agreed that forsooth it is much alike, in the marble mansions of the rich and in the hillside cabin of Mr. and Mrs. Deeyahkatchee.

Katch recently had been "tipped off" that the three Ruffs had fled together across the state line and were hiding out in the Sugarlands. So he had brought his troubles to the detective. That gentleman already had federal warrants for the fugitives, but, to provide further against contingencies, he had our sheriff swear him in as a local deputy and give him state warrants as well. He also bore papers for one or two other citizens of North Carolina who were supposed to be enjoying the innocent hospitality of Tennessee.

My own status in the affair was not yet defined. I had not been sworn in as an officer. Yet Mr. Quick had provided me with a .45 Colt automatic and a pair of handcuffs. I did not assume that he meant me to eat soup with them. Probably the swearing business could be attended to at his convenience. Anyway, I was with the bunch; and "bunch it" I surely would. This was a sporting proposition.

It is a little over nine miles uphill from Smokemont to a crossing of the divide that we Carolinians call Collins's Gap, marked Indian Gap on the government map. This is the only pass that is practicable on horseback in more than thirty miles of the Smoky range. On the Carolina side there is a wagon road, of fairly easy grade, to the top. Beyond, down the Tennessee side—but we will come to that.

A logging railroad was being pushed up through the wilderness, along this route. Some time it will cross the Smokies and send feeders down the razorback ridges to haul up timber from the far side.

At the second construction camp we found a gang of Indians working on the grade. All of them knew Katch and his troubles, many of them knew me, and we could tell from their sly glances and grins that they identified Quick as the Snake-Stick Man, and that they felt something was in the wind.

A red athlete on my right sang out to us *"Bon jour."*

It was startling to hear French from a full-blooded Cherokee; but I remembered that he and many of his tribesmen had seen hot service, and acquitted themselves well[,] in the World War.

We stopped for luncheon at a mossy springside in the Beech Flats. It was a cold bite and a bad one, but we were ravenous and down it went.

Soon we entered the balsam zone. It was an abrupt change from the world we had emerged from; real mountains now, and a forest reminiscent of the far North.

At a few minutes past 3 p. m. we "topped out" in the Gap. This is probably the deepest sag in twenty miles of divide from Clingman Dome [to] Mt. Guyot. The government map indicates its elevation to be 5,300 feet above sea-level.

If you had before you the Knoxville and Mt. Guyot sheets of that map (U. S. Geological Survey) you might get some idea of the kind of country we were in. You would observe from the contour lines that we were surrounded on all sides by high and steep mountains (uninhabited they are, and heavily forest-clad), and that we stood upon the state line that marks the end of North Carolina, the beginning of Tennessee.

The map of this upper zone is very faulty. It shows a 5,700-foot "Mt. Mingus," on our right, that does not exist. It places the sharp pinnacle[s] of the Chimney Tops directly on the state line (*i. e.*, the backbone of the divide) whereas in reality they are on a ridge that leads off and away into Tennessee.

The courses of Alum Cave Creek and the head of Little Pigeon River are misdrawn. In fact, most of the headwaters along the Smoky divide are sketched in by guesswork, where they happen to be marked at all. Whosoever, being a stranger, relieth on that map for guidance shall infallibly lose his way.

At this time of year the Gap was a luxurious place on which to lounge and view and dream. We cast ourselves on the grass and took a good smoke as we rested our tired limbs.

Ahead of us was the descent into Tennessee. The road had abruptly ended. Beyond was a steep and rocky trail, going down, down along a torrent into the gloom of narrow gulfs that were choked with laurel and spruce and balsam.

This was the beginning of the Sugarlands, a country of ill-fame, hidden deep in remote gorges, difficult of access, tenanted by a sparse population who preferred to be a law unto themselves. For many a year it had been known on our side of the mountains as Blockaders' Glory, which is the same as saying Moonshiners' Paradise, and we all believed it to be fitly named.

Thus doth sinless North Carolina look down upon sinful Tennessee.

Katch was the only one of us who had ever been down that trail. Quick might as well have been on the moon, for all he knew of the land; and it is safe to wager that he would be equally [un]concerned in either situation.

As for me, all I knew of the Sugarlands by actual observation was what I had now and then glimpsed from afar, standing on some peak of the divide. I recalled my first impression. It was years ago, of a bitter cold winter evening, that I looked down from the north front of Siler's Bald into a great triangular gulf that is formed by the Miry Ridge and the Sugarland Mountain with the main Smokies as a base.

That was a weird and forbidding land. Vast labyrinths of rhododendron covered those profound and dismal depths, impenetrable, sunless, dead but for the murky evergreen of shrubs and spruces. The place was unearthly in its dreariness and desolation. I turned to my companion mountaineer and asked him if it had a name.

"No: not as a whole."

"Let us call it Godforsaken."

"A good name: it is fitten."

"What lies off beyond that Sugarland Mountain to the northeast?"

"Down on the lower reaches," he replied, "there's a settlement where they mostly make liquor and honey, but they call it the Sugarlands."

"And the upper reaches?"

"Hell itself, perpendic'lar."

I recalled now that description of his, and at the same time looked dubiously at the smooth-soled street shoes with which both Quick and I were shod. But this was a sporting proposition.

We started down from the Gap at 4 o'clock, passing two recently abandoned browse camps and the ruins of a burned log camp. The trail was what remained of a military road that had been made across the Smokies in the Civil War. What sort of road it must have been, in its prime, may be judged from the fact that cannon had to be dismounted from their carriages and dragged over the bare rocks and clay.

On down we passed through the balsam zone and thence into a forest of great hardwood trees of many species. The trail meandered along the bottom of deep and narrow glens, with great cliffs above, and dense laurel on either side. Seldom could we see out to right or left. There were no side trails.

We slipped and slid. The toes of our street shoes punished us. They were broad enough, being of army pattern, but for this kind of work they should have been a half-size longer.

Rocks of all sizes, everywhere. Any boulder less than a house we called a "pebble."

Quick asked the Indian: "How do they bury people in this country?"

"Guess they criminate them," answered Katch, and he misunderstood our laughter.

Down, down, down! And never a sign that man had ever been here before us, except along the narrow track we followed. The torrent alongside us dashed over ledges and boulders with hiss and roar. The crossings became difficult. There was nowhere a footlog, so we had to jump from one waterworn rock to another. Those that did not project high were slippery as grease. If one of us had fallen, the others might have had to make a litter to bear him out.

Five miles from the Collins Gap, and fourteen from where we had started afoot, we came to the first evidence of settlement. It was a bit of cornfield, perched above the trail at a slope so steep that it must have been dug up with a mattock and hoed on hands and knees. A pumpkin broke loose from its vine, as we came along, fell out of the field and burst on the trail like a bomb.

Why would anyone plant corn on such a place? Because the Sugarlanders were a little behind the times; they had not yet learned to make whiskey out of anything more lethal than honest corn.

We passed through a couple of old clearings, very small ones, in each of which stood an abandoned cabin—just a log pen covered with clapboards, a dirt floor, and a pile of rocks shoulder-high for a chimney.

Then the trail wound tortuously through dense laurel that grew twelve to twenty feet high, gnarled and twisted and with interlocking limbs. We were following it, Indian file, of course, when Katch, who was in the lead, suddenly stopped as if shot.

"Two or three men have come this way," he whispered, pointing to fresh footprints, "and they dodged aside when they heard us coming toward them."

It was true. The tracks showed that the men were advancing in our direction; that they had heard us at thirty or forty yards and had instantly vanished in the laurel on our left-hand side. No one would do that unless he had reason to dodge all comers.

We parted the laurel carefully and squirmed through it to a little opening diagonally to the rear. There on the ground lay two burlap sacks of rations and clothing, a haversack, a shotgun, and a small rifle, hastily abandoned by men who had plunged on into the farther laurel. In such a mizmaze of tough and tangled vegetation they would have to crawl. In all probability they were now lying flat in it, facing toward us, not twenty yards distant, and with pistols drawn. We, on our side, could not see ten feet into that jungle.

There we stood at gaze, listening, for several minutes. Not a twig cracked. It was certain that the fugitives had not stirred. They were awaiting our move.

It was a rather ticklish situation. If we advanced upon them we could not help but make enough noise for them to locate us. They would see us before we saw them. If they chose to fire, they could do so with certain aim. If they were residents of the country, and killed one or more of us, they could readily fix up a story that would clear them in their own court. We were interlopers if we made the least hostile move.

And yet these might be the very men we had come so far to seize. If we let them slip by, they would be gone for good and all. Why should residents of this district fly from the very sound of travelers along the trail?

We consulted in whispers. Then Quick decided to advance. Being on the left, I stepped out to the trail to head off the men if they turned to flee; for in that case they would have to break for the trail.

Quick and Katch started to move forward into the thicket. It was a tense moment. Then my ear caught a faint sound from *behind*. I wheeled, and there stood a tall youth of eighteen, in the trail, bending forward on the alert, his shotgun poised, his eyes straining at my comrades. He was pale but resolute. I well remember the grim set of his jaw.

I spoke, and he was startled; for he had not seen me.

"Are those your things in there?"

"[N]o; they belong to some fellows I'm with."

"Who are you?"

He flushed angrily, as though that were none of my business, but gave me a name.

My companions had heard us, and they came out of the thicket.

"What are you doing here?" demanded the detective sternly.

"Going fishing." The lad's reply was ready, but defiant. Of course he was lying, and he knew we knew it; but every mountaineer is schooled from boyhood to meet such an emergency as this. Where was our evidence?

He was put through a quiz that developed nothing. [Quick and] Katch described the men we were after, but the fellow denied all knowledge of them, and we were satisfied that in this he was telling the truth. He and his party no doubt were on the way to some still-house, where they would stay until the "run" was made. But that was none of our present business.

So we moved on. It was plain enough that we would have some queer experiences in the Sugarlands, where the very first people we met were "on the dodge." Very well: this was a sporting proposition.

(*To be continued.*)

Roving with Kephart

IS MAN-HUNTING "THE GREATEST SPORT IN THE WORLD?"

CHAPTER III

Blockaders' Glory

Looking backward it seemed a long time since we had breakfasted. Our luncheon up in the Smokies had not counted for much: canned meat and crackers are poor fuel for mountaineering.

The shades were deepening to twilight in this cleft between the cliffs. So we pressed on eagerly to find some lodging place for the night, and a hot supper, God willing, to put strength back into our weary limbs.

The lad with the shotgun had told us that the first house would be Old Man Warne's.[19]

We came to it in about half an hour. It was the usual log house of the backwoods, set in a small rocky clearing against a background of towering wooded mountainside.

Through a gap opening southeastward we got our first long-range view of a bit of the country we had descended through. More than three thousand feet above us rose those sheer pinnacles of rock that they call the Chimney Tops. They protrude like tusks from the top of a ridge that is so narrow that a man can sit down astraddle it and toss a pebble a thousand feet down through the air. Yet such is the nature of rock and climate in this region that wherever a cliff is not quite vertical it will hold moisture and vegetation. So the Chimney Tops are not bare, but clothed with little tough shrubs and bracken, or with balsam and spruce and rhododendron where the slopes will permit their roots to grapple.

To the northeast of us was a face of Bullhead Mountain that was vertical, or even

---

From *All Outdoors,* March 1921

overhung; and here was naked rock, hundreds of feet high, in which we could see the mouths of small caves like portholes in an old-fashioned man-of-war.

From Warne's yard came several hounds and curs, bristling and bellowing the alarm. Immediately two or three men appeared, among them a stout old fellow, red-faced, essaying to smile, but evidently more anxious than pleased at our sudden advent.

Katch did most of the talking for us. He told the Warnes what men we were after, and why, but did not give them our own names nor credentials. I felt that this was a blunder. In the mountains it is the stranger's first duty to tell who he is, where he is from, and whom he knows that might turn out to be a mutual acquaintance.

Old man Warne said at once that he had seen no one answering the description of our fugitives from justice. He was plainly nervous. He had instinctive doubts that we were telling him our real business. We had come into his neighborhood suddenly as it were through the back door. We were armed (Mr. Quick's automatic Winchester, at least, was conspicuous to everyone), and neither of us, I fancy, was reassuring as to "cut of jib."

When strangers come to a mountain home, and have told who and what they are, then, if the owner likes their appearance, even a little bit, he will invite them in to rest. Mr. Warne did not invite us in; nay, he promptly directed us to the next house farther on.

We could fairly feel the flutter of the women and children of his family, who remained indoors, peeping out through cracks, and no doubt sighing with relief when we turned and went on down along the Little Pigeon.

Soon we came opposite another cabin on the far side of the stream from where the trail ran. It was set in a remarkable location.

In front was the wild torrent, now grown in volume, that boiled and roared between large rocks. Two loose planks, end to end, served as rude drawbridges across the chasm. The rocks were too far apart for a man to leap from one to the other, save at peril of falling stunned or broken into the brawling water, which immediately would sweep him away. With the planks withdrawn, the house would be secure from sudden frontal attack. Behind it rose the steep Sugarland Mountain, across which, as we were to learn on the morrow, there ran but a single difficult trail.

"A natural fortification," remarked Quick to me.

"Yes; we will call it The Castle."

Neither of us three adventurers knew any residents of the Sugarlands. Katch had been advised by someone to seek out a certain Jasper Fenn "who don't fool with liquor and likely will tell you the truth."

When we came to where the trail broadened into a wagon road, and a footbridge crossed the stream, we knew we were near Fenn's home. Presently it was to be seen: a prosperous looking place, with a fenced front yard in which stood over a hundred bee-gums (hives made of cuts from hollow logs).

"Looks more civilized," one of us remarked. "Here, surely, they will ask us in."

The usual challenge came from a dog. The master of the house appeared. Again Katch explained our business, and Quick reinforced him with details.

Mr. Fenn's expression changed from calm to perplexity, and then to embarrassment. He did not invite us in. He protested that he had neither seen nor heard anything of fugitive rogues from North Carolina, and we could plainly see that he did not want to mix in our business. It was also plain that he suspected we might be rogues ourselves, putting up a false story as a blind while nosing into the home affairs of Sugarland.

I happened to stand behind him, as he talked with my companions, and was whittling a groove around my walking-stick to shorten it. The groove completed, I tapped the end of the stick on the ground and snapped it off. Fenn jumped as if a gun had been cocked behind him and wheeled around. A man so nervous as that may be either cowardly or dangerous. There are mighty few cowards in the mountains, and he was not one of them.

Night was coming on. We finally asked Fenn if he would let us have something to eat. He muttered an excuse, but consulted his wife. She did not welcome the suggestion, but said she could give us a "cold bite." And she did not even warm the coffee.

Now I have had years of association with mountain people of every degree. This was the first time I ever was made to feel unwelcome. But it was also the first time I had ever appeared among them in the role of a man-hunter.

When we offered to pay for our food the Fenns would not take a cent. They directed us to the next house, but made no suggestion as to where we might find lodging.

We plodded on down the road in gathering darkness.

"Folks around here seem jumpy," I observed.

"Guess we won't get much out of them," said Katch.

"Not much information," answered Quick, "and it looks as if we'd have to stand hitched all night."

"It isn't us they're afraid of: it's each other. When a man fleeing from North Carolina takes refuge in the Sugarlands, it's a cinch that he knows somebody here. He must make a living somehow. The natural occupation for him is blockading or whiskey running. No doubt the Ruffs would be as welcome at that as anybody. Warne may not know them; Fenn may not know them; but some of their neighbors may be hiding and employing them at this moment. Hence the theorem: Don't tell anything about anybody, or you'll get in Dutch with your neighbors."

The next two miles were weary ones, and black night had fallen upon us by the time we came to a place where we thought it might be worth while to apply for shelter.

Dogs rushed at us with fangs glistening and hair on end. When the owner appeared there was the same old round of question and answer. We were not asked to stop for the night.

This man, however, did not seem perturbed. He was smooth and easy in manner; but his eyes betrayed secret amusement at our night-bound plight.

He hinted that a neighbor living back on the mountainside might know something to our advantage, if anybody did.

So we stumbled on over the back fields, picking our way with flashlights, and finally came to a shack not much bigger than a piano-box. Dogs, as usual. We helloed. A lamp was lighted within the house, and a man came out in his bare feet.

No; he knew nothing. But if our scalawags were anywhere in the country they would probably be at one of the lumber camps, several miles on the far side of Sugarland Mountain. A place for us to spend the night? Well, we might try Old Man Tuckett's; he kept visitors sometimes.

Scene at Old Man Tuckett's

10 P. M.

Two narrow beds: Katch in one of them; a boy of the household in the other.

One wide bed: Quick and Kephart inspecting it. This bed is a trough in the center. Straw mattress underneath, feather mattress on top, quilts over all.

Kephart enters and tries to lie down on far side. Feather mattress slides down with him into trough.

Quick gets in on near side. Mattress slips and piles him on top of Kephart.

Sundry remarks. Each man grabs his edge of bed, wriggles toward it, and holds on.

10:10 P. M.

Slap. Scratch. "This damned hole is alive with [fleas]!"

4 A. M.

"Say, Quick, are you awake?"

"Haven't slept a wink all night."

"Neither have I; but man-hunting is the finest sport in the world."

"Shut up; you'll get a cold bite for breakfast pretty soon."

He guessed wrong. We had things served smoking hot on the table, soon after daylight. Hot corn bread, hot black coffee, and hot *groundhog*.

I'll wager my flint and steel and tinder-box that the groundhog's ghost danced a joyful jig around that breakfast table. They're all in cahoot, in Sugarland.

Out again on the road, we turned back along our previous day's line of march, and then went to a house set in a field. No one was at home but an old lady. She was a motherly looking soul, neat, handsome, and with gracious manner. But the moment we announced our mission she fell into a fidget of fear.

She tried bravely to smile, but her mouth twisted awry. Her clasped hands trembled, and her fingers wove in and out like a bashful schoolgirl's.

I pitied her. She dared not tell anything at all—though evidently knowing nothing useful to us—dared not say more than yes or no, lest she should get in wrong with her neighbors. Poor soul! She had to live here. I was ashamed of myself for bothering her, and so were the other men. We said little, and passed on.

Then we met a man coming with eager announcement in his eyes. He was one we had noticed the day before. He said that a lumberjack, passing in the night, had told him of a fellow who matched our description of Jake Ruff, and who was "dodging." He had been seen recently at Barra[n]dale's upper logging camp on Rough Creek.

Yet when our informant was through with this, his manner suddenly changed. He lifted his hand as though taking an oath, his eyes flashed, and he fairly trembled with earnestness as he exclaimed: "Now, men, if you ever breathe who it was told you this, I'll follow you to your graves or I'll kill you!"

I was astounded at the folly of such a threat. Here we stood, three armed men confronting him, and he knew that one of us was a Federal officer with the whole power of the Government backing him. And yet, if we should tell where we got this information, he swore to our faces that he would follow us up and kill us, though it should take a lifetime for him to do it.

You who read these lines may scoff and say that the man was bluffing. I who write them know that he meant just what he said. Subsequent events, that have nothing to do with this story, proved full well the man's character and nerve.

Rough Creek is a branch of Little River, on the far side of Sugarland Mountain, and it drains that dismal gulf which, you may remember, I had named Godforsaken. To get there we had to go back upstream to that place we called The Castle, cross over, and follow a trail—a mere footpath—that marks a long diagonal up the precipitous side of the ridge. For Sugarland Mountain is, in fact, a "razorback" ridge, rising 1,500 feet above The Castle, and running for about eight miles down from the Smoky divide, without a single gap along the crest. It forms a rampart hard to scale from either side.

The top of this ridge, where we crossed it, is only five feet wide. The descent is as steep as the other side, but instead of thick woods it is mostly burnt-over ground, grown up in fire-cherry, except where the laurel had shielded it. We were well winded by the time we reached a cabin at the foot of the trail.

We followed an old logging road about a mile and half up Rough Creek to Barradale's camp. It was a new location, with flume, portable mill, and cook house just finished, and shacks under construction.

I introduced my companions to Barradale, whom I happened to know, and told him what we were after. He said that the description of Jake might fit some one of his hands; we would see when the men came in to dinner.

Soon they began to arrive. Down below us, about a hundred and fifty yards, I espied a fellow from the Carolina side who was also a bond-jumper and for whom Quick had a warrant. We watched him giving a hand at some odd job, but let him alone for the present lest our more important quarry should take alarm. Presently he saw us, straightened up for an instant, and then plunged into the laurel and was gone.

The cookee banged his poker on a piece of iron swung from a string, to call all hands to dinner. The word got about that we were hunting somebody. Several of the men became nervous[,] having unpleasant pasts of their own, no doubt. Some were "mean looking," some sullen, some indifferent, many joyful at the prospect of a row.

We took places with them at the long table. There were grins back and forth, and scowls, but the crew ate in a silence that would have seemed ominous to one unaccustomed to logging camps. In some camps all unnecessary talk is prohibited at meals. I asked a woods boss, once upon a time, why he had such a rule. He answered:

"If you had to run a hell-roarin' bunch like mine, you'd know why. Their idea of conversation is an argument; their idea of argument is a rumpus. I can't afford that where there's three hundred dollars' worth of crockery lyin' handy."

All the men were in, and not a Ruff among them. The suspect proved to be another man from Lufty—not our Jake at all.

We left the camp and started back toward the Sugarlands, disappointed and silent. Finally Katch remarked: "This is as slow as poking butter into a hen's mouth with a hot awl to cure the throat-pip."

Quick asked me: "How do you like man-hunting?".

"Bully; for a chap who is bone-weary, flea-bitten and groundhog-fed."

"Do you always win at any game?"

"Who would play if he did?"

At the foot of the mountain, where our trail met the road, there was a shack, and here we made inquiry once more. The man and his wife assured us that two young strangers and an old one had passed them hurriedly on the way to the "works" on Fish Camp Prong, three miles below.

It was a slender chance; but Quick and Katch decided that they would follow it out, if I would return to the Sugarlands and make arrangements for lodging. I felt sure I could do so at Fenn's if I went alone. And so we parted.

I climbed the mountain and rested a bit on the narrow top. Starting then to descend, I stepped far down on a mossy stone that slipped and threw me. In regaining balance I wrenched my right knee. It began to puff up immediately, and I found that I could not walk downhill but had to hobble sidewise, with the help of a staff.

It took me two hours to reach the bottom of the ridge. I stripped partially and bathed my game leg in the cold water of the torrent. Then painfully I made my way to Jasper Fenn's. He saw me at a distance and came to meet me at the gate. I told him of our ill luck, and he invited me to come and rest on the porch.

We chatted there in the grateful sunlight. I told some of my early adventures in the Hazel Creek country, and, so doing named several of my old neighbors, among them Quill Rose (this is a real name), who has been famous for half a century, in western Carolina, as a blockader and an original character. Fenn exclaimed: "Why, I saw a picture of him and his wife and two of Jake Rose's daughters, one time, in a book."[20]

"Where did you get the book?"

"Some women from outside came in here and started a settlement-house. They had the book, and they lent it to us to read. It was called *Our Southern Highlanders*."

"How did you like it?"

"Fine. Did you ever see it?"

"I wrote it."

Fenn's eyes nearly popped out of his head. For a moment he was dumbfounded. Then he seized me by the arm and half dragged, half carried me, crippled as I was, back to the kitchen, crying to his wife: "Mary—Mary—here's the man who wrote *that book!*"

From this moment all suspicion was banished. I was welcome. And Mary proved herself a most excellent cook. The feast that evening will always be a joy to remember.

By an hour after dark I gave up expecting Quick and Katch. They had only one flashlight, and I knew that its battery was about played out. As my leg was quite stiff and painful, I went early to bed. Two or three hours later I was aroused by my comrades' hellos and Fenn's welcome at the door. They had found their way back through the darkness, after all, but were empty-handed, and exhausted by the hard day's tramp.

Next morning I tried to take up the trail on our return journey, but it was too much for the game leg. My companions hired a mule for me to ride, and a boy to bring it back.

We were joined by seven Knoxville boys, from a large camp of young people in the woods of the Sugarlands. Their party had run short of rations. No more supplies were to be had in the neighborhood, and so this squad of stalwarts decided to cross the mountains with us to Smokemont, load themselves down with food, and carry it back—a twenty-six-mile [round] trip for the day, and a continuous climb each way. They were jolly lads, and we enjoyed their company.

There is no more to add, save that the three Ruffs did not long enjoy the freedom of the woods. They were captured on the Carolina side; and so Katch did not lose either his money or his better half.

(The next chapter of this series will show a more serious aspect of "the sport" of man-hunting. It will deal with The Killing of Hol Rose.)

Roving with Kephart

IS MAN-HUNTING "THE GREATEST SPORT IN THE WORLD?"

CHAPTER IV

The Killing of Hol Rose

Among the boarders at the old Cooper House, in my time, there have been some interesting characters. One of them was a United States deputy marshal, suave, dignified, a keen judge of human nature, who had the knack of arresting men without trouble. There was something in his look and manner that soothed wild fellows instead of infuriating them. He would say:

"Jim, I have a paper to serve on you. I'm sorry; but of course it has to be done. Now if you'll come along quietly, and behave, I'll treat you like a gentleman. I don't want to put handcuffs on such a man as you."

The average hill-billy, when he is at all sober, respects such treatment and will go along without any fuss.

One day this officer, returning from a tour of duty, came to me and said: "Kep, I had to serve a paper on one of your kinsfolk, down on Hanging Dog, last week."

"The deuce you did! I didn't know I had any relatives in North Carolina."

"Well, they spell the name just as you do and pronounce it the same way."

"What kind of people are they?"

He answered mischievously:

"Nicest kind of people: they make *good* liquor."

"Well, Charlie, if you find any of my kinsfolk making bad liquor, just hang them, with my compliments; but when they're making pure double-distilled corn I want you to treat them right."

From *All Outdoors,* April 1921

"I did. I told the old man that I wouldn't arrest him at all if he'd give me his word to appear before the Unites States Commissioner at two o'clock the next Wednesday; and he said 'All right.'"

"Well, did he show up?"

"Sure, he showed up, punctual to the minute, and he made bond. Then he invited me to come and stay with him any time I'm down there. We're the best of friends."

This was seven or eight years ago, when moonshining was only an offense against the internal revenue law—a form of tax dodging—and trading in this contraband liquor was a sort of smuggling.

Many backwoods farmers were so situated that all profit in raising corn would be eaten up by the cost of transporting it, unless they concentrated the grain into liquid form. Their output of whiskey was too small to bear a distiller's license fee. So they made the stuff on the sly, sold it on the sly, and got enough ready money out of it to keep the family in groceries, clothing, and the like. "Blockade" in those days brought only two to three dollars a gallon.

Such men knew they were breaking the law, of course; but they considered it an unjust law. They believed that every man had a natural right to do as he pleased with the grain he raised on his own field, and that a heavy tax on home-made whiskey was as iniquitous as one on home-made bread.

So long as they were not caught with the goods their conscience was as serene as that of the lady of fashion who smuggles jewels past the customs officers when arriving from Europe. And in fact their crime was the same as hers.

Old-time blockaders of this sort were shown a good deal of consideration by the better class of federal officials, who made allowance for environment and tradition. When a man, otherwise of good repute, was haled before a court in spring or summer, for illicit distilling, and it was found that he had no one left at home to look after the farm, it was customary for the judge to parole him until the following winter, so that he could go back and "make his crop." This being done, and his family provided for, the man would return without escort, give himself up, and serve his term.

Still, even in the old days, there always were some moonshiners in the mountains who had to be handled with severity, if they were caught at all. They were not amateurs, but professionals. Among them were some desperadoes, men already stained with blood and reckless or ruthless about shedding more.

It was among such a class that Hol Rose spent a part of his young manhood. By nature and by training, Rose was something of a bravo. He had to be such, so long as he mixed with the wild crew that made a business of blockading. I do not mean that he was particularly quarrelsome or underhanded; but he had the mountaineer's pride of "nerve" developed to the point of arrogance, and that was sure, sooner or later, to strike a spark of fierce resentment in someone of temper similar to his own. In the mountains they do not settle such affairs with fist fights but with knives or pistols.

Hol told me himself that he had killed two men in Georgia, but I have forgotten how he said the fracas arose. He said he "had it to do."

Later in life, Hol settled down, quit drinking, and made a fair name for himself. He seemed to have an ambition to aid in law enforcement, and was appointed deputy sheriff in our county.

It was at this time that I became acquainted with him. He boarded for a while at the Cooper House, and we saw a good deal of each other. Among his friends he was a jolly fellow, fond of chaffing, and yet with a certain reserve that impressed one as a dead-line.

As soon as he became an officer he displayed more than usual activity in running down offenders. He would take more trouble and run greater risks than the average county officer. Man-hunting, for him, was a sport. He thoroughly enjoyed it.

One day he went after a man who, so he told me, had sworn to resist arrest, and who was known to be a powerful fellow with plenty of "nerve." Rose testified in court, when the case came up for trial, that when he started to read his warrant the man slapped him in the face and ran away; that he ran in pursuit of the fugitive, fell, and his gun was accidentally discharged. Anyway, the aforesaid runaway is now minus a leg. Rose lost his job as deputy for having displayed excessive zeal.

In various cities that I have lived in it is a common practice for policemen to shoot at men who try to run away from them, and I never knew one of them to be disciplined for doing so. But here in the mountains the law and the custom are that an officer must catch his man by running him down, if he can; he must not shoot unless dangerous resistance is offered.

After the passage of the eighteenth amendment, and the Volstead act, Rose was appointed deputy prohibition enforcement officer under the Federal Government. He at once began to display an ambition to make a record for rigorous enforcement, and he lived up to it. He made many raids, captured many stills, arrested blockaders and bootleggers and anybody that he found with liquor in his possession. He went the limit of his authority in doing so.

He used to ask me sometimes to help him with his official reports, as he had no typewriter and the papers had to be made out in duplicate. He kept a pocket diary, and from it he filled in the reports, stating for every day in the month just where he was, how many miles he traveled, and what he did in an official way. From this I know how active the man was and to what pains he went to carry the law unto the lawless.

It is my business, as a writer, not to praise nor to criticize, but simply to narrate facts. It is a fact that Rose's methods in searching and seizing were, in some cases, considered high-handed by a large part of the community. It was common talk that he searched men, or their belongings, not only without warrant, but with an overbearing manner that was bound to excite bitter feeling and resentment. It was common to hear men say to each other: "It wouldn't surprise me any day to hear that Hol Rose had been killed."[21]

Rose came in to town, one day last fall, with an unusually fine specimen of copper still, and a photographer took his picture with it standing beside him. Hol brought me one of the photographs—the one here printed—knowing that I was making a collection of such things.

I had been hearing a good deal of gossip about him and the risks he ran. So I remarked, just to see how he would take it:

"Hol, one of these days some fellow is going to plug you." He did not ask why, nor laugh the warning aside. His face fell, as though it were no idle thing I had said, and he answered sadly:

"Well, if they do, it will be from behind or from the bushes."

There was something in the tone that pierced my heart. It was the voice of one confronting death, and realizing it, but game to die with his boots on, face to the front.

A few weeks later—it was on the 25th of last October—as I was going for the afternoon mail, a neighbor asked me: "Have you heard of the killing?"

"No. Who?"

"Babe Burnett has killed Hol Rose, over on Brush Creek. Charlie Beck, who was with Rose, has 'phoned in to the sheriff. Reed, at Asheville, has been notified, and he has called out all his men in this district. He is coming himself, with Lyerly's bloodhounds."

The first of the federal officers came in on the seven o'clock train from Dillsboro. I was invited to go out in his car, with three others. It is eighteen miles from our town, Bryson, the county seat, to Burnett's farm on Brush Creek. There is a good road most of the way, though it has many hairpin curves along the edge of precipices. We made fast time for a while.

My thoughts went back to the previous week, when "Babe" Burnett had been in to the county fair and had stayed at the Cooper House. He complained that although he had a good orchard the apples were going to waste because it would not pay to haul them to market.

Burnett was a man of 55 to 60 years, tall, spare-built, dark, wrinkled, with determined expression and quick, nervous, movements, a vigorous talker, with snapping eyes.

There is record that about six years ago he had an altercation with a mail-carrier, whom he stabbed with a pitchfork and left for dead. He escaped to Canada and thence to the State of Washington, but returned to his old home here a couple of years ago. He told us he was dissatisfied and wanted to sell his farm and move west again.

I thought of him now: a wild-eyed fugitive among the rocks and thickets, slipping about with gun in hand, prepared to sell his life dearly if his hiding place were found. I thought of his anguished wife, alone in her desolated home, with a murdered man lying in her dooryard, and an armed posse with bloodhounds coming to take her husband dead or alive.

And I thought of Hol Rose: yesterday a mountain cavalier, handsome, well groomed, debonair, proud of his daring, vain of his record as a hunter of men; but tonight lying stark and stained in his own blood, done forever with his gallantries and his ambitions.

The men beside me had their minds on the work ahead. The deputy marshal on my right, leaning forward on his high-power rifle, exclaimed: "I'd rather do this than anything else I ever did in my life."

And the local officer on my left smiled back, with a glint in his eye, as if to say: "You're right, comrade, man-hunting is the finest sport in the world."

I could appreciate their feeling. It was as though one's hunting companion had been killed by a wild beast and it was up to his partners to stalk and slay it; except that a murderous man is more cunning and more dangerous than any beast, and so the stimulus is greater.

But my mind went back again to that forlorn woman on the mountain, and her desperate broken heart. In the face of such tragedy it would be sacrilege to speak of sport.

We came finally to a rough and narrow by-road up which we had to turn, driving the big car carefully, feeling our way around the twists and among the rocks. A couple of miles further we discovered the cars of the sheriff's posse, and a rude little sled such as highlanders use where wheeled vehicles cannot go. Around the sled was clustered the group of men, conversing solemnly in low tones.

Rose's body had just been brought down off the mountain on this sled, and there it lay face up, the hands bound together so they would not dangle in going over the rocky ground. The face was calm and unmarred. On Hol's breast there was a group of shot-holes, centered over the heart, and tinged with red.

Charlie Beck was there: he who had been Rose's companion on the raid. Charlie was a veteran of the Philippine war, where he had been captured by savages and held prisoner for a month in the wilds of the interior, fed on nothing but rice and little of it. Of late years, here at home, he had often been employed as deputy by local or federal authorities when "bad men" were to be taken.

Beck told us that Rose had asked him, this morning, to go along on a raid after blockade stills. He had answered: "Wait a bit; I have only eight cartridges." Rose said that would be plenty, as he did not expect any trouble. Rose himself was in the habit of carrying a shotgun when he thought there was danger of resistance, and Beck, at such time, would take his Winchester rifle. But this time they set forth with nothing but their side arms.

They traveled southward among the Alarka Mountains to the home of Burnett, where Rose suspected there was some distilling going on. They found a lot of apple pomace in or about the house. Mrs. Burnett protested that she was preparing it to make vinegar. Rose decided, however, that it was for apple brandy, and he destroyed the stuff.

The officers then went away and searched other places in the neighborhood. They finally returned to Burnett's place for further investigation, believing that there was a still somewhere on the premises.

As they approached the house they caught sight of Burnett himself running away from it. They gave chase. As they ran around a corner of a barn, Rose being in the lead, a shot was fired from a strawstack about thirty paces away. Beck said he could not see the man who fired it, as the fellow was behind the stack or hugging close to its side, but he saw the straw blown aside by the blast of the gun.

He heard Rose cry out: "Babe, you have killed me!" Then, in a moment: "I believe I'm rallying." A few seconds later, Beck by this time having advanced a little ahead of Rose, Beck was half deafened by a pistol shot close to his ear. Turning quickly, he saw Rose sagging down with his pistol pointed upward. Hol evidently had fired wild in his death struggle. He expired in two or three minutes.

Meantime Beck had plenty to occupy him. He expected to be fired at, himself, by the man behind the strawstack, or by others, for there might be several of them in ambush. He watched for a head to appear from behind the strawstack.

It developed, however, that Burnett, immediately after firing, had run along a gully straight away from the strawstack, and Beck did not see him until he emerged about seventy yards away, running through bushes as high as his waist. Beck fired his eight cartridges at the man, but he told us he did not think he hit him, as he had only a small revolver.

He said that Mrs. Burnett protested: "He didn't do it," meaning her husband; and "I didn't see anything." Beck replied: "If you'll come and look at this man lying dead here you'll see something."

Beck then went about the neighborhood trying to get someone to go to the nearest telephone and call up the sheriff. But no one would stir. He had to go himself, leaving his comrade where he had fallen. The first telephones that he tried were not working (perhaps the wires had been cut), and he had to walk seven miles before he found one that was in order. Then he returned alone to the Burnett house, which was now deserted, and waited there in the darkness through the long hours until the sheriff arrived.

Anyone who knows these mountains, and the character of moonshine bands, will understand that there was no sport in that lonely vigil. It took nerve, all right, but the strain must have been anything but pleasant.

I have told the story as Charlie Beck told it to us, to the best of my recollection. It may be that there is another side. No doubt, if the case ever comes to trial, there will be contradictory testimony. That is the usual way in murder cases. If I had heard the other side I would report it with the same care for accuracy as is my habit at all times.

That night, in the mountain glen, Rose's body was transferred to a motor truck, and most of us came back with it, arriving in town about midnight. Several officers accompanied Charlie Beck back to the Burnett house and waited there for the reinforcements they knew were on the way.

At three in the morning I was awakened by the deep bellow of bloodhounds. These animals are silent when trailing, but they exercise their throats sometimes when idle or when being transported. Reed's men from Asheville were passing in their car, on the way to Brush Creek, carrying the dogs with them.

The animals took up the trail at Burnett's and followed it straight to the home of a neighbor, three-quarters of a mile away. The neighbor's wife said that Burnett had come there wounded by bullets through one leg and in the side. She dressed his wounds with turpentine and bound them up to staunch the blood.

Charlie Beck's marksmanship must have been better than he had given himself credit for. It is not unlikely that some of the turpentine found its way to Burnett's feet. That would account for the failure of the dogs to trace the man scent beyond this house.

Burnett is still at large, at the time of this writing (December 18th). If he should be captured he will have to be tried in our local court, under State laws; for it is a curious fact that although our Federal laws provide drastic punishment for those who assault Government officers, yet they cannot punish those who kill such officers. The reason is that the United States, in their national capacity, have no common law, and Federal courts have no common-law jurisdiction in criminal cases.

Rose was buried by his lodge in the little cemetery on a hilltop overlooking our town. Hail to adventurers all; and to those who fall, Farewell! May the Higher Justice rate them by the chances [that] they have had and the strains they have undergone.

(*The End*)

Roving with Kephart

MEMORIES AND COMMENT ON OLD AND THE NEW— THE SNAKE-STICK MAN IS BACK WITH A BULLET HOLE IN HIS HAT

RED BLOOD IN OUR DAY

It's many a year since I received that wire from a dear old friend asking me to meet him in New York for a little chat before he should sail back to Italy. There were two of us young fellows to dine with him, both of us formerly companions of his in Europe. He chose a favorite corner at Delmonico's where, in the old days, he had enjoyed the company of many a famous man now dead and gone.

I knew what was on his mind when the first course was served.

My old accustomed corner here is,
The table still is in the nook:
Ah! vanished many a busy year is
This well-known chair since last I
took.
When first I saw ye, cari luoghi,
I'd scarce a beard upon my face;
And now, a grizzled, grim old fogy,
I sit and wait for bouillabaisse.

He listened to our chatter, and took his part in it, but there was a sad and far-off look in his eyes, reminiscent, while still he spoke of present affairs.

From *All Outdoors*, July 1921

Where are you, old companions trusty
  Of early days, here met to dine?
Come, waiter! quick, a flagon crusty—
  I'll pledge them in the good old
wine.
The kind old voices and old faces
  My memory can quick retrace;
Around the board they take their
places,
  And share the wine and bouillabaisse.

We did our best, we two youngsters, to fill the void, and the old man responded bravely. Other courses followed, and more cheering wines. But it was a sad parting, for all that. We three never met again. And I have not been in New York City from that day to this.

Horae, et dies, et menses, et anni cedunt.[22] Now I, in turn, am the grizzled, grim old fogy; but the old corner is gone. I wouldn't even know the town if I should return to it. Imagine me seeking a quiet nook there and ordering a bowl of "bouillabaisse," a bottle of "the Cham[b]ertin with yellow seal"! To be stared out of countenance, and made to feel I'd done a rude and monstrous thing, instead of (as I would be doing) only coming to give decent burial to my dead.

NEW TIMES, NEW MANNERS

I take a New York paper, and here is something I read in it, the other day:

(U. S. Chief Prohibition Supervising Agent, speaking to Herald reporter):

"Take the household situation—the private still. How many men do you know that are making their own booze, either distilling hard liquor or brewing beer?" Langley asked.

"A number," the interviewer said. "One of them, by the way, is a very prominent banker. Another is a well-known lawyer. I wouldn't be surprised to hear of a preacher."

"Nor would I," said Langley. "I haven't a doubt that thousands of stills are running in this city, many thousands in the private homes. These contrivances are being manufactured enormously, and there is no doubt that they have a wide sale. One can buy a very classy still for about forty dollars, copper and everything. It might amaze the community if we could get a look at all the good people who are moonshining thus in utter contempt of the law and their country."

I had to laugh. Here I've been, away back in one of the most primitive communities in all America, writing about the picturesque survivals of ancient customs that still are practiced here—among them, moonshining—which have literary value simply because they are odd, or because they show red-blooded men in action (bad action, doubtless, but still interesting, just as murder is interesting in a detective story). While writing about the raw but pure liquor made in some of those backwoods stills, my thoughts would sometimes go back wistfully to Delmonico's, and Fiske's grunt of disapproval when they brought on a Chateau Yquem that was below the standard of what he was used to. Imagine, now, the sort of hooch those blundering city amateurs must be turning out in their kitchens! Why, if I went back to New York, now, they'd pizen me.

NEW ART

When the April ALL OUTDOORS came to our little town there was a rush for it. Everybody here knew the *dramatis personae* in flesh and blood. Charlie Beck, who did the rest of the shooting after Hol Rose was killed, now has Rose's job. He was in my office when the magazine showed up. He opened it, and stared—stared at the queer wriggly picture of a humped man in a long-tailed coat (supposed to be himself) glaring at an emaciated female (supposed to be Mrs. Burnett) and pointing from her to the crumpled body of Rose.

I said to him, "Charlie, when your wife sees that picture, she'll sue for divorce."

He answered grimly, "Maybe she won't have to; I had two pistols drawn on me yesterday."

And there was no joke about it; it was so.

Here in the mountains, where "revenuers" used to go anywhere (often only one of them by himself) with no thought of carrying any weapon but a revolver, the prohibition agents now never stir out of town without their repeating rifles, and they always go accompanied by a posse. And when a fugitive "hides out," they send for bloodhounds.

New art? Why, we are learning new arts, lots of 'em.

I can't say that I like any of them. But then, who am I? An old fogy.

HOSPITALITY, A LOST ART

One day last fall I had a visit from my old partner, Bob Barnett, and his wife. He is the big, fat Bob who figures in the books "Camping and Woodcraft" and "Our Southern Highlanders." He came, years ago, to the old mine site where I'd been living alone with the bobcats and hoot-owls, and became caretaker for the company that had possession. It was an abandoned place—that is, no one else lived near there—and I welcomed a neighbor. Soon I shifted quarters to his house. We lived together, in various necks of the woods, for several years. Bob now is at Aquone, N. C., on the upper Nantahala, where he keeps open house for all comers.

Well, Bob and Mrs. Bob kidded me a good deal, this time about having been taken in by the Snake-Stick Man.

Then, last month (April) I returned the visit and spent a week with Bob, trout fishing.

But when I got to Aquone, I found things in a pretty mess. As Mrs. Bob explained the situation: "There came two men here to board, in February, and they stayed a month. Kep, they were the nicest kind of men, and everybody liked them. They were looking for a large tract of cut-over land for sheep ranching. Bill Latham, the super, showed 'em all over Lord-knows-how-many thousand acres, and offered it to 'em for thirty-five thousand dollars. They weren't willing to pay quite that much.

"They were interested in mineral, too. Bob has a fine mica prospect, and they all got excited over it, and Bob was goin' to be a millionaire, and he dug his fool self to death for 'em.

"They were such sociable folks! Would sing, and play games, and dance, and have a good time with everybody. They liked liquor—it was a sight how they'd buy it—but nary one of 'em ever got too gay with it. We don't keep any, as you know; but there's folks as does, and these strangers got acquainted with every last one of 'em.

"Then, finally, they came to leave—and, Lord bless my soul, Kep, they'd turned up twenty-seven men and women for sellin' moonshine, and one of 'em a preacher-man!

"Now everybody around here is suspicious of everybody else, and we're in bad with our neighbors for havin' harbored the critters."

After this episode, I was informed, the people "acrost the ridge" installed telephones (a private line) in every house, and wires have even been run back into the big woods, scouts are posted, and no outsider can now get into that country without being announced all down the line. The schoolmaster told me, "No stranger need come in here, now, and ask for a night's lodging. The door will be slammed in his face."

Yet this was hitherto one of the most hospitable regions in the world.

ANXIOUS READERS

The "Man-Hunting" series that ended in the April number of ALL OUTDOORS brought me a good many letters. I am glad to get such correspondence. There have been no criticisms, but there have been some questions, and I will answer them here, to forestall repetition.

No, dear brethren, I am not writing for the sake of any "moral" to be drawn. If there be any, the reader is supposed to be intelligent enough to draw it for himself. Anyway, that is his business, not mine. As a writer I accept any interesting episode or character as "material," regardless of whether the person be saint or sinner.

No, again, there is no fiction whatever in that series. The printer made some bad blunders in the first three chapters, but that is not my fault. I said at the outset that all of the characters *but one* were still living; the printer left out the words here italicized. Since that was written, two more have departed; one killed in a gun fight, the other drowned.

"Mr. Quick" has checked up two errors in the story—(1) When he carries only one pistol, it is on the right side, [below] the suspender, butt to the rear. When he packs two, the one on the left, likewise with butt to rear, always has the safety thrown off. (2) He did not mention whom or what we were after when we met the first young man with the shotgun—said nothing about it till we got to "Jasper Fenn's." It was "Katch" who mentioned it first.

A correspondent who has been in the Sugarlands and up on the divide says there *is* a Mount Mingus. Well, what I meant was that there is no such mountain where my old government map placed it.

The man who dodged into the laurel from us at "Barradale's" camp was brought in here by a posse night before last, after nearly two years of hiding out in the mountains.

NEWS FROM THE SNAKE STICK MAN

"Mr. Quick" wrote me from Muskogee, Okla., under date of January 15, 1921:

> On December 17, 1920, I had the *misfortune* to lead a raid—so I consider it in this instance, for prior to this time I had never been in one wherein a man was actually killed. I was proud of that record, inasmuch as I have participated in very many raids, arrests and chases involving the capture of desperate men, and although I have shot and wounded, not until this time have I ever had to carry out a prisoner with his face covered out of respect for the dead. It is not pleasant, not a matter fit to boast of. . . .
>
> We left Hugo, and proceeded to a big lumber camp, from which point we intended to leave for the main drive. We timed our trip so as to reach Wright City well in the night, in order to avoid advertising our presence in the vicinity.

About an hour before daybreak I drove our car out into the hills, and concealed it as best I could, and we started on our walk just at sunrise. . . .

I had been in the locality before, and knew the lay of the land, and where Merritt's house was located. . . . We made a circuitous reconnoitre, looking for the road, and a place to cross the Glover River. . . .

The water was too deep to wade, very swift, and exceedingly cold; but frequent rapids caused by the large rocks promised a means of crossing. . . . The rocks were slippery as an eel's skin.

One of my partners—there were four of us—found a place narrow enough to risk a leap, and he landed safely on the opposite rock. I followed, then returned, and found a cedar log up on the cliff side, which I brought down for the other two men to cross on. Again I leaped the stretch between the rocks, and dragged the log into position for the other two; but they could not make up their minds to cross on the unsteady bridge.

About this time my progressive partner slipped on a slimy rock and went down into a whirlpool of unknown depth. He caught with his hands on a rock, and kept his head above water. He threw his rifle up on the rock and tried to pull himself up after it, but could not make the top.

We dared not make any unnecessary noise; so I hastily took off my shoes, rolled up my trousers above my knees, and started to his rescue; but he managed to pull himself up on the rock and climb out. He was dressed in a heavy suit of corduroy and his clothing almost weighted him down. . . . He was nearly freezing after the cold clothing began to take effect, and we dared not wait very long. Finally the other two men got across. . . .

From the ford we took the wagon road and hurried up the mountainside. About a mile farther the road made an abrupt turn and ran down into a canyon. We knew that the still was near, and we proceeded with great caution. Then one of the men looked down into the canyon and discovered a large white tent.

We knew the still was there. Soon we could hear the moonshiners talking, and we crept on down among the loose stones and dead leaves until we came within forty yards of the still. Then one of the boys and I started a charge, the other two following closely. At about a hundred feet the moonshiners heard us, and we gave the command *"Hands up!"*

One man whirled and drew a .45 Colt automatic pistol. A rifle cracked from our party. The moonshiner started away on a run, I after him, firing at his legs. Another rifle crack from our party, and a moonshiner fell headlong. It later developed that *he* was not hit, but, just as the officer pulled the trigger, the moonshiner had tripped on a root and fell, saving his life. . . .

> I followed the wounded moonshiner up the creek for perhaps 200 yards before he fell. He was shot through the breast, and soon died. I was very much upset at having the killing occur in one of my raids, but it was better to have it so than that one of our party should be killed by the moonshiners.
>
> We cut two saplings, made a stretcher, and carried the dead man back to the still, where I found we had captured a preacher named B. S. Walker, well known as "Preacher Walker" (one of the most notorious moonshiners in the Kiamichi district), and T. A. Rudolph, known to us as a most dangerous character. They had a high-power rifle in the tent, but did not have a chance to use it. . . .

The Kiamichi Mountains, in southeastern Oklahoma, are part of a rough country that has been a harborage for desperadoes since the days of the James and Younger gangs, and long before. The name is locally pronounced "Ky-mish," with accent on the last syllable.

Innocent readers may imagine, from this officer's letter, that the battles in these cases are all one-sided. It is true that the raiders generally have the advantage, but it is not always so. Sometimes they are bushwhacked. An attempt of that sort was narrowly avoided in my county a couple of months ago. The blockaders, having learned through their own spies that a posse was seeking them, lay in ambush in a spot so favorable that there would have been a massacre if the officers had not shrewdly taken another course.

"Mr. Quick," replying recently to a letter of mine telling of the shooting of a man here by our town marshal, said:

> That shooting of the jitney driver by Sam Beck brings up another incident. I am sitting here now, and, as is my abominable custom, wearing my hat in the house. That hat has a neat round hole in the turned-up edge of the brim, and a ragged hole in the base of the crown. Said holes were made by exactly the same sort of bullet (soft-point from a .32-20 revolver) as that which passed through the jitney driver and the window sash.
>
> This bullet was fired from a Colt revolver, and struck my hat, passed through the brim at the edge, cut the lower edge of a woven hair hatband of Mexican make, passed through that and the hat crown, sweat-band, etc., and into my head to the bone. There, finding itself up against a solid green bone proposition, it bounced off my premises and has not been seen since. And it did not even

> knock me senseless. Perhaps there is a good reason for that—but it didn't. The sensation, as nearly as I can describe it, was just as if some unfeeling person had knocked away about half of my head with a sledge hammer. It did not hurt much at the time, but later on it *did*.

If things of this sort had happened back in the 'seventies or 'eighties of the last century, in cow towns of the western border, we would be seeing movie pictures of them today. But they are going on around us right now, East and West, North and South. I suppose there will be movies of them some day, staged by people who knew nothing of the real thing. And the audiences will thrill, and say "What red-blooded men they did have in those days of old!"

Roving with Kephart

SOME DOPE ON THE QUICK "DRAW" AND THE DISAPPEARANCE OF A SUITCASE

"MR. QUICK'S" PISTOL HOLSTER

A jinx has pursued me when trying to describe the suspender holster in which our "Snake Stick Man" carries his pistol. In our July number I said: "When he carries only one pistol it is on the right side, below the suspender," and so on. What I meant was *down* below, not underneath; but the way I put it was so clumsy that the detective came at me instanter, by mail, in this wise.—

"Now, Kep, dad gum it! 'What [for] on earth' would a man want to carry a gun in a holster UNDER his SUSPENDER? Hey? So's he could get the dad burned thing tangled up with his gun, and give the other fellow a chance to drill him?

"Primarily I carry my guns in that position for the simple reason of speed in drawing and presenting. The reason I have evolved this particular kind of holster is that the position in which it is worn admits of a much quicker draw, and that the holster itself, in the way it is made and attached to one's person, REMOVES EVERY POSSIBLE OBJECT WITH WHICH IT MIGHT BECOME ENTANGLED AND THEREBY GET A MAN KILLED.

"If you will just reflect a moment, you will remember that the suspender is attached to the top of the holster, and that the holster thereby becomes a component part of the suspender; but the 'gallus' business goes no farther down than the TOP of the holster, the holster proper forming the lower portion of the suspender. This leaves nothing whatsoever on the outside for the gun to become entangled with."

I knew perfectly well how my friend carries his gun, and could see the advantages ten seconds after I first spied where and how he toted 'em. One unfortunate little word bungled my description of the dingus.

From *All Outdoors,* October 1921

Here is a drawing that will make the thing clear to anybody. But let me hasten to add that "Quick's" pet gun for everyday wear is a 9 mm. (.354 caliber) Luger, loaded with hollow point bullets. I drew a Remington butt in the sketch because it is the only pistol I happen to have at hand with this sort of holster fitted to it. And "Quick's" holster is not cut away in a downward and outward curve from rear sight to trigger (upper *e* of sketch) but runs rather in a straight slant.

This holster is quicker on the draw than any other I know of, except the well-known cowboy pattern of belt holster that is carried on a slack belt and well down on the leg, just above where the hand naturally hangs. The last named kind is best when one travels mostly on horseback; but it is a poor contrivance for a pedestrian, as it is much in the way of walking.

"Quick's" suspender holster, fitted, as it is, for buttons *inside* the trousers waistband (instead of for outside ones, like Heiser's patterns) is ideal for a man afoot. It is best adapted to pistols of medium size; but Charlie Beck is every day carrying a .45 Colt military pistol in a "Quick holster, [*sic*] and he says it is the best scheme he ever struck.

THE TRIAL OF "BABE" BURNETT

Readers of "The Killing of Hol Rose," in our April number, will probably be interested in the subsequent fate of his slayer, "Babe" Burnett.

It will be recalled that Rose was a Federal prohibition enforcement agent who, accompanied by Charlie Beck, attempted to arrest Burnett, on the 25th of last October, at Burnett's home in the Alarka Mountains, Swain Co., N. C., on a charge of moonshining; and that Burnett killed Rose, and escaped amid a rain of bullets from Beck's pistol.

Burnett, after hiding out in the laurel thickets until the posse and bloodhounds had given up the chase, slipped away to another county where he had friends who would help to keep his whereabouts unknown. So he stayed out all winter and until late spring. On the 15th of last May he came in to our town and gave himself up to the sheriff, having evidently acted on advice of counsel. He was put in jail to await trial in July. While he was there, other prisoners on two occasions broke jail and escaped. He could have done the same, if he had wanted to do so.

Meantime, in the old Cooper House, where I stay, there was developing an extraordinary romance. Two of Burnett's sons came from Idaho, soon after the old man got into his trouble. One of them, Verlin, stayed on, and appeared to be in communication with his father. He boarded, off and on, at the Cooper House.

Our cook was Ima Rose, daughter of Hol Rose, well named and blooming. Truth to tell, she was one of the prettiest mountain girls I ever saw.

Verlin Burnett was a dashing ex-marine.

The whole countryside wondered what would happen when these two young and vital representatives of the two warring clans had to meet daily in the same house.

What did happen was so unexpected that it made everybody gasp. Verlin and Ima fell in love with each other. They went abroad together. One of Ima's cousins, a man with "a record," came to town and (so I was credibly informed) bluntly told Verlin that he would kill him if he did not stop "running with Ima."

But the young folks merely stopped promenading and took to automobiling. Ima tried to learn how to drive the car. She knocked two wheels off a car that stood opposite our hotel, ricochetted across the street, hit our telephone pole, broke it short off at the butt, and alighted smiling and unhurt.

Next day (I think it was the 25th of May) the loving couple eloped. My suitcase disappeared at the same time. Within a few days we learned that Verlin and Ima were married in an adjoining county. Sometime later they were reported to have been seen in the mountains, both of them carrying guns. My vagabond suitcase has not been heard from. And I'll be darned if I ever taught it such tricks.

On the morning of July 28th, in our court-house, was opened the case of State of North Carolina *vs.* J. E. ("Babe") Burnett, charged with the murder of James Holland Rose, F. P. A.

The Grand Jury at first refused to send in a true bill; but, on instructions from the Court, finally returned one.

The prisoner entered a plea of not guilty. A special venire of one hundred men was drawn from the jury box. A jury was secured next day, and the case proceeded to trial. The Solicitor was assisted in the prosecution by the U. S. District Attorney and three other lawyers. The defense was conducted by three of the ablest attorneys in our section.

Charlie Beck was the only eyewitness for the State. His testimony was substantially what he told us on the night after the killing, when we went out after Rose's body, and as I reported it in the April ALL OUTDOORS, but with certain additions brought about by examination.

Being asked if Rose carried a warrant for the arrest of Burnett, he replied:

"If he did, I didn't know it."

"Did you have a warrant yourself?"

"No."

"When you were shooting at Burnett, after Rose was killed, did you try to kill him?"

"Yes, I tried to kill him."

"Why did you try to kill Burnett when you had no warrant for him?"

"Because he had killed my friend."

"Were you ever indicted for trying to kill Burnett?"

"No."

Beck swore positively that the first shot in the fight was the one that killed Rose; that Rose fired only once, and that was in his death struggle; that he (Beck) did not see the man firing at Rose, but only saw the straw blown aside by the blast of the gun; that Burnett ran away, from behind the strawstack, and that he (Beck) emptied his .45 Colt pistol at the fleeing man, but did not observe Burnett flinch or show other sign of being hit.

Counsel for the defence tried repeatedly to inject into the evidence the question of the right of the officers to search the premises of Burnett, and to arrest him, without a proper warrant. The State attempted to show that Rose did have a warrant, but this effort completely broke down. It then contended that the officer had a right to search, seize, arrest, without a warrant, under the provisions of the Lever Act, a war-time anti-profiteering and food conservation statute, which made it a felony to ferment fruits or grains.

Burnett took the stand in his own defence. He was calm throughout the ordeal, answered promptly, and did not get tangled up. The issue became one of veracity between him and Beck, who had been equally cool and straightforward under keen examination.

Burnett admitted that he fired the shot that killed Rose, but he set up a plea of self-defence. He swore that he found the officers at his house when he returned from work; that Rose said: "I am a revenue officer and am hunting your whiskey;" that neither of the officers showed any warrant; that he voluntarily assisted them in searching the premises, and even directed them to some barrels of apple pomace in the orchard that were near an old still furnace that he had repaired. He admitted that he had intended to make brandy of his surplus apples, but said that someone had stolen his still, and that he then determined to make vinegar from the pomace. The officers found the still-place, but did not thereupon arrest him, but went away.

Burnett testified that he had been squirrel hunting early in the morning, and, on his return, had left his shotgun at the strawstack while doing work around the barn. He said that when the officers came back the second time he was starting from near the barn to go and help the boys build a sledding road; that the officers started after him on the run, with their pistols drawn; that he had heard that Rose was a violent and dangerous man; that he became alarmed by their attitude, and ran; that Rose fired and shot him in the leg; that he fell over some rails and rolled against the strawstack, where his gun stood; that when he looked back, Rose was aiming his pistol at him with both hands; and that he then rose, seized the gun, and fired quickly from his hip, to save his life, and Rose fell.

Mrs. Burnett corroborated her husband's testimony that Rose fired the first shot.

A medical expert who examined Burnett's wound testified that the bullet entered his leg from behind, and that the wound was of such nature that it would stun the leg and impede locomotion.

Various witnesses testified that Rose's "character" (reputation) was that of a violent and dangerous man. Nothing was offered in rebuttal.

The evidence was completed on the afternoon of the second day.

The State in its arguments insisted that Burnett was guilty of murder in the first degree, the fact that Burnett had his gun at the strawstack, and that he ran toward it at the approach of the officers, and killed Rose as soon as he had secured the gun, showing premeditation; that in the act of secreting the gun and shooting from behind the stack, Burnett was making a secret assault upon the officers and committing a felony, and that he could not therefore claim self-defence; that the officers were using no more force than was necessary in making the arrest; and that, at the time of the killing, the Lever Act was in force, making it a felony under Federal statute to make alcoholic drinks of food products; that the officers found evidence that such a felony had been committed, and that therefore they had a right to arrest without warrant.

The defence claimed that the officers had no warrant for the arrest of Burnett; that the Lever Act was discredited by having been subsequently declared unconstitutional; that Rose had the reputation of being a violent and dangerous man; that the officers were engaged in an unlawful assault upon Burnett, and that he, fearing for his life, had a right to shoot.

The judge, in his charge to the jury, instructed them that the Lever Act was in effect at the time of the killing, and that under its provisions the officers did have a right to arrest Burnett without a warrant.

The jury, under our law, could bring in either one of four verdicts: murder in the first degree, murder in the second degree, manslaughter, or acquittal. Its first vote stood nine for acquittal and three for murder in the first degree. But at 11 o'clock on Sunday morning it returned a verdict of murder in the second degree.

The judge sentenced Burnett to serve twelve years in the state prison at hard labor. Burnett is 60 years of age.

The defence gave notice of appeal. Bonds were fixed at $7,700 aggregate.

Burnett, I understand, is also under indictment in the Federal court for this same act, the shooting of Rose, the charge here being "assault on a Government officer," and, if released under bond given the State court, will be held under $6,000 bond for appearance at the Federal court.

How can a man be twice put in jeopardy for the same offence, when the 5th Amendment to the Constitution expressly forbids it?

Well, here is what happened at this same term of our court at which Burnett was tried. A young cripple named Nation had been tried in the Federal court on a liquor case. Prayer for judgment was continued, and the defendant released under bond. He was promptly arraigned for the same act and tried in our State superior court, the same witness (a Federal prohibition agent) appeared against him, he was convicted by said witness's testimony, and sentenced to 18 months on the roads. The local court held that one and the same act constituted two separate offences: one against Federal law and the other against State law.

Coming back to the Burnett trial: to so ignorant a layman as myself, this has been an interesting case in more ways than one. The United States Supreme Court has repeatedly ruled that under no circumstances has a Federal officer the right to make searches and seizures without due process of law, as defined in the Fourth Amendment to the Constitution. In the case of Gouled *vs.* U. S., decided February 28, 1921, the Court declared:

"It would not be possible to add to the emphasis with which the framers of our Constitution and this Court (cases cited) have declared the importance to political liberty and to the welfare of our country of the due observance of the rights guaranteed under the Constitution by these two amendments (4th and 5th). The effect of the decisions cited is:

"That such rights are declared to be indispensable to the 'full enjoyment of personal security, personal liberty and private property;' that they are to be regarded as of the very essence of constitutional liberty; and that the guaranty of them is as important and as imperative as are the guaranties of the other fundamental rights of the individual citizen—the right to trial by jury, to the writ of habeas corpus, and to due process of law.

"It has been repeatedly decided that these amendments should receive a liberal construction, *so as to prevent stealthy encroachment upon or 'gradual depreciation' of the rights secured by them, by imperceptible practice of courts or by well-intentioned, but mistakenly overzealous, executive officers.*"

Yet there seems to be no protection against the passage of laws that the legislators well know are unconstitutional; nor against their stringent and oppressive enforcement, until, maybe years afterward, the Supreme Court, on appeal, rules them to be unconstitutional. Nor is there any redress for acts of tyranny perpetrated by officers of the law under color of such a statute.

In the judgment of many lawyers, as well as laymen, the provisions of one amendment to the Constitution have, in numerous cases, been enforced by systematically violating other sections of the same Constitution. Thus, by the lawless hands of those entrusted to wield the law, are seeds of revolution sown.

But tut, tut! And O fie, O foh, O fum! Amid a conflict of laws such as lawyers themselves get hopelessly entangled in, how can a mere layman know what the law is or is not? How can he obey, even if he does know them, laws that are self-stultifying or contradictory? Here is a hypothetical case—and it would not surprise me any day if it turned out to be an actual one:—

Suppose that, one o' these mornings, I should arise from bed, make my toilet, and start for the breakfast table. But as I open my bedroom door, there stands directly in front of it MY RUNAWAY SUITCASE!

I stop and pick it up. I give it an angry shake. And from within that leathern bag there comes to my ears, like the plea of a returned prodigal, a propitiatory GLUG—GLUG—GLUG.

There is no scrap of paper, no sign whatever to suggest in whose company that vagabond suitcase has been roaming through the long months since last I saw it. But inside I find three half-gallon fruit jars full of moonshine whiskey.

What shall I do?

Under our present law, if I keep that gallon and a half of illicit spirits, I am guilty of "retailing," even though I do nothing with it. If I carry it out to pour it into the river, I am guilty of "transporting."

There is one thing I might *lawfully* do: I might stand there in my tracks and drink every drop of it, and the law could do nothing at all to me; but I am physically restrained from that—my belly is too small and my head too weak.

But I might report the matter to the sheriff or the prohibition agent. Yes: in my case it would be safe to do so; for I have never made or sold liquor. Just one little query enters here—bad little query, shameful query, but it will come in—namely: What would become of that liquor if I turned it over?

You will try in vain, in our town, to get a few ounces of whiskey for a sick person, from all that is confiscated and stored in jail. What ever does become of that stuff? Nobody seems to know, though everybody thinks he "as good as knows." Should I encourage such practices?

O fie, O foh, O fum!

[front of brochure]

Trips in the Smokies
1929

BY

HORACE KEPHART, AUTHOR

Our Southern Highlanders and *Camping and Woodcraft*

PUBLISHED BY

THE BRYSON CITY DRUG CO.

THE REXALL STORE

Make Our Store Your Headquarters
Bryson City, N. C.
1929

[middle of brochure]

At present, 1929, the best approach to the Smoky divide, on the N. C. side is from Bryson City by car or bus to Smokemont on Ocona Lufty River, 18 miles. Cars can go 2 miles farther to "Doc." Connor's, which is the best place to get guides and horses.

From Connor's, supplies can be carried by pack horses to Indian Gap, on crest of the divide (see Knoxville and Mt. Guyot sheets of gov't topographic map—U. S. Geological Survey, Washington D. C., 10c each). Guides about $3.50 a day; horses $2.00.

From the Gap all travel must be afoot.

MAPS—The topographic sheets mentioned above are all we have at present. They are reliable in the settled districts but very inaccurate in the wild upper ranges. Anyone going without a guide and relying on these maps is almost sure to get lost for a few hours, if not days. They are good to locate main peaks and general direction of watercourses, but useless for details.

Last year the Geological Survey sent a hundred men in here to begin a new official map of the Smoky Mts. National Park area. It will be finished next year (1930). Scale 2 in. to 1 mi., countour [*sic*] intervals 20 ft., and very accurate.

EQUIPMENT—Depends, of course, on size of party and length of trip. Go light, for the climbing is hard and the way is rough, in many places.

A good pack-sack makes the trip much easier. The best, for this country, is the Poirier or Duluth pack, with leather (not web) shoulder straps, 26 × 28 in., 2½ lbs. It is big enough so that all equipment stows inside and then there are no stick-outs to catch in brush or impede one when climbing or crawling. Sold by
Poirier Tent & Awning Co., Duluth, Minn., $6.00

One good wool blanket, about 5 lbs., per man, is enough from May to September.

A light shelter cloth should be carried, as there may be a rainy night any time. Just a rectangle of thin but loosely woven cloth waterproofed. The so-called "balloon silk" is good (sold by camp outfitters and some tent makers), but the best material is "Vivatex army shelter cloth," sold by the Metacloth Co., Inc., Lodi, N. J., about 50c a yard. Have a tent maker make it up in rectangle with grommets (not brass eyelets) about every 18 in. along all four sides, to tie out as inclined roof (lean-to). Sizes: for one or two men, 8 × 10 ft., 4 lbs; for three for four, 10 × 12 ft., 6 lbs.

Boy Scout cook kit good for one man going alone. For party: frying pan and coffee pot with folding handles (camp outfitters), and a plate, knife, fork, spoon, seamless pint cup, apiece.

One of the party should carry a hunter's hatchet for getting firewood. Plenty of matches in waterproof can or box. Compass. Strong pocket knife. Flashlight.

These, besides food, are the essentials. Anything else a luxury and a burden, unless a trip of several days is taken, in which case a regular camping outfit is required.

Shoes must be hobnailed; small cone-headed Hungarian nails best.

TIME—April likely to be rainy. May, bracing and delightful, but cold nights in high ranges. June, perfect, with rhododendron and azalea blooming. July, Aug., first half of Sept., warm, usually dry; but showers may be looked for any time.

No mosquitoes. Gnats troublesome at times. Fleas in the old cabins or lean-tos that native hunters use for shelters. Carry insect powder if you stop in mountain cabins. Most of the country, however, is uninhabited.

ROUTES—Indian Gap best for base camp, with excursions Tenn side.

From Indian Gap to summit of Clingman Dome and return to Gap, fairly good trail for hikers, one day. Same to Collins, or a little beyond, and return, one day. Same to Le Conte and return, two hard days (spend night in occupied cabin on top of Le Conte) but scenery sublime.

Northwest from Collins is the "Sawtooth range," exceedingly rough. None but seasoned mountaineers should attempt it. A mile an hour good time in part of it. Carry water here in canteens.

Southwest from Clingman and west to [Little] Tennessee River, trail along divide (state line); but hard to follow in some places. Stranger should have a guide; otherwise likely to stray off on abutting ridge and get lost, especially if foggy. Country west of Clingman has been logged and not nearly so interesting as it used to be; but superb views from Siler's Bald (northwest side) and Thunderhead.

From Indian Gap a trail goes down into Tennessee to Gatlinburg which can be followed on horseback. Another crosses the Smokies to Townsend and to Cade's Cove at Spencer cabin, just west of Thunderhead. No other horse or mule trails across Smokies.

Mt. Guyot difficult to approach. Best way probably from head of Enloe Creek along crest of divide.

SHORT TRIP—A very interesting trip would be (1) to Connor's by car or bus; (2) to Indian Gap with pack horse, to avoid tiring oneself out by doing his own packing that far; (3) afoot (next day) from head springs of right fork of Deep Creek (Indian Gap) by trail down the whole length of Deep Creek, to Bryson City (no guide needed). This takes one through some of the most varied virgin forest in the park area.

A good hiker can make the trip from Indian Gap to Bryson, by this route, in one day; but it will put him to the proof. If tired out, spend night at Bryson Place cabin, 1½ mi. south of main fork of Deep Creek (you can't miss it, as it is the only house near creek). Then the remaining 10 mi. to Bryson next day.

[*back of brochure*]

Having made this trip, one gains a good idea of Smoky Mt. conditions, and he can then put in spare time to good advantage in other similar excursions.

Bryson City Drug Co.
one block north of
Highway No. 10, at the bridge
Is headquarters
For tourist information to all points
In the Smokies, Nantahala Gorge
and surrounding country.
Distributors of Cherokee Indian
Crafts and Curios.
Ask Bennett—He Knows.

Trips in the Smokies 1930.

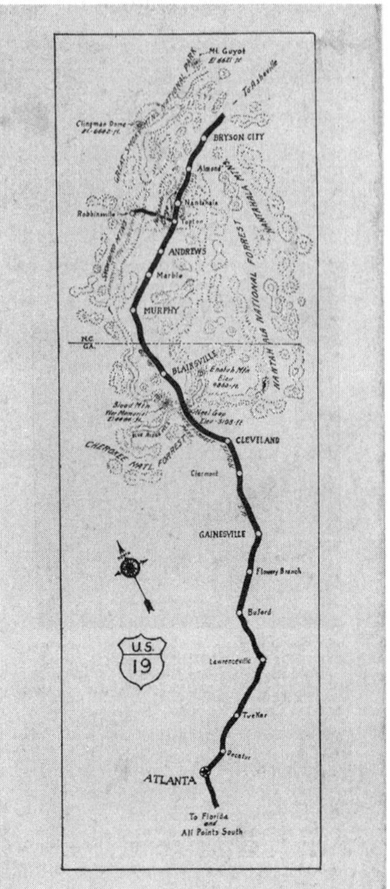

Trips in the Smokies map 1930.

[front of brochure]

Trips in the Smokies
1930

BY

HORACE KEPHART

PUBLISHED BY
BRYSON CITY DRUG COMPANY
THE REXALL STORE

Official Tourist Information

[middle of brochure]

The Smoky Mountains National Park lies half in North Carolina and half in Tennessee. The state line runs along the crest of the great divide, from the Pigeon River on the northeast to the Tennessee River on the southwest.

The best way to reach the "top o' Smoky," and the center of the Park, is from Bryson City 5 miles east on N. C. 10 to Oconaluftee River, thence north 13 miles on N. C. 107 to Smokemont, passing through the Cherokee Indian Reservation on the way. North from Smokemont light cars can go to the Indian Gap, 9 miles, which is on top of the Smoky range (5265 ft. above sea-level).

From Indian Gap is a good foot trail along the summits 6 miles southwest to top of Clingman Dome (6642 ft.).

Eastward from the Indian Gap, along the top of the divide, is hard travel for experienced and well equipped mountaineers. Here, in the "Sawtooth" county [*sic*], is the most rugged region east of the Rocky Mountains. The scenery is sublime. In some places one can straddle the mountain, as in a horse's saddle, and cast pebbles hundreds of feet down on either side.

About a mile before coming to Indian Gap a new road forks off to the right, over which a light car can be driven into Newfound Gap, where it joins a good highway from the top of the Smokies down to Gatlinburg and Sevierville, Tenn. This is the only crossing of the Smokies, for cars, except on N. C. 288 at Deal's Gap near the Tennessee River.

Swain County, of which Bryson City is the county-seat, has more trout streams and forests than any other county in North Carolina.

It is a paradise for campers. April is the best month for trout fishing, but likely to be rainy. May is bracing and delightful, but with cold nights in the high ranges. June is perfect, with rhododendron and azalea blooming over thousands of acres. July, August and the first half of September are warm and usually dry, but showers may be looked for at any time. Climate, here, is a matter of altitude. In the upper mountains one must have blankets every night.

THERE ARE NO MOSQUITOES

Most of the Park area is quite uninhabited. Campers should bring their own equipment. Guides about $3.50 a day; horses $2.00.

Nowhere else in the temperate zones can be found so many species of trees, shrubs and plants growing native to the soil, and in such luxuriance, as in the Smokies. Botanists are still making new discoveries here. In climbing a few miles from the Tuckaseegee River to the high mountain tops, one passes through a succession of floral belts, from Mid-South to Sub-Arctic climes, each with its characteristic vegetation and animal life. Along the main divide we are in the home of the black spruce and the balsam, the eagle, the raven and the black bear. From gaps in the great forest, here and there, we can look out over endless vistas of floral beauty, wild gardens where hundreds of acres are abloom with azalea, rhododendron, laurel, and innumerable other flowering shrubs and plants.

Five miles east of Bryson City, turning from N. C. 10 to N. C. 107, we enter the reservation (60,000 acres) of the Eastern Band of Cherokees. These Indians are descended from the refugees of their nation who, at the time of Removal in 1838, hid out in the wilds of the Great Smoky Mountains and refused to leave their ancient homeland.

There are 3000 Indians on the reservation, all of them self-supporting. The Government maintains a school for them at Cherokee, on N. C. 107, ten miles from Bryson City. In October of each year, on the school campus, the Indians hold a fair that attracts thousands of visitors from all over the Union. They have exhibits of native arts and crafts and perform daily contests in the aboriginal "ball-play," archery, blow-gun shooting and Indian dances.

Seventeen miles west of Bryson City, on N. C. 10, the highway runs for eight miles along the crystal-clear Nantahala River, at the bottom of a profound gorge, with exceedingly steep but thickly forested mountains on either side. On the far bank of the river will be noticed the black mouths of caves that have been used as refuges since prehistoric times.

This canyon is marked by an extraordinary variety of unusual shrubs, plants, ferns and mosses. The best view of the gorge as a whole, and of the still higher mountains all round about, is from a look-out platform on N. C. 108, two miles off from N. C. 10, near Topton, N. C.

[*back of brochure*]

BRYSON CITY DRUG COMPANY

One block north of Highway
No. 10, at the bridge, is

Headquarters for Tourist Information

to all points in the Smokies, Nantahala Gorge,
and surrounding country.

CURB SERVICE

"Ask Bennett—He Knows."

Basketry, Bead-work, Pottery, Bows
and Arrows, Carved wood

and other crafts and curios of the
Cherokee Indians, on sale

FISHING TACKLE SPECIALLY SUITED
TO MOUNTAIN STREAMS

Autographed copies of Horace Kephart's books:
"OUR SOUTHERN HIGHLANDERS,"
"CAMPING AND WOODCRAFT."

Ladies' Parlor

Atlanta to Asheville Via Neel Gap-Smoky Mt. Park

0.0 Leave Peachtree St. at Georgian Terrace Hotel, go east out Ponce de Leon Ave. U. S. Route 19, Ga. Route 8, follow car line.

6.8 Decatur, one block east of Court House, turn left at Hotel Candler follow pavement. U. S. Route 19, Ga. Route 8.

30.0 LAWRENCEVILLE, far corner of Court House square turn left, follow pavement, U. S. 19, Ga. 13.

60.0 GAINESVILLE, Hotel Dixie Hunt corner public square straight ahead, one block east of public square turn left at Service Station, at two blocks bear right up Green St., U. S. 19, Ga. 11.

85.5 CLEVELAND, straight ahead on pavement. U. S. 19, Ga. 11, north from old Court House center of Public Square.

100.0 ENTER BLOOD MOUNTAIN GORGE, all paved. DeSota Falls on left at 102.5 miles. Gorge heads up to Blood Mt. on left, summit 4464 ft. elevation.

104.0 NEEL GAP, top of Blue Ridge Divide, elevation 3108 ft. Highest point on Georgia State Road system. Vogel State Forest-Park, observation point 200 ft. on right, all paved route. Hiking trail along Ridge top 2,000 miles to Maine.

104.5 STATE PARK on right, free camp site on left. Notalee Falls on right at 104.7 mi. North slopes Blue Ridge Divide on right sky-line.

110.0 CHOESTOE VALLEY, Mt. Enotah on right, elevation 4800 ft. Blue Ridge sky-line in rear on right.

118.0 BLAIRSVILLE, turn left at Court House, follow paved highway, U. S. 19, Ga. 11, Christopher Hotel on left, Akins Hotel on right. A. S. H.

129.0 NORTH CAROLINA-GEORGIA STATE LINE. N. C. Route 10.

139.0 MURPHY, Hotel Regal corner of public square, straight ahead on concrete U. S. 19, N. C. 10. A. S. H. following Valley River.

155.0 ANDREWS, straight ahead on pavement U. S. 19, N. C. 10. (156.0 Junaluska Terrace right) follow pavement. Snowbird Mts. left, Valley River Mts. right.

163.9 TOPTON, Straight ahead down Nantahala Gorge, paved U. S. 19, N. C. 10. Second highest railroad point in Eastern America. (side trip 2½ mi. to Observation point, view of Gorge and Nantahala River, turn left at Topton across bridge.)

174.0 GREAT SMOKY MOUNTAINS NATIONAL PARK, Carolina-Tennessee boundary along sky-line on left. Clingman Dome, 6642 ft. elevation, second highest peak east of Rocky Mountains.

191.0 BRYSON CITY, Straight ahead. Court House on left. U. S. Route 19, N. C. Route 10. (Entrance to Fryemont Inn, turn right at Court House, follow signs on winding road.)

196.0 Side trip to CHEROKEE INDIAN RESERVATION, turn left for 5 miles. Appalachian Scenic Highway straight ahead, all paved, U. S. 19, N. C. 10.

266.0 ASHEVILLE, U. S. 19 north to Bristol; U. S. 70 west to Knoxville; U. S. 70 east to Raleigh; all paved to Quebec, Detroit, Chicago, etc.

Changing Mountaineers of South

AFTER YEARS ON ISOLATED FARMS THEY ARE CAUGHT BY TIDE OF INDUSTRIALISM

The visits of President Hoover to his mountain camp in Virginia and his direct contact with natives of that region have drawn national attention to a puzzling and picturesque element of our population—the Southern highlanders.

For a long time it has been known that the Appalachian Mountains south of the Potomac and Ohio Rivers were inhabited by a class of people distinct from the lowland Southerners, differing from them in tradition as well as in manners and mode of life. They also differ in many ways from the people of the North and West. Occupying a vast landlocked region that had little communication with the outer world until recent years, they have dwelt apart and developed marked characteristics of their own.

The Southern Appalachian highlands spread over parts of eight States. They take in one-third of Virginia, from the Blue Ridge westward; more than half of West Virginia, the eastern quarter of Kentucky, one-fifth of North Carolina, west of the Piedmont, three counties in the northwestern tip of South Carolina, one-seventh of Georgia, in the Northern section, and the northern quarter of Alabama.[23]

This is the housetop of the South. Its area equals that of England and Scotland combined. Its population, at present, is close to 4,000,000, nine-tenths of it is rural, and it has a few large towns.

Within the borders thus defined there are some thickly settled lowlands that are not properly mountain territory. Residents of the Shenandoah Valley, as a class, are not mountaineers; nor are those of the broad Appalachian Valley that separates the Unaka ranges from the Cumberland Plateau. Asheville and Roanoke, Knoxville and Chattanooga, are rated as mountain cities because of their locations; but a great part of their people are unrelated to the mountaineers.

Early in the seventeenth century there came into the highland region a few white

---

From *New York Times*, February 9, 1930

adventurers—traders with the Indians, explorers, soldiers; but they left no permanent settlements. Those of them who stayed were absorbed by the Indians.

PIONEERS FROM THE NORTH

About the middle of the eighteenth century Pennsylvania frontiersmen began to overflow southwestward into the Shenandoah Valley and thence into the Carolina Piedmont, both of which regions were mainly settled from this northern source. The pioneers of that time were not yet blended into a homogeneous stock. They were still readily distinguished as English, Irish, "Scotch-Irish," French Huguenot and "Pennsylvania Dutch." Among the men who took this long trek were Daniel Boone and ancestors of David Crockett, Sam Houston, John C. Calhoun, "Stonewall" Jackson and Abraham Lincoln.

After the Pennsylvanians had occupied the pick of the land in Western Virginia and adjoining parts of North Carolina, their own overflow of adventurous spirits began moving westward, across the Appalachian Mountains, to fertile but disputed valleys in what are now Tennessee and Kentucky. They did not tarry in the mountains, but went on to where game abounded and crops were easy to raise.

For a long time the mountains were regarded only as barriers in the way of westward expansion. At last, when Tennessee and Kentucky were fairly well settled, there came a backwash from contiguous lowlands both east and west. So the conquest of the Southern mountains was accomplished by members of this same frontier stock, mainly Anglo-Celtic, that had peopled the valleys and foothills on either side.

NO COLONISTS FROM ABROAD

Later accessions of population have come, in like manner, chiefly from the adjoining regions. The mountains have had no colonists from abroad. Very few highlanders trace their descent to former residents of the tidewater and coastal plains of the South, or to far northern or western sources. Leaving out of account a few large towns, Summer resorts, mining camps and the like, there has been no marked change in the strain of the mountain folk.

At the beginning of the twentieth century the Southern Appalachian Mountains were occupied by 3,000,000 people. Eighty-eight per cent of them were whites. Only one-third of 1 per cent were foreign-born. Only 9 per cent lived in villages or towns of 1,000 inhabitants and upward.

There were no navigable rivers, no surfaced highways. There were many counties without railways or newspapers. Most of the highlanders had little contact with the outer world; many of them had none at all. As a class they were unbelievably removed from, and independent of, modern civilization. It was a commonplace to say, in those days, that the Southern highlander[s] were the most isolated large group of people in America.

More than nine-tenths of the mountaineers were farmers. Most of their land was steep, rocky and hard to till. Of course there were some good valley farms whose occupants lived in the style of comfortable husbandmen; but the great body of the people were in the backwoods, on sterile hills, where they struggled for a bare existence. As a rule, every one, from childhood to old age, had to do without many things that he actually needed; he had to make shift with something else, however inadequate it might be.

Most of the families were widely scattered. It was every man for himself, with his back against the wall. Isolation bred a fiery individualism, a sense of equality before all men, a fierce passion for self-government, with corresponding suspicion and resentment of restraints imposed from without. Habituated to the independence and aloofness of backwoods life—where every man is lord of himself and his immediate surroundings, ready at all times to defend his honor and his possessions with arms in hand—the mountaineers saw little use in police expenditures. Often they were insubordinate to the law. Crimes of violence were common, but crimes against property were rare. The average mountaineer was a quick-tempered fellow, but he was an honest man.

Where there is little community life there can be hardly any civic or social consciousness. The mountaineers were unused to team-work; they had never heard such a word as cooperation. They seemed incapable of concerted effort, save as kinsmen against rival clans or as partisans against a common enemy. Bitterly clannish they were, not only in family matters, but in politics and in religion; yet outside of these emotional interests they were hard to combine. What they lacked most was a trained and sympathetic leadership.

In the old days there was slight chance for such leadership to develop among themselves. In the mountain counties of the South, in the year 1900, 18 per cent of the native whites 10 years old and upward were illiterate. Few of those who could read and write pursued any studies of cultural value. Many parents neglected to send their children to school; some even forbade them to go.

At bottom the problem of the Southern highlanders has always been an economic one—how to make a bare living. In their case it was doubly difficult, because most of them were far from towns, on almost impassable roads, with no market but interfamily trading. For such a people there can be no progress—they stand still or retrogress, unless there comes help from without.

Then, shortly after the twentieth century opened, there swept into the highland region a mighty tide of commercialism. Lumbermen and miners and hydroelectric companies came, overturning everything with their axes and saws, picks and shovels and dynamite. The mountaineers were shocked out of their Rip Van Winkle sleep. To their amazement the old order was wrecked and a new dispensation was forced upon the old-fashioned folk of the backwoods.

As late as 1916 Professor Eugene C. Branson of North Carolina asked: "Will our highlanders adjust themselves advantageously to new economic and social conditions? Will they surrender a sturdy manhood for the subservience that industrialism demands? Will they be content to stand quite discrowned in the presence of invading aliens? Will they withdraw into their shells like periwinkles, or in remote coves seek freedom from the annoyance of an impious new order of things? Or will they decline the struggle for adjustment and drop into chronic apathy or develop the dependency that afflicts modern civilization like creeping paralysis?"

The answer is now forthcoming from the loom of events. Wherever the mountaineers have been left to their own devices, neglected by their own Commonwealth as if alien to it, they have been unequal to the task of adjustment. But wherever the State has done its plain duty by them the mountaineers are forging ahead. For example, in Western North Carolina about fifteen years ago compulsory education was introduced. There was some opposition at first. Yet most of the people were tractable when the new system was explained to them. The State went quietly ahead. The courts obliged all recalcitrant citizens to submit.

So the schools were modernized. Not only that, but they have been consolidated. Motor buses collect the children, bring them to graded schools and return them safely home. A much larger proportion of young mountaineers are now getting high school education. Many are going outside to college, to technical schools, to universities. In due time they will supply an educated and progressive leadership of mountain stock.

At the same time the North Carolina State Board of Health is teaching, even enforcing, sanitation in the mountain communities. It sends welfare workers and medical examiners into every school district. The improvement in health of the mountain children is already apparent.

But education alone will not suffice to modernize 4,000,000 primitive people. The mountaineer must learn better ways of making a living. And so the State Board of

Agriculture, by cooperation with the counties, maintains farm demonstrators and veterinarians who are introducing improved methods of farming and stock breeding. The farm agents are also leaders in cooperative marketing.

AN IMPROVED ROAD SYSTEM

About eight years ago the admirable highway system of North Carolina was extended into the remotest mountain counties. Every county seat is now connected with every other, and with the outside world, by a network of graded and surfaced roads. The day of the harnessed steer, slowly dragging a little dry-land sled along a rocky road to market, has passed away forever. Our mountain farmers in large numbers have automobiles. They are going out and seeing the world.

In the mechanical arts the mountaineer is quick to "catch on" and learn a new trade. Even the women of the hills are adept after short training. One corporation, which is now building, near Asheville, a rayon plant that will employ more than 4,000 hands, will use none but native labor, notwithstanding that our mountaineers never heard of rayon until a year or so ago.

The influx of new people with new ideas, so far from being resented, is really welcomed by those mountaineers who have most influence among their own people. It helps mightily in organizing the mass for economic, civic and social efficiency. The newcomers bring not only fresh opportunities that hillsmen are quick to seize but also a buoyant spirit of optimism that is contagious.

The old apathy of fatalism, the hopelessness of bettering one's condition, that hovered like a fog over the worn-out rocky farms of Appalachia, is now rising and fading away under the cheerful rays of a new era.

Kephart Writes of Odd Names in Smoky Mountains

EVERY MOUNTAIN, CREEK, BRANCH, COVE AND "LEAD" HAS NAME KNOWN ONLY TO FEW ADVENTURERS

This is the first of a series of Sunday articles, written especially for *The Times* by Horace Kephart, of Bryson City, noted author and authority on the Great Smoky Mountains, on subjects of great interest relating to the Great Smokies. This story on "Odd Names in the Smoky Mountains" will be followed next Sunday by "Panthers in the Great Smoky Mountains" and the following Sunday by "The Language of the Cherokees."—EDITOR.

When I first came into the Carolina mountains I had no guide but an old "tope sheet" atlas of the U. S. Geological Survey. In poring over those maps my eyes were caught and held by many queer names that amused or puzzled me. I could grasp the significance of Standing Indian, as applied to a mountain—the term was picturesque and dignified—but what quirk of imagination, what ribald streak of humor, had dubbed a fine summit of the Blue Ridge with such a name as Chunky Gal? Nor was my wonder much abated when I learned, from the Indians, that Chunky Gal is the white mountaineer's delicate way of interpreting the original Cherokee name, which means Pregnant Woman.

On the way up Shooting Creek to the Chunky Gal, one goes parallel with Drowning Creek and passes Licklog Branch, Jack Rabbit Mountain, Fleaback Mountain, Hothouse Branch, Pounding Creek, Burnt Cabin and Thumping Creek, all in the course of ten miles.

As I had never seen or heard of a "bald" mountain, in the sense of a heavily wooded dome topped by an unaccountable open meadow of wild bluegrass, such names on the map as Parson Bald and Warrior Bald (properly Wayah, meaning wolf) caused

---

From *Asheville Times,* March 2, 1930

me to break out laughing. I thought they were inversions of Bald Parson and Bald Warrior. But when I came upon Burning-town Bald and Wine-spring Bald I was quite confused. What, in the name of sanity, could such names mean?

Later, when I went to live far back in the wilderness, not in the Blue Ridge but in the Great Smoky Mountains, where no map showed accurately the features or the names of that rugged country, I had to learn everything, from the ground up, by my own exploring and from the lips of the few pioneers who had ventured there.

The settlements, such as they were, extended in a fringe of scattered cabins along the southern border of the Smokies, and along their northern border in Tennessee. The great mass of the Smokies was quite uninhabited, as most of it still is today. Often, in that wilderness, while going on my lone exploring trips, I met no human being for several days, nor saw any sign of man save here and there a foot-trail left by wandering hunters or fishermen, or herdsmen who came into the high ranges, now and then, after their half-wild cattle and razorbacks.

VIVIDLY DESCRIPTIVE

And still, every creek and branch and "lead" and gap, west of Clingman Dome, had a name by which it was known to the few adventurers who quested the woods. And such names! Vividly descriptive, if one understood the backwoods lingo; often unintellible [*sic*] if he did not. Whimsical names. Sometimes profane or indecent names—but with good cause, as one realized when he tried to bore his way through the laurel "slicks" or found himself trapped in a gulch where the only way out was by edging along cliffs and perilously sliding down the slippery, precipitous courses of mountain torrents. To be caught there in fog, that is to say, in clouds, when one could not see a tree ten feet away, was a dismal predicament indeed; or when steady rain set in and the drench[ed] bushes rubbed the water right through duxbak, leather, or any other material that one could wear in mountain climbing.

No wonder we have such names in the Smokies as Ripshin and the "Harricane," the Devil's Den and Huggin's Hell, the Defeat and Desolation branches of Bone Valley, the Rough Arm and the Blowdown, Tear Breeches and Long Hungry Ridge. Aye, worse names, that may not be put in print until some stripling of the intelligentsia comes from a big city and whoops over his discovery of some new and bizarre specimen of smut.

Names there are, in plenty, that express the raw virility of the backwoodsman, his literal-mindedness, his whimsical humor that makes a sport of hardship and privation. Pictur[e]s, showing in a word or two, the features of places, or celebrating some incident of the rough life of the woods, or recalling some person who one time was somehow identified with a given place.

On the watersheds of Twenty Mile and Eagle Creek are Judy Branch and Genes Camp Branch, Big Tommy and Little Tommy, the Shuckstack, Big Swag Ridge, Proctor's Sang Branch (ginseng), Lawson Gant-lot Branch (once a cattle corral), Painter (panther) Branch, Bear Pen (a log trap), Coon-town Branch, Pawpaw and Soapstone, Pinnacle Creek.

IN HAZEL CREEK COUNTRY

In the Hazel Creek country we have Blockhouse and Thunderhead mountains, Brier Knob, Indian Camp, Woolly Range, the Chestnut Bald, the Raven's Den, Owl Cove, Old House Branch, Slick Rock. When one turns up from Bone Valley to the Locust Gap he comes to the Nigh Long Big [F]lats Branch, then to the Main Long Big Flats Branch, beyond which, as a head stream, is the Fur Long Big Flats Branch.

Crossing the high Welch Divide to the eastward of Hazel Creek, and trailing down from Bear Wallow Bald, one reaches Forney Creek. Proceeding upstream, the first branch he comes to, on the left, is Ad Valorem. No native mountaineer could have given it such a name. Some outsider, God knows who and God knows why, christened a trout stream with that abominable reminder of custom-houses. But, with this sole exception, all the names are genuinely backwoodsy. The next branch, on the same side, is Slab Camp, and the next is White Man's Glory! Up the right fork, toward Clingman Dome, we pass Board Camp (not a boarding place, but a lean-to of clapboards split with a froe), Buckhorn and Steel Trap branches.

On the waters of Deep Creek, and the mountains from which they spring, are some peculiar names. Easy Ridge is a satiric term; for it is anything but easy to ascend with a pack on one's back. Nick's Nest refers to the Old Nick. The Keg Drive is a favorite for bear-driving, probably called after an Indian family named Keg, of whom the noted, if not notorious, Modi Keg is a living specimen. A gap at the head of Bee-Tree Creek is known as Turkey-fly-up, because old Indians remember that wild turkeys were always to be found there—and there are still some of the big birds in that neighborhood.

ALONG OCONA LUFTY

Proceeding eastward, we come to the Ocona Lufty River. The left fork of Horse Camp Creek is called Sweat Heifer. You may learn what it means from old Dock Connor or his son Charlie. The creek that bears this extraordinary name runs parallel with Fuzzy Top Ridge and is joined by prosaic Mud Creek, which heads in the exceedingly wild and steep region of the western Sawtooth, just under Dry Sluice Gap and Charlie's Bunion. The last-mentioned name dates back no longer than last summer, but it has struck the fancy of the mountaineers and it will probably stick. When George Masa was photographing this difficult country, Charlie Connor pointed out a protruding knob and said: "That looks just like a bunion on Old Smoky's foot."

Many of the branches thereabouts are named after individuals: for instance, Huskey, Jake Bradley and Jim Mac Branch (after James McMahan). In some cases the family name is omitted, as in Ted's Branch and Dan's Creek. The Loorie Camp Branch is called after an old Indian hunter, Loorie Owl, who used to go there every year for bear-hunting. And, by the way, there are plenty of bears around there now. Some of the names on Bradley Fork are self-explanatory, as Gold-mine branch, Washout and Bear-wallow; but Tow String gets its odd designation from the industry of an old white woman who used to live there and made tow string for the settlers.

NAME COVE FOR "RAMPS"

In the very wild country above Big Cove, on the Raven Prong of Lufty, are some strange names. Bull Die (both creek and ridge) commemorates, in Indian-English, a place where a more or less valuable bull perished. Breakneck Ridge, Little Niagara, Bear-foot and Setback are obvious enough; but Ramp Cove will not be understood by anyone from outside these mountains until it is explained to him that "ramps" are rampions, otherwise known as wild garlic.

On Straight Fork we have Turkey Pen (not an enclosure for keeping tame turkeys, but a trap to catch wild ones), Stillhouse (must this be explained today?), Raven's Roost and 'Tater-hill Bald. In the Catalooche country is the Big Butte (pronounced Butt by the mountain folk) at the head of a ridge between Lost Bottom and Pretty Hollow. There is a Bunk Ridge (logger's bunk, not slang) and a Shanty Mountain, a Wolf Cove Creek and a George Ira Creek, a Sheep-back Knob and a Maggot Spring Branch, a Little Bald Knob and a Tough Ridge, a Winding Stair Branch, and, of course, a Hell's Half-acre.

LOCAL NAMES ON NEW MAP

George Masa has reduced the big official map of the North Carolina Park Commission's survey to a scale of one inch to the mile. He and I have corrected it in spots, from personal knowledge of the topography, and we have added the local names of nearly all mountains, streams, gaps and other natural features, so far as possible. We got these names mostly from old residents on the respective watersheds, when we did not already know them or find them on any map.

It is a pity that Tennessee has no such accurate map showing the topography of its half of the National Park. If there were one, and it bore the local names as ours does, it would be sprinkled all over with quaint and interesting native names, similar in general character to those of the Carolina side.

When the U. S. Geological Survey's new topographic map of the park area is published, which I suppose will be within a couple of years, it will delineate with accuracy the contours and heights of peaks, as well as the features that appear on the map George and I have worked on.

Kephart Tells of Panthers in Smokies

SPECIES IS KING OF ALL CATS IN AMERICA

This is the second of a series of Sunday articles, written especially for *The Times* by Horace Kephart, of Bryson City, noted author and authority on the Great Smoky Mountains, on subjects of great interest relating to the Great Smokies.—THE EDITOR.

Three species of native cats were formerly common in the southern mountains, namely: the wildcat, the lynx and the panther. The wildcat or bobcat is still a too plentiful nuisance in the Smokies. It is generally less than three feet long and weighs under twenty pounds. Like all the cats it is very furtive. A man hunting without dogs will never run across a wildcat in our woods except by rare accident. I have done so but once; and then both the cat and myself were absorbed in stalking the same pheasant, which had been drumming on a fallen tree.

The lynx is very rare in our region. It stays in the sub-arctic or Canadian zone of the high Smokies, among the spruces and balsams. It is a bit over three feet long, weighs up to thirty pounds, has an even shorter tail than the bobcat, tufted ears, and very large feet. Our native hunters call this animal a "catamount."

The panther is king of cats in the United States. Our mountaineers call him a "painter." In the West he is known as mountain lion. In Spanish America his name is puma. Scientists know him as the cougar. But it is the same beast, by whatever name. His total length is from seven to nine feet, including a three-foot tail. He weighs from a hundred and fifty to two hundred pounds.

MANY FANCIFUL YARNS

There are many fanciful yarns about panthers stalking human beings and attacking them unprovoked. The truth is that they are naturally sneaking and wary beasts, afraid of armed men, but, for all that, there have been individual exceptions. Under

---

From *Asheville Times,* March 9, 1930

rare circumstances, under the urge of hunger or fright, a panther may attack a man—perhaps one chance in a thousand. A buck deer may do the same thing.

In the spring of 1916 I heard that Tom Sparks had been set upon and badly injured by a panther in the Smoky Mountains. I was inclined to [doubt] the tale, notwithstanding that it was told me by old neighbors of mine and fellow hunters in the Smokies.

So far as I knew, the last panther seen in the Smokies was one that was treed by Dan Cable's dogs, in 1911. Dan had no gun with him. He cut the tree and the beast ran away. The dogs would not follow it. Jess Cable and Bill Cope, who are still living and with whom I have hunted, tracked what was probably the same animal, at different times, but it eluded them.

TOM VERY MODEST

But the time came when I had to put more credence in the Sparks story. In the spring of 1917, Tom himself came to see me in Bryson City. He was very modest about his adventure, saying he was not dead sure the thing was a "painter"; but he told me the following story—

"In February, 1916, I was herdin' on Thunderhead and tharabouts, and was livin' alone in the Spence cabin—you know the place. I had sheep on the mountain. One evenin' I went out jest to look around a bit. Didn't take my gun or dog along, for I didn't aim to stay out long. Hit was gittin' dark as I kem back along the trail, gradin' by Thunderhead. I heered what seemed to be somebody hollerin'. Soon I heered it agin, close by. Then I suspicioned hit mought be some wild critter follerin' me. I got out my pocket-knife.

"Then, all of a suddenty, somethin' bigger 'n a dog jumped me and knocked me back'ards. Hit was a survigrous beast and bit me in the left elbow and the left wrist. I stobbed the thing twicet and hit jumped off inter the thicket. The night, by now, was too dark for me to see more'n the bulk of the beast. I didn't know, for sure, was it a painter or a wolf or what; but hit was bigger'n ary hound. When I kem to think, I knowed in reason 't wa'nt no wolf; for a wolf don't holler thataway.

GOES FOR GUN

"I made tracks for the cabin, to git my gun; but the critter kem back and jumped me agin. This time hit seized me by the coat and clawed me. I stobbed it deeper, I think, than before, and hit run off. Then I burned the wind and got to camp. But by now I was bleedin' purty bad and had myself to take keer of.

"Next mornin' I tracked the thing in the snow, along with my dog. There was blood on the trail till I kem to whar the beast had wallowed in the snow. Then the tracks led into that devilish laurel on Killpeter Ridge, and the dog wouldn't foller. No more would I."

Sparks showed me the scars on his arm and body. They were made by large teeth and claws, beyond doubt. I was impressed by his sincerity and I believe his story, just as he told it.

Poor fellow! He was to meet a worse fate, a few years later. He was murdered in this same Spence cabin.

As late as last summer, if anyone had asked me whether there were still any panthers in the Smokies, I would have said: "I think not. Probably the last of them left when the deer were dogged out of this range."

But I learned better from my friend Roy Ozmer, of Erwin, Tennessee. He and Granville Hunt, of Knoxville, came down off the Smokies, last September, and dropped into my office. Roy had been scouting the Appalachian Trail, from Mt. Oglethorpe, Georgia, northward, choosing a route and marking it with the official copper disks. He came as far as Siler's Bald, in the Smokies, but had to lie up for a time on account of an injured back. Later in the season, he and Hunt tackled the Smokies from the opposite direction and tied in, on the trail, at Siler's Bald.

Coming up Big Creek, north of Cataloochee, toward Mt. Guyot, they encountered a blow-down and a sandbar formed by a cloudburst. On the damp, level sand they discovered many tracks made by a large beast, or maybe a pair of them, and these were certainly not bear tracks. Hunt made a half-scale drawing, true in outlining and proportions, of one of the tracks. They showed it to me.

This track was four-toed, four and a half inches wide across the pad and five and a half across the spread of toes; but only four and half inches from hollow of heel to tip of toe. It was a cat's track, beyond question. There is only one North American animal that makes such a huge cat track, namely: the panther.

six

FICTION

Horace Kephart 3482 57

CRIME-- Detection.

The mysterious criminal May, having succeeded in concealing his identity in spite of all cross-examinations and ruses of detectives, is allowed, as a last resort, to escape, or is being shadowed by detectives in the hope of running him to his den. May, knowing all this, is leading the sleuths a dance. But he is penniless. Fails in attempt to sell his clothes for a cheaper suit and a little money. Dares not go near his accomplices, knowing that it would cost him his secret.

"Undoubtedly, at that moment, he [May] gave himself up for lost. Alone, in the midst of Paris, without a penny, what was to become of him?---

[Lecoq to fellow detective]—"The moral of this is that there is a vast difference between theory and practice. Here is a man who has made the most discerning believe that he is a poor devil, a low buffoon; so much has he prated of the misfortunes and the hazards of his existence.— He is free; and this so-called Bohemian does not know how to go to work to sell the clothing that he wears upon his back. The comedian who could play his part so well upon the stage, disappears; the man remains— the man who has always been rich, and who knows nothing of the vicissitudes of life!"

(Gaboriau, Monsieur Lecoq.)

Last week at dinner she had sat beside Judge Allison in his home and heard him denounce the police in biting tones. He had said that eighty per cent. of all the murderers went uncaught and that less than two per cent. got punished.

"Insight, Wit, Nerve"—the three winning cards in the game of crime—had been Judge Allison's pronouncement. Insight to divine the road the pursuer would take; wit to extricate one's self when cornered; nerve to play the game through to the end, making no admissions, conceding no points, proclaiming innocence in the face of an army of accusers. Insight, wit, nerve,—she would have these, because *she must have them!*

(Maravene Thompson. The Woman's Law.)

See also Law, Inadequacies of.

Gunshot Wounds.

See Murder (Elwell Case) Firearms 4°, 935.

Well, I knew now who had committed the murder up in Room 309 in the Palace Hotel. His apparent alibi in the fact that he was taking part in Elaine's performance at the theater at the time when the murder occurred puzzled me for a minute or two; but then I worked it out. He had come on during the first act, but only in the early part of it and not at all in the second. Indeed, his only subsequent appearance had been in one of Elaine's later dances in the third, one that followed my own return from the lobby.

He must have dressed after his first appearance and left the theater in his proper person. But his crutch? That was what the loop of cord was for! He could hang it round his neck and button it up under his overcoat.

Somewhere between the theater and the hotel he had made the transformation which had just taken place under my eyes. And it was as a hunchback that he walked boldly into the hotel and rode up in the elevator to Room 309.

The act showed an almost satanic precalculation that was more horrifying than anything else about it. He must have meant to commit the crime, or at least have foreseen its possibility, when he left the theater with his crutch.

But, granting that, it was one of the most perfect things of its kind I had ever heard of. I recalled what Elaine had said that very morning. If you wanted to keep people from thinking of one thing you must give them something else to think about. He saw to it that he gave us a hunchback to think about and then went his ways in complete security.

Horace Kephart

Crime—Detection. Page from Kephart's journal.

Introduction

MAE MILLER CLAXTON

"But, for God's sake, don't send out stories that will make the world think we're all that way. Our southern highlands have been cursed by yarn spinners who reported little but feuds and moonshining and 'quare' people."

KEPHART, "The Trail of a Bullet," *Flynn's*, April 18, 1925

In his account of a "man hunt" in the Sugarlands in Tennessee, published in *All Outdoors* in 1921, Kephart writes about encountering a mountaineer who had read his book *Our Southern Highlanders*. As they sat chatting on his porch, Kephart mentioned a friend of his named Quill Rose, a neighbor from his days in Hazel Creek. The mountaineer mentioned that he had seen a picture of Rose once in a book. Kephart asked what book, and the man replied, "'Some women from outside came in here and started a settlement-house. They had the book, and they lent it to us to read. It was called *Our Southern Highlanders*.'" Asked how he liked it, the mountaineer replied, "'Fine. Did you ever see it?'" Kephart answered, "'I wrote it.'" He continues, "'Fenn's eyes nearly popped out of his head. For a moment he was dumbfounded. Then he seized me by the arm and half dragged, half carried me, crippled as I was, back to the kitchen, crying to his wife: 'Mary—Mary—here's the man who wrote *that book*!'" (See "Roving with Kephart," Chapter III, in chapter five).

In this story, Kephart was clearly gratified to receive the approval of the people he was writing about in "*that book*." *Our Southern Highlanders* continues to be consulted by writers in fiction and nonfiction genres as an insightful and sympathetic portrayal of the people and customs of this region. In it, Kephart displays the knowledge he obtained over many years from books and universities during his career as a student and eminent librarian. At the same time, he came to the Smoky Mountains to receive a kind of "learning" that could not be found solely in books, one that could only be obtained from listening to stories and folklore from the mountain people and from tramping many hours in the woods. *Our Southern Highlanders* is nonfiction, but it is written in an engaging narrative style, combining stories and anecdotes with information. His meticulous research can be seen in his journal pages, which obsessively document his extensive reading and notes on various topics such as footgear and moccasins, rations, blowguns, and "domestic affection."

While Kephart brought to his writing a respect for the mountain people and meticulous research, he was also an outsider to the region and thus open to criticism as yet another "furriner" exploiting the resources of the locals, albeit stories and information rather than timber or land. As Gary Carden eloquently puts it in his review of *Our Southern Highlanders*, "As a native of the region that Kephart describes, I have always had an acute sensitivity to 'outlanders' who define, appraise and judge my culture. I always read Kephart with a clenched jaw, anticipating some flagrant offense in the next sentence."[1] Carden disagrees with some aspects of Kephart's portrait of the mountain people, for example his focus on more isolated mountain people and not "the valley people" who lived in towns and shopped at stores on Main Street. He also complains about Kephart's "bleak assessment on the role of women in mountain culture."[2] Carden admits, though, with these reservations, "I must conclude that I endorse and even applaud most of his observations, finding that they coincide with the world that I inhabited as a child."[3] In his play *Outlander*, Carden provides another perspective on the Kephart story and the subsequent creation of the national park.

It is perhaps the "literariness" of *Our Southern Highlanders*, and of Kephart's work in general, that makes it attractive to contemporary poets and fiction writers, who have cited it as influential for their own work. Poet Robert Morgan opens his volume *At the Edge of the Orchard Country* (1987) with a poem entitled "Horace Kephart" in which he describes the writer sitting at a desk "Outside the tent on the Little Fork / of the Sugar Fork of Hazel Creek" (1–2).[4] Morgan continues, "His table boards / on upended kegs, he drafts meticulously clear / paragraphs and weights the finished pages / with a shotgun shell" (3–6).[5] Later in the poem, a "loose / hog crashes through the brush into his camp," interrupting his writing, just as real life often interrupts art (25–26).[6] But the poem mostly talks about sacrifices—those in Kephart's family who released him from responsibilities so that he could seek the career and life he wished and, less obviously, Kephart's own sacrifices. He would, necessarily, always be an outsider and thus often separated from close relationships.

More recently, Ron Rash included a similarly conflicted fictional version of Horace Kephart in his best-selling novel *Serena* (2008).[7] In this work, Kephart acts as a moral contrast to the capitalistic Pembertons in his determination to preserve the land for a national park, but Rash also portrays his loneliness along with his drinking problem. Another possible literary connection that calls for more research is the long-held belief of George Ellison, Kephart biographer, that William Faulkner might have read Kephart's chapter "A Bear Hunt in the Smokies" from *Our Southern Highlanders* and used it as inspiration for his story "The Bear," originally published as "Lion" in *Harper's Magazine* (December 1935). It later appeared in the *Saturday Evening Post* (May 1942) and then in his collection *Go Down, Moses* (1942). While no one has found a copy of *Our Southern Highlanders* in Faulkner's personal library, there are several first edition copies at the library at the University of Mississippi in Oxford frequented often by Faulkner.[8]

Kephart's debts to his literary ancestors are easy to trace. For a variety of reasons, including the lack of international publishing rights that permitted widespread pirating of more famous European novelists, American writers struggled to achieve success until well into the nineteenth century. Notable exceptions were the wildly popular captivity narratives, nonfiction accounts written by Anglo Europeans who were captured by Native Americans and spent time among them before returning to the precarious border settlements. These narratives could be justified as morally edifying, but they often contained a riveting plot. Kephart edited a collection of these narratives for *Outing* entitled *Captives Among the Indians* (1915). These works were perhaps the first to capture the American "frontier" and portray the unique interdependence of the individual with his or her environment along with complex interactions with the indigenous inhabitants.

Kephart was also hugely influenced by the Romantic writers, both English and American. In his famous speech later entitled "The American Scholar," Ralph Waldo Emerson called vehemently for American thinkers and writers to "study nature," to understand themselves in relation to "this spectacle."[9] This challenge was taken up by many writers who were already beginning to see civilization impacting the landscape. Just a few years before Emerson's speech, Washington Irving had embarked on an extended journey into the American West. He published three works based on these travels. Beginning in 1823 with *The Pioneers*, James Fenimore Cooper published a number of books that proved incredibly popular well into the twentieth century. George Ellison mentions Kephart's reading of Wordsworth, Shelley, Goethe, Emerson, Thoreau, and Whitman in his introduction to *Our Southern Highlanders*.[10] The first chapter in Kephart's earlier work *Camping and Woodcraft* (1906) urges men (and he does mean men primarily) to leave the confines of the city and head out to the freedom of nature: "This instinct for a free life in the open is as natural and wholesome as the gratification of hunger and thirst and love. It is Nature's recall to the simple mode of existence that she intended us for."[11] Kephart writes at the end of the chapter of the "proud self-reliance of one who is absolutely his own master, free to follow his bent in his own way."[12] According to George Ellison and Janet McCue, Kephart in *Camping and Woodcraft* is very much influenced by a writer (George Washington Sears) with the pseudonym of "Nessmuk," who also borrows from writers such as Thoreau in wishing to " lure the clerk and workingman out of the degrading city and into the soul-cleansing wilderness."[13]

Like Twain and Faulkner, and many other late nineteenth and early twentieth-century Southern writers, Kephart was greatly influenced by a pre-Civil War literary subgenre known as "Southwestern humor" and named after the "old Southwest": Georgia, Alabama, Tennessee, and Mississippi.[14] In his 1976 introduction to *Our Southern Highlanders*, George Ellison claims that Kephart's readable, entertaining book is a "direct descendant" of this subgenre.[15] Southwestern humorists wrote sketches, anecdotes, and tales and published either in local newspapers or in "sporting papers" with a national audience such as William T. Porter's *Spirit of the Times*. Johnson Jones Hooper, George Washington Harris, and Thomas Bangs Thorpe all wrote for Porter's magazine. Many of these stories followed a type with an "educated" narrator who tells the story and a humorous local who speaks in dialect and teaches the more traditionally educated narrator something about common sense and the foibles of human existence. These stories could be called "slice of life"—they were realistic in setting and written about everyday people, characteristics often associated with the later literary genre of realism. Louis Rubin also notes that the writers of Southwestern humor would likely be from the Upcountry, where manners, literature, and customs were less set in stone than in the coastal eastern region. Unlike writers from more settled areas, he must retain his ability to critique the social and political customs of his community.[16] These "border" places, newly open to settlement due to the Louisiana Purchase and, later, Indian Removal, were societies still in flux, and the writing reflects uncertainties and upheaval in language, class, and morality.

These early publications were the prototypes for magazines Kephart wrote for, such as *All Outdoors*, *Forest and Stream*, *Field and Stream*, and *Outing*. They appealed to a kind of nostalgia for a frontier America by a post-industrial rising middle class audience that often lived in urban areas but longed for outdoor adventure and recreation. For example, *Forest and Stream*, founded in the early 1870s, created great interest in rifle matches, an activity that Kephart participated in for many years before his move to the Smokies. F. Phillips Williamson writes in the foreword to *American Sporting Books Series*, "Ranges were built in every state and most cities had a rifle club. Ads were run in *Forest and Stream* for 100 and 200 yard underground rifle ranges (under Broadway Avenue in New York, for example)."[17] Ironically, the same industrialism bemoaned by outdoor writers such as Nessmuk (George Washington Sears) created a demand for outdoor publications and the ability to mass produce them cheaply. Gerald Hallock, editor of *Forest and Stream*, writes in the first issue of the magazine:

> The object of this journal will be to studiously promote a healthful interest in outdoor recreation and to cultivate a refined taste for natural objects. We especially desire to make *Forest and Stream* the recognized medium of communication between amateurs and professional sportsmen. All of us have something to impart, which, if made available to each other, will in time render us proficient in all those several branches of physical culture which are absolutely essential to our manhood and well-being, both as individuals and as a nation.[18]

In this passage, Hallock suggests a kind of egalitarian exchange of information for those with similar interests, amateur and professional alike.

Other literary influences are more difficult to trace. In his article "The Man Who Has Lived Two Lives" (see chapter one), F. A. Behymer (*St. Louis Post-Dispatch*, October 31, 1926) lists the twenty books that Kephart states that he brought to western North Carolina to his cabin on Hazel Creek "in the order in which they usually stood on a shelf on his soap-box cupboard"[19]:

English Dictionary.
Roget's Thesaurus.
My sister's Bible.
Shakspeare. [*sic*]
Burns. Poems.
Dante (in Italian).
Goethe. Faust.
Poe. Tales.
Stevenson. Kidnaped.
Stevenson. David Balfour.
Stevenson. The Merry Men.
Fisher. Universal History.
Pilcher. First Aid.
"Nessmuk." Woodcraft.
Frazer. Minerals.
Jordan. Vertebrate Animals.
Wright. Birdcraft.
Mathews. American Wild Flowers.
Keeler. Our Native Trees.
Lounsberry. Southern Wild Flowers and Trees.

Of this list, it is significant that eight out of the twenty are works of fiction, three by Robert Louis Stevenson. Also important is the complete absence of Appalachian writers of fiction. Kephart was later able to expand his "library" when he moved to Bryson City in 1910 and rented an office. Jason Brady's list of titles in Kephart's collection (see appendix to this volume) reveals an eclectic mix of genres, from westerns such as Owen Wister's *Lin McLean* and Edna Ferber's *Cimarron* to G. K. Chesterton's *The Man Who Knew Too Much* and H. G. Wells's *The Invisible Man*. Thomas Hardy, the stories of Guy de Maupassant, and Percy Bysshe Shelley's poetry also occupied space on Kephart's shelves along with, interestingly, a copy of D. H. Lawrence's 1922 *Women in Love*. Dates of these books range from 1899 to 1929.

Brady also lists a good number of Appalachian works, both fiction and nonfiction, including three books by Lucy Furman along with Emma Bell Miles's important 1905 book *The Spirit of the Mountains*. Furman worked at the well-known Hindman Settlement School with Katherine Pettit and May Stone for seventeen years teaching, gardening, writing, and acting as housemother.[20] Emma Bell Miles lived most of her life in east Tennessee but died at the age of thirty-nine in a county tuberculosis sanitarium in 1919.[21] There is no evidence that she and Kephart ever met, but he did save a clipping of a review Miles wrote for the *New York Times Saturday Review of Books* in one of his journals. Other works Kephart owned were by Elizabeth Madox Roberts, a Kentucky writer; Margaret W. Morley, who wrote *The Carolina Mountains* (1913); and John Fox Jr., who wrote the bestseller *The Trail of the Lonesome Pine*, which had multiple lives on screen and stage in addition to print. Fiswoode Tarleton also deserves mention because he became friends with Kephart and, tragically, died in the car crash that killed both in 1931.

Kephart's interest in writing fiction goes all the way back to 1907, when he published "A Magistrate of Skull Creek" in the magazine *Puck*. *Puck* was a unique magazine published by Joseph Keppler beginning in 1871. It was originally published in St. Louis, where 50,000 Germans had immigrated in the 1860s, making it the fourth largest city in America behind only New York, Brooklyn, and Philadelphia. This influx greatly impacted publications in St. Louis in the latter half of the nineteenth century. Keppler was trained in drawing and painting in prestigious academies in Vienna and worked as a successful actor before joining his father in America in 1867. After making his way to St. Louis, Keppler joined a group of intellectuals that included Joseph Pulitzer and Udo Brachvogel, librarian at the Mercantile.[22]

Keppler began creating cartoons for *Frank Leslie's Illustrated Newspaper*, a rival of *Harper's Weekly*, where Thomas Nast, another famous political cartoonist, worked. While still working for Leslie's newspaper, Keppler re-launched *Puck* in New York

City as a German-American humor magazine.[23] By 1886, the magazine had become well-established, suggested by the seven-story Puck building on Houston Street and Mulberry, complete with a nine-foot-high statue of Puck.[24] It brought intellectual ideas to the masses via political cartoons produced according to the latest printing methods.[25] Kephart's "Magistrate" is noteworthy as an early example of the writer's interest in fiction. Its placement in a national magazine specializing in illustrations and political cartoons is also interesting. Given the story's publication date in 1907, soon after Kephart's departure from St. Louis, it is possible that connections with former Mercantile librarian Udo Brachvogel and the German press in St. Louis led to this unusual publication.

Kephart followed up his publication in *Puck* with "The Rock Hunter," published in *Field and Stream* in December 1909. It is the lead story for the magazine and contains the subtitle: "A Pen-Picture of Life among the 'Blockaders' of the Great Smokies." The table of contents for this issue shows the mix of writing genres common to outdoor magazines during this time period. Kephart's illustrated story is published along with articles on "Black Sea Bass Fishing," "How to Organize a Gun Club," several poems, photographs, drawings, and letters from readers. A piece entitled "A Talk With Our Readers" at the end reminds readers of the mission of the magazine: "The sportsmen's magazine of to-day must be, above all things, instructive and helpful. Its mission is to bind sportsmen together in closer brotherhood, to teach them the higher meaning of sportsmanship, and to help one and all to a more perfect enjoyment of the outdoor life."[26]

Nine years later, Kephart published "The Girl with the Turquoise Eyes" in *Field and Stream*.[27] See "Fiction for April" (pg. 422). The editors suggest that the challenge for outdoor magazines that wish to publish fiction is to find good writers who can successfully combine a good plot with an outdoor setting. Hy Watson was an editor for *Field and Stream* from 1918 to 1924 who also did illustrations.[28]

In a weekly magazine called *Flynn's*, Kephart published two long parts of a story entitled "The Trail of a Bullet."[29] The cover features Kephart's story title with a nameplate that reads "Flynn's Issued Weekly" and then states, "William J. Flynn, Editor, Twenty-Five Years in the U. S. Secret Service." The illustration shows a man dressed like a mountaineer, complete with floppy black hat, holding a rifle with a scope. The opening page of the story reads, "A novel by the greatest living authority in the country on woodcraft and small arms you will agree is an unusual event. *Flynn's* has secured just such a thing for its readers." The story, it asserts, is a "regular mystery-action story." However, *Flynn's* lets its readers know that "Trail of a Bullet" is much more than a conventional story: "There isn't a remark in the story,

RIGHT
Field and Stream March 1918.

BELOW
Table of Contents *Field and Stream,* December 1909.

In the Mule Deer Country of Squaw Butte 909

"He was requested to shoot the next deer a little nearer sea level"

FICTION FOR APRIL

Good outdoor fiction is the hardest of all to get. To find trained authors who can write a real short story in a fishing or hunting setting, yet have the details technically correct—so we outdoorsmen will see no error—is a harder task than any of the "literary" magazines have to face. But Field and Stream has done the impossible. Honest, weren't those stories, illustrated by a regular magazine artist, Hy Watson, as good as any you ever read? And we've been running them monthly for nearly a year now, and will keep right on doing so. Next month Clarence Mulford, the famous author of the "Hopalong Cassidy" series, will be with us with a corking cow country tale, "The Invasion." Don't miss it!

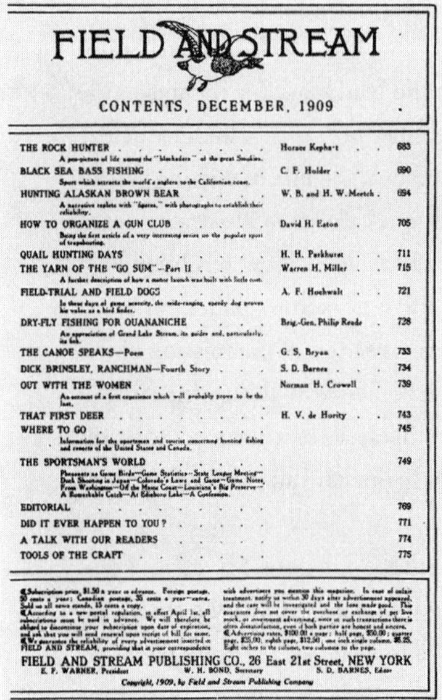

FIELD AND STREAM

CONTENTS, DECEMBER, 1909

FIELD AND STREAM PUBLISHING CO., 26 East 21st Street, NEW YORK

however simple, on firearms or on woodcraft that may not be accepted as the last word. . . . This is the creation of an expert" (see chapter six). The introduction also claims, "Small town life in the mountains is made as realistic as life. The characters portrayed are masterpieces. The mystery set up and finally solved doesn't require any encomium."

"Trail of a Bullet," then, combines Kephart's factual knowledge of guns and woodcraft with a more conventional mystery complete with a romance. Whether it succeeds, readers must determine for themselves. It is, however, significant in comparison to his full-length novel, *Smoky Mountain Magic*, also written in the 1920s. "Trail" is over 40,000 words; thus, Kephart had time and space to write more description and create more complex characters. The story is set in Oakvale, clearly a town very like Bryson City (or Kittuwa, the town in *Smoky Mountain Magic*), where Kephart had lived since about 1910. It also uses speech and dialect to distinguish among the characters. There are local, well-educated professionals; there is Parilla Dreem, self-described as "a hillbilly with a town school veneer," and there are outsiders and true mountaineers who live outside the town. In his journal, Kephart devotes separate sections to most of the main characters in the story. While Kephart does include a great amount of detail about the various firearms that appear in the story, there is enough plot to keep the reader interested. Significantly, the great majority of the action occurs in town, not in the surrounding mountains. One chapter, entitled "Backwoods Sleuthing," involves two of the characters venturing into the mountains. There, of course, they have a dangerous encounter with some moonshiners. Fortunately, Dr. Mando, a "town" character, had saved the baby of the mountaineer, and the father had never forgotten it. After implicating a conniving widow and her accomplice, the story ends with a romantic scene of the two young lovers in the story.

Continuing his adventure into fiction writing, according to a letter sent to his son Leonard, Kephart completed "Mr. Pinwell Breaks Jail" on March 31, 1929. While no evidence exists at this time that this manuscript was published or where it was sent, the long story provides another interesting window into Kephart's continued development as a fiction writer. As in his previous fictional works, Kephart develops his plot mostly with dialogue, using dialect to capture the speech of the mountaineers he portrays in his works. Mr. Pinwell is a humorous character, a bookkeeper and a "gaunt, near-sighted, stoop-shouldered man, near forty and unmarried." Pinwell has been recruited, with much trepidation on his part and on the part of his boss, to purchase a stand of timber in the Carolina mountains that the company has optioned. Pinwell, a resident of Baltimore, "has no first-hand knowledge of the southern mountaineers. But he had fared far over land and sea by the medium of books, and he was a movie fan." Equipped with an ancient pistol carried by his grandfather, Pinwell must channel the adventurous spirit of his ancestor and embark on a mission into the wilderness. He encounters various adventures, which ultimately land him in the Kittuwa, North Carolina, jail. Predictably, Pinwell rises to the occasion and manages to stop a jailbreak, saving the day. He is then informed that the man he was accused of killing is, in fact, hale and hearty and ready to do business. There will be a buggy sent the following day to fetch him. Kephart ends the tale of his reluctant yet brave hero: "'Thank God!' exclaimed Pinwell. 'Then I don't have to ride a horse!'"

Kephart's books, journals, and letters to his son Leonard during this time period provide evidence that Kephart approached fiction with the same methodical discipline that he applied to all of his writing. He probably saw that, although he had achieved success as an "expert" in the fields of camping and woodcraft, the articles published in outdoor magazines were not going to ensure solid financial success, and much of his energy and writing in the 1920s went to advocate for the establishment of the Great Smoky Mountains National Park. As noted by George Ellison in his introduction to Kephart's novel *Smoky Mountain Magic*, Kephart also encountered Hollywood in 1925 as he was writing his novel.[30] Writer-director Karl Brown, a former student of D. W. Griffith, arrived in Bryson City to film a silent picture called *Stark Love*. Brown came in search of the author of *Our Southern Highlanders*, and Kephart introduced him to people in the area who could assist him. In his account of the making of the film, Karl Brown notes that he went over "every phase of the film with Kephart, who had been on hand much of the time."[31] Clearly, the making of this movie would have influenced the novel he was writing during the same time period.

Strengths of the novel would be Kephart's meticulous rendering of the Deep Creek area portrayed in the novel along with the town setting of Kittuwa (Bryson City). As Ellison notes, "The descriptions of the natural world encountered along Deep Creek are accurately drawn—and they are sometimes beautifully rendered, particularly during Cabarrus's initial exploration of Nick's Nest."[32] Kephart also, fittingly, took great interest in preparing his main character for his time in the woods. Several pages of Kephart Journal 25 are devoted to "John's Outfit," with lists of clothing, camping gear, weapons, and food, complete with total poundage and cost. Thus, for the novel he uses his deep knowledge of place and woodcraft. The characterization and story line are somewhat conventional, but the plot is interesting. In 1919, Kephart had published a series of articles about the Eastern Band of Cherokees, and he includes an intertwined subplot with a magic Ulunsuti, an egg-shaped orb of crystal, passed down among the Cherokees and believed to contain special powers. This section, like all of his writings on the Cherokees, is very dependent on James Mooney. While some of the portrayals are stereotypical, he does convey respect for the Cherokee characters and their beliefs.

Kephart also includes several well-drawn female characters and a romantic main character, Marian Wentworth. Marian wears breeches, has bobbed hair, and fearlessly rides horseback through the woods gathering plants for the herbarium at her college. She quickly becomes friends with Sylvia Burbank, a more traditional but also independent, strong mountain woman.

Unfortunately, Kephart had no luck finding a publisher for *Smoky Mountain Magic* and died in 1931. The present text was printed in 2009 from a 1929 typescript of nearly 73,000 words. While Kephart clearly will be known more popularly for his nonfiction works, his fiction rewards thoughtful examination for its vivid portrayal of a unique time and place. In turn, Kephart's nonfiction rewards analysis from a literary perspective.

A Magistrate of Skull Creek

Splits in politics sometimes work wonders; and so it came that Peter Ponder—"Old Pete" of the milky eyes and uptilted nose—fell into the chair of magistracy in our "settle*ment*." Pete, by the way, kept store for Wilkins at the forks of Skull Creek, where four counties all but meet. Some days he traded a little coffee and snuff and calico for "sang"[33] or coonskins; other days he whittled and brooded alone amid his scanty furnishments.

Pete's manœuvres for the office had been a joke to everybody but himself; for he was never known to have an opinion worth repeating, except for its utter irrelevance to the matter in hand. So, when the news came by mail-rider that Pete had actually "won out," there was a stir in the neighborhood. Some were disgusted, and sneered; others were amused, and gibed. As for Pete himself, the joy of winning over all his detractors was too much, even for the stoicism of a Carolina mountaineer: he had to retire to the rear room and sip from the bottle of cinnamon extract, in default of anything better.

Next day the old man sent over to Redbird and borrowed from 'Squire Pruitt a book of legal forms. Day after day he spelled out forms, night after night he dreamed of "jedgments;" and so time passed, but no cases came to be tried—not even an affidavit for him to sign and seal. The burden of Pete's actual office became more of a joke than his aspirations had been—until, one day, there came trooping up to the store six armed and swearing men leading a prisoner bound with hickory withes.

"He stole my gilt," declared the spokesman; "my black gilt that I was fattenin' for winter, 'Squire—stole it right outen the pen. Me an' Bill an' Little John found whar he'd butchered it in the woods; we tracked him right to his own home place; and we done found the hams hid up in his loft. He hain't never denied 't, and he cayn't deny 't."

Pete regarded the prisoner sternly over his spectacles, then demanded, "Did you ste[a]l that pig, Jim Beechfield?"

Jim deigned no answer, save by a curl of the lip.

From *Puck,* December 24, 1907

"'Pears like you-un's 'd know better 'n to do the like o' that. I know in reason that you did know better. Pig-stealin', Jim, is jest about the meanest sin—crime—that a man can commit agin his neighbor. Now you-uns go right along with these six men to jail in Mica City, and I don't want nary 'nother word outen you. Men, take this thievin' varmint straight to old baldy Jedge Potter, and tell him *I* said to make Jim Beechfield work out three months in the chain-gang for the betterment of public morals and public roads."

Accusation, trial and sentence had taken barely five minutes, mostly consumed in pauses. Seven men took a round of drinks together, and one went dry-throated, speechless, to his doom.

"There hain't no sorter sense in prodjectin' around about sich as that," proclaimed Pete to the hastily gathered crowd. "Jestice on Skull Creek useter hang fire, mebbe, but now, feller-citizens, hit's as quick and sure as a cap-shootin' gun." Then, for the first time in his life, our new magistrate reveled in public applause.

Alas! next day came another armed and swearing man—came to the store with menace in his eye.

"Are you 'Squire Ponder?" he challenged, in a big bass voice.

"I am."

"Did you send Jim Beechfield to Mica City, yestiddy, fer pig-stealin' ?"

"Yes, *sir*, I did."

"Do you know whar the crime was committed?"

"Right over yan ridge in Tucker's Cove."

"Well, do you know what county that's in?"

"Gray-ham, of course."

"Yes; and do you know what county you're livin' in, here?"

"Swain, you plumb fool!"

"Fool, eh? You p'int-blank fizzle! What right have *you* got to jail a citizen of Macon county for crime committed in Graham? I'm high sheriff of Graham. *I've* got oblige to capture that feller and turn him over to court at Robbinsville. I've rid twenty-three mile over here to git a lawbreaker what you've done gone and packed twenty mile furder on. You're a purty speciment of a magistrate, you are! What brains you've got, if 't was dynamite, 't wouldn't blow your nose!"

And then the sheriff set off charge after charge of verbal high explosives, to the infinite enjoyment of the rabble, who momentarily expected "shootin' words."

Pete turned from angry white to embarrassed red.

"Now, see here, sheriff: jedgmatically that critter was nearer to me than he was to you—right over yan ridge."

"Nearer hell! Next time you pick up a stray yearlin', keep it penned up at home till called for."

Pete stuttered, stood the jeers of the crowd as long as he could, then, with a parting "Go peel your own polecats!" he fled to the back room and [took] solace in a bottle taller than those containing "cinnyment."

For three days our magistrate remained in seclusion. His wife gave out that he was sick. Rumor had it that he was intoxicated. Probably both dames were right.

But on the fourth day Peter had to emerge. There came a couple to be married—urgent duty, he simply must appear. So, with sudden resolution, he straightened himself out. Tucking the book of forms under his arm, he led the pair and their escort over to the store. Squared for the new ordeal, Pete vowed there should be no error of technique now. Age, residence, birthplace, and descent, of both parties, were sworn to and confirmed by witnesses. Similar facts as to their parents and "foreparents" were likewise determined and put on record. It turned out that no party concerned, or even remotely implicated, had ever been out of Swain county in his or her life. Then Ponder adjusted his spectacles with an air of finality and declared:

"Sam Jones and Polly Higgins, I do now pronounce you-uns man and wife—so long as you remain within my jurisdiction!"

The Rock Hunter

A PEN-PICTURE OF LIFE AMONG THE "BLOCKADERS" OF THE GREAT SMOKIES

Aunt Victory bent to her cooking over the open fire. A scarred old bear-dog drowsed beside her with nose snuggled between his paws. The woman molded and patted her cornbread into small loaves, the while crooning to herself in mournful cadence a snatch from some mountain ballad:

"La-a-ay down, boys,
        Le's take a nap;
Thar's goin' to be trouble
        In the Cumberlan' Gap!"

Both doors were closed and barred. The cabin walls had no window, and such light as streamed in through chinks between the logs was too dim to dispel the gloom at the woman's back. Her face glowed red in the glare of the fire. Her beady black eyes had a peculiar glister, as though filmed over with thoughts remote.

A step sounded lightly from without. Like a startled wild thing the woman stood instantly alert, glancing at old Dred for warning or reassurance. The hound merely opened his eyes for a second and wriggled an ear.

A low whistle. Victory answered by thrusting back the stout oaken bar from the door, admitting a young man whose coat glistened with moisture. He stood his Winchester in a corner, muzzle-down, to drain. Shaking himself as though chilled, the man exclaimed:

"Ey, but the fog is thick out thar! I could nigh stick in my dirk and hang up my shot-pouch."

He was a swarthy fellow, raw-boned, but withy, nervous in action, slouching in repose. The broad brim of his hat sagged forward, screening bloodshot and feral eyes.

From *Field and Stream*, December 1909

"Durn me if I prize standin' gyard in the clouds! They rolled down offen the top o' Smoky, a spell ago, and you can't see much fernent the end o' your gun-barrel. This gorge o' Poundin' Creek is a right joyful place to 'still whisky in; but hit shore is a master trap to ketch fog and hold it!"

The woman offered no comment.

"Fixin' to git dinner, Aunt Vic?"

"B'ilin' 'taters and makin' bread. Whar's Wolf?"

"Over yan at the still-house, playin' cyards with Big Matt Corder."

"Good lawsy me! You tell me—"

"Oh, you-uns needn't look so! Matt'll play shet-mouth; you can gamble on him. He gin out, down 't the settle*ment*, that he was goin' coon huntin'. I'm right proud he's come. We're goin' to make a run o' liquor to-night, and hit'll take wood a-plenty for the furnace. Dry wood that won't smoke nor spark is gittin' furder to fotch every day; and that feller Matt can man-power more at a load, on his own wethers, than a mule can pull downhill on ice."

"Mount McVey, have you been drinkin'?"

"Nothin' but still-beer. Why?"

"Don't!"

"Shucks! I got *oblige* to stay sober. Thar's sixteen gallon to be peddled out acrost the mountain, to the lumber camps, to-morrow. Reckon a man can afford to have bumblings in his head at sich a time?"

"Wal, do be keerful! No dare-dev'lin' and showin' off." The dame came close to him with uplifted finger. "I dreamp', los' night, o' muddy water!"

"Ey, godlings!"

Mount paled, fidgeted, and stared at the floor. Something clutched at his throat. He sank heavily into a chair.

For several minutes no word was spoken. Then, in low, serious tones, the young man addressed his mentor:

"Aunt Vic, they claim that your dreams jes' never was knowed to fail. Wal, hyur's wuss tidings, and more of 'em: I dreamp' me a dream my own self; I seed bloody meat that the dogs was chawin'. You reckon that was a warnin', too?"

"Hit denotes blood o' man; and you'll see it afore the moon fulls!"

Victory sank to the floor and threw her apron over her face.

Mount glared at her in silence. Tardily the color came to his brow. Seeing the woman still crouched in the keen misery of fear, he arose with a show of bravado.

"I don't hold much to signs and warnin's," he declared. "We-uns can't afford to git narvish in this business of our'n. Anyhow, 'whut must be, will be,' as the devil said, when the pig's tail bruk in his hand. I'll go now a wood-gittin', and don't you-uns fret no mo'!"

He picked up his rifle and sneaked forth into the fog. Once out of sight, he dropped the lever of his weapon an inch and peered within the breech, to make sure that a cartridge was in the chamber.

"Indictments agin me in four counties, right now," he muttered, "to say nothin' of the govern*ment*. A third term 'd go hard with Mount McVey! That blood business may come true; for I swar to man I won't be tuk alive this time!"

Following a trail for fifty yards back of the house, Mount came upon a spring which emptied into a shallow brook. Here the trail ended. The farther bank rose straight up for twenty feet, and was crowned with briars. Mount stepped directly into the brook. The swift water washed out his footprints as soon as made. He followed downstream toward an every-increasing clamor of brawling waters.

Rounding the point of a bluff, he reached a narrow creek which was chin-deep, and which rushed so impetuously over slippery rocks that a horse, had he been forced to enter, would have been swept to his death. On all sides a tall forest loomed dimly through the milky vapor. Mazes of laurel and rhododendron crowded the banks of the stream. The branches of this tough underbrush sprangled in every direction, twisting and interlocking until it seemed that no large creature save a bear or a wild hog could force a passage. Here and there a sinuous grapevine dangled across the creek from tree to tree.

McVey seized a certain vine and tugged hard upon it. Then a queer thing happened. What had stood on the farther bank like the dead stub of a tree now leaned toward him and steadily descended until it spanned the chasm. Its upper side bore the print of hobnails. On this slender footlog Mount crossed as nimbly as a cat. Parting the undergrowth with experienced hands, he reached out to where the counterpoised log was pivoted over a pit, and then swung the rude drawbridge back into upright position. Thence crawling on all-fours where the ground was bare under the dense shade, he soon arose upon a blind trail. This led some fifty paces to a cliff, and there swerved sharply aside, following the base of the rock.

To right and left of the trail, evergreen shrubbery of rhododendron was matted like steel-wool. Mount advanced halfway to the turn of the path, then thrust the bushes aside, and unmasked a low door of riven boards. He whistled a tremolo like the opening notes of the screech-owl. The door opened inward to his touch, creaking noisily on wooden hinges.

Mount entered a hut of small logs—a pen about twelve by fourteen feet, barely high enough for a tall man to stand upright beneath the rafters. It was roofed with shingles that had been split with a froe. The hut was so thickly enveloped in bushes and laurel, so screened by young hemlocks, that no passing stranger's eye could have detected the structure.

A sour odor pervaded the place. It came from tubs of mash that was passing through the last stages of fermentation. In one corner stood a crude apparatus which, save for its copper work, had evidently been fashioned on the spot with the simplest tools. A small furnace of rough rocks, partly embanked in earth, supported a twenty-gallon still. A pipe connected the cap of the still with a jacketed worm that descended into a condenser and thereby led to a receiving barrel.

Beside the furnace two men were playing the favorite game of the mountaineers, "set-back," or pitch. Both were giants, but of sharply contrasted types. Corder was plump and brawny over an ample frame. He passed for a fat man, and hence an oddity, in this Highland Dixie, where gauntness of man and woman is a racial cast. His humorous eyes, his ruddy face, and his practice of keeping smoothly shaven, were likewise defiant of mountain standards. Opposite Corder sat he who was known from Tuckaleechee to the Little Tennessee, from the Balsams to Hiwassee, as the King Blockader. Wolf Woody was extraordinarily tall, lean as a panther, bushy whiskered, sallow and wrinkled from his indulgences; and, still, at sixty, a man of iron. Although he had followed his perilous calling for forty years, no officer had ever served a warrant on him. It was a proverb that no officer ever would.

Mount dipped a gourd into the "beer," and drank.

"Ugh! Sour enough to make a pig squeal."

"Wal, you needn't spill it about," growled Woody. "What make [*sic*] you shake so? Got the weak trembles, or have you seed a ha'nt?"

"Been on the look-out till the fog chilled me. 'Bout time to git in some wood, ain't it?"

Matt volunteered: "I'll go he'p you, soon as this game is done."

"All right. You'll hear me cuttin', right up thar along the creek, whar there's a main big white ash tree that died on the stump."

Mount exchanged his rifle for an axe, and started up the trail. The fog had settled thicker than ever. He could scarce see a tree ten paces distant.

The still-house thicket covered a narrow flat at the base of Warrior's Ridge. This ridge arose first as a low cliff, then less and less abruptly, under heavy timber and matted laurel, until it rounded to its summit five hundred feet above Pounding Creek. As Mount reached the turn of the trail and wheeled to the right, he heard a great thrashing and crackling in the bushes above him. Startled, and staring upward, he made out the form of a man hanging by one arm to a laurel branch while struggling for foothold on the sheer face of the cliff. The branch threatened to snap. The man struck viciously into the mossy rock with a small pick.

The sight of that pick drove Mount's blood coldly back into his heart, which throbbed in spasm.

"Ey, God, the revenue! Her dream's kem true!"

The whisky peddler dropped his axe, thrust a hand under his shirt, and drew a revolver from his shoulder-holster.

The stranger was clad in khaki. An army knapsack perilously overbalanced him in his predicament. No soldier had been seen in the Carolina mountains since the civil war, but Mount had seen khaki at the recruiting station at Knoxville. Revenue officers do not wear such a garb; but this might be only a disguise. The fog was too thick for him to distinguish facings, if there were any.

That one-hand pick! What could it be but a "revenuer's 'devil,'" expressly made for cutting up stills? As the man struggled, a holster dangled from his belt. Whatever the fellow might be, deputy or soldier, he could have no innocent business here!

Mount had swift vision of years in the penitentiary, or worse—of years spent in cracking rocks for the state authorities, down in the sultry lowlands, where mountain men could not stomach the water nor breathe with ease.

"I'd ruther be killed right hyar, and done with!"

Holding his revolver in both hands, after the mountain practice, the left hand around the right, he aimed at the dim form as carefully as he would have sighted a rifle, and fired.

The stranger screamed. He strove desperately for foothold, and missed it; drove his pick hard against the rock, but struck no crevice; his grasp relaxed. So, with crash of bushes and clatter of small stones, he plunged downward and sprawled lifeless beside the trail.

McVey did not hesitate a second. Springing aside, he wriggled like a blacksnake into the thicket.

When the shot was heard at the still-house, both players sprang to their feet so abruptly that they upset the table. Wolf flashed a formidable forty-four.

"Hit's kem at last! Now, by the 'tarnal, we'll see who's the master man of Pounding Creek!"

The old moonshiner's face was pale, but resolute.

"You can run, if you wanter," he addressed Corder. "I'm goin' to circle above the rock-clift and head 'em off. Whar there's one wasp, there's several. I surmise that there'll be a frolic."

Alas, for the good-natured, truant Matt! Motives more powerful than fear of death grappled and strove within him. He to commit felony, he to disgrace his name, ruin his future, overwhelm wife and kindred—only to stretch hemp[34] or languish in some foul lowland prison! Yet what could he do? Desert those with whom he had touched cups and broken bread? Run away from them in their extremity? A coward might do that, but no man who bore the name of Corder. The law and the obligation of hospitality are as binding in Appalachia to-day as ever they were in the Highlands of old Scotland. Matt Corder was a mountaineer. His code was the mountain code.

"Reckon Mount won't keer if I borry his gun," he answered steadily.

"Don't go up the trail, then," ordered Woody; "you'd be right whar they want ye. Le's surround the varmints!"

So, crawling through a hole in the rear of the hut, and along a "belly trail" that led therefrom, the two men found a cunningly screened exit to the top of the cliff. Cat-like, on all-fours, snapping no twigs, they scouted hither and yon. A blundering track they found, scored by big hobnails slipping. No other sign. They listened, minute after minute. No sound. It was queer. A band of revenue officers would have made a rush.

Finally Wolf ventured to the very brink of the cliff and peered over. Directly under him lay the body of the fallen man. Beyond the trail a bared head peeped from under a clump of bushes. There was no mistaking that frowsy poll.

"You, Mount! Whut you been a-doin'?"

"Got me a revenuer," answered that worthy, standing. "All safe up thar?"

"Yes. Le's see your man."

Wolf scrambled down to the trail, followed by Corder. The victim lay as he had fallen. He was warm, but deadly pale, and bled slightly from a puncture in the left forearm. His face, untanned by exposure, had a refined and gentle cast.

"He ain't dead; he's stunned," asserted Woody.

"Le's finish him, then—dead men don't carry no tales." Mount snatched up the sharp double-bitted axe.

"I be whupped if you do!" cried Corder, squaring himself in the pathway, his eyes flashing fire. "I'll fight ary man fair and squar, but I won't stand here and see murder done!"

"You-uns peacify yourselves, right now!" commanded Woody. "I misdoubt if this is ary revenuer at all. What fer a new-fangled gun is this?"

He opened the curiously flat holster and drew forth—a tiny hatchet with folding guard.

"*Good* la! This trick hain't never been on a grindin'-rock. Looks like a kid's play-purty. He'd look smart cuttin' up mash-tubs with sich as that!"

"Then whut do you name this?" demanded Mount, producing the pick.

"Cur'ous—cur'ous! Who ever seed a 'devil' with a hammerhead? S'arch him!"

The stranger's pockets produced a purse, compass, jackknife, keys, a notebook bearing unintelligible marks, and a folding lens. The lens passed from hand to hand as the men speculated.

"I seed one o' them make-big things las' summer," asserted Matt. "That furriner had it who was up on the mountain studyin' bugism."

The knapsack was overhauled. In its bottom were some small bags, hastily labeled, containing specimens of freshly broken rock. With bitter scorn Wolf turned upon McVey as if he would throttle him.

"Now, you've got us all in one tormentin' mess, fer shore! Have you eyes in your head, or are they bar'l bungs? This feller hain't nothin' but a travelin' rock hunter!"

Mount expostulated, stormed, and squirmed with embarrassment. The fog, the man's queer actions, the pick, the holster, and finally—out it came—the dream!

It was Corder who first fully recovered his wits.

"See here, men; we can't have no ructions atwixt ourselves. This feller may come alive ag'in. The thing is to git him outen here quicker'n 'scat.' He mustn't see the trail, nor that walk-log over the creek."

"Right!" admitted Woody. "This is no time for blackgyardin'. Git me a pair o' saplin's."

Quickly they lopped some poles and withed them into a rude, but practicable, litter. Matt and Woody bore the stricken man down the path, wormed their way out through the laurel, delicately bore their burden across the swaying footlog, and thence straightway to the cabin. Mount followed with his rifle and the stranger's duffel.

Aunt Victory was snatching hot pones of bread from the Dutch oven. She suppressed an exclamation as the downcast group entered her door. Dred growled, bristled, then sniffed in curiosity. The wounded man was laid upon a bed. McVey slipped silently out of doors, and hovered close to a convenient chink in the wall.

Wolf in few words laid bare the situation. "Fotch me the bottle, till I give him a rub," he suggested.

"No," answered his spouse, with unwonted sternness, "I'll see to the lad myse'f."

Loosening the stranger's collar, she slipped up the sleeve of his shirt and examined the wound. It had stopped bleeding.

"The ball's clus under the skin on the fur side. There don't 'pear to be no bones bruk."

She propped up the head of the bed with an extra pillow. Then, having nothing else for her purpose, she wrapped two scorching hot loaves of cornbread in her shawl and applied them to the man's feet. Wringing out a cloth in cold spring water, she packed it around his forehead.

"Now, Wolf, whut's in your mind to do with him when he gits his sense?"

The reply was slow and dubious.

"Things is all in a mixtry. Fust, we'll see who he is, what he knows, and what he aims to do about it. This has kem at a main bad time. The run's got to be made to-night, and the liquor carried out, or I'm plumb ruined. We'll haffter shift everything, then, to another hide-out, afore he gits stirrin' in the mornin'. When he pines to travel, Matt'd better wingle him around in the woods, and see that he makes no way-marks to git back by."

"S-st!"

The stranger stirred. His eyes opened. He stared wildly at the cobwebbed rafters, and then blankly at the group around him. He essayed to rise.

"Lay still a bit, mister," soothed the woman; "you'll pearten up d'reck'ly. Then you can git up and look about."

For some time the man lay quietly, gathering consciousness. No one spoke until he rose on his elbow and addressed them:

"I fell off the rock—didn't I?"

"Yes," answered Victory. "The men folks done found you and fotched you to the house."

"How far is it to the post-office at Lost Cove?"

"I call it eight mile," replied Woody.

"Where did I fall?"

"Hit mought be a mile from here, eh Matt?"

"I don't know, raelly, to measure, if it is a mile."

"What mought your name be, mister?" inquired Woody. "How kem you up this 'way-off branch?"

"My name is Avery. I remember, now—I was lost in the fog. They told me to cross the divide at Thunderhead, and take the Deep Gap trail for Lost Cove. I had no trouble until clouds settled on the mountain. Then I strayed off on the wrong ridge. The government map must be inaccurate, for I followed it by compass. Soon I was on a mere cattle-trail, and finally it faded away. The brush and briars grew so thick that I could make no headway on the crest of the ridge. So I tried to descend to a creek bottom and make my way to some house or river. I came to a low ledge of rock, and was crawling down, when some one shot me. Why did he do it?"

Woody looked hard at the man before him. In the calm gray eyes that confronted him he read neither fear nor guile.

"Matt nor me wasn't thar at the doin's; but I've figgered the thing over, and seems like, how kem it, mought a-been this[-]away. Thar's herders on the mountain comes prodjectin' down here sometimes, lookin' for cattle that's strayed. Then again, once in a while some ballhooter from the lumber camps in Tennessee makes a short-cut through here for the river. Whoever 'twas, likely enough he didn't count on meetin' nobody human in sich a wild and lonesome gorge. The fog was thick as curdled milk, and he p'intedly couldn't see much afore his nose. Somethin' stirred and clawed on the rock-clift. Nobody in reason'd a-thought to find a man grabblin' up thar, with a plain trail right below him. The feller took hit for a varmint. So he shot. You couldn't handily blame him. Then, seein' what he'd done, he was sceert, and run. Hit mought a-been that; and, then, ag'in, hit moughtn't."

"Such mistake might be made, under the circumstances, and could be forgiven. But, for running away, and leaving me there—for that I can 'right handily blame him.'"

"Jes' so."

"Let me see what my arm looks like."

Avery examined his wound, and laughed with relief.

"A romantic reception, truly! Lucky my sleeve had slipped down—there won't be any trash to pick out of the hole."

The stranger thrust his right hand into his trousers pocket. Finding nothing, he looked nonplussed.

"Here's your things, mister," offered Matt. "They was scattered some about." He blushed furiously.

"Count your money," suggested Wolf.

"Oh, that's all right, I'm sure. Hand me my knife, please, with the sharpest blade open."

Avery slit open his own skin—he was surprised to find how thick and tough it was—and the bullet dropped on the bed.

"I'll keep this little missile for a souvenir," he remarked. Aunt Victory bandaged his arm, while Woody proceeded to quiz him.

"You was 'lowin' to go to Lost Cove; got ary friends thar?"

"No; this is my first trip into your mountains. I am a geologist, from Baltimore. I came down here to study the formation of the Smokies. Can you recommend a boarding place?"

"Aimin' to stay some time?"

"A month or two. I'll need a guide to show me over the mountains. Especially," he laughed, "in case of fog."

"If you l'arn who shot you, you'll lay information ag'in him?"

"No. I'll just hunt him up and give him the best beating he ever had in his life. That will be for running away."

"Huh! I don't generally offer advice that ain't asked for; but, you bein' a stranger, I'll just sujjest that you don't go atter ary mountain man with your bare han's. We ain't much for knock-fightin'. Hit looks childish. If you don't shoot the other feller, he'll shoot you."

"So it seems. We'll cross the next river when we come to it. I don't believe I was mistaken for a wild beast—do you?"

"Who do you reckon you was tuk for?"

Avery returned the stern gaze without moving an eyelash.

"At the Maryville Hotel I was advised to give up this trip. They warned me that the mountains were full of moonshiners who would shoot on sight."

"Moon-shiners," purred Woody, stroking his beard. "That's a furrin word. Here in North Car'lina we call 'em blockaders. What mought be your sen-ti-ments about blockadin'?"

"I believe the government has a right to levy an excise tax, and to collect it. Personally, I am neither a tax collector nor a meddler."

"S'pose you suspicioned that a sartain man was 'stillin' ' without a license—would you set the officers on him?"

Big Matt squirmed in his chair at this amazing question. Aunt Victory held her breath. The eavesdropper outdoors cocked his rifle.

Avery's answer was sharp and decisive: "No. At home I suspect certain men of not paying taxes on their personal property; but I do not report them."

"Mister," declared Woody, "that word they gin you at Maryville was fool talk. I've lived in these mountains, man and boy, for sixty year. I've seed a sight of blockadin'—a sight of it! Yit never but wunst did I hear tell of blockaders misusing a stranger who happened in on 'em."

"Tell me about it."

"Thar was a feller had a sour stummick, and he dreamp' him a dream. That dream warned him the revenue was comin'. Nex' day he seed a revenuer in every bush and knot-hole. Every narve in his body was like a holler tooth. So, the fust man he kem ag'in unexpected, he shot, without axin' who or what. He'd a-shot his grandmother if she'd come suddent around a corner."

"Did the victim die?"

"Him? No; he was up, eatin' 'taters afore sundown."

"Are those potatoes that I smell?"

"I reckon *so*. You-uns calls 'em pottaters when they're biled, eh? That's cute. Vict'ry, us men's all sp'ilin' for somethin' to eat. Draw up, mister—draw up! We ain't got much, but, sich as it is, thar's a-plenty—and you're right p'intedly welcome! Matt, set you a cheer!"

The Girl with the Turquoise Eyes

We met so abruptly at a hidden fork of the road that I started in my saddle. Under the tall trees grew a thicket of laurel and leucothoe that no eye could pierce. From a byway behind it emerged a gentleman riding a mettlesome black mare. He was a fine giant of a man, whose face I took for a passport.[35]

We were headed in the same direction, and in a moment were riding side by side. I laughed at my own unwariness.

"Our horses almost touched noses before I saw you. Capital place for an ambuscade," I observed, waving my switch at the jungle on either side.

He returned my smile. "Travelers on this mountainside are few and far between. I dare say there has been a blue moon or two since any stranger ventured so far up Panther Creek."

"Are strangers unwelcome in these mountains?"

"N—no; but the roads discourage them."

"I certainly have seen better roads."

"You will soon see worse. This one turns up yonder ridge, and it is impassable for wagons beyond the bend."

"How do the mountaineers get to market?"

"Few of them ever see a market. The storekeeper at The Forks drags his goods from this point in a little sled hitched to a steer."

"Summer and winter?"

"Summer and winter."

"How strangely isolated these people are! I presume some of them have never been out to the railroad."

"There are old folks on Panther Creek who have never been ten miles from home. They have never seen a well, a sewing machine, a two-story house, a railroad, a church, or a negro. They will call you a 'furriner,' simply because you are from beyond the

---

From *Field and Stream*, March 1918

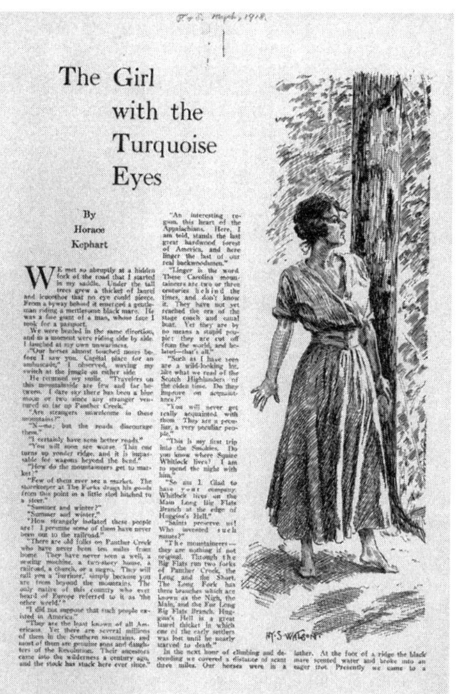

The Girl with the Turquoise Eyes

By Horace Kephart

We met so abruptly at a hidden fork of the road that I started in my saddle. Under the tall trees grew a thicket of laurel and leucothoe that no eye could pierce. From a byway behind it emerged a gentleman riding a mettlesome black mare. He was a fine giant of a man, whose face I took for a passport.

We were headed in the same direction, and in a moment were riding side by side. I laughed at my own unwariness.

"Our horses almost touched noses before I saw you. Capital place for an ambuscade," I observed, waving my switch at the jungle on either side.

He returned my smile. "Travelers on this mountainside are few and far between. I dare say there has been a blue moon or two since any stranger ventured so far up Panther Creek."

"Are strangers unwelcome in these mountains?"

"N—no; but the roads discourage them."

"I certainly have seen better roads."

"You will soon see worse. This one turns up yonder ridge, and it is impassable for wagons beyond the bend."

"How do the mountaineers get to market?"

"Few of them ever see a market. The storekeeper at The Forks drags his goods from this point in a little sled hitched to a steer."

"Summer and winter?"

"Summer and winter."

"How strangely isolated these people are! I presume some of them have never been out to the railroad."

From *Field and Stream*, March 1918.

mountains. The only native of this country who ever heard of Europe referred to it as 'the other world.'"

"I did not suppose that such people existed in America."

"They are the least known of all Americans. Yet there are several millions of them in the Southern mountains, and most of them are genuine sons and daughters of the Revolution. Their ancestors came into the wilderness a century ago, and the stock has stuck here ever since."

"An interesting region, this heart of the Appalachians. Here, I am told, stands the last great hardwood forest of America, and here linger the last of our real backwoodsmen."

"Linger is the word. These Carolina mountaineers are two or three centuries behind the times, and don't know it. They have not yet reached the era of the stage coach and canal boat. Yet they are by no means a stupid people; they are cut off from the world, and belated—that's all."

"Such as I have seen are a wild-looking lot, like what we read of the Scotch Highlanders of the olden time. Do they improve on acquaintance?"

"You will never get really acquainted with them. They are a peculiar, a very peculiar people."

"This is my first trip into the Smokies. Do you know where Squire Whitlock lives? I am to spend the night with him."

"So am I. Glad to have your company. Whitlock lives on the Main Long Big Flats Branch at the edge of Huggins's Hell."

"Saints preserve us! Who invented such names?"

"The mountaineers—they are nothing if not original. Through the Big Flats run two forks of Panther Creek, the Long and the Short. The Long Fork has three branches which are known as the Nigh, the Main, and the Fur Long Big Flats Branch. Huggins's Hell is a great laurel thicket in which one of the early settlers was lost until he nearly starved to death."

In the next hour of climbing and descending we covered a distance of scant three miles. Our horses were in a lather. At the foot of a ridge the black mare scented water and broke into an eager trot. Presently we came to a brook that poured across the road from a dark and heavily wooded gulch.

The mare plunged her muzzle deep into the sparkling stream. Then she withdrew it quickly, as if astonished, whisked her nose contemptuously over the surface, and refused to drink. My own nag gulped greedily at first, but soon ceased, and hung a stupidly dejected head.

"Hello!" I exclaimed. "Is this sulphur, or—what?"

A queer look came into my companion's face. He checked a rising exclamation, and peered intently into the thicket on the upstream side. I was puzzled, first by the incident, then by his demeanor; but I held my peace.

"There is better water beyond," he simply announced.

We rode a few hundred yards to another brook. Here the animals drank until we had to check them.

My chance acquaintance seemed to be debating inwardly some matter of grave concern. Finally he turned to me with a nonchalance that I felt was assumed.

"I have business with a man in yonder woods," he announced. "There is no trail that a horse can follow. Will you be kind enough to lead my mare to Whitlock's? You can't miss his house, for it is the first one you will come to on this road. I will cross afoot by a short-cut and rejoin you this evening."

This was sudden and mysterious. Plainly the man must have seen astonishment written on my face. Yet he offered no explanation, and I could not very well refuse. Was he not entrusting a valuable horse to me, a stranger, in a wild land?

"As you say?" I replied. "What name shall I give Squire Whitlock for you?"

"Blake, of Asheville. He knows me, and it will be all right."

As Blake swung from the saddle his coat flew open, revealing for an instant the butt of a service revolver under his left armpit. Without further word he gave me the bridle-rein, slapped his mare on the rump, parted the bushes, and disappeared.

I rode away with my head bent in quandary. "This is no common man," I reflected. "Carries himself like a major-general. Evidently expecting trouble for he is armed. Sheriff, perhaps, going to serve a subpœna on somebody up there in the woods. But what has bad water to do with sheriffs and subpœnas? He knows this country like a book; yet that water surprised him as much as it did his horse. If it had been mineral water he would have said so. Strange!"

The notion that Blake was a sheriff stuck to me like a burr. Suddenly an unpleasant fact burst upon me. "If he is a sheriff, by George, I'm queered with the natives! It puts me in a false position. I am here to negotiate a delicate land deal. The people are suspicious, clannish, and lawless by nature. It is my business to propitiate, not to antagonize them. Yet here I come among them leading an officer's horse. Confound it! I'll be shunned like a bailiff in Donegal."

Thus brooding over one predicament, I incontinently ran into another.

A girl's expletive announced it. My horse stopped as if at command.

A slight, graceful figure confronted me, barring the way. I sat looking into a pair of blue eyes big with alarm. They were turquoise eyes—too light for beauty, I thought, yet rare and memorable of their kind. Quickly they narrowed into what seemed a glint of defiance.

She was a girl of sixteen, hatless and barefoot as Maud Muller[36] dressed in a faded cotton gown that was cut with painful economy of material. Her face was sunbrowned, but flushed red with mingled anger and shyness. High cheekbones betokened a Scotch-Irish ancestry. Straight black hair showed some interfusion, and contrasted sharply with the blue of her eyes. Her hands and feet were small for one who plainly toiled in the field as well as at the hearth. She stood straight as a young Indian, so poised that she could spring lightly from either foot and in any direction. At my lifted hat she stared as though not comprehending the courtesy. No Southern mountaineer ever lifts his hat to a woman.

"I beg pardon! Did I startle you?"

Instead of answering, she let out a scream—nay, it was a succession of musical notes, lifting, falling—a hunter's yodel, clear and piercing as any bugle call among the hills.

What did the girl mean?

We were silent for half a minute. She bore my puzzled stare without wincing. Fire flashed beneath the turquoise, as in an opal. If the creature was rude, she was no less a mountain beauty.

Comeliness among the mountaineers is exceedingly rare. Their men generally are uncouth and fierce of expression; their women, bent, sallow, and either bold-eyed or melancholy; their youths and maidens commonly awkward or even loutish. Yet occasionally there appears among them a freak of reversion to the physical type of some well-born vagabond cavalier who cast his fortune into the wilderness a century or two ago. Nature sometimes revolts from perpetuating common folk, and, from crudest materials, fashions a superman. So a Napoleon springs up in Corsica, a Lincoln in the backwoods of Kentucky, a queenly woman in some secluded hut.

"I am going to Squire Whitlock's. Can you tell me. . . . ?"

Another yodel, even clearer, wilder than the first. Yet never a word did the young woman deign. Was she bewitched? Some passion that I could not fathom was overmastering her. She seemed oblivious of my presence, looking far beyond me to the hazy sky-line, and rapt as though listening for an answer. So I, too, listened, but heard no sound.

"My name," I began again. . . .

The third yodel.

And with that for my pains of politeness, this incomprehensible creature darted from before my horse, dashed away into the underbrush, and vanished with even less ceremony than had my late companion on the highway.

I recalled Blake's words: "They are a peculiar people!"

Then the truth flashed upon me with a vividness that struck me dumb. This girl's cry, reiterated at regular intervals, was a signal, a call to arms, a tocsin to her clan!

What it might signify in regard to myself and the black mare's master I could scarce conjecture. All the wild tales I had heard of this region—tales of feud and assassination from ambush—swarmed upon me like hornets, urging all speed to refuge on the Main Long Big Flats Branch. I proceeded in dignified leisure, for all that; but I am honest enough to own that the chill of impending death did not leave my spine until I dismounted at Squire Whitlock's gate.

To my host I delivered Blake's message as briefly as that worthy had put it. The squire grunted "Huh!" then apparently found some strange new thing at the base of his left thumbnail.

I spoke half humorously of the tongue-tied but silver-throated maiden, describing her by her remarkable eyes, and asked what he supposed she was shouting about.

Whitlock compared thumbs, backward and forward, for full a minute, spat tobacco-juice on an inoffensive toad at three yards range, and finally delivered a helpless "Wal, now I wonder!"

"Who is she?" I inquired.

"Old Pap Meredith's daughter, Marjy. A *re*markable peart gal. Anybody 'd note her, like she was a pieded colt, bekase of them sky-blue eyes and coal-black ha'r."

Promptly at noon our dinner was served by a grim-faced silent housewife, who refused my suggestion that she sit at table and let us help ourselves. I had yet to learn that it is mountain "manners" for women to wait until their lords are filled.

Whitlock ate with voracious haste, and soon dashed away for his pipe. I joined him, later, on the piazza. We took up the land business, which seemed to afford him much satisfaction.

Far up the hill opposite Huggins's Hell a rifle cracked.

The squire stopped in the middle of a sentence to call indoors: "Fotch me my gun, Mare Yellin!"

His wife appeared speedily with an old muzzle-loading rifle of preposterous length, also with a bullet-pouch to the strap of which a horn of powder was attached by a running thong. Whitlock replaced the percussion cap with a fresh one, and stood the rifle within arm's reach.

"Mought see a hawk from hyur, 'most any time," he explained.

Again that absurd chill mounted my backbone. The squire, settling his feet comfortably on the piazza rail, resumed "timber and mineral" with imperturbable calm.

It was two o'clock in the afternoon ("evening" they call it in the South) when Whitlock's feet came down with a thump. Following the aim of his eyes, I sighted three people descending the ridge in front of us. First came a lithe figure that I recognized at once as the girl with the turquoise eyes. Next, a little weather-bitten old man with patriarchal beard. Bringing up the rear, a tall man of military bearing—Blake himself—carrying a yellow-brown globe of metal on his extended arm.

The old man was bent forward, handcuffed. The girl was expostulating in the high key that denotes tears welling or flowing.

Whitlock heaved a sigh of relief. "That shot wa'n't nothing but some feller squirrelin'," he affirmed, as though he had expected worse.

At sight of us the girl came bounding on ahead with the grace of a doe.

"Squire!" she called with a sob, "that thar man's a-goin' to put my ole pappy in jail! Don't you let him do it, squire! He *couldn't* do it if Jim and Jake was home; but they're all off at Camp Seven, on Little River, ballhootin' with the timber gang."

"What's your pa been and gone and done, Marjy?"

"Stillin'. But, oh squire! He done it jes' to pay his taxes. There hain't nary 'nother way to *git* money 'round hyur, and you *know* there hain't!"

"I'm shore right sorry for you, Marjy, and for your mother and the leetle fellers; but I ain't got no more say about this than yan joree-bird."

"Hain't you to do with the law? What's a squire fur?"

"County matters and State law, yes. But these doin's is agin the federal law. Now don't you worry. Mr. Blake hain't no common dep'ty—he's a big man in the Government. He'll treat your pappy squar."

"He won't—he don't! He's got arns on pappy's pore thin wrists right now—can't you see? Make him take 'em off, squire! Hit'll ruin pappy! He's too old to go to jail! He'll plumb sulter[37] down thar in the valley, and die o' the bad water!"

"Not him. He'll git a fair trial, and we-uns'll see what can be done. Mr. Blake, I've knowed old man Meredith all my life. He ain't never done no wrong afore. If you'll take the arns offen him, I'll be responsible that he don't cut and run."

Blake deposited upon the ground a spherical copper vessel of about ten gallons capacity, and planted beside it a stick sheathed with a copper tube which had been straightened from a coil in this manner. From the woodpile he procured an axe, with which he chopped holes in the still and clipped the worm into short pieces. Then he unlocked the handcuffs from Meredith and politely bade the old man take a chair. Turning to me the officer said:

"I owe you an explanation, sir. I am United States Collector for the tenth district of North Carolina. For some time I have had reason to believe that my deputies have not been doing their full duty in this remote region. So I came to investigate for myself. Circumstances have obliged me to take a different hand. You remember where my mare refused to drink. Well, she is dainty and detests the taint of still-slops. There is this peculiarity about the refuse from a whisky-still: cattle like it, hogs love it, but horses scorn the stuff. The moment my thirsty mare whisked her nose over that spring-branch I knew there must be a blockade still not far upstream. I could not well explain matters to you on the spot. So I left you—rather cavalierly, I fear—and this is the result."

Margery resumed her pleading; but Blake cut her short.

"This is no spite work, young woman. I am sorry for you and your people. I am merely doing my sworn duty. As this is your father's first offence, he will get off with a light sentence. . . ."

"I don't want none o' your 'sorry for me!'" cried the girl, blazing into sudden wrath. "You great big overgrown thing! To put arns on my pappy when he's old and might' nigh crippled! I've a mind to take one o' God's biscuits and bust your brains out!" She stooped and snatched up a stone.

"Marjy!" commanded her father, "you drap that rock and git right on home!"

The girl burst into violent sobbing, but soon dried her eyes on her apron and turned to obey. With hands clenched, she sped swiftly away into the forest.

All afternoon we men sat on the piazza, Whitlock and I debating timber and land boundaries, Blake adding a remark now and then, old Meredith preserving a gloomy silence.

About five o'clock we heard the door open from the kitchen and a shrill voice calling for Whitlock.

"Oh, I can't come now, Mare Yellin; I'm busy," replied the squire. "What you want?"

"There's a Indian gal back hyur wants to sell peaches, seems like, but I can't make nothin' of her gibberish. Come see what she sells 'em at: I want some for pies."

"Send her out hyur. Meredith talks Indian; don't you, Pap?"

"Yes," sighed the prisoner. "I useter live over on Luftee."

"Indians in this neighborhood!" I exclaimed.

"About eight hundred of them have a resarve right acrost yon ridge. They're called the Eastern Band of Cherokees. The United States army druv out all the rest, away back some'ers in the thirties, and tuk 'em acrost the Mississippi—what didn't die on the way. These on Luftee is descended from what hid back in the roughs of the Smokies, whar army, nor devil, nor Gineral Winfield Scott hisself, couldn't smoke 'em out. The Government finally gin it up, and let 'em alone."

We all turned to survey a shrinking female form, baggy with ill-fitted gingham and topped off with a red bandanna. Her face was almost as dark as a Seminole's. We seemed fated to meet peculiar eyes this day. The Indian girl's were the blackest eyes I ever saw in a human head—not a dull coal-black, but glistening jet. Their expression—they had no expression at all, but were vacuous, like the eyes of one walking in his sleep. For a moment I judged that the girl was blind; but I was mistaken.

Meredith started perceptibly when he observed her. In a moment they were conversing in a strange tongue, with oddly explosive sounds at which their chests heaved.

"She wants ten cents a dozen," he interpreted.

Mrs. Whitlock, who had followed the Indian to the porch, haggled over the price until Meredith announced that the girl would take five cents if they gave her supper. A bargain was struck.

"What is the gal's name?" inquired Whitlock.

"Annie Kalana, from the Raven Fork. She ain't quite right in her head; but she's harmless, and her folks is pore."

Mrs. Whitlock took the girl back into the kitchen, and we resumed business.

Supper was served in the living room, which opened upon the porch in front and into the kitchen in the rear. Blake and Meredith were seated opposite Whitlock and me, the prisoner being nearest the kitchen door. I will not soon forget that supper!

We had finished the fat pork and beans, the corn pone, the yellow biscuits, and Mrs. Whitlock was standing directly behind Blake in the act of serving some sort of peach cobbler that she called a "pie," when old Meredith kicked his chair backward, leaped through the kitchen door, slammed it shut, and was off!

Whitlock roared "Shoot!"

Blake dashed at the door, found it fastened by a thumb lock on the far side, burst it open with one shove of his powerful shoulder, but was balked by the rear door, which opened inward and had been locked with a key from the outside. Both Meredith and Annie Kalana had escaped.

Blake, raging, was forced to turn and follow Whitlock in the opposite direction. The squire flew across the piazza, around the corner of the house, tripped over a hog-trough that some schemer had placed directly across the path, and went speedily to grass. I arrived over my host in time to see the heads of old Meredith and Annie bobbing above the bushes a hundred yards up the steep ridge behind the house. Blake, bareheaded, flew in hot pursuit. In a moment the fugitives were lost to view in the thick woods.

Twenty minutes later, Blake returned, panting and disgusted.

"Your innocent Indian girl had a horse saddled and bridled on the trail at the top of the ridge. Meredith got it, and went north on the run."

"The gal?" cried Whitlock.

"Vanished down the far side of the ridge. She flies like the wind. She is no Indian at all; she's white."

"White! Are you crazy?"

"No; I'm only a fool. So are you. That girl, I tell you, is white, with her face and hands stained with walnut juice, or something. The bushes tore her dress half off of her, and—she's white."

"She's the one locked the doors—that hussy!" shrilled the squire's wife. "Who can she be? Nobody from this settlement, I'll lay; for I hain't never sot eyes on the likes o' that critter!"

"If she doesn't belong here, how could she have learned, within three hours, that Meredith had been arrested?"

"Wal, if this ain't the beatenest!"

"If 't wasn't for her shiny black eyes, I'd swar she was Marjy Meredith," declared the squire.

"Marjy Fiddlesticks!" retorted his wife. "Hain't I knowed that pieded thing ever since she was a leetle set-along child on the flo'?"

"It was nobody but Marjy," affirmed Blake. "I heard her cry 'Gallop, Pappy—gallop ole Britt for Tennessee!"

"Old Britt is Meredith's own hoss," spoke Whitlock. "He's a reg'lar billygoat for climbin' the roughs. That thoroughbred o' you'rn, Mr. Blake, couldn't ketch him in these hills between now an' Christmas."

"How, in the name o' sense, could Marjy Meredith change the sight of her eyes?" demanded the woman, who now was crying with vexation.

We looked to each other for answer, for a theory, even for a guess; but speculation was paralyzed.

Three years later I was sent by my firm into the Ozark Mountains of western Arkansas, on another timber-buying venture.

Far back from the railroad, in a region almost as wild as the Great Smokies, and tenanted by a similar people, I was asked, one day, to see what I could do for the sick child of a settler. As there was no physician within twenty miles, I took my emergency case and proceeded on the errand of mercy.

In a new cabin, rather neatly kept, I found a distraught mother with—turquoise eyes. She was Margery Meredith plus another name. I succeeded in relieving the baby, and was fairly overwhelmed by the parents' gratitude.

"We-uns is pore," said the mother, "but you're right welcome to ary thing we got."

"I would not and could not take pay for my services," was my answer; "but you can do one thing for me."

"Name it."

"Show me how you change the color of your eyes."

Mistress Margery laughed. "Come out to the gyarden," she bade.

I followed her to a wee plot back of the house, where the chief crop that I could see was jimson weed.

Margery plucked a bit of jimson leaf and handed it to her husband. "Squeeze a drap into my eye," she directed, tilting her head.

He squeezed out a small drop of the jimson juice and let it fall on the side of her eyeball. I took out my watch.

Within fifteen minutes her jet-black pupil had expanded like that of a cat's eye in the dark, leaving a rim of blue iris so thin that no one would notice it unless he looked closely for it.

"How long will that last," I inquired.

"About three days."

"Doesn't it affect your eyesight?"

"Things glimmer a leetle in the sun; that's all," she assured me.

"How in the world did you ever learn this trick?"

"From a gal back in North Car'lina who useter blacken her eyes thisaway whenever she dressed up to go to meetin' or sich. She thought black eyes was purty."

"Did no one tell her that she would ruin her eyes if she kept that up?"

"Hit don't do no hurt—only smarts a bit, an' that's soon gone. Anyhow, she 'lowed black eyes was purty."

Mr. Pinwell Breaks Jail

"O Lord!" sighed McNab. "Here's a mess!"[38]

The junior partner of Dyer & McNab, lumbermen, leaned wearily back in his pivot chair and stared at a telegram. His stenographer looked up expectantly.

McNab chewed the stub of a cigar, rolled it from side to side, thought hard for a minute, and then barked: "Call Pinwell here."

Miss May arose and went into the outer office. The bookkeeper was perched on a high stool, posting a ledger. He was a gaunt, near-sighted, stoop-shouldered man, near forty and unmarried.

At the summons, Mr. Pinwell dropped his pen, untangled his long legs, descended from the stool, stretched himself to take out the kinks, and followed the girl in a dazed way, wondering if the boss was going to raise his salary or fire him.

McNab looked up from his telegram as the two entered.

"Pinwell," he snapped.

"Yes, sir," answered the clerk, with a propitiatory but doubtful smile.

McNab half closed his eyes and silently regarded his employee with the air of one contemplating a fly and wondering what it was made for. He stared so long that Pinwell felt guilty of something, he knew not what.

"Have you ever traveled?" asked McNab.

"Traveled?" repeated Pinwell, taken by surprise. "Why—not very much, sir. I—I went down the Bay, once, as far as Crisfield."

"Crisfield—er—umph—Crisfield! Ever been out of this State?"

"Only to Washington, at Wilson's inauguration."

McNab clucked with a sound of suction in the side of his mouth.

"Are you a horseman, Pinwell?"

"Sir?"

"Ever ride a horse?"

"N-no, sir."

"A sportsman? Ever go bird-hunting—that sort o' thing?"

"No: but I'm very fond of dogs. I have a collie, a most intelligent animal—"

Pinwell was about to expand on his favorite topic; but McNab cut him short.—

"Gun shy?"

"I—I don't know. He's never been shot over."

"Hell, I don't mean the dog—I mean you."

"Me? Gun shy?" Pinwell was shocked. Had the boss taken a drop too much? What was he driving at? "Why—I'm not—not accustomed to firearms, if that's what you mean, sir."

"Ever been in a fight?"

"N-not since I was a schoolboy."

McNab made a gesture of hopelessness. He drummed the desk with his fingers. He coughed and snorted. Then, with sudden and desperate decision, he brought down his big fist and bellowed: "We've got to do it!"

"Fight? Who?" asked the embarrassed clerk.

"Sit down, Pinwell. It's like this.—"

McNab sighed, rubbed the stubble on his chin, and proceeded to outline the situation.—

"Last March we took an option on a tract of timber in the Carolina mountains. That option will expire next Monday, June 16th. Today's Friday, the 13th. Huh! Just the day for bad luck. And right now I got a wire that if we're not on hand, Monday, with the cash, the Hiwassee Company will snap up that land and cut us off from a larger tract that we have in view."

McNab drummed again on the desk, then continued: "Dyer was to have attended to this in person; but now he's down with the flu, threatened with pneumonia. And here I am, up to my ears in office work. Pinwell, there's no way out of it but for you to make that trip."

The bookkeeper swallowed a lump that rose to choke him. He stuttered: "Ah—um—b-but w-what's it to do with riding and f-fighting?"

McNab exploded: "The land belongs to a damned old fool, named Hoke, who'll have nothing to do with banks, but hoards his money at home. He won't touch commercial paper, nor trust anyone on time payments. The only way to trade with him is with currency in hand, right in his own house."

"I understand, sir," nodded Pinwell. "There are such people."

"Well," explained McNab, "Hoke lives away back from the highway, where no car can go. So you've got to ride horseback, over a lonesome mountain road, with ten thousand dollars of real money in your jeans. And you must go alone; for we don't know anybody down there that we'd trust as guard. Now, have you the g-g-grit—have you got the grit to do it?"

McNab's cold gray eyes bored through Pinwell's skin like X-rays searching his interior.

The bookkeeper shrank; he felt himself shrivel. My God, what an assignment! To go alone, with ten thousand dollars of the firm's money, into such a country! It would be risky enough on the streets of Baltimore—but to ride up into those wild mountains, infested, as everybody knew, with bushwhacking bands of desperadoes, and with no police within a hundred miles—

Pinwell, of course, had no first-hand knowledge of the southern mountaineers. But he had fared far over land and sea by the medium of books, and he was a movie fan.

In novels, in magazine stories, but more vividly in pictures on the screen, he had learned about those fierce clansmen of the Cumberlands, the Blue Ridge and the Great Smokies. They were feudists, moonshiners who shot at sight, hard-drinking lumberjacks who fought at the drop of the hat, wild women who "bloused their waists a-purpose to kerry pistols."

And he must ride a horse! Pinwell was more afraid of a horse than he was of an elephant.

"Well?" blared McNab.

Pinwell's eyes roved as if seeking a way of escape. And so, roving, they caught a smile on the plump lips of the stenographer. It was a derisive though pitying smile. Miss May was trying to hide it by averting her face.

In a flash the bookkeeper seemed to read the meaning of that smile.

"Poor Pinwell!" it said. "Nervous, sensitive, timorous Pinwell! Home-loving, church-going, choir-leading Pinwell! Untraveled, innocent, unworldly Pinwell! To see him buckle on a gun and straddle a horse—O dear, O dear!"

The old clerk stiffened in his chair. The blood that had left his face surged back in an angry flush. He raised his hand in awkward imitation of a military salute and looked straight into McNab's eyes.

"What train shall I take, sir?" he asked with terse simplicity.

The boss consulted a time-table. Pinwell felt Miss May's bright eyes regarding him with sudden interest; but he disdained to look her way.

"You will take the Southern," said McNab, "at 8:12 tonight. Change at Asheville for a small town called Kittuwa, in the Smokies. You'll get there for supper tomorrow evening. Then, Sunday morning, hire a horse and ride east to Wildcat Branch. Hoke lives near the mouth of that stream. Stay with him. You'll have Monday to fix up the deed in Kittuwa, the county-seat."

"Very well, sir."

"Go home, now, and pack your grip. I'll have funds and tickets ready for you, here at the office. And, by the way, don't dress up in your Sunday clothes. Go just as you are. The commoner you look, the less notice you'll attract."

Pinwell did not like that last piece of advice. He would be on an important mission and had a right to carry himself accordingly. Still, there was worldly wisdom in McNab's order. The poorer Pinwell dressed, the less he would look like something profitable to rob.

When the bookkeeper arrived at his boarding place he bathed, shaved, and got back into his old street garb. But he stowed his Sunday best in a big suitcase, so he might put on a few airs when it came to the return trip.

Having packed up, Pinwell dove down to the bottom of his trunk and brought forth a japanned metal box to which he tremulously fitted a key.

His eyes grew misty as he lifted the lid. In the box were some old letters and faded photographs; a medal, now tarnished, that he had won at school; a bit of ribbon and a lock of hair.

Gently he moved these aside and took from the bottom of the case an old derringer, a pocket pistol of antique type, very short and light but of large bore. It had lain there undisturbed this many a year.

He stood and gazed at the little weapon for several minutes. On its curved wooden stock were two notches that someone had cut there, long, long ago.

There is said to be a skeleton in every family's closet. The Pinwells—reputable and godly people for the most part—were no exception. There had been a black sheep in the flock: a gambler, a desperado, who died with his boots on, in the Far West, half a century ago. He was the clerk's grandfather. And this derringer, with the sinister tally cut on its handle, was all the keepsake he had left to his descendant.

Pinwell opened the diminutive gun and extracted a cartridge that had been there since the old man died. Its shell was green with verdigris, its bullet gray with incrustation.

The clerk sighed; then he replaced the cartridge, closed the breech and put the pistol in his hip pocket. For the first time in his life he was going armed.

Returning to the office, he found McNab ready and waiting for him. From a cloth envelope the boss drew out ten banknotes of a thousand dollars each. He displayed them to Pinwell and asked: "Have you an inside vest pocket?"

"Yes, sir."

McNab put the bills back in the envelope and with his own hands stowed the packet in the clerk's inmost pocket, securing it there with a safety-pin. He gave Pinwell his tickets and expense money. Then he took from his desk drawer a formidable .45 automatic pistol and offered it to his messenger.

"Never mind," said Pinwell confidently: "I have a gun."

"Oh—all right, then."

Had McNab known that his clerk's "gun" was a single-barrel derringer loaded with a rim-fire cartridge that was fifty years old, he would have had a fit. But, taking for granted that the fellow was adequately armed, he led Pinwell out to supper, entertained him with pointers on travel, and saw him off on the train.

Once aboard the Pullman and among well dressed people, Pinwell felt ill at ease. As soon as the porter had shown him his berth, he retired to the smoking compartment and effaced himself in a corner. There he stayed until everyone else had gone to bed.

Even after he had turned in, he lay awake. Now and again he would raise the window shade and peer out over a level monotony of cotton and tobacco fields that spread stark and bare in the pale moonlight. He was being hurried farther and farther into a region as alien to his former life as the shires of Argyll or Aberdeen.

At last, insensibly, he sank into a stuffy purgatory where he was followed by stealthy shapes that threatened and alarmed him.

When Pinwell came to himself again it was broad day. Some of the berths were already made up and ladies were sitting in them. He got back into his shiny old black suit and stumbled out, ashamed of his disheveled condition. He had to pass through nearly the whole length of the aisle to gain the wash-room.

Breakfast in the dining car restored him to an easier state of mind and body. He returned to his seat in the Pullman and began to enjoy the scenery, which was rapidly changing from piedmont to mountain type.

He felt that they were climbing. The locomotive labored up hard grades and around sharp curves where the wheels sang on the rails. The air was noticeably cooler and it had a tonic quality. Soon the outlook was narrowed by steep wooded ravines where cataracts dashed over great boulders and tossed their spray along banks thickly blooming with laurel and rhododendron.

They came to the crossing of a divide where the passengers looked out over an immensity of wooded peaks and ridges sweeping to the sky-line. It was a sublime but gentle and luring landscape. Every mountain was clad in living green and spangled with brilliant flowers. It was a friendly country that seemed to offer hospitable hands to a stranger and bid him tarry and rest at ease.

Pinwell had an hour and a half in Asheville, between trains. He checked his suitcase through to Kittuwa and went out to stretch his legs.

When the time came for his train, he followed a gateman's direction and went up the track to where an old locomotive panted before a baggage car and two rusty day coaches. Relics, these, turned over from the main division to the country spur.

Pinwell climbed into the rear coach. Not half the seats were taken. The passengers were mostly country folk. They were of stern visage, slow moving, silent, but with an air of dignity and independence. He regarded them curiously. Here were his southern mountaineers, in the flesh; but not like those of the movies.

Then in came one who did look the part. He was a very tall, lank, big-boned man, with cadaverous cheeks and an enormous mustache that he could have tied behind his neck. He was dressed as black as an undertaker. His broad-brimmed felt hat sagged toward his shoulders. He wore high laced boots, with thick soles studded with hobnails, that clumped like a dray horse plodding over concrete. His piercing black eyes were set close to a beak of a nose and were shaded with heavy brows.

Here was one who would command instant attention in a picture show. Nature had framed him for the heavy villain's part.

The tall newcomer scanned everybody in the car, as if taking inventory of damaged goods and marking them down to near zero point. Then his eyes fell upon Pinwell. Without betraying emotion of any kind, he fixed the clerk with a deliberate, unwinking stare.

The object of this impudent scrutiny turned red with resentment and yet he shivered. No one with ten thousand dollars on his person could afford to treat such inspection haughtily. The self-conscious clerk felt that something in his own bearing must have given him away. Nor was he reassured when the tall mountaineer took a seat directly in front of him and, for the time being, turned his back upon Pinwell.

They drew out from the station, crossed a river, and headed westward. This was a slow train, very slow. The schedule gave it three hours to cover seventy miles. Even at that, it lost time. There were long waits at sidings.

Pinwell was uncomfortable. The afternoon sun slanted into the car with a grilling heat that made him wriggle and perspire. Cinders blew in through the open window and he got one in his eye.

He reached for his handkerchief. It stuck in his tight hip pocket and he gave it a jerk. The derringer, which he had forgotten, was entangled in the kerchief. It flew out with the sudden tug, sailed across the aisle, and dropped plump in the lap of a fat woman who occupied a reversed seat facing her husband and a sleeping child.

The woman squawked like a frightened hen. Her man, after a momentary stare of amazement, snatched up the pistol from her lap and turned on Pinwell with murder in his eye.

The clerk was horrified, both at the blunder he had committed and at its possible consequences. He stuttered an apology, whereat the countryman, with never a word of acknowledgment, stuck the derringer out through the open window, fired it in the air, and then tossed it contemptuously back into the aisle.

The flustered owner picked up his empty pistol from the floor and hastily pocketed it, wondering if the conductor would be summoned to arrest him for carrying a concealed weapon on the train.

The hillsman, however, had no thought of such proceeding. He was competent to skin his own skunks. So he sat silently glaring at Pinwell and waiting for him to make the next move.

The clerk's predicament was all the more humiliating from the tears that were streaming down his face. The cinder was still in his eye.

He felt other people's eyes boring into his back; but, strange to say, he heard never a comment nor a snigger. These mountaineers were either a remarkably stolid folk or they disdained to show any emotion that they did feel.

Ahead of him in the car, no one had observed the incident save the fellow with the big mustache. He turned half about, threw one long leg over the arm of the seat, and took in the situation with grave and impartial calm. He neither smiled nor frowned nor uttered a syllable. He just sat at ease and looked the clerk over as if he had discovered some strange but harmless and mildly interesting bug.

Pinwell tried to assume a stony stare in return; but no one can do so with a cinder in his eye. Anyway, it had no more effect on the hirsute pirate than the cocked eye of an inquiring chicken.

The clerk gave it up. He succeeded, at last, in getting rid of the cinder. Then he raised a newspaper and pretended to read. Still he felt the fat woman, her indignant husband, and the villain in front of him, all gazing hard at the figure behind the paper.

It was unendurable. He was relieved to hear the engine whistle for a station. Pinwell arose and left the car, as if this were his stopping place. Slamming the door behind him, he went on into the smoking car.

The smoker was crowded, but he was lucky enough to drop into a seat just vacated by two mountaineers who were getting off. He had no more than congratulated himself, however, when a new passenger arrived at his side. This was a small man, very dirty and unkempt, who bore a gunny-bag that was stuffed with something heavy.

The newcomer glanced about with an uncertain air. Seeing no other place vacant, he gave Pinwell a friendly look and asked "Can I set hyur?"

Pinwell rather ungraciously made room for him. He even squeezed up to the window, so as not to touch the fellow's soiled and ragged coat. Then he sniffed. There was a new and penetrating smell in the air—something reminiscent of stables, kennels or sties. He wondered what was in that big bag. Why had the trainmen permitted so disreputable a piece of luggage to come aboard?

His seat-mate was pleasantly disposed and sought to strike up a conversation. To this the fastidious clerk responded with little more than a "yes" or "no."

Presently the gunny-bag seemed to move, of its own accord. Could Pinwell believe his eyes? Yes: the thing did move. There was something alive and smelly in that abominable carryall. He tried to hunch still farther away from the phenomenon. Then the countryman calmly explained:

"The best way to carry a pig is in a tow sack, with a hole cut for its nose, ensurin' it to breathe."

Pinwell sighed to himself "My God!" He had fled from the rear coach to escape hostile eyes—must he now go on into the baggage car to get away from a damned pig?

But suddenly his thoughts were diverted to what was going on outside. The mountains had fallen into shadow and there was a keen chill in the air. Almost without warning there came a crashing thunderstorm, with violent wind and rain that made the passengers jump to pull down their windows. In a moment all surroundings were blotted out and there was nothing to see but the interior of the gloomy car.

At a flag station, a few miles farther on, the man with the pig got out and disappeared in the tempest. Then other passengers dropped off, at one small station after another, until Pinwell was left alone, save for two ragged hillsmen and the dozing "news butch."

The storm beat on. The streams had swollen into torrents. One of the hill-billies turned to his companion with an anxious look and said something about "slides." The other nodded and muttered "dangersome."

Pinwell, being new to mountain travel, did not comprehend just what they meant; but he felt uneasy on his own account. His position seemed precarious. Those ragged men looked "dangersome" themselves. Here was he, alone and now quite disarmed, at the mercy of two scurvy rogues, if they chose to assault him. They could overpower him in a trice, steal his ten thousand dollars, jump off the poky train, and disappear in the blinding storm without leaving a trace.

What a fool he had been, not to have brought with him some spare cartridges!

A gust of cold wind swept in from the rear. Pinwell started up, thinking the door had blown open. But no—there was a man coming forward from the other coach.

He was a very tall person, raw-boned, stoop-shouldered, but of powerful build. As he turned from closing the door he revealed the sinister features of the brigand with the long mustache!

The huge fellow took a seat diagonally opposite Pinwell, lit a pipe, and then looked around. At once he recognized the gentleman of the derringer. He cocked his head and stared; but never a word did he say to anybody.

The clerk was now thoroughly alarmed. His imagination needed no prompting from the movies to realize that here was a trap. Somehow these mountain desperadoes had got wind of the fact that he was carrying a large sum of money. Perhaps he had betrayed it himself by nervously fingering his breast to make sure that the precious packet was still there.

But it would never do to show timidity. So Pinwell pulled down his travelling cap, half closed his eyes, and yawned as if bored or drowsy.

By and by the rain ceased and the late afternoon sun broke through a cloud. Pinwell was rising to look out over the sodden landscape when there came a terrific crash and the train almost buckled with the jar of a violent stop. Part of the roof of the smoker was crushed in and some rocks fell into the car. The man with the big mustache slumped over into the aisle. A spot of blood showed on his forehead.

Pinwell was bruised and choked with dust. He staggered to his feet and managed to get out into the open air. A dozen other passengers scrambled out of the train and looked about in a dazed way.

A slide from a cliff alongside had ditched the engine and battered the two forward cars. The conductor said it would take all night to clear the track. He sent a flagman back half a mile to a way station where there was a telegraph. The man returned, by and by, with the report that there was a washout near Kittuwa and no relief train could get through until morning.

Among the passengers there was one, a drummer, who reacted promptly to the situation. He told Pinwell that there was a small town three or four miles ahead, where they could get a car to carry them on to Kittuwa. So the two started together up the railway track. They soon got well ahead of the slower moving country folk.

They had gone nearly a mile when they came to a trestle. A muddy torrent was rushing underneath it which made the clerk's head swim. The drummer, offering a hand, remarked that this was Wildcat Branch.

"Oh," exclaimed Pinwell. "Do you happen to know a man named Hoke—Sebe Hoke—who lives up this branch?"

"Yes," answered the drummer: "I've been to his place."

"He's the very man I have business with," said Pinwell.

"Well, it's only a mile up yonder to his house. You could make it before dark."

"Just follow this wagon road?" asked Pinwell, pointing to a rough byway leading up the branch.

"Yes. You can't miss Hoke's place, for it's the only house up there, and the road ends at his farm."

"Would he put me up for the night?"

"Certainly. Everybody in the mountains is hospitable to strangers, even if they're not on business. Of course, you'll have to fare just as Hoke does himself. He's a tight-fisted old widower and has nobody with him but a nephew who's drunk half the time. They do their own cooking. The fleas will eat you up; but I reckon you can stand one night of it."

Pinwell shivered. However, there was one compensation: in a place so rude as all that, his lack of a suitcase and a change would be no embarrassment. And, after all, this railway accident might prove a godsend in disguise; for it saved the actual dread and probable torture of riding a horse next day.

So Pinwell said farewell to the friendly drummer and he turned aside, following the muddy, deep-rutted road that wound up into drear back hills.

It was a lonesome tramp up the narrow, heavily wooded glen. There were abrupt turns, between steep high banks, where he thought anything might be encountered, from a panther to a hold-up man. The sun had set, half an hour ago. The dark arched shadow of the earth was mounting high in the east to meet the western twilight glow.

At last the gorge spread out into a wide cove of bowl-shaped cultivated land. Here, amid a small orchard, was a log house of the "double-barreled" kind: two duplicate cabins separated by an entry like a hallway that was open at both ends, the whole joined by a single swaybacked roof of riven clapboards. There was a stone chimney at each end of the house.

No smoke rose from either of the flues. No housedog challenged the visitor. A dead silence brooded over the place and its surroundings.

Apparently there was no one at home. Pinwell feared that he had got out of one predicament only to fall into another. Would he have to go back down that dismal road, cross the dizzy trestle in the dark, and stumble along the poorly ballasted railway track to the next town?

The custom of the mountain country requires a visitor to call out "hello" before stepping on a man's porch, if there be no one out to receive him. Pinwell did not know that, and so he went forward into the wide-open entry. There was a door on either side. The one on the right was shut, but the other stood ajar.

He rapped on the half-open door, but there was no response. He knocked again, louder. Still no answer. Then, emboldened by his night-bound plight, he pushed the door inward, disclosing the whole room.

A mellow twilight flooded the interior and it revealed a ghastly thing outstretched on the cabin floor.

"My God!" cried Pinwell, shrinking back in horror.

His heart stopped and the blood drained from his countenance. His staring eyes were fixed upon the figure of an old man inanimately sprawled on the bare boards in front of the fireplace. The stricken one had fallen forward on his face. Beside his head was a small pool of blood, so recently shed that it was not yet fully clotted.

"Dead!" whispered Pinwell. "Dead! Alone in the house—dead!"

For a time he stood rooted to the spot, awed by the frightful spectacle of death and the sinister silence of the darkening room.

At last he mustered up courage to step over the threshold, his eyes darting from side to side in apprehension of he scarce knew what. There was no living thing in sight, but the aura of a passing spirit seemed to touch him like a chilling vapor.

Near the fireplace was a small iron safe. Its door stood open with damnatory evidence of crime. Papers were strewn over a desk, apparently tossed aside by someone picking out things negotiable.

"Robbery!" gasped Pinwell. "Murder! O, what shall I do?"

The stark and bloody form that lay tumbled on the floor was doubtless Hoke himself. Poor old Hoke! A miser who mistrusted all mankind and would not even deal with banks. So this was all his sordid saving had come to!

This, too, was all that Pinwell's adventurous mission had come to. What a report to carry back to McNab!

In the dull routine of Pinwell's sheltered life there had been no experience comparable to this. He had read of such things, of course; he had seen robberies and murders acted on the stage; he had followed the quick interplay of crime and justice in imaginary scenes of violence with avid interest and pleasureable thrills. But never had the sickening brutality of the real thing come home to him; never the awfulness of a human being coming to such an end.

He had often fancied himself in a detective's rôle. How cool and cunning and observant he had been! When everyone else was blind with terror or dumb with perplexity, he, Pinwell, went calmly to work on the evidence in the case, piecing together the telltale clues, divining motives, following up leads, with the infallible precision of a master mind.

But here, with the thing itself before his eyes in naked reality, he could do nothing but gulp and stare and feel his wits going all astray. Beyond noting that the room showed no sign of struggle, and that the victim had probably been struck or shot from behind, Pinwell saw nothing but the enormity of the crime and the futility of trying to do anything for a man who was already dead.

All he could think of was to flee from the sickening sight and spread the alarm. The murderer could not have gone far—the blood from the old man's wound was still partly liquid. Ugh!

Night was fast coming on. So he hurried away, leaving everything in the forlorn farmhouse as he had found it. He recalled that there was a hamlet within view of the trestle where he had parted from the drummer.

Pinwell had gone scarce two hundred yards when he heard what sounded like back-firing from an automobile. It came from around a bend of the lane, ahead of him. The noise puzzled him, as it did not seem possible for any car to come up so rough a road.

At the turn of the lane he came abruptly on the cause of the disturbance. Approaching him were two hard looking young men, both of them drunk, and one firing a revolver in the air for jollification. Probably Hoke's dissolute nephew and a boon companion.

They stared at the stranger, then broke out in ribald jokes and laughter. There was a dog with them. It bristled and snarled.

"Go to the house—quick!" cried Pinwell. "Something awful has happened!"

He started to explain, but the drunken fools would not listen to him. One of them fired three shots in quick succession over Pinwell's head. Then the two carousers reeled against each other and laughed boisterously.

"Make the dude dance!" cried one.

A shot struck the ground in front of the clerk's feet and splattered mud over him.

Pinwell did not dance, but he broke past them and fled down the lane. A wild rage boiled within him; but what could he do against two armed ruffians who were too drunk to listen to reason or understand what was meant by "something awful" in the house?

In his hurry to get out of range he slipped on the slick wet clay, fell, tore his trousers and got very muddy. He picked himself up and sped away, as fast as a bruised knee allowed him.

Soon he heard loud cries of men in pursuit and the barking of an excited dog. The revelers had been to the house, they had taken one look, and now they were chasing after Pinwell, intent on vengeance.

He was aghast at the cruel sufficiency of evidence against himself, if they caught him before he reached some rational people who would listen to his explanations.

Running at top speed, he came, ere long, to Wildcat Branch. Here was a path leading to a foot-bridge that he had not noticed on his way to the house. That saved him the dreaded passage over the trestle.

On the outskirts of a hamlet he caught up with a few farmers returning from the scene of the railway wreck. He stumbled in among them, breathless, pale as a ghost, all muddy and tattered from his flight.

The mountaineers stared at him in amazement, then looked from one to another as if asking "Is he crazy? What can be the matter?"

The pursuers, fairly sobered by now, were hard on his heels. They came dashing around a bend of the trail with loud cries of accusation.—

"Grab him! Hold him! He's a robber! He killed Uncle Sebe!"

Two men seized Pinwell by the arms. They had no need to restrain him from breaking away; for he was all spent and they had to support him lest he fall to the ground.

"I didn't do it!" he gasped. "They're drunk. Take me to a magistrate. I can prove what I say."

But the men paid no heed to his protestations. They took for granted that anyone in such a plight would try to lie out of it. And the boys were known—Pinwell was a suspicious stranger.

Some loiterers at a wayside store came out to meet them. There was a buzz of shocked surprise, then a growling undertone.

"Lord, Lord!" exclaimed an old man, wagging his beard. "Sixty-five years I've dwelt in this county, man and boy, and this is the fust murder for money, in my time, savin' old Nimrod Larkin that Red Jerry Kyrkland killed. You mind, Amos," he said to another patriarch, "how they hung Red from the bridge, with a tow-rope, and shot him to bits as he dangled thar."

A constable and a preacher took charge of proceedings and they put Pinwell through a quiz. His hurried explanations were not convincing, in the light of what the young men told.

"Me and Jim," said Hoke's nephew, "met this feller as he was slippin' out o' the house. He looked skeered and guilty as a dog. We-uns passed by and went in the house. Thar lay Uncle Sebe, dead on the floor, with fraysh blood runnin' out o' his head. Thar was his safe, wide open, and his papers scattered about."

"How much money did he keep in the safe?" asked the preacher.

"I dunno. Hunderds—thousands o' dollars. You-uns all know he was rich."

"Did you look to see if it was gone?"

"No—of course it was gone. We didn't tetch ary thing. We jist run hot-foot atter this thievin' varmint, not losin' a minute o' time. He's got the money. Sarch him!"

The constable went through Pinwell's pockets. One of the first things produced was the derringer. The officer opened its breech and took out an empty cartridge shell. He smelt of it and gave a grunt of discovery.

"This gun has been shot today," he announced.

He spread out his fingers, showing the smudge of freshly burned black gunpowder from handling the fired cartridge.

To the preacher he passed the other contents of Pinwell's pockets, one by one. Presently he came upon the cloth envelope pinned fast inside the stranger's vest. He opened it and drew out ten banknotes of a thousand dollars each.

"That settles it!" cried the nephew. "He's the man! That's Uncle Sebe's money he was arnin' and savin' for fifty years."

The crowd surged. It was convinced and thoroughly angry, now. Men whispered to each other and exchanged significant gestures.

The preacher plucked the constable by the sleeve and muttered in his ear: "Get him out of here at once, or they'll lynch him. My car's the nearest. Take it and go, quick!"

"I deputize you as gyard," replied the officer. "Come on!"

Before Pinwell fully realized the hopelessness of his plight, he was handcuffed and hurried away. A menacing mob followed and reviled him. His two guards had all they could do to get him into a car. Then they sped away up the highway, heading for the county-seat.

They arrived at Kittuwa about nine o' clock. They got out in front of a red brick building, shabby and old, that was secluded on a back lot behind the court-house. It was hemmed in by stores and offices that presented their backs to the ugly thing. Only to the rear, where a river ran through the town, was there an outlook from its barred windows and free space for cleansing winds to reach this hidden shame, the jail.

In the presence of the jailer, Pinwell tried once again to explain how innocently he came to be such [*sic*] predicament. But he was curtly told to "keep that for the jury."

He demanded that a lawyer be called, so he might get in communication with his employers and arrange to give bond.

"Bond nothing!" answered the jailer. "You're charged with a felony, a capital crime. The sheriff's out of town and won't be back till morning. I've no call to run around after a lawyer. It's for me to lock you up—that's all. And it's bedtime in this place. Come on upstairs."

He took from his belt a great bunch of old-fashioned keys that looked like relics from the Bastile [*sic*]. Unlocking an iron door, he shoved Pinwell ahead of him and they climbed a dark winding stairway to the upper floor. Here he opened another iron door and quickly relocked it as they entered a big room that took up more than half of the second story.

Originally this room had been the common place of imprisonment for all except women and lunatics. Twice, however, within the past year, desperadoes had escaped from it by digging through the wall. So, to put a stop to jail-breaking, a steel cage had recently been set up inside the main room. This cage was known in prison slang as the "killers' pen."

Six pallid and dirty men had the relative freedom of the big room. They were moonshiners, bootleggers, car thieves, and the like.

The cage had only one occupant, a newcomer, brought in just a few hours ago. He had killed a prohibition agent, in the presence of witnesses, and his doom was considered sealed. He lay on a bunk, with his head averted, apparently asleep.

The jailer unlocked the cage door, thrust Pinwell inside, slammed the door shut with a loud click, and went his way.

Pinwell sat down on the edge of a bunk, with his head between his hands. The shame of his position seared and tortured him. Its injustice choked him with helpless rage. Why wouldn't they call a lawyer for him? Why wouldn't they let him wire or telephone McNab?

Tomorrow would be Sunday: the hardest day in the week to get anything done. But the newspapers never rest—they would get the story. His relatives and friends would be aghast. And McNab, knowing that his clerk had no motive for killing Hoke, would say to himself: "The papers got it all messed up. Pinwell was trying to skip with our money. He made a boggle of it and got caught. He's no murderer; but he's a thief."

The unfortunate clerk groaned and dug his nails into his palms.

But what was this, coming?

Pinwell's sensitive nose detected the approach of a fellow jail-bird before he looked up to see whom it might be. A rasping voice offended his ear.—

"We-uns collect fifty cents initiation in this club."

Pinwell raised his head and saw a greasy face leering at him from outside the cage bars. A grimy paw was extended with significant open palm.

"What do you mean?" asked the new arrival.

"Hit's for the common fund, to buy cigarettes and things."

"Oh," acknowledged Pinwell, seeing light. He reached in his pocket, where the jailer had considerately left him some loose change. "Here's a dollar," he said, passing it out.

The ragamuffin shuffled away and consulted his fellows. Soon he came back to the cage and spoke sympathetically.—

"Feelin' purty bad?"

"Of course," sighed the clerk.

"How'd you like some beer?"

"Beer!" exclaimed Pinwell. "What's the use talking about it in such a place as this?"

"Oh, we've got some. That's what the club dues is mainly for."

"How can you get beer in here?"

"Make it. They's a trusty that has liberty, part time, outside. We give him the money for meal and 'east [*sic*]. We all got stomach trouble, you know," grinned the prisoner, "and eat lots o' 'east." He laughed at the implied joke.

"But where can you make beer here?"

"In the bug-room."

"Bug-room?"

"Yeah, whar the crazy ones is put, when there is any. The room's been empty a long time. We-uns made a key out o' a bit o' wire."

The fellow moved over to a door at the rear of the big room. He fussed with the lock, turned it, went in, and soon reappeared with a can that had been squeezed flat enough to pass between the cage bars. He gave it to Pinwell, saying: "Drink hearty—hit's got the kick."

Pinwell looked dubiously at the stuff. It was like cloudy water and bore no froth. He took a mouthful, but spat it out.

"What trick is this you're playing me?" he demanded.

One of the prisoners laughed.—"You're sure green," he jibed.

The bringer of the cup explained: "This is still-beer—what whisky's made of. We ain't got no still to bile it in, of course; but this beer has the vengeance, all right. Hit'll make hair grow on your chist."

Over on the other bunk, the killer stirred. He rolled, sat up, saw what was going on, and blared out a demand: "Give me some o' that!"

"Drink it all," whispered the cup-bearer.

The clerk did so. The stuff tasted like watered vinegar; but he took a chance. If there was any surcease in this jail-brewed stuff, he felt that he deserved it.

They brought a can of beer for Pinwell's cell-mate. He was a slender, pasty-faced young man, with a shock of red hair that stood up in a belligerent pompadour. He drained the can at a draft and then addressed the room.—

"See here, you fellows: I'm booked for the chair."

He paused, and all eyes were on him with sympathetic interest.

"They think they've got me," he continued; "but they don't know who they're dealing with." His voice rose in contemptuous bravado. "There's no hick jail can hold me!"

The killer's hard eyes searched every man's face in turn.

"I'm going out of here tonight," he declared. "Do you get that?"

The men outside the cage solemnly nodded.

"Any objections?" rasped the speaker.

"No," answered an eager chorus.

"Needn't ask you, I reckon," added the desperado, turning to Pinwell with a grim smile. "Who did you kill?"

"Nobody," answered the clerk.

"Of course," leered the other. "Cook up an alibi and stick to it. Me, I haven't any. But, fellows, the job starts at midnight. All you have to do is tie your blankets together and keep still, till I'm out o' this pen."

One of the prisoners warned him: "That cage is the last word in hardened steel. I done heered the contractor brag that no file or hacksaw in the world could cut it."

"Bunk!" spat the red-head. "Watch me go through it tonight."

The next two hours dragged interminably for the excited prisoners out in the big room. Each had his own problems of route to take and refuge to seek if he succeeded in winning clear of town.

Strange to say, the only cool heads in the place were those of the two occupants of the "killers' pen."

One of them, to be sure, was no novice at this sort of thing. He was contemptuously confident of success. So he lay in his bunk and dozed, resting before going into action.

But Pinwell, too, was no longer worrying. Somehow he was relaxed, now, and quite at ease. A pleasantly soothing sensation was stealing through his body, very welcome and comforting after the nervous strain of the day's adventures.

Of course, he had not the least idea of breaking jail. His case, bad enough as it was, would be utterly ruined by such folly. But neither would he interfere with the others. Nobody could reasonably chide him for not springing an alarm and getting beaten to a pulp for his pains.

His head swam with exhilirant [*sic*] optimism. Everything would be all right on the morrow. He would get a lawyer, prove his identity, establish his innocence, and go free. Meantime he would just take a snooze.

That sour, watery still-beer was deceptive stuff.

The court-house clock was striking midnight when Pinwell was roused by a vigorous shaking. His cell-mate stood over him.

"Get up!" said the killer. "What's your name?"

"Pinwell."

"Mine's Beckel. Now you're going to see what a little forethought is good for."

Beckel unbuckled his belt. It was a cheap, inconspicuous thing—not a solid strap, but made of two strips of split leather sewed together along the edges. He seized a projecting end of thread on the under side and gave it a tug. The belt ripped apart. Within it, as in a long pocket, were several hacksaw blades broken into half-lengths.

Beckel set to work, slowly, daintily, at first, sawing on one of the hard steel rods.

The other prisoners were all agog. When Beckel tired, another man took his place, working from the outside. Presently two of them were at work, one on each of the two bars that had to be cut away. A lookout listened at the stairway door.

Dawn was approaching when the last cut was made. Beckel crawled through the narrow aperture. Pinwell followed; for he had to pretend, up to the last moment, that he was "with the gang."

They made short work of the old rusty bars at the rear window. The knotted blankets were tied to a bunk and were ready to be lowered. Then Beckel suggested: "Let's drink up the rest of that beer before we go."

With one mind the gang hurried to the "bug-room." He who had the key unlocked the door, leaving the key in the lock, as he would have no further use for it. Beckel went in first, the others crowding eagerly behind him, save Pinwell, who took the listener's place at the stairway door.

Beckel had not finished his can of beer when Pinwell's straining ears caught a grating and squeaking of the door to the office below. Then the steps of two persons coming upstairs.

Now hell would break loose!

The jailer would be in upon them before any prisoner could squeeze out through the wrecked window. He would be obliged to shoot; for Beckel, certainly, and probably others, would fight to the death. The room would be a slaughter-pen.

Though Pinwell habitually shrank from violence, yet at heart he was far from being a coward. If he had really been one of the gang, he would have fought with them, barehanded, and let come what may. He did not fear death. He was game to take a chance.

But he was overwhelmed with the thought of something worse than death—the fear of being eternally disgraced. If he were killed now, in a jail riot, before anything could be done to clear him of the abominable charges hanging over him, he would be forever branded as a murderer and a thief.

The jailer was at the top of the stairs. He had but to reach out and unlock the door.

Pinwell sprang like a cat to the door of the little room where the men were lined up for drinking. He seized the handle, jerked the door shut, heard the click of its spring lock, pulled out the key and stuck it in his pocket.

Instantly there was a furious buzz in the "bug-room" like that of a disturbed swarm of bees. Through the heavy door he heard, faintly, the hoarse, muffled curses and threats of the trapped gang.

Pinwell turned to face the expected officer. But the door of the main room did not open. Instead, the jailer and some other person crossed the corridor. The door of the women's compartment opened and shut. The jailer, having locked up some female vagrant, returned downstairs.

The harassed clerk was now confronted with a new problem. Should he unlock the door of the "bug-room" and let the gang out?

If he kept them fast in the trap that he himself had sprung, was he not betraying the confidence of men who, however bad they might be, had trusted him as one of themselves?

That would be treachery, indeed, if he were one of them. But he was not, and he had never pretended to be of their own ilk. It was through no fault of his own that he was confined among common criminals and judged accordingly.

In the welter of conflicting interests, one fact stood out as plain as a pikestaff: if he opened the door now, to that enraged mob, they would listen to no explanation. Pinwell's life would not be worth a brass button. And that settled it.

He went over to the open window in the rear, where the rope of blankets hung ready to be thrown outside. He wiped his wet brow and drank in the pure fresh air that blew up from the river. Out over the eastern mountains rose the first glow of dawn. He stood and watched it spread over the firmament.

The court-house clock struck five. The sun rose over the distant hills. Yet nothing stirred in the town. Sunday morning. Everyone would sleep late.

Pinwell had never been so horribly lonesome in his life. He thought of home.

Not much of a home, to be sure; but it was all he had. A fusty cubicle in a back-street boarding house. The tenants, rather seedy people who slaved at monotonous tasks and whose minds were blanks. Not a soul in the house who cared two straws for him, nor who failed to bore him whenever they did condescend to chat. But it was one of those rare places where the landlady allowed him a kennel in the back yard for his dog. No matter about the people—there was one creature at home that always welcomed and worshipped him. Pinwell's troubled eyes grew misty as he thought of his dog. It was waiting, wondering what had become of him.

And now, by a strange irony of fate, there came to the prisoner's ears a terrible choking sound from the alley alongside the jail. He rose on tiptoe, leaned out between the remaining bars of the window, and saw what was causing the disturbance.

In the rear of a provision store a barrel had been set up for garbage. A little dog had tried to sate its hunger from the waste. One of the staves was broken at the top. The dog had slipped and was caught by the neck in a V-shaped notch. It was not big enough to extricate itself or overturn the barrel. The poor, starved creature was strangling to death.

That was something that Pinwell simply could not stand. Without a thought of consequences, he crawled out through the window, slid down the knotted blankets, and ran and released the dog.

The forlorn little animal gratefully licked his hand and followed him with adoration.

"Come on, kyoodle," said Pinwell. "I'll get you something fit to eat."

Then, with quixotic bravery, Pinwell strode straight to the front of the jail and hammered on the door.

Presently he heard someone growling within and shuffling along the floor. The sleepy jailer appeared, in shirt and trousers, barefoot and with tousled hair. He took one amazed look at the prisoner abroad, then seized him by the collar and ejaculated: "What in thunder are you doing here?"

"Well," explained Pinwell, "I—I suppose that, technically, I've broken jail."

"How the technical hell did you do it?" roared the jailer.

"Why, the other prisoners sawed the bars and—"

"Wha-a-at! Good God A'mighty!"

The jailer jerked Pinwell into the front room, locked the door, sprang to the wall where his pistol belt hung, seized his big bunch of keys, opened the iron door, and ran upstairs, two steps at a jump, swinging a big revolver in his right hand.

In a moment he was back again. Snatching up the telephone, he cried: "Give me Asheville, quick—Hartwell, master of the bloodhounds—quick!"

"Ah—er—wait!" interrupted Pinwell.

"Shut your mouth!" snapped the jailer.

"But you don't need bloodhounds," persisted Pinwell. "The prisoners are all here. I locked them up in the bug-room."

"Bug-room!" cried the distracted jailer. "Are you bugs, yourself?"

"Go and look," said Pinwell curtly. "Here's their wire key."

The jailer flew up the stairs once more. Pinwell heard him open the door of the lunatics' cell; heard an explosion of curses; heard the door slam shut again with a click.

Down, then, came the jailer, looking like a man with sense adrift. He sank into a chair and stared at the prisoner—the only one—who had actually broken jail. The keeper was breathing heavily and sweat rolled from his forehead to his chin.

"For the love o' Mike," gasped he, "how did you do it?"

Pinwell started at the beginning, in Baltimore. It was a long story. Breakfast was ready before he had finished. The jailer led Pinwell as an honored guest into the dining room. He selected for him the choicest cuts and pressed more and more upon him. He whistled for the little dog that stood timorously at the doorway and he gave it a big plateful on the floor.

By and by the sheriff came to the jail. Pinwell had to tell his story over again. When he was through, the sheriff took him by the hand and complimented him; then he said: "Let's go to my office; there's a man over there who wants to see you."

They went to the court-house. The sheriff stepped aside, at his office door, and bade Pinwell enter.

There sat the "pirate" with the long mustache, whom Pinwell had suspected on the train.

"Mr. Harrod, this is Mr. Pinwell," said the sheriff.

"I'm Hoke's brother-in-law," said Mr. Harrod. "He told me about your firm sending a man out to trade with him. As I was in Asheville, on business, I kept a lookout for him, and I figgered you was the one. I sat by, to see you didn't git off at the wrong station, or anything. But I got knocked out, temporarily, when them rocks kem through the car roof. When I got to my feet, you was up and gone."

"Why didn't you introduce yourself, on the train?" asked Pinwell.

"W'y, you're from the city, whar they's lots o' confidence men. You'd a-tuk me for one."

The sheriff was opening his safe. "Here's your money and other things," said he, handing them to Pinwell. "I'm right sorry you were put to all this trouble, by mistake. If I had my way, the county would pay you a reward for preventing all those prisoners from breaking jail. It was a nervy thing to do."

Pinwell, with human weakness, failed to enlighten the sheriff as to why he had done it. There was something of more importance to discuss.—

"Am I free of those absurd charges?" he asked.

"Yes, and with the apologies of the community," answered the sheriff.

"But have you learned who did kill Mr. Hoke?"

The sheriff turned, with an odd smile, to Mr. Harrod, and said: "You tell him."

"Well," began the tall man, "you see, Hoke takes spells, sometimes. He had one last evenin', jist afore you kem to his house. When he got the wire from Mr. McNab that you was comin', he had some preparations to make. So, in the evenin', he opened his safe and was sortin' out papers. He drapped one on the floor, and, as he was stoopin' to pick it up, he was tuk with a head-swimmin'. He pitched forrad and hit his head agin' a corner of the safe. Then he lay thar, in a manner dead, for awhile."

"Good God! Then he isn't dead—he recovered?"

"Yeah: he's up and peart agin."

"And wasn't robbed?"

"Nary a brownie gone. But them fool boys, both of 'em drunk, never stopped to 'zamine nothin'. I'm rael hurt that they all got you in sich a mess. Hoke, he's all cut up about it. But, you see, our people ain't used to robberies. We do fight over grievances. Mountain folks kill each other, now and then, over women, dogs, boundary lines, cyard games, and sich as that; but they ain't thieves."

Mr. Harrod paused, to let this sink in. Then he continued:

"Still and all, we read the papers. Every paper tells about the goin's-on in cities: the hold-ups and burglaries and daylight bank robberies and murders for money. So you cain't handily blame us for suspicionin' city folks, till we git to know 'em personal. So that's how you come to be run in and sont to jail."

Pinwell heaved a vast sigh of relief. Then, remembering his errand, he asked: "Is Mr. Hoke ready to trade that timber land?"

"Yeah. He'd be pleased to have you come now and take dinner with him. You can wind up the business tomorrow. I've a rig, out hyur in the yard, to fotch you."

"A rig?"

"My buggy."

"Thank God!" exclaimed Pinwell. "Then I don't have to ride a horse!"

The Trail of a Bullet

A novel by the greatest living authority in the country on woodcraft and small arms you will agree is an unusual event.

FLYNN's has secured just such a thing for its readers. Horace Kephart is the author. "The Trail of a Bullet" is the story.

It is not a dissertation on any of the subjects in which this remarkable man is an authority. It is a regular mystery-action story of the type you have come to look for in FLYNN's. But coming from the hand of Horace Kephart it is much more than that.

There isn't a remark in the story, however simple, on firearms or on woodcraft that may not be accepted as the last word. Captain Wayne's detective work may be taken without question. There isn't anything, important or trivial, in his work that Mr. Kephart and FLYNN's won't vouch for.

This is the creation of an expert.

The story itself, to those who are not interested in technical details, is a remarkable work. Small town life in the mountains is made as realistic as life. The characters portrayed are masterpieces. The mystery set up and finally solved doesn't require any encomium.

"The Trail of a Bullet" begins in this number of FLYNN's. And this rare opportunity to read the fiction of Horace Kephart makes this a banner issue.

We invite your comments on Captain Wayne's work. Pick holes in it if you think you can. Perhaps you have had experiences of a sort that will enable you to corroborate or enlarge upon this unusual type of detective sleuthing.

But in any case don't miss this novel by the man who has to his credit any number of handbooks on camping, woodcraft, and small arms, each of which says the last word on its respective subject.

[signed] William J. Flynn

From *Flynn's* April 18, 1925

TOP
Flynn's
Issued Weekly
April 18, 1925.

BOTTOM
Flynn's "The Trail of a Bullet"
by Horace Kephart
April 18, 1925.

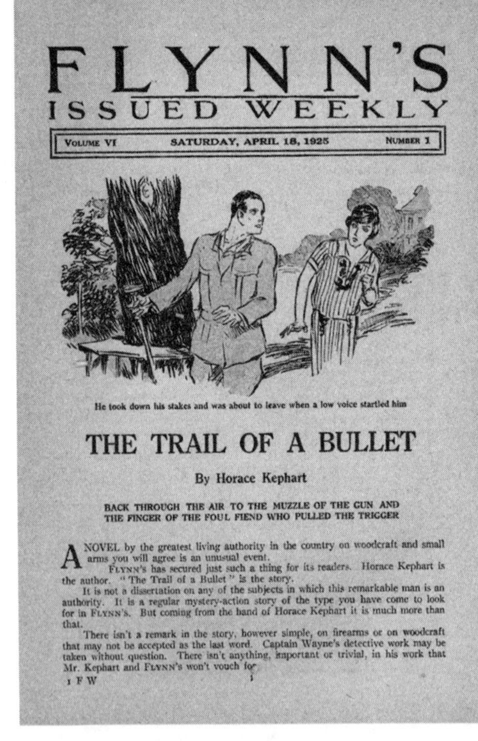

FLYNN'S
ISSUED WEEKLY

VOLUME VI — SATURDAY, APRIL 18, 1925 — NUMBER 1

He took down his stakes and was about to leave when a low voice startled him

THE TRAIL OF A BULLET

By Horace Kephart

BACK THROUGH THE AIR TO THE MUZZLE OF THE GUN AND THE FINGER OF THE FOUL FIEND WHO PULLED THE TRIGGER

A NOVEL by the greatest living authority in the country on woodcraft and small arms you will agree is an unusual event.

FLYNN'S has secured just such a thing for its readers. Horace Kephart is the author. "The Trail of a Bullet" is the story.

It is not a dissertation on any of the subjects in which this remarkable man is an authority. It is a regular mystery-action story of the type you have come to look for in FLYNN'S. But coming from the hand of Horace Kephart it is much more than that.

There isn't a remark in the story, however simple, on firearms or on woodcraft that may not be accepted as the last word. Captain Wayne's detective work may be taken without question. There isn't anything, important or trivial, in his work that Mr. Kephart and FLYNN'S won't vouch for.

1 F W — 1

CHAPTER I

A Girl as Dangerous as a Cocked Gun

It was on a hot afternoon in the last week of June that Mr. Blotter, editor of the local paper, set out from his print-shop to see the heads of committees in charge of the celebration that Oakvale was planning for Independence Day.

He would make it his business to "put pep in 'em," get them to pull together, and see that they did not shirk, overlap, or forget any detail. Oakvale had not worthily observed the national holiday since before the war. It was now to be shown something worth while.

Mr. Blotter was a born boomer. In the southern mountains this term has a double meaning. There, as elsewhere, a boomer is a persistent and noisy promoter of something or other; but in mountain dialect the word also stands for the common red squirrel, who, by the way, is a frisky chatterbox himself.

Now the red squirrel or "boomer" of the South is found only in the cool upper zone of the mountains. He is emblematic of Highland Dixie. So the Carolina highlanders often call themselves "mountain boomers."

When Blotter took over the moribund *Oakvale Weekly Gazette* he at once changed its name to *The Mountain Boomer*. Thus by a deft and persiflant touch he achieved, in three words, a double success with his subscribers. The happy phrase not only announced the paper's mission of boosting the interests of the community but it also flattered the country folk by adopting their own pet nickname.

The editor hurried along Oakvale's main street and crossed the river on the concrete bridge. At the southeast corner of the bridge is an old landmark known as the Ames Building. It is a long wooden structure that stands broadside to the river and rises on piers almost from the water's edge.

Here Mr. Blotter climbed a flight of outside stairs to a narrow balcony that runs back along the river side of the building and gives entrance to several suites of office rooms.

A summer tourist stood leaning against the rail and gazing through a clear space between the big sycamores that shaded the porch. He looked down at the clear, swift river that cuts the little town of Oakvale in two. Its deep current swirled under the arches of the bridge. The farther bank was lined with trees. The foliage there was so dense that he could see little of the town itself, save a glimpse here and there of a broad avenue that ran along the opposite river front.

From it he raised his eyes, looking out over roofs and tree tops, to a background of mountains, all forest clad, that rose in green undulations, higher and higher in the distance, till the farthest ones touched the clouds.

"Beautiful!" he exclaimed to the approaching citizen. "One would not know he was in the midst of a town. I've seen nothing so charming in a month of travel. And your Oakvale got it a free gift from Nature herself!"

"Not quite as it is," said the editor. "That new avenue across the river is the work of man. It is Judge Eldon's creation. He used to say that Oakvale had been built 'wrong end to.'

"There was no street along the river bank. A block back of it the houses fronted to the north, with their back yards to the river. Along that bank, which is now so clean and attractive, there was nothing but outhouses and trash scattered among the trees. It was a bare and filthy dumping ground.

"The judge said that the view from the bridge, upstream or down, was made beautiful by nature but abominable by man."

"So he got the town to clean it up and improve the river front?"

"No; he did it himself. When he retired from the bench, he bought up all the property along the north bank, tore down the ramshackle sheds, laid out that avenue, and put up some neat residences fronting toward the river.

"If you look through this opening between the trees, diagonally across the bridge, to that wide lawn, you will see a corner of the new mansion he built there for himself."

Blotter nodded, waved his hand in parting, and went on into an entry that was inset from the balcony at the head of the stairs. The door at the right bore the sign of Fiske & Field, attorneys at law. It was hospitably open to all comers. The editor entered.

He found no one present but a young person with bobbed hair and rouged cheeks who was clicking a typewriter and chewing gum.

"Ah, Miss Parilla! Alone in your glory?"

"Alone, alone—all, all alone; alone on a wild, wild spree," chanted that flippant miss.

"Your estimable employers?"

"Gone, all gone—gone to referee's court."

"Then do you know, perchance—just perchance, Parilla—whether that handsome bachelor across the entry, Mr. Venrick, is busily engaged?"

Parilla tossed her head. "I'm no bachelor's keeper; but I know, perchance, that he went out, all dolled up, tea-party style, an hour ago."

"Pert but intriguing creature! Is your next neighbor, Doctor Mando, likely to be in a mood for conference on matters pertaining to the public weal?"

"He's fixin' to go a-gunning. You're a likely mark."

"Thanks. You have the gift of prescience, Parilla; he is in his apartment, on murder bent. But I, Blotter the boomer, have the gift of gab; I will disarm him with my honeyed tongue. A false metaphor, perhaps, and a sticky one. But I go."

Blotter swept the young lady a profound bow.

Parilla whirled about on her swivel-chair.

"Isn't he the queerest?"

"Mando? Queer? In what way?"

"Every way, from his name to his neckties. He isn't one of our people. What brung him here?"

"Mountain climate, cool nights, absence of mosquitoes, glorious scenery—"

"Stop it! He's a doctor: he come here to practice. Well, why don't he?"

"Are you crazy? He does practice. Doctor Mando is a noted specialist in diseases of the eye, ear, and nose."

"Then why didn't he set up in Asheville? What brung him away out to this neck o' the woods, where there ain't enough cases of that sort to keep him busy? If he likes this burg so much, then why don't he go into general practice?"

"Doesn't have to. Mando has an independent income."

"Uh-huh. Where does it come from?"

"None of my business. The bank knows."

"Well, he's rich. He's fitted up his rooms with oriental rugs and swell pictures and shay-doovers that cost him thousands. But why did he put 'em in such an old shell as this Ames building?"

"He likes the view from his windows, out over the river and the trees to the mountains. Here he's right in the heart of town, but there's a silent river before him, instead of a noisy street, and there are no high walls or back yards to offend him."

"He's rich, I say. Then why does he do his own cooking, half the time?"

"Mando has dainty tastes, a gourmet's palate, a chef's skill, and he prides himself on his special dishes. No country restaurant or boarding house could satisfy such a man. He gets choice supplies by express from New York and Boston."

"Why don't he marry a prize cook, then?"

"Ah-ha! I knew that was what you were leading up to. Why don't you vamp him?"

"That fish! I wouldn' take him on a Limoges platter with sauce Tartare. What makes his face so haggard, at times, and sickly pale? Do you reckon he dopes?"

"Shame on you! He drinks, now and then."

"Lookee here! Mando is two people in one. He's all smiles and politeness, one day, and plays love melodies on his violin in a way that would make you fall down and worship him for a god. Next morning he looks like he'd been hag-ridden all over hell, and he spits at you like a mad cat."

"Temperament."

"Why does he buy every new-fangled gun that comes out, and fool away hours and hours monkeying with powder and bullets? He seldom goes hunting."

"Mando's a scientific experimenter; probably inventing some improvement in firearms or ammunition."

"Do you know who shoots so many cats from our porch here, and makes no noise doing it? Maybe that's one o' his scientific improvements."

"Everybody hates a night-prowling cat. He uses a Maxim silencer on a twenty-two rifle."

"He hypnotizes folks for fun. Is that science?"

"How do you know he does?"

"Seen it. That gangly fool of a sick John Pringle come to town, one day. He lives over on Pant'er Creek, where I was principally raised. He brung his miseries to me. Said he had 'the chronics.' The only thing chronic about him is darned laziness and lack of sense about what he eats.

"I had to get shet of him. For a joke, I sent him to Mando, thinking he'd get a first-class blowing up. Well, pretty soon, I slipped around there and spied through the portière. Hope I may die if there wasn't John in the chair, eyes bulging, cold-sweating, seeing a spook.

"There was Doc holding one o' them petrified fossils o' his'n right before Sick John's nose, and saying, in a tone would curdle your blood: '*It's quickening! It's alive! See its heart beat through the stone skin!*' John couldn't move, no more than if his legs was glass—I beat it back here, and nigh fainted!"

Blotter roared.

"Served the beggar right!" cried he. "That's the treatment a malingerer needs."

Parilla shrugged her shoulders.

"Well, now tell me this," she continued, looking keenly at the editor through half-closed eyes. "Why is Judge Eldon's new wife so darned intimate with Mando?"

Blotter was thunderstruck.

"Pa-ril-la!"

"Oh, I don't mean all you think; but I've noticed some things my own self. She comes here to see him two—three times a week." The girl said it carelessly; then changed to a meaning note: "Nobody ever seen anything the matter with her eyes, ears, or nose."

Blotter still stood with eyes distended, and mouth open.

Parilla paused long enough for her hint to sink in. Then she took a reflective pose, as if considering without bias how this affair had come about.

"The judge was a widower for a long, long time. His own children died young. He adopted Mary, his brother's daughter, and she come to live with him in the old house. He educated her in a swell college, and they say he made her his sole heir. Nobody dreamed of him marrying again.

"Well, then he got that notion of public improvements, and he built the avenue and the big house. That changed things, and it changed him, too. He needed a wife to manage such a place. When spring opened, this year, there came a party of tourists to the new Ivy Inn.

"There was a spry young widow with 'em, a Mrs. Chester, from Washington, D. C. She was a humdinger. The judge never was much for the big society doin's; but now, somehow, he tuk a notion to limber up a bit. He went to every party and ball and musicale at the Inn. Reckon he first noticed her when she sung in church; and from there to the Inn ain't far.

"I read a book wunst, that had all that in it: old man, humdinger, and all. It said: 'He felt the urge of renewed youth.' What's a urge, Mr. Blotter?"

The distracted editor scarcely heard her prattle. He was pacing the floor with his head bowed, frowning and silent.

Miss Parilla Dreem, quite unabashed, bent her head mockingly, closed one eye, and slowly nodded twice at the editor's back.

"Well," she continued, "the judge felt it—whatever it is—and they were married in three weeks. That was in May. Now it's most July. If I tell you something, will you promise not to breathe it to a living soul?"

Blotter, still inarticulate, nodded an affirmative.

"Day before yesterday, for once in my life, I peeked. Mando was alone in his back office, the consulting room, when she flung herself in on him and ripped out: 'Doc, for God's sake, give me a drink! This restraint is wearing me to the bone.

"'Why, I can't even smoke a cigarette in my own house without having to burn incense, wash my hands, and gargle my throat. If he scents the smoke, or the odor about me, he looks as reproachful and discouraged as a sick calf!'"

"He?" inquired Blotter feebly.

"Yes, silly: the old judge."

Blotter resumed pacing the floor. He crossed his hands and fidgeted with his fingers. Finding such exercise ineffective, he rubbed his chin. He cleared his throat, as if about to speak, but reconsidered, and stroked his nose.

Parilla sighed. "There'll be the Old Scratch to pay, around here, one o' these days," she predicted.

Blotter hesitated; but he had to learn more.

"What happened after she mentioned the cigarettes?"

"Doc laughed. Then I heard him moving toward the portière. I sloped."

"Sloped," repeated the editor. Then with sudden resolution he exclaimed: "Parilla, the Old Scratch will surely be to pay if you don't stay where you belong, and—I hate to say it to a lady, but—keep your mouth shut!"

Miss Dreem defiantly made a very pretty pout with two red and enticing lips. But Blotter did not so much as notice it. He sloped.

The stenographer spun round to her machine, drew a melodramatic sigh, lifted her sparkling blue eyes toward the ceiling, and besought: "O tell me, what does make men such fools over poor little me?"

Then she tossed her arms and broke into ripples of laughter at herself.

"You're nothin' but a hillbilly, sister—a hillbilly with a town school veneer. What'd such a highbrow as Blotter want with the like o' you? You spilled your little secret on him, and he jumped as if it was hot coffee on his pants!

"All righty: I know as well as he does how to keep my mouth shet to other folks. I only wanted to ketch his in-in-terest. I thought a con-confidence would seem friendly."

Her voice broke into little sobs.

But Blotter, retiring through the vestibule, did not hear them. He went muttering to himself: "I wonder if that girl has a line on every man in town. Hell's bells! She's as dangerous as a cocked gun!"

CHAPTER II

The Doctor and the Judge's Wife

The editor passed out along the balcony, determined to erase from his mind all trace of the gossip he had been weak enough to listen to. Nothing in it! Nothing but a streak of jealousy, and the guesswork of an idle minx.

He pushed open the screen door of the doctor's reception room.

If this had been Blotter's first visit to the apartment he would have been startled by the sudden contrast of stepping from a squalid porch into a neat and tastefully furnished chamber that might have been the study of a scholarly millionaire.

As it was, he gave not a glance at the rugs, the rare books, the curios, or the etching on the walls. He called out "O, Doc!" as if expecting an answer from the inner consulting room. There was none.

"In his den, then," Blotter assured himself. He went out to the last entrance from the balcony and rapped on the screen door. A surly voice bade him come in.

This room was severely plain. It was cluttered with apparatus that did not remotely suggest the owner's profession. The left side of the room was fitted as a kitchenette, with oil-stove, table, dresser, and sink. A refrigerator stood in a corner. Through a doorway in the partition could be glimpsed a tidy bedroom in the rear.

The other wall space of the den was filled with shelves of books and cabinets of guns and tools. Many handsome weapons, all bright as new, showed behind the glazed doors of the gun cabinets. The eccentric doctor was evidently a connoisseur of arms.

At a work bench facing one of the windows, and looking out over the river, sat the man himself. He was a very tall and thin person of forty, or thereabouts, with a fine head and scholarly face. Mando at one time might have been strikingly handsome, but his features now were drawn.

He gave the impression of one who had suffered from mental anguish, and had sought to drown it at times in dissipation. His keen eyes had a challenging look, as though he were accustomed to censure, and met it with flat defiance. One who crossed him must take the consequences.

The doctor did not look up as Blotter entered the room. His finely molded hands worked deftly at a singular task.

On his right was a tray of the empty shells of rifle cartridges that had been fired, and which he was now reloading. Mando took one of them, put it in a queer-looking tool, punched out the old fired primer, resized the neck of the shell, and seated a new primer in its pocket.

He held the brass shell under the funnel of a self-measuring powder charge, turned the lever, and so dropped a load of smokeless powder into the shell. He picked up a jacketed bullet from another tray, put it in the neck of the shell with his fingers, and then, with the reloading tool, seated it to the proper depth and crimped the mouth of the shell securely upon it. The cartridge was loaded.

Not until then, did he look up and gruffly say "Hello."

"Still bent on the science of extermination!" exclaimed Blotter mockingly. "And you a man pledged to preserve life!"

"Uh!" grunted the doctor.

"The irony of professions! It was a monk, Schwartz, I believe, who gave Europe firearms, and another monk, Roger Bacon, who made gunpowder famous."

"Huh!"

"Flintlocks wouldn't work well in wet weather, and so a Scotch clergyman, Forsyth, invented the percussion lock, that they might fight on in the rain."

"Humph."

"Dynamite wasn't deadly enough; so the President of the World's Zionist Association produced that superior man-killer T.N.T."

"Pooh!"

"Marat, the most bloodthirsty monster of the French Revolution, was a physician. When the headsmen of Paris couldn't chop fast enough, another doctor of medicine devised the guillotine. The inventor of the Gatling gun was a physician."

"Oh, shut up! I'm working on a machine to kill off all the meddlers and bores in the world. When that's done, I'll turn monk myself and grow sweet herbs in a cloistered garden."

Mando stuck a cigarette in his mouth, and fumbled at his pockets as if hunting a match.

"Say!" exclaimed Blotter, hastily backing toward the door. "If that damned powder blows up, I don't want to be here."

"You won't," remarked Mando coolly. He removed the cigarette, and laughed.

Blotter edged back. "I want to talk about the Fourth. You're chairman of the fireworks committee—"

"Wait a bit. You spoke of the irony of professions. What you meant was hypocrisy. Well, what is more hypocritical than for one who murders the king's English to profess to write it? Last week you reported a gun fight at a lumber camp. You said a man was shot with an 'automatic revolver.'"

"Well, he was."

"He was not. There is no such thing as an automatic revolver."

"What was it, then?"

"An automatic pistol."

"Oh, what's the odds?"

"Simply that you made an ass of yourself. A revolver is a pistol with a revolving cylinder holding the cartridges. An automatic is a self-loading arm with no revolving mechanism at all."

"The public doesn't know the difference."

"The deuce it doesn't! There are not less than ten million men and women in this country who own pistols of one sort or other. Most of them know the difference."

"All right; then I'm an ass; but I want to know what you've done about those fireworks."

"Bought five hundred dollars' worth. The stuff is here, and the shooting will be superintended by a man named Mando, who knows that a rocket is not a pinwheel."

"Good Lord! You were authorized to spend only two hundred."

"I know it. And that would have provided a hick entertainment. *The Mountain Boomer* would have had to make up for the parsimony with hot air. Five hundred dollars' worth of fireworks will make an impression. It will bring such a crowd as you've never seen here.

"The country folks will remember the Big Fourth at Oakvale, and they'll date things from it. Well, I took the extra sum out of my own pocket; so don't get a bellyache, Blotter."

"By Jove! I'll make a spread of that all over the front page! I'll placard it in red, white and blue, over five counties! Trust a crank to head a committee on his own hobby!"

Blotter was going off into rhapsody when there came an interruption. The screen door opened quietly behind him. A fuzzy little white dog came bounding into the doctor's den. Some one called "Tiptoe! Come, Tiptoe! Don't play mischief, Tiptoe!"

The voice was a cooing contralto.

Blotter turned and made an embarrassed bow to Mrs. Judge Eldon. Whatever had been on his mind was shunted into oblivion.

The lady had entered without knocking; indeed almost in a furtive manner. For a second her eyes widened with surprise at encountering another visitor in the doctor's sanctum. But immediately she recovered perfect poise.

"Mr. Blotter." She slightly acknowledged his presence [*sic*]

The editor felt insignificant and *de trop*.

"Tiptoe! Come here, booful."

The dog was a creature of consequence.

Blotter, being a country editor on a very small paper, was perforce his own reporter. Being a reporter, he was not thin-skinned. Politely he stepped aside for the lady to take the stage, while he, as from one of the wings, calmly inventoried her personality.

Cordelia Eldon was one of those voluptuously mature women whom boys in their 'teens worship but fear to address, and whom old men covet and pursue. She was a creature of beautiful curves who moved with the vigor and lithe grace of a leopardess.

There was a suggestion of the jungle about her, despite her cultured accents and sophisticated air. She dressed strictly in the mode, but had not sacrificed to it the glory of her tawny hair. She had Pagan eyes, untroubled by any delicacy of dissimulation.

Toward people who interested her they sparkled with a charm that bore sympathy and understanding. So she beamed now upon Mando; and Blotter said to himself, in cool detachment: "She has the 'glamor-gift.'"

"Oh, doctor," she prettily complained, "why do you hide yourself in this horrid den so patients do not know where to look for you? If dear little Tiptoe hadn't trailed you, doctor, I never could have found you. My tonsils are inflamed. Can you spare me a moment from—Good gracious! What is all this? Explosives? Come, Tiptoe! Why, darling, the man would blow us up!"

"It's safe as sand," assured Mando, smiling at the lady's alarm. "Mr. Blotter will excuse us, I am sure, and I'll take a look at those tonsils. Let us go into the office."

"Oh, I can wait there. Don't let me interrupt your business. Mr. Blotter, really, my case is not urgent."

"I was on the point of leaving," lied Blotter gallantly. Then he told her of the doctor's handsome contribution for the Fourth, and was rewarded by a compliment from the lady on his own public spirit. She sought to make amends for any pique or hauteur he might have observed at the moment of her entrance; so now she granted him a smile of blandishment.

"We are giving a lawn party on the afternoon of the Fourth. You are invited, in particular, Mr. Blotter. I do hope you'll come."

He accepted.

"She wants me to be a 'good fellow,'" said Blotter to himself. "To be sure, I will. This is no affair of mine." So he shook hands and departed.

It was no affair of his. Yet, on his way home, Blotter could not dismiss it. That little cat of a Parilla was right—But how far had the thing gone?

Was the judge's new wife already infatuated with another? Ridiculous! And yet—she was a woman of the world. None knew better than she the thinness of the ice she was venturing on.

A woman of the world, accustomed to the freedom of society in large cities, but now bored beyond endurance by the pettiness of small-town life and the old fogy notions of an elderly county judge.

Did she seek a wild hour, betimes, for relief? With Mando she could smoke to her heart's content, use any freedom of speech or choice of topic that she chose—drink, if she felt like it, and let herself go.

Blotter half sympathized with her; yet, inconsistently, he censured Mando for granting her the opportunity.

Then his thoughts flew to the sinister aspect of the case. This was not Paris, nor London, nor New York. It was Oakvale.

Oakvale: a sequestered village in the mountains, hide-bound by immemorial conventions, censored by a puritanical religious caste, bored by the monotony of its own narrow round of affairs, eager for the thrill of gossip—withal, a place of so few people that cynics said: "Everybody knows every one else's business and takes small shame in attending to it."

It could not be long till Judge Eldon got wind of this affair. He was a gentleman of the old school, proud, chivalrous, sensitive, vehement, and strong-willed. A churchman and a jurist, to be sure; but one who, if the very soul of his honor were defamed, would be stopped by no law of God or man from taking vengeance with his own hand.

And opposed to him was Mando: sardonic, wise, formidable; a man experienced in handling difficult situations; one skillful and tremorless with the trigger as with the scalpel; one who held creeds and conventions in contempt, who suffered no illusions and feared no hell.

If it came to a clash, the result was easily foreseen. Mando would meet the judge's furious assault with cold sarcasm and scientific accuracy of ripost.

Blotter shrank from considering the likelihood of such catastrophe. He tried to reassure himself that there was nothing in Parilla's tale.

But there came in answer, like a thrust of steel, his own instant certitude when Mrs. Eldon had made her hasty explanation: "If Tiptoe hadn't trailed you, doctor, I never could have found you."

That good-for-nothing lapdog showed the way?

The hell he did!

Blotter drew a deep breath and expelled it forcibly through his mouth, like one pining for relief from torrid heat. He walked on up the street in a maze of perplexity.

CHAPTER III

All Set for the Fourth

The Sherwood home is a rambling old white house on the edge of town, set at the base of a wooded ridge that rises abruptly from the river valley like a promontory from the sea. It stands on a terraced lawn, near the end of a street upon which the new highway from Asheville, rounding a steep hill, suddenly debouches. Tourists scarce know they are approaching a town until, spinning around this sharp turn of the road, they see a courthouse directly before them.

The house is shaded from a westering sun by a great maple tree. Beyond the tree are rows of flower-beds along the street front. Back of them an evergreen hedge screens off a vegetable garden that skirts a rocky cliff in the rear.

At the base of the cliff a spring gushes from the freestone and is caught in a cement basin covered by a rustic roof. There is a bench beside the pool and shrubbery all round about. Hugh Venrick found it very pleasant here, on this hot June day, under the shadow of the cliff, by the bubbling pool, embowered in the bloom of rhododendron and the verdure of tall ferns.

He was a man of full habit, though not corpulent. who [*sic*] had passed forty without getting a wrinkle or a gray hair. His skin was as smooth as that of a fat boy. He had a massive head, crowned by a thick growth of soft black hair.

A long mustache was trained in an upward curve, like a drawn bow, to which the cleft of his chin was as an arrow. His nose was straight and full, with sensitive nostrils. His plump under lip expressed satisfaction with life as he found it. A man of artistic temperament, one would say, and a gourmet.

Yet the firm set of his rather heavy jaw bespoke a sturdy masculinity. A competent person, this: a doer as well as a dreamer, and one who would welcome difficult tasks.

Something difficult seemed just now to occupy his thoughts; for his brow was knit and he bent forward drawing lines upon the gravel walk with his cane. But on hearing steps approaching from the rear he straightened to an easy posture and at once assumed an air of pleasant meditation. And so Blotter found him, an immaculate figure in white flannels, handsome, good tempered, sociably inclined. To the tired and worried editor he was a relief.

"Has the colonel got back from Asheville?" Blotter inquired.

"An hour ago," answered Venrick. "What a dear old chap he is! Don Quixote of the Smoky Mountains! What do you suppose he has been up to, now?"

"Something crazy, of course, or charming."

"Both. You know he drew his precious little annuity the other day. So his wife sent him to Asheville to get himself some new clothes. She said he went about, weekdays, so shabby she was ashamed of him. He must go to a tailor who would give him a good turn out. Did he do it?

"No, sir; he ran all up and down Patton Avenue and Haywood Street, buying presents for the family, till that immense luggage bag of his was crammed full. Then, with purse nearly empty, he stepped into a Jew clothing store and got himself a suit of hand-me-downs."

"What did Aunt Margaret say?"

"She said plenty. But the old scamp showed her an extra buttonhole in the waist-coat, a vertical one, that he had the Jew work in, and he said: 'That is for my watch chain; nobody else has such a buttonhole in his vest; and you see for yourself, my dear, how it takes "the shop" out of it! Everybody will think my suit was made to order.'"

Blotter chuckled. "Just like him—and he was perfectly sincere. There never was such a man! Always buoyant, always visionary as a child, always going broke over some one else."

"He thinks the world of Donald, and the lad deserves it. Did the colonel ever have any children of his own?"

"No. Donald is his sister's son, and was left an orphan. They adopted him. The colonel and Aunt Margaret met rather late in life. I never saw a couple more happily married; but I fancy he must have had an earlier romance, woven out of boyhood's moonbeams, and that the girl died, or jilted him, or something.

"Anyway, whenever he sees a pair of young lovers together, he slips away to croon old love songs and have a good long moony spell by himself. It makes such an old bachelor as I feel quite castaway."

"You have lived with the Sherwoods a good while?"

"Twelve years. They have but few boarders, the table and service are good. It is homelike—well, you have been here six weeks, and already you have seen for yourself."

"An oasis in life! I wish I had found it years ago."

A shadow passed, like a fleeting cloud, over Venrick's face.

"You are interested in mines?"

"Yes; I am agent for a northern syndicate. They sent me here into virgin territory to examine prospects. It's pioneer work. I am having to fit up a rude laboratory in my back room at the Ames Building, to test samples brought me by the backwoodsmen. That's somewhat out of my line; but I save time by it."

"There's our new boarder, Captain Wayne."

From beyond a corner of the piazza came strolling a tall young man of fine figure who walked with the easy resilience of an athlete. He paused at the edge of the terrace and gazed at the summer sky and the vista of green hills.

"He is a writer, is he not?" inquired Venrick.

"Yes; short stories, mostly of the outdoor sort."

"I thought from his conversation at breakfast that he was of scientific bent."

"He is, in a way; but an artist in letters, too."

"Versatile, eh? Where is he from?"

"Detroit. Son of a Michigan lumberman and brought up in the big sticks; but he took a classical course in some western college and then a technical one at Cornell. He was a senior in forestry when we entered the war. His class was graduated two months ahead of time, so they could enlist instanter.

"They did it, to a man. Wayne joined the artillery, having been in the battery as a cadet. He was wounded; then transferred to the ordnance department at Washington. After a couple of years of that, he resigned and went to Europe, with our embassy at Rome.

"He is here now to examine timber lands for his father."

A small bell tinkled from the hallway.

"Heavenly sound!" exclaimed Venrick, rising. "Kamama with the supper bell. I intrigued that Indian maid into telling me a charming secret: we are to have a salad of lettuce, sliced tomatoes and cucumbers, with Italian oil and French vinegar, thank God! The colonel brought the condiments to-day.

"There is nothing like a salad dressing made from the cold-pressed oil of Lucca and the wine vinegar of Bordeaux!"

They filed into the dining room and there found an old gentleman with glistening bald head and an enormous mustache who was busily engaged in what seemed a trick of jugglery with table glasses. He was quickly shifting tumblers from beside the plates into a basket and replacing them with others from a tray.

"A surprise for Margaret," he explained in a stage whisper. Then, with an air of grandeur, "thin blown ones cut in the optic pattern, to take the place of those cheap old thick ones."

Colonel Sherwood twirled the ends of his mustache and drew them out straight till they projected stiffly beyond his ears. With a courtly bow he bade the gentlemen be seated. His nephew Donald came trailing in behind.

Kamama, a Cherokee girl from the nearby reservation, waited on the table. Aunt Margaret put a finishing touch on some dish in the kitchen, then came in and took her seat at the foot of the table. The colonel punctiliously asked a blessing. In the midst of it his good wife, glancing out of the corner of downcast eyes, caught sight of the new tumblers and visibly started. The colonel, concluding, beamed upon her.

She bowed to him. "They're beautiful, dear; but what an extravagance!"

The old man lifted his glass of spring water. "Nothing is extravagant for your table, Margaret. Behold the iridescence of the rainbow! The water of Sherwood Spring comes to us from a mountain's heart, not over the hot surface through a vulgar pipe, but filtered through the clean, cool depths of the rock. It is crystal clear, and should be served in crystal."

"Oh, Julian, you should have been born a millionaire."

"Not so," he protested. "I knew one of 'em, once, and I hope Beelzebub will get him! If I had my way, we'd all have just enough to be comfortable—no more.

"I'd be most comfortable, myself, if they'd let me dress in bright colors. Wish I were a Turk, so I could be robed in crimson and gold! The Lord made me a lover of pretty things."

"Then why didn't you get yourself a pretty present, instead of spending all you had on the rest of us?"

"Margaret, I—I did."

"O-o-o! Show it to us!" cried Donald.

The colonel coughed, then straightened himself and said: "Very well, go get it; the leather case on my chiffonier."

Donald ran, and was quickly back.

The old gentleman opened the case and exhibited a pair of ivory-backed hair-brushes of the round, military pattern.

"Good heavens, Julian!" exclaimed his wife. "Why, you haven't a spear of hair above your ears! What do you want with such gewgaws?"

"Gewgaws? Nothing is a gewgaw if it delights the eye. I bought those brushes because they were so confounded pretty I couldn't help it. I passed Fields's window three times, praying to be delivered from temptation; but they got me.

"I paid ten dollars for that set. Look at 'em! There's the British sign-manual on them: the lion and the unicorn!"

"But who can admire your magnificence in this out-of-the-way place?"

"I can. On a Sunday morning, when I've had Jim polish my shoes till you can see your face in 'em, and have got into my dress shirt and broadcloth, I can sit around all day and feel like a gentleman. And my dog Don appreciates it.

"When he sees me brushing what hair I've got with these brushes, he'll wag his tail and his luminous eyes will say: 'Those bristles never came from a common razorback; they grew on a gentleman pig.' It makes a better dog of him.

"I tell you, a fellow should put on style sometimes for his dog's sake. The dog feels then that his master is somebody, and that he's somebody, too, by Jeremy!"

"There, there, Julian! To-morrow is your birthday: you're entitled to your fling."

"So it is, by the way. Let me see: Hippocrates held that multiples of seven and nine were fateful years in a man's life. I am seven times nine. I have reached the grand climacteric."

"You're the nimblest man of your years that I know," declared Blotter.

"Ah, sir, I have the secret of continuous youth. Let me tell you how to live to be a hundred: get you a wife who can cook like my Margaret."

"There never was better advice, colonel; but there is only one Aunt Margaret. I am happy to be one of her boarders."

Mrs. Sherwood smiled. "Tell me," she asked, "is it true that Doctor Mando is such a wonderful cook?"

Blotter turned red. That infernal Mando again!

"One of his eccentricities. But, like all the rest of them, he does it well."

Wayne, the newcomer, now saw a chance to add his mite to the table talk. "I was introduced to Doctor Mando ysterday [*sic*]. He has some of the finest guns I ever saw. He showed me a dozen, or more, American and foreign, that were made after his own specifications.

"There was one in particular that I covet, a Springfield remodeled to a sporter, with Pope barrel, stocked by Hoffmann, and fitted with a Noske telescope sight. It will hit a silver dollar nine times out of ten, at a hundred yards, and would drill my hat at five hundred. Mando showed me the test targets."

"Ah," exclaimed Venrick, "but the colonel here has a gun that I'd wager would beat it. It's such a beauty!"

The colonel choked, blushed, glowered at Donald, and explained: "Mine is a shotgun, Mr. Venrick, made for bird shooting on the wing, and not meant to drill hats, or men, at five hundred yards. But it is, indeed, as you say, a beauty. Old-fashioned, to be sure—a hammer gun—and I still prefer them to the hammerless—but there never was more perfect workmanship in wood and metal.

"Purdey made only one grade of gun, in those days: the highest. He had but one price: one hundred guineas. With duty and all, I paid seven hundred dollars for that gun, and I had to wait a year for it.

"When it was assembled, the barrels and the standing breech fitted so perfectly that one almost needed a magnifying glass to find the joint between them. That was forty years ago. I have used it hard in the field, but it is as good to-day as it ever was. I would not trade it for the finest modern arm in all the world."

"Then still I don't see why it isn't as good as Mando's," persisted Venrick.

The colonel sighed and gave it up. It was not until Wayne explained that a rifle is a weapon of precision, using a single bullet and driving it with great force to a long distance, while a shotgun uses a scattering charge of small shot and is ineffective beyond fifty to eighty yards, that Venrick got the point, and laughed at himself.

"I have never used a gun," said he. "I don't like the idea of killing things."

The doorbell rang. Kamama answered it, and two ladies followed her into the dining room with the informality of old acquaintance.

"Please don't get up," cried Mrs. Eldon breezily, as the gentlemen rose from their seats. "Mary and I just dropped in with an invitation. We'll be gone in a moment."

Wayne was presented to the ladies. On the younger one his eyes lingered till he felt himself almost guilty of staring. There was something so winsome in her expression, so ladylike in her poise. She was a lovely girl, fair-skinned, with large dark eyes and raven hair.

"We want you all on the afternoon of the Fourth. We're giving a lawn party to our choicest friends and their summer guests. Yes, you too, Donald, tousle-head," said the young matron laughingly, as she ran her slender fingers through the boy's hair.

"No, no; we can't stop for tea; the judge is waiting outside in the car, and we must hurry home. We've just been up on the Indian reservation for a cool drive."

Venrick alone declined the invitation. "I cannot get away from work on the Fourth," said he. "It is too bad; but I'm remodeling and setting up some apparatus with which to make a test before some gentleman [*sic*] who are coming Saturday morning. It is an important matter that I cannot escape."

"Oh, I'm so sorry! We don't see much of you, Mr. Venrick. I'd been counting on your musical talent to help us out. Doctor Mando has not accepted, either. He is so busy with rockets and bombs for the evening display—bah! That man is mentally only ten years old when there are guns or fireworks to play with. He'd rather do that than flirt with the prettiest girl in town."

"I hope so," declared the colonel; "for that would be our Mary, who is reserved for Apollo, and only to be worshiped by common clay."

"Blarney, humbug, blague!" cried Mary. "I'd tousle your hair, if you had any, you old dear!"

"These musicians are never dependable," complained Mrs. Eldon. "With Mr. Venrick and the doctor both sending regrets, and Apollo retired to the skies, I don't know what we shall do. Do you sing, or play any instrument, Captain Wayne? Do help us out!"

"I play the jewsharp adorably, Mrs. Eldon, and can sing 'Casey Jones Went Down on the Robert E. Lee.'"

"Oh, that is the judge's favorite air! Tune up your jewsharp, and our musical divertisement will be a success after all. Now don't get temperamental and fail us."

The callers ran away, laughing, and Wayne helped them into their car.

CHAPTER IV

A Mountain Fourth

On the morning of the Fourth of July everybody in Oakvale got up early. Sleep was out of the question. Small boys had been abroad since daybreak, without stopping to wash their faces, and the spiteful crackle of their activities was incessant. Big boys were busy with giant crackers or jarring the earth with cannon-like explosions from loaded anvils.

The hot spell of the past week had been followed by a cool wave. The mists of the morning were rising and fading away, revealing a clear blue sky.

"Who wouldn't be a boy on such a day as this?" exclaimed the colonel. "Old fogies may growl at the noise and the risk of fire; but my heart goes out to the kids. What are a few burned fingers to a fellow who's making things go *chuh-boong*?

"Anyway, it's safer around here than it was when the old fogies were young. They didn't have firecrackers. They did their celebrating with ball cartridges fired at random.

"It's disconcerting for a young gentleman promenading with his girl to have wild bullets go *ping, ping-g-g* overhead. It gets his mind off the proper subject."

The words were hardly out of his mouth before there came from across the river the staccato reports of a six-shooter that some one emptied as fast as he could work his finger.

Venrick laughed. "One of your old fogies renewing his youth," he rallied the colonel.

"Oh, that's just some young chap deviling the police. If they run after him, his chum will let fly from some other direction."

Sure enough: soon there was a similar fusillade from another quarter.

"That will stop when the athletic contests begin," said Blotter. "Boys don't misbehave when there's legitimate fun to see. We have a surprise in reserve. An aviator will be here from Knoxville. He will come flying across the Smoky Mountains. There's hardly a mountaineer west of the Balsams who ever saw an airplane, except the boys who were in the war."

"Airplanes and radios and automobiles have changed our own lives," said the colonel; "but imagine, if you can, what a jolt they give to the log cabin people of the far back places.

"When I came into this county there were old folks here who had never been on a railway train, nor owned a wheeled vehicle, nor used a cook stove or a sewing machine, nor seen a graded road, or a brick house, or a town of two hundred inhabitants. The stage coach and the canal boat were improvements they had never dreamed of.

"They were as isolated and primitive as their ancestors in the days of Daniel Boone."

"I wish there were some of that kind left," said Wayne. "I'd give anything to meet one of the Boone type in flesh and blood."

"You can have your wish," answered the editor. "Go up yonder into the wild mountains, away from wagon roads, and you'll find them to-day.

"But, for God's sake, don't send out stories that will make the world think we're all that way. Our southern highlands have been cursed by yarn spinners who reported little but feuds and moonshining and 'quare' people."

Wayne laughed, and Blotter frowned, and the subject was dropped.

Wayne went down town soon after breakfast. The streets were filling up with respectable farmer folk whose cars were parked around the courthouse square and along the side streets. There were many well dressed townsmen and tourists in the throng. None of them specially interested him.

He found suggestions, though, among the dare-devil young horsemen from the back country who had sprigs of balsam from the high mountains stuck in the bands of their rakish black hats; in the hard-faced families of "branch water people" who came in shackly wagons, or afoot; in the Cherokee squaws who wore bright bandannas around their heads and carried papooses in shawls slung on their backs. These were picturesque.

He came to the railway station just as the morning train arrived. From an extra coach there piled out a band of lumberjacks from the mountain camps. They were burly fellows, gnarled and tough as oak knots, and they swaggered with a sense of power. They sported new shirts of bright blue denim, or flaring Mackinaws.

Their "stagged" trousers barely met the tops of heavy Cutter boots that had high heels and enormously thick soles studded with steel spikes that left marks on cement sidewalks. They swung masterfully through the crowd, which everywhere gave way before their massed weight and brawn.

The town marshal quietly signaled to several deputies, who, with a pair of prohibition agents, fell in behind the good-humored but devil-may-care woodsmen as they trooped uptown. Wayne sensed possibilities in that bunch. Whatever they did, it would not be a bore. Their blood ran too fast for that.

A bugle blew. The local battery of National Guardsmen advanced at the head of a procession of floats and decorated cars, followed by a line of athletes stripped for the games, among whom were a number of Indian youths.

Wayne followed the crowd till he came to the far corner of the bridge. Here he climbed some stairs to a balcony that would give him a vantage point. Hearing some one sawing wood and driving nails, he looked back through an open window and saw Venrick, in shirt sleeves, working in the laboratory behind his office room. Wayne called to him "That's a pretty way to enjoy 'the day we celebrate!'"

"Hard luck!" panted Venrick. "But I must fit up some apparatus for a demonstration to my visitors in the morning. Come in."

Wayne entered and was shown some samples of copper ore.

"That stuff carries enough gold to pay the cost of mining the copper," said Venrick.

Another blare came from a bugle.

"The foot races are starting," said Wayne. "Come along out and see them."

"Sorry, but I can't spare a minute. This is one of the things that must be finished on time."

Wayne returned to the balcony. Through a gap between the sycamores he saw the same vista of river and avenue and mountains that had charmed the tourists whom Blotter had met here a few days before. Diagonally across the bridge he saw a corner of the Eldon mansion, and the lawn where the party was to be held.

He was enjoying the view when a pretty girl stepped out from the front office into the vestibule and spoke to him.

"Pardon me; you are a guest at the Sherwoods', are you not?" asked Parilla in her best manner.

"Yes; my name is Wayne."

"Oh, Captain Wayne, I have heard of you through Mr. Blotter. I am Miss Dreem. You can't see the races from here. There's a good view of the whole course from our front balcony. Won't you let me give you a chair there?"

"That is very kind of you." And Wayne went with her.

They sat comfortably, side by side, and saw the hundred yard dash, the obstacle race, the relay race, the tug of war, the jumping and vaulting, the high diving from the bridge. Wayne paid little attention to the sports, having found Parilla an animated and interesting talker.

Her comments on the passing throng were shrewd and original. She did her best to avoid the bad grammar that was natural to her, and partly succeeded; but now and then she would unconsciously let drop a quaint idiom of the hill country, or some ancient English survival, that thrilled Wayne as though he were meeting one of Chaucer's or Shakespeare's characters in the flesh.

The girl was quick to feel that she interested the handsome young outlander, and she responded with deft wit and pretty gestures. She was all life and spirits. Nor was her success in any wise chilled by the inspection she saw they were getting, through opera glasses, from an upstairs window across the way.

So they passed the time very pleasantly until noon, when Wayne bade her adieu and went to the Sherwood home for dinner.

When he came back down town the crowd had thinned out. Most of the country folk had gone to the high school hill to eat their lunches in the grove and to hear speeches or listen to the music of singing societies. There would be a lull in the athletic sports until four o'clock, when games were to be played at the baseball park.

Some uneasy scamps were firing pistols again from alleys and back windows, knowing that the police were concentrated about the railroad restaurants, where the lumberjacks and town roughnecks were slyly drinking and openly milling about.

Wayne met Blotter at the bridge, and together they strolled over to the avenue and turned to the left, along a terrace faced with rubblework of smooth stones set in cement. They went up a short flight of stone steps and were on the Eldon Lawn.

The big house was glaringly new. The shrubbery and vines were so lately planted that they looked artificial. But there were several large old trees left on the place that helped to subdue the rawness that otherwise would have been offensive. Under the shade of the trees were lawn chairs and settees and tables, and here the company was gathering.

Mrs. Eldon came quickly to greet them. She was all smiles, but her eyes roved restlessly as she talked with them and her manner betrayed anxiety. Wayne thought she was nervously eager to entertain.

Blotter, knowing her better, saw that she was under some unusual strain. He wondered if she and the judge had been having a tiff. In the back of his mind lingered the sinister shadow of Mando.

She presented Wayne to some of the guests, and then led him to where her husband was seated under one of the big trees. She introduced him as "the prominent young author of whom you have heard so much"—a form of address that he particularly detested.

Judge Eldon looked tired, as if he had been overexerting himself or had been losing sleep. He shook hands with Wayne, excused himself from rising, and invited the young man to share his settee.

He was a portly, well preserved man of sixty-two or three, with a resolute bearing and self-sufficient air. His features were homely, particularly the long, flat nose, the thick underlip that was always moist, the large ears and pendulous jowl.

His small black eyes, sunken under beetling brows, seemed to search the young man as though doubtful of him and bound to take nothing for granted. He ignored the conversational opening that his wife had given him, and only made some trifling remarks about the day's festivities.

Wayne, seeking to thaw the old man out, spoke appreciatively of the beauty of Oakvale, nestled among its hills and trees, and especially of the new avenue along the riverside as a unique gift of a public man to his home town.

"I get credit for it," answered the judge, "but I am not the author of it at all. It was Mary's idea—my niece's. She pleaded and cajoled it out of me. Mary has great faith in the civilizing influence of beautiful surroundings. Well, I gave in at last, and—here is the avenue. The town won't pave it, or even sprinkle it to lay the dust!"

Wayne was shocked by the abruptness of that cynical, bitter comment. It voiced a disappointment gnawing at the old man's pride. There was an awkward pause.

Then Wayne said cheerily: "All towns have bad administrations at times. Surely your progressive citizens will not tolerate such neglect: they will put new men in office."

The judge changed the subject. But whatever they talked about, he did not warm up to it. Eldon seemed a man weary with disillusion; as one who had sampled all things and found nothing to his taste.

Presently, to Wayne's relief, another party arrived and claimed the judge's attention. Then Mary Eldon came, with a winning smile, to ask Wayne's advice about a boat landing she was planning for the grounds.

They strolled down to the river bank. A crowd was hurrying across the bridge, from the courthouse square, all looking up at the sky. From high in the air came the drone of a fast running motor. An airplane was circling above them as though seeking a landing place.

"What a novelty that must be for most of the mountain folk," said Wayne. "I should think they would cheer."

Mary laughed. "That is not their way. They are too proud to show any surprise or enthusiasm. Really, they marvel at the sight, but they'd die before they'd let us know it. We asked three old women one evening to come in and listen to the radio.

"They sat still as graven images, without a flicker of interest on their faces, for a long time. Finally one of them said sarcastically to the others: 'They're gittin' mighty *smart* nowadays!' That was all the comment they made."

Wayne was amused. "I dare say, when they got back home they talked many a day about the miracle they had witnessed."

"To be sure," said Mary. "Those poor old women realized how far they were behind the times. But there is another side: they knew, as most of us do not, that in some ways we town folks are more ignorant than they.

"Many a young couple in the mountains have started married life with nothing in the world but an ax, a rifle, a frying pan and an iron pot, a few home-made quilts, a cow, a pig, two or three chickens, a few bushels of corn, and some garden seeds. They took this pitiful outfit into the wild forest, made a little clearing there, and built their house and furniture from the trees they cut down.

"They planted their little plot. They fought the savage wilderness almost with bare hands. And they lived; they thrived. In the same situation we would have starved to death."

"Yes," said Wayne, "they are wise. And I like their pride: there is something noble back of it."

Then Mary asked him what he had written. She admitted frankly that she had never seen any of his work.

"I'm glad you don't pretend that you should have seen my stories," said he. "Most people think they must flatter a writer. Really, I have had little published and much rejected."

"But, tell me, what do you hope to do?"

Wayne flushed, but as he looked in the girl's eyes he saw that she was not merely trying to make conversation. She was putting herself in his place, with understanding, with genuine fellow feeling, and in a charming way. Before he was aware of it, he was opening his heart to her.

CHAPTER V

Sudden Death through the Air

It was very pleasant tarrying there by the wooded riverside with this genial girl, so frank but modest, and withal so beautiful. As she stood looking down at the water, listening to his plans, he was fascinated by the exquisite curves of her profile, so expressive of refinement, and of gentleness, of tenderness.

The young man caught himself feeling, rather than thinking, that she would be sweet to live with.

At that he consciously checked himself and turned the conversation back to their surroundings. But when he spoke of her uncle, he was surprised to see a shadow pass over the girl's countenance. Her brow was knit and her underlip quivered for a moment.

It set Wayne wondering what evil thing haunted the new Eldon home. And instantly his protective instinct was aroused.

Mary exclaimed that they were staying too long. She must hurry back and see that refreshments were served.

As they climbed the river bank and crossed the avenue to the terrace, the airman overhead finished his exhibition flying and descended to the ball ground on the other side of town. The crowd followed, leaving no one but the sheriff and the fire chief standing on the bridge.

When Wayne and Mary came out upon the lawn, they found that Mrs. Eldon was already having ices and punch served. The ubiquitous Mr. Blotter was making himself useful as a waiter. Mary hurried on to the house. Wayne chatted a while with the Sherwoods and other guests. Judge Eldon was still sitting on his settee, under the big tree, facing the river. He was conversing with several guests who had lawn chairs grouped about him at intervals. Wayne moved toward them. Blotter was coming up from behind the judge, bearing a tray.

When Wayne was within thirty feet of the judge there came a sudden, sharp *spat*, as of some hard-driven missile striking the tree. His trained ear instantly knew it for a bullet's impact.

He expected to see a bit of bark fly from the tree; but instead of that he observed a leaf flutter from a shrub directly behind the judge. Then, to his horror, he saw Judge Eldon's head sink slowly forward.

There was a sinister red spot on his forehead. His eyes were staring, his lips parted as if in wonderment at something he could not understand.

Wayne, in the instant of the shock, scarcely noticed that Blotter, in the background, screamed and dropped his tray.

In a couple of seconds the judge's body began to sag forward. The near-by guests made no move to catch the falling man, nor did they utter a sound. They were frozen stiff with horror.

But Wayne, with soldierly instinct, reacted in a flash. He sprang forward and caught the stricken man by the shoulders, as if to brace him against the seat; but the body collapsed in his arms, and he lowered it gently to the ground.

Some one cried: "Oh my God!" Another: "Judge Eldon has been shot!"

Immediately there was panic among the guests. Two women fainted. Mrs. Eldon came shrieking and fell upon her husband's body. Mary, running from the house, threw herself upon her knees beside them, sobbing so bitterly that Wayne yearned with pity.

One of the guests was a physician. He examined the judge's wound. A glance was enough, and he said simply: "He is gone."

Blotter came, white-faced and limping, asking: "Is Eldon killed?"

"Yes," answered Wayne, "shot through the brain." Then he saw blood trickling down Blotter's leg and running over his shoe. He exclaimed: "Why, man, you're hit yourself!"

"It's nothing much," said Blotter bravely. "Got it in the thigh; but I can walk."

The sheriff came at a hard run. He had seen, from the bridge, the commotion on the lawn. He pushed his way through the excited throng, examined the body, noted the position in which the judge had been sitting, and cast a glance backward to the bridge, the farther end of which was visible through a gap between the trees.

He learned that Blotter, too, had been struck by the same missile, after it had passed through the other man's head. He shivered and called Blotter to him, bidding him show exactly where he had been at the time. The fallen tray marked the spot.

It was directly in line with that part of the bridge which showed between the trees and with the end of the settee where Eldon had sat. Beyond the bridge was nothing but the Ames Building, with a steep wooded hill towering above it in the distance.

"The shot was not fired from the bridge," declared the sheriff. "I was there myself with the fire chief, and there was not another soul thereabouts. It was not fired from the Ames Building, for we were close to it, and we heard nothing but Mr. Venrick driving nails in his laboratory. It was a stray bullet, fired by some infernal fool away back yonder on that hillside. I will send out deputies to investigate at once."

Judge Eldon's body was carried to the big house, which was at once closed to all but a few intimate friends of the family.

Wayne started to assist Blotter to the nearest physician's office, which was Dr. Mando's. On the bridge they met Mando and Venrick, excitedly led by Parilla Dreem, who, having heard on the street that Eldon was shot, had run to summon her neighbors in the Ames Building.

All of them turned back with the wounded editor and went with him and Wayne to Mando's apartment. The men took him into the operating room, and Parilla hovered within earshot in the reception room.

Blotter was stripped and put on the operating table. His wound was in the upper part of the left thigh, near the outer edge, and the bullet had stopped there. Mando said, in his cool, professional way: "If that were my leg, I'd slit the wound wide open throughout its length, so as to give it immediate and thorough sterilization. The ball is not far below the skin."

"Go to it," said Blotter gamely. "I don't need any anæsthetic."

Mando selected a knife with a long and slender blade, stropped it to razor keenness, sterilized it, and ran it straight along the bullet channel with its edge up. He gave a quick, upward cut, laying the wound open. Blotter had scarcely time to grit his teeth.

The doctor removed the bullet, cleansed the wound of fragments of clothing that had been driven into it, and proceeded to sterilize and dress the injury.

Wayne picked up the bullet and examined it.

"This is a full jacketed Luger pistol bullet," said he, "of 7.65 millimeters, which is thirty caliber by our measurement: that is to say, its diameter is thirty-hundredths of an inch."

Venrick stared in surprise. "How can you tell that without measuring?" he asked.

"I used to be in the small arms division of the Ordnance Department," answered Wayne. "I was engaged in experimental work and comparative tests of ammunition. I could distinguish the various bullets, blindfolded, just by rolling them between thumb and finger.

"A trained sense of touch can detect a difference of a hundredth of an inch, or less. But, anyway, the Luger bullet is easily told from any other by its peculiar shape, and by its weight."

Blotter was listening. He asked: "The Luger is a foreign weapon, is it not?"

"Yes, made in Germany and Austria, and used by many of their officers during the war. Our own country has been flooded since the war with old Lugers refurbished and sold cheaply by mail order houses. The Luger pistol, of either caliber—there are two—uses a cartridge of such dimensions that it will not chamber in any other gun; so this bullet must have been fired from a Luger—well, I'll be damned!"

Wayne's sudden cry of surprise made Mando look around. "What's the matter?" he asked sharply.

The young ordnance expert did not answer. He went to the window, held the fatal missile up to a strong light, and examined it intently, his brow frowning. At last he said gravely:

"Mr. Blotter, you must keep this thing where it cannot be lost or exchanged. Don't let any one have it out of your sight. Put a private mark on it."

"It is a gruesome souvenir," said Blotter.

"It is more than a souvenir. It is a mystery!"

The portière stirred with a slight rustle. Wayne glanced toward it and caught Parilla's startled eyes peeping from the front room.

Mando paused in the act of bandaging and asked: "What is mysterious about it?"

Wayne nodded significantly at the portière as though to say "Hush!" He replaced the bullet on the instrument stand. He moved mechanically to the set basin, washed his hands, and then sat down, with bowed head, and ran the fingers of both hands through his hair. His features were set and pale.

"You look as if you had seen a ghost," muttered the doctor in an undertone. "What the devil is wrong?"

"Oh, I'm just overwrought by the tragedy over there," answered Wayne with a gesture toward the Eldon home.

"We are all in a state of nerves," declared Blotter. "Tragedy is bad enough when we only read about it in the newspapers, but when it strikes down a lifelong friend—ah, it is hard, indeed!"

Then they talked about Judge Eldon's life and character until the editor was ready to be taken home. Venrick called a car, and he and Wayne went their sorrowing way to their boarding place.

They put Blotter to bed. Venrick said he would go now to the Eldons' and see if Colonel and Mrs. Sherwood needed him as a messenger or otherwise. When he had gone, Blotter at once asked Wayne what he meant by the mystery of the bullet.

"Mr. Blotter," answered the young man, "this must go no further. There is much to learn before we dare make it public. But this much I already know: that Judge Eldon was killed by this Luger pistol bullet, but that it never was fired from a Luger or any other kind of pistol. It was shot from a rifle."

"*A rifle*!"

"Yes: it certainly was fired from a rifle."

"But you said, yourself, that it could not have been shot from anything but a Luger."

"Neither could it, if a Luger cartridge had been used, as I, of course, assumed. But there is a way—just one way—by which this bullet could have been fired from a rifle, a high-power rifle. The devil of it is that nobody but an expert, a scientific experimenter with arms and explosives, would know how to do it, and succeed as this fellow did succeed."

"My God!" exclaimed Blotter, striving to rise in bed.

"Lie still!"

"But don't you see what that means?"

"Hush! It means nothing against any man until we have learned much more than we now know."

They were silent a long time, their minds groping and harnessed with evil forebodings.

Finally Wayne spoke; but it was [as] if he were talking to himself:

"The trail of a bullet through the air! Back to the muzzle of the gun. It is hard to trace; but perhaps it can be done. By Heaven, it shall be done!"

Letters to and from Leonard and family re: Writing of Smoky Mountain Magic 1928–1929

September 25, 1928.

Dear Dad; [*sic*]

I have just seen "Caty" (J. Sidney Cates) and he says by all means let the Curtis Publishing Co. have the first chance at your mms. Between the Saturday Evening Post, the Ladies Home Journal and the Country Gentleman they are the largest buyers of high grade fiction inAmerica [*sic*]. The three publications work independently and in fact bid against each other but on the other hand if one gets ahold of something that it cannot use it turns it over to one of the others. Consequently, if you get entre to one you have to all.

Caty says that the process of getting the most possible return from a mms. is to have it appear serially in a magazine, followed by publication as a book and that, in turn, by the sale of the movie rights. Practically all books are submitted first to the magazines, except in the case of writers, of whom there are quite a few, who have contracts with book publishers.

At any rate Caty said that he would be delighted to hand the mms. to the chief editor of the Country Gentleman with a personal letter of recommendation. Provided of course that the story is as good as I said it was. Since he has long been an ardent admirer of yours through Our Southern Highlanders there is not much question of his approval. He wanted however to ask your permission to make small tentative changes or additions to the story or the wording if he thought it would add to the "saleability" of the mms. He would of course not do anything radical to the mms. but simply fix it up lightly in places if he thought it desirable. Since he is an experianced [*sic*] and very skillful writer himself his opinion would be invaluable.

If you think favorably of this scheme send me a copy of the mms. by registered mail and I will give it to Caty to read. If he approves it it will get a direct entre to the highest paying editors in the country. He wont send it in without returning it to you first for approval of any changes that he may have made. If he does not think that the Curtis people will take it he will say so frankly and tell you why.

He would like very much to get it for the Country Gentleman because he is on the staff of that magazine. I told him however that the mms, was not merely a "story", it was an authentic picturization of a community that is going to be prominently in the public eye, and that this feature, togeather [*sic*] with the high literary style in which it is written, would be more or less wasted on the readers of a farm magazine. It is good enough from a purely literary and historical standpoint for the most sophisticated audience and it ought to have a chance to reach them. Consequently the editors of the Saturday Evening Post ought to have a chance to see it.

So far as the price paid is concerned the three Curtis papers would pay about equally. But the Sat. Post would carry the largest literary prestige, and would give it the largest book value.

Of course it is entirely possible that the story is not a "magazine" story and the Curtis people may not want it. But it certainly would do no harm to try and if they did accept it it would be the most profitable market in America for the writer.

This then seems to be the first step. It [*sic*] it does not work there will still be time to try the brokers and the book publishers.

Leonard

Sep. 25, 1928

My dear Leonard:—

By this mail I am returning the book you loaned me. It is very interesting, on account of the subject; but it's a pity the author was not more of a writer.

Perhaps that's what they'll say about my novel. I have finished it, all but the last chapter. Am calling it

MOUNTAIN MAGIC.

That fits the theme, it's unhackneyed, and, I think, rather catchy.

Please get in touch with Mr. Cates as soon as you can and ask him to recommend a literary agent.

Dad

Bryson City, N. C.
Sept. 27, 1928.

My dear Leonard:—

I will mull over my MSS. a few days, putting on some finishing touches, and then send it to you for Mr. Cates's inspection. Provisionally I am calling it "Mountain Magic;" but the title will be changed if someone suggests a better one.

If it should turn out that the Curtis Co. accepts it, I can then handle the sale of book rights by myself. But I realize the odds against such luck, and will turn the MSS. over to an agent if it fails to land in a magazine.

You are very kind to take so much interest in the Old Man's effort, and I feel encouraged by it; for your comments show that you have unusual literary taste yourself.

Of course, I would rather get into the POST than any other periodical; but I will not be cast down if they refuse it. No doubt they reject car-loads of MSS., including many of more than ordinary quality.

Anyway, it does no harm to "shoot at the moon."

I would be glad to profit by any suggestions Mr. Cates may make about changes in the book.

Bryson City, N. C.
Oct. 3, 1928.

My dear Leonard:—

I am sending you today, by Southern express, the MS. of my novel "Mountain Magic." I will be very grateful if you will turn it over to Mr. Cates for examination.

Dad.

Bryson City, N. C.
Oct. 3, 1928.

My dear Leonard:—

On my carbon copy I see that there is an error on page 261, line 7, which begins "his holy place." It should read "this holy place."

Please insert a t before his.

Dad.

Bryson City, N. C.
Dec. 3, 1928.

Dear Leonard:—

I am not much disappointed at the Curtis Co. turning down my MS., for I felt in my bones that the story was not well balanced. The defects you mention were quite apparent, and there are others. Big Tom should have more to do; so should Marian. I am going to recast the thing, cut out half of the Indian myth, add several chapters, and run the story up to about 100,000 words.

Please return the MS. by express, collect, and I will turn out something worth while [*sic*].

I thank you very much for the interest you have taken and I wish you to thank Mr. Case [*sic*] for me.

Bryson City, N. C.
Dec. 3, 1928.

Dear Leonard:—

Your telegram came just after I had mailed a letter to you. As I stated in the letter, I want to recast the story before another publisher sees it. The Doubleday-Doran people wrote me a good while ago asking to see the MS. when ready, and I promised to send them a copy. The Viking Press and the Macmillans also asked for it. I will have to make several copies.

Thanks, very much, for your help. I believe the thing will go through, O.K., when revised.

Dad.

December 4, 1928.
Miss May Massee,
Doubleday, Doran and Co., Inc.
Garden City, N. Y.

My dear Miss Massee,

I am sending you today Mr. Horace Kephart's manuscript entitled, tentatively, "Mountain Magic."

The story is draggy in spots but it has some fine characterizations and the descriptions of the country where the new Smoky Mountain National Park is to be located are most accurate.

I shall be most appreciative of any suggestions that you can make as to the character of the manuscript and its disposal.

Your enthusiasm for manuscripts was so infectious that I going [*sic*] to work on mine again and I may burden you with them before long.

Sincerely,
L. W. Kephart,
Senior Agronomist,
Clover Investigations.

Title— "Mountain Magic" not sufficiantly [*sic*] distinctive. Does not intrigue the interest and does not describe the setting. It needs a title with a local place name, like "The Little Shephard of Kingdom Come," "The Bridge of San Luis Ray" etc. For example "The Magician(s) of Clingman's Dome," "High Smoky Magic" etc.

10 —"Oakvale" is a little too soft, too bucolic a name for the Great Smoky Mountains. It should be something a little more rugged, i.e. "Blowing Rock," "Black Mountain" or a personal name like "Booneboro," "Waynesville" or even Bryson itself though its [*sic*] better not to be too specific.

21 —Delete "new." It rather spoils the picture to bring in too much newness. Better just hint at it.

23 —Delete "NC 10" for same reason and because is too specific for a piece of fiction. Same for "city limits." These references to urbanity rather jar.

76 —3rd paragraph. Begin "These extra-terrestrial aff___[39] attended to, Youlus put some ground coffee etc."

140 —Dagataga's conversation here is too sophisticated to be realistic. We dont [*sic*] expect an Indian, even a well-educated chief, to have facile use of words like subtle, denote, terror (in this sense), revere etc. If it is a fact it should be brought out strongly by Col. Fielding when discribing [*sic*] the chief to Marian some time earlier, in order to prepare us for it.

145 —148 —The chiefs [*sic*] account of the legend is fine but had better be boiled down. Casual readers are interested in folk-lore and legend only up to a certain point. Beyond that they get bored and think the story drags.

151 —154 —Same as above. If readers skip much of this, as they are apt to do, they will miss the point of what follows.

197 —The language is a little melodramatic and unreal. Better and more natural to say, "Shoot me down in cold blood, will you. You damned murderer."

202 —Next to last paragraph. "Mr. Jack Dale" is melodramatic. I "Mr. Jack Dale Cabarrus" is derision. Delete "with your life."

252 —Skiddoo is archaic slang. Better use "Beat it."

262 —The wind-up ought to be a fairly strong love scene. Suggest the following in place of the last two paragraphs.

"John turned his back upon the jewel-studded wall. All the years of his life were in his eyes as he looked into Marion's [*sic*] face. Then trembling with an emotion that he could not suppress he drew her gently to him. Reverently he raised his hand in salute to the invisible genii of the grotto.

"Little People" he said, "This is what I want. I want—to take—this."

Bryson City, N. C.
Jan. 11, 1929.

Dear Leonard:—

I have been laid up, sick and miserable; but am out once more and eager to recast the bloomin' novel. The MS. has not come—I inquired both at the post-office and the express-office.

Your suggestions will be studied with care. Meantime I have decided to cut out some of the Indian myth, give Big Tom more to do, mix the girl up in something exciting, turn the gem discovery into a thriller, and perhaps kill Matlock.

Dad.

January 14, 1929.

Dear Dad,

Sorry to hear that you have been under the weather. Was it the flu? Hope that you are feeling fit again. Be sure to take it easy if it was the flu for the after effects are worse than the disease at times.

The mms. was forwarded several days ago. I cant [*sic*] say the exact date for the receipt is out at the house but it certainly should have reached you by the time this letter does. If it hasn't let me know and I will trace it at once.

The Doubleday-Doran people did not, of course, send it to me as soon they said they would but it arrived eventually.

I included the suggestions with the mms. Most of them were trivial. I do believe however that your plans will strengthen the yarn. The big chance it seems to me is to play up the local people and the local color. Big Tim is fine.[40] I'd like to see him get mixed up with Matlock and nearly, but not quite, kill him. Perhaps in defense of the girl. That would be quite in keeping with Matlock's character and would not be pure mellow dramer [*sic*]. But in any event there ought to be more of Big Tim's conversation. Bupply is also good and he gives the necessary humorous touch. Matlock's passing is a little too tame. He just quietly disappears, which is a little too easy after all his devilment. He ought to get hissn [*sic*] somehow.

I have thought several times that there is a chance here to work in some of the experiances [*sic*] that you had in the caves below St. Louis. Could not the girl, in prospecting around, come across an opening in the ground from which came a draught of air. Of course the Smokies are not limestone country and it would have to be a different kind of a cave. But, she has heard what's-his-name (the hero) tell about his hopes of finding a gem mine. By that time she has begun to be pretty keenly interested in him. So, without admitting even to herself, that that is the reason, she begins to watch for gem mines rather than botanical specimens. Finally, late on [*sic*] evening, while returning to Big Tim's for the night, she comes across this cave. Its [*sic*] too late to do anything that night, but she tells Tim about it and in the morning goes back to investigate. Tim had rather laughed at her, and piqued she had not told him exactly where the cave was. She finds the cave alright and starts to investigate. She slips down into the hole —and the [*sic*] she gets stuck. Do you remember the Flloyd [*sic*] Collins case of the chap who got stuck in a cave. [*sic*] The whole U. S. followed the efforts to release him and it gives me the shivers yet to think of the horror of it.

When Marion does not return that night Tim scents disaster. Taking his dog (which is a good tracker) he starts after her. After some difficulty he finds her. But not before Matlock, attracted by her calls for help, has also found her. Finding her helpless Matlock refuses to help her unless she tells him all she knows about our hero. She refuses scornfully, of course, and Matlock says "All right you can stay right here till you do tell me. You wont [*sic*] die overnight but you will be mighty darn uncomfortable. Maybe by morning you will have some sense." So he leaves her. When Marion tells Tim what Matlock did Tim nearly boils over. But Marion makes him promise not to say anything about it. If he tells our hero the latter will probably proceed to smear Matlock all over the landscape and be arrested [for] murder, and if he tells anyone else the story will be garbled and twisted and her reputation damaged. So Tim reluctantly agrees to keep quiet. But after Marion is safe in bed he goes back up the mountain and proceeds to lie in wait for Matlock. In the morning when the villain appears Tim is waiting for him. Thereupon Matlock gets properly beat up.

This of course does not improve Matlock's feeling for the hero and gives added[41] reason for his vindictiveness later on when he has the hero in his power.

It seems to me that some such action would be substituted for some of the rather drawn-out material where the hero is wandering around his camp looking for the mine. I forgot to mention it before but that is also a rather draggy place. If that could be shortened it would be better. Have just enough to show that the hero made a detirmined [*sic*] effort to find the mine but failed. Then when the girl finds it, more or less by accident, it gives her a sort of proprietary interest in it too and heightens her keenness about it. It becomes their mine rather than his mine and paves the way for their eventual love scene.

Well I've been rambling on as though I could not stop. But I do think that, in order to be distinctive and definately [*sic*] a story of the Great Smoky Mountains and not "just another novel" it ought to have more action by local people. It sure is a darn good yarn. But keep outsiders out as much as possible.

Bryson City, N. C.
Jan. 19, 1929.

Dear Leonard:—

The MS. came today. Your criticisms are sound. Some of them I had anticipated; others hit the mark where I would have missed completely.

When I was writing this thing I was under severe strain, partly mental partly physical. A good rest from the theme has given me new pep and a fresh point of view. Now, I'm confident, I'll do better.

The title never pleased me—it was only provisional. How would this do? "Red Magic in the Smokies." We are familiar with black magic and white; but red (Indian) is out of the ordinary. Most people don't know where or what the Smokies are; but the combination will catch almost anybody's attention.

Dad.

Circular Letter to the Family (so far as I have present addresses)

Bryson City, N. C.
Feb. 16, 1929.

Dear Folks:—

As you will see from enclosed copy of notification from the U. S. Geographic Board, we Kepharts are now among the "Higher-ups."

At this same meeting of the Board a mountain in South Dakota was named for President Coolidge. Cal's hill is only 6,000 ft. high; ours is 6,255. So we can't help looking down on him; but let's not be supercilious about it.

I am recasting "Smoky Mountain Magic," the novel I'm[42] trying to perpetrate, and feel confident that it will hit a mark somewhere above ground level.

Love to all of you.

Dad.

Bryson City, N. C.
March 11, 1929.

Dear Leonard:—

I sent the recast novel to Doubleday, Doran on the 7th. Aside from changes in diction and the like, the following major changes have been made.—

(1). Title is "Smoky Mountain Magic."

(2). Oakvale becomes Kittuwa (actual name of ancient capital of the Cherokees, which, before the white men came, extended from mouth of the Lufty to well within present town limits of Bryson).

(3). Cabarrus does not fall off cliff at the Alcove. Not quite so much description of forest growth, etc.

(4). First love scene improved.

(5). Youlus Lumbo's superstitions elaborated, showing cause of his following Cabarrus to Degataga's.

(6). Uktena myth condensed into one chapter.

(7). Cabarrus back at the Alcove after fight—elaborated. He goes alone into the rift. Falls into abyss and is entombed in utter darkness.

(8). Marian and the Burbanks alarmed because C. does not show up at 9 a.m. next day as promised. Big Tom, Marian and the hound go into Nick's Nest. They eventually rescue Cabarrus. Much new matter here.

Total: 73,000 words, instead of scant 70,000.

Dad.

Bryson City, N. C.
March 31, 1929.

My dear Leonard:—

That is a very well written story of yours in the COUNTRY GENTLEMAN on your African trip. You have the talent for writing interesting stories and I hope you will give us more. My friends here are quite elated over the success of your expedition and the way you tell about it.

I suppose I will hear from Doubleday within a week or two. Yesterday I finished a short story (9,000 words) "Mr. Pinwell Breaks Jail," being some adventures of a

Baltimore clerk, who had never been south of Washington, when he was sent off into our wild hills with $10,000 currency in his jeans.

In the last Sat. Evening Post is a story, "Treat You Clever," by Maristan Chapman, who published not long ago a novel of Tenn. mountain life that was a "best seller." I have not seen the novel; but this story in the S.E.P. is pointless, written in a made-up dialect that never has been heard on land or sea, and she cribbed one of the episodes almost bodily from my narrative of the bear hunt in "Our Southern Highlanders." In adapting her own lingo to it she botched it.

Maybe if my novel goes over, I may be able to "place" any old thing; but I'll be darned if I'll crib.

Dad.

seven

THE CHEROKEES

Cherokee stickball game.

Cherokee stickball game.

Introduction

ANDREW DENSON

When Horace Kephart moved to western North Carolina in search of "a free life in the open air," he made his new home in Cherokee country.[1] The Smoky Mountains formed the heart of the traditional Cherokee homeland, and the region's valleys and forests were familiar territory for the Cherokee people who still resided there. For Cherokees, this area was not "the back of beyond," but the center of the world, a landscape rich in cultural and historical meaning. Kituwah, the ancient site Cherokees identify as their people's "Mother Town," was only three miles east of Bryson City, Kephart's base of operations for much of his time in the region. The Qualla Boundary, the principal landholding of the Eastern Band of Cherokee Indians, was located nearby. In his travels through the mountains, Kephart met Cherokee people and observed the contemporary tribal community. He read the available literature on Cherokee history and culture. In time, he worked Cherokee themes into his writing, applying his distinctive vision of the southern highlands to the region's indigenous people.

THE CHEROKEES OF NORTH CAROLINA

At the time of Kephart's arrival, the Eastern Band of Cherokee Indians numbered around 1,400 members. The majority lived on the Qualla Boundary, the 78,000 acre "reservation" in Swain and Jackson Counties.[2] Other Cherokees resided on parcels of tribal land farther west, such as the Snowbird community in Graham County, while a small number lived in non-Indian towns and settlements. According to the federal Indian Bureau, most Cherokees residing on tribal lands supported themselves through small-scale agriculture supplemented by wage work in regional industries like logging. The majority of tribal members spoke Cherokee as their principal language, although census takers in 1900 counted some 500 Cherokees who could speak English. Many Cherokees attended Christian churches, with the Baptists forming the largest denomination. Christian services often retained elements of traditional Cherokee religious practice and were conducted in the Cherokee language. The federal government operated a boarding school in the town of Cherokee, the tribe's administrative center on the Qualla Boundary. In 1900, around 150 Cherokee boys and girls attended the school, which emphasized vocational education and agricultural training. Cherokee was also the home of the tribal government, consisting of an elected chief, vice-chief, and fifteen-member council. These officials oversaw the Eastern Band's relationships with state and federal authorities while managing tribal lands, which the Eastern Band owned collectively under a North Carolina corporate charter.[3]

This small tribal community descended from Cherokees who had avoided forced removal from the Southeast. In the early nineteenth century, the Cherokee Nation held territory in western North Carolina, east Tennessee, northern Georgia, and northwestern Alabama supporting a population of around 15,000. In the 1830s, the United States compelled the majority of these Cherokees to relinquish their land and migrate to present-day eastern Oklahoma in the episode later remembered as the Cherokee "Trail of Tears." Under the Indian Removal policy, the United States pressured Indian nations to accept treaties exchanging tribal lands in the East for territory west of the Mississippi River. In the case of the Cherokee Nation, federal authorities imposed the removal policy through a fraudulent treaty negotiated with an unrepresentative minority of tribal leaders. When Cherokees rejected the treaty and refused to move, the United States deployed troops to the Cherokee country, uprooting Indian communities by force. Several thousand Cherokees died during removal as a result of disease and exposure suffered during the military operation and on the long journey west.[4]

Employing several methods, a small number of Cherokees in North Carolina managed to avoid deportation. Cherokees living at Quallatown, the future location of the town of Cherokee, convinced the United States to exempt them from the removal policy. The Cherokee Nation had ceded the territory around Quallatown in treaties negotiated before the removal era in 1817 and 1819. Some Cherokees remained in this territory after its sale under a treaty provision that allowed individuals to take land "reserves" and become state citizens. While most of the Indian people who made use of this provision lost their land, many chose to stay in what was now a part of North Carolina. They formed new communities, with Quallatown among them. When the United States pressed the Cherokee Nation to make a removal treaty, the Quallatown Cherokees asked to be excluded from its provisions. Working through William Holland Thomas, a white merchant and self-taught lawyer, they persuaded federal authorities that their community had separated from the Cherokee Nation under the 1817 and 1819 treaties. They were North Carolina citizens, they insisted, and thus should not be bound by a removal treaty forced upon the Cherokee Nation.[5]

Outside of Quallatown, meanwhile, Cherokees adopted other strategies in the hope of remaining in the East. Some managed to secure individual exemptions by convincing federal agents that they were "civilized" enough to join the non-Indian population of North Carolina. Others chose to flee into the mountains when the troops arrived to enforce removal, hoping that if they could avoid capture the army would eventually give up the search and leave. Some of these "fugitive" Cherokees received aid and information from Indians who had permission to stay and from non-Indians living in the region.[6] When the army finally departed in the autumn of late 1838, around 1,100 Cherokees remained in North Carolina. About 700 lived in the vicinity of Quallatown with the remainder residing in small communities to the west and southwest.[7]

In the years immediately following removal, individual Cherokee communities in North Carolina seem to have exercised a high degree of local autonomy rather than operating as a single tribe.[8] William Holland Thomas continued to represent the Quallatown Cherokees in many of their dealings with non-Indians. During this time, he also helped them purchase land, a process that began the creation of the Qualla Boundary.[9] After the Civil War, North Carolina Cherokees developed new political institutions, creating a tribal government designed to bring all of the remaining Cherokee communities in North Carolina under a single chief and council. By the end of the nineteenth century, the United States recognized the North Carolina Cherokees as a distinct Native American polity officially identified as the Eastern Band of Cherokee Indians.[10]

Kephart's career in Southern Appalachia spanned a period of significant change for the Eastern Band. In 1904, when Kephart arrived, Cherokee communities were as isolated as many of the white mountaineers who so captured his attention. By the time of Kephart's death, in 1931, improved roads and the expansion of the mountain tourism economy had reduced that isolation significantly, at least when it came to the town of Cherokee and the Qualla Boundary. The designation of the Great Smoky Mountains National Park, in particular, brought new attention and growing numbers of visitors to the Cherokee lands. The park was located on the edge of the Qualla Boundary, and the town of Cherokee became the park's principal North Carolina entrance.[11] These developments placed the Eastern Band at the center of the region's most important industry, and the Cherokee community's significance to Appalachian tourism would continue to grow throughout the rest of the 1930s and then after World War II. Kephart witnessed the beginning of this change before his death. Indeed, as a writer and tourism promoter, he contributed to the transformation.

NORTH CAROLINA CHEROKEES IN KEPHART'S WRITING

Kephart took an active interest in the Eastern Band from the start of his time in the southern mountains. He visited the Qualla Boundary just a few months after his arrival, and his photos from this early period include a collection of candid shots of Cherokees from the Birdtown community. His research journals from the 1910s and 1920s contain observations on Cherokee life and culture as well as notes on tribal history and the Cherokee language.[12] This curiosity should not surprise us. The history of the American West formed one of Kephart's great passions. He counted among his favorite authors writers like Francis Parkman, who published dramatic histories of Indian wars, pioneers, and westward expansion. Kephart moved to Appalachia, in part, so that he could recapture something of the frontier experience. The Indian presence likely confirmed his idea of the region's frontier authenticity.[13]

In his published writing, however, Kephart's great subjects were the Appalachian landscape and white mountaineers rather than the region's Indian population. In his most famous work, *Our Southern Highlanders*, he displayed his familiarity with the Cherokee community of western North Carolina, but he described little of the Cherokees' history, culture, or contemporary existence. As he recounted his adventures in the mountains, he occasionally cited an Indian place name, and he made offhand references to the Qualla Boundary and the contemporary Cherokee community. He sometimes framed his descriptions of the landscape with references to "Indian times," suggesting the Smokies had changed little since the frontier era. In the second edition of the book, the chapter titled "A Raid into the Sugarlands" features a Cherokee guide ("Katch"), who helps Kephart and a federal agent track down liquor dealers charged with bringing moonshine onto Cherokee land. For the most part, however, Kephart's Indian neighbors remained in the background. They were present in *Our Southern Highlanders*, but they played only ancillary roles in the story of Kephart's discovery of the mountain environment and its isolated white communities.[14]

In a similar way, Kephart scattered references to the Cherokees in his writings promoting the Great Smoky Mountains National Park while focusing most of his attention on the grandeur of the region's natural landscape. Like many tourism advocates, he noted the presence of the Qualla Boundary just outside the proposed park's borders, suggesting that the Eastern Band might help attract visitors. In a 1926 essay "The Last of the Eastern Wilderness" (reproduced in this volume), he explains that the tribe's "ancient capital" had been located in the Smokies, an allusion to the Cherokee "Mother Town" of Kituwah, adding that several thousand Cherokees still resided in the region. In a letter to Congress, he even suggested (erroneously) that Sequoyah, whose statue stands in the US capitol, invented the Cherokee syllabary while living in the vicinity of the park. These references were brief and perfunctory, but they served to heighten the exoticism of Kephart's portrayal of the Smokies. Like his rapturous descriptions of mountain scenery, they marked the region as special, distinctive enough to merit the government's protection. A national park in Southern Appalachia, Kephart implied, would offer unexpected human interest as well as surprising natural beauty.[15]

On several occasions, Kephart produced magazine and newspaper articles that focused specifically on the Cherokee past and present. In these writings, he exchanged his usual superficial references to the Indian community for more sustained discussion. In 1928, for instance, he published an article titled "The Indian Blowgun" in *Boys' Life*, the magazine published by the Boy Scouts of America (reproduced in this volume). The article describes a visit to the Cherokee Fall Fair, an annual event established in 1914 by Cherokee community leaders and the tribe's federal agents. The fair began as an agricultural exposition, but by the late 1920s, organizers included a growing number of events that involved Cherokees demonstrating elements of the traditional culture such as stickball games and exhibitions of Cherokee dance.[16] In the *Boys' Life* article, Kephart describes a marksmanship competition among Cherokee men using cane blowguns, a traditional weapon used to hunt small game. He describes the fashioning of the guns and the darts they fired, and he compares the Cherokee blowguns with those used by tribal peoples in other parts of the world. He frames this material with a general description of the fair, which he notes had become a popular attraction for tourists. He also gives a brief synopsis of Cherokee history, explaining that North Carolina Cherokees descended from the "Indian mountaineers who escaped to the high Smokies" to avoid removal. He regrets that Cherokee ability with the blowgun likely fell far below that of their ancestors, but he hopes that the competitions at the fair might lead to improvement and a revival of this ancient skill.[17]

Kephart's most extensive treatment of Cherokee themes came in the form of a series of essays published by the sporting magazine *Outing* in 1919. Kephart's family later republished the articles as a short book titled *The Cherokees of the Smoky Mountains* (presented here). In this work, Kephart provides a historical sketch of the tribe, paying special attention to the Cherokees' resistance to the Indian Removal policy, their suffering on the Trail of Tears, and the origins of the Eastern Band of Cherokee Indians. Much of the material came from the writings of James Mooney, the pioneering anthropologist who includes an overview of tribal history in his influential volume

Myths of the Cherokee (1900). Kephart quotes Mooney extensively, and the basic structure of Kephart's narrative mirrors that of the earlier work. Kephart, however, managed to frame this history in ways that highlighted some of his own enduring themes, in particular his image of the Smokies as remote and sheltered from modern times. For the Cherokee, Kephart writes, the mountains provide a sanctuary, "a refuge for their people in case of disaster."[18] Possession of such a refuge explains Cherokee persistence in the Southeast, he suggests, much as the isolation of white communities preserved the pre-modern distinctiveness of Kephart's southern highlanders. In the *Outing* essays, then, Kephart locates the Cherokee within his familiar conception of Southern Appalachia.

Kephart begins his tribal history by describing early Cherokee contact with the Spanish, relations with colonial empires, and the tribe's uneasy alliance with the British in the eighteenth century. On this last subject, he offers a distinctly sympathetic account of Cherokee involvement in the Revolutionary War, presenting the Cherokees' decision to side with the British as a logical response to pressure from frontier settlers. Backcountry whites, he explains, were quite as savage as any Indian warrior, and Cherokees allied with the British in the hope of ridding themselves of these threatening neighbors. The result, however, was a brutal war of extermination in which pitiless frontier whites destroyed Cherokee towns, killed any Indians they could find, and drove the survivors into hiding in "the wildest recesses of the mountains."[19] These murderous backcountry riflemen, of course, were the ancestors of the white mountaineers Kephart celebrated in much of his other writing. In the Cherokee essays, however, he notes few of the positive traits he generally ascribed to white highlanders. Here, the image is solely one of primitive violence, unleavened by Kephart's usual humor and romantic anti-modernism.[20]

The Cherokee removal crisis provides the dramatic center of Kephart's narrative. In the early nineteenth century, he explains, the Cherokee managed to recover from the destruction of the Revolutionary War and made "rapid progress in the arts of peace."[21] Surrounding white communities, however, pressed them continually for land. Cherokees developed a republican government and written law in emulation of their white neighbors. Through Sequoyah's miraculous invention of the Cherokee syllabary, they became a literate people in their tribal language. Yet nothing would satisfy the states bordering the Cherokee Nation but the cession of all Indian lands. Kephart describes the Cherokees' peaceful resistance to removal, and he credits their determination to their devotion to the landscape of Southern Appalachia. "The Cherokees were the mountaineers of the South," he explained. "Like all highlanders, of whatever race, they were passionately attached to the rugged but healthful and picturesque land that gave them birth."[22] They could not imagine leaving their mountain homes.

Most Cherokees, of course, suffered removal, despite their spirited resistance. Borrowing liberally from Mooney, Kephart recounts the signing of the removal treaty, the arrival of the military, and the forced deportation of the Cherokee majority. Back in North Carolina, however, another drama unfolded. The Cherokees in western North Carolina were "the purest blooded and most conservative of the Cherokee Nation," Kephart explains.[23] When soldiers arrived to enforce removal, many of these "pure" Cherokees fled into the deep secluded sections of the mountains, just as their ancestors had during the American Revolution. Here, Kephart offers a description of the Smokies that might have come directly from his travel writing. He notes the ruggedness of the terrain and the thick forest cover. This area remained wild in modern times, he observes, and it readily sheltered moonshiners and other contemporary outlaws. It was even wilder during the time of the removal. The soldiers pursued the fugitive Cherokees as best they could, but they captured very few.[24]

Here, Kephart pays special attention to one particular fugitive, an old man named Tsali, whose story Mooney also highlights.[25] A detachment of soldiers captured Tsali and his family during the latter stages of the removal campaign. Tsali and his sons attacked their captors, killing two before taking flight. In Mooney's version, which Kephart echoed, this incident offered American military commanders an opportunity to strike a compromise with fugitive Cherokees to end the removal operation. Working through William Holland Thomas, the army offered the fugitives a deal. If they would capture Tsali and his sons, the military would depart the mountains, leaving the remaining fugitives alone. Thomas brought this message to Tsali, who agreed to surrender rather than suffer the indignity of being hunted by his own people. Cherokees then executed him, along with his adult sons, near the mouth of the Tuckasegee River. Following Mooney, Kephart treats this episode as an origin narrative for the Eastern Band. Cherokees survived in western North Carolina thanks to Tsali's heroic sacrifice, which came to symbolize the Cherokees' love for their homeland in the Smokies.[26]

As several historians have noted, this story, which Mooney's work made famous, contains some significant inaccuracies. Tsali and his family seem not to have surrendered but rather suffered capture by Cherokee pursuers. If true, this detail undermines the image of Tsali as a heroic martyr, a man who willingly sacrificed his life for his community. More importantly, the Tsali story does not accurately explain the origins of the Eastern Band. As noted earlier, Cherokees at Quallatown, along with some individuals and families elsewhere, gained exemptions from removal.

The Eastern Band emerged both from these "citizen" Cherokees and from groups of fugitives who avoided capture. In *The Cherokees of the Smoky Mountains*, Kephart suggests that the people of Quallatown fled from the soldiers when in fact they defeated removal through careful legal maneuvering. Military leaders did pardon a small number of fugitive Cherokees in return for help in capturing Tsali and his family, but, by itself, the Tsali story can not adequately explain the persistence of Indian people in western North Carolina.[27]

The story of Tsali's heroic sacrifice, however, proved irresistible to non-Indian writers, especially those, like Kephart, who wanted to promote travel to the Smoky Mountains. For Kephart, the legendary Tsali exemplified the Cherokees' attachment to their homeland, a love that he shared, in his own way, and that he hoped to cultivate in his readers. The idea of the Smokies as a Cherokee refuge, moreover, suited Kephart's basic image of the southern highlands as an isolated place existing outside of modern time. For Kephart, white mountaineers were members of a "sequestered folk," racially pure Anglos with "primitive ancient ways."[28] North Carolina Cherokees had a similar status as "pure" Indian people who managed to remain in the Southeast. They were "a little band that has stood against the white tide," as the subtitle to *The Cherokees of the Smoky Mountains* observes. For Kephart, the landscape of the Smokies explained the continued existence of both of these peoples. The mountains inspired unshakable devotion in its human communities while creating a rugged barrier to hold the modern world at bay.

Kephart was not the only travel writer and tourism advocate to embrace the Cherokee removal episode in this manner. In fact, the story of Cherokee resistance and Tsali's martyrdom appeared frequently in tourism promotions during the interwar period. Travel writers covering the creation of the Great Smoky Mountains National Park often included references to removal and Eastern Band persistence in their descriptions of the region's natural environment. As one writer put it, "tourists bask in history as well as grandeur when they visit the Great Smoky Mountains National Park," and the saga of Cherokee resistance provided one of the Smokies' greatest stories.[29] During the 1930s, tourism festivals in Cherokee, Knoxville, Asheville, and Chattanooga featured historical pageants that dramatized the removal story, among other episodes. Around the same time, tourism promoters in east Tennessee went so far as to create a public memorial to Tsali, which they placed in Gatlinburg, on the road leading into the national park. Like Kephart, these tourism advocates recognized that Cherokee history provided dramatic stories to match the Smokies' majestic natural landscape. "We have everything in the Smokies from the standpoint of scenic splendor and beauty but we need more attractions from the standpoint of human interest and tradition," remarked a Knoxville resident in discussing the Tsali monument. "This unique case of heroism provides that opportunity."[30] After World War II, the story of Cherokee removal (and Tsali's resistance and supposed martyrdom) would become the centerpiece of one of the mountain region's most popular tourist attractions, the outdoor historical drama *Unto These Hills* performed in Cherokee each summer beginning in 1950.[31] The articles in *Outing*, then, reflect not only Kephart's idea of Southern Appalachia but a trend toward the embrace of a particular kind of Cherokee history in the culture of mountain tourism.

While Kephart dealt with Cherokee subjects only occasionally in his writing, his articles on the Eastern Band deserve attention for the extent to which they echoed the major concerns of his larger body of work on Appalachia. In the North Carolina Cherokees, Kephart identified another "sequestered folk," a people whom the mountains had sheltered from some of the currents of modern American life. Like his white mountaineers and the landscape itself, the Cherokees became reminders of another time. Kephart met Cherokees at the heart of their people's homeland. In his writings, he drew them into his own, imagined Appalachia.

The Strange Story of the Eastern Cherokees

A LITTLE BAND THAT HAS STOOD AGAINST THE WHITE TIDE FOR THREE HUNDRED YEARS

In the southwestern corner of North Carolina, near my present home, is a band of Cherokee Indians who, alone of a once powerful tribe and by a strange freak of fate, have been left in possession of a fragment of their ancient realm. They hold what is known as the Qualla boundary, approximately ninety square miles of rough country on the southerly slope of the Great Smoky Mountains. From time immemorial this natural fastness has been a refuge of their people in case of disaster.

The Cherokees are of Iroquoian stock or affinity, and apparently of northern origin, but at some remote period they migrated southwestward along a route long afterward followed by the first white settlers of western Virginia and Carolina. With the high Appalachians as a center and stronghold, they spread over the adjoining lowlands in seven of our present States.

The original nucleus of the tribe, in the South, seems to have been the Kituhwa settlement, near the lower edge of what is now the Qualla boundary, adjoining the site of Bryson City, North Carolina. Their national capital was Echota, just above the mouth of Tellico River, in south[eastern] Tennessee.

It was a quest for gold that first led white men into the Cherokee country, and three centuries later it was another gold-fever of the whites that wrought the Cherokees' undoing.

In 1540 the Spanish explorer, De Soto, came to an Indian town on the lower Savannah that was governed by a woman chief or "queen." Here he was shown implements of copper that appeared to be mixed with precious metal. These, he was told, came from a mountain province on the north.

De Soto seized the Indian queen as a prisoner and compelled her to go with him as guide. She, however, led him astray over mazy courses and finally made her escape, leaving him in a bare wilderness with his men and horses fairly worn out with hunger.

From *Outing*, March 1919

De Soto turned westward crossing "very rough and high ridges," to the upper waters of the French Broad, thence southerly until he reached some Cherokee settlements, where he was hospitably received. Still no gold was found, and the only treasure that he carried back was a dressed buffalo skin, the first ever seen by white men.

Long before their discovery by Europeans, the Cherokees had developed for themselves the rudiments of civilization. They were not roving hunters but dwelt in villages of log huts and cultivated the soil. They raised corn, beans, potatoes, squashes, fruits, and practiced various simple industries. Their tribal organization, though looser than the confederacy of the Iroquois, was yet coherent enough for the whites to recognize as the "Cherokee Nation."

Scotch and Irish traders began to traffic with the Cherokees about the middle of the 17th century. Some of them remained and intermarried with the Indians, gaining much influence over them. Yet whatever tendency such mingling may have had toward bringing the Cherokees into friendly relations with the British was neutralized by the haughty bearing and ruthless policy of the border settlers and provincial governments.

It is a commonplace of history that our own colonists, wherever they encountered Indians, stirred up bad blood and then proceeded to spill it. The French generally got along better with the natives because they were, for the most part, only traders, and relatively few in number, who were content to let the Indians live their own life in their own way. The English, on the contrary, came in swarms, with greed of land and a fixed purpose to seize and hold. So it resulted that when war broke out between the French and English in America, most of the native tribes sided with New France.

In this crisis the Cherokees found themselves in a pinch between conflicting interests. Their hearts really were with the French, but they were constrained to ally themselves with the English for protection against their hereditary foes, the neighboring Indian tribes, who had promptly gone over to the French side.

They were destined to rue the bargain, for they fell out with the English long before the war was over, were attacked by them and overrun, half their warriors were killed, and the survivors were brought to such extremity by smallpox and starvation that they had to sue for peace on any terms. This involved of course, large cessions of land.

In spite of this experience the Cherokees again joined sides with England when the struggle came between Colonies and Crown. Their reason was that American frontiersmen had already begun surging westward and taking everything they could hold by force of arms. Tennessee and Kentucky were partly occupied by them. The Cherokees found themselves almost surrounded by whites of a class that regarded red men simply as vermin to be exterminated. Against this encompassing death England offered them protection.

The Americans quickly mobilized their riflemen, in the summer of 1776, and struck from four different directions at once, in overwhelming force. They destroyed nearly all the Cherokee towns, granaries, orchards, and growing crops, killed or drove off the cattle and horses, slaughtered all Indians who resisted, and scattered the wretched remnant into the wildest recesses of the mountains, where there was no sustenance but roots, chestnuts, acorns, and such few wild animals as harbor in those dreary roughs.

It is not nice to recall, but it is naked truth, that our backwoodsmen, regarding the Indians as mere heathen and cumberers of the earth, displayed the same ferocity in fighting them as is shown by savages and by whites gone wild with fanaticism. They slew without regard for age or sex. They scalped the victims, and collected bounties for those scalps from their own governments. They did not consign captives to death by torture, after the Indian fashion, but they coolly murdered the feeble and carried away the strong to be sold into lifelong slavery.

One of the members of Col. William Christian's army of Virginians, named Ross, has left a journal of their expedition against the Cherokee towns in western North Carolina. I quote his own words in describing a personal encounter during one of the battles:—

> "A stout Indian engaged a sturdy young white man who was a good bruiser and expert at gouging. After breaking their guns on each other they laid hold on one another, when the Cracker had his thumbs instantly in the fellow's eyes, who roared and cried '*canaly*'—enough, in English. 'Damn you,' says the white man, 'you can never have enough while you are alive.' He then threw him down, set his foot upon his head, and scalped him alive; then took up one of the broken guns and knocked out his brains. It would have been fun if he had let the latter action alone and sent him home without his nightcap, to tell his countrymen how he had been treated."

That a white savage should do such a thing to a red savage is not so strange, but that a fairly educated man of some standing should be capable of such comment is hideously illuminating to those who seek true pictures of 18th century border life.

Some of the Cherokees continued to fight the colonists until the close of the Revolution, but the main body succumbed after the first disaster and surrendered to the adjoining States a great part of their territory.

The first treaty with the new government of the United States was concluded in

1785. All of the Cherokee lands east of the Blue Ridge, and much of the northern boundary, were ceded to the whites. But the ink was hardly dry on the parchment before there began a conflict between State and Federal authority as to the remaining Indian land. Intruders swarmed into it. The Indians protested in vain. Bloody forays and reprisals were followed by open war in 1792.

Six years later another peace treaty was concluded, with more cessions of land, and with the usual guarantee on the part of the United States that thereafter the Cherokees should be left in possession of their country forever.

The retirement of the British to Canada, and the abandonment by Spain of claims east of the Mississippi, left both the northern and the southern tribes without any foreign backing; but the second war with Great Britain gave them a fresh opportunity. The Shawnee chief Tecumseh, whose confederacy had been shattered at Tippecanoe, now rallied his forces and made common cause with England in the north. The Creeks in the south took to the warpath in 1813.

In this contest the Cherokees sided with the Americans. It was largely due to their help that General Andrew Jackson won a final victory over the Creeks at the Horseshoe Bend (Tohopeka), as a result of which most of the Creek territory passed over to the United States. How Jackson requited their aid will be seen in the sequel.

At the opening of the 19th century the Cherokees had recovered from the ravages of war and were making rapid progress in the arts of peace. Their number had increased to about 20,000. Their fields and orchards were well cared for and prolific. Nearly every Indian had two or more horses, some of them owned cattle, and there was an abundance of hogs and poultry. The Federal government was encouraging industry by introducing plows and spinning wheels and looms.

There were some able men in the Nation, educated and quite as fit to lead or represent their people as the officers or politicians of the neighboring whites. Many were of mixed blood, descended in part from resident traders of the pre-Revolutionary period, who were not shiftless adventurers of "squaw-man" type but more like the Hudson Bay factors, men of good stock and character, who married regularly into the tribe and sent their children away to be educated or brought in private teachers from the outside.

Such were the Daughertys and the Adairs, the Rosses and the Woffords. Nancy Ward, a woman of great influence who was friendly to the Americans, was the daughter of a British officer by the sister of Atakullakulla, principal chief of the Cherokee Nation. General Samuel Houston, it may be remembered, took for his second wife the daughter of a Cherokee chief.

The Cherokees still remained in recognized possession of a region as large as Ohio, about half of it being within the present limits of Tennessee, and the rest in Georgia, Alabama, and the southwestern corner of North Carolina. This is marked on the old maps "Cherokee Country" or "Cherokee Nation," the United States claiming no jurisdiction over it.

If the Indians had had nothing but the Federal government to deal with they might perhaps have secured just treatment. President Jefferson acknowledged their title and sovereignty within the limits fixed by treaty. It was a region very desirable for the future expansion of the whites, and coveted by them, but to which they had neither legal nor moral right, because it had been guaranteed to the Indians in perpetuity by the Government.

But our own Union in those days was loosely knit. The boundaries of those States bordering on the Cherokee country had been run without regard for Indian claims. Georgia, which then included all of what are now Alabama and Mississippi, claimed everything within its chartered limits, under the doctrine of State sovereignty, regardless of treaties negotiated by the Federal government.

Among the Cherokees themselves there was a disturbing element—a conservative, irreconcilable group that disdained civilization and dreamed of a free hunting ground far away where they should never be molested by the whites.

Taking advantage of this split between Indian factions, our Government then sought to compromise by proposing that the conservative Cherokees cede their proportionate share of land in return for a tract in the West, where they could enjoy the unfettered life of hunters and follow their primitive ancient ways. A treaty was negotiated, not with the Cherokee Nation but with a few chiefs of these malcontents, whereby considerable areas in Georgia and Tennessee were given in exchange for a western reservation, to which some of the Indians emigrated.

The main body of the Cherokees bitterly protested that this treaty had been effected by improper means and influences, without authority of their Nation, and could only be regarded as another move toward driving them from the land of their fathers. They pointed to the evidences of their own progress in civilization and begged that they be not forced to abandon this hard-won status and exiled to a wild land where stress of environment, and the hostility of native western tribes, would tend to make them revert to savagery.

Their pleas fell on deaf ears. Still another treaty was virtually thrust upon them by which they lost more than one-fourth of their territory, and this was declared to be a "final adjustment" of all claims and differences.

In the face of such discouragements, or perhaps stimulated by them, the Cherokees now made extraordinary efforts to win recognition as a civilized and independent people. In 1820, at the suggestion of Thomas Jefferson, they formed a republican government modeled after that of the United States, and seven years later they adopted a constitution.

This was an assumption of distinct nationality, and their sovereignty was recognized by the United States. They passed laws for the collection of taxes, for repairs on roads, for the support of schools, for the suppression of intemperance and polygamy, and for preventing the sale of lands to the whites without consent of the national council.

And now occurred among these Indians, from within, an astounding development of culture which for originality and swiftness of accomplishment has no precedent nor parallel in the history of the human race.

There was a Cherokee of mixed blood named Sequoya (Se-qua[w]-yah) who through an accident in hunting had become a cripple for life. Being unable to follow the chase, he took to sedentary occupations and developed considerable mechanical skill, especially in silver-working. He never learned to speak English, and of course could neither read nor write.

Sequoyah had observed that the whites had a way of "talking on paper" whereby messages were sent and records were preserved. It set him to brooding over a project for devising a similar system for his own people. Being an old-fashioned Indian, true to his own religion, he did not seek help from the missionaries, and they in turn discouraged him. But by himself he pondered long and earnestly over the mystery of the talking paper.

Like every other inventor of writing he began by trying to make a separate symbol for every word or idea. This proved an utterly hopeless scheme. In Cherokee there were thousands and tens of thousands of words. Even if so many symbols were designed yet no man could remember half of them.

After years of hard study, in the face of ridicule and repeated failures, Sequoya finally got to analyzing his language into its component sounds. He had no conception of vowels and consonants, but he picked out the distinct syllables of his mother tongue and found there were only one hundred and fifteen.

Then came the brilliant solution of his problem; he would assign a separate character to each syllable, and any word in the Cherokee language could be written. For example, *kalanu* (raven) would be expressed by three symbols standing respectively for *ka*, *la* and *nu*.

From an old spelling-book he took the English alphabet and numerals, without the least idea of their sound or significance, and finding there were not enough characters for his purpose he devised others of his own. Most of the double consonants in Cherokee being formed with the hissing sound of *s*, he made a separate mark for it (when used as the initial of a syllable) and so reduced his syllabary to eighty-five characters. The mark for *s* and the one for the nasal *u* (like *un* in hung) are the only actual letters in his system, as the vowel characters are used only when they form separate syllables.

The effect of this invention was amazing. Any one who could speak Cherokee, having once learned the sight and sound of these eighty-five marks, could at once read and write the language with precision. There was no arbitrary spelling to learn. Any Indian could pick up in a few weeks what it takes our own children at least two years of hard work to acquire. A bright child or adult could master the art of reading and writing in a few days.

As if by magic the education of the Cherokees became an accomplished fact. Thousands of them became literate, through this invention of an illiterate, without one school being established or one teacher hired.

Although Sequoyah himself was a pagan, and remained one to the end of his days, the first literary fruit of his writing system was a translation of a part of St. John's gospel, made by a native convert.

In 1827 the Cherokee Council resolved to establish a national newspaper in their own language. Types for that purpose were cast in Boston. The press, types, and paper were laboriously transported to the capital at New Echota, an office was set up in a log hut, and the *Cherokee Phoenix* began publication, under the editorship of Elias Boudinot, a young Indian who had been educated in Connecticut by the American Board of Commissioners for Foreign Missions. The type cases and other furniture were made on the spot.

Meantime the formation by the Cherokees of a national government caused a rupture between Federal and State authorities. President Monroe approved the suggestion of the Indian agent that the Cherokee lands be allotted, the surplus sold for their benefit, and the Indians invested with full rights of citizenship in the States where they resided. But Tennessee, North Carolina, and Georgia refused to allow any Indians to live within their boundaries on any pretext whatever. Georgia further demanded cession of all Indian lands within the limits of her charter.

Naturally the Cherokees protested that their own limits were defined by treaties with the United States, and they declared that "It is the fixed and unalterable determination of this Nation never again to cede one foot more of land."

The Governor of Georgia in reply blamed the missionaries for the refusal of the Indians to "move on," and informed the Federal government that if it backed up the

Indians and resisted occupancy of their lands by Georgians it would have a fratricidal war on its hands.

The thread of Indian tenure thus strained was soon snapped by an unexpected turn of affairs. Gold was discovered in the Cherokee country, and the white man's greed burst all bonds of law or morality. At the same time Andrew Jackson, an out-and-out Indian hater, became President of the United States. From that moment the doom of the Cherokees was sealed.

How the Cherokee Nation was then driven at the point of the bayonet to the far West, and by what strange means a few hundred of their people, starving in the gulfs of the Great Smoky Mountains, but still indomitable, were at last permitted to retain a fragment of their ancient birthright, is one of the most dramatic episodes in American history. I will try to tell the story in the next issue of this magazine.

The Strange Story of the Eastern Cherokees

II. THE LURE OF GOLD LEADS TO THE UNDOING OF THE INDIAN AND THE DISHONOR OF THE WHITE

(Note: boxed text in top middle of page says, "Last month Mr. Kephart told the story of the earlier years of the Cherokees' contact with the white man in the Southern mountains. An important part was the account of Sequoya, the cripple, who invented the Cherokee alphabet, bridging at a stroke the gap that the white race was thousands of years in crossing. This picture of Indian brains, courage, endurance and character, contrasted with the rapacity, cruelty, and ignorance of the white invaders is not a pleasant one for the white race to consider, but we should study it for the good of our souls.")

The existence of gold in theCherokee [*sic*] country was well known to Spanish adventurers who followed after De Soto in the last half of the sixteenth century. There is evidence that they carried on some mining operations in that region. But they kept their knowledge secret, and it perished when they left the country. Then a century went by before the English appeared on the scene, and another century before any gold finds were reported in the South.

In North Carolina the first mint returns appeared in 1793. Six years later a 17-pound nugget was discovered on the Reed plantation in Cabarrus County, and in 1823 one was found that weighed 28 pounds. Here and in adjoining districts the placer ground was vigorously worked, and much nugget gold was taken out.

From 1804 to 1827 all the gold produced in the United States came from North Carolina. It was from the Piedmont region, east of the mountains, and not within the Cherokee country.

In 1828 gold was discovered in the mountains of Burke County, North Carolina, and the auriferous belt was at once traced south-westward along the edge of the Indian territory. About the same time some of the precious metal was found near the present

---

From *Outing*, April 1919

Dahlonega, within the boundary of the Cherokee Nation, but in the part claimed by Georgia. Then the Georgians went wild.

In December, 1828, one month after Andrew Jackson's election to the presidency of the United States, the Georgia legislature passed an act annexing that part of the Cherokee country within her chartered limits. It was further ordained that after the first day of June, 1830, all laws, usages and customs of the Cherokee Indians should be null and void within that region; that all Indians remaining within it should be subject to such laws as Georgia might enact; and that no Indian, or descendant of an Indian, should be deemed a competent witness or a party to any suit in any court where a white man was a defendant.

The confiscated territory was then mapped out by state surveyors into "land lots" of 160 acres each, and "gold lots" of 40 acres, which were put up at public lottery, each white citizen of Georgia being given a ticket.

A caustic but truthful writer of the time remarked that "intrusive mining ceased then and there, and swindling mining commenced." So far as gold was concerned, most of the supposed mineral veins proved to be barren; but the land lottery was a different matter.

By laws passed later every Cherokee head of a family was nominally granted an allotment of 160 acres; but other laws made it impossible for the Indian owner to defend his right in any court, or to prevent the seizure of his homestead, or even of his own dwelling house, by any white who saw fit to oust him. If he resisted he was subject to imprisonment.

Any contract between a white man and an Indian was declared invalid unless established by the testimony of two white witnesses. This virtually canceled all debts due from white men to Indians. An Indian was forbidden to dig for gold on his own land. Armed bands of Georgians now swept over the country, seizing or destroying Indian property and assaulting any of the owners who resisted.

There were among the Cherokees some white teachers, missionaries and printers, who had been sent there by permission of the President of the United States. In order to get rid of them, or at least shut their mouths about the spoliation, Georgia demanded that they take a special oath of allegiance to the State. Those who refused were sent to the penitentiary.

In 1832 the Supreme Court of the United States, of which John Marshall was Chief-justice, decided that the Cherokees formed a distinct community in which the laws of Georgia had no force, declared the act of Georgia in seizing their lands to be void, and ordered the release of the imprisoned missionaries.

With regard to Georgia's claim that the land in question was within her chartered limits, the Supreme Court ruled that a charter granted by the King of Great Britain to one of his colonies merely regulated the rights of the discoverers among themselves, but could not affect the rights of those already in possession as aboriginal occupants. It simply conferred the exclusive right of purchasing such lands as the natives were willing to sell. The treaties with the Cherokees bound them as a dependent ally of the United States, claiming and receiving the protection of a powerful friend and neighbor, but without involving a surrender of their national character.

It is said when the action of the court was announced President Jackson remarked "John Marshall has made his decision, now let him enforce it." The Governor of Georgia had defied the summons, with threat of rebellion. He now ignored the Supreme Court's decision, and kept the imprisoned missionaries at hard labor among felons for more than a year.

The Cherokees were staring ruin in the face. As a last resort they submitted to Washington a memorial proposing to satisfy Georgia by ceding to her part of their lands, they to be protected in possession of the remainder for a definite period to be fixed by the United States, after which, having disposed of their surplus lands, they should become citizens of the various States within which they resided.

Their plea might as well have been addressed to the North Star. Bluntly they were told that the only way out of their troubles was for them to give up the land of their fathers and emigrate in a body to the far West.

One wishes he could say that then and there an end was made to subterfuge and that the bayonets of the ejectors were frankly bared. No doubt that would have been Jackson's way if he had been dictator. But some pretext of bargaining with the Indians had to be found to give color of legality to their banishment. And now a sly politician, in the garb of a Christian minister, steps into the plot.

Among the Cherokees there was a small faction that favored the idea of emigrating. With the leaders of this faction a commissioner, in the person of the Reverend J. F. Schermerhorn, drew up the terms of a treaty binding the Cherokee Nation to surrender their whole territory and move west, in consideration of a sum of money and a new territory beyond the Mississippi. The deal, however, could not be concluded until ratified by the Nation in full council assembled.

Schermerhorn then visited the Cherokee country and tried for six months to induce the national council to approve this treaty; but he completely failed. The reverend emissary then suggested to the Secretary of War two alternative propositions: (1) to get the signatures of influential Cherokees by buying up their personal improvements at their own valuation, if in any degree reasonable; or (2) to make a treaty with a part of the Cherokees and compel the rest to accept it.

Jackson, although ruthless himself in dealing with Indians could not stomach this. He replied pointedly that the treaty, if concluded at all, must be procured on fair and open terms, with no special inducement to any individual, high or low, to win his aid or influence, and without sacrificing the interest of the whole to the cupidity of a few.

In October, 1835, the national council of the Cherokees, led by their great chief John Ross, unanimously rejected the treaty framed by Schermerhorn, even the original signers repudiating it. The commissioner concealed his chagrin by reporting "I have pressed Ross so hard by the course I have adopted that although he got the general council to pass a resolution declaring that they would not treat on the basis of the five million dollars, yet he has been forced to bring the Nation to agree to a treaty, here or at Washington. They have used every effort to get by me and get to Washington again this winter. They dare not yet do it."

He explained the defection of the minority leaders by intimating that they feared for their personal safety. "But," he piously added, "the Lord is able to overrule all things for good."

The reason for heading the Indians away from Washington was that Ross was a man of such high character, ability, and impressive personality that his influence was feared if he could get in touch with Congress, and there was already a powerful opposition to the administration's Indian policy.

At the October meeting of the council, notice was served on the Cherokee Nation to meet Schermerhorn and the Governor of Tennessee, as commissioners, at New Echota in the following December, for the purpose of negotiating a treaty, and it was declared that all who failed to attend would be counted as assenting to whatever treaty might be made.

But these commissioners were not empowered to deal on any other basis than the one that the Cherokees had already rejected. Therefore Ross determined to carry their case direct to Washington. He had moved his home to Tennessee, to escape persecution by the Georgia authorities; but they, hearing of his intended visit to Washington, sent a body of Georgia militia across the line into Tennessee, arrested Ross, confiscated all his private papers and the proceedings of the council, and carried him into Georgia, where he was held for a time without charge.

The poet John Howard Payne, author of *Home, Sweet Home,* was stopping with Ross at the time, collecting scientific data relating to the Indians. He likewise was seized, and his manuscripts were taken from him. At the same time the national newspaper, *The Cherokee Phoenix*, was suppressed.

By such acts as these, in plain defiance of the law of the land, the Cherokees, at the most critical time in their history, were deprived of their teachers, their national press, and the one spokesman whose voice at the seat of government might have won them a hearing.

When the time came for the assembling at New Echota, not over 300 Cherokees, men, women and children, were present, out of a population of over 17,000. The Governor of Tennessee was absent. Schermerhorn, on the one side, and a dozen Indians as committeemen, on the other, negotiated a treaty that sealed the doom of the whole Cherokee Nation.

This instrument provided that the Cherokees cede to the United States all their remaining territory east of the Mississippi for the sum of five million dollars and a common joint interest in the region already occupied by those Cherokees who had gone west at an earlier date, situated within what are now Oklahoma and Kansas. Improvements on the eastern lands were to be paid for, and the Indians removed at the expense of the Government and subsisted for one year after their arrival in the West.

A confidential agent, Major W. M. Davis, who was sent into the Cherokee country by the War Department soon after this farce had been enacted, reported:

> "Sir, that paper, . . . called a treaty, is no treaty at all, because not sanctioned by the great body of the Cherokees, and made without their participation or assent. I solemnly declare to you that upon its reference to the Cherokee people it would be instantly rejected by nine-tenths of them and I believe by nineteen-twentieths of them. There were not present at the conclusion of the treaty more than one hundred Cherokee voters. . . . The most cunning and artful means were resorted to to conceal the paucity of numbers present at the treaty. No enumeration of them was made by Schermerhorn. The business of making the treaty was transacted with a committee appointed by the Indians present, so as not to expose their numbers. The power of attorney under which the committee acted was signed only by the president and secretary of the meeting, so as not to disclose their weakness. . . . Mr. Schermerhorn's apparent design was to conceal the real number present and to impose upon the public and the Government upon this point. . . . I now warn you and the President that if this paper of Schermerhorn's called a treaty is sent to the Senate and ratified you will bring trouble upon the Government and eventually destroy the Cherokee Nation. The Cherokees are a peaceable, harmless people, but you may drive them to desperation, and this treaty can not be carried into effect except by the strong arm of force."

Chief Ross and a body of national delegates sent protests to Washington with signatures representing nearly 16,000 Cherokees. Resolutions denouncing the treaty were presented to General Wool, commanding United States troops who had been sent into the Cherokee country "to look down opposition," and he forwarded them to Washington. The General received for his pains a stinging reprimand from President Jackson, who declared that no communication whatever would be held with Ross, and that no council would be permitted even to discuss the treaty.

The outrageous injustice suffered by the Cherokees, without one retaliatory act on their part, excited the sympathy of decent people everywhere. And yet the "treaty," so infamously concocted and so brazenly sustained by the administration, passed the Senate, by the margin of one vote, and was proclaimed by the President on the 23rd of May, 1836. The Indians were given two years from this date in which to abandon the land of their fathers and move a thousand miles to the western wilderness.

Some of the ablest leaders in Congress, northern and southern, were bitterly opposed to the treaty. It was denounced by Daniel Webster, Edward Everett, Henry A. Wise and Henry Clay. A few years earlier Jackson's Indian policy had been scathingly rebuked by sturdy old Davy Crockett, who cried shame upon it as unjust, dishonest, cruel and short-sighted. "I had considered a treaty," said he, "as a sovereign law of the land, and now I hear it considered as a matter of expedience!"

Crockett's own constituents were immediately interested in the removal of the Indians, he had been elected to Congress from Tennessee as a Jacksonian Democrat, and he had been threatened that if he did not advocate the forcible removal of the Cherokees his public career would be summarily cut off; but he declared on the floor of the House that he could not permit himself to please his constituents and his colleagues at the expense of his honor and his conscience. Jackson never forgave him; and the threat to eject Crockett from politics was carried out.

False reports were now circulated that Chief Ross and other leaders were seeking to excite the Cherokees to war, and the militia of the surrounding states were put in the field to prevent or suppress it. General R. E. Dunlap, commanding the East Tennessee volunteers, found on the contrary that it was the Indians, and not the whites, that needed protection. In a speech to his brigade at their disbandment he said:

> "My course has excited the hatred of a few of the lawless rabble in Georgia, who have long played the part of unfeeling petty tyrants, and that to the disgrace of the proud character of gallant soldiers and good citizens. I had determined that I would never dishonor the Tennessee arms in a servile service by aiding to carry into execution at the point of the bayonet a treaty made by a lean minority against the will and authority of the Cherokee people . . . I soon discovered that the Indians had not the most distant thought of war with the United States,

notwithstanding the common rights of humanity and justice had been denied them."

General Wool was ordered to disarm the Cherokees and overawe them by a display of force. While going about this work he was manifestly disgusted with the role and sick at heart. In one of his letters he declared:

> "If I could (and I could not do them a greater kindness) I would remove every Indian to-morrow beyond the reach of the white men, who, like vultures, are watching, ready to pounce upon their prey and strip them of everything they have or expect from the Government of the United States. Yes, sir, nineteen-twentieths, if not ninety-nine out of every hundred, will go penniless to the West."

Nemesis fell heavily upon the very men who signed the treaty at New Echota as Indian committeemen. Their leader, Major John Ridge, who had negotiated the first treaty with Schermerhorn, was obliged to appeal to President Jackson for protection against the harpies who beset him and his neighbors:

> "They have got our lands and now they are preparing to fleece us of the money accruing from the treaty. We found our plantations taken either in whole or in part by the Georgians—suits instituted against us for back rents for our own farms. These suits are commenced in the inferior courts, with the evident design that, when we are ready to remove, to arrest our people, and on these vile claims to induce us to compromise for our own release, to travel with our families. Thus our funds will be filched from our people, and we shall be compelled to leave our country as beggars and in want.
>
> "Even the Georgia laws, which deny us our oaths, are thrown aside. . . . The lowest classes of the white people are flogging the Cherokees with cowhides, hickories and clubs. We are not safe in our houses—our people are assailed by day and night by the rabble. Even justices of the peace and constables are concerned in this business. This barbarous treatment is not confined to men, but the women are stripped also and whipped without law or mercy. . . . Send regular troops to protect us. . . . If it is not done we shall carry off nothing but the scars of the lash upon our backs, and our oppressors will get all the money. We talk plainly, as chiefs having property and life in danger."

A few of the Indians accepted outfits and moved voluntarily to the West, but the main body sternly refused to go. It took all of Ross's influence to preserve the peace, and military officers on the spot reported that he alone stood between the whites and bloodshed. In February, 1837, General Wool called the Cherokees together and made them a speech counciling [*sic*] prudence and submission to the inevitable. The result he reported to the Adjutant-General at Washington:

> "It is, however, vain to talk to a people almost universally opposed to the treaty and who maintain that they never made such a treaty. So determined are they in their opposition that not one of all those who were present and voted at the council held but a day or two since, however poor and destitute, would receive either rations or clothing from the United States lest they might compromise themselves in regard to the treaty. These same people, as well as those in the mountains of North Carolina, during the summer past preferred living upon the roots and sap of trees rather than receive provisions from the United States, and thousands, as I have been informed, had no other food for weeks."

Soon after making this report, General Wool was relieved from command at his own request.

Meantime Jackson had been succeeded in the presidency by Martin Van Buren. Word having reached Washington that the mass of the Cherokees did not intend to move to the West, Van Buren ordered General Winfield Scott to assume command of the troops already in the Cherokee country, and to add to them a regiment of infantry, a regiment of artillery, and six companies of dragoons. Scott was further authorized, at his discretion, to call upon the governors of the four neighboring States for militia and volunteers, not exceeding four thousand in number, to aid in moving the Indians.

But public feeling was now so deeply stirred in sympathy with the Indians that Van Buren sought a compromise by proposing to allow them two years further time in which to remove. To this suggestion Governor Gilmer, of Georgia, responded:

> "... It is necessary that I should know whether the President intends by the instructions to General Scott to require that the Indians shall be maintained in their occupancy by an armed force in opposition to the rights of the owners of the soil. If such be the intention, a direct collision between the authorities of the State and the General Government must ensue. My duty will require that I shall prevent any interference whatever by the troops with the rights of the State and its citizens. I shall not fail to perform it."

Van Buren hastily explained that no such action was contemplated, and he proceeded to carry out the original schedule.

On the 10th of May, 1838, General Scott issued a proclamation to the Cherokees in which he announced that:—

> "The President of the United States has sent me with a powerful army to cause you, in obedience to the treaty of 1835, to join that part of your people who are already established in prosperity on the other side of the Mississippi. Unhappily the two years . . . allowed for that purpose you have suffered to pass away . . . without making any preparation to follow, and now . . . the emigration must be commenced in haste. . . . The full moon of May is already on the wane, and before another shall have passed away every Cherokee, man, woman, and child . . . must be in motion to join their brethren in the far West. . . .
>
> "I have come to carry out that determination. My troops already occupy many positions, . . . and thousands and thousands are approaching from every quarter to render resistance and escape alike hopeless. . . . Will you then by resistance compel us to resort to arms? . . . Or will you by flight seek to hide yourselves in mountains and forests and thus oblige us to hunt you down? Remember that in pursuit it may be impossible to avoid conflicts. The blood of the white man or the blood of the red man may be spilt, and if spilt, however accidentally, it may be impossible for the discreet and humane among you, or among us, to prevent a general war and carnage."

Let us now briefly summarize the situation:—

The Cherokees of the South, by a census taken in 1835, numbered 16,542, exclusive of 1,592 negro slaves, and 201 whites intermarried with the Indians. They were entirely self-supporting. They grew bountiful crops of corn, wheat, oats, cotton, potatoes, indigo and tobacco. Their apple and peach orchards were prolific. Much attention was given to gardening. They had plenty of cattle, horses, sheep, goats and swine. Many families made butter and cheese.

Cotton and woolen cloths and blankets were manufactured by the women. Considerable trade was carried on with the neighboring States. The Cherokees exported much cotton, in boats of their own, to New Orleans. The Nation had no debt, and the revenue was sufficient for public purposes. The roads were in good condition, and inns were kept by natives at convenient distances along the routes.

Nearly all Cherokees could read and write their own language. Schools were increasing every year. There was a national press (or had been until the Georgians destroyed it). Some of the leading men of the Nation were highly educated, according to the standard of the time, and could hold their own in discussion with statesmen anywhere.

The Cherokees were the mountaineers of the South. Like all highlanders, of whatever race, they were passionately attached to the rugged but healthful and picturesque land that gave them birth. The promise of a far-away wilderness, encompassed and disputed by savages, in exchange for their ancient villages and cultivated fields, held no allurements for a people that was prosperous in the arts of peace and asked nothing better than to be let alone.

They had been at peace with the United States for forty years. The last war in which they had been engaged was when they fought shoulder to shoulder with the Americans against the Indian allies of Great Britain. If it had not been for their charge against the enemy's rear at the battle of the Horseshoe Bend it is probable that General Jackson would have been obliged to retire, instead of winning that decisive victory.

The nationality of the Cherokees, and their clear title to the soil they occupied, had been confirmed by the Supreme Court, which ruled that the sea-to-sea charters of the British gave the States that had succeeded to them merely exclusive rights to buy land from the Indians, but no right to force such sales. The territory of the Cherokees was separated from that of any State within whose chartered limits they might reside by a boundary line established by treaties, and within that boundary the Indians possessed rights with which no State could interfere. The Federal Government had guaranteed the Cherokees by treaty that their territory should remain inviolate forever.

And yet President Jackson, with a frontiersman's contempt for Indians, and an arrogance that brooked no opposition from any quarter, disputed the ruling of the Supreme Court and forthwith proceeded to violate it. His weak-kneed successor, seeking to temporize, was shaken back into direct action by the threatening hand of a State executive. And now came a force of 7,000 troops, with artillery, to round up and drive out the Cherokees, who, if they had wanted to fight and had possessed arms to fight with, could not have mustered more than half as many men, to say nothing of the myriads that were at the call of the President if reinforcements for Scott's army had been needed.

One can feel to-day the sting in the words of the old chief Junaluska; "If I had known that Jackson would drive us from our homes, I would have killed him that day at the Horseshoe."

(*To be concluded in the May* OUTING)

The Strange Story of the Eastern Cherokees

III. THE LONG FIGHT ENDS IN THE WESTERN EXILE OF ALL BUT A REMNANT OF THE TRIBE

The Cherokees preserved to the end an unwavering devotion to their great chief Ross and a pathetic trust in his ability to persuade Congress to let them remain in their old home. He did all that a wise and brave leader could do to preserve the peace and rescue for his people at least a moiety of what was by right and in honor due them.

On the advice of Ross, the Indians had given up their arms to General Wool, so that no suspicion of ill intent could be harbored against them. They did this even though it left them defenceless against the rabble who harried and robbed them behind the backs of the Federal troops.

Despite repeated rebuffs at Washington, and threats against his person and property at home, Ross once more sent to Congress a protest and memorial in the name of the Cherokee Nation. This was delivered in March, 1838. At the same time a memorial from citizens of New York was submitted calling for an inquiry into the validity of the treaty of 1835.

The ensuing debate in both houses of Congress was "characterized by a depth and bitterness of feeling such as had never been exceeded even on the slavery question." Henry A. Wise, who was a member of the House of Representatives from Virginia, declared "without fear of contradiction" that there was not one man in that House or out of it, who had read the proceedings of the case, who would say that there had ever been any assent given to that treaty by the Cherokee Nation. In replying to Mr. Halsey of Georgia he told him that an ex-governor of Halsey's own State, who had declared that Georgia must and would have the Cherokee lands, would not gain greatly by a comparison, either in civilization or morals, with the Cherokee chief, John Ross.

This chief Ross, by the way, was only one-eighth of Indian blood. His father and

---

From *Outing*, May 1919

maternal grandfather were born in Scotland, and his mother was only a quarter-blood Cherokee. From 1809 until his death in 1866 he was in the constant service of his people. He was adjutant of the Cherokee regiment that turned the tide of battle for General Jackson at the Horseshoe Bend. He was a member, and then president, of the national committee of the Cherokee council.

In 1827 he was president of the convention that framed and adopted the constitution of the Cherokee Nation, "the first effort at a regular government, with distinct branches and powers defined, ever made and carried into effect by any of the Indians of North America." In the following year he was elected principal chief of the Cherokee Nation, and he held this office continuously until his death.

After a hard fight in Congress both the Ross memorial and the one from New York were tabled. In May, President Van Buren made his belated proffer of a stay of proceedings, but then immediately backed down before the bristling Governor of Georgia. John Ross then submitted another project for the negotiation of a new treaty as a substitute for that of 1835, but the last day of grace for the voluntary emigration of the Cherokees was only one week off, and the Government declared that it could not consider any further negotiations.

Meantime General Scott had built a number of stockade forts throughout the Cherokee country and had disposed his troops in them. There were six of these forts in southwestern North Carolina, five in northern Georgia, one in northern Alabama, and one in southeastern Tennessee. When the last hour had struck he began the round-up.

To my knowledge there is but one reliable and full account of the Cherokee removal. It is by Mr. James Mooney, of the U. S. Bureau of Ethnology, who is not only a master of the Cherokee language but a competent historian. The facts were collected by him directly from men, white and red, who were themselves participants in this tragic affair. Let me quote a few paragraphs from Mr. Mooney's narrative:—

> "Squads of troops were sent to search out with rifle and bayonet every small cabin hidden away in the coves or by the sides of mountain streams, to seize and bring in as prisoners all the occupants, however or wherever they might be found. Families at dinner were startled by the sudden gleam of bayonets in the doorway, and rose up to be driven with blows and oaths along the weary miles of trail that led to the stockade.
>
> "Men were seized in their fields or going along the road, women were taken from their wheels and children from their play. In many cases, in turning for one last look as they crossed the ridge, they saw their homes in flames, fired by the lawless rabble that followed on the heels of the soldiers to loot and pillage. So

keen were these outlaws on the scent that in some instances they were driving off the cattle and other stock of the Indians almost before the soldiers had fairly started their owners in the other direction.

"Systematic hunts were made by the same men for Indian graves, to rob them of the silver pendants and other valuables deposited with the dead. A Georgia volunteer, afterward a colonel in the Confederate service, said: "I fought through the Civil War and have seen men shot to pieces and slaughtered by thousands, but the Cherokee removal was the cruelest work I ever knew."

In this manner, within a few weeks, nearly 17,000 of the Indians were corraled in the various stockades. The rest, about a thousand, mostly natives of the high mountains of southwestern North Carolina, fled and hid out in the trackless wilds of the Great Smoky divide.

Early in June the work of removal began. Several parties, aggregating about 5,000, were dispatched under direction of officers of the Army to landings on the Tennessee River, where they were put aboard steamboats, sent down the Tennessee and the Ohio, to the further bank of the Mississippi, and then marched afoot across Arkansas to the recently established Indian Territory (now Oklahoma).

This removal, in the hottest part of the year, of a mountain-bred people unaccustomed to the scorching lowlands, unused to the kind of food given them, nauseated by the warm drinking water, and crowded together like sheep on the steamboats, was attended by much sickness and mortality. The Cherokee national council pleaded that they be allowed to remove the rest of their people overland, in parties led by their own chiefs, after the summer heat and sickly season had passed. This was permitted, and the remaining 13,000 started on their long trek, from their assembly place at Rattlesnake Springs, Tennessee, in October, 1838.

"It was like the march of an army, regiment after regiment, the wagons in the center, the officers along the line, and the horsemen on the flanks and at the rear. . . . The route lay south of Pikeville, through McMinnville and on to Nashville, where the Cumberland was crossed. Then they went on to Hopkinsville, Kentucky, where the noted chief White-path, in charge of a detachment, sickened and died. His people buried him by the roadside, with a box over the grave and poles with streamers around it, that the others coming on behind might note the spot and remember him.

"Somewhere also along that march of death—for the exiles died by tens and twenties every day of the journey—the devoted wife of John Ross sank down, leaving him to go on with the bitter pain of bereavement added to heartbreak at the ruin of his nation. The Ohio was crossed at a ferry near the mouth of the Cumberland, and the army passed on through southern Illinois until the great Mississippi was reached opposite Cape Girardeau, Missouri.

"It was now the middle of winter, with the river running full of ice, so that several detachments were obliged to wait some time on the eastern bank for the channel to become clear. In talking with old men and women at Tahlequah [Mr. Mooney] found that the lapse of over half a century had not sufficed to wipe out the memory of the miseries of that halt beside the frozen river, with hundreds of sick and dying penned up in wagons or stretched upon the ground, with only a blanket overhead to keep out the January blast."

At last the crossing was made, and the sad procession passed on through southern Missouri. In March, 1839, they reached their destination in Indian Territory, after nearly six months' travel and agonizing hardships. It is estimated that over 4,000 Cherokees perished as a direct result of the removal, or nearly one-fourth of all those who were driven into exile. A war with an enemy of anything like their own number would not have taken so heavy a toll.

The struggles and trials of the Cherokees in their new western home do not concern our present topic. Let us go back now to the scattered and desperate refugees, those pitiful few hundreds who were left outlawed in the forests of their native mountains.

I have already mentioned that the original nucleus of the Cherokees was the Kituwha settlement on the Tuckaseegee River, near the mouth of the Okona-lufty, in the present Swain County, North Carolina. The Indians of this and the neighboring settlements on Lufty and Soco were the purest-blooded and most conservative of the Cherokee Nation. Their chief, Yonaguska ("Drowning Bear"), was a man of fine presence, six feet three inches in height and of powerful build. He was a noted orator. His people revered him not only as a leader but as a prophet.

Yonaguska counseled peace and friendship with the white man, but he was immovably opposed to a western migration. He declared that his people were safer from aggression in their steep and rocky mountains than they would ever be in a fertile land that would sooner or later be coveted by the westward-moving whites. He was a firm upholder of ancient customs and of the aboriginal religion. The white missionaries he regarded with suspicion.

When a Cherokee translation of St. Matthew was published at New Echota, and a copy was brought to the Kituwha country, Yonaguska would not allow it to be circulated until it had first been read to himself. After listening to a few chapters the old chief dryly remarked: "Well, it seems to be a good book—strange that the white people are no better, after having had it so long."

When Scott's soldiers began to seize the Indians and drive them to the stockades, most of Yonaguska's band fled in advance and secreted themselves in the high mountains. Here they were joined by others who had escaped from Calhoun and other collecting stations, until upwards of a thousand Indians were hiding in the roughs. About half of them were under command of a leader named Utsala ("Lichen"), who disposed them along the head waters between Clingman Dome and Mount Guyot of the Great Smoky range.

Having spent several years in that region myself, and being acquainted with many whites and Indians descended from those who were there at the time of the man-hunt, I can visualize the situation in which the fugitives were placed.

It is a wild country to this day, although lumbermen have recently begun to invade it. Nearly all of it is very rough and rugged. Most of the divide (which forms the State line between North Carolina and Tennessee) is over 5,500 feet above sea-level, and the abutting ridges for several miles each way are but little lower. The sides of the mountains have steep slopes that begin at the very banks of the streams.

There are extensive areas strewn with great fragments of rock, although there is a heavy forest mantle everywhere. Cliffs and precipitous banks are so frequent that the only thoroughfares are a few carefully chosen trails. For several miles east of the Porter Gap the crest of the Smoky divide is almost knife-edged, so that footing is precarious, the rock being covered with slippery moss or by dense, low, iron-like bushes that are very hard for a man to push through. A misstep might send one hurtling and sliding five hundred feet or more into North Carolina on one side or Tennessee on the other, unless some tree-top caught and held him.

On the slopes of the mountains there is a heavy stand of hardwoods and chestnut and hemlock; on the upper reaches there is dense spruce and balsam. Labyrinths of laurel keep many of the watercourses in perpetual gloom. On some slopes and ridges, particularly on the Tennessee side, are great tracts of stunted rhododendron that a man can only flounder over. Dogs cannot go through such a thicket at all.

So far, then, as configuration and natural cover are concerned this region is almost ideal for men hiding out, and it is a refuge for moonshiners, deserters, and outlaws, to this day. But the problem of getting food in such a country is serious, unless the fugitive has clandestine help from outside.

There is little animal life in the upper zones, other than small brook trout, chipmunks, red squirrels, and a few birds. Bears harbor there, but they are wily and almost impossible to find without a pack of dogs. Formerly there were deer, and at that time a small party of hunters might have been able to feed themselves for a week or two on products of the chase. But when a thousand fugitive Indians swarmed up into the roughs of the mountains, all game animals must have fled before them, leaving an empty solitude.

It was summer-time; so there were no nuts nor acorns. Edible roots are seldom to be found in such a highland. There was little sustenance but toads, snakes, insects, berries, and the inner bark of trees. Many of the Indians starved to death. And yet the survivors stayed out, defying every effort of the troops to capture them.

General Scott found himself confronted by a problem similar, on a small scale, to the one that was giving so much trouble to our army operating against the Seminoles in the Everglades of Florida. To dig the Cherokees out of their warrens would require a large force operating simultaneously from both the Tennessee and the Carolina sides, and beating through a country so difficult that the "drive" might last all summer. At this juncture there occurred an incident that gave him an opportunity for compromise.

Among the Indians who had been seized was an old man named Tsali (Cherokee pronunciation of Charley). He was taken with his wife, his brother, his three sons and their families. His wife being unable to travel fast, the soldiers prodded her along with their bayonets. Charley, boiling with rage at this brutality, gave the word to the other men, in Cherokee, to strike down the guard and make a dash for liberty. They sprang upon the unsuspecting soldiers, killed one of them, stampeded the others, and made their escape to the mountains.

Scott sent for the white man Thomas, who was the Indians' most trusted friend, and authorized him to seek out the leader Utsala and propose to him that if he would seize Charley and the others concerned in the "murder," and deliver them to headquarters for punishment, the General would call off the pursuit, secure a respite for the main body of refugees, and use his influence at Washington to get a special dispensation permitting the band to remain unmolested in their native hills.

Thomas accepted the commission. With one or two Indian guides he made his way over secret paths to Utsala's hiding-place. Here he stated his mission, and argued with the chief that if Tsali and his few companions were delivered to justice there was good hope that the Government would make an exception in favor of the band [on] Lufty and allow them to remain in their own country.

Utsala's heart was bitter, for his wife and little son had starved to death on the mountain side. "But he thought of the thousands who were already on their long march into exile, and then he looked round upon his little band of followers. If only they might stay, even though a few must be sacrificed, it was better than that all should die—for they had sworn never to leave their country. He consented, and Thomas returned to report to General Scott."

I have heard various and conflicting tales about the Charley episode, some of them mere legends, evidently colored by prejudice, and others the recollections of very old people who were not actors in the event. On the other hand Mr. Mooney got the story directly from Colonel Thomas himself, and from Wasituna, Charley's youngest son, who alone was spared by General Scott on account of his youth. His relation can be accepted as historic fact.

> "It was known that Charley and his party were hiding in a cave of the Great Smokies, at the head of Deep Creek." (There is no real cave in that region, but there are shelving rocks sufficient to shelter a few men, and that is what is evidently meant.) "But it was not thought likely that he could be taken without bloodshed and a further delay which might prejudice the whole undertaking. Thomas determined to go to him and try to persuade him to come in and surrender.
>
> "Declining Scott's offer of an escort, he went alone to the cave, and, getting between the Indians and their guns as they were sitting around the fire near the entrance, he walked up to Charley and announced his message. The old man listened in silence and then said simply, 'I will come in. I don't want to be hunted down by my own people.'
>
> "By command of General Scott, Charley, his brother, and the two elder sons were shot near the mouth of Tuckaseegee, a detachment of Cherokee prisoners being compelled to do the shooting in order to impress upon the prisoners the fact of their utter helplessness."

A year later (September 12, 1839) the Commissioner of Indian Affairs reported that the Indians scattered throughout the mountains of North Carolina and Tennessee numbered 1,046. They were in a distressing condition, mere landless aliens, staying under respite that might be cancelled at any moment, and kept alive mostly by the white settlers out of pity or in return for labor they performed. If they had been left to their own devices it is more than probable that they would have been gradually gathered up and sent to join their brethren in the West. In fact a commissioner was appointed in the spring of 1840 to enroll them for such removal.

But Colonel Thomas went to Washington, and stayed there continuously for three years, working with all the energy of a devoted friend to induce the Government to let the Eastern Band remain in its old home and to secure for them their fair share of moneys due for reservations and improvements confiscated. And he succeeded.

In 1846 the Eastern Cherokees were admitted to participation in the benefits of the treaty of 1835, and Thomas was authorized at various times to buy back from the whites enough land in western North Carolina to serve as a permanent home for the Band. This he did: but since the State of North Carolina persisted in refusing to recognize Indians as landowners, until 1866, Thomas held the deeds in his own name, as their authorized agent under the Government. The Indian title was finally adjudicated by the United States during the period from 1875 to 1894.

The present legal status of the Eastern Band of Cherokees is indeterminate and anomalous. It has been ruled by the courts that they are citizens of the United States, and again that they are wards of the Government. They are under discipline of a resident Indian agent, but never have been reservation Indians. They are citizens of North Carolina, and at the same time a body corporate and politic. They have a tribal constitution, and are governed in tribal matters by chiefs and councillors elected by themselves.

Their lands were purchased by themselves, or by the Government from funds due them, but they cannot make free contracts nor alienate the lands that they hold in severalty. They pay taxes, except poll tax, perform road service, and are amenable to the local courts, save in land matters. Male Cherokees of voting age who can read and write English are allowed to vote—sometimes, and sometimes not.

There are about 1,800 of these Indians in the Qualla boundary, and about 500 more scattered in other parts of western North Carolina. More than half of them are full-bloods, a much larger percentage than among their kinsmen in Oklahoma.

Nearly all of the men, and many of the women, can read and write their own language. About half of them can use enough English for ordinary intercourse. The Government training school at Cherokee postoffice affords an excellent education to the boys and girls, and, under the present Superintendent, is doing fine work among the adults by demonstrating modern methods of farming and stock raising.

I was surprised and delighted to see the prompt and generous response of the Eastern Cherokees to our Government's calls for subscriptions to liberty bonds and war saving stamps. In proportion to their ability they more than equalled the whites. Their young men went into the war willingly and fought gallantly. Only one slacker was reported in the whole tribe, and he was immediately brought to book by his own people. The Indian children in the Cherokee school are supporting a war orphan in France.

The sacrifice of poor old Tsali and his kinsmen was not made in vain.

eight

SCOUTING

BSA Handbook (1920) in Kephart Library.

Introduction

MAE MILLER CLAXTON

"A Scout chooses as his motto 'Be Prepared,' and he seeks to prepare himself for anything—to rescue a companion, to ford a stream, to gather firewood, to help strangers, to distinguish right from wrong, to serve his fellowmen, his country and his God—always to 'Be Prepared.'"

FRANKLIN K. MATHIEWS, ed., *The Boy Scouts Own Book* (New York: D. Appleton, 1924), 206

As previously noted in the introduction to chapter three on camping and woodcraft, Kephart joined a number of outdoor writers who advocated for the middle and working classes along with the more wealthy leisure class to seek out the "soul-cleansing wilderness" as a respite from growing industrialism and city life.[1] At the turn of the century, several boys' organizations sprang up that echoed similar ideas about the need to spend time in the wilderness and learn necessary camping and outdoor adventure skills. However, these organizations created goals that moved far beyond an appreciation for nature or respite from city life. They believed that boys who spent time in the wilderness achieved skills that cultivated leadership, good citizenship, and an ability to succeed in a rapidly changing society.

Many of these early organizations were associated with both the church and the military. In *Sons of the Empire: The Frontier and the Boy Scout Movement, 1890–1918*, Robert H. MacDonald writes that William Smith began the Boys' Brigade in Scotland in 1883. It was a church-sponsored organization that advocated for a kind of "Christian manliness," combining religious teaching with military drill. By 1890, the group had over eleven thousand members in Scotland and five thousand in England and Wales.[2] During the same time period, in the United States, clubs formed such as the Young Men's Christian Association (YMCA), the Boys' Club, and the Big Brother Movement. These groups sought to create good American citizens out of working class immigrant children, mostly in urban areas.[3] Meanwhile, Ernest Thompson Seton began his Woodcraft Indians organization in 1902 based on romanticized notions of

Native Americans and the study of woodcraft.[4] Seton wrote a series of articles for the *Ladies Home Journal* in 1902 and then a handbook.[5] In 1905, Daniel Beard founded the Sons of Daniel Boone, which idealized the American pioneer.[6] He developed his ideas from his late nineteenth-century *American Boy's Handy Book* and from 1905 writing for *Recreation Magazine.*[7]

The Boy Scout movement, begun in England in 1907, the year after Kephart published *Camping and Woodcraft*, soon surpassed all of these organizations in popularity. It advocated for the virtues of the wilderness experience and stressed the need to train boys to survive outdoors. It was also aimed at the middle and working class in addition to wealthier boys.[8] During the 1920s, Kephart became associated with the Boy Scouts of America (BSA), publishing at least five articles for *Boys' Life*, the Boy Scout magazine, and likely submitting another. He was also elected as a member of the National Council of the Boy Scouts. Even without considering the best-selling BSA handbook, an entire body of literature grew up around scouting during this time. Examining Kephart's BSA articles from *Boys' Life* in context with his other writing provides an important perspective on the outdoor movement in general and Kephart's contributions to this growing body of scouting literature in the early decades of the twentieth century.

About the same time that Horace Kephart moved to western North Carolina in 1904, the scouting movement was taking off in Britain and the United States following paths already laid out by the previously mentioned boys' organizations. Robert Baden-Powell, the founder of the Boy Scouts, went to India in 1876 as an army officer and worked in scouting, map-making, and reconnaissance. He soon began training other soldiers. He developed a specific strategy that emphasized small units or patrols working together under one leader with recognition for those who succeeded. Later, he helped defend the town of Mafeking in Africa using the skills he had honed earlier. To his surprise upon his return home to England, a small handbook written for his solders, "Aids to Scouting," was being used by youth leaders and teachers all over the country to teach observation and woodcraft. After the success of the famous weeklong camp at Brownsea Island in August 1907, Baden-Powell released *Scouting for Boys* in six parts in 1908.[9] In 1910, Baden-Powell visited the United States, where the Boy Scouts of America had already started. At a speech at the Waldorf Astoria Hotel in New York City, Baden-Powell acknowledged Seton and Beard as "uncles" of the BSA. But BSA membership soon eclipsed these earlier youth organizations.[10] Membership topped 100,000 in 1913 and 481,084 boys and 86,737 men in 1918. Membership topped 1,000,000 in 1919 and reached 4,277,833 by 1930. By 1927, there was one active Scout for every eight boys.[11]

The pervasiveness of Scouting is evident in Benton MacKaye's 1921 treatise "An Appalachian Trail: A Project in Regional Planning." In this document, he describes values he associates with scouting and integrates them with his new idea for a connected trail from New England to Georgia. MacKaye emphasizes the problem of a civilized society that renders its citizens "potentially helpless as canaries in a cage."[12] "The ability to cope with nature directly," he maintains, "unshielded by the weakening wall of civilization—is one of the admitted needs of modern times."[13] MacKaye explains that the Scouting movement is an attempt to address this need. It is good to learn to sleep and cook in the open, but MacKaye believes that Scouting can achieve even greater goals—encouraging the cooperation and community of the Scouting camp rather than "every-day worldly commercial life," an alternative to the competitiveness of an increasingly commercial and industrial society.[14] He writes that in the camp community, "Cooperation replaces antagonism, trust replaces suspicion, emulation replaces competition."[15] Along with the establishment of the Appalachian trail, which would encourage health, volunteerism, and cooperation, MacKaye states that "the care of the country side," which Scouting also encourages, is an important goal for the entire country.[16]

Like MacKaye, who chose writing as a way to make his case for this important project, the Boy Scouts, too, used various forms of writing as an important tool for disseminating their values. The first key piece of writing was the BSA handbook written in 1910 entitled *The Official Handbook for Boys: A Handbook of Woodcraft, Scouting, and Life-craft*, co-written by Ernest Thompson Seton and Baden-Powell.[17] By 1920, the handbook was 492 pages, a manual covering information about the Boy Scout oath, merit badges, and other "scoutcraft" in the first chapter but also including chapters on chivalry and patriotism and citizenship. It also contains chapters covering woodcraft; wildlife and conservation; campcraft; signs, symbols and signaling (written by Daniel Carter Beard); health and endurance; and prevention of accidents, first aid, and lifesaving. At the end, an appendix entitled "Every Boy's Library" contains a list of recommended books with the admonishment to "Please order through our Book Department." The list includes fiction by authors such as James Fenimore Cooper, Jack London, Jules Verne, and three books by Robert Louis Stevenson.[18] In "The Boy Scouts of America and Literature for Youth: 1910–1935," Corry Kanzenberg, Curator of Collections and Exhibitions at the National Scouting Museum, notes that book publishers soon began to profit from the popularity of Scouting. He writes that Scouts "were featured in over one hundred full-length novels published between 1911 and 1914."[19] Many of these books were published without any kind of official endorsement from the BSA. Often, they were "nickle-novels" featuring Scouts in stories "of adventure, heroism, and bravery."[20] Many of the leaders of the BSA organization did not approve of how Scouting was portrayed in these books. Thus, they hired a Baptist minister, Franklin K. Mathiews, to oversee the newly formed Library Department. A Library Commission was formed to select books to comprise the *Every Boy's Library*. The books were issued at a cost of twenty-five cents with an introduction by the Chief Scout Executive James E. West. Later, the commission hired authors to produce new fiction serials.[21] Kanzenberg concludes that millions of both authorized and unauthorized books on scouting circulated from 1910 to 1935. He writes, "The influence of the Boy Scouts of America on children's literature cannot be underestimated during the early years of the twentieth century. From the phenomenal success of the Boy Scout handbook to the fictional literature produced and endorsed by a focused and determined Library Department, the sheer volume of their output in this realm is impressive."[22]

Kephart's own collection of books, many of them archived in Special Collections at Western Carolina University, contains several books related to Scouting, including one entitled *Scout Notebook* by O. N. Hurd. The list contains books such as the *Boy Scout's Hike Book* (1915) and other books on the outdoors for boys in general, including two by Daniel Beard.[23] In *Camping for Boys* (1913), by H. W. Gibson, the writer explains that he has run a boys' camp for twenty-three years and notes, "If this book will help some man to be of greater service to boys, as well as to inspire boys to live the noble life which God's great out-of-doors teaches, the author will feel amply repaid for his labor."[24] He also mentions Kephart in a list of "apostles of outdoor life."[25] Notably, two of the books in the collection deal with women and the outdoors: *Woodcraft for Women* (1916) and *Scouting for Girls* (1920), published by the Girl Scouts.[26] *Woodcraft for Women* mentions Kephart's *Camp Cookery* as "an inspiring and exhaustive treatise which opens up all sorts of possibilities."[27] In the chapter "Camping for Girl Scouts" in *Scouting for Girls*, a footnote states that the passages in this section are from Kephart's *Camping and Woodcraft*.[28] Both books contain large sections gleaned from Kephart's writing. The presence of this many books for young people in Kephart's library demonstrates the popularity and ubiquity of outdoor literature for the younger generation.

Kephart published his works in *Boys' Life*, a publication which began in 1911 and still continues. A series of two articles appeared in April and May 1914 entitled "How to Cook in the Open: An Expert's Advice Which Will Help Scouts to Pass the Cooking Merit Badge Test." The introduction to the second article states that "Mr. Kephart knows Cooking from A to Z" and mentions his *Camp Cookery* book published by the Outing Company. A quote from the book is included: "The less a man carries in his pack, the more he must carry in his head. A camper cannot go by recipe alone. It is best for him to carry general principles in his head, and recipes in his pocket. The simpler the outfit, the more skill it takes to manage it, and the more pleasure one gets in his achievements."[29]

The April article discusses how to build a proper cooking fire and prepare camp stew and corn batter cakes. It also contains a list of the amounts needed for "Four Boys, Three Meals."[30] The May article contains more detailed advice on what foods to bring and how to prepare them properly. One section, for example, covers eggs—boiled, fried, and scrambled. Another section discusses how to make "Army" bread.[31]

The April 1923 issue features a picture of Kephart in front of his tent with the caption reading "This is Horace Kephart, the famous camper, in a camp of his own" and states that *Boys' Life* has "secured the service of Horace Kephart, nationally famous as a camper, and the author of campcraft books that are classics, to write a series of two articles on Camping for the Camping issues."[32] The first article is entitled "Hiking Rations—What to Take" and is illustrated with a picture of a brawny man carrying a large sack through tall trees. This article mainly discusses the best kinds of foods to carry along on a three-day camping trip along with necessary equipment.[33] The June 1923 article contains a picture of Scouts cooking over an open fire and details food preparation from boiling water for tea and cocoa to cooking meat stew, flapjacks, and creamed salmon.[34]

Interestingly, the April and May 1914 articles are reprinted, with some minor changes, in a collection entitled *The Boy Scouts Own Book* edited by Franklin K. Mathiews, Chief Scout Librarian, BSA. In this book, Kephart's cooking articles accompany a wide range of literature ranging from poetry, "Top o' the Morning!," to "How to Clean and Repair Your Bicycle," "Winter Hiking," stories, games, and an article entitled "What's a Boy Scout?" The book is dedicated to "The Millions of Boys *Waiting* to Become Boy Scouts." The book reflects the organization of *Boys' Life*, which is also a collection of nonfiction, stories, photographs, illustrations, poetry, how-to articles, and many other genres of writing targeted to the audience.[35]

Kephart contributed another article to *Boys' Life* in August 1928, three years before his death in 1931. Entitled "The Indian Blowgun," the article begins with an account of the narrator, presumably Kephart, having a conversation with a journalist from the Raleigh *News and Observer* who had come up to visit the "Indian fair" at Cherokee. As part of this account, readers learn how blowguns are made and how they work. The last part of the article details a blowgun match. Kephart lists the names of the contestants and their success or non-success in hitting the target. He notes that this was an attempt to resurrect an ancient sport and that in the past the blowgun would

BOY SCOUTS OF AMERICA

ORIGINALLY INCORPORATED FEBRUARY 8, 1910

GRANTED FEDERAL CHARTER BY CONGRESS, JUNE 15, 1916

HERBERT HOOVER, HONORARY PRESIDENT
WILLIAM H. TAFT, HONORARY VICE PRESIDENT
CALVIN COOLIDGE, HONORARY VICE PRESIDENT
COLIN H. LIVINGSTONE, HONORARY VICE PRESIDENT
DANIEL CARTER BEARD, HONORARY VICE PRESIDENT
WILLIAM G. McADOO, HONORARY VICE PRESIDENT
WALTER W. HEAD, PRESIDENT, CHICAGO, ILL.
MORTIMER L. SCHIFF, VICE PRESIDENT, OYSTER BAY, N. Y.
MILTON A. McRAE, VICE PRESIDENT, DETROIT, MICHIGAN
CHARLES C. MOORE, VICE PRESIDENT, SAN FRANCISCO, CAL.
BOLTON SMITH, VICE PRESIDENT, MEMPHIS, TENN.
JOHN SHERMAN HOYT, VICE PRESIDENT, NEW YORK
DANIEL CARTER BEARD, NAT'L SCOUT COMMISSIONER, SUFFERN, N.Y.
MORTIMER L. SCHIFF, INTERNATIONAL COMMISSIONER

GEORGE D. PRATT, TREASURER

NATIONAL COUNCIL OFFICES
PARK AVENUE BUILDING
2 PARK AVENUE
THIRTY-SECOND TO THIRTY-THIRD STREETS
NEW YORK CITY
TELEPHONE LEXINGTON 3200

MEMBERS OF THE EXECUTIVE BOARD

DANIEL CARTER BEARD	WILLIAM D. MURRAY
NEWCOMB CARLTON	JOHN M. PHILLIPS
BARRON COLLIER	GEORGE D. PORTER
CHARLES E. COTTING	GEORGE D. PRATT
ALFRED W. DATER	FRANK PRESBREY
JOHN H. FINLEY	G. BARRETT RICH
LEWIS GAWTRY	VICTOR F. RIDDER
HOWARD F. GILLETTE	THEODORE ROOSEVELT
WALTER W. HEAD	MORTIMER L. SCHIFF
CLARENCE H. HOWARD	BOLTON SMITH
JOHN SHERMAN HOYT	ROBERT P. SNIFFEN
JEREMIAH W. JENKS	CHARLES L. SOMMERS
COLIN H. LIVINGSTONE	DANIEL A. TOBIN
MILTON A. McRAE	JOHN P. WALLACE
CHARLES C. MOORE	NELL R. WILKINSON

JAMES E. WEST, CHIEF SCOUT EXECUTIVE

May 15, 1929.

Mr. H. Kephart,
Bryson City,
N. C.

Dear Mr. Kephart:

It is a source of special pleasure to me to inform you that at the meeting of the National Council just concluded you were unanimously re-elected as a member of the National Council. Because of the actions taken, it was the most important meeting in the whole history of Scouting. A special communication has already been sent to you transmitting printed matter and information regarding one of the important matters acted upon.

Under separate cover we have mailed you a copy of the Annual Report and invite special attention to my summary report of the activities of the whole Organization for the year. Please note that in the year 1928 there were 1,183,105 Scouts and Scout Officials registered as members. Please feel free to ask questions, or make suggestions, or call upon us for conference at any time.

Rejoicing in the progress that is being made through the Scout Program in our efforts to contribute to America's greatest need, character development and citizenship training, I am,

Sincerely and cordially yours,
BOY SCOUTS OF AMERICA
James E. West
Chief Scout Executive.

JEW/MVC

"BE PREPARED"

ALL COMMUNICATIONS SHOULD BE ADDRESSED TO THE BOY SCOUTS OF AMERICA, 2 PARK AVENUE, NEW YORK CITY.

"DO A GOOD TURN DAILY"

Boy Scout letter informing Kephart of his re-election as a member of the National Council.

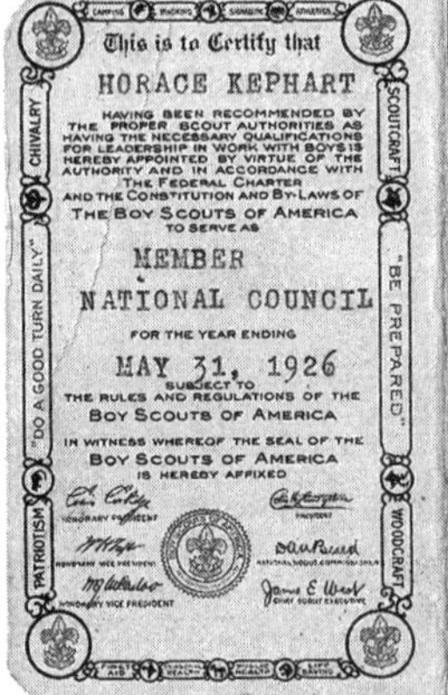

This is to Certify that
HORACE KEPHART
HAVING BEEN RECOMMENDED BY THE PROPER SCOUT AUTHORITIES AS HAVING THE NECESSARY QUALIFICATIONS FOR LEADERSHIP IN WORK WITH BOYS IS HEREBY APPOINTED BY VIRTUE OF THE AUTHORITY AND IN ACCORDANCE WITH THE FEDERAL CHARTER AND THE CONSTITUTION AND BY-LAWS OF THE BOY SCOUTS OF AMERICA TO SERVE AS
MEMBER
NATIONAL COUNCIL
FOR THE YEAR ENDING
MAY 31, 1926
SUBJECT TO THE RULES AND REGULATIONS OF THE BOY SCOUTS OF AMERICA
IN WITNESS WHEREOF THE SEAL OF THE BOY SCOUTS OF AMERICA IS HEREBY AFFIXED

Member National Council BSA card May 31, 1926.

not have been "just a toy to play with but a weapon to put meat in the empty pot."[36] Kephart also discusses how blowguns are used by other indigenous groups and ends with a description of the Cherokee stickball game. He notes that the Eastern Band of Cherokees is composed of some 2,500 descendants of Cherokee people who remained in the Smoky Mountains: "The refugees in the Smoky Mountains were so hard to dislodge that they were finally allowed to return to their home, buy back their own lands with money due them from the United States, and there in the beautiful valley of the Okona Luftee we now find their descendants, more than half of them full-bloods, holding their land by tribal ownership in the ancient way, supporting themselves by their own labor, but schooled and supervised by the federal Government. Their land adjoins the high ranges and primitive forests that are now being acquired for the Smoky Mountain National Park."[37] In contrast to his previous *Boys' Life* articles, which are strictly informational, in "The Indian Blowgun" Kephart tells a story but also manages to convey information in a style that is engaging and approachable.

Special Collections possesses one other Kephart manuscript possibly submitted to *Boys' Life* but with no record of publication. The envelope attached to the manuscript is postmarked March 10, 1928. This typewritten article, entitled "Mountaineering in the Appalachians," contains advice about appropriate clothing and equipment for mountain climbing, animals a troop might encounter, and medical intervention for blisters, poison ivy, and snake bite. The article is a very practical, how-to piece of writing, but Kephart does suggest that the group should spend "at least one night in the open. Sunset and sunrise, viewed from the mountaintop, are the chief rewards of the trip, never to be forgotten."[38] He also warns them about maintaining a strict time schedule since the southern mountain trails are not always well marked and clouds may descend at any time. No stranger, Kephart states, should venture into this "uninhabited wilderness" without a native guide.[39]

Kephart's writing for the Boy Scouts is important for several reasons. First, he clearly was seen as an expert in the field and was thus sought after by the most popular youth organization in the country to write for its publications. In addition, his election to the National Council shows his support of the values of Scouting. His card as a member of the National Council for 1926 has pictures of Boy Scouts in church, cooking over an open fire, and "doing a good turn" by carrying the luggage of an elderly woman. The other side reads "Be Prepared" and states, "Boy scout leaders are producing for the nation its greatest need, men of character trained for citizenship. 'Do a Good Turn Daily.'"

When Kephart died in a car accident in 1931, Boy Scouts from the Bryson City troop were in attendance at the funeral. According to Ken Wise, librarian in Special

Collections at the University of Tennessee at Knoxville, the Scouts hauled in a millstone from nearby Elliot Cove Branch and placed it at Bryson Place on Deep Creek where Kephart often camped in the summers. On the stone is a brass plaque bearing the inscription: "On this spot Horace Kephart, Dean of American Campers and one of the principal founders of the Great Smoky Mountains National Park pitched his last permanent camp. Erected May 30, 1931 by Horace Kephart Troop, Boy Scouts of America, Bryson City, North Carolina."

How to Cook in the Open

AN EXPERT'S ADVICE WHICH WILL HELP SCOUTS TO PASS THE COOKING MERIT BADGE TEST

All Scouts know Horace Kephart. He is a top-notch out-of-doors man. His articles on life in the woods have been appearing in high-class magazines for years, and "The Book of Camping and Woodcraft," which he wrote and which was published by the Outing Company, is the pocket companion of pretty nearly everyone who likes to live in the open.

The cooking article printed in this issue was specially prepared by Mr. Kephart to help Boy Scouts in their camp life and in obtaining the Merit Badge in Cooking. Another article by him, giving more recipes, will appear in the May Boys' Life.

It is not expected that the processes of baking, roasting, stewing or protracted boiling will be undertaken on a marching trip. Bread should be carried from home. If flapjacks are wanted, for variety and for the fun of "flipping" them, it is best to use the corn batter which will be described later. Plain flapjacks of wheat flour (without eggs or milk) are indigestible and unpalatable.

The main thing, in camp life, is to learn to prepare a few simple but wholesome and sustaining dishes, and to cook them *right*.

A boy's stomach is one of his most precious possessions. Nothing else in his body will do more to make or mar his success in life. Therefore, it should have good treatment. When you are marching or camping is the very time that you need good food properly cooked.

Do not eat canned meats. At the best they are unappetizing, and at the worst they are dangerous. Canned fish, such as salmon and sardines, are not quite so unwholesome, but they afford very little nourishment for their weight and bulk. Choose food that is not bulky, not heavy, but that will taste good and "stick to the ribs."

From *Boys' Life*, April 1914

Beware of dishes that are sodden with grease or soggy with half-baked flour. In hot weather, carry some lemons.

THE COOKING FIRE

Half of the art of cooking is in making a proper fire. For a quick meal, when you have only to boil coffee and fry something, a large fire is not wanted.

Drive a forked green stick in the ground, lay a longer green stick across it, slanting downward to the ground, and weight the lower end of this dingle stick with a rock, or peg it down with an inverted crotch. The slanting stick should have the stub of a twig left at upper end to hold pot bail in place (or you can notch it), and should be set at such angle that the pot swings a foot or so clear of the ground.

Then gather a small armful of sound, dry twigs from the thickness of a lead pencil to that of your thumb. Take no twig that lies flat on the ground, for such are generally damp or rotten. Choose hardwood (oak, hickory, maple, etc.), if there is any, for it lasts well and makes good embers. Soft woods burn quickly to dead ashes.

Select three of your best sticks for kindling. Shave each of them almost through, except at top and bottom, leaving the frills attached. Stick these in the ground, under the hanging pot, in tripod form, with curls down. Around them build a conical wigwam of the other sticks, standing each on end and slanting to a common center. Leave free air spaces between the twigs. Fire requires plenty of air, and it burns best when it has something to climb on. Now touch off the shaved kindling, and in a moment you will have a small blast furnace under your pot of water, which will get up steam in a jiffy.

Then get some flat rocks, or two sticks of wood about five or six inches thick, to support the frying pan. The firewood will all drop to embers soon after the pot boils. Toss out the smoking butts, leaving only clear, glowing coals. Put your rocks or bedsticks on either side, parallel and level. Set the pan on them, and fry away. So, in fifteen or twenty minutes from the time you drove your stake, the meal will be cooked.

When going into camp, start a large fire the first thing, and set kettles of water over it. Then you will have coals and boiling water ready when you begin cooking, and the rest is easy.

For baking, roasting, or stewing, a good bed of hard coals is needed. To get them in a hurry, split your wood into small sticks. Remember, it takes hardwood to make good coals.

Stewing cannot be hurried. It is essential that the water should not boil hard, but merely simmer, after the meat and vegetables are put in. The time varies according to materials used; just cook until tender. Do not use any fat meat.

The simplest stew, but not the best, is made by gently simmering pieces of meat, and, a half hour before meat is done, add potatoes, onions, rice and seasoning.

A better way is to cut some lean meat or game into small pieces, brown it with some hot fat in a frying pan, shuffling the pan so as to sear the surface of the meat, but not burn it. Then drop the meat into a kettle of boiling water and set kettle to one side or hang high over fire, so as to simmer. Add sliced onion, other vegetables as above, salt, pepper, and a little sugar. This stew may be thickened by rubbing up a little flour in the grease left in frying pan, add about a pint of water, stir, and let the mixture boil a little; then stir this thickening into the stew a short time before it is ready.

Almost any meat, vegetables, and cereals can be used in a stew.

Corn Batter Cakes

Mix up, before starting on the trip:

- 1 pint yellow corn meal
- ½ pint flour
- 2 heaped teaspoonfuls baking powder
- 2 heaped teaspoonfuls sugar
- 2 level teaspoonfuls salt.

These should be sifted thoroughly together and put up in a moisture-proof bag of cloth or parchment paper. When ready to bake, take half of this quantity, add cold water, a little at a time, stirring briskly, until a rather thick batter results, with no lumps.

Set frying pan level over thin bed of coals, get it quite hot, and grease it with a piece of bacon in the split end of a stick. The pan must be hot enough to make the batter sizzle as it touches. Pour in batter.

When the cake is full of bubbles and the edges have stiffened, shuffle the pan to make sure that the cake is free below and stiff enough to flip.

Then hold pan slanting in front of and away from you, go through preliminary motion of flapping once or twice, to get the swing; then flip boldly, so that the cake will *turn a somersault* in the air, and catch it upside down. Beginners generally do not toss high enough. Grease pan anew and stir batter every time before pouring.

This recipe is improved by using milk instead of water, and adding two eggs, if these can be procured.

Hiking Rations

For Four Boys, Three Meals.

Four pounds breadstuffs, in bag or waxed paper.

One pound bacon, sliced thin, without rind, in waxed paper.

One pound cheese, in waxed paper.

One dozen eggs, in carton.

One can evaporated milk, not sweetened.

One-half pound butter, in tin.

One-half pound sugar, in bag.

One-half pound dried fruit, in waxed paper; or lemons.

One-quarter pound ground coffee, in bag.

One can jam.

One-sixth pound salt, in joint of bamboo, corked.

Pepper, in waxed paper.

Utensils

Frying pan, large, with folding handle.

Stew pan.

Cover to fit both of above.

Coffee pot, small, or covered tin pail.

Canvas water bucket, folding.

Four each of [cups,] knives, forks, spoons, plates.

Large spoon.

Dish cloths, soap, matches, candle.

How to Cook in the Open

AN EXPERT'S ADVICE WHICH WILL HELP SCOUTS TO PASS THE COOKING MERIT BADGE TEST

This is the second of a series of articles on Cooking which Mr. Kephart has prepared for Boy Scouts.

Mr. Kephart knows Cooking from A to Z. In his book entitled "Camp Cookery," published by the Outing Company, he tells far more than we can give in this series. One thing from that book we want you to read and remember—it is this:

"The less a man carries in his pack, the more he must carry in his head. A camper cannot go by recipe alone. It is best for him to carry general principles in his head, and recipes in his pocket. The simpler the outfit, the more skill it takes to manage it, and the more pleasure one gets in his achievements."

Never fry over a flame; the fat will easily catch fire.

Frying requires little heat. If your fire is too big, take a stick and rake some coals off to one side to fry over. Get your pan quite hot before you grease it. Then put in just enough grease to keep the fish or beef or flapjack from sticking to the pan. Too much grease, or grease that is not hot enough, makes the stuff sodden and indigestible.

FRIED BACON

Slice quite thin. Remove the rind, or cut through it in two places to prevent curling in the pan. Put pan half full of water on fire; when water is warm, drop the bacon in and stir around until water begins to simmer. Then throw out the water, fry bacon and turn often. Remove slices just before they would turn brown. They will get crisp as they cool.

From *Boys' Life*, May 1914

FRIED FISH

If the fish is too large for the pan, cut steaks from it, slicing down on either side of the backbone (in this case the fish need not be cleaned). Small fish, to be fried whole, should have the backbone severed to prevent curling.

Rub them with cornmeal or flour before putting in the pan—this browns them and prevents them from absorbing grease. Fry to a golden brown, sprinkling lightly with pepper and salt just as the color turns. If fish are fried in butter, do not salt them. Fish should be wiped dry before frying and the grease should be quite hot.

FROG LEGS

These are best if, after skinning, they are soaked for an hour in cold water with a little vinegar added; or put them for two minutes into scalding water that has vinegar or lemon juice in it. Then drain, wipe dry, roll in flour or bread crumbs seasoned with salt and pepper, and fry rather slowly, preferably in butter.

BROILING

Fresh meat of any kind that is tender enough is better broiled than fried.

This may be done on a forked stick or by inserting the slice in the cleft of a split stick. Beef or venison should be cut at least an inch thick.

Have a clear, flaming fire, and rake a good bed of hard coals from it to one side. Sear the outside of the meat first by thrusting it for a moment right into the flame and turning. This seals up the juices. Then broil over the coals or in front of them, catching drippings in a pan underneath. Do not season until done.

Bacon will be broiled in three or four minutes; a steak one inch thick in five minutes, one and a half inches thick in ten minutes.

Serve steak on hot plates with drippings and butter.

To broil in a frying pan, clean the pan thoroughly and get it almost red hot so as to seal the pores of the meat instantly and keep the juices in. Grease pan very lightly, put meat in and cover; turn often, without jabbing the fork.

BOILED RICE

To cook rice so that each grain will be plump, dry and separate, instead of making a mushy and tasteless mess, first get a quart of water to boiling furiously. Meantime wash a half-cupful of rice in cold, *salted* water, and drain. When the unsalted water in the pot is boiling as hard as it can, add the rice a little at a time so as not to check the flurry.

Keep the pot boiling hard for twenty minutes, but do not stir. This keeps the grains dancing around instead of gluing to each other.

Then strain off the water, hang the pot high over the fire, uncovered, and let it swell and dry for half an hour, if you have time. Remember that rice swells enormously in cooking.

Wild rice is better than the ordinary kind.

RICE PUDDING

Mix a pint of cold, boiled rice (see recipe for boiling rice) with a quart of milk. If you have a couple of eggs, mix them up with the milk and then stir in the rice. Some seeded raisins may also be mixed in. Sprinkle nutmeg or cinnamon over the top. Place in a well-greased pan and bake until done.

If you have no milk, boil the rice in salted water, add cinnamon, butter and sugar and cook fifteen minutes longer.

FRIED POTATOES

If raw, peel and slice into pieces half an inch thick. Drop into cold water until frying pan is ready. Put enough grease in the pan to completely immerse the potatoes and get it very hot. Dry the slices of potatoes in a cloth and drop one at a time into the grease, so as not to check the heat.

When the potatoes turn a faint brown, remove them, salt them, turn out the grease and brown a little in the dry pan. The outsides then will be crisp and the insides deliciously mealy.

Boiled potatoes that have been left over can be sliced one-quarter inch thick and fried in a little grease.

BAKED POTATOES

Scoop out a depression in the ashes and embers of the camp fire to a depth of three or four inches. Lay the potatoes in it, side by side. Cover with hot ashes, topped with a heap of glowing coals. In about forty minutes begin to test them with a sliver; when this will pass readily through them they are done.

ROASTING EARS

Remove the outer husk, stripping off the skin, and twist end of husks tightly down over the broken end. Then bake for about an hour in the ashes and embers, as directed for baked potatoes.

If in a hurry, cut off but [*sic*] of ear until pith is exposed, ream it out a little, impale the cob lengthwise on the end of a hardwood stick and turn over the coals until grains are browned.

EGGS

BOILED—Bring water to a hard boil. Then leave eggs in the water two and a half minutes, if small, or three minutes if large. When utensils are limited, it is all right to boil eggs in the same water you are to make coffee in, provided you wash them first. If you have no watch, put the eggs in cold water, set over fire and remove as soon as the water begins to boil. If wanted hard, boil at least twenty minutes.

FRIED—Be careful not to break the yolks. Run knife under eggs as soon as they go into the pan to prevent sticking, and separate each from the other. Use only enough grease to make the pan "slick." Do not fry more than two or three minutes.

SCRAMBLED—The easiest way, and as good as any, is to put in a well-greased pan as many eggs as it will hold separately, each yolk being whole. When the whites have begun to set, stir from bottom of pan until done (buttery, not leathery). Add a piece of butter, pepper and salt. Turn out on a warm plate.

"ARMY" BREAD

I call this "army" bread because I learned the process from a soldier; because it keeps fresh longer than yeast bread, does not dry up in a week nor mould, is more wholesome than biscuit and is the only baking-powder bread I know of that is good to eat cold—in fact, it is best that way. It is easier to make than biscuit dough, since there is no grease to rub in, but it takes longer to bake.

One quart flour.
One teaspoonful salt.
One tablespoonful sugar.
Two heaped teaspoonfuls baking powder.

The amount of baking powder will vary with quality (the best grade is here assumed—cheap powder requires about twice this amount). Mix the dry ingredients thoroughly. Then stir in enough cold water (about 1½ pints) to make a thick batter that will pour out level. Mix rapidly with spoon until smooth and pour at once into bake pan. Bake about forty-five minutes or until no dough adheres to a sliver. Above quantity makes a 1½ pound loaf (say 9 × 5 × 3 inches).

Any dough that is made with baking powder will get "sad" if kneaded or if left standing around before baking. Get it into the hot pan as soon as you can after mixing.

OATMEAL PORRIDGE

Rolled oats cook much quicker than the old-fashioned oatmeal; the latter is not fit to eat until it has been boiled an hour or more.

To a quart of boiling water add half a teaspoonful of salt, stir in gradually half a pint of rolled oats and boil until it thickens, and then ten minutes more, stirring constantly, unless you have a double boiler.

TEA

Never allow tea to boil; that would make a liquor that would tan skin into leather.

Put one heaped teaspoonful of tea in a pot, pour a pint of boiling water over it, let it steep away from the fire for just four minutes, settle with cold water and pour the clear fluid off into a separate vessel.

If you leave it a couple of minutes longer on the grounds your tea will be ruined.

COFFEE

Put one heaped teaspoonful of freshly ground coffee in a [p]int of cold water, stir it down and hang over fire. Watch it, and when water begins to bubble, remove pot from fire and let it stand five minutes. Settle grounds with a tablespoonful of cold water poured in.

CHOCOLATE AND COCOA

Follow directions on can. There is an "instantaneous cocoa" that only needs to be brought to a boil and requires no milk, as there is milk powder incorporated with it; but it is rather expensive.

Cover of *Boys' Life* May 1923.

Horace Kephart's Camping Articles

BOYS' LIFE has secured the service of Horace Kephart, nationally famous as a camper, and the author of campcraft books that are classics, to write a series of two articles on Camping for the Camping issues. There are few other men in the country who have made the reputation that Kephart has made as a writer of camp information and the articles he has contributed to this magazine are fine examples of his work. No scout who wants to know how to live in the woods can afford to miss reading "Hiking Rations—What to Take" and "Hiking Rations—How to Cook Them." They will appear in the Camping issues of BOYS' LIFE along with a lot of good camping stories and articles.

There will be articles on canoeing, hiking and biking. There will be special features on the camera in camp, and radio in camp. There will be camping fiction stories too by some of the best writers of boys' stories in the country and every one of the three camping issues is going to be worth buying, reading and keeping for reference. Don't miss one of them.

From *Boys' Life*, April 1923

Hiking Rations—What to Take

Suppose we are going for a hike in the big woods or waste lands, where there are no stores or farms to get supplies from. Everything must be packed along: shelter, bedding, food and all. We are to spend three days and two nights in the open. The materials for seven meals must be taken with us, and the utensils to cook them in.

Hard work in the open air (and that's what hiking is) can not be done on mere picnic lunches. It calls for three hot and hearty meals a day.

Everybody who has ever done any marching despises a big pack and a heavy one. The motto is "Go light." Cut the equipment down to what you really must have to keep up strength and spirits: plenty of good food and sound sleep o' nights. *It does not pay to go too light on those things.*

Soldiers operating far from camp sometimes have to subsist on hardtack and coffee, "bully-beef" and "goldfish." But they don't do it for fun. They have been known to rob henroosts at such times.

Sailors of the olden time went for months and months, all over the seven seas, on a diet of lobscouse and slumgullion, salt horse, dunderfunk and skilligalee. (You don't know what those words mean, Johnny Jones! My goodness! where were you fotch up? Go to the landlubbers' lexicon, thou numbskull! Get thee to the unabridged dictionary, and dig 'em out.)

Well, those hardy old salts sometimes would mutiny; and nearly every case of mutiny I ever read of was due to bad grub.

We don't want to encourage chicken stealing or mutiny among the Boy Scouts. So let's feed 'em well.

If we were buying supplies at a big city outfitting shop we might find there some wonderful patent grub that had been simmered down, desiccated, mummified and shrunk till the original twenty-pound cubic foot had been reduced to perhaps a one-pound chunk the size of your fist. But let us not worry over what we miss by that. I have sad memories of tabloid dinners. Some of them were tasteless, and others I can taste yet.

From *Boys' Life,* May 1923

There are a few, very few, concentrated foods that are good—that is, good for special service. Admiral Peary made his Arctic expeditions on a daily ration of one pound of pemmican, one pound of hardtack, four ounces of condensed milk and half an ounce of compressed tea: about two and a quarter pounds of food per man per day, besides the weight of the tin containers. An admirable ration for explorers in the Arctics; but who could use it down here in summer? And the pemmican I once bought from a New York outfitter cost me $1.40 a pound, pre-war price.

Well, let's see what we can get right here at Smith's corner grocery.

First, the staff of life: bread. The baker's loaf is bulky. Pound for pound, it does not go as far as hardtack or flour. But it is a mighty good thing to have for the first few meals. We can find room for one loaf per man. Some self-raising flour for flapjacks, and some rice, will serve for the rest of the trip. I am omitting other cereals from this list merely because we can't try everything in a three days' trip, and I want to show how to use some good foods that have no directions for cooking printed on the package.

Second, butter. It is *the* concentrated food. Bread and butter make a good snack by themselves; but leave out the butter and you have—dark cell diet. Pack the butter in pry-up tins; then if it melts, let it melt. Cool it in the spring, when you reach camp, or in running water, or in a hole in the ground.

Third, jam. It is another form of concentrated nourishment that is wholesome and makes the ration go. Mother may have misgivings about the mess that Son will produce in his frying pan, but Mother is sure that Son knows exactly what to do with bread and butter and jam. Pack the jam, too, in pry-up tins. These tins, by the way, are hard to find on sale in small quantities. The Department of Scout Supplies ought to keep them in stock, of various sizes, as many dealers do, and a few of them should be included with every cooking kit.

Fourth, cured meat. We can't carry fresh meat on a hike. We might take along some roast chicken, roast beef or boiled ham, if preparation had been made in advance; but here we are supposed to be off on the spur of the moment, with just what Smith's grocery can supply. Wrap and tie up your bacon and ham in waxed paper, such as creamery butter is wrapped in. Do the same with dried beef; for a small tumbler of sliced beef is 3½ ounces meat and 6½ ounces glass—and you can't eat the glass. Corned beef and salmon will stay in their cans.

Fifth, evaporated milk. Milk is a very concentrated and necessary food item, useful in cooking, as well as for cocoa and by itself. Get the smallest cans, so there will be no partly emptied ones to mess with on the march (though you can close the two punched holes with adhesive plaster, after wiping the surface perfectly dry).

Sixth, cheese. Enough for one meal, for variety's sake. Wrap in waxed paper.

Seventh, vegetables. You could save a lot of weight here by using dehydrated vegetables. But Smith does not keep them. Well, let's have some real potatoes and onions: they pay for their freight, taste better than dehydrated ones, and can be used in lots of ways that the others can not—fried, baked in the ashes, and so on.

Canned tomatoes, corn, peas, and the like, are out of the question. They are mostly water—and the best flavored water that ever came in cans weighs a pound to the actual ounce after you've carried it all day.

But canned baked beans are something else. They are mostly solid nourishment; so the can pays its freight. You could not bake beans in camp without a bulky heavy pot, and then you could only have them for breakfast, on a marching trip, because it takes all night to cook them. But canned beans may be heated in a jiffy in the frying pan, or in boiling water with the can unopened.

It is the same way with canned spaghetti—no oven needed. Experiment at home with different brands till you find the kind you like best: they differ a great deal. I prefer Heinz or Purity Cross. This precaution holds good for all other canned groceries, even baked beans.

I spoke of tin cans that pay their freight, and others that do not. For instance, you might think of sardines as an item in the marching ration; but consider the tin: it weighs from half as much to fully as much as the fish and oil contained. On the other hand, Miss North's jams, put up in enamel-lined tins, run fourteen ounces of jam to two ounces of tin can.

Eighth, fruits. Stewed fruit is needed in the ration for the sake of the acid, and to correct the clogging tendency of concentrated foods. Dehydrated fruits are best, but plain dried ones will do. They should be soaked overnight in cold water before using. That makes them "plum up"; then they stew quickly and are tender and better flavored than if put to stew without soaking. A few lemons will be needed for the Russian tea I am going to brag about.

Ninth, beverages. Parents and physicians differ among themselves about coffee and tea for growing boys. I assume that we will use cocoa for breakfast and supper, and my sort of tea in the middle of the day.

Tenth, condiments. Just sugar, salt and pepper. Fresh air and exercise supply all the rest.

So we have picked out our food materials; but how much shall we get of each item? It depends on the menus, and these may vary a great deal, even with the simple materials here listed. I am a firm believer in *variety* for the campers' bill of fare. Here is just one example: seven meals, and no two alike.

FIRST DAY

(Breakfast at home)

Dinner
Fried Ham
Spaghetti
Bread, Butter, Jam
Tea

Supper
Meat Stew
B. B. J.
Cheese
Cocoa

SECOND DAY

Breakfast
Fried Bacon
Baked Potatoes
Stewed Apples
Toast, Cocoa

Dinner
Corned Beef
Fritters
Flapjacks
Tea

Supper
Dried Beef
Rice and Beef Gravy
Cocoa

THIRD DAY

Breakfast
Fried Bacon
Potatoes and Onions Hashed
Stewed Apricots
Flapjacks, Cocoa

Dinner
Creamed Salmon
Baked Beans
Leftovers (?)
Tea

(Supper at home)

Recipes for these dishes will be given in the next article.

In planning this menu I have had in mind actual field conditions. The dishes are simple for you to prepare. None of them, except the baked potatoes, take more than half an hour to cook, from the time the water boils. They can be cooked with only a few utensils that are small enough and light enough for back packing.

The amount of each food item listed below is ample. The total foots up 9½ pounds per boy, for the three days' trip, *including the weight of tins*. Seems quite a load? Well, it grows less from meal to meal. But why so many items? Couldn't the list be simplified? Of course it could, but the total weight would be about the same. It is my purpose here to show how a pleasant variety in the camp menu can be had, even with marching rations and with materials that can be bought at any common grocery. Also, it is well to teach the readers as many ways of handling the marching rations as can be shown on so short a trip.

Bread, 4 loaves @ 12 oz.	3	—
Flour, self-raising, 2 packages @ 20 oz.	2	8
Rice	—	8
Spaghetti, 2 cans @ 10½ oz. net	1	10
Breakfast Bacon, sliced	1	8
Ham, sliced	1	—
Dried Beef, sliced	—	4
Corned Beef, 2 cans @ 12 oz. net	2	—
Salmon, 1 can, 1 lb. net	1	4
Butter, 2 lbs. in pry-up tins	2	8
Cheese	1	—
Evaporated Milk, 10 cans @ 6 oz. net	4	6
Potatoes, 16 medium	6	—
Onions, 2 large	1	4
Baked Beans, 2 cans @ 11 oz. net	1	12
Dried Apples, Apricots	2	—
Lemons, 6 medium	1	—
Sugar, in bag	2	—
Jam, in pry-up tins	2	4
Cocoa, 1 can, ½ lb. net	—	11
Tea, English Breakfast	—	3
Salt, Pepper	—	4
	38	14

The flour, rice, potatoes and onions, dried fruit and lemons, sugar, tea, salt, are to be packed in small muslin bags.

Utensils needed for the squad cooking are simply:

2 Frying Pans, 9-inch, with folding wire handles.
Aluminum Bucket, with tin cover, holding 3¼ qts.
Aluminum Bucket, with tin cover, holding 1¾ qts.
4 each Tin Plates, Pint Cups, Knives, Forks, Spoons.
Butcher Knife, Cooking Spoon, Can Opener.
Cheese Cloth, washed, 2 pieces about a foot square.
Towel, Dish Cloths, Steel Wool, Soap.

There is a practical limit to the size of kettle that can comfortably be carried on the march. It is reached in the larger one mentioned above, which is 8½ inches wide, including projections of bail, and 6½ inches high to top of lid knob. The smaller kettle nests within it. The two together weigh two pounds, and the frying pans 14 ounces each.

There should be two such cooking outfits for each patrol of eight boys.

The larger kettle is to be used for stewing, mixing batter, soaking fruit overnight, or sometimes just for heating water. The smaller one is for tea and cocoa. No other utensils than those here listed will be needed, thanks to our simplified cookery.

When making camp, two boys of each squad will rustle wood while the other two are setting up forked stakes and a cross-pole over the fireplace and cutting and notching the wooden hooks to hang kettles on. They will take turns from meal to meal at playing cook and cookee, under direction of the scout master, so that all may learn the essentials of good camp cookery.

With such an outfit as here described, you can lay it all over the hiking doughboys with their bully-beef and goldfish. Yes, and all over the dunderfunk and lobscouse crews.

Hiking Rations—How to Cook 'Em

Horace Kephart, the recognized authority on Camping, learned his wisdom of the woods through actual experience. His health failed him. He was forced to go into the out-of-doors and rebuild. For three years he lived alone in the Virgin Woods of the Great Smoky Mountains of North Carolina.[40] *Here he found the health he was looking for and learned first hand much of the information that he is writing here in* BOYS' LIFE *for you readers.*

To cook the noonday meal we need a fire that will get up a quick blaze to start the water boiling, and and [sic] then soon burn down to a neat bed of smokeless red-hot coals to fry over.

For the squad fire get hardwood sticks, if possible; for they make much better coals than softwood. Hickory, oak, maple, beech, birch or ash is good. Seasoned wood is best, but green wood will do if there is plenty of dry kindling to get it going.

Split the wood into sticks about an inch thick. Lay down two of them for bed-sticks, cross these near the ends with two others, forming a square, and so on up until you have a pen to enclose the kindling. Start a fire in the pen. Then cover it with a layer of parallel sticks an inch apart. Cross this with a similar layer at right angles, then with another crossing it. The free draft makes a roaring fire at once, and all burns down to coals together.

Put two unopened cans of spaghetti in the larger bucket, fill it with water to within an inch of the top, and hang it over the fire. Put three pints of water in the smaller bucket and hang it up to boil, while the fire is flaming.

When the fire has burned to coals, level them out so that two frying pans can be used together. Lengthen the handle of each pan by fitting a stick in it, so the cooks can keep a comfortable distance from the fire.

From *Boys' Life*, June 1923

TEA

As soon as the smaller kettle boils, take it off the fire. Remove the cover, spread the foot-square piece of washed cheese-cloth over the top, letting it sag in the center. Put into it four teaspoons of tea. Let the cloth sag down so that the tea will be immersed. Put the cover back on the kettle, over the cloth, so as to hold the cloth in place. Set the kettle near the fire where it will keep hot, but *do not let the tea boil* or even simmer. The tea brewer will guard this pot with watch in hand, as if he were boiling eggs, and when the tea has steeped exactly four minutes he will remove the cloth containing the tea leaves and throw the latter away. Longer steeping would dissolve tannin from the leaves and produce a bitter decoction that is ruinous to digestion. He will now put eight heaped teaspoons of sugar in the tea, stir it till dissolved, then squeeze the juice of a whole lemon into it, add a snip of peeled rind, and return the tea kettle to its place beside the fire till wanted.

There is nothing so heartening on the march as tea made in this manner. The lemon juice is valuable not only for the acid but for the vitamins it supplies. Never use cream in tea: it is, as the pharmacists say, incompatible.

FRIED HAM

While this is going on, other boys are frying the ham. Heat the dry pan, put in the slices of ham, brown them quickly on one side, turn and brown slightly on the other side, and repeat the turning until the meat is cooked through, but not hard and dry. Both sides should be dappled with golden brown. If the ham is very salty, it should first be parboiled a few minutes with water in the pan, to draw out the salt, then wiped dry and fried.

Two pans are supposed to have been in action with the ham business. When the meat is done, put it all in one pan, and into the other empty the two cans of heated spaghetti. The squad has spread its bread and butter and jam, and will now do the rest.

When dinner is over, clean all utensils, using the hot water in the larger kettle. A little swab of steel wool will make it easy to get rid of anything that sticks to the pans, and to clean plates with only a little hot water. Rinse off the cheesecloth and save it.

The following recipes follow the order in which they occur in the menu:

MEAT STEW

Put several slices of bacon in the bottom of the larger kettle. Set it over the fire until the grease has fried out and the bacon is browned. Drop into the hot fat a sliced-up onion and let it brown. Then add sliced potatoes till the kettle is half full. Pepper it well, and salt. Pour in a cup (half-pint) of hot water. Cover the kettle and let the vegetables steam over a slow fire for about twenty-five minutes. Cut corned beef into inch cubes, lay them on top of the vegetables, cover again, and put back on the fire until beef is heated through. Serve all together.

COCOA

Boil a quart of water in the small kettle. Mix four teaspoons of cocoa with three tablespoons of sugar and a small pinch of salt. Rub it up to a smooth paste with a little of the boiling water. Turn this into the kettle and boil gently five minutes. Meantime mix a can of milk with a scant pint of water and scald this in a clean frying-pan, bringing it just to a simmer. At the end of the five minutes, take the kettle from the fire, pour the scalded milk into the boiling cocoa, and stir it vigorously with a big spoon until it froths.

FRIED BACON

If the rind has not been removed, cut through it in two places to prevent curling in the pan. Have the pan hot, lay the slices in it, and when they turn clear, turn them over. If not wanted crisp and dry, turn the slices before they look clear, and remove before all the fat is tried out. Fry enough bacon for breakfast to make half a panful of grease, and save this, in a pry-up tin, for the fritters mentioned below.

BAKED POTATOES

If a night fire has been kept up there will be a deep bed of hot ashes and embers. Scoop out a depression three or four inches deep. Lay the potatoes in it side by side. Cover them with hot ashes and then with glowing coals. Build the breakfast fire on top. In about forty minutes try the potatoes with a pointed sliver. When this will pass through them they are done and should be raked out and eaten at once before they can get soggy.

STEWED FRUIT

The night before, put the fruit in the larger kettle, pour in enough cold water to cover the fruit, and let soak overnight. This "plumps it," as described in the former chapter. In the morning, stew until tender, season with sugar and thin shavings from the rind of a lemon.

CORNED BEEF FRITTERS

Open large end of can. Punch a hole in the other end to admit air, then the meat will drop out. Slice it with a sharp knife into slabs a quarter of an inch thick. Make a batter as for flapjacks. Cover slabs with batter and fry them brown in a pan half full of sizzling hot bacon grease. After you once try this you will not again be guilty of eating corned beef cold out of the can.

FLAPJACKS

Mix the batter stiff enough so it will drop lazily from a cooking spoon, like thick molasses. Heat the frying-pan quite hot and then grease it lightly with a piece of bacon in the split end of a stick, just enough to keep the cakes from sticking. If you used too much grease the cakes would be soggy with it and would not get crisply brown.

Stir the batter rapidly till it froths. Fill the big spoon and turn it into the pan. When the bubbles in the middle of the cake burst, run a thin-bladed knife under the cake and shuffle it loose from the pan. When the under side is browned, turn the cake with the knife.

Or, to flip the cake, hold the pan slanting away from you, go through the preliminary motion of flipping, once or twice, to get the swing. Then flip boldly, so the cake will turn a somersault in the air, and catch it upside down. Beginners generally do not toss high enough.

Grease the pan anew and stir the batter every time before pouring. Two pans should be going at once, as the cakes are not good unless eaten piping hot.

DRIED BEEF AND GRAVY

I am indebted for this recipe to Mrs. J. L. Hancock, in *Outing*:

"Put into your frying-pan, for each person to be served, a tablespoonful of butter, a well-heaped tablespoonful of flour, and an ounce, or a trifle over, of dried beef, separated into small pieces and with strings and fat removed. The mixture should be stirred over the fire until the meat gives off a savory odor and until the flour and butter are distinctly browned, but not hopelessy [*sic*] burned. This will ensure flavor for the resulting dish and keep the gravy from looking like an unwholesome flour-and-water paste. Even a little burning before the milk is added is preferable to adding the liquid before the proper browning is accomplished.

"Then add, a cupful or less at a time, condensed milk diluted with water according to the taste of the company, stirring constantly until you have a moderately thick, smooth gravy, slightly brown in color and of appetizing smell. On the average about one cupful (one-half pint) of liquid will be required for each person to be served. The entire process of cooking should not take much more than ten minutes.

"When your gravy reaches the thickness and smoothness that you desire, you had better remove it from the fire until you are ready to use it, and then quickly reheat it; otherwise it will become too thick, and perhaps burn."

The gravy is excellent to use on bread, biscuit, flapjacks, potatoes, cereals, and so on. Its particular use in this present menu is on the boiled rice, the recipe for which follows.

BOILED RICE

In the larger kettle get two quarts of water boiling furiously. Meantime wash half a pint of rice in cold *salted* water, and drain. When the unsalted water in the pot is boiling as hard as it can, add the rice a little at a time, so as not to check the flurry of bubbles.

Keep the pot boiling hard for twenty minutes (brown rice takes thirty or thirty-five), but do not stir. The hard boiling water keeps the grains dancing around instead of gluing to each other. This will make them plump, tender and separate, instead of producing a mushy, tasteless mess.

When done, the rice should have the water strained off, by covering with a piece of cheesecloth and tilting the kettle, and then should be hung high over the fire, uncovered, to swell and dry, while you are making the dried beef gravy described above, which is to be used on it as a sauce.

Those who, like myself, have never relished either dried beef or rice by themselves, will find this combination one of the best rough-and-ready camp dishes they ever tried.

POTATOES AND ONIONS HASHED

Slice two potatoes to one onion. Put them in a pan of salted water and simmer them together about fifteen minutes. Pour off water, and drain. Meantime be frying some bacon. When it is done, remove it to a hot side-dish, turn the vegetables into the frying-pan with the hot grease, and fry them to a light brown.

CREAMED SALMON

Cut the salmon into dice. Melt into the frying-pan a tablespoon of butter, rub into it a tablespoon of flour and half a teaspoon of salt. Take off the fire and stir into it half a pint of evaporated milk diluted with hot water. Return to the fire and cook up the flour and milk. Turn the salmon into it and cook together until the fish is well heated through.

—

Mountaineering in the Appalachians

In any of the eastern mountains, from Maine to Alabama, the Scout uniform, without blouse, is a good climbing rig until cold weather sets in; provided the breeches are loose enough at the knee so as not to "pull" and provided a few small hobnails are added to the shoes.

Stand near a chair, set one foot on the chair seat, then rise on that foot. Do this several times. If the breeches draw so tight over the kneecap that you feel the cloth drag or bind the knee, then they are not fit for mountain climbing. It wears one out to have such a pull constantly repeated ove[r] the knee.[41]

Ordinary trousers do very well for a trip of only a fe[w] days in the mountains. Knickers are better, provided they do not go to the other extreme of being too full at the knee. If they are baggy they will catch in brush and briers, tear, and will be uncomfortable when wet. One's legs always get wet in the mountains, whether from rain or from the morning dew on the bushes, which rubs right through the best cravenetted duck.

Hobnails are a necessity in mountaineering. Without them one will be slipping on rocks, on leaves, and particularly on pine needles. Even if one escapes a fall he will at least be handicapped by so much lost motion.

Do not let a shoemaker put large, flat-headed hobnails in the shoes. They soon wear smooth and then are treacherous on rocks; besides, they do not hold so well in the soles as smaller nails, unless riveted in.

There is no need of studding the whole surface of sole and heel with nails. Too many nails add unnecessary weight, make the sole too stiff and cause it to ball up with mud or snow. Ten nails in the sole and six in the heel are enough, set as here shown in the sketch. When these have worn down so that they no longer grip there is room left between them to insert new ones.

Unpublished MS. Accompanying envelope is from *Boys' Life*, 200 Fifth Avenue, New York, N. Y. It is addressed to Mr. Horace Kephart, Bryson City, North Carolina, First Class Mail. The envelope is postmarked March 10, 1928.

Cone-headed Hungarian nails are better than round-headed ones, because they still "bite" even after the points have worn blunt. If the shoemaker does not have them, go to a sporting goods store and get some screw calks and a wrench for setting them. Calks for Scout shoes should be no large[r] than No.1 size. Longer ones may be used in the heels, but they pick up more trash in forest travel and have little or no advantage over No.1s in the long run.

The two nails under the arch of the foot are useful when crossing streams on small logs. Nails in the middle of the sole are uncomfortable when the leather is of moderate thickness. Soles thicker than those of the standard Scout shoe are heavy, stiff and clumsy. They are not needed unless one goes in for alpine work high above timber line. In the latter case there should be some Swiss edging nails along the outer edges of the shoe sole and heel, with small nails over the face of the leather.

In the southern Appalachians, or in any other mountains where there is much underbrush and greenbrier, leggings are needed, unless high-topped boots are worn. Leather leggings are too heavy and they have the serious fault of cutting one in the arch under the knee whenever he bends his leg as much as he must do in steep climbing.

The leggings should be of heavy canvas, not too long, fastened with a spiral puttee strap that is quick to adjust, or with a lace over a single stud in front. Leggings that lace at the side are nuisances, as the numerous studs are always catching in grass or twigs and getting bent out of shape.

Spiral puttees that wrap around the legs like bandages have some points over leggings. They keep water from trickling down into the shoes. But they should be of closely woven wo[ol] or gabardine, not knit. Knitted puttees and uncovered long stockings snag easily, collect burs, and they are no protect[ion] against wet or snakes.

The same fault is to be found with knitted sweaters. A lumberjack shirt, carried in the pack when climbing, is better than a coat to put on when the breeze-swept summit is reached, or when resting, and to sleep in if one stays overnight on the mountain.

A short rubber cape is the best protection against rain. A raincoat or long poncho is in the way of the legs, when climbing, and is likely to be torn by laurel or other undergrowth.

When pushing through brushy places where there is no trail, tie the hat on with the neckerchief. It looks, then, like a poke bonnet; but woodsmen call it a "stay-put."

To do any mountaineering worth while it is generally necessary to spend at least one night in the open. Sunset and sunrise, viewed from the mountaintop, are the chief rewards of the trip, never to be forgotten.

The tent should be as light as practicable and only high enough to sit up in. A low tent, securely pegged and guyed, will stand staunchly in storms that would knock down a bigger one. The Scout featherweight shelter tent is a very good model for mountaineering.

Blankets are more comfortable than sleeping bags, when two sleep together, and they carry better in the pack. A ground blanket is needed under them. Make a bed of browse or dried moss or whatever soft stuff may be found on the camp site. Such a mattress is needed not only to rest one's bones but [also] to insulate him from the chill of the ground.

One member of the party should carry a full-size axe. [A] hand axe swinging from the belt is very much in the way when climbing or when boring through thicket. So is a canteen. When I carry a canteen it is on the back of the pack sack. The less weight carried on the belt, the better. The fewer flopping articles, the better.

Cooking utensils will be of the simplest, parceled out among members of the party. If there be a trail to the summit, or near it, that is practicable for horse or mule, it is best to have the camp equipment carried by one or more pack animals.

Each member of the party should carry in his pack a lumberjack shirt, a suit of woolen underclothes or pajamas to sleep in, spare handkerchief and socks or stockings, waterproof cape, toilet articles, [lunch, cup,] map, compass, jackknife and waterproof match box filled.

A good staff is a great aid in climbing and in fording streams. The Scout stave and guard rope are fine for mountaineering.

When going up into the mountains do not depend on keeping a time schedule. You will reach a certain destination when Nature allows you do [*sic*] do so. Cloud may descend on the mountain, or rise up from the ravines and encompass it. At times the cloud is so thick that one can not see a tree until he nearly butts into it. At such a time travel is hazardous unless there is a plain and well-known trail to follow. In most of the northern Appalachians there are good trails and many signs to guide one; but in the southern mountains, up to the present year, there are comparative[ly] few trails and no finger-posts. The Smokies, for example, are [an] uninhabited wilderness, thickly forested to the summits, and [no] stranger should venture into them without a native guide.

The wild animals of the mountains are harmless if let al[one]. The black bear is the only formidable beast that ranges in the Appalachians, and he always minds his own business. There are rattlesnakes and copperheads, to be sure; but the chance of being bitten by one is as remote as that of being struck by lightning. I have spent twenty-four years in the Smokies and in all that ti[me] I have known only two cases of people being bitten by dangerous snakes, though I have known and experienced some "close calls."

Never let a blister form on the foot. Stop, the moment you feel a tender spot, put a very small piece of absorbent cotton over the spot, fix it in place with a piece of adhesive tape, and you will not hear from it again.

Shoes for mountaineering, or for any long hikes, should be a half-size longer and wider than your street shoes, to allow for the swelling of the feet that always comes from long walks. If the shoe is of common length your toes will be severely punished in going downhill.

The squad leader should carry in a small vial, or in the hollow rubber handle of a snake-bite lancet, some potassium permanganate in crystals. It has been found that this is a specific for ivy poisoning. Apply a 5 per cent. [*sic*] solution as a lotion (3 grains to a teaspoon). When buying a snake-bite lancet be sure to get one with a long, narrow blade, instead of the short, stubby ones sold by some dealers. The last named are too short for the work and are hard to sharpen. The kind recommended costs 75 cents, including the permanganate, and may be found in some outfitting shops.

The Indian Blowgun

It was early on the third day of the Indian fair at Cherokee, in the valley of the Okona Luftee. On a turfy meadow below the school a group of old Indians was giving the Green Corn Dance. Here I ran across Ben Dixon MacNeill, who had come up from Raleigh into the Smoky Mountains to get a story for the *News and Observer*.

When the dance was over, he and I strolled to the upper end of the field where Jack Gloyne and some Indians were setting up an archery target. One of the Cherokees bore in his hand a long cane tube, something like a big fishpole with the flexible upper part cut off.

"What is that thing he carries?" asked MacNeill.

"A blowgun."

"Blowgun? What is it for?"

"To shoot with. They kill birds, squirrels and rabbits with it."

"I never heard of such a thing."

"Blowguns are common weapons among the savages of the Amazon and the Orinoco, also in the Malay Archipelago and the Philippines; but I never heard of them, myself, among North American Indians until I came here and found these Cherokees using them."

"How can they kill game with such reeds?"

"Well, when you were a boy, didn't you have a pea-shooter or a putty-blower?"

"Yes, but—"

"The blowgun works on the same principle, but it is far more powerful. It shoots darts, instead of pellets, and an Indian can drive one of them through the panel of a door. The blowgun has points over a .22 rifle, for it is cheaper to use and it is noiseless."

"But I don't see—"

"Show him, Too-nigh," said I to the Indian.

Too-nigh lowered his tube and puffed two darts out of it to the ground, the gun itself being his quiver. Then he pushed one of the darts into the breech of the gun, raised the long tube vertically, gave a strong puff, and the dart flew straight up into

---

From *Boys' Life*, August 1928

the air a good two hundred feet. It turned gracefully, came down point-foremost, and stuck in the sod near the shooter's feet.

MacNeill took the weapon and examined it. The cane was a fine specimen from the southern lowlands, colored by age and use until it resembled a dark bamboo. It was a treasured heirloom, nobody knew how old. Too-nigh's father had inherited it from his father, and so on back to a time beyond record. The cane that grows on the river banks in the high country of western North Carolina is too small for blowguns; so the mountain Cherokees had to journey far southward for their material. That is why blowguns are scarce among them now and highly prized.

This gun was ten or eleven feet long, about an inch in diameter at the breech and a little over half-inch at the muzzle. Looking through it, one saw that the bore was almost as smooth and true as that of a shotgun, with an even taper from breech to muzzle.

One thing had long puzzled me, and here was a chance to get information.

"How the dickens were the joints of this cane bored out so neatly?" I inquired.

The young Indian did not know; but a very old man answered: "Not bored—burnt."

Then I got details. The Indian gunmaker, having procured a suitable cane, straightened it, while green, by heating at the joints and bending over his knee. Then he got a piece of iron rod six or eight inches long and smaller in diameter than the desired bore. This he heated to redness and dropped it down into the cane, which was held vertically, thus burning out the joints. Then he got a straight wooden rod of somewhat more than half the tube's length. He tapered the rod at one end like a reamer. Round the pointed end he fitted a piece of tin in which small holes had been punched, like a nutmeg grater. This was his round rasp. He worked it, first from one end of the cane, then from the other, until all joints were rasped out to the required bore. Finally he glued sandpaper (or sand itself, if the paper could not be procured) to the rod and smoothed out the bore of the gun.

The darts—but no Indian uses that word; he calls them arrows—are of hickory, much larger and heavier than a novice would expect to see in a blowgun. Some Indians employ darts as long as thirty inches and half the thickness of a lead pencil. Others prefer shorter and slenderer shafts, down to twelve inches in length. The average seems to be about two feet long and three-sixteenths-inch gauge. In service the dart gets battered or broken at the end, and that may be why very long ones are used at the start.

All Cherokee blowgun darts are "feathered" in the same way—if we may use such a term for a thing that has no feathers. Around the butt of the dart is a swab of dried thistle-down, wrapped on with thread, from four to six inches long. This is somewhat larger than the bore of the gun, but it is so smooth and elastic that it slips easily through the tube, adjusting itself automatically to the gradually increasing "choke" of the tapered hole, and preventing windage.

A sudden and powerful puff drives the missile swiftly and silently on its mission. The range is determined partly by the force of this puff and partly by the degree of elevation of the gun's muzzle. It is noticeable that these long cane tubes, when in aiming position, bend upward in the middle and sag somewhat at the muzzle.

The two teams of contestants in the blowgun match began to line up, three men on a side. Sampson Welch, Karl Standing Deer, Runaway Swimmer, Joe Too-nigh, Ranz Swaney, a "breed" with a peg leg, and old Going Bird, who was past sixty but still going strong.

They shot first from the fifty-foot line, then from seventy-five. The first man up was a young fellow. He was plainly nervous. It was his first appearance before a crowd. A stage-struck Indian! But why not? On rifle ranges I have seen more than one good marksman go to pieces before a crowd, just from over-anxiety to break a record.

He puffed too hard, and overshot the whole target. The crowd jeered. The Indian sweated. He shot again. The dart struck viciously into the white ring at the top of the target—a line shot, but still much too high. The third shot was better, a blue, counting five, but low. The nervous fellow retired, abashed by the chaffing crowd and mad at himself. He had my sympathy. Not half an hour before, I had seen this same boy pick up his blowgun, and, without a second's hesitation, drive the dart *crack!* through a small candy carton at forty or fifty feet.

The next shooter was the quarter-breed with the peg-leg. He had a square jaw and no nerves to speak of. *Spat!* went his dart into the red. *Spat!* went another into the blue. *Spat!* and the third dart pierced the gold.

"Bull's-eye!" cried the crowd. And the team stiffened up.

So it went on. Better work was done at seventy-five feet than at fifty; for the teams were getting over their embarrassment, and the boy who had led off so ingloriously had now recovered poise and was shooting for blood.

Still, at no time did these exhibitors equal the skill they display when shooting little matches for fun among themselves. And it is a fact that when hunting in the woods they often bring down squirrels out of tall trees. That means center shots; for a tough old gray squirrel, if hit anywhere but through the head or heart, and not knocked off the tree by impact, will bite the offending dart in two and pull it out.

It stands to reason that the marksmanship of present-day Cherokees with the blowgun is nothing compared to what their ancestors could do. A moment's thought will show why. In the old days everybody had his blowgun and practised with it continually from the time he was a little boy. It was not just a toy to play with but a weapon to put meat in the empty pot. That is what makes marksmen. And there were hundreds of blowgunners then to one now. Naturally there would be more in the expert class.

I believe, though, that if this first attempt to revive an ancient sport at the Cherokee fair is encouraged, so that the young Indians find it worth while to practice and shoot matches frequently among themselves, they will soon develop a creditable mastery of this singularly interesting weapon. If someone would ship them a bundle of selected large canes or bamboo, such as can be bought at an anglers' supply store in the city, it would start them. A few modest prizes would do the rest.

The extreme range of the blowgun dart, fired by an expert, is probably about 150 yards, possibly 200. Its effective range as a game-killer depends, of course, on the size of the animal. Scientists and other credible travelers who have seen blowgun shooting by the Macusis of Guiana or the Dyaks of Borneo say that fifty or sixty yards is an almost certain distance.

Dr. H. H. Furness got some Dyak headhunters to give an exhibition of their shooting. He took a potato about an inch and a half in diameter, set it up on a pole, and stepped off fifty paces. A native shot with his blowgun, at that range, and hit the potato with six darts out of ten. That would be pretty fair work for a rifleman, shooting offhand.

Both the Bornean and the South American blowguns are fitted with a bell-shaped mouthpiece and with front and rear sights. The rear sight can be of no use in determining angle of fire, as it does not come up to the level of the shooter's eye, but it may help to get a line shot.

The Cherokee blowgun has neither of these accessories. The shooting is done by instinctive pointing aided by sighting over the elevated muzzle. The way of holding the gun is a surprise to visitors. A novice would naturally extend his left arm to support the long tube, just as he would with a rifle; but the Cherokee grasps it at the end of the breech, with both hands tight together, and he presses the right hand firmly against his mouth, in cup shape, thus making his own hand the mouthpiece.

In South America, as in Borneo and the Philippines, the blowgun is used in warfare and in hunting big game. For such service the darts are steeped at the point in curare or other quick-acting contact poison. This is fatal to men or animals of any size. When this poison enters the circulation it paralyzes the motor nerves and soon kills by suffocation. Our Indians could easily poison their darts, if they wanted to do so, but there is no record or tradition of their using the blowgun for any more serious purpose than hunting small game.

The Indian fair is held every autumn, after the harvest is gathered, on the grounds of the Government school at Cherokee, N. C. It is primarily an exhibit, and a very creditable one, of agricultural and domestic products, basketry, pottery, wood-carving, bead-work, needlework and other Indian crafts. The ancient dances, the ball-play, archery, blowgun shooting and other games are picturesque features that draw crowds from far and near. Two thousand cars were parked on the athletic field when MacNeill and I were there, many of them bearing license plates from far distant States.

The ball-play is an exciting game, the original of lacrosse, which is still played by the Cherokees with all the ancient ceremonials of dancing, fasting, scarifying, anointing, drinking of sacred potions and prayer by the medicine-man. MacNeill wrote of it: "Indian ball is the oldest game in America. It combines all the best features of a dozen games and some virtues of none of them. Indian ball is like polo; it is like football; it is like baseball; it is like boxing; it is like wrestling; it is like tennis; it is like basket-ball. But nothing is barred short of sheer murder. Probably only the Indians could be permitted to play it: they are the best sportsmen in the world."

The Eastern Band of Cherokees, as they are officially titled, is composed of some 2,500 descendants of those Indian mountaineers who escaped to the high Smokies and hid out, starving but indomitable, in 1838, when Andrew Jackson, in defiance of the United States Supreme Court, seized the territory of the Cherokee nation and drove its owners into permanent exile beyond the Mississippi. The refugees in the Smoky Mountains were so hard to dislodge that they were finally allowed to return to their home, buy back their own lands with money due them from the United States, and there in the beautiful valley of the Okona Luftee we now find their descendants, more than half of them full-bloods, holding their land by tribal ownership in the ancient way, supporting themselves by their own labor, but schooled and supervised by the federal Government. Their land adjoins the high ranges and primitive forests that are now being acquired for the Smoky Mountain National Park.

nine

PARK AND TRAIL

A NATIONAL PARK
In The
GREAT SMOKY MOUNTAINS

SUNRISE IN THE SMOKIES

Published by
The Swain County Chamber of Commerce
Bryson City, North Carolina
1925

Promotional brochure 1925.

Introduction

ANDREW DENSON

In 1931 the United States Geographic Board named a 6,200-foot peak in the Smoky Mountains for Horace Kephart. Part of the high ridge that forms the North Carolina-Tennessee border, Mt. Kephart recognizes the writer's long service to the campaign that led to the establishment of the Great Smoky Mountains National Park. Over the last decade of his life, Kephart devoted much of his work to the park movement, joining an alliance of civic and business leaders who hoped a national park might provide permanent economic benefit to Southern Appalachia. In myriad writings (some reproduced here), Kephart argued for the preservation of the Smokies landscape while endorsing a booster's vision of an abundantly prosperous tourism economy. When supporting the park campaign, he reiterated many of the most prominent themes from his earlier works, such as *Our Southern Highlanders*. In particular, he emphasized the distinctiveness of the Smoky Mountain landscape, presenting the region as an Edenic wilderness that had survived in spite of the nation's industrial progress. The National Park Service, in turn, drew upon Kephart's portrayal of mountain communities when interpreting Appalachian cultures. Although Kephart died before the national park's completion, his work played a significant role in both establishing the park and shaping its approach to preservation and tourism development.

A PARK FOR SOUTHERN APPALACHIA

The idea of creating a national park in Southern Appalachia first arose in the late nineteenth century. During this period, Congress established the earliest national parks in mountain areas of the West, like Yosemite and Yellowstone. The protection of these western landscapes encouraged civic leaders in the Southeast to contemplate a park for their own mountain region. In 1899, a group of politicians, journalists, and businessmen launched the first organized park campaign, establishing the Appalachian National Park Association in Asheville, North Carolina. Members worked to raise public interest, and the association lobbied Congress, arguing that the federal government had ignored the South in its efforts to protect the nation's natural beauty. Within a few years, however, the campaign faltered due to resistance from the timber industry and a lack of support among federal authorities.[1]

Despite this setback, the idea of an Appalachian park remained popular among regional leaders, and, in the 1920s, a new campaign evolved. By this time, the United States possessed more than a dozen national parks, and Congress had created the National Park Service (NPS) to manage these federal assets. Visitor numbers had grown steadily, encouraging tourism boosters around the country to suggest new units for the park system. Residents of Knoxville, Tennessee, formed the Great Smoky Mountain Conservation Association to push for a Southern Appalachian park while business leaders in Asheville launched a similar effort. In 1924, Secretary of the Interior Hubert Work established a committee to study proposals for parks in the East with a particular focus on the southern mountains. In its report, the committee recommended the creation of two new national parks, one in Virginia's Shenandoah region and a second in the Smokies, along the Tennessee-North Carolina border.[2]

For most advocates, tourism provided the main reason for creating a national park in the Smoky Mountains. From the start, the campaign focused on economic development, as well as the protection of the mountain landscape. As the historian Daniel Pierce explains, boosters hoped that a national park would become a great economic engine, bolstering and expanding a tourism industry that was already important to the region. A song sung by park promoters (to the tune of "My Old Kentucky Home") captured the spirit of the campaign:

> The sun shines bright on the Smoky Mountains Park
> In summer the tourists are gay
> By'n by good roads will bring millions to our Park
> And then all will prosper every day[3]

This commercial focus complemented the goals of the Park Service, which emphasized outdoor leisure, as well as preservation. NPS intended the national parks to provide recreation opportunities for a broad range of American consumers and not merely protect distinctive environments. This outlook, in fact, provided a particularly strong argument for a park in the Smokies. Most of the existing national parks were located in the West, far from the nation's population centers. A Smoky Mountains park, on the other hand, would lie within easy reach of the nation's biggest cities. Park promoters continually raised this point, illustrating it with maps that placed the Smokies at the center of a great network of tourist routes. Once designated, a park in

Southern Appalachia could become a "playground" for a great multitude of ordinary Americans.[4]

In 1925, Congress established a commission to determine park boundaries while authorizing boosters to begin gathering donations of money and property. Timber companies and other private landowners held most of the area suggested for the park, which made its creation a complicated endeavor requiring more than a decade to complete. While federal authorities had established earlier national parks on public land, the creation of a park in the Smokies would require multiple purchases of private property. In response to the 1925 law, organizations in Tennessee and North Carolina launched extensive fund-raising campaigns and began working to secure the necessary real estate. By May 1926, boosters had gathered around $1 million in pledges while drumming up significant public support for the project. These results convinced Congress to approve the creation of the park, but this act only marked the beginning of the campaign to secure the land. Timber companies relinquished their holdings only after difficult negotiations and sometimes condemnation suits while some individual landowners resisted as well. A donation of $5 million from the Laura Spellman Rockefeller Fund helped to sustain the campaign, and, by 1930, park commissions in North Carolina and Tennessee had amassed around 150,000 acres. As land purchases continued, large numbers of travelers began visiting the park area. After 1933, and the arrival of the New Deal, the federal government increased its support for the project. By 1934, the state commissions had assembled enough property that Congress chartered the park, allowing its completion and the construction of public facilities. Six years later, President Franklin D. Roosevelt led the formal dedication in a ceremony at Newfound Gap, a mountain pass situated at the center of the Smokies on the border between Tennessee and North Carolina.[5]

KEPHART AND THE PARK CAMPAIGN

Horace Kephart supported the park campaign throughout the 1920s and early 1930s, becoming one of its most visible public advocates. He wrote numerous magazine and newspaper articles in favor of the national park while contributing to the promotional literature produced by groups like the North Carolina Park Commission. During this same period, he also supported the creation of the Appalachian Trail, the long hiking path from Georgia to Maine first proposed in the early 1920s. He wrote essays promoting the trail project and participated in discussions of how to route the trail through the Smokies and northern Georgia. He joined his friend the photographer George Masa in blazing specific trail sections. When completed, the Appalachian

Trail would include a substantial leg passing through the area designated for the Great Smoky Mountains National Park.[6]

In his promotional writings, Kephart explained his enthusiasm for the park by referring to his personal history in the Smokies. He had moved to Southern Appalachia to start his life over, he explained, escaping the city in search of freedom, health, and a more authentic existence. "Twenty-four years ago I was a nervous wreck," he wrote in the late 1920s, "with no hope of recovery unless I gave up my profession, quit city life, got out into the open and stayed there."[7] Life in the mountains, he recalled, had restored him in body and soul. He favored the creation of a national park because it promised to make a similar experience available to others. "I owe my life to these mountains," he remarked, "and I want them preserved that others may profit by them as I have."[8] Logging and other extractive industries, however, threatened the Smokies' natural environment and, by extension, its potential value to the American people. Kephart himself had been forced to abandon his famous camp on Hazel Creek when a lumber company began operating in the area. In an essay published in the *Asheville Times* and circulated as a pamphlet, he recalled the experience, contrasting the grandeur of the unspoiled forest with the destruction caused by logging. "I am not a very religious man," he explained, "but often, when standing alone before my Maker in this house not made with hands, I bowed my head in reverence and thanked God for his gift of the great forest to one who loved it." Irresponsible logging transformed Kephart's forest home, destroying its spiritual value in the name of immediate profit. "Not long ago I went to that same place again," he continued. "It was wrecked, ruined, desecrated, turned into a thousand rubbish heaps, utterly vile and mean. Does anyone ever thank God for a lumberman's slashing?"[9]

This concern for preservation could potentially place Kephart at odds with other boosters given most park advocates' focus on tourism. Kephart surely understood that many of his allies in the park campaign took economic development as their primary goal. Yet he seems to have partnered easily with the more commercially minded promoters. He found in tourism an industry preferable to logging or mining, and he anticipated that the national park would lead to construction of better roads through the region, a traditional concern of mountain residents. He endorsed the grand economic visions of the tourism boosters, predicting that, if the park campaign proved successful, "the mountain counties of far Western North Carolina would emerge from obscurity and become gems in the old State's crown."[10] It is worth remembering, meanwhile, that Kephart had long contributed to the culture of commercial leisure. His writings on camping had always represented a form of tourism promotion, and *Our Southern Highlanders*, whatever else it achieved, served as an advertisement for travel to the mountains. Kephart may have had conservation more thoroughly in mind than did other park advocates, but he was well-suited to the role of tourism booster.[11]

In promoting the national park, Kephart argued that the Smokies held the last wild places in the East. "Here are large areas of superb wilderness, practically uninhabited," he wrote in 1925. "Here are the highest and most massive mountains in eastern America. . . . [and] the last survivals of the magnificent primeval forest that covered the eastern part of the continent when the first white men landed in the New World."[12] This wilderness remained intact because the ruggedness of the mountains kept all but the heartiest people from venturing there. As a consequence, the Southeast now possessed a spectacular region of unspoiled beauty located just a short distance from many of the nation's largest cities. "The Smokies stand in the center of Eastern America, midway between the Atlantic and the Mississippi, midway between the Great Lakes and the Gulf," Kephart wrote. "And yet, to this day the Smokies remain a land of mystery, unknown save by long-range view, not only to tourists but even to most of the people who live round about."[13] In Kephart's writings, the Smoky Mountains were both remote and available, exotic but close at hand.

A national park in the Smokies, he argued, would preserve the region's unique landscape while reducing its remoteness. With good roads and proper facilities, a park would allow Americans to experience this unlikely paradise firsthand. In his promotional writing, Kephart assembled long descriptions of the Smokies' natural wonders: the stunning views, lush forests, and abundant wildlife. He then assured his readers that a national park would both maintain this wilderness and make it accessible to the American people. "There are thousands of people in cities and on prairie farms who would realize one of the darling ambitions of their lives if they could get away to some new and rugged and untamed region where they could feel the explorer's thrill," Kephart observed. "And here it is, unknown to them, almost at their very doors!"[14] Opening this wilderness to travelers would provide an inestimable public service by offering urban Americans much-needed contact with nature. "The East is swarming with industrial centers," Kephart wrote. "The millions of people hived in the cities have learned that it is a matter of self-preservation for them to have wing-room, every now and then, in the open air."[15] With a national park in the Smokies, ordinary Americans could gain some of the benefits of outdoor living that had transformed Kephart's own life.

The nation would only realize this public good, however, if the federal government and park promoters saved the Smokies from the timber industry. In promoting the national park, Kephart warned that logging would soon destroy the Smokies if the park campaign failed. Americans could not simply ignore the region, allowing it to remain remote and obscure, if they hoped to see the mountain forests continue. The timber industry already menaced the Smokies, and it would ruin the mountains if given the chance. "In the old days I saw the Smokies in their primal glory," Kephart recalled in 1929. "Then came the lumbermen with their mills and logging trains," and soon large sections of his "Eden" disappeared, reduced to desolation. "The grandest forest in Eastern America would be utterly destroyed," he wrote, "unless the power of the Federal Government itself was enlisted and the primeval woods that still remained were preserved forever as a national park."[16] Even the creation of a national forest in the Smokies, Kephart argued, would leave the region vulnerable. In the political debates over the national park, some participants argued that the US Forest Service should oversee the Smokies rather than the Park Service, which would exclude many forms of commercial development from the region. Kephart rejected this idea, noting that the Forest Service managed its lands for the benefit of logging companies. "A National Forest is first and last a commercial enterprise," he wrote. While Forest Service supervision might be preferable to unregulated logging, it would not save the Smokies from industrial exploitation.[17] In his writings for the park campaign, Kephart portrayed the Smokies as a wilderness that had miraculously survived into the twentieth century only to be threatened at the very moment that Americans were waking up to the value of wild places. Under these conditions, he argued, a national park provided the sole alternative to the destruction of the mountain forest.

In these essays, Kephart employed some of the same images of Appalachia he had broadcast in *Our Southern Highlanders*. The Smokies were a "mysterious realm" in Kephart's famous book, a wilderness so remote that it formed "terra incognita" for the great majority of Americans.[18] His rhapsodic descriptions of the Smokies' abundant plant and animal life in the national park writings might have come directly from his earlier work. In *Our Southern Highlanders*, this image of the unknown mountain paradise served to establish Kephart's authority as a guide who would explain this strange place to his readers. Later, in the essays supporting the national park, it helped him highlight the region's distinctiveness and its desirability as both a candidate for preservation and a potential tourist destination. Visitors to a national park in the Smokies would enact a version of Kephart's own adventures. Like him, they would discover the ancient wilderness in America's backyard.

INTERPRETING APPALACHIAN CULTURE, DISPLACING APPALACHIAN PEOPLE

In the essays about the national park reproduced in this volume, Kephart concentrates on the landscape and environment, writing relatively little about the people who lived in the Smokies. Other park promoters, however, interpreted Appalachian cultures, suggesting that visitors would encounter distinctive communities as well as a unique landscape. In discussing Appalachian people, the promotional literature echoed the images of white mountaineers Kephart helped to popularize in works like *Our Southern Highlanders*. As the historian C. Brenden Martin observes, park boosters and the NPS depicted Southern Appalachia as a "land forgotten by time."[19] Like Kephart in his best-known work, they suggested that the more remote areas of the Smokies had never advanced beyond a frontier state. Locked in isolation, white mountaineers represented living artifacts of an older America. "In this national mountain museum are many quaint people," the *New York Times* explained in an article describing the park campaign. "They still guard their heritage and reveal in their present-day customs many characteristics of a hundred years ago."[20] White highlanders lived in cabins and scratched a subsistence living from the land, boosters suggested. They hunted bears, drank moonshine, and sang centuries-old folksongs that, like the rest of their ways, had become frozen in time. The park would offer tourists contact with this preserved mountain culture, forming a link to a vital era of national history. Here lived "the American frontiersman," a guidebook said of the Smokies. "They belong to that homogeneous racial group that produced such men as Boone, Sevier, Clarke, Robertson, Admiral Farragut, Shelby, Houston, Andrew Jackson, Lincoln, Crockett, and Sergeant York."[21] This image of mountain people mirrored the idea that the environment of the Smokies formed a "primeval" wilderness, preserved as the rest of the nation advanced. In the national park, boosters promised, visitors would consume both a landscape and a culture from the past.

Kephart was not the only writer to broadcast this image of white mountaineers as isolated from modernity. On the contrary, he belonged to a long line of travel authors, reformers, and "local color" writers who claimed to have discovered the southern mountains and their rural white communities. Long before Kephart arrived, these authors fed a public fascination with Americans' "contemporary ancestors." Park promoters and the NPS, however, appear to have relied heavily on Kephart's writings for their cultural interpretation of the Smokies. Martin, in fact, argues that *Our Southern Highlanders* provided NPS with its main guide for depicting and explaining mountain life.[22] While Kephart's park essays concentrated on the natural environment, his overall body of work shaped how other park boosters and the national park itself depicted the history and culture of mountain people.

Relying on Kephart's conception of mountain whites sometimes led the Park Service to distort Appalachian history. At the national park's popular Cades Cove destination, for instance, the NPS dismantled structures that appeared too modern to fit its preferred image of mountain whites as frontiersmen. At Cades Cove, the Park Service took a settlement that had maintained a variety of connections to the modern industrial South and transformed it into an isolated mountain hamlet. The agency followed a similar approach in its cultural preservation efforts. It worked to collect craftwork, folklore, and music that represented what it considered Appalachia's "pioneer culture" purified of any modern influences. It froze Appalachian culture in a way that mirrored Kephart's depiction of white mountaineers as a people trapped in the past.[23]

As the Park Service adopted this interpretation of mountain culture, it removed actual mountain communities from the lands within the new park's borders. Timber companies owned most of the property targeted for the park, but the area also held around 1,200 farms and numerous other private landholdings. Communities like Cataloochee in North Carolina and Greenbriar in Tennessee were home to hundreds of residents each, and the park area hosted an overall population of around four thousand. Boosters generally depicted the park campaign as a boon to these landowners who would receive good prices for their property and have the opportunity to start over in better circumstances. Not all residents agreed. Landowners in several communities resisted selling or demanded prices much higher than the park commissions were willing to contemplate. John Oliver, of Cades Cove, fought the Tennessee park commission for years before a condemnation suit forced him to sell. Others parted with their land but insisted on retaining access to cemeteries or community churches. To this day, some in western North Carolina and east Tennessee remember the creation of the park with considerable resentment. The people of these communities provided the model for Kephart's romantic image of the white mountaineer, but there was little room for them in the park that Kephart's writing helped to create.[24]

Kephart died in late 1931, years before the completion of the Great Smoky Mountains National Park. Before his death, however, the park movement had raised enough money that he could be relatively certain of its ultimate success. By the end, Kephart understood that the national park, while preserving some of what he valued about the Smokies, would also transform the place he loved. "It was a big undertaking, and beset with discouragements of all sorts; but we've won!" he wrote. "Within two years we will have good roads into the Smokies, and then—well, then I'll get out."[25]

The Last of the Eastern Wilderness

AN ARTICLE ON THE PROPOSED GREAT SMOKY NATIONAL PARK

Two national parks for the East are proposed—one, of about six hundred square miles in the Great Smoky Mountains on the North Carolina-Tennessee boundary, and the other, of about four hundred thousand acres, in the Blue Ridge Mountains of Virginia. This article deals with the Great Smoky proposal, and is by the foremost authority on the history, traditions, customs, and folklore of the region.[26]

Nobody knows who named them the Great Smoky Mountains. On the North Carolina side of the range was the ancient capital of the Cherokee Nation, and there, on the Lufty River, about two thousand of the Indians are still living. If you ask one of them what is the Cherokee name for the Smokies he will probably answer "Giuk-sus-*tee*," meaning smoke. But that is only their translation of the English word.

The older Indians have assured me that the Cherokees have no native name for the Smoky range as a whole. They give a name to each and every peak, ridge, gap, stream, waterfall, or other definite location. Ahaluna is "the place of the ambush"; Atagahi, "the enchanted lake"; Datsiyi, "where the water-monster lives," and so on.[27] But the Smokies as a whole are not distinguished from neighboring ranges of the Unaka system.

The white mountaineers of this region never say "Great Smoky." To them the range is simply "the Smokies." Now and then they use the word in the singular, as when a bear hunter says: "I've seed the wind blow on top o' Smoky till a hoss couldn't stand up agin it."

Some time, if I get the chance, I shall dig into the old records and the old maps in the Library of Congress to find out how far back the poetic title of the Great Smokies goes.

Any visitor in the Smokies can see for himself what suggested the symbolism.

From *World's Work*, April 1926

Nearly always there hovers over the high tops and around them, a tenuous mist, a dreamy blue haze, like that of Indian summer, or deeper. Often it grows so dense as almost to shut out the distant view, as smoke does that has spread from a far-off forest fire. Then it is a "great smoke" that covers all the outlying world; the rim of the earth is but a few miles away; beyond is mystery, enchantment.

Mysterious, indeed, this Smoky Mountain region has been ever since the first white explorer, De Soto, heard of it, nearly four centuries ago. At intervals of many years a few adventurous botanists and geologists have roamed through its great forest—Bartram, Michaux, Gray, Buckley, Mitchell, Guyot, and others—but their reports reached none but scientific circles. When Miss Murfree published a novel entitled "The Prophet of the Great Smoky Mountains" it was commonly supposed that she had invented the striking name. The wildest and most picturesque highland east of the Rockies remained virtually unknown until about ten years ago. Even to-day there are gulfs in the Smokies that no man is known to have penetrated; and seven of the capital peaks, all of them higher than any point in the Blue Ridge, remain to this day unnamed!

In fact, so little is known of the Smokies that newspapers generally misplace them by calling them a part of the Blue Ridge. A recent textbook of advanced geography, prescribed for use in the high schools of North Carolina, has repeated this blunder. It is like confounding the Alleghanies with the Blue Ridge in Pennsylvania.

Let us get it right. In western North Carolina the Blue Ridge is the southeastern rampart of the Appalachian mountain zone. It fronts toward the Piedmont and part of it borders on South Carolina. The Smokies are a segment of the Unaka system, corresponding to the Alleghanies farther north. The Smoky range runs parallel with the Blue Ridge, some forty to fifty miles away. It is part of the northwestern escarpment of the Appalachians, overlooking the great valley that spreads thence westward to the Cumberland plateau. The crest of the Smokies is the state line between North Carolina and Tennessee.

The Smokies are unknown to the world of tourists simply because there are no roads through them, nor even trails in the wilder and rougher parts. Fully six hundred square miles of this region consist of uninhabited forest wilderness. Last summer it was necessary to make an accurate map of the district for use of the Appalachian Park Commission. The work could not be done on the ground in time for the commission's report, and so an army aviator, Lieutenant Williams, flew back and forth over the Smokies for many weeks, making a photographic map from the air. He did not see a house or a human being, except in a few spots where some lumbermen were at work.

What a strange survival of primitive conditions, what astonishing isolation! For the Great Smoky Mountains are not on the other side of the earth or somewhere remote in tropic or arctic solitude: they are midway between the Atlantic and the Mississippi, midway between the Great Lakes and the Gulf, and nearer the center of population of the United States than any other mountains that have scenic attraction.

And they are the mountain climax of eastern America, the master chain of the Appalachian mountain system. From eastern Canada to the southwestern boundary of Virginia—three fourths of the length of the Appalachian zone—there is only one summit that rises as high as six thousand feet above sea-level: it is Mt. Washington (6,293 ft.) in New Hampshire. In the Great Smoky Mountains, within the proposed boundary of the new national park, there are eighteen peaks and many miles of divide that are six thousand feet or more above sea-level. In the Black and Craggy ranges, northeast of Asheville, there is a similar uplift; but these two ranges together cover only eighty-five square miles, whereas the Smokies cover more than seven hundred square miles with their giant ridges and profound gulfs.

Elevation above sea-level is, of course, no adequate measure of a mountain's majesty. It is the "relief," or height above the surrounding country, that impresses a beholder. In this respect the Great Smoky Mountains worthily compare with any in our far western parks. The Rockies rise from an elevated plateau and not many of them exceed in visual height the chief peaks of the Smokies: Clingman Dome, Mt. Guyot, and Mt. Le Conte, which tower a mile in air above base level.

The scenery of the Smoky Mountains is typically Appalachian: steep-sided ridges gradually rounding off toward their crests, the tops gently undulating in outline like billows of the sea, and every mountain covered with a forest mantle. There are no bare rocks rising coldly above a timber-line. There are few jagged peaks, few jutting crags. The Smokies are among the oldest mountains in the world and the erosion of untold ages has worn off the sharp pinnacles that originally rose above the rounded tops that now remain.

Because of this peculiarity it will be no great engineering feat to build along the top of the main divide a skyline highway from the Indian Gap to the Tennessee River, about thirty-five miles, most of which would be from four thousand to five thousand feet above the adjoining country. It is the intention of the Appalachian Park Commission to have this road constructed and to connect it with three transmontane roads running from the Tennessee border to the Carolina border of the park. From many points on the skyline road there will be vistas of a hundred miles out over the Appalachian Valley to the blue Cumberlands on the western horizon, while to the eastward the visitors will behold a sea of wooded mountains as far as the eye can reach. At times the touring parties will be above the clouds; at times they may witness the strange phenomena of thunderstorms or rainbows far below them in the mountain gulfs.

East of the Indian Gap, on the way from Mt. Collins to Mt. Guyot, there is a different formation. Here is the roughest and wildest mountain region in all eastern America. The divide here is saw-toothed and so sharp-edged that an adventurous mountaineer is dizzily poised above slopes so steep on either hand that a misstep might plunge him hundreds of feet down into Tennessee or North Carolina, according to which way he slipped. So rugged is this part of the Smokies that no road will ever be built over it, nor even a bridle path. It is better so. Let its crags and peaks remain forever inviolate for the enjoyment of those hardy and daring climbers who wield the alpenstock and carry their bed and board upon their own backs.

The most luring feature of the Smoky Mountains is their extraordinary variety of trees and plants. Botanists, from Bartram in 1791 to Trelease in 1924, have found here the richest collecting ground in the United States. In a two-day ramble and scramble among the Smokies one may see more species of indigenous trees and shrubs than in a cross-continent trip from Boston to the Pacific Coast. The forests of all Europe have only eighty-five species of native trees; the Smoky forest has one hundred and twenty-seven, not counting many shrubs that here assume arborescent form. There is a huckleberry tree that grows twenty to thirty feet high; the mountain laurel and the great rhododendron reach thirty to forty feet, with trunk diameter of twelve to eighteen inches.

Going from a neighboring river valley up to "the top o' Smoky," one passes successively through the same floral zones, in a twenty-mile hike, as he would view in a trip from mid-Georgia to southern Canada. He starts amid sycamores, elms, willows, black gum and sweet gum, holly, hackberry, hornbeam, persimmon, mulberry, oaks, chinquapin, and box-elder. The near-by ridges have been cut over and are now mostly covered with second-growth oaks, hickories, black pine, locust, and dogwood. If the traveler be lucky at the start he may chance upon a fine specimen of that rarest of eastern trees the *Cladrastis*, or yellowwood.

A few miles from the river town he will pass the last settler's cabin. Thenceforth he is in forest primeval, from which nothing has ever been taken except the big poplars that grew near the creek that he is following as his guide in the upward climb.

In the first ten miles he has ascended perhaps only a thousand feet, but he is already in a different zone of vegetation from that of the river valley. The creek is bordered with black birch and yellow birch, red ash and green ash, butternut and walnut, beech, holly, magnolia, witch hazel, maples of sundry species, giant hemlocks, and chestnut trees of mighty girth. On the steep encompassing ridges are many kinds of oaks, several species of hickories, red maple, white and black pine, yellow locust, sourwood, dogwood, chestnut, gum, and "sarvis" or serviceberry.

A dashing trout brook lures the wanderer aside into one of the rich mountain coves. Here there is no trail and he must push his way through dense thicket of leucothoe higher than his head, squirm under laurel and rhododendron, and zigzag his way amid shrubs and vines of so many kinds that he is bewildered by their tropical variety and luxuriance. In such a place, if he should chance to meet another wayfarer, it will be so unexpectedly and at such close quarters that it will give him a jolt, as if he had stumbled upon a bear—and, in fact, he is as likely to meet the one as the other. But the ragged fellow, himself startled, will probably turn out to be only some harmless "yarb hunter" who prowls here with his "sang hoe" seeking ginseng, snakeroot, cohosh, bloodroot, Indian physic, and other old-fashioned simples. He may tell you of strange things, unknown to the sophisticates of cities.

"Rub horse-sorrel in a pewter platter; the sour eats the pewter and makes a likker that eats away cancer, and hit's done cured fer good an' all. . . . Thar's a plant in these woods—hit ain't common—that we'uns calls North-and-South. Hit resembles wild verbena, grows thigh-high, and is ginerally found in hollers amongst the rocks on the south side o' mountains, near leetle spring-branches. Hit has a toothed leaf, with purple heart, yaller edges, and the rest a bright red. The root allers grows *north and south*. You think I'm a liar; but hit's so!"

Mosses and ferns and mushrooms are everywhere, and in delightful variety, amid the fallen and decaying trunks. There is not a cranny in the rocks, not a foot of the wild glen, but harbors something lovable or rare. Here are the unimproved works of God. These flowers that spring up under the dense canopy of the ancient forest are such as defy cultivation. They can exist nowhere but in the untouched wildwood, which has been left to itself these many thousands of years and provides a mold rich in organic matter and so spongy as to hold moisture at all times. The decaying trunk of a fallen tree, despised by foresters, is really a priceless thing, giving life and sustenance to forms of beauty that nothing else can nourish.

Leaving the cove, a steep climb of a couple of thousand feet brings the visitor to the top of one of the ridges that lead on up to the main divide. From here, as far as one can see in every direction, are wooded mountains without a clearing or other trace of man's activity. On the drier slopes, especially on the south side, the prevailing growth is oak and chestnut, with considerable locust interspersed. The ridge tops have many pines. Hemlocks crowd the deep, cool recesses at the heads of small tributary streams.

Beech, yellow birch, buckeye, and chestnut are found within a wide range of altitude, persisting to the edge of the sub-arctic zone, which begins at about five thousand feet in the region east of Siler's Bald.

The natives of this region do not consider that one knows anything about the Smokies until he has been "up among the balsams." A spray of balsam in his hatband, or a climbing staff of peeled balsam, shiny white and with whorls of clipped stems protruding at intervals around it, is the young mountaineer's proof that he has "been somewhere," that he is travel-tested.

And it is indeed a strange world for a lowlander to visit, this kingdom of the high Smokies, with its dense stand of black spruce and feathery sprayed balsams, its thick moss and waist-high beds of ferns, its snowbirds, vireos, warblers, winter wrens, ravens, eagles, and hawks. Here is the refuge of the black bear, which, in the Smokies, grows larger, I believe, than anywhere else in the country. Panthers no longer haunt the Smokies, but wildcats are numerous, though one seldom sees the furtive things.

At this altitude, mingled with the conifers, there are few species of deciduous trees. There is some striped maple or moosewood, some aspen, and considerable red cherry, which the natives call "Peruvian," owing to its bitter bark that is used as a substitute for quinine. They have curious names, by the way, for several other trees: black spruce is "he-balsam," Fraser's balsam is "she-balsam," hemlock is "spruce-pine," and the curious smoke-tree is "chittimwood."

In May and June the mountains are a vast flower-garden, with laurel and rhododendron and the fiery azalea in full bloom. There are places where for hundreds of acres nothing grows but the rhododendron. There are several species of this showy shrub, some with flowers of lilac-purple, others rose-pink, while the splendid bloom of the great rhododendron is waxy-white.

The wild animals of the Smokies have abundant food. Untold thousands of bushels of blackberries, dewberries, wild raspberries, strawberries, gooseberries, huckleberries, buckberries, service-berries, haws, and grapes supply them in summer. In autumn there is inexhaustible "mast" of acorns, chestnuts, hickory-nuts, beechnuts, and edible seeds.

The charm of the Smokies, and their economic value to the nation as well, is due in great part to their abundant stream-flow. Here are the springheads of wild rivers whose feeders come tumbling down over their rocky beds, rollicking, bubbling, splashing along, taking roaring plunges over the waterfalls. They are crystal-clear and alive with trout—brook trout in the upper reaches, rainbow trout in the lower courses where they have been introduced. There is scarcely any standing water in this whole region—and, by the by, there are no mosquitoes.

Last summer I was called to Asheville to meet Robert Sterling Yard, executive secretary of the National Parks Association. He said to me: "Our association is pledged to defend the high standards of the national parks system and to promote the recreational use of public lands. We have an affiliated membership of more than four million Americans who work together for these ends. I have been sent here to visit the Smoky Mountains and report back to the association whether this area is worthy of being included among our national parks; whether, in its own way, it measures up to the standard set by the Yellowstone, the Yosemite, the Grand Canyon, and the other parks in the Far West.

"I came here skeptical," he continued, "fearing that your Smokies had been overrated by enthusiasts."

"Well," I replied, "you have seen them. What is your verdict?"

"Kephart, I have become one of those enthusiasts myself. Nobody can overrate the Smokies. They are supremely worthy. And they have one quality that is unique."

"What is that?"

"Charm. The Smokies are natural wonders; but they are more than that. One can see a stupendous phenomenon of nature that awes one with its majesty; but when he has seen it once—well, he has seen it. But the Smoky Mountains have enduring charm. Having seen them once, they lure you back to them again and again. I love them. I am coming back."

The charm of the Smokies depends on its living mantle, the tall old forest that covers even the steepest slopes with verdure and fills the woods with living forms that win one's interest and affection. Without that virgin forest the Smokies would be arid rocks. The stony bosom would be cold.

Here to-day is the last stand of primeval American forest at its best. If saved—and if saved at all it must be done at once—it will be a joy and a wonder to our people for all time. The nation is summoned by a solemn duty to preserve it.

Letter from Arthur Perkins to Kephart, April 19, 1929

750 Main Street,
Hartford, Conn.,
April 19, 1929.

Mr. Horace Kephart,
Bryson City, North Carolina.

My dear Mr. Kephart:

I do not know whether you have heard of the project called the Appalachian Trail which is intended to be a mountain trail along the Alleghenies from Maine to Georgia. Such an enterprise is on foot, however, under the management of an organization called the Appalachian Trail Conference, which is composed of mountain clubs through whose territory the proposed trail is to run, together with those in control of state and national forests and parks on the route and a number of interested individuals besides.

Your friend, Mr. Paul Fink of Jonesboro, is one of the enthusiastic workers for this plan, as are also the supervisors of the National Forests in your neighborhood.

Mr. Fink suggests that you might be interested in becoming a member of this Conference, and the Committee in charge of the organization would certainly feel very gratified if they could include your name.

In order that you may get some idea of the organization I am enclosing you a copy of a proposed constitution which will be presented for action at the next annual meeting of the Conference. This draft has been somewhat corrected already, and may be changed more when it is finally adopted.

You will notice that there is a provision for a Board of Managers consisting of three individuals from each section, the southern section consisting of the states through which the Trail runs, south of the Virginia line.

On the list of proposed officers you will find that the managers for your section will be Mr. Fink and Mr. Thompson, (the president of the Smoky Mountain Hiking Club,) and the third name is that of Col. David Chapman of the Smoky Mountain Park, but he will be unable to act on account of his other interests, and it would give us great satisfaction if you would be willing to allow your name to be presented as a substitute for him on the Board.

There will be no expense connected with the membership in this Conference or on the Board, except, of course, traveling expenses in case you wish to attend meetings, etc.

The annual meeting this year will be held at Easton, Pennsylvania which I fear will be too far for you to come, but we hope to have a meeting, shortly, somewhere in the South at which I hope you can be present.

The location of the Trail in southern Virginia is not as yet established, and there may be room for discussion as to its location through the Great Smokys also.

I have in mind a trip south next Fall to look over the situation especially in Virginia, and I think it may be a good plan if we could get together those especially interested in the matter south of that point. We might, at such a meeting, be able to determine on some point for the southern terminus of the Trail, though I am rather amused to find thateverybody [*sic*] down that way who is interested has a different suggestion to make about it.

I shall be very glad to keep you informed in case any such meeting is planned, for of course, we should want your advice and assistance.

Yours very truly,

Arthur Perkins.
Acting Chairman

AP:L

Letter from Arthur Perkins to Kephart, January 22, 1930

750 Main Street,
Hartford, Conn.,
January 22, 1930.

Mr. Horace Kephart,
Bryson City, N.C.

My dear Mr. Kephart:

I have yours of January 15th the contents of which is [*sic*] extremely interesting to me.

I had heard of your trip to Mt. Oglethorpe from George Masa, but he gave no details as he said he thought you would write me fully about it, as you certainly have done.

This question of the route of the Trail in the Great Smoky Mountains and to the south of them, seems to me can be solved by having the route divide at Silers Bald into two parts, both of which shall be the main trail, one going down the Ridge to the southwest, crossing the Little Tennessee River, and continuing over a little private land and through the Cherokee National Forest to Cohutta Mountain, which, on the map, at any rate, looks like an abrupt termination and is near enough Cohutta Springs to furnish railroad and automobile connection. I agree with you that there is no particular reason for the plan to continue from here to Chattanooga or Lookout Mountain. This suggestion probably originated in the north where that Mountain is about the only one which the average northerner ever heard of. This [to Cohutta], by the way, was the route which was formerly adopted by the Appalachian Trail Conference before we had as much information about the southern end as we have now.

As the mountains in your neighborhood are by far the most interesting on the whole Trail, and many of them are higher than any others on the Trail, it seems to me that there is quite room enough for two main trails, branching from each other at Silers Bald and [one] going down over Forney Ridge and through the Nantahala and Cherokee Forests (eastern division) to Mt. Oglethorpe as you suggest.

After the new club in Asheville is organized, I hope it will be willing to take over the supervision of this route which will not involve very much work, as the two Forests and the Tate Estates are so much interested that I am quite sure they will undertake the necessary construction and maintenance of the parts already not in existence.

As to the other branch of the main Trail the Knoxville Club have already agreed to see to that, as I said before, Mr. Smith, the Supervisor of the Cherokee Forest is only too glad to do his part.

It might be possible also in a conference between the two clubs to divide up some sections of the Trail to the north of this point assigning to each club the part more readily accessible to it.

I also had a long letter from Mr. Fink which I have not yet had time to read carefully, telling about your meeting at his house which seems to have been extremely satisfactory.

He enclosed a letter from Mr. Broadbent and a map showing the suggested location of the Trail in the Unaka Forest, and I need hardly say that his statement that there are already in existence about 350 miles of available trails there is extremely interesting and satisfactory to me.

When all routes available are added together, both north and south, I should say that there will probably not be more than 200 or 300 miles to be arranged for, and as the whole trail approximates 1,300 miles, it seems to me that we are making extremely good progress.

I noticed in the Press a day or two ago that the deeds of the Tennessee side of the Smoky Mountain Park are ready for delivery to the United States government, and will actually be delivered in the course of a few weeks which is very satisfactory news. I heard about the trouble with the Champion Fibre Company on the North Carolina side when I called on Mr. Verne Rhodes.

At that time he hoped to make some friendly adjustment with them but evidently has been unable to do so, and I regret that it will be necessary to resort to condemnation proceedings, which, of course, will take a good while.

I am delighted to hear that you and Mr. Masa hope to attend the annual meeting at Skyland, Virginia, the last of May. The place was selected for the meeting largely on account of the hope that the members from the southern end could be present and get acquainted with the northern enthusiasts, which I think is very desirable.

If you want something to get busy on, I suggest that you try to get as many as possible to come up and attend the meeting. Mr. Rhodes certainly ought to be there, and also Mr. Wood, the Supervisor of the Nantahala Forest, and Mr. Smith of the Cherokee. The latter attended the meeting of the Conference in Washington two years ago, and I think will make every effort to be present. I am pretty sure Paul Fink will be there unless prevented by business, and we certainly ought to have a good delegation from the Knoxville Club, though I presume that is a little out of your range of influence.

Yours very truly,

Arthur Perkins.

AP:L

Letter from Kephart to Arthur Perkins, February 21, 1930

HORACE KEPHART
Bryson City, N.C.
Feb. 21, 1930.

Judge Arthur Perkins,
Chairman of the Board,
Appalachian Trail Conference,
Hartford, Conn.

My dear Judge Perkins:-

From Mr. E. B. Stone, Jr., Assistant State Forester of Georgia, stationed at Gainesville, I learn that Georgia strongly disapproves of running a fork of the Appalachian Trail via the Frog Mountains to Cohutta Mountain, and that they will do nothing to open or maintain it; but that they will heartily cooparate [*sic*] on a main trail to Mt. Oglethorpe.

On the other hand, I understand that the Knoxville Hiking Club desires the Cohutta route, largely, I suppose, because it would carry the Trail through the whole length of the Smoky Mountains National Park and give them direct access to the A.T. from any point on their side.

I have given this matter much study, and believe that I have found a way to satisfy both parties by a modification of the Ozmer trail that is outlined on the enclosed map. I also think, from person [*sic*] familiarity with the country, that the suggested course through to Gregory Bald and out to the Ozmer trail at Tellico Gap, via Tapoco and Santeetlah lakes and the Nantahala Gorge, has much more scenic attraction than the short cut from Siler's Bald via Bushnell.

In all probability the Aluminum Company of America, through a subsidiary, will begin before long the construction of large dams for hydro-electric purposes below Bushnell, or near it, which will completely flood the small towns in that region with a deep lake extending upstream to Bryson City. In that case there would be no crossing at Bushnell nor anywhere near it. But there will always be a crossing at Rymer's Ferry.

My suggestion is to continue the A.T. westward along the crest of the Smokies (state line) from Siler's Bald to Gregory Bald, through the National Park. From Gregory Bald the trail would run down Twenty Mile to the main forks of the creek, then east to Rymer's Ferry on Tapoco Lake. The scenery all along this route is very fine. At Rymer's Ferry the crossing would be by ferry boat or small power boats. Entering Graham County, the trail would follow the old wagon road around the point of the mountain to Yellow Creek, where a surfaced highway runs thence, along the beautiful shores of Santeetlah Lake, to Robbinsville, where one can rest and get supplies.

From Robbinsville we would follow the state highway to the lookout at the head of the Nantahala Gorge, where the vistas are sublime. Leaving the highway at this point, we would descend to an old wagon road, below the railroad, that goes on down to Nantahala station on the Southern Railway. Here begins a good road recently built by the National Forest Service, which goes up the breath-taking Winding Stairs, from which even better views of the Gorge are afforded than on the opposite side. This road would be followed to Partridge Creek. Then an old wagon road would be taken up into Tellico Gap, where the Ozmer trail is struck. There would be no change in the Ozmer route from Tellico Gap to Mt. Oglethorpe.

I am thoroughly convinced that Mt. Oglethorpe is the natural and most fitting southern terminus of the A.T., as I wrote you some time ago. Cohutta Mountain is isolated and gets one nowhere. Neither is it the true southern end of the Appalachian Mountain system, which Oglethorpe really is. The scenic attractions of Oglethorpe and its surroundings are superior, its accessibility from everywhere in Georgia is all that could be desired, and both the State authorities and the local people heartily support the A.T. project, whereas, if there is any corresponding sentiment for Cohutta I have not heard of it. Anyway, it is up to Georgia to make the choice, as the opening and maintaining of the Trail in their State requires their support and is their own affair.

I am sending copies of the enclosed map to Paul Fink and to Mr. Stone, to get their opinions on the suggested relocation of the part of the Trail marked on the map.

I hope to be with you at the May meeting at Skylands, Va. Recently I spent a week in Washington, D.C., attending the transfer to the Federal Government of the first block (150,000 acres) of Smoky Mountains National Park land by North Carolina and Tennessee, then doing some historical research in the Library of Congress. I was entertained at the Cosmos Club by scientists of the Dep't of Agriculture, to whom I showed about 60 of George Masa's photographs. These gentlemen were quite enthusiastic about the Park and several parties of them will visit it, botanizing, this coming spring and summer.

Sincerely,
Horace Kephart.

Afoot and Awing in the Great Smokies

THE MOST PICTURESQUE SECTION OF THE EAST, WHERE OUR LATEST NATIONAL PARK IS LOCATED

My office windows overlook a clear, swift river—the Tuckaseegee—which runs through the middle of our town. The old building in which I write stands directly on the river bank. It is on the same block with the court-house and the post-office; yet if some big sycamores were not in the way, I could cast a line from the upstairs porch in front of my windows and catch small-mouth bass or redhorse or spotted channel catfish. That is too handy for any but a lazybones; so I am glad that the trees spread over the waterside and thwart such trifling.

I look up from my typewriter and out across the river, over the roofs of stores and houses, to a pine-clad ridge less than four hundred yards away, and up to ranges of wooded mountains that tower to the sky-line among the clouds. There is something remarkable about that piny ridge in the foreground—something that sets it apart and personifies it among all the thousand ridges that surround it in these highlands of North Carolina and Tennessee.

Abruptly the hill rises just across the track from the railway station. The morning train from Asheville is now coming in. If a whimsical passenger or a fugitive should hop off on the wrong side of the train, he could disappear at once among the pines. He could travel northward for two days through thick forest, where there is no road nor habitation of man. He would then be across the border in another state. And in those two days, from the time he scrambled up the front of my piny ridge, there is slight chance that any human eye would glimpse him.

Such an adventurer would cross a wilderness of high mountains—the most massive range east of Dakota. He would pass over one of the most picturesque but least known parts of Eastern America. On the map it is called the Great Smoky Mountains, a name suggested by the dreamy blue haze that generally hovers over the peaks like smoke—a great smoke—from some far distant forest fire.

From *Field and Stream*, January 1929

Bryson City.

The Smokies stand in the center of Eastern America, midway between the Atlantic and the Mississippi, midway between the Great Lakes and the Gulf. A railroad runs along their southern border. Beside it, within the past year, a hard-surfaced highway has been finished, which is a link of the Appalachian Scenic Highway from Montreal to Miami and New Orleans. And yet, to this day the Smokies remain a land of mystery, unknown save by long-range view, not only to tourists but even to most of the people who live round about.

Four years ago, at a meeting of our local Chamber of Commerce, I talked about a project that had long been in my mind and heart—the preservation of the superb forest of the Smokies by its rescue from the lumbermen who threatened utterly to destroy it. There were sixty-five men present at that meeting, most of them born or bred in the shadow of the Smokies.

I knew all of these men personally. Looking them over, I said: "There are only three men in this room who have ever been on top of any one of the fifteen capital peaks of the Smoky Mountains. Yet the chief of those summits, old Clingman Dome, center and apex of the proposed park area, is only nine and a half air-miles from this table where we are eating dinner."

The peaks I referred to are all in the 6,000-foot class, higher than any mountains of the Blue Ridge in its whole range from Pennsylvania to Georgia; yet seven of those giants are to this day without a name on any map. I know no other region in the civilized world that is at once so majestic, so picturesque, and yet so little known as the Smokies. Though right in the center of the most populous half of our country, and now accessible by train and automobile to its portals, this is still virgin ground where sportsmen may feel the thrill of exploration and naturalists may discover new species of animals and plants.

The astonishing isolation of the Smokies in the very midst of civilization—the fact that they still preserve the charm and lure of the Unknown—is due simply to lack of roads up from the valley highways into the mountains themselves. Hundreds of tourists now pass daily in their cars. From the highway (N. C. 10) they see Clingman Dome and other majestic peaks of the Smokies on the horizon; but they can have no idea of the wonders and beauties in the seven hundred square miles of wilderness, all wooded, uninhabited by man, in which those mountains stand.

It is only the native bear hunter, the timber cruiser, the venturesome naturalist or the true mountain lover, who packs his equipment on his own back and goes where no horse can travel, that really knows the Smokies.

Twenty-four years ago I was a nervous wreck, with no chance of recovery unless I gave up my profession, quit city life, got out into the open and stayed there. I knew that I could not stand the monotony of farm life nor make a living there. But I loved the wilderness and was used to going alone.

So I picked out the Smokies for my roving. It was a country without screed and almost without hearsay. I knew no one who had ever visited it. All I could learn about it was that there were high mountains covered with the finest mixed forest in America; that there were trout and bear; that the people were as primitive as the ancient Gaels. So there I went, far back into the wildest part of that unknown land, and started life over again, alone in a log hut.

At that time Caspar Whitney had charge of *Outing* and Emerson Hough was editing FIELD AND STREAM. They induced me to write for their magazines. In a year or so I was strong again, scarcely knowing what nerves were. I could have gone back to the city grind, but—never again! I had found a more satisfying, wholesome[r] way of living.

So in the old days I saw the Smokies in their primal glory, ere ever a stick of timber had been cut or a stream polluted. Then came the lumbermen with their mills and logging trains. Far back in the mountains they established camps with their big horses and hell-roaring crews of "jacks." I saw them fell the old forest giants over thousands of acres, tearing up the very earth with their skidders. Mile after mile of my Eden was left a desert of stumps and slashings, where briers sprang up so thickly that nothing but fire could travel through them.

So went the watersheds of Hazel and Eagle Creeks, Forney and Twentymile; so went the prongs of Little River; so went a good part of Lufty and Cataloochee. Within a few more years, all the rest would go. The grandest forest in Eastern America would be utterly destroyed unless the power of the Federal Government itself was enlisted and the primeval woods that still remained were preserved forever in a national park.

I preached, and in my heart I prayed for such intervention. But here in the backwoods, mine was but a feeble voice. The native people would give no ear at first, for they were making day's wages in camps and mills. They resented criticism of the lumber interests as a quarrel with their bread and bacon. "What are trees for, anyway?"

Yet the good old wilderness has friends, not only in low but in high places. All over the nation, scattered but linked together by ties of mutual tastes and ideals, are loyal and zealous friends of the woods and streams—sportsmen and nature lovers, artists and scientists, writers and editors, statesmen with vision, women devoted to the country's welfare, men of wealth who use their fortunes for the public good.

By the persistent team-work of all of these, in the last three years, ten million dollars have been raised to buy up the seven hundred square miles of the Smokies and present the land to the Federal Government, which in turn has agreed to maintain that area forever as a Smoky Mountains National Park. Half of the fund was raised in North Carolina and Tennessee by state appropriations and private subscription, and this was matched, dollar for dollar, by the Laura Spellman Rockefeller Foundation. The surveys are now nearly completed, and the purchasing has begun.

This new national park lies half in North Carolina and half in Tennessee. The state line follows the crest of the Smoky range. On the sketch-map printed here, only a few of the peaks are marked. The whole region is a labyrinth of mountains. An official map of the park area, on a scale of two miles to the inch, with contours showing elevations above sea-level, may be procured from the Director, U. S. Geological Survey, Washington, D. C.

The boundary shown by a heavy black line on the sketch-map extends somewhat beyond the actual limits of the park. For example, it takes in the reservation of the Cherokee Indians, of whom some 2,500, two-thirds of them full-bloods, live near the site of their ancient capital on the Okonalufty River. The chief area of primeval forest is on Deep Creek, beginning five miles north of Bryson City, North Carolina.

When the park area is taken over by the Government, a few roads for automobiles and many bridle-trails will be made among the Smokies, but the greater part will doubtless be left as it is—aloof and sacred from unappreciative crowds, but open to genuine nature lovers who do not disdain to walk. The cut-over lands, now rapidly reforesting themselves with a dense new growth, will be game sanctuaries, from which the surrounding country will get the overflow. No hunting will be allowed in the park itself, but fishing will be permitted under the usual regulations. Camp sites will be furnished in the more level places, mostly where there are now some mountain farms.

The scenery of this superb region, the luxuriance of the virgin forest, of which about a hundred thousand acres has been rescued inviolate, the streams and waterfalls are described and pictured in booklets that may be obtained free from the Knoxville and Asheville Chambers of Commerce, along with travel guides. The character of the country and its native inhabitants I have described in one of my books, *Our Southern Highlanders*.

Year after year, since 1904, I have tramped and camped in the Smoky Mountains, and still there are many parts of that wild and rugged land that I have never been in. There are cliffs and gulfs that no man is known to have scaled. In fact, I know only half a dozen men who have even followed the full length of the Smoky divide.

There are parts of it, between Collins and Guyot, two of the chief peaks, that are so sharp-edged that one can straddle the state line and cast a pebble down either side, hundreds of feet, into North Carolina or Tennessee.

I have worn out many a blanket and knapsack in the Smokies, many a pair of hobnailed shoes. For weeks on end I have climbed their rugged heights, seldom if ever meeting a human being.

It was hard toil, but glorious; never monotonous, often thrilling. Sometimes I would make ten miles a day, or even fifteen; sometimes only three or four. It made no difference; I was there to observe, not to hurry. I would camp where night found me, on some summit that touched the clouds, or deep in a fairy glen beside the waterfalls.

Often, in such situations, there came to me through the mist of years a whisper of verses from old Nessmuk, my tutor in woodcraft, now in the Happy Hunting Ground. He wrote them in the Adirondacks when I was a boy:

Only to him whose coat of rags
  Has pressed at night her regal feet
  Shall come the secrets, strange and sweet,
Of century pines and beetling crags.

For him the goddess shall unlock
  The golden secrets which have lain
  Ten thousand years, through frost and rain,
Deep in the bosom of the rock.

The world of man has passed through some mighty changes since those lines were penciled by the old woodsman back in the far-away 'eighties. It is a fast age now.

One day last week an airplane came to Deep Creek and settled on a landing field that some of my friends have made on the very edge of the Smoky Mountains National Park. The pilot invited me to see the mountains from the air. We glided from the field, nosed upward over the valley, spiraled above the town of Bryson nestling amid its hills as at the bottom of a bowl, sailed westward following the winds of the Tuckaseegee River that glinted like a silver ribbon so far below, turned and came back to Deep Creek, ever mounting higher and higher, then swerved and darted over the pinnacle of Sharptop, heading toward Clingman Dome.

Hitherto I had scarcely realized how far we were above the earth, for there was nothing near enough alongside to measure by. If one stuck his head out over the cockpit to look straight down, he got such a blast of air in the face that he ducked back before there was time to get dizzy. But now, as we shot over Sharptop, we were in a few seconds over a vast gulf, with exceedingly steep mountains on either side. From the trees on the mountain flanks, one could estimate what a drop there was into that mighty chasm below.

Still we were nosing upward, pointed straight toward the summit of the highest peak of them all. The pilot shouted something that I could not hear above the roar of the engine and through the thick leather of the helmet strapped down over my ears. He idled the motor to silence it, so we might chat a moment, and we glided along without effort, like a sailing red-tailed hawk.

"Five thousand feet," said he, reading the altimeter.

"Then we're still sixteen hundred and eighty below the top of Clingman," I remarked.

He opened the throttle, and we kept on climbing; but we only went close to Clingman, not over it, and turned back the nose of the plane at the head of the Noland gorge.

It is a tremendous experience, this flying over such rugged mountains and close to their bristling sides. At an elevation of five thousand feet, one's range of vision on a clear day is ninety-four miles in every direction; or it would be so over a sea or plain. Here, of course, it was restricted by a mountainous horizon. And to whatever point of the compass we looked, however the plane might turn in its bird-like soaring, there was a chaos of tree-clad mountains, like a cosmic sea with mile-high waves turned rigid and set for all eternity in the postures of its last upheaval.

CAMPING DEPARTMENT

HORACE KEPHART

EDITOR

Then and Now

This month and henceforward, Horace Kephart, the most respected living authority on camping, will write and edit your favorite department.—Ed.

When I was a boy, in the old West, we often camped out, as a matter of course. But cooking in the open and sleeping under the stars were only incidental to the main business in hand, which was hunting or fishing or moving from place to place. Camping for its own sake, as a recreation or a means of rejuvenation, was a thing unheard of. Special equipment for such purpose would have been gawked at and ridiculed. We just took along some simple things that everybody had at home. We could be ready for a trip in half an hour.

And why not? More than three-fourths of the population of the United States, at that time, was rural. Nearly everybody was still endowed with the poineer [*sic*] spirit. Nearly everybody was accustomed from childhood to pioneer ways of life. When a boy entered his 'teens he already knew how to shoot, how to catch fish, how to chop wood, how to make a proper fire in the open. There would have been no sense in reading about such things in books or magazines.

So camping had no literature. The nearest approach to a camping manual was "The Prairie Traveler," by General Marcy, which was a guide to overland travel in covered wagon and wild Indian days; but not one actual "mover" in a hundred ever saw or heard of such a book.

Over in Europe conditions were different. The Old Country had been urbanized for a long, long time. There was a leisured class that went in for all sorts of outdoor sports—among others, yachting. And there was a white-collar class of moderate means that felt the strain of confinement within city walls and loved to spend vacations in the open.

From *National Sportsman,* April 1931

For the multitude of shopkeepers, clerks and professional men there came a godsend in the "poor man's yacht"—the canoe. John MacGregor set the fashion, in 1865, when he began making long voyages, alone, in his *Rob Roy*, a decked canoe that could be either sailed or paddled and was light enough for portaging. He carried a minimum of equipment and slept aboard.

The New York Canoe Club, following British precedent but soon modifying it to suit American conditions, was founded in 1871. At first our city folk did most of their cruising in near-by waters and their sport was chiefly racing. But gradually they took more to open paddling canoes, modeled after the Indian's birch-bark masterpiece. This was the craft for the wilderness, and it took them thither. Away off into the wild back-country, where there were no inns nor markets nor even farmsteads to depend on for supplies. So the adventurers took along grub for a week, or a month and they slept ashore in little tents.

Thus the sport of camping that is camping for its own sake—was born. Thus did the city-worn take to gipsying. Good old "Nesstnuk," [*sic*] the cobbler-poet, the canoeist and woodsman, showed them how, in his fascinating little book on "Woodcraft." That was in 1888. Camping began to have a literature.

By that time one-third of our people were living in cities. The urban population was feeling the nerve-strain and bodily exhaustion that are the penalties of a hurrying, high-tensioned civilization. To ease it there came an urge to break away from it all, now and then, and get back to Mother Earth—"back to Nature," as we were fond of phrasing it. City folk were finding out that the best of all restoratives is to cruise the woods and waters, fend for ourselves, and camp out.

The thing came like a wave. In 1906 there appeared three more books on camping, simultaneously written: one by Stewart Edward White, one by Charles Stedman Hanks, and the other by myself.

There was a suddenly born passion for contriving new sorts of camping gear. Sportsmen's magazines welcomed new "kinks" in that line. Specialists went into the camp equipment business on a large scale and soon had orders from the ends of the earth.

And now—how it all has grown! Today considerably more than half the people of the United States are town or city dwellers. Even the farms are mechanized. The old handicrafts of the pioneers are forgotten. Not one house-builder in a thousand today knows how to use a frow in riving shingles. The nerve-strain has increased; the chests have flattened; the urge to get out of doors, away from the hurly-burly, is no longer an idiosyncrasy but a commonly recurrent passion.

Canoeing and motor-boating are more popular than ever. Hiking and mountaineering clubs have thousands of active members. Hunters and fishermen who go far and camp out are now a prodigious army. Automobiles speed us away from the city to pleasant camping grounds, wherever we choose to go. The number of automobile campers runs into the millions.

Correspondingly, the literature of camping has grown until two long shelves in my den are crowded with books on that subject that have appeared within the last twenty years.

A LOOK AHEAD

In this department we will discuss, from month to month, all sorts of things interesting to campers. The old, old topics are yet ever new. The last word has been said on none of them. Conditions change and call for fresh adaptations. Another generation is always springing up, with tastes and requirements more or less peculiar to a new age.

And even the old-timers do not lose interest in new aspects of camping. It is, perhaps, the outstanding merit of our sylvan sport that it keeps the brain young, no matter if the hand has lost its cunning and the eye is too dim to align rifle sights. One of the most enthusiastic "fans" that I know is a gentleman now well in the eighties who, though no longer nimble enough to wade the rocky trout streams, still finds a heaven on earth when camping in the wild forest of the Smokies.

THE LONG, LONG TRAIL

One of the topics that is forever new is *Where to Go?*

Let us start this, our first month's camp-chat, with the outline of a project, now well under way, to provide outing places for the millions, where they may go at little expense, each on his own and following his own bent.

It is the Appalachian Trail from Maine to Georgia. Not a road, but a crestline path that winds for 1,500 miles through the wild back-country of the Appalachian system and links up the various segments with each other. Much of the country that it traverses is genuine wilderness. Yet it is easily reached by half of the people of the United States, and particularly by those who live in congested districts.

The idea of such a trail was first suggested in 1920 by Benton MacKaye. He said: "The project is one for a series of recreational communities throughout the Appalachian chain of mountains from New England to Georgia, these to be connected by a walking trail. Its purpose is to establish a base for a more extensive and systematic development of outdoor community life."

It is a hikers' trail, with shelter camps located at convenient distances so as to allow a comfortable day's walk between each. The camps are to be equipped for sleeping, so that the hiker need not burden himself with a heavy pack, and some of them will serve meals, after the fashion of the Swiss chalets.

The foundation for such a scheme had been laid a long time ago, when the Appalachian Mountain Club, the Green Mountain Club, and twenty-one other outdoor organizations formed the New England Trail Conference that built and cared for a thousand miles of trails in New Hampshire, Vermont, Massachusetts and Connecticut.

Thence the movement spread to the central and southern states. The federal and state governments began to cooperate through their forest and park services. In 1925 a body of those interested was formed under the name Appalachian Trail Conference. In 1928, in Washington, D. C., a formal and permanent organization was effected and active work began. By the end of 1929 some 500 miles of the trail had been constructed, other hundreds of miles had been scouted, and new hiking clubs had been formed to look after respective sections.

The most remarkable outcome has been the quick and energetic response in the South, where hiking heretofore has been almost as rare a form of recreation as it was among the old-time cowmen of the West. The Smoky Mountains Hiking Club, of Knoxville, the Carolina Appalachian Trail Club, of Asheville, the Georgia Appalachian Trail Club, of Gainesville, all are at work scouting and placing the copper markers of the A. T. along the high mountain ranges of their states. The Potomac Appalachian Trail Club, of Washington, has been especially active and has already finished over a hundred miles of the trail in Virginia.

A glance at the accompanying sketch-map shows where the trail runs. Beginning at Mt. Katahdin, in the Maine wilderness, it goes to the foot of Moosehead Lake and thence to Grafton Notch where it joins the excellent trail system of the Appalachian Mountain Club. At Moosilauke, N. H., it links with the trail of the Dartmouth Outing Club, which in turn meets the Long Trail of the Green Mountain Club of Vermont. At Mt. Greylock and on through to Mt. Everett in the southwest corner of Massachusetts the work has been done by local groups, and I presume it is finished by this time. So also in western Connecticut, where the trail was located by Judge Arthur Perkins, chairman of the board of the Appalachian Trail Conference.

From the Connecticut-New York line the trail is looked after by the New York chapter of the Appalachian Mountain Club to Bear Mountain bridge over the Hudson River. It then enters the Palisades Interstate Park and has been extended by way of Greenwood Lake and the Kittatiny Ridge to the Delaware Water Gap.

Through Pennsylvania and along the Blue Ridge to the Susquehanna River the trail is in charge of the Blue Mountain Club, the Blue Mountain Eagle Climbing Club and the Linglestown Appalachian Trail Club. Thence it will probably cross the Cumberland Valley near its northern end and follow the ridge of South Mountain, through a state park, and cross Maryland to Harper's Ferry.

From the Potomac to the southern end of the Shenandoah National Park the work is rapidly nearing completion by the Potomac Appalachian Trail Club. It extends by a sky-line trail through the Natural Bridge National Forest.

From the Peaks of Otter, at the southern edge of the last-named forest, there are two alternative routes: one following the Blue Ridge to Grandfather Mountain and thence westward over the Yellow Mountains and the Roan to the main Unakas; the other, from the Peaks of Otter through the Unaka National Forest to the point where the first-named loop would top out on the Unakas. From this point to the Big Pigeon River, on the North Carolina-Tennessee boundary, considerable scouting must be done before the route is definitely located.

At the Big Pigeon River begins the Great Smoky Mountains National Park. The Smookies [*sic*] are the wildest, most massive and ruggedest segment of the whole Appalachian system. Here the peaks rise to from 5,000 to 6,600 feet above sea-level, some of them a full mile above their bases, and a good part of the way is through virgin forest, as there is no tree limit. At present the going is difficult in places; but the National Park Service is beginning to build what will eventually be an admirable system of trails throughout the whole Park.

The trail will run almost the length of the Smokies, leaving them at either the Gregory Bald or the Parson Bald, thence turning down to the Little Tennessee River, crossing it at Rhymer's Ferry, skirting Santeetlah Lake, running out to and across the upper end of the Nantahala Gorge, up the Winding Stairs, along a forest road to the top of the Nantahala Range, then through the Cherokee National Forest and along the Blue Ridge to the southern terminus at Mt. Oglethorpe, fifty miles north of Atlanta, Georgia.

It is rather inspiring to see the A. T. markers already nailed to the trees all along the Georgia end of the trail. A few months ago there was erected on the summit of Mt. Oglethorpe a tall monument to the founder of the state after whom this fine peak was named. On the occasion of the dedicatory ceremony a squad of Georgia Boy Scouts who had just finished their hike from the North Carolina line, along the Appalachian Trail, arrived in time to salute the national colors flying from the top of the marble shaft.

Yes, it is a long, long trail, this Appalachian. It goes up and down, up and down over a thousand hills and slopes. It would take an athlete, and a determined one, to

The Gypsy Caravan Cartoonist Records His Mountain Impressions

Illustrated trip from Columbus, Ohio, to the Great Smokies.
Kephart is featured at lower right.

follow its course from end to end—take him three months, probably, to make the trip. In the high ranges of the South he would have to carry full equipment, with a week's rations, on his own person, and he might not meet a human being for days on end.

Few will atempt [*sic*] such a feat; for the pleasure of a walking trip is not in breaking records for endurance but in the scenes and surprises of it, the fresh air and the exhiliration [*sic*] of lusty muscular movement, the enjoyment of unspoiled natural surroundings, the peace of mind and relaxation from common everyday affairs: so the sensible walker goes till he is tired and then stops for the day.

But all along that trail, from Maine to Georgia, there is something new and interesting, or even marvelous, or quaint and lovable, for anyone with an open mind and a free soul. And so, all along its sinuous course, in every state, in every county, through the greater part of the year, there will be people rambling over its wooded and flower-decked hills and dells, each pursuing his fancy and having a good time in his own way.

It will do them more good than sitting still in a stadium and watching a few other folks play the game. And it will cost them nothing but their lunches and the sole-leather they wear out. This is recreation—*re-creation*—for everybody who is not blind or lame of body or soul.

Words of an enthusiast? Well, why should not one be an enthusiast who, at sixty-eight, is still climbing the highest hills of the Trail Country, and sleeping out o' nights, just for the sheer enjoyment of it, although twenty-five years ago that same man could not have climbed Bunker Hill Monument without halting now and then to regain his breath?

What the mountains and forests did for me they can do for other run-down folks—and then they, too, will be enthusiasts; for one just can't be stolid or despondent when his lungs are full of mountain air and his blood is coursing free.

APPENDIX I

Horace Kephart's "Index to Diary"

GEORGE FRIZZELL

Kephart's handwritten two-page "Index to Diary" is an intriguing glimpse into his first months in western North Carolina. The index is not a chronology, but when matched with his photo album, it presents a general overview of his experiences and research inclinations. Notations from his extensive journals provide additional contextualization. The diary itself has not been located and may have been destroyed on purpose or by accident over the intervening years. Lacking the diary's full text, the index entries are open to conjecture and interpretation. Still, they reveal a Kephart who is expressing his feelings, his impressions, and a restless desire to observe and document the western North Carolina he sought out upon his arrival in the town of Dillsboro in the summer of 1904 and his subsequent relocation to the Medlin community in the Great Smoky Mountains later that autumn. Images of the "Index to Diary" are reproduced in this volume to highlight their stark brevity and the precision of his penmanship that cannot be captured in a transcription. Also, Kephart's photo album and journals have been digitally reconstructed and are available online for comparison.[1]

The index and photo album are not random assemblages. Rather, they feature Kephart's thoughtfulness in arrangement and show a concise attention to preparation. This may be because Kephart initially intended only a six month reconnoiter of western North Carolina for a potential publication and was using them as research materials.[2] While the index is undated, the notations focus heavily on events from 1904 to 1905. Kephart used numbered sections to group his summations, often with multiple entries and frequently incorporating an ampersand (used in the transcript as "&") to make cross-references to the diary. The photo album in its final form primarily covers the years from 1904 until about 1909 and exhibits the "rage for photos" that Kephart expressed. The album was rearranged, as seen in the erasure of original captions on many pages and changes in photograph placement. This may help explain the correlations in the text of the index and several photo captions. For instance, among the entries in the index with corresponding photograph captions in the album are "Addio!," "The Mail Rider," and "Visitors." In addition to photographs, Kephart interspersed the album with pictures cut from publications, notably his personal copy of a 1902 government report on Southern Appalachia that he invoked as the only source that met his requirements to discover, as he called it, a *terra incognita* in the mountains.[3] Even so, he seems to have sought out a Southern Appalachia that met his preference for an eighteenth-century frontier, as embodied by Daniel Boone, and a people trapped in a "Rip Van Winkle" sleep that preserved a lifestyle unsullied by urbanization and industrialization.

All the while, the index reflects Kephart's immersion in a new cultural landscape and physical environment and is replete with references to weather, plant and animal life, geographic locations, and the people. Scattered throughout are notes about his explorations, from fishing trips to high mountain tops, and to his interactions with individuals. Tantalizing references are found to his personal side that range from the private to the mundane. For instance, given his emotional state after abandoning a professional career and undergoing a family crisis, the first entry invokes "New Freedom." Also, Kephart remarked on the practicalities of setting up camp on Dicks Creek, such as coping with incessant rain and "Cooking in the wet," but also mentioned "Isolation. (Camping alone)" and "Insomnia." Some references indicate the difficulties of relocating to a new home. While he may have been traveling light upon his arrival in western North Carolina, Kephart seems to have had additional items sent separately given comments referring to his persistent trouble with "delayed freight" and its eventual arrival. In addition, some entries were woven into his publications, such as the notation "The man whose eyes shine," which became a short feature in *Forest and Stream,* and the comment on the "Blizzard of April, 1900" that appeared in *Our Southern Highlanders*.

The transcript presented here of the "Index to Diary" features it in its entirety, though with endnotes to provide context or clarity. Also, a selection of photographs from Kephart's album, along with their captions, has been included in this volume that illustrates the text. However, readers are encouraged to compare the sparseness of the index with the photo album and journals to draw independent conclusions. Nonetheless, while the index is brief and sketchy, it speaks volumes on an often private individual and on the research interests that shaped his classic works *Our Southern Highlanders* and *Camping and Woodcraft*.

IX

Index to Diary.

Vol. I.

1. "New Freedom."
Hand luggage.
Muddy streams.
White trash.
Asheville.
Prospects.
Outfitting.
Dillsboro. Could have outfitted here.
"Grandma" & "Uncle Bob."

2. Lumbago.
A new Swedish movement.
Mica.
"Notice".
A scouting base.

3. Steep corn-fields.
Chiggres.
Hunting a camp-site.
Dick Creek.
Corn mill. + [illegible] (Toting, &c.) + 25, 50, 51.
Turpin's. + 13.
Camp.
Delayed freight.

4. Storm.
Vicissitudes.
Fixing camp.

5. Rain everlasting.
Cooking in the wet. + 6, 7.
(Rained every day but one in the first two weeks.)

6. Leaky tent.
Isolation. (Camping alone.)

7. Cleared.
Visitors.
Freight arrived.

8. Ham stolen.
Honesty of natives.
Cider mill.

9. Rage for photos.
Fence. + 11, 12.
(Razorbacks & Pepper Pie.)
Temperatures. + 10, 12.
Insects.

10. Illness. (No colds.)
Night line.

11. "Do you like this sort of thing?"
Green pitch pine.
Camp work. Also previous pp. & 14.
Winter underwear.

12. Sun time.
Whippoorwill.

13. Candler with papers.
Fishing N.G. + 16, 19, 22.
Boy dropped on Indian bed.

14. Irv. the porter driven away by mob.
(Attitude of mountaineers toward negroes.)
Photography. + 29, 41.

17. Black Rock trip.
Fatigue of climbing.
Insomnia. [illegible]

18. Sled. + 56, 59.

21. Fox grapes. + 33.

Vol. II.

23. Trout-fishing at the Falls.
Sourwood turning, &c.

24. Gate without a nail.
Indian turnip root.
Black alder berries.
Cold at night.
Rock fire-place.
Smoky tent.

25. "Corn cracker."

26. Cherokees.
Stella Turpin peddling buttermilk.

27. Lodging-house at Whittier.
Stock-law gate.

28. Indian Association.

~~29~~. Merle.

30. Pistol match.
(Another negro driven out of town.)
First frost.

33. Milk sickness. + 36.

34. Snowbird Mts.
Bryson City & its newspaper.
Cold.

35. Harking on moonshiners.
Rise in river without rain. (The drought.)
Parshall playing solitaire. Counting a million pine.
Indian summer in mts.
Addio!

36. Off for Medlin.
Second-class travel.
Grade at Nantahala. + 77.
Tramway.
Delayed freight.
Barefoot Kid. (Chores, barefooted in snow.)
Blacksmith (no batteries).
Trip to Medlin.
Ginseng. + 53 & 56.
Buzzards and hog cholera.
Holly, mistletoe, "ivy." + 45.
The mail-rider.

37. The Everett mine.
The cabin.
Prices of hauling. + 38 & 56.
Forest fires.
Ownership of lands. + 57.
The man whose eyes shine.
Josh Calhoun & the burnt shoe.
Levying on ground-hogs.
Working on cabin. + 38.
Dearth of provisions.

38. Recovered strength. + 40, 48.
Prices.
Small economies.
Mice.
Cold. + 39.
Fuels.
Hard work. + 39, + 50.

39. Blazes.
Inquisitiveness.
Dilly-dallying.
Distaste for beef.
Snow.
"Waterproof" shoes.
Solid comfort.

---

22. Genealogy.
27. Rustic work.
28. Dimensions of old tent.
30. Calling on neighbors with a club.

Index to Diary

X

40. Short days.
Cold.
Cabin.
Wormy pork.
Pinnacle trip.
Hawk. + 47.
No wood-cutters.

41. Bear hunt. + 58.
Temp. of spring in summer 47°
(Song mentions one of same.)

42. do. Dogs. + 47 + 50.

43. do. Vegetation on N. + S.

44. do.

45. Outfit needed. + Vol. II.
Xmas decorations. + 58.
Long-lost goods reached B.

46. New hunting-party.
Goods arrived at mine.
Washing flannels. + 47.
Details of distilling.

47. Cold night.
The Snowbird ranger.
Matt. Hyde's vicissitudes in Godforsaken.
A culinary chef d'oeuvre.

48. Shrubs near cabin.

49. Uniformity of temperature.
Cold.
Corn-feeding hogs.
Shiftlessness. + 57.
Water froze on stove.
Sheriff collecting taxes.

50. Jores-bird.
Wood-cutters came.
Wages. + 58.

51. Winter temperatures.
Juncos.
Cat hunting. + 58.
Prevailing growths in Godforsaken.
+ 52, 54, + inside cover.

52. Mountain scenery in winter.
Berry-times.
Dream lore.
Old pioneers to interview.

53. Projected hunting club.
Long hair.
Blizzard of April, 1900.
Bill Cope's. "Sprouted corn." + 60.
Coburn on ginseng.
Bill Jenkins + the panther.

54. Panther hunt.
Cold.
Frozen fog.
Trip to Siler's Bald.

Bee keeping.
Foot-logs.
Breathing above 4000 ft.
Wildcat tracks.
Stunted beeches.
The Cabin. [crossed out]. + 56.
Wood mice.
View from summit. + 52 + 56.
Godforsaken. + 51.
Cutting frozen beech.

55. Clingman's Dome. Trees.
Rabbits.
Uninhabited strip.
Straight-handled axe.
Mauls. Gluts.
Cold. + 58.
Fire-place. Illus.

56. Trapping ravens and eagles.
To test straight-grained and curly trees.
Cattle-weighing and dehorning.
Distance from Medlin to Siler's Meadow.
Cost of cabins.
Team Trade from Bushnell.
Return.
Abstemiousness.
Petition for pardon of Indian.
Stalled horses and brutal driver.
Eggs!
Sled-building. + 59, illus. + 18.

57. Granville's gold.
Ritter Co. Taylor + Crate.
Big trees in Horse Cove.
How to skin a squirrel. Ill.
Notches on blaze.

58. Improvement on leggings.
Mistletoe.
Bear-hunting season.
Grant-lots.
Immersion.
Share of bear's hide.
Packed up.
Queer names.

60. Bill Cope's.
Good camp site.
Trip to Townsend.
Trail on Spencer Field.
U.S. Foresters.
Royal feed.
U.S. Revenue officers.

Dose of Sow Cholera mixture. (Inside cover.)
Pace, 27 in.
77. Trade at Balsam.
Lat. + long. of Medlin.
Length of N.C. + I, 41.

Index to Diary

Vol. I.

1. "New Freedom."
Hand luggage.
Muddy streams.
White trash.
Asheville.
Prospects.
Outfitting.
Dillsboro. Could have outfitted here.[4]
"Grandma" & "Uncle Bob."
2. Lumbago.
A new Swedish-movement.
Mica.
"Notice."
A scouting base.
3. Steep cornfields
Chiggers.
Hunting a camp-site.
Dick Creek.
Corn mill. & =[5] (Toting, &c.) & 25, 50, 51
Turpin's. & 13.[6]
Camp.
Delayed freight.
4. Storm.
Vicissitudes.
Fixing camp.
5. Rain everlasting.
Cooking in the wet. & 6, 7
(Rained every day but one in the first two weeks.)
6. Leaky tent.
Isolation. (Camping alone.)
7. Cleared.[7]
Visitors.[8]
Freight arrived.
8. Ham stolen.
Honesty of natives.
Cider mill.

"Turpin's House" and "Mr. and Mrs. Turpin, Dick Creek"
(Album, p. 7)

"Pantry Tent" (Album, p. 1)

" 'Big Laura' Davis spinning. The Widow weaving." (Album, p. 3)

"Visitors"
(Album, p. 1)

9. Rage for photos.
Fence. & 11, 12.
(Razorbacks & Pepper Pie.)
Temperatures. 10, 12.[9]
Insects.
10 Illness. (No colds.)
Night line.
11. "Do you like this sort of thing?"
Green pitch pine.
Camp work. Also previous pp. & 14.
Winter underwear.
12. Sun time.
Whippoorwill.
13. Candler with papers.
Fishing N.G. & 16, 19, 22.[10]
Boy dropped on Indian bed.[11]
14. Irv. the porter driven away by mob.
(Attitude of mountaineers toward negroes.)[12]
Photography. & 29, 41.
17. Black Rock trip.[13]
Fatigue of climbing.
Insomnia. The book. A devil's tattoo in my head.[14]
18. Sled. & 56, 59.
21. Fox grapes. & 23.

TOP

"Trout Fishing, Falls of the Tuckaseegee (upper and higher falls not shown)"
(Album, p. 9)

BOTTOM

"Stella Turpin"
(Album, p. 7)

"Annual Association of the Eastern Band of Cherokees, Birdtown on Ocona Lufty, Oct. 2, 1904." (Album, p. 11)

"Addio! Sunday, Oct. 30, 1904" (Album, p. 10)

Vol. II.

23. Trout fishing at the Falls.[15]
    Sourwood turning, &c.[16]
24. Gate without a nail.
    Indian turnip root.[17]
    Black alder berries.
    Cold at night.
    Rock fire-place.
    Smoky tent.
25. "Corn cracker."[18]
26. Cherokees.
    Stella Turpin peddling buttermilk.[19]
27. Lodging-house at Whittier.[20]
    Stock-law gate.
28. Indian Association.
29. Merle.
30. Pistol match.
    (Another negro driven out of town.)
    First frost.[21]
33. Milk sickness.[22] & 36.
34. Snowbird Mts.[23]
    Bryson City & its newspaper.
    Cold.
35. Harkins on moonshiners.[24]
    Rise in river without rain. (The drought.)
    Parshall playing solitaire. Counting a million pins.
    Indian summer in mts.
    Addio![25]
36. Off for Medlin.
    Second-class travel.
    Grade at Nantahala. & 77.[26]
    Tramway.
    Delayed freight.
    Barefoot kid. (Chores, barefooted in snow.)[27]
    Blacksmith (no butteris).[28]
    Trip to Medlin.
    Ginseng. & 53 & 56.[29]
    Buzzards and hog cholera.
    Holly, mistletoe, "ivy." & 45.[30]
    The mail-rider.

"The Mail Rider."
(Album, p. 15)

37. The Everett mine.
The cabin.
Prices of hauling. & 38 & 56.
Forest fires.
Ownership of lands. & 57.
The man whose eyes shine.[31]
Josh Calhoun & the burnt shoe.
Levying on ground-hogs.
Working on cabin. & 38.
Dearth of provisions.

38. Recovered strength. & 40, 48.
Prices.
Small economies.[32]
Mice.
Cold. & 39.
Fuels.
Hard work. & 39, & 50.

39. Blazes.[33]
Inquisitiveness.
Dilly-dallying.
Distaste for beef.
Snow.
"Waterproof" shoes.
Solid comfort.

---

22. Genealogy.[34]
27. Rustic work.
29. Dimensions of old tent.
30. Calling on neighbors with a club.

40. Short days.
Cold.
Cabin.
Wormy pork.
Pinnacle trip.[35]
Hawk. & 47.
No wood-cutters.
41. Bear hunt. & 58.
Temp. of spring in summer 47.°
(Gray mentions one of same.)
42. do. Dogs. & 47 & 50.
43. do. Vegetation on N. & S.
44. do.
45. Outfit needed. & Vol. III.
Xmas decorations. & 58.
Long-lost goods reached B.[36]
46. New hunting-party.
Goods arrived at mine.
Washing flannels. & 47.
Details of distilling.
47. Cold night.
The Snowbird ranger.
Matt Hyde's[37] vicissitudes
in Godforsaken.[38]
A culinary chef d'overe.
48. Shrubs near cabin.
49. Uniformity of temperature.
Cold.
Corn-feeding hogs.
Shiftlessness. & 57.
Water froze on stove.
Sheriff collecting taxes.[39]
50. Joree-bird.[40]
Wood-cutters came.
Wages. & 52.
51. Winter temperatures.
Juncos.[41]
Cat hunting. & 52.
Prevailing growths in Godforsaken.
& 52, 54, & inside cover.
52. Mountain scenery in winter.
Berry-times.
Dream lore.
Old pioneers to interview.

"A Caller at my Door (X$^{\underline{mas}}$, 1904)"
(Album, p. 21)

53. Projected hunting club.
Long hair.
Blizzard of April, 1900.[42]
Bill Cope's "Sprouted corn." & 60.[43]
Coburn on ginseng.[44]
Bill Jenkins & the panther.
54. Panther hunt.
Cold.
Frozen fog.
Trip to Siler's Bald.[45]
Bee Keeping.
Foot-logs.
Breathing above 4 000 ft.
Wildcat tracks.
Stunted beeches.
The Cabin. Spring. & 56.
Wood mice.
View from summit. & 52 & 56.
Godforsaken. & 51.
Cutting frozen beech.

"Clingman Dome (6,619 ft.) from the summit of Siler's Bald (5,594 ft.) Jan., 1905" (Album, p. 24)

55. Clingman's Dome. Trees.
Rabbits.
Uninhabited strip.
Straight-handled axe.
Mauls. Gluts.
Cold. & 56.
Fire-place. Illus.

56. Trapping ravens and eagles.
To tell straight-grained and curly trees.
Cattle-weighting and dehorning.
Distance from Medlin to Siler's Meadow.
Cost of cabins.
Team loads from Bushnell.
Return.
Abstemiousness.
Petition for pardon of Indian.
Stalled horses and brutal driver.
Eggs!
Sled-building. & 59, illus. & 18.

57. Granville's gold.[46]
Ritter Co. Taylor & Crate.[47]
Big trees in Horse Cove.[48]
How to skin a squirrel. Ill.
Notice on blaze.

58. Improvement on leggings.
Mistletoe.
Bear-hunting season.
Grant-lots.
Immersion.
Share of bear's hide.
Packed up.
Queer names.[49]

60. Bill Cope's.
Good camp site.
Trip to Townsend.[50]
Trail on Spencer Field.[51]
U.S. Foresters.
Royal feed.
U.S. Revenue officers.

Dose of sun Cholera Mixture.
(Inside cover.)[52]
Pace, 27 in.

77. Grade at Balsam.[53]
Lat. & long. of Medlin.
Length of N.C. & I, 42.

APPENDIX 2

Horace Kephart's Library

JASON BRADY

A large portion of Horace Kephart's personal library is housed in Hunter Library's Special Collections at Western Carolina University. The Kephart collection, which includes Kephart's library, papers, and other items, is substantial, being one of the largest in Special Collections by any measure. It is consistently one of the most requested and referenced collections by patrons. Where most other collections are narrow in scope and specialized in content, the Kephart collection contains writings and research on a broad array of topics, from culinary arts to firearms, from botany to Southern Appalachian dialect. Kephart's library can fairly be called a complete, stand-alone library within Hunter Library.

Shortly after Kephart's death, his library, a number of his possessions, and some of his papers were on loan to the Great Smoky Mountains National Park as a potential collection for a proposed museum. While under the care of the park, the collection was cataloged by Hiram C. Wilburn (1880–1967) in his capacity as acting park historian. Each item in the Kephart collection was described on its own catalog card. From this inventory of the entire collection, Wilburn created an incomplete, albeit lengthy, list of the books and periodicals that made up Kephart's library. An April 24, 1936, letter from Wilburn to Horace Kephart's son Leonard indicates that Wilburn was nearly finished with his examination of the Kephart library.[1] On his list, Wilburn loosely categorized the works in Kephart's library by subject, e.g., "Guns and Gunlore," "Plant Life," "Reference Books," and so on. The following list retains these headings, which bear a striking resemblance to the table of contents of this book.

The "List of Monographs" presented here describes primarily the monographic works in Kephart's library. In the original Wilburn list, most titles were abbreviated and, therefore, complete and correct titles were not always readily apparent without consulting Wilburn's index cards. All efforts have been made to ensure that the following version contains complete titles, including subtitles.

Books that were part of Kephart's library but were missing from Wilburn's list have been included in the following list. Magazines, journals, and newspapers mentioned on Wilburn's list have been placed in a "List of Periodicals" that follows the monographs. Reports, brochures, catalogs, and other non-monographic publications from the original list have been omitted because they number in the thousands. In cases where a particular book was published in two or more editions, I have endeavored to give the date of the edition that Kephart owned. Kephart's personal copies, which survive and are part of WCU's Kephart Collection, are indicated with an asterisk (*) and were stamped by Wilburn as being property of Horace Kephart.[2]

LIST OF MONOGRAPHS

Human History, Southern Appalachian Mountains

A Mountain Boy's Life Story. J. Dean Crain, 1914*.
The Galax Gatherers: The Gospel Among the Highlanders. Edward O. Guerrant, 1910*.
The Spirit of the Mountains. Emma Bell Miles, 1905*.
The Quare Women: A Story of the Kentucky Mountains. Lucy Furman, 1923*.
The Glass Window: A Story of the Quare Women. Lucy Furman, 1925*.
The Lonesome Road. Lucy Furman, 1927.
The Way to the West, and the Lives of Three Early Americans, Boone—Crockett—Carson. Emerson Hough, 1903*.
The Carolina Mountains. Margaret W. Morley, 1913*.
Geographic Influences in American History. Albert Perry Brigham, 1903*.
Kentucky Superstitions. Daniel Lindsey Thomas and Lucy Blayney Thomas, 1920*.
The Land of Saddle-bags: A Study of the Mountain People in Appalachia. James Watt Raine, 1924*.
The Southern Frontier, 1670–1732. Verner W. Crane, 1928.
The Southern Highlander and His Homeland. John C. Campbell, 1921*.
Our Southern Highlanders. Horace Kephart, 1913*.
Our Southern Highlanders. Horace Kephart, 1921*.
Our Southern Highlanders. Horace Kephart, 1922.

Guns and Gun-Lore

Manual for Rifle Practice. Including Suggestions for Practice at Long Range and for the Formation and Management of Rifle Associations. Gen. Geo. W. Wingate, 1878*.
Pistol and Revolver Shooting. A. L. A. Himmelwright, 1915*.
The Modern Rifle. J. R. Bevis and Jno. A. Donovan, 1917*.
Sporting Firearms. Horace Kephart, 1912*.
Automatic Pistols. Captain Hugh B. C. Pollard, 1920*.
Sporting Firearms of Today in Use. Paul A. Curtis Jr., 1922*.

Handloading Ammunition: A Handbook Covering All Phases of the Loading of Metallic Ammunition for Revolvers, Pistols and Rifles. J. R. Mattern, 1926*.

Sporting Rifles and Rifle Shooting. John Caswell, 1920*.

Modern Sporting Gunnery: A Manual of Practical Information for Shooters of To-day. Henry Sharp, 1906.

Guns, Ammunition, and Tackle. Captain A. W. Money, Horace Kephart, W. E. Carlin, A. L. A. Himmelwright and John Harrington Keene, 1904*.

Bullet Holes: A Record of Records. Douglas B. Wesson, 1915*.

Firearms in American History. Vol. 1–3. Charles Winthrop Sawyer, 1910–1920*.

The American Shotgun. Charles Askins, 1910*.

The Gun Book for Boys and Men. Thomas Heron McKee, 1918*.

The Gun and its Development. W. W. Greener, 1910*.

The American Rifle: A Treatise, a Text Book, and a Book of Practical Instruction in the Use of the Rifle. Major Townsend Whelen, 1918*.

American Small Arms: A Veritable Encyclopedia of Knowledge for Sportsmen and Military Men. Edward S. Farrow, 1904*.

The Kentucky Rifle: A Study of the Origin and Development of a Purely American Type of Firearm, Together with Accurate Data Concerning Early Colonial Gunsmiths, and Profusely Illustrated with Photographic Reproduction of Their Finest Work. Captain John G. W. Dillin, 1924.

Plant Life

Field Book of American Wild Flowers: Being a Short Description of their Character and Habits, a Concise Definition of their Colors, and Incidental References to the Insects Which Assist in their Fertilization. F. Schuyler Matthews, 1902.

Field Book of American Wild Flowers: Being a Short Description of their Character and Habits, a Concise Definition of their Colors, and Incidental References to the Insects Which Assist in their Fertilization. F. Schuyler Matthews, 1927.

Field Book of American Trees and Shrubs: A Concise Description of the Character and Color of Species Common throughout the United States, Together with Maps Showing Their General Distribution. F. Schuyler Mathews, 1915*.

Poisonous Plants in Field and Garden. George Henslow, 1901*.

Ginseng and Other Medicinal Plants: A Book of Valuable Information for Growers as well as Collectors of Medicinal Roots, Barks, Leaves, Etc. A. R. Harding, 1908*.

The Complete Herbalist, or The People Their Own Physicians by the Use of Nature's Remedies: Describing the Great Curative Properties Found in the Herbal Kingdom. O. Phelps Brown, 1897.

Useful Wild Plants of the United States and Canada. Charles Francis Saunders, 1920*.

Studies of Trees in Winter: A Description of the Deciduous Trees of Northeastern America. Annie Oakes Huntington, 1902.

Our Native Trees and How to Identify Them: A Popular Study of Their Habits and Their Peculiarities. Harriet L. Keeler, 1900*.

How to Know the Wild Flowers: A Guide to the Names, Haunts, and Habits of Our Common Wild Flowers. Mrs. William Starr Dana [Frances Theodora Smith Dana Parsons], 1900.

Southern Wild Flowers and Trees, Together with Shrubs, Vines and Various Forms of Growth Found Through the Mountains, the Middle District and the Low Country of the South. Alice Lounsberry, 1901*.

How to Know Wild Fruits: A Guide to Plants When Not in Flower by Means of Fruit and Leaf. Maude G. Peterson, 1905*.

The Vines of Northeastern America: Fully Illustrated from Original Sketches. Charles S. Newhall, 1897*.

Grasses, Sedges and Rushes of the Northern United States. Edward Knobel, 1899*.

The Travels of William Bartram. William Bartram and Mark Van Doren, 1928.

An Ecological Study of the Heath Balds of the Great Smoky Mountains. Stanley A. Cain, 1930.

An Illustrated Flora of the Northern United States, Canada and the British Possessions. Vol. 1–3. Nathaniel Lord Britton and A. Brown, 1896–1898.

Message from the President of the United States Transmitting a Report of the Secretary of Agriculture in Relation to the Forests, Rivers and Mountains of the Southern Appalachian Region. United States Department of Agriculture, 1902*.

The Southern Appalachian Forests. H. B. Ayres and W. W. Ashe, 1904–1905*.

Studies of American Fungi: Mushrooms; Edible, Poisonous, etc. George Francis Atkinson, 1901*.

Surveying and Mapping

Landscape. Philip Gilbert Hamerton, 1890*.

Topographic Surveying: Including Geographic, Exploratory, and Military Mapping, with Hints on Camping, Emergency Surgery, and Photography. Herbert M. Wilson, 1900.

Rapid Reconnaissance Sketching including Contouring. Captain C. O. Sherrill, 1912.

Elements of Military Sketching and Map Reading. Captain John B. Barnes, 1917*.

Estimating Distance Tables. Captain Edwin Bell, 1904*.

Pioneering and Map-Making: For Boy Scouts and Others. C. Reginald Enock, ca. 1910*.

Military Maps Explained. Henry Edgar Eames, 1909*.

The Art of Reconnaissance. Major-General Sir David Henderson, 1914*.

Military Map-Reading: Field, Outpost and Road Sketching. Wm. D. Beach*.

Geology and Mineralogy

College Physiography. Ralph Stockman Tarr, 1914*.

Geology of the Tate Quadrangle, Georgia. W. S. Bayley, 1928*.

Field Book of Common Rocks and Minerals: For Identifying the Rocks and Minerals of the United States and Interpreting Their Origins and Meanings. Frederic Brewster Loomis, 1925.

A Pocket Handbook of Minerals: Designed for Use in the Field or Class-Room with Little Reference to Chemical Tests. G. Montague Butler, 1911*.

Practical Instructions in the Search for and the Determination of, the Useful Minerals including the Rare Ores, for the Prospector, Miner, and as a Ready Reference for Everybody Interested in the Mineral Industry. Alexander McLeod, 1917*.

Introduction to the Rarer Elements. Philip E. Browning, 1917*.

Medicine and Surgery

Medical Diagnosis: A Manual for Students and Practitioners. Austin Wilkinson Hollis, 1905.

Tabular Diagnosis: An Aid to the Rapid Differential Diagnosis of Diseases. Ralph W. Leftwich, 1913.

Nervous and Mental Diseases: A Manual for Students and Practitioners. Joseph Darwin Nagel, 1904.
A Pocket-Book of Treatment. Ralph Winnington Leftwich, 1914.
Handbook for Ship's Medicine Chest. George W. Stoner, 1904.
First Aid in Illness and Injury: Comprised in a Series of Chapters on the Human Machine, Its Structure, Its Implements of Repair, and the Accidents and Emergencies to Which It Is Liable. James Evelyn Pilcher, 1899*.
Squibb's Materia Medica. E. R. Squibb & Sons, 1906.
Wellcome's Excerpta Therapeutica. Burroughs Wellcome Company, 1906*.
A Manual of the Practice of Medicine: Prepared Especially for Students. Arthur A. Stevens, 1898.
Chemistry in Medicine: A Cooperative Treatise Intended to Give Examples of Progress Made in Medicine with the Aid of Chemistry. Julius Stieglitz, 1928.
Secret Nostrums and Systems of Medicine: A Book of Formulas. Charles W. Oleson, 1894.
A Compend of Human Anatomy. Samuel O. L. Potter, 1903*.
A Compend of Human Physiology, Especially Adapted for the Use of Medical Students. Albert P. Brubaker, 1902*.
A Compend of Gynecology. William Hughes Wells, 1903.
A Compend of Surgery. Orville Horwitz, 1904.
The Dispensatory of the United States of America. Geo. B. Wood and Franklin Bache, 1894*.

Travel

1924 Atlas of the World and Gazetteer. Funk & Wagnalls Co., 1924.
The Happy Traveler: A Book for Poor Men. Frank Tatchell, 1923*.
Secrets of Polar Travel. Robert E. Peary, 1917*.
Comfort in Small Craft: A Practical Handbook of Sailing and Cookery. S. J. Housley, 1911*.
The Cabin Boat Primer: Containing Descriptions and Diagrams, Photographs and Chapters on the Construction, Navigation and Use of House-Boats for Pleasure and Profit. Raymond S. Spears, 1913.
The Canoe: Its Selection, Care and Use. Robert Eugene Pinkerton, 1914*.
Canoe Handling: The Canoe, History, Uses, Limitations and Varieties, Practical Management and Care and Relative Facts. C. Bowyer Vaux, 1888*.
Dictionary of Sea Terms. A. Ansted, 1898.
The California and Oregon Trail, Being Sketches of Prairie and Rocky Mountain Life. Francis Parkman, ca. 1900*.
Shewey's Pictorial St. Louis, Past and Present: A Sketch of St. Louis, Its History, Resources, Chronological Events, Table of Information, and Points of Interest. Arista C. Shewey, 1892*.
The Adirondacks. T. Morris Longstreth, 1917*.
The Catskills. T. Morris Longstreth, 1918*.
Narratives of the Career of Hernando de Soto in the Conquest of Florida, as Told by a Knight of Elvas, and in a Relation by Luys Hernandez de Biedma, Factor of the Expedition; Translated by Buckingham Smith, Together with an Account of de Soto's Expedition Based on the Diary of Rodrigo Ranjel, His Private Secretary, Translated from Oviedo's Historiea General y Natural de las Indias. Vol. 1 and 2. Edward Gaylord Bourne, 1904*.
The Frontiersman's Pocket-Book. Council of the Legion of Frontiersmen, 1914*.
Handbook of Travel. Harvard Travelers Club, 1917*.
Glories of the Carolina Coast. James Henry Rice Jr., 1925*.

Notes on Sports and Travel. George Henry Kingsley, 1900*.
Memoirs of a Sportsman. Ivan Turgenieff, 1920*.

CAMPING AND WOODCRAFT

The Book of Camping and Woodcraft: A Guidebook for Those Who Travel in the Wilderness. Horace Kephart, 1915*.
The Book of Camping and Woodcraft: A Guidebook for Those Who Travel in the Wilderness. Vol. 1 and 2. Horace Kephart, 1916–1917*.
Camp Cookery. Horace Kephart, 1910*.
Holidays in Tents. W. M. Childs, 1921*.
Camping in Comfort. John A. Donovan, 1919*.
Out of Doors. Emerson Hough, 1915*.
Canoe Cruising and Camping. Perry D. Frazer, 1897*.
The American Boys' Handybook of Camp-Lore and Woodcraft. Dan Beard, 1920*.
Pioneering. Frederic Shelford, 1909.
Camp and Trail Methods: Interesting Information for All Lovers of Nature, What to Take and What to Do. Elmer Harry Kreps, 1910*.
Harper's Camping and Scouting: An Outdoor Guide for American Boys. George Bird Grinnell, 1911*.
The Way of the Woods: A Manual for Sportsmen in Northeastern United States and Canada. Edward Brek, 1908*.
The Camper's Handbook. T. H. Holding, 1908*.
Camp Kits and Camp Life. Charles Stedman Hanks, 1906*.
Wilderness Homes: A Book of the Log Cabin. Oliver Kemp, 1911*.
Winter Camping. Warwick Stevens Carpenter, 1913*.
Camp and Trail. Stewart Edward White, 1915*.
The Book of Camping. A. Hyatt Verrill, 1917*.
The Boy Scout's Hike Book: The First of a Series of Handy Volumes of Information and Inspiration. Edward Cave, 1913*.
The Boy's Camp Book: A Guidebook Based upon the Annual Encampment of a Boy Scout Troop; the Second of a Series of Handy Volumes of Information and Inspiration. Edward Cave, 1914*.
The Camper's Own Book, for Devotees of Tent and Trail. George S. Bryan, 1912*.
The Camper's Own Book, for Devotees of Tent and Trail. George S. Bryan, 1913*.
The Field and Forest Handy Book. Daniel C. Beard, 1915*.
Camping for Boys. H. W. Gibson, 1913*.
Outdoorsman's Handbook (formerly The Angler's Guide). Warren H. Miller, 1916*.
Camp Craft, Modern Practice and Equipment. Warren H. Miller, 1915*.
Going Afoot: A Book on Walking. Bayard H. Christy, 1920*.
Touring Afoot. Dr. C. P. Fordyce, 1922*.
Packing and Portaging. Dillon Wallace, 1912*.
Horse Packing: A Manual of Pack Transportation. Charles Johnson Post, 1914.
Trail Craft: An Aid in Getting the Greatest Good out of Vacation Trips. Claude P. Fordyce, 1922*.
Vacation Tramps in New England Highlands. Aleen Chamberlain, 1919*.
On the Trail: An Outdoor Book for Girls. Lina Beard and Adelia Belle Beard, 1915*.
Woodcraft for Women. Kathrene G. Pinkerton, 1916*.
Scouting for Girls: Official Handbook of the Girl Scouts. Girl Scouts of America, 1920*.

Camp-Fire Verse. William Haynes, Joseph Le Roy Harrison, and Stewart Edward White, 1917.
Shifts and Expedients of Camp Life, Travel, and Exploration. W. B. Lord and T. Baines, 1876*.
Land Cruising and Prospecting: A Book of Valuable Information for Hunters, Trappers, Land Cruisers, Prospectors and Men of the Trail—Tells How to Locate One's Self on the Map, etc. A. F. Wallace, 1908*.
The Forest. Stewart Edward White, 1904*.
The Cabin. Stewart Edward White, 1911*.
Log Cabins and Cottages: How to Build and Furnish Them. William S. Wicks, 1920*.
Handbook for Rangers and Woodsmen, etc. Jay Laird Burgess Taylor, 1917.
Alone in the Wilderness. Joseph Knowles, 1913*.
Games and Recreational Methods for Clubs, Camps and Scouts. Charles F. Smith, 1924*.
Nature's Program. Gaylord Johnson, 1926*.
Autocamping. F. E. Brimmer, 1923*.
The Motor Camping Book. Elon Jessup, 1921*.
Woodcraft. "Nessmuk" [George Washington Sears], 1888*.

Foods and Cooking

Cooking for Two: A Handbook for Young Housekeepers. Janet McKenzie Hill, 1921*.
Better Meals for Less Money. Mary Green [Marietta McPherson Greenough], 1917*.
The A B C of Cooking: For Men with No Experience of Cooking on Small Boats, Patrol Boats, in Camps, on Marches, etc. Moffat, Yard and Co., 1917*.
Kitchenette Cooking. Anna Merritt East, 1918*.
The Boston Cooking-School Cook Book. Fannie Farmer, 1921.
The Stag Cook Book, Written for Men by Men. C. Mac Sheridan, 1922*.
The Century Cook Book: With a New Supplement of One Hundred Receipts of Especial Excellence. Mary Ronald [Augusta Arnold Foote], 1909*.
The Wild Foods of Great Britain, Where to Find Them and How to Cook Them. L. C. R. Cameron, 1917*.
Manual for Army Cooks. United States Army Subsistence Department, 1896*.
Manual for Army Cooks. United States Army Subsistence Department, 1914*.
Manual for Army Bakers. United States Army, 1910.
Mess Officers' Manual. United States Army, 1919*.
The Milk Diet: How to Use It. Bernarr MacFadden and Charles Sanford Porter, no date given.

Animal Life

American Food and Game Fishes. David Starr Jordan and Barton Warren Evermann, 1902*.
Streamcraft: An Angling Manual. Geo. Parker Holden, 1919*.
Fine Art of Fishing. Samuel G. Camp, 1911*.
Science of Fishing: The Most Practical Book on Fishing Ever Published. Lake Brooks [A. R. Harding], 1912*.
The Art of Worm-Fishing: A Practical Treatise on Clear-Water Worming. Alexander Mackie, 1912*.
American Trout-Stream Insects: A Guide to Angling Flies and Other Aquatic Insects Alluring to Trout. Louis Rhead, 1916.
*Fisherman's Lures and Game-Fish Food, with Colored Pictures from Life of Various Creatures Fish

Eat and New Improved Artificial Imitation Floating Nature Lures and Chart-Plans to Show the Haunts Where Fish Feed on Them in Lake and Stream. Louis Rhead, 1920*.

Fly Fishing Up to Date: Or, The Evolution of a Fisherman. Malcolm D. Whitman, 1924*.

Fishing Tackle. Perry D. Frazer, 1914*.

Fishing, Tackle and Kits: Practical Information on Game Fish. How to Land Them, the Correct Tackle and How to Use It. Dixie Carroll [Carroll Blaine Cook], 1919*.

The Angler's Workshop. Perry D. Frazer, 1908*.

Fishing Kits and Equipment. Samuel G. Camp, 1910*.

Book of the Black Bass, Comprising Its Complete Scientific and Life History, Together with a Practical Treatise on Angling and Fly Fishing and a Full Description of Tools, Tackle and Implements. James A. Henshall, 1881*.

The Small-Mouthed Bass. W. J. Loudon, 1910*.

More about the Black Bass. James A. Henshall, 1889*.

The Log of the Sun: A Chronicle of Nature's Year. C. William Beebe, 1906*.

Nature's Calendar: A Guide and Record for Outdoor Observations in Natural History. Ernest Ingersoll, 1900*.

Birds of North Carolina. T. Gilbert Pearson, C. S. Brimley, and H. H. Brimley, 1919*.

Birdcraft: A Field Book of Two Hundred Song, Game, and Water Birds. Mabel Osgood Wright, 1897*.

Field Book of Wild Birds and Their Music: A Description of the Character and Music of Birds, Intended to Assist in the Identification of Species Common in the U.S. East of the Rocky Mountains. F. Schuyler Mathews, 1921*.

Field Book of North American Mammals: Descriptions of Every Mammal Known North of the Rio Grande, Together with Brief Accounts of Habits, Geographical Ranges, etc. H. E. Anthony, 1928*.

Field Book of Insects, with Special Reference to Those of North-Eastern United States, Aiming to Answer Common Questions. Frank E. Lutz, 1921.

American Animals: A Popular Guide to the Mammals of North America North of Mexico. Witmer Stone and William Everett Cram, 1902.

Wild Animals of North America, Intimate Studies of Big and Little Creatures of the Mammal Kingdom. Edward W. Nelson, 1918*.

The Black Bear. William H. Wright, 1910*.

Snakes: Curiosities and Wonders of Serpent Life. Catherine C. Hopley, 1882.

Reptiles of the World: Tortoises and Turtles, Crocodilians, Lizards and Snakes of the Eastern and Western Hemispheres. Raymond L. Ditmars, 1927.

Fahrten und Spuren: Eine Anleitung zum Spuren und Ansprechend fur Jager und Jagdlibhaber. Eugen Teuwsen and Carl Schulze, 1920?

Taxidermy. Leon L. Pray, 1913*.

Home Manufacture of Furs and Skins: A Book of Practical Instructions Telling How to Tan, Dress, Color and Manufacture or Make into Articles of Ornament, Wear and Use. Albert Burton Farnham, 1916*.

Wilderness Hunting and Wildcraft, with Notes on the Habits and Life Histories of Big Game Animals. Lieut. Colonel Townsend Whelen, 1927*.

Hints and Points for Sportsmen. "Seneca" [H. H. Soule], 1895*.

Science of Trapping: Describes the Fur Bearing Animals, Their Nature, Habits and Distribution, with Practical Methods for Their Capture. Elmer Harry Kreps, 1909*.

Fox Trapping: A Book of Instruction Telling How to Trap, Snare, Poison and Shoot, a Valuable Book for Trappers. A. R. Harding, 1906*.

Mink Trapping: A Book of Instruction Giving Many Methods of Trapping, A Valuable Book for Trappers. A. R. Harding, 1906*.
Night Hunting. Joseph Edward Williams, 1911.
Twenty Years Hunting and Fishing in the Great Smoky Mountains. Samuel J. Hunnicutt, 1926*.
Deadfalls and Snares: A Book of Instruction for Trappers about These and Other Home-Made Traps. A. R. Harding, 1907*.
3001 Questions and Answers: Containing Much Valuable Information for Hunters, Trappers and Outdoor People in General and Could Properly Be Called an Encyclopedia of Useful Information. A. R. Harding, 1913*.
The Grizzly Bear: The Narrative of a Hunter-Naturalist, Historical, Scientific and Adventurous. William H. Wright, 1909*.
The Grizzly, Our Greatest Wild Animal. Enos A. Mills, 1919*.
The Moose Book: Facts and Stories from Northern Forests. Samuel Merrill, 1916*.
The Romance of the Newfoundland Caribou: An Intimate Account of the Life of the Reindeer of North America. A. A. Radclyffe Dugmore, 1913*.
The Wild Turkey and Its Hunting. Edward A. McIlhenny, 1914*.

Mountain History, Southern Appalachia

Mountain Songs of North Carolina. Susannah Wetmore and Marshall Bartholomew, 1926.
Ballads and Songs of the Southern Highlands. Mellinger E. Henry, 1929.

Mountain History

"Pennsylvania's Part in the Winning of the West: An Address Delivered before the Pennsylvania Society of St. Louis, December 12, 1901." Horace Kephart, 1902.

Cherokee Indians

Itse Kanohedv Tetlohisdv Ugvwiyuhi Igatsetseli Tsisa Galone Utseliga [*Cherokee New Testament*]. 1860*.
Handbook of American Indians North of Mexico. Vol. 1 and 2. Frederick Webb Hodge, 1907.
Physiological and Medical Observations among the Indians of Southwestern United States and Northern Mexico. Ales Hrdlicka, 1908*.

Fiction

The Works of Edgar Allan Poe. Vol. 1, Tales. Edited by John H. Ingram, 1899.
The Time of Man, a Novel. Elizabeth Madox Roberts, 1926.
Don Quixote. Miguel de Cervantes Saavedra, 1910.
The Best Stories in the World. Thomas L. Masson, 1922.
Mountain Blood: A Novel. Joseph Hergesheimer, 1919*.
Jurgen: A Comedy of Justice. James Branch Cabell, 1919.
Cardigan. Robert W. Chambers, 1901.
The Maid-at-Arms: A Novel. Robert W. Chambers, 1902.

The Spoilers. Rex Beach, 1905.
The Settler. Herman Whitaker, 1906*.
Lin McLean. Owen Wister, 1907.
Santa Fe's Partner: Being Some Memorials of Events in a New-Mexican Track-End Town. Thomas A. Janvier, 1907.
King Spruce. Holman Francis Day, 1908.
The Barrier: A Novel. Rex Beach, 1908.
Cimarron. Edna Ferber, 1930*.
Joe Pete. Florence E. McClinchey, 1929.
The Man Who Knew Too Much. G. K. Chesterton, 1922.
Through the Shadows with O. Henry. Al Jennings, 1921.
Treasure Island. Robert Louis Stevenson, 1900*.
Drums. James Boyd, 1925*.
The Story of the Outlaw: A Study of the Western Desperado, with Historical Narratives of Famous Outlaws; the Stories of Noted Border Wars; Vigilante Movements and Armed Conflicts on the Frontier. Emerson Hough, 1907*.
The Return of the Native. Thomas Hardy, 1917.
Prisoner at the Bar: Sidelights on the Administration of Criminal Justice. Arthur Train, 1918.
Bloody Ground: A Cycle of the Southern Hills. Fiswoode Tarleton, 1929.
The Invisible Man. H. G. Wells, 1897.
The Island of Elcadar: A Pilgrimage to Novel-Land. Icarus de Plume, 1921*.
The Trail of the Lonesome Pine. John Fox Jr., 1908.
Jungle Gods. Carl Von Hoffman, 1929.
Kidnapped. Robert Louis Stevenson, 1905*.
The Death Maker. Austin J. Small, 1926.

Classical and General Literature

The Collected Novels and Stories. Guy de Maupassant, 1922.
Shakespeare: A Critical Study of His Mind and Art. Edward Dowden, 1897.
The Complete Works of William Shakespeare. W. J. Craig, 1919.
A New and Complete Concordance or Verbal Index to Words, Phrases, and Passages in the Dramatic Works of Shakespeare: With a Supplementary Concordance to the Poems. John Bartlett, 1894.
Shakesperian Synopses: Outlines or Arguments of the Plays of Shakespeare. J. Walker McSpadden, 1902.
Synopses of Dickens' Novels. J. Walker McSpadden, 1909.
The Poems and Songs of Robert Burns. Robert Burns and Andrew Lang, 1899.
Percy Bysshe Shelley, Poet and Pioneer: A Biographical Study. Henry S. Salt, 1896*.
The Poetical Works of Percy Bysshe Shelley. Edited by Edward Dowden, 1890*.
Fromont Junior and Risler Senior. Alphonse Daudet, 1895.
South-Sea Idyls. Charles Warren Stoddard, 1901.
Representative American Dramas, National and Local. Montrose Jonas Moses, 1925.
The Inward Light: A Drama in Four Acts. Allan Davis and Anna Reese Stratton, 1919.
Selected English Short Stories. Hugh Walker, 1916.
The Virginian. Owen Wister, 1918.
Nature Studies: Selections from the Writings of John Ruskin. Rose Porter, 1900*.

Nature for Its Own Sake: First Studies in Natural Appearances. John Charles Van Dyke, 1898*.

The Pageant of English Prose: Being Five Hundred Passages by Three Hundred and Twenty-five Authors. Edited by Robert Maynard Leonard, 1912.

Cyrano de Bergerac: An Heroic Comedy in Five Acts. Edmond Rostand and Bryan Hooker, 1927.

Heart Throbs in Prose and Verse Dear to the American People. Vol. 1 and 2. National Magazine, 1904–1905.

Canticles of the Corn Patch. Clee Kernstaff, of Inglenook [Arthur Middleton Huger], 1923*.

War Letters of Kiffin Yates Rockwell: Foreign Legionnaire and Aviator, France, 1914–1916. Kiffin Yates Rockwell and Paul Ayres Rockwell, 1925.

The Note Book of Elbert Hubbard: Mottoes, Epigrams, Short Essays, Passages, Orphic Sayings and Preachments, Coined from a Life of Love, Laughter and Work, by a Man Who Achieved Greatly in Literature, Art, Philosophy and Business. Elbert Hubbard II and the Roycrofters, 1927.

Critical Literature

A Gentle Cynic: Being a Translation of the Book of Koheleth, Commonly Known as Ecclesiastes, Stripped of Later Additions, Also Its Origin, Growth, and Interpretation. Morris Jastrow Jr., 1919*.

Human Motives. James Jackson Putnam, 1917.

Back to Methuselah: A Metabiological Pentateuch. Bernard Shaw, 1921*.

Why We Behave like Human Beings. George A. Dorsey, 1925.

The Doctor Looks at Love and Life. Joseph Collins, 1926.

The Dance of Life. Havelock Ellis, 1923.

Women in Love. D. H. Lawrence, 1922.

Arts and Crafts

The Craftsmanship of Writing. Frederic Taber Cooper, 1911.

Shorthand for General Use. William Timothy Call, 1911.

Authors and Publishers: A Manual of Suggestions for Beginners in Literature, Comprising a Description of Publishing Methods and Arrangements . . . Together with General Hints for Authors. George Have Putnam and John Bishop Putnam, 1900.

A Measuring Scale for Ability in Spelling. Leonard Porter Ayres, 1915.

The Only Two Ways to Write a Story. John Gallishaw, 1929.

The Technique of the Mystery Story. Carolyn Wells, 1913.

The Universal Plot Catalog. Henry Albert Phillips, 1916.

The Policeman's Art: As Taught in the New York State School for Police. George Fletcher Chandler and Albert B. Moore, 1922?

The Police Recruit. Arthur W. Wallander, 1923.

Woodworking for Beginners: A Manual for Amateurs. Charles G. Wheeler, 1899*.

Outdoor Photography. Julian A. Dimock, 1912*.

Pictorial Photography: Its Principles and Practice. Paul L. Anderson, 1917*.

The Fine Art of Photography. Paul L. Anderson, 1919*.

Miracle Mongers and their Methods: A Complete Exposé of the Modus Operandi of Fire Eaters, Heat Resisters, Poison Eaters, Venomous Reptile Defiers, Sword Swallowers, Human Ostriches, Strong Men, etc. Harry Houdini, 1920.

Conjuring Tricks with Cards, from 'Modern Magic'. Professor Hoffman, no date given.
Clouds and Weather Phenomena: For Artists and Other Lovers of Nature. C. J. P. Cave, 1926*.
Weather Lore: A Collections of Proverbs, Sayings, and Rules Concerning the Weather. Richards Inwards, 1898*.
Manufacturing and Laboratory Tests to Produce an Improved Cotton Airplane Fabric. Fred Taylor and D. E. Earle, 1920.

History and Political

Outlines of Universal History. George Park Fisher, 1886?
Liberty in the Modern World. George Bryan Logan, 1928.
National Ideals and Problems: Essays for College English. Maurice G. Fulton, 1918.

Reference Books

New Standard Dictionary of the English Language. Funk & Wagnalls, 1929.
An Etymological Dictionary of the English Language. Walter W. Skeat, 1884.
Encyclopedia Britannica, 11th ed. 1910.
World Almanac. Robert Hunt Lyman, 1923.
World Almanac. Robert Hunt Lyman, 1925.
World Almanac. Robert Hunt Lyman, 1926.
World Almanac. Robert Hunt Lyman, 1928.
World Almanac. Robert Hunt Lyman, 1930.
World Almanac. Robert Hunt Lyman, 1931.
A Concordance to the Old and New Testament, or A Dictionary and Alphabetical Index to the Bible. Alexander Cruden and Charles Stokes Carey, no date given.
Thesaurus of English Words and Phrases Classified and Arranged So as to Facilitate the Expression of Ideas and Assist in Literary Composition. Peter Mark Roget and John Lewis Roget, 1910.
The Happy Phrase: A Hand-Book of Expression for the Enrichment of Conversation, Writing, and Public Speaking. Edwin Hamlin Carr, 1915.
Bartlett's Familiar Quotations. John Bartlett, 1900.
Putnam's Phrase Book: An Aid to Social Letter Writing and to Ready and Effective Conversation, with over 100 Model Social Letters and 6000 of the World's Best English Phrases. Edwin Hamlin Carr, 1919.
Putnam's Handy Law Book for the Layman. Albert Sidney Bolles, 1921.
What to Talk About: The Clever Question as an Aid to Social, Professional, and Business Advancement. Imogene B. Wolcott, 1923.
The Best Books: A Reader's Guide to the Choice of the Best Available Books (*about* 100,000) *in Every Department of Science, Art and Literature, with the Dates of the First and Last Editions, and the Price, Size and Publisher's Name* (*Both* English and American) of Each Book; A Contribution Towards Systematic Bibliography. William Swan Sonnenschein, 1910*.
A Dickens Dictionary: The Characters and Scenes of the Novels and Miscellaneous Works Alphabetically Arranged. Alex J. Philip, 1909.
A Thomas Hardy Dictionary: The Characters and Scenes of the Novels and Poems Alphabetically Arranged and Described. F. Outwin Saxelby, 1911.

The Devil's Dictionary. Ambrose Bierce, 1925.
Cornell University Alumni Directory. 1922.

English Language

Principles of English Grammar, for the Use of Schools. George R. Carpenter, 1900.
A Working Grammar of the English Language, Designed to Give in Simple Statement the Principles and Methods of Correct English Speech and Writing. James Champlin Fernald, 1908.
Connectives of English Speech: The Correct Usage of Prepositions, Conjunctions, Relative Pronouns and Adverbs Explained and Illustrated. James Champlin Fernald, 1904.
The Practice of Typography: Correct Composition, a Treatise on Spelling, Abbreviations, the Compounding and Division of Words, the Proper Use of Figures and Numerals . . . with Observations on Punctuation and Proofreading. Theodore Low De Vinne, 1901.
English Compound Words and Phrases: A Reference List, with Statement of Principles and Rules. Francis Horace Teall, 1892.

Foreign Languages

Practical French Taken from the Author's Larger Grammar, and Supplemented by Conversations and Idiomatic Phrases. William Dwight Whitney, 1887.
All the French Verbs at a Glance: With Practical Elucidations of All the French Sounds, and Comprehensive Table of Pronouns. Etienne Lambert and Alfred Sardou, 1874.
A Latin Grammar: Founded on Comparative Grammar. Joseph Henry Allen and J. B. Greenough, 1880.
Italian Conversational Course: A New Method of Teaching the Italian Language, Both Theoretically and Practically. Giovanni Toscani, 1883.
A Compendious German Grammar. William Dwight Whitney, 1871.
Dictionary of the English and German Languages. Vol. 1 and 2. Christoph Friedrich Grieb and Arnold Schroer, 1894.
Faust. Goethe, 1876*.

Army and Navy

Fundamentals of Military Service. Captain Lincoln C. Andrews, 1916*.
Self-Helps for the Citizen Soldier: Being a Popular Explanation of Things Military. James A. Moss and M. B. Stewart, 1915.
Training for the Trenches: A Practical Handbook Based upon Personal Experience during the First Two Years of the War in France. Captain Leslie Vickers, 1917*.
How to Live at the Front: Tips for American Soldiers. Hector Macquarrie, 1917*.
Practical Instruction in Security and Information of Non-commissioned Officers of Infantry. E. K. Massee, 1914*.
The Service of Security and Information. Arthur L. Wagner, 1903.
Manual of Instruction of the Non-commissioned Officers of a Troop of Cavalry in Security and Information, with a Scheme for Progressive Instruction in That Subject. First Lieut. Jno. J. Boniface, 1904*.

Manual for Non-commissioned Officers and Privates of Infantry of the Army of the United States. United States War Department, 1917.
Field Service. Capt. James A. Moss, 1912*.
Privates' Manual. Capt. James A. Moss, 1911.
Trench Warfare: A Manual for Officers and Men. Joseph S. Smith, 1917.
Hand-to-Hand Fighting: A System of Personal Defense for the Soldier. A. E. Marriott, 1918*.
Manual for Privates of Infantry of the Organized Militia of the United States. United States War Department, 1909.
Field Service Regulations, United States Army. United States War Department, 1914*.
Suggestions to Military Riflemen. Lieutenant Townsend Whelen, 1906*.
Small Arms Firing Manual. United States War Department, 1913*.
Infantry Scouting: A Practical Manual for the Use of Scouts in Training at Home and at the Front. L. C. R. D. J. Cameron, 1916*.
Drill Regulations and Outlines of First Aid for the Hospital Corps, United States Army. United States War Department, 1908*.
Drill Regulations for the Hospital Corps, United States Navy. United States Navy Department, 1907.
Our Navy at War. Josephus Daniels, 1922.

Outing Adventure Library

Adrift in the Arctic Ice Pack, from the History of the First U. S. Grinnell Expedition in Search of Sir John Franklin. Elisha Kent Kane, edited by Horace Kephart, 1915*.
Adventures in Mexico. George Frederick Ruxton, edited by Horace Kephart, 1915*.
Captives among the Indians: First-Hand Narratives of Indian Wars, Customs, Tortures, and Habits of Life in Colonial Times. Edited by Horace Kephart, 1915*.
Castaways and Crusoes: Tales of Survivors of Ship-Wreck in New Zealand, Patagonia, Tobago, Cuba, Magdalen Islands, South Seas and the Crozets. Edited by Horace Kephart, 1915*.
First through the Grand Canyon. Major John Wesley Powell, edited by Horace Kephart, 1915*.
The Gold Hunters. J. D. Borthwick, edited by Horace Kephart, 1917*.
Hobart Pasha: Blockade-Running, Slaver-Hunting, and War and Sport in Turkey. Augustus Charles Hobart-Hampden, edited by Horace Kephart, 1915*.
The Lion Hunter. Ronaleyn Gordon-Cumming, edited by Horace Kephart, 1915*.
Wild Life in the Rocky Mountains. George Frederick Ruxton, edited by Horace Kephart*.

List of Periodicals

Adventure
All Outdoors
American Amble
American Angler
American Motorist
American Review of Reviews
American Rifleman
Appalachian Scenic Highway Bulletin
Arms and the Man
Atlantic Monthly
Audobon
Author and Journalist
Biblical Recorder
The Bookman
Boys Life
Bulletin of the American Game Protective Association
Campfire

Carolina Skyline
Cassier's Magazine
Century
The City Builder
Colliers
Country Life in America
Dearborn Independent
Engineering and Mining Journal
English Times
The Epicure
Field and Stream
The Field
Flynn's
Forest and Stream
Good Housekeeping
Harper's
Hearst's International
Hunter-Trader-Trapper
Hunting and Fishing
The Independent
Ladies Home Journal
Liberty
Literary Digest
McClure's Magazine
Magazine of American History
Magazine of History
Manufacturer's Record
Nation
National Geographic
National Sportsman
New York Times
North Carolina Historical Review
North Carolina Law Review
North Carolina Library Bulletin
North Carolina Education
Ohio Journal of Science
Oregon Country
Outdoor America
Outdoor Life
Outdoor World and Recreation
Outer's Book
Outer's Life
Outer's Recreation
Outing
Outlook
Outlook & Independent
Publisher's Weekly
Recreation
Rod and Gun
Saturday Evening Post
School and College World
Shooting and Fishing
Science
Scientific American
Scouting
Scribner's Magazine
Seapower
Skyland Magazine
South Atlantic Quarterly
Southern Baptist
Sporting Goods Dealer
Sporting Goods Gazette
Sportsman's World
Time
Tours: Weekly News Magazine of the Great Smokies
Travel
Vacation Manual
Watchword
Water Motoring
World's Work

APPENDIX 3

Bibliography of Horace Kephart

GEORGE FRIZZELL

This bibliography had its origins in my years of working with the Horace Kephart collection housed in the Special Collections of Western Carolina University. From my first days in the office, beginning in the early 1980s, it quickly became apparent that Kephart held a unique attraction to researchers. His collection was a fount of information for those interested in Southern Appalachian life or outdoor activities. In the ever-flowing stream of questions on a myriad of topics that Special Collections received over the years, Kephart remained a constant fixture. At the same time, fully half of the patrons sought to learn about the personal life of this individual who became so indelibly identified with the region.

In 2004, due to his immense popularity with researchers, Suzanne McDowell, former director of WCU's Mountain Heritage Center, and I collaborated to create a website devoted to Kephart using his manuscripts, photographs, and artifacts, which we called "Horace Kephart: Revealing an Enigma." At the time, Kephart was a mysterious figure whose name might invoke praise, raise eyebrows or comments about his perceived family relations, or spark inquisitiveness as to the accuracy of his observations on mountain life. As seen in chapters of this book, he remains a topic of debate—often divisive—that will likely not reach a conclusion. To some extent, that is part of his appeal. The prominence he achieved in his writings about Southern Appalachia in the first half of the twentieth century helped shape national perceptions of the region, whether correct or not. The consummate researcher, he could not help but dispense his findings into his own words and his own opinions. And yet, there remained another Kephart—one who wrote fiction, was an expert on firearms, enjoyed providing recipes for campers, and (to my delight) published advice on librarianship. In recent years, donations of more intimate materials divulged a continuing bond with his family that was long unacknowledged. And yet, an aura of mystery remained about the sheer range of his interests, which led to a desire to document his published and unpublished works.

The foundation of this bibliography is based upon materials that are available in the WCU Kephart holdings, as they contain hundreds of his books, magazines, news clippings, and ephemeral publications. As a result, some citations may lack a full bibliographic entry as Kephart did not always include all details, such as page numbers. However, research was conducted to locate additional Kephart items or to verify an entry. In some instances, authorship by Kephart has been attributed to his handwritten notes on personal copies. I also must acknowledge the contributions of colleagues who provided citations or copies in our shared interest.

While the bibliography attempts to provide an overview of Kephart's articles, books, and unpublished works, it is not presented as definitive. Kephart had a penchant for making submissions to a wide variety of publications, some not now widely available and some submitted anonymously. Readers will immediately note that the list is arranged chronologically rather than alphabetically. This was done so as to highlight the development of Kephart's career—from his first days writing library science articles to an early interest in writing fiction, a noticeable change in 1896 to outdoor activities and firearms, and eventually to his work as an advocate in the 1920s of a Great Smoky Mountains National Park.

Though I never knew Kephart, I felt an affinity to a fellow researcher, a fellow librarian. Throughout his publications, he would make handwritten corrections on the wording of a sentence or on a typographic error even after it appeared in print. He would have corrected me here on the bibliography, and rightly so, but perhaps others will consider his works.

1887 "Fumagalli's Rules for Cataloguing." *Library Journal* 12, no. 12 (December 1887): 547–48.

1888 "The Proposed National Library, Florence, Italy." *Library Journal* 13, no. 5 (May 1888): 139.

"A New Library Journal." *Library Journal* 13, no. 7 (July 1888): 205–06.

1889 "Italian Libraries." *Library Journal* 14, no. 4 (April 1889): 108.

1890 "Being a Librarian." *Library Journal* 15, no. 11 (November 1890): 330–32. (An attribution indicates the article was reprinted from the August 30, 1890, issue of *Harper's Weekly*.)

"The Rifle in Colonial Times." *The Magazine of American History* 24, no. 3 (September 1890): 179–91.

1891 "Fumagalli, Giuseppe. Utilita, storia ed oggetto dell' insegnamento bibliografico," in the column for "Reviews." *Library Journal* 16, no. 3 (March 1891): 83–84.

1892 *Catalogue of the St. Louis Mercantile Library. Section 1. English Prose Fiction*. St. Louis: Nixon-Jones Printing Co., 1892.

"Classification." *Library Journal* 17, no. 7 (July 1892): 228.

1893 "Paste for Labels, with a Word about Writing Inks." *Library Journal* 18, no. 1 (January 1893): 8–9.

"Bindings in Libraries." *Library Journal* 18, no. 3 (March 1893): 82–83.

"Inks." *Library Journal* 18, no. 4 (April 1893): 122–23.

"The Sacconi Binder." *Library Journal* 18, no. 6 (June 1893): 184–85.

"Classification." *Library Journal* 18, no. 7 (July 1893): 240–42.

Wm. H. Brett, Edith E. Clarke, and Horace Kephart. "Report of the Co-operation Committee, 1893." *Library Journal* 18, no. 9 (September 1893): 68–71.

1894 "Combined Receipt and Cash Register." *Library Journal* 19, no. 3 (March 1894): 86–87.

"Tree-Climbing Snakes." *Forest and Stream* 42, no. 12 (March 24, 1894): 246.

Contribution from the Mercantile Library, St. Louis, on "Inks for Library Use." *Library Journal* 19, no. 3 (March 1894): 84–86.

"Report on Gifts and Bequests to Libraries." *Library Journal* (Lake Placid Conference) 19, no. 12 (December 1894): 61–63.

1895 "Shall a Librarian Aid Personal Interests?" *Library Journal* 20, no. 1 (January 1895): 4.

"Reviews." "Manchester (Mass.) City Library. Catalogue of English Prose Fiction." *Library Journal* 20, no. 1 (January 1895): 27.

"Missouri Rifle Notes." *Forest and Stream* 44, no. 9 (March 2, 1895): 178.

"Notes from Camp Nessmuk. I.—Mincke." *Forest and Stream* 44, no. 18 (May 4, 1895): 343; "Notes from Camp Nessmuk. II.—House-Building." *Forest and Stream* 44, no. 21 (May 25, 1895): 408; "Notes from Camp Nessmuk. III.—Snakes and Presentiments." *Forest and Stream* 44, no. 22 (June 1, 1895): 440; "Notes from Camp Nessmuk. IV.—'Roots and Yarbs.'" *Forest and Stream* 44, no. 23 (June 8, 1895): 460.

Horace Kephart and George Kennedy. "A Few Remarks about a Live Western Town.—I." *Forest and Stream* 44, no. 25 (June 22, 1895): 506; George Kennedy and Horace Kephart. "A Few Remarks about a Live Western Town.—II." *Forest and Stream* 45, no. 1 (July 6, 1895): 2; George Kennedy and Horace Kephart. "A Few Remarks about a Live Western Town.—III." *Forest and Stream* 45, no. 2 (July 13, 1895): 24.

"Lost in the Swamps.—I." *Forest and Stream* 45, no. 5 (August 3, 1895): 90-91; "Lost in the Swamps.—II." *Forest and Stream* 45, no. 6 (August 10, 1895): 112-13.

"How about Turtles and Gars?" *Forest and Stream* 45, no. 10 (September 7, 1895): 208.

1896 "Classification." In *World's Library Congress,* edited by Melvil Dewey. Washington, DC: Government Printing Office, 1896.

"Cyclone-Stricken: Former Ithacans Imperiled at St. Louis." *The Ithaca Daily . . .*, June 2, 1896. (Clipping, Kephart collection, MSS 80-24, Western Carolina Univ. The introduction notes "Mr. Horace Kephart Describes Some of the Freaks and Ruin of the Besom of Destruction—A Prairie Home and Family Annihilated.")

"Nitro Powder in Rifles." *Shooting and Fishing* 20, no. 21 (September 10, 1896): 406.

"The Backwoods Rifle." *Shooting and Fishing* 20, no. 24 (October 1, 1896): 472.

"Sic Transit Gloria Arkansae!" *Shooting and Fishing* 21, no. 11 (December 31, 1896): 231.

1897 "Rustless Rifles." *Shooting and Fishing* 21, no. 12 (January 7, 1897): 249.

"The Rifle in the Revolution, I." *Shooting and Fishing* 21, no 16 (February 4, 1897): 327; "The Rifle in the Revolution, II." *Shooting and Fishing* 21, no. 17 (February 11, 1897): 345–46; "The Rifle in the Revolution, III." *Shooting and Fishing* 21, no. 18 (February 18, 1897): 365–66; "The Rifle in the Revolution, IV." *Shooting and Fishing* 21, no. 19 (February 25, 1897): 385–86.

"The First American Rifle." *Shooting and Fishing* 21, no. 20 (March 4, 1897): 406–7.

"A Card from Mr. Kephart." *Shooting and Fishing* 21, no. 23 (March 25, 1897): 469.

"A Poor Shot." *Forest and Stream* 48, no. 15 (April 10, 1897): 283.

"The Rifle and the Redskin." *Shooting and Fishing* 21, no. 26 (April 15, 1897): 529.

"Another Old Rifle's Story." *Shooting and Fishing* 22, no. 2 (April 29, 1897): 26.

"Camp Cutlery." *Shooting and Fishing* 22, no. 4 (May 13, 1897): 69.

"German Sharpshooters in the Revolution." *Shooting and Fishing* 22, no. 9 (June 17, 1897): 166.

"My Knife." *Shooting and Fishing* 22, no. 14 (July 22, 1897): 269.

"Accuracy of Backwoods Rifles." *Shooting and Fishing* 22, no. 17 (August 12, 1897): 328.

"Mr. Kephart's Reply." *Shooting and Fishing* 23, no. 1 (October 21, 1897): 10.

"A Notation for Books." *Library Journal* 22, no. 12 (December 1897): 739–41.

"Reply to Captain Meyrick, I." *Shooting and Fishing* 23, no. 8 (December 9, 1897): 147–48; "Reply to Captain Meyrick, II." *Shooting and Fishing* 23, no. 10 (December 1897): 203–4.

1898 "Some Old Rifle Literature, I." *Shooting and Fishing* 23, no. 17 (February 10, 1898): 342; "Some Old Rifle Literature, II." *Shooting and Fishing* 23, no. 18 (February 17, 1898): 366.

"A British Expert on American Backwoods Rifle Shooting, I." *Shooting and Fishing* 23, no. 19 (February 24, 1898): 382–83; "A British Expert on American Backwoods Rifle Shooting, II." *Shooting and Fishing* 23, no. 20 (March 3, 1898): 402–3; "Some Old Rifle Literature, III." *Shooting and Fishing* 23, no. 24 (March 31, 1898): 482–83.

"To the Sharpshooters of St. Louis, and Others Interested." [1898]. (A two-page flyer calling for a meeting in St. Louis for May 5, 1898.)

"The M'Bean Telescope Sight." *Shooting and Fishing* 24, no. 14 (July 21, 1898): 270–71.

"Let Us Organize." *Shooting and Fishing* 24, no. 17 (August 11, 1898): 329.

Horace Kephart and Perry D. Frazer. "A National Association." *Shooting and Fishing* 25, no. 2 (October 27, 1898): 27–28.

1899 "The Rifle for Sharpshooters." *Shooting and Fishing* 25, no. 14 (January 19, 1899): 288.

"Missouri Rifle Club." *Forest and Stream* 52, no. 6 (February 11, 1899): 116.

"Monkey, Man and Hog." *Forest and Stream* 52, no. 6 (February 11, 1899): 108.

"The Birth of the American Army." *Harper's New Monthly Magazine* 98, no. 588 (May 1899): 961–70.

"The Great Eye Theory Again." *Forest and Stream* 52, no. 20 (May 20, 1899): 385.

"Cooking without Utensils." *The Youth's Companion* 73, no. 31 (August 3, 1899): III.

1900 "Ruxton's 'Life in the Far West.'" *Forest and Stream* 54, no. 1 (January 6, 1900): 4–5.

"'Life in the Far West.'" *Forest and Stream* 54, no. 4 (January 27, 1900): 64.

"Scientific Sharpshooting." *Cassier's Magazine* 17, no. 5 (March 1900): 418–22.

"Requirements of Sharpshooting." *Springfield Daily Republican* (Springfield, MA) (March 29, 1900): 11. (An introductory note indicates the article is from *Cassier's Magazine*).

1901 "Rifles for Big Game." *Outing* 37, no. 4 (January 1901): 382–86.

"The A, B, C of Marksmanship." *Outing* 37, no. 5 (February 1901): 609–11; "The A, B, C of Marksmanship—II." *Outing* 38, no. 2 (May 1901): 234–36; "The A B C of Marksmanship—III. (Conclusion)." *Outing* 39, no. 2 (November 1901): 245–47.

"Telescopic Rifle Sights." *Outing* 37, no. 6 (March 1901): 728–29.

"The Autumn Camp." *Outing* 39, no. 2 (November 1901): 151–53.

1902 "Pennsylvania's Part in the Winning of the West: An Address Delivered before the Pennsylvania Society of St. Louis, December 12, 1901." St. Louis, Bureau of Publicity of the Louisiana Purchase Exposition, 1902.

Fifty-Sixth Annual Report of the St. Louis Mercantile Library Association, 1901. St. Louis: Commercial Printing Co., 1902.

"Cave Hunting in Missouri Stirs Love for Adventure." *The Republic*, May 11, 1902.

"Forest and Stream Day in St. Louis." *Forest and Stream* 59, no. 1 (July 5, 1902): 5–6.

"Can the Rattlesnake Poison Itself?" *Forest and Stream* 59, no. 8 (July 19, 1902): 45.

1903 "How to Tell Direction in Forest and on Prairie." *Outing* 42, no. 1 (April 1903): 79.

"Practical Hints to Campers." *Field and Stream* (April 1903): 840–43

"Cave Exploration." *Forest and Stream* 61, no. 21 (November 21, 1903): 395.

1904 "The Hunting Rifle." In A. W. Money, Horace Kephart, W. E. Carlin, A. L. A. Himmelwright, and John Harrington Keene. *Guns, Ammunition, and Tackle*. New York: Macmillan Company, 1904, 115–87.

"Camping and Woodcraft. I—Camping Out," *Field and Stream* 9, no. 7 (November 1904): 49–54; Camping and Woodcraft. II—The Sportsman's Clothing," *Field and Stream* 9, no. 8 (December 1904): 171–76; "Camping and Woodcraft. III—Personal Kits," *Field and*

Stream 9, no. 9 (January 1905): 270–75; "Camping and Woodcraft. IV—Tents and Tools," *Field and Stream* 9, no. 10 (February 1905): 359–64; "Camping and Woodcraft. Chapter V—Utensils and Food." *Field and Stream* 9, no. 11 (March 1905): 439–46. (Chapter VI is included in this article beginning on page 443.); "Camping and Woodcraft. VI [sic, VII]—The Camp." *Field and Stream* 9, no. 12 (April 1905): 542–46. (An erratum note in the following issue states that "'The Camp" in the April number was meant to be Chapter VII.); "Camping and Woodcraft. VIII—The Camp-Fire," *Field and Stream* 10, no. 1 (May 1905): 38–42; "Camping and Woodcraft. Chapter IX—Forest Travel—Getting Lost—Bivouacs," *Field and Stream* 10, no. 2 (June 1905): 149–54; "Camping and Woodcraft. Chapter X—Dressing and Keeping Game and Fish." *Field and Stream* 10, no. 3 (July 1905): 245–51; "Camping and Woodcraft. Chapter XI—Camp Cookery." *Field and Stream* 10, no. 4 (August 1905): 359–66; "Camping and Woodcraft. Chapter XII—Emergency Foods." *Field and Stream* 10, no. 5 (September 1905): 461–66; "Camping and Woodcraft. Chapter XIII—"Axemanship—Qualities of Woods and Barks." *Field and Stream* 10, no. 6 (October 1905): 590–95; "Camping and Woodcraft. Chapter XIV—"Accidents: Their Backwoods Treatment." *Field and Stream* 10, no. 7 (November 1905): 697–702; "Camping and Woodcraft. Chapter XV—Marksmanship in the Woods." *Field and Stream* 10, no. 9 (January 1906): 912–15.

1905 "Camping Out." *Forest and Stream* 64, no. 25 (June 24, 1905): 491.

"Hunting Wild Bees." *New England Magazine,* n.s. 32, no. 5 (July 1905): 542–49.

"Eyes that Shine in the Dark." *Forest and Stream* (September 2, 1905):.

"Compass Trees, Feathered Worms and Mudchucks." *Forest and Stream* 65, no. 18 (October 28, 1905): 350.

"On Getting Lost." *Forest and Stream* 65, no. 25 (December 16, 1905): 487–88.

"The Runaway from Nature." *Sports Afield* 35, no. 6 (December 1905).

1906 *The Book of Camping and Woodcraft; A Guidebook for Those Who Travel in the Wilderness.* New York: Outing Publishing Company, 1906.

"Missouri's Blue Springs." *Forest and Stream* 66, no. 13 (March 31, 1906): 501.

"A New-Found Land of Promise." *Forest and Stream* 66, no. 19 (May 12, 1906): 747–48.

"The Mountain Moonshiner. I—Getting Acquainted." *Forest and Stream* 67, no. 11 (September 15, 1906): 408–10; "The Mountain Moonshiner. II—Ways that are Dark." *Forest and Stream* 67 (September 22, 1906): 448–50; "The Mountain Moonshiner. III—A Leaf from the Past." *Forest and Stream* 67, no. 16 (October 20, 1906): 608–10; "The Mountain Moonshiner. IV—The Revenue." *Forest and Stream* 67 no. 18 (November 3, 1906): 689–91; "The Mountain Moonshiner. V—A Few Hard Facts." *Forest and Stream* 67, no. 19 (November 10, 1906): 728–30.

"'Morgan's Men.'" *Forest and Stream* 67, no. 21 (November 24, 1906): 811.

1907 "The Bullet of the Future." [*Arms and the Man*] (August 1, 1907).

"A Magistrate of Skull Creek." *Puck* 62, 1608 (December 24, 1907): 4–5.

1908 "Marvels, Old and New. Some Fiction in the Guise of Fact." *Arms and the Man* (March

5, 1908); "Marvels, Old and New. Backwoods Marksmanship According to Fenimore Cooper." *Arms and the Man* (March 12, 1908).

"Looking for a New Place." *Recreation* (December 1908): 278–79.

1909 "What Goes Up Must Come Down." *Rochester Democrat and Chronicle,* May 15, 1909.

"Bear Hunting in the Smokies: Strenuous Sport with Mountaineers on the Tennessee–Carolina Border." *Field and Stream* 14, no. 5 (September 1909): 435–40; *Field and Stream* 14, no. 6 (October 1909): 521–27.

"A Month in the Woods for $30: You Can Get All the Fun and Sport You Want on an Amount Within the Reach of All." *Collier's* 44 (November 13, 1909): 20.

"The Rock Hunter: A Pen-Picture of Life among the 'Blockaders' of the Great Smokies." *Field and Stream* 14, no. 8 (December 1909): 683–89.

"Sharp Point Penetration." *Outer's Book* (December 1909).

1910 *Camp Cookery.* New York: Outing Publishing Company, 1910.

"How to Build a Camp Fire." *The Outing Magazine* 56, no. 5 (August 1910): 528–34.

"Clapboards and Puncheons." *The Outing Magazine* 57, no. 3 (December 1910): 285–90.

1911 "Route Sketching." *The Outing Magazine* 58, no. 3 (June 1911): 297–301.

"Rifles and Ammunition: The Kind of Cartridge to Use to Get the Highest Shooting Efficiency Out of Your Gun." *The Outing Magazine* 59, no. 2 (November 1911): 184–88.

"The Flight of Bullets: What Trajectory Means and What It Is for Some of the Best Known Sporting Cartridges." *The Outing Magazine* 59, no. 3 (December 1911): 348–53.

1912 *Sporting Firearms.* New York: Outing Publishing Company, 1912.

"Killing Power of Bullets: Energy That the Various Types Develop at the Point of Impact for Different Ranges." *The Outing Magazine* 59, no. 4 (January 1912): 481–86.

"Real Pistol Practice." *The Outer's Book* (July 1912): 70–71.

1913 *Our Southern Highlanders.* New York: Outing Publishing Company, 1913.

"Sane Remarks on Pocket Arms for Defensive Purposes." *Outdoor Life,* August 1913: 162–63.

"The Southern Highlander. I—'Something Hidden; Go and Find It.'" *The Outing Magazine* 60 [actually v. 61], no. 3 (December 1912): 259–70; "The Southern Highlander. II—'The Back of Beyond.'" *The Outing Magazine* 61, no. 4 (January 1913): 396–406; "The Southern Highlander. III—The People of the Hills." *The Outing Magazine* 61, no. 5 (February 1913): 548–54; "The Southern Highlander. IV—The Land of Do Without." *The Outing Magazine* 61, no. 6 (March 1913): 703–14; "The Southern Highlander. V—The Outlander and the Native." *The Outing Magazine* 62, no. 1 (April 1913): 89–95; "The Southern Highlander. VI—The School of the Wilderness." *The Outing Magazine* 62, no. 2 (May 1913): 210–12.

1914 "Emergency Rations: Their Good and Bad Points and the Real Nature of the Problems that Experts Are Trying to Solve." *Outing* 64, no. 1 (April 1914): 84–88.

"How to Cook in the Open: An Expert's Advice Which Will Help Scouts to Pass the Cooking Merit Badge Test." *Boys' Life* 4, no. 2 (April 1914): 24; *Boys' Life* 4, no. 3 (May 1914): 26–27. (These articles are reprinted, with minor changes, in a collection entitled *The Boy Scouts Own Book*, edited by Franklin K. Mathiews.)

"Woodcraft Tips Worth Knowing: Something about All Sorts of Things from Tents for Mountaineers to Fly Dope." *Outing* 64, no. 2 (May 1914): 207–9.

"Going Alone: A Plea for the Man Who Wants to Go His Own Way and Do His Own Thinking." *Outing* 64, no. 5 (August 1914): 601–2.

"Featherweight Camping in England: Things That Our English Cousins Can Teach Us in the Art of Going Light." *Outing* 64, no. 6 (September 1914): 715–22.

"Adventures in a Cavern: What Two Men Found in One of Earth's Secret Places among the Ozark Hills." *Outing* 65, no. 1 (October 1914): 83–89.

"Sport of Cave Hunting: Where Caverns May Be Found and How They May Be Explored in Safety and Comfort." *Outing* 65, no. 2 (November 1914): 165–72.

1915 Gordon-Cumming, Ronaleyn. *The Lion Hunter: In the Days When All South Africa Was Virgin Hunting Field*, edited by Horace Kephart. New York: Outing Publishing Company, 1915.

Hobart-Hampden, Augustus Charles. *Hobart Pasha: Blockade-Running, Slaver-Hunting, and War and Sport in Turkey*, edited by Horace Kephart . New York: Outing Publishing Company, 1915.

Kane, Elisha Kent, M.D. *Adrift in the Arctic Ice Pack: From the History of the First U.S. Grinnell Expedition in Search of Sir John Franklin*, edited by Horace Kephart. New York: Outing Publishing Company, 1915.

Kephart, Horace, ed. *Captives among the Indians: First-Hand Narratives of Indian Wars, Customs, Tortures, and Habits of Life in Colonial Times*. New York: Outing Publishing Company, 1915.

Kephart, Horace, ed. *Castaways and Crusoes: Tales of Survivors of Shipwreck in New Zealand, Patagonia, Tobago, Cuba, Magdalen Islands, South Seas and the Crozets*. New York: Outing Publishing Company, 1915.

Powell, John Wesley. *First through the Grand Canyon; Being the Record of the Pioneer Exploration of the Colorado River in 1869-70*, edited by Horace Kephart. New York: Outing Publishing Company, 1915.

Ruxton, George Frederick. *Adventures in Mexico: From Vera Cruz to Chihuahua in the Days of the Mexican War*, edited by Horace Kephart. New York: Outing Publishing Company, 1915.

Ruxton, George Frederick. *In the Old West: As It Was in the Days of Kit Carson and the*

"Mountain Men," edited by Horace Kephart. New York: Outing Publishing Company, c1915, 1916.

"Wall Tents and Their Fittings: How to Set Up and Equip the Tent That Is More Used than Any Other." *Outing* 65, no. 5 (February 1915): 555–60.

"The Sportsman's Clothing: Materials That Will Achieve the End of Keeping the Heat In and Letting the Moisture Out." *Outing* 66, no. 6 (September 1915): 668–73; "The Sportsman's Clothing: Taking Care of the Feet. II." *Outing* 67, no. 1 (October 1915): 25–29.

"How Horace Kephart Aims a Rifle," *All Outdoors* 3, no. 1 (October 1915): 41.

"Camp Bedding: The Relative Merits of Blankets, Sleeping Bags, Carryalls, and Mattresses." *Outing* 67 (November 1915): 135–39.

"Outfit for Walking Trips: The Things That a Man Must and Can Take with Him on the Road." *Outing* 67 (December 1915): 259–66.

1916 *Camping and Woodcraft: A Handbook for Vacation Campers and for Travelers in the Wilderness.* Volume I: Camping. New York: Outing Publishing Company, 1916. Volume II: Woodcraft. New York: Outing Publishing Company, 1917.

Ruxton, George Frederick. *Wild Life in the Rocky Mountains: A True Tale of Rough Adventure in the Days of the Mexican War,* edited by Horace Kephart. New York: Outing Publishing Company, 1916.

"Camp Sites and Tent Pitching: How to Select a Safe, Healthful Place and Then to Make the Tent Secure and Comfortable." *Outing* 68 (April 1916): 35–43.

1917 Borthwick, J. D. *The Gold Hunters: A First-Hand Picture of Life in California Mining Camps in the Early Fifties,* edited by Horace Kephart. New York: Outing Publishing Company, 1917.

"A Word-List from the Mountains of Western North Carolina." *Dialect Notes* 4, pt. 6 (1917): 407–19.

"Building a Log Cabin: Making Your Home in the Wilderness Out of the Material the Wilderness Offers." *Outing* 70, no. 2 (May 1917): 218–27.

"The Outing Legion: For Those Who Want to Be Fit and Ready When Uncle Sam Calls." *Outing* 70, no. 3 (June 1917): 385–88.

"The Outing Legion: The Need of the Day Is for Men Who Know a Rifle and Can Shoot." *Outing* 70, no. 4 (July 1917): 532–36.

"The Outing Legion: Ways in Which You Can Measure and Improve Your Powers of Observation." *Outing* 70, no. 5 (August 1917): 676–80.

"The Outing Legion: How to Keep Your Gun in Shape to Do the Hard Work You Expect of It." *Outing* 70, no. 6 (September 1917): 813–16.

"Winter Clothing." *Outing* 71, no. 1 (October 1917): 40.

"The Outing Legion: The Only Road to Skill with the Rifle Is through Practice." *Outing* (November 1917): 118–19, 154–56.

"The Outing Legion: How to Read the Map Pictures Uncle Sam Makes of This Country of Ours." *Outing* (December 1917): 195, 230–233.

1918 "'The Primitive Woman,'" *Asheville Citizen-Times*, January 27, 1918.

"Gas Hand-Weapons." *All Outdoors* (January 1918): 123-26.

"Did a Panther Attack Tom Sparks?" *All Outdoors* (February 1918): 167.

"Pemmican: The Only Food for Hard Travel." *All Outdoors* (February 1918): 167–68.

"Rifles and Battle Sights." *All Outdoors* (February 1918): 168–69.

"The Pistol in the Trenches." *All Outdoors* 5, no. 6 (March 1918): 203–5.

"The Girl with the Turquoise Eyes." *Field and Stream* (March 1918): 910–14.

"The Eastern Cherokees." *All Outdoors* 5, no. 7. (April 1918): 243–45.

"Imaginary Crusoes—and Some Real Ones." *All Outdoors* 6, no. 8 (May 1918): 283–85.

"Over the Camp Fire in the Woods: The Essentials of Wholesome Camp Cookery." *Motor Life* (June 1918): 37.

"Inside Dope for the Hemale Camper." *Los Angeles Times,* June 30, 1918.

"Some Useful Types of Pyramidal Tents." *All Out*doors 5, no. 10, (July 1918): 363–65.

"The Backwoods Rifle. I. Types of Guns That Our Forefathers Used in Colonial Times." *Outing* 72, no. 5 (August 1918): 298–300; "The Backwoods Rifle. II. Types of Guns That Our Forefathers Used in Colonial Times." *Outing* 72, no. 6 (September 1918): 368–70, 395; "The Backwoods Rifle. III. How Our Forefathers Laid the Foundation for the High Speed and Flat Trajectory of To-day." *Outing* 73, no. 1 (October 1918): 23–25, 56–57; "The Backwoods Rifle. IV. How The Old Guns Would Shoot in the Hands of Men Who Knew Them." *Outing* 73, no. 2 (November 1918): 88–90, 117.

"The Story of the Gun. Chapter I. The Early Smooth Bores." *All Outdoors* 6, no. 1 (October 1918): 3–6; "The Story of the Gun. Chapter II. American Backwoods Rifles." *All Outdoors* 6, no. 2 (November 1918): 43–47; "The Story of the Gun. Chapter III. Early Breech Loaders and How They Were Made." *All Outdoors* 6, no. 3 (December 1918): 83–87; "The Story of the Gun. Chapter IV. Story of the Remington-U.M.C. Companies and the Development of Modern Breech Loading Rifles." *All Outdoors* 6, no. 4 (January 1919): 123–27; "The Story of the Gun. Chapter V. The Evolution of the Famous Six-Shooter Revolvers and Pistols." *All Outdoors* 6, no. 5 (February 1919): 163–67; "The Story of the Gun. Chapter VI. The History of the Invention and Development of Magazine Guns, from the Repeating Crossbow down to Modern Sporting Arms." *All Outdoors* 6, no. 6 (March 1919): 203–8; "The Story of the Gun. Chapter VII. Old Fowling Pieces and the Development of Modern Double-barrel Shotguns." *All Outdoors* 6, no. 7 (April 1919): 251–53, 280–81; "The Story of the Gun. Chapter VIII. The Ithaca, Fox, Davis-Warner, Iver Johnson and Marble Arms Companies" *All Outdoors* 6, no. 8 (May 1919): 298–301.

1919 "The Strange Story of the Eastern Cherokees: A Little Band That Has Stood Against the White Tide for Three Hundred Years." *Outing* 73, no. 6 (March 1919): 312–15; "The Strange Story of the Eastern Cherokees. II. The Lure of Gold Leads to the Undoing of the Indian and the Dishonor of the White." *Outing* 74, no. 1 (April 1919): 28–31; "The Strange Story of the Eastern Cherokees. III. The Long Fight Ends in the Western Exile of All But a Remnant of the Tribe." *Outing* 74, no. 2 (May 1919): 89–91.

"An Outfit for Trips Afoot." *Field and Stream* 23, no. 12 (April 1919): 923–27.

"Ask Outing, Tell Outing." Horace Kephart, ed. *Outing* 74, no. 2 (May 1919): 101.

"Ask Outing, Tell Outing." Horace Kephart, ed. *Outing* 74, no. 3 (June 1919): 165.

"Roving with Kephart: Being Two Pages of Observations, Hints and Hunches Gathered Through Many Years of Outdoor Living and Writing." *All Outdoors* 6, no. 9 (June 1919): 346–47.

"Roving with Kephart: Did Bloodhounds Really Chew Slaves?—Nature's Medicines—Your Fishing Rod—Do You Order 'Steak Rare'?—Ever Try It 'Straight'?—A Map to Guide You." *All Outdoors* 6, no. 10, (July 1919): 394–95.

"The Best Fuel." *All Outdoors* 6, no. 10 (July 1919): 388.

"Echoes from 'The Story of the Gun.'" *All Outdoors* 6, no. 10 (July 1919): 404.

"Ask Outing, Tell Outing." Horace Kephart, ed. *Outing* 74, no. 4 (July 1919): 233, 261–65.

"Ask Outing, Tell Outing." Horace Kephart, ed. *Outing* 74, no. 5 (August 1919): 299, 324–30.

"Roving with Kephart: 'Une arme terrible'—Carnivorous Horses—False Beliefs about Bears— 'Concealing' a 'Pump Gun.'" *All Outdoors* 6, no. 11 (August 1919): 442–43.

"How to Rig a Neckerchief Hood." *All Outdoors* 6, no. 11 (August 1919): 454.

"North Carolina Trails." *All Outdoors* 6, no. 11 (August 1919): 470.

"Roving with Kephart: The Sport of Still Hunting (Moonshine Stills)." *All Outdoors* 6, no. 12 (September 1919): 490–91.

"Ask Outing, Tell Outing." Horace Kephart, ed. *Outing* 74, no. 6 (September 1919): 363, 382–83.

"The Acquittal of Poor Lo." *All Outdoors* 7, no. 1 (October 1919): 5.

"Roving with Kephart; Where You May Find Some Adventures in North Carolina—We Talked Moonshine Last Month, But Here's a New Drink." *All Outdoors* 7, no. 1 (October 1919): 10–11.

"Why I Live in North Carolina." *All Outdoors* 7, no. 1 (October 1919): 12. (Kephart's submission to a section titled "In the Blue Ridge Playground," on pages 12–15, and subtitled "Those who live in any particular place are best qualified to tell about it. Here are bits about Western North Carolina and Eastern Tennessee from those who live there and like it.")

"Ask Outing, Tell Outing: Questions and Answers on Problems That Spring Up in Camp and along the Trail." *Outing* 75, no. 1 (October 1919): 33, 56, 57, 58, 59.

"Roving with Kephart: The Twenty-two as a Training Weapon." *All Outdoors* 7, no. 2 (November 1919): 62–63, 80; "Roving with Kephart: The Twenty-Two as a Training Weapon." *All Outdoors* 7, no. 3 (December 1919): 102–03; "Roving with Kephart: The .22 as a Training Weapon. Part III." *All Outdoors* 7, no. 4 (January 1920): 150–51.

"The Best Form of Bullet: Objections to the Square Base and Arguments in Favor of the Boat-Tailed Variety." *Outing* 75, no. 2 (November 1919): 81–83.

"Ask Outing, Tell Outing." Horace Kephart, ed. *Outing* 75, no. 2 (November 1919): 119–21.

"A New Bolt Action .22: Outing's Firearms Expert Reports on the New Savage Match Shooting Arm." *Outing* 75, no. 3 (December 1919): 148–49, 180–181.

"Ask Outing, Tell Outing." Horace Kephart, ed. *Outing* 75, no. 3 (December 1919): 165, 185–89.

1920 "Primitive Mills in Southern Mountains: The Pounding Mill Still in Use, Presents the Earliest Know Application of Power." *Outing* 75 (January 1920): 220–22.

"Roving with Kephart: This Month It Is Your Tent." *All Outdoors* 7, no. 5 (February 1920): 190–91.

"The Hawken Rifle." *Saturday Evening Post*, February 21, 1920.

"Ask Outing, Tell Outing." Horace Kephart, ed. *Outing* 75, no. 5 (February 1920): 293.

"Guns, Ammunition, and Equipment." Horace Kephart, ed. *Outing* 75, no 6 (March 1920): 353.

"Roving with Kephart: Spring Is in the Offing, Mr. Kephart Had the 'Feel' and Here He Is with Fishing with the Worm, More about Mate, Wool vs. Cotton." *All Outdoors* 7, no. 6 (March 1920): 230–31.

"Roving with Kephart: The Compass and the Map: How to Use Them." *All Outdoors* 7, no. 7 (April 1920): 278–79, 283.

"Guns, Ammunition, and Equipment." Horace Kephart, ed. *Outing* 76, no. 1 (April 1920): 31, 52–55.

"Guns, Ammunition, and Equipment." Horace Kephart, ed. *Outing* 75, no. 8 (May 1920): 83, 122–25, 127.

"Roving with Kephart: Sighting the .22 for Field Work." *All Outdoors* 7, no. 8 (May 1920): 326–27, 364.

"The Chef in the Wilderness." *Vacation Manual,* no. 1 (Summer of 1920): 4–8.

"Guns, Ammunition, and Equipment." Horace Kephart, ed. *Outing* 76, no. 3 (June 1920): 156, 186–91.

"Roving with Kephart: The Days When Everybody Shoots Are Here. If You Didn't

Know it—Read. If You Didn't Know Where—Read. If You Didn't Know How—Here's How." *All Outdoors* 7, no. 9 (June–July 1920): 374–75.

"The Fisherman and His Tackle (A Plea of the Kanahti): The Case of a Simple-Minded Folk Who Find These Arid Days Bad for Fish." Horace Kephart, trans. *Outing* 76, no. 4 (July–August 1920): 223.

"Guns, Ammunition, and Equipment." Horace Kephart, ed. *Outing* 76, no. 4 (July–August 1920): 217, 246–57.

"Roving with Kephart: The Wild Turkey: Premier Game Bird of the World." *All Outdoors* 7, no. 10 (August 1920): 438–39.

"Watermelon Mysteries." *New York Times,* August 21, 1920.

"A New Lyman Sight: For the Savage Model 1920 Rifle .250-3000." *Outing* 76, no. 5 (September 1920): 294, 296–97.

"Roving with Kephart: Round Ball: What It Can Do in Breechloaders." *All Outdoors* 7, no. 11 (September 1920): 476–77, 487.

"Guns, Ammunition, and Equipment." *Outing* 76, no. 5 (September 1920): 292, 309–10.

"Guns, Ammunition, and Equipment." Horace Kephart, ed. *Outing* 77, no. 1 (October 1920): 32, 34, 36, 38, 40, 42.

"A New Bolt Action Rifle: What Careful Testing by OUTING's Gun Expert Showed about the 1920 Savage .250-3000." *Outing* 77, no. 1 (October 1920): 23–25.

"Camping and Cooking in Italy: How You Can Be Your Own Italian Chef on Your Next Trip into the Woods" *Outing* 77, no. 1 (October 1920): 30–31.

"Roving with Kephart." *All Outdoors* 8, no. 1 (October 1920): 10–11.

"A New Rifle Book." *Outing* 77, no. 1 (October 1920): 50, 52–53. (A review of John Caswell's book *Sporting Rifles and Rifle Shooting.*)

"Roving with Kephart." *All Outdoors* 8, no. 2 (November 1920): 50–51, 80.

"Caches and Masked Camps: How to Hide Your Duffle from Prowlers—Both Two and Four Footed." *Outing* 77, no. 2 (November 1920): 74, 96, 98.

"Guns, Ammunition, and Equipment." Horace Kephart, ed. *Outing* 77, no. 2 (November 1920): 88–90, 92–95.

"Guns, Ammunition, and Equipment." Horace Kephart, ed. *Outing* 77, no. 3 (December 1920): 138–43.

"Roving with Kephart: Some Observations on Keeping Dry When Out in the Wet—Further Suggestions as to the Possibilities of Fireproof Paper." *All Outdoors* 8, no. 3 (December 1920): 90–91.

"Camping in Winter: Proving That It Is Possible to Live Comfortably under Canvas below Zero." *Outing* 77, no. 3 (December 1920): 112–14.

"A New High-Power Cartridge: The Last Word on the Cartridge for the Bolt-Action .250-3000 Savage." *Outing* 77 (December 1920): 119–20.

1921 "Roving with Kephart: Is Man-Hunting 'The Greatest Sport in the World?'. Chapter I—The Snake-Stick Man, Being the First of a Series of Southern Moonshine, Unusual Detective Work, and a Raid into the Sugarlands of Tennessee." *All Outdoors* 8, no. 4 (January 1921): 130–31, 158–59; "Roving with Kephart: Is Man-Hunting 'The Greatest Sport in the World?' Chapter II—A Raid into the Sugarlands." *All Outdoors* 8, no. 5 (February 1921): 170–71, 197–98; "Roving with Kephart: Is Man-Hunting 'The Greatest Sport in the World?' Chapter III—Blockaders' Glory." *All Outdoors* 8, no. 6 (March 1921): 210–11, 224–25; "Roving with Kephart: Is Man Hunting 'The Greatest Sport in the World?' Chapter IV—The Killing of Hol Rose." *All Outdoors* 8, no. 7 (April 1921): 250–51, 260–61.

"How Shot Is Made: They Made It in Colonial Days, but We Have Improved on Their Method." *Outing* 77, no. 4 (January 1921): 179.

"Guns, Ammunition, and Equipment." Horace Kephart, ed. *Outing* 77, no. 4 (January 1921): 182–185.

"Some Aids to Correct Aiming." *Outing* 77, no. 4 (January 1921): 189–90.

"Guns, Ammunition, and Equipment." Horace Kephart, ed. *Outing* 77, no. 5 (February 1921): 222–24.

"Guns, Ammunition, and Equipment." Horace Kephart, ed. *Outing* 77, no. 6 (March 1921): 266–72.

"A New Automatic: A New Gun That Is Primarily a Weapon for Quick and Effective Use." *Outing* 77, no. 6 (March 1921): 264, 278, 280.

"Guns, Ammunition, and Equipment." Horace Kephart, ed. *Outing* 78, no. 1 (April 1921): 32, 34–37.

"Roving with Kephart: The Winchester .410 Bore Sport-Gun—Killing Grizzlies with Bow and Arrow." *All Outdoors* 8, no. 8 (May 1921): 290–91, 298.

"Guns, Ammunition, and Equipment." Horace Kephart, ed. *Outing* 78, no. 1 [actually no. 2] (May 1921): 80, 84–85.

"How High Was the Tower of Babel?" *Arms and the Man* 68, no. 18 (May 1, 1921): 423.

"Guns, Ammunition, and Equipment." Horace Kephart, ed. *Outing* 78, no. 3 (June 1921): 126–27, 129–31, 133.

"Roving with Kephart: The Hunter Has His Troubles Cut Out for Him, Particularly with Small Bores. Some Helps over the Rocky Road." *All Outdoors* 8, no. 9 (June 1921): 330–31, 346.

"Roving with Kephart: Memories and Comment on Old and the New—The Snake-Stick Man Is Back with a Bullet Hole in His Hat." *All Outdoors* 8, no. 10 (July 1921): 370–71, 377.

"Guns, Ammunition, and Equipment." Horace Kephart, ed. *Outing* 78, no. 4 (July 1921): 174–75, 184, 190.

"Guns, Ammunition, and Equipment." Horace Kephart, ed. *Outing* 78, no. 5 (August 1921): 224–29.

"Roving with Kephart: When You're Killed, Call a Policeman." *All Outdoors* 8, no. 11 (August 1921): 410–11.

"Roving with Kephart: Good Meals in Camp—Some New Utensils and Some Old Ways of Savory Cooking." *All Outdoors* 8, no. 12 (September 1921): 450–51.

"Guns, Ammunition, and Equipment." Horace Kephart, ed. *Outing* 78, no. 6 (September 1921): 267, 275–83.

"Arms for Defense of Honest Citizens: An Answer to Mr. Thompson of Chicago and All Others Who Agree with Him." *Outing* 78, no. 6 (September 1921): 259, 286.

"Guns, Ammunition, and Equipment." Horace Kephart, ed. *Outing* 79, no. 1 (October 1921): 34, 36, 38.

"Roving with Kephart: Some Dope on the Quick 'Draw' and the Disappearance of a Suitcase." *All Outdoors* 9, no. 1 (October 1921): 10–11, 24. (Contents include "'Mr. Quick's' Pistol Holder" and "The Trial of 'Babe' Burnett.")

"Roving with Kephart: New Outputs in Firearms." *All Outdoors* 9, no. 2 (November 1921): 56, 68–69.

"Guns, Ammunition, and Equipment." Horace Kephart, ed. *Outing* 79, no. 2 (November 1921): 81–82, 84–90.

"Guns, Ammunition, and Equipment." Horace Kephart, ed. *Outing* 79, no. 3 (December 1921): 128, 130–33.

"Early American Rifles De Luxe: Some Remarkable Specimens in the Collection of Marc Woodmansee." *All Outdoors* 9, no. 3 (December 1921): 96, 105, 115, 119.

1922 *Our Southern Highlanders: A Narrative of Adventure in the Southern Appalachians and a Study of the Life among the Mountaineers.* New and enl. ed. New York: Macmillan Company, 1922.

"Roving with Kephart—A Pocket Tent." *All Outdoors* 9, no. 4 (January 1922): 124–25, 147–48.

"'It Is Time'" contribution to "The Outdoor League of America," *All Outdoors* 9, no. 4 (January 1922): 131.

"Guns, Ammunition, and Equipment." Horace Kephart, ed. *Outing* 79, no. 4 (January 1922): 178–84.

"Guns, Ammunition, and Equipment." Horace Kephart, ed. *Outing* 79, no. 5 (February 1922): 228-232.

"A Mystery of the Mountains: What Became of a New York Sportsman Who Disappeared in the Mountains of North Carolina?" *All Outdoors* 9, no. 5 (February 1922): 163, 175–76, 185.

"All Outdoors All Indoors, Department for Readers." *All Outdoors* 9, no. 5 (February 1922): 172. (Kephart quoted in "The Small Camp Fire.)

"Roving with Kephart: A Packet of Letters." *Outing* 79, no. 6 (March 1922): 270–71, 285, 288.

"Guns, Ammunition, and Equipment." Horace Kephart, ed. *Outing* 79, no. 6 (March 1922): 274–75, 277–79.

"Guns, Ammunition, and Equipment." Horace Kephart, ed. *Outing* 80, no. 1 (April 1922): 320–22, 333.

"The Right to Bear Arms: The Real Safeguard against Anarchy Lies in 'Millions of Good Civilians Who Have Arms and Know How to Use Them.'" *Outing* 80, no. 2 (May 1922): 70–71.

"Guns, Ammunition, and Equipment." Horace Kephart, ed. *Outing* 80, no. 2 (May 1922): 78–85.

"Guns, Ammunition, and Equipment." Horace Kephart, ed. *Outing* 80, no. 3 (June 1922): 128, 130–31.

"Horace Kephart, by Himself." *North Carolina Library Bulletin* 5, no. 3 (June 1922): 49–52.

"Easily Prepared Camp Meals: Some Suggestions for the Guidance of the Camp Cook." *Vacation Manual*, no. 3 (Summer 1922): 8–11, 69.

"Guns, Ammunition, and Equipment." Horace Kephart, ed. *Outing* 80, no. 4 (July 1922): 176–79.

"The New Game-Getter." *Outing* 80, no. 4 (July 1922): 185–89.

"The Man-Trap on Thunderhead." *Arms and the Man* 69, no. 21 (July 15, 1922): 9–10, 20.

"Guns, Ammunition, and Equipment." Horace Kephart, ed. *Outing* 80, no. 5 (August 1922): 230–36.

"Guns, Ammunition, and Equipment." Horace Kephart, ed. *Outing* 80, no. 6 (September 1922): 278–282.

"When Gun Men Meet." *Arms and the Man* 69, no. 24 (September 1, 1922): 9-11.

"A Man of Nerve." *Arms and the Man* (Sept. 15, 1922): 15.

"Guns, Ammunition, and Equipment." Horace Kephart, ed. *Outing* 81, no. 1 (October 1922): 38–42.

"Improved High-Power Rifle Ammunition." *Outing* 81, no. 1 (October 1922): 32–33.

"A Gun for the Home and the Highway." *Outing* 81, no. 2 (November 1922): 70, 95.

"Guns, Ammunition, and Equipment." Horace Kephart, ed. *Outing* 81, no. 3 (December 1922): 134–38.

"In the North Carolina Mountains." *Arms and the Man* 70 (December 15, 1922): 202.

1923 *The Camper's Manual: For the Novice and the Expert.* Chicago: Outer's Book Company, 1923.

"Arms for Self Defense and Home Defense." *Arms and the Man* 70, no. 8 (January 1, 1923): 225, 232.

"Guns, Ammunition, and Equipment." Horace Kephart, ed. *Outing* 81, no. 4 (January 1923): 182–85.

"Guns, Ammunition, and Equipment." Horace Kephart, ed. *Outing* 81, no. 5 (February 1923): 230, 234.

"Revolvers and Pistols." *New York Times,* March 25, 1923.

"The Awakening." *Arms and the Man* (March 1, 1923): 335–36, 346.

"Hiking Rations—What to Take." *Boys' Life* 13, no. 5 (May 1923): 5, 41.

"Hiking Rations—How to Cook 'Em." *Boys' Life* 13, no. 6 (June 1923): 30–31.

"Likes Times Editorials." *Western North Carolina Times,* September 28, 1923.

1924 "Fried Fish." In *Games and Recreational Methods for Clubs, Camps and Scouts,* by Charles F. Smith, 327–29. New York: Dodd, Mead and Company, 1924. (In Chapter XI, "Hike Cooking.")

"The Hawken Rifle." *The American Rifleman* (April 15, 1924): 703–5.

"Our Highland Playground." *Bryson City Times,* June 6, 1924.

"A Backwoods Riflemaker." *The American Rifleman* 72, no. 4 (July 15, 1924): 9–10, 20; "An Old-Fashioned Shooting Match. Part I." *American Rifleman* 72, no. 5 (August 1, 1924): 7–8, 14; "An Old-Fashioned Shooting Match. Part II." *The American Rifleman* 72, no. 6 (August 15, 1924): 9–10, 17.

"A New Winchester." *American Rifleman* 72 (September 1, 1924): 200, 206.

"A Practical Gun for the Handbag or Knapsack." *American Rifleman* 72 (November 1, 1924): 337, 345.

1925 Dunraven, Windham Thomas Wyndham-Quin, 4th Earl of Dunraven. *Hunting in the Yellowstone: On the Trail of the Wapiti with Texas Jack in the Land of Geysers,* edited by Horace Kephart. New York: Macmillan Company, c1917, 1925.

"The Smoky Mountain National Park." In *A National Park in the Great Smoky Mountains,* published by the Swain County Chamber of Commerce. Bryson City, NC: 1925.

"Why Great Smoky Mountains Bid Fair to Become National Park." *Bryson City Times,* March 6, 1925.

"What the Tourist Trade Amounts To." *Bryson City Times,* March 13, 1925.

"The Trail of a Bullet." Flynn's 6, no. 1 (April 18, 1925): 1–32; "The Trail of a Bullet." [Part 2.] Flynn's 6, no. 2 (April 25, 1925): 213–40.

"Reasons Given by Kephart for His Chair Opposition." *Asheville Citizen*, July 14, 1925.

"The Smoky Mountain National Park." *Bryson City Times*, July 17, 1925.

"Great Smoky Mountains Are Well Adapted for Locating a National Park." *Asheville Times*, July 19, 1925.

"Last Survivals of Forests in Appalachians." *Asheville Times*, July 19, 1925.

"National Park in Great Smokies Would Be of Inestimable Benefit To W.N.C. Counties, Kephart Says." *Asheville Citizen*, September 14, 1925.

"The Smoky Mountains National Park." *The High School Journal* 8, nos. 6–7 (October–November 1925): 59–65, 69.

1926 "The Great Smoky Mountains and the National Park." *Charlotte Observer*, February 16, 1926.

"The Last of the Eastern Wilderness: An Article on the Proposed Great Smoky National Park." *World's Work* 51, no. 6 (April 1926): 617–32.

"What We Do." *Asheville Citizen*, December 15, 1926.

1928 "The Indian Blowgun." *Boys' Life* 18, no. 8 (August 1928): 35, 48.

1929 *Trips in the Smokies 1929*. Bryson City, NC: The Bryson City Drug Co., / The Rexall Store, 1929.

"Afoot and Awing in the Great Smokies." *Field and Stream* 33, no. 9 (January 1929): 26–27, 75.

"The Beginning of Swain County." *Bryson City Times*, May 17, 1929. (An introduction notes "The following address was delivered before the Women's Club, Bryson City, N.C., May 7, 1929.")

"The Last of the Eastern Wilderness." *The Carolina Skyland* 1, no. 9 (July 1929): 5, 9, 12, 15, 18. (Introduction indicates "Courtesy of 'The World's Work.'") (This issue contains an article by Arthur Johnson, "Good Roads Lead Ohio Gypsy Caravan into Great Smokies" on pages 4, 10, 16, which mention Kephart along with a cartoon featuring him.)

"Kephart Tells of Search in Smokies. Indian Writings Object of Jaunt into Wilderness. Noted Author Compares Smokies of Today with Smokies as He First Learned Them Score of Years Ago." *Asheville Times*, September 22, 1929.

1930 *Trips in the Smokies 1930*. Bryson City, NC: The Bryson City Drug Co. / The Rexall Store / Official Tourist Information, 1930.

"Changing Mountaineers of [the] South: After Years on Isolated Farms They Are Caught by Tide of Industrialism." *New York Times*, February 9, 1930.

"Autos Climb Trail to Cross Smokies. Feats Lead to Road Building to Indian Gap." *Asheville Times*, February 19, 1930.

"Kephart Writes of Odd Names in Smoky Mountains. Every Mountain, Creek, Branch,

Cove and 'Lead' Has Name Known Only to Few Adventurers." *Asheville Times,* March 2, 1930.

"Kephart Tells of Panthers in Smokies. Species Is King of All Cats in America." *Asheville Times,* March 9, 1930.

"Cherokees' Language Discussed by Kephart; Vast Difference Is Found in Speech of Various Tribes." *Asheville Times*, March 16, 1930.

"Roadside Cookery." *Ladies Home Journal* 47 (August 1930): 76.

1931 "Then and Now." *National Sportsman* 65, no. 4 (April 1931): 52–54, 56–57.

1932 Bryson, Anne D. "Rifle Which Killed Tsali, Noted Cherokee Indian Rebel, Is Given to College." *Asheville Citizen-Times*, January 24, 1932. (The article contains a letter written by Kephart to Mr. Coburn, November 3, 1919, providing a physical description of the rifle in question and background history of rifles in the United States.)

1936 *The Cherokees of the Smoky Mountains: A Little Band That Has Stood Against the White Tide for Three Hundred Years.* Ithaca, NY: The Atkinson Press, 1936; 1971 printing, Silver Spring, MD: Westland Printing Co.

"Early Spring Flowers of the North Carolina Mountains." *The Journal of the Southern Appalachian Botanical Club* 1, no. 7 (November 1936): 77–83. (A note indicates "The material for this paper, from the original notes of Horace Kephart, deceased, of Bryson City, N.C., was kindly supplied by Robert G. Stone, Milton, Mass.")

2009 *Smoky Mountain Magic*. Gatlinburg, TN: Great Smoky Mountains Association, 2009.

UNPUBLISHED MANUSCRIPTS AND UNDATED

"Backward, Turn Backward, O Time, in Thy Flight!" (Three pages, typescript).

"The Cherokees of Olden Time" talk by Horace Kephart presented to the NCLHA in December 1930. 22 typescript pages. Located in the North Carolina State archives.

"The Great Smoky Mountains and the National Park."

"The Great Smoky Mountains: Origin of the Name." (Eleven pages, typescript. Based upon its content, the manuscript was written about 1930).

"The Joys of Barbarism." Compiled by "H. K.," St. Louis, 1901. (One hundred pages, handwritten.)

"Meig's Post." (Two pages, typescript).

"Mr. Pinwell Breaks Jail." (In a letter to his son Leonard dated March 31, 1929, Kephart comments that he has finished this short story the day before).

"Mountaineering in the Appalachians." (An accompanying envelope for the typescript is postmarked March 10, 1928.)"

Pedestrian Equipment." (Twelve pages, handwritten).

"The 'Peruvian Tree.'" (Undated clipping to "Editor of The Times.")

"Smoky Mountain Magic." (Drafts of the book that was published in 2009).

Untitled manuscript on firearms consisting of a "Preface," "Chapter I" and Chapter II." A cover sheet notes "To My Sons Leonard and George I dedicate this chapter from the long record of American Patriotism and Manliness." (Nineteen pages, typescript).

Notes

GENERAL INTRODUCTION

1. Horace Kephart quotes Jane Barlow at the beginning of chapter two of *Our Southern Highlanders* defining the "Back of Beyond" to mean travel to a place "'inaccessible to any wheel or hoof that ever was shod.'" Kephart clearly saw his own decision to move to western North Carolina as a similar journey to a distant world. He writes, "When I went south into the mountains I was seeking a Back of Beyond."
2. "Camping Out," *Forest and Stream*, June 24, 1905.
3. "Camping Out," *Forest and Stream*, June 24, 1905.
4. The southern terminus of the Appalachian Trail was later moved to Springer Mountain in Georgia.

I. BIOGRAPHY

1. "Widow Says Kephart was Student, First, Last and Always," *Asheville Times*, November 26, 1935.
2. Horace Kephart, "Horace Kephart, by Himself," *North Carolina Library Journal* 5, no. 3 (June 1922): 49.
3. Kephart, "Horace Kephart, by Himself," 49.
4. C. J. Kephart and Rev. William R. Funk, *Life of Rev. Isaiah L. Kephart, D.D.* (Dayton, OH: United Brethren Publishing House, 1909).
5. Kephart, "Horace Kephart, by Himself," 50.
6. Morris Bishop, *History of Cornell* (Ithaca, NY: Cornell Univ. Press, 1962).
7. Horace Kephart, "Being a Librarian," *Library Journal* 15, no. 1 (November 1890): 330–332.
8. Horace Kephart, "The Rifle in Colonial Times," *Magazine of American History* 24, no. 3 (September 1890): 179–191.
9. Clarence Miller, "Horace Kephart, a Personal Glimpse," *Missouri Historical Society Bulletin* 16 (1959): 307.
10. Charles Brown, "Moments in Mercantile History, Horace Kephart: A Calling for Books and the Wilderness," *News of Note: A Quarterly Publication of the St. Louis Mercantile Library* 1, no. 3 (Spring 1987): 19.
11. Horace Kephart, "Notes from Camp Nessmuk, II," *Forest and Stream* 64, no. 21 (May 25, 1895): 408.
12. Horace Kephart, "Pennsylvania's Part in the Winning of the West: An Address Delivered to the Pennsylvania Society of St. Louis, Dec. 12, 1901," St. Louis: Bureau of the Publicity of the Louisiana Purchase Exposition, 1902, 9–10.
13. Miller, "Horace Kephart," 307.
14. Kephart, "Horace Kephart, by Himself," 51.

15. "A Biographical Sketch of the Life, and a Tribute to the Memory of Elizabeth Belle Kephart, [s.l.: s.n.]
16. Variant spellings for the river flowing through Bryson City: Tuckaseegee, Tuckasegee, Tuckaseigee.
17. Kephart, *Our Southern Highlanders* (Gatlinburg, TN: Great Smoky Mountains Association, 2014), 13.
18. Horace Kephart, *Camping and Woodcraft*, vol. 2, "Woodcraft" (Gatlinburg, TN: Great Smoky Mountains Association, 2011), 11.
19. Kephart, *Our Southern Highlanders*, 13.
20. Horace Kephart, "Woodcraft," 12.
21. Horace Kephart, "Roving with Kephart: Memories and Comment on Old and the New—The Snake-Stick Man is Back with a Bullet Hole in His Hat," *All Outdoors* 8, no. 10 (July 1921): 370.
22. Kephart's "Journals" are encyclopedic compilations of quotes, observations, clippings, etc. Examples of Barnett's expressions can be found in Journals 1–4, which are available in the Special and Digital Collections area of Hunter Library, Western Carolina Univ. or online: http://www.wcu.edu/hunter-library/find/special-and-digital-collections.aspx.
23. Kephart, "Woodcraft," 12.
24. Kephart, *Our Southern Highlanders*, 24.
25. Horace Kephart, *Camp Cookery* (New York: Outing Publishing Co., 1910), v.
26. Kephart, "Horace Kephart, by Himself," 52.
27. Horace Kephart, "Afoot and Awing in the Great Smokies," *Field and Stream*, January 1929, 26.
28. Horace Kephart, letter to the editor, *Asheville Times*, December 15, 1926.
29. Leonard Kephart, "An Experienced Generation," [unpublished manuscript], 2–32.
30. Kephart to Julius Stone, July 18, 1929.
31. Stearns to Uncle Fred (Frederick S. Jordan), May 17, 1923.
32. *Asheville Times*, September 22, 1929.
33. Helen Topping Miller, "The Man from Back of Beyond," *American Motorist*, October 1926, 113.
34. "Authors Die Instantly in Wreck Near Bryson City," *Asheville Times*, April 3, 1931.
35. "Southern Authors Are Buried Together," *New York Times*, April 6, 1931.
36. Editorial, *Bryson City Times*, April 10, 1931.
37. "Tribute Is Paid to Kephart in Final Services," *Asheville Citizen*, April 6, 1931.
38. *Civis* is from the Latin meaning "a citizen." In this case, Kephart seems to be referring to the extent to which a librarian should assist a man or woman in the pursuit of monetary profits or social standing.
39. S. D. Barnes was a friend of Kephart in St. Louis and the editor of the periodical *Outdoor Sports*.
40. The front log in a wood fire, as in a fireplace. An Americanism dating back to 1785–95. See *Dictionary.com*, s.v. "forestick," accessed April 15, 2018, http://www.dictionary.com/browse/forestick.
41. Kephart's offensive language here reflects the racism of the day. We have chosen to keep the original.
42. Noun: 1. any of various alloys of copper containing up to 40 percent nickel. Adjective: 2. containing copper and nickel. See *Dictionary.com*, s.v. "cupronickel," accessed April 15, 2018, http://www.dictionary.com/browse/cupronickel.

43. Emerson Hough (1857–1923) was a noted editor and writer whose works included *Covered Wagon*. In his biography of Kephart, Clarence Miller noted that Hough was one of the writers who would consult with Kephart at the St. Louis Mercantile Library (Miller, "Horace Kephart," 307). In his own "Afoot and Awing in the Great Smokies," Kephart indicated that Hough "induced me to write" for his magazine.
44. A reference to the settlement of Ohio by New Englanders in the latter eighteenth century, including the founding of the community of Marietta, OH.
45. A quote from James Russell Lowell's poem "The Pioneer."
46. Istituto di Studi Superiori di Firenze.
47. Miller is incorrect on the publication dates of *Our Southern Highlanders*. The book first appeared in 1913 and then as an expanded and revised edition in 1922.

2. FAMILY AND FRIENDS

1. For more information on Isaiah, see Cyrus J. Kephart, *Life of Rev. Isaiah L. Kephart* (Dayton, OH: United Brethren Publishing House, 1909).
2. "Horace Kephart, by Himself," *North Carolina Library Bulletin* 5, no. 3 (June 1922): 49.
3. Libby Kephart Hargrave, "Foreword," in *Smoky Mountain Magic* by Horace Kephart (Gatlinburg, TN: Great Smoky Mountains Association, 2009), x-xi.
4. Horace Kephart and Laura Mack Kephart Family, MSS 16-01, Special Collections, Hunter Library, Western Carolina Univ., Cullowhee, NC.
5. Hargrave, "Foreword," vii-xiv.
6. Horace Kephart collection, MSS 80-24, Special Collections, Hunter Library, Western Carolina Univ., Cullowhee, NC.
7. Laura Kephart to Harry Koopman, May 26, 1931.
8. Other important Kephart collections are found at Pack Library in Asheville, NC; Cornell Univ., Ithaca, NY; the Mercantile Library of St. Louis; and the Great Smoky Mountains National Park archives in Townsend, TN.
9. Kephart's article "The Indian Blowgun" from *Boys' Life*, August 1929, comments on the Cherokee ballgame.
10. "Kephart Tells of Search in Smokies," *Asheville Times*, September 22, 1929.
11. The "Snake-Stick Man" is identified as W. W. Thomason in a newspaper clipping found in the Kephart collection, MSS 80-24, Western Carolina Univ., Journal 3, page 951.53, "W. W. Thomason Is Subject of Two Chapters in New Edition of Book on Mountain People," which has a handwritten citation "Hugo (Okla.) Daily News. Jan. 28, 1923."
12. Horace Kephart, "Roving with Kephart," *All Outdoors* (July 1921): 370.
13. For more information on George Masa see: William A. Hart Jr., "George Masa: The Best Mountaineer," in Robert S. Brunk, *May We All Remember Well*, vol. 1 (Asheville, NC: Robert S. Brunk Auction Services Inc., 1997), 249–275; Paul Bonesteel, *The Mystery of George Masa*, video recording (Asheville, NC: Bonesteel Films, 2002); and Rose Houk, *Pictures for a Park: How Photographers Helped Save the Great Smoky Mountains* (Gatlinburg, TN: Great Smoky Mountains Association, 2016), 78–89.
14. "Hundreds of Friends Pay Final Tribute to Kephart and Tarleton," *Bryson City Times*, April 10, 1931, clipping in George Masa collection, MSS 80-29, Western Carolina Univ. Special Collections, Notebook 4, "Horace Kephart."
15. For more information on Stearns and his relation to the Kephart family, see George Ellison

and Janet McCue, introduction to *Camping and Woodcraft*, by Horace Kephart (Gatlinburg, TN: Great Smoky Mountains Association, 2011), xxx.

16. F. A. Behymer, "Horace Kephart, Driven from Library by Broken Health, Reborn in Woods," *St. Louis Post-Dispatch*, October 31, 1926; reprinted in the *Asheville Citizen*, December 12, 1926.
17. Harry Lyman Koopman, friend of Kephart's, fellow Cornell graduate student, and library assistant at Cornell who later became director of Brown University Library.
18. Willard Fiske, former professor of North European languages and university librarian at Cornell Univ. then residing in Italy. Kephart spent a year in Italy cataloging Fiske's Petrarch collection.
19. The German is something along the lines of "So I give myself to magic" Line 377 from Goethe's *Faust* https://www.poetryintranslation.com/PITBR/German/FaustIScenesItoIII.php
20. Ettore Sordi was Fiske's secretary in Florence.
21. Harry Lyman Koopman, friend of Kephart's, fellow Cornell graduate student and library assistant at Cornell, who later became director of Brown University Library.
22. Fellow student at Cornell.
23. The new University Library.
24. Louis Hampton, friend of Horace Kephart.
25. Older son of Laura and Horace Kephart.
26. Bob Barnett, friend of Kephart.
27. Wife of Leonard Kephart.
28. Older son of Laura and Horace Kephart.
29. This paragraph is indented, and so a word appears to have been intended at the beginning. Perhaps an "A."
30. Harry Lyman Koopman, friend of Kephart's, fellow Cornell graduate student, and library assistant at Cornell who later became director of Brown University Library.
31. Unknown. According to Janet McCue, biographer, best guess is a pseudonymous name for attorney involved in Kephart's estate.
32. George Ellison and Janet McCue, in their *Camping and Woodcraft* introduction, claim that Fernow also disguised her sister's name by using "Cordelia" instead of Cornelia. However, in checking the original, it is difficult to tell, and the "d" is handwritten.
33. Possibly one of Lucy Kephart Fernow's hidden allusions. From the wording, it seems Lucy is referring to Kephart's creditors and the payment of his debts. "Solomon" would then seem to be a reference to Kephart.
34. Unclear reference.
35. In her letter, Lucy Kephart Fernow, daughter of Laura and Horace Kephart, thinly disguised her name and locations by spelling them backwards, for instance "Wonref" for Fernow, "Wen Kroy" for New York and "Auqappahc" for Chappaqua. She also made thinly veiled references, such as using Troy for the family hometown of Ithaca, NY.
36. Irving Kip Stearns, friend of Kephart and his executor.

3. CAMPING AND WOODCRAFT

1. "Horace Kephart: Revealing an Enigma," Hunter Library Digital Collections, accessed November 4, 2017, http://www.wcu.edu/library/DigitalCollections/Kephart/.

2. Horace Kephart, *Camping and Woodcraft* (Gatlinburg, TN: Great Smoky Mountains Association, 2011), v.
3. George Ellison and Janet McCue, introduction to *Camping and Woodcraft*, by Horace Kephart (Gatlinburg, TN: Great Smoky Mountains Association, 2011), xxii-xxiii.
4. Nessmuk, *Woodcraft*, 3.
5. Nessmuk, *Woodcraft*, 2.
6. "Frederick Jackson Turner: The Significance of the Frontier in American History 1893," National Humanities Center, accessed November 4, 2017, http://nationalhumanitiescenter.org/pds/gilded/empire/text1/turner.pdf.
7. Kephart, *Camping and Woodcraft*, 18.
8. Kephart, *Camping and Woodcraft*, 18.
9. Kephart, *Camping and Woodcraft*, 18.
10. Kephart, *Camping and Woodcraft*, 18.
11. "Travel Western North Carolina," Hunter Library Digital Collections, accessed November 4, 2017, http://www.wcu.edu/library/DigitalCollections/TravelWNC/.
12. Worth Mathewson, "The Roots of Outdoor Magazines," *Outdoor Life*, December 1988, 63, Proquest Central.
13. Mathewson, "The Roots," 63, 84.
14. Mathewson, "The Roots," 84.
15. Mathewson, "The Roots," 86.
16. Mathewson, "The Roots," 86.
17. M. Deborah Bialeschki, "We Said, 'Why Not?'—A Historical Perspective on Women's Outdoor Pursuits," *Journal of Physical Education, Recreation and Dance* 63, no. 2 (1992): 52, Proquest Central.
18. Bialeschki, "We Said, 'Why Not?,'" 52.
19. Bialeschki, "We Said, 'Why Not?,'" 53.
20. Bialeschki, "We Said, 'Why Not?,'" 54.
21. Anne LaBastille, *Women and Wilderness* (San Francisco: Sierra Club, 1980), 67.
22. LaBastille, *Women and Wilderness,* 70.
23. LaBastille, *Women and Wilderness,* 71.
24. LaBastille, *Women and Wilderness,* 73.
25. LaBastille, *Women and Wilderness,* 73–74.
26. Anna M. Sanford, "Wardrobe Essentials for the Woman Camper," *Field and Stream*, August 1912, 366–367.
27. Sanford, "Wardrobe Essentials," 366.
28. "Gypsy," "The Sportswoman and Her Clothes," *Field and Stream*, 527, Kephart collection, MSS 80-24, Folder 214, Western Carolina Univ.
29. Warren H. Miller, "Taking the Family Along," *Field and Stream*, August 1913, 362.
30. Mathewson, "The Roots," 86.
31. *Vacation Manual*, Summer 1920, 62.
32. Horace Kephart, "*Guns, Ammunition, Equipment*," *Outing*, May 1922, 80.
33. *Vacation Manual* (1922), 49.
34. *Vacation Manual* (1922), 5-7, 53-55.
35. Cargill, Fedelia, "Two Women in the North Woods," *Outing*, May 1919, 73-76.
36. Horace Kephart, "Guns, Ammunition, Equipment," *Outing*, March 1920, 376–77.
37. Benton MacKaye, "An Appalachian Trail: A Project in Regional Planning," Appalachian Trail Conservancy, accessed November 12, 2017, https://www.appalachiantrail.org/docs

/default-document-library/2011/04/16/An%20Appalachian%20Trail-A%20Project%20in%20Regional%20Planning.pdf, 9, 4.

38. Albert Britt, "Let's Clean Up the Mess," *Outing*, May 1919, 71.
39. Britt, "Let's Clean," 71.
40. Britt, "Let's Clean," 71.
41. Jim Casada, introduction to *Camping and Woodcraft*, by Horace Kephart (Knoxville: Univ. of Tennessee Press, 1988), viii, xxxii.
42. George Ellison and Janet McCue, introduction to *Camping and Woodcraft*, xxiii.
43. Horace Kephart, *Forest and Stream*, June 24, 1905 [clipping].
44. Horace Kephart, "Adventures in a Cavern," *Outing*, October 1914, 84.

4. GUNS

1. *Outing* (June 1911): 297–301.
2. *Camping and Woodcraft: A Handbook for Vacation Campers and for Travelers in the Wilderness* (Knoxville: University of Tennessee Press, 1988), 68-70.
3. Famed gun book publisher Thomas Samworth, who worked for the NRA before venturing out as a publisher in his own right, changed the title to *American Rifleman* during his tenure as the magazine's editor.
4. Kephart actually was referring to the Second Amendment of the US Constitution concerning the right to bear arms.
5. The title is from a popular nineteenth century poem entitled "Rock Me to Sleep" by Elizabeth Akers Allen.

5. SOUTHERN APPALACHIAN CULTURE

1. Michael Ann Williams, *Great Smoky Mountains Folklife* (Jackson: Univ. Press of Mississippi, 1995), 17–18.
2. While Kephart's two-page "Index to Diary" is part of his Journal 1, ix–x, the diary itself has yet to be located. The journal is part of the Horace Kephart collection, MSS 80-24, Special Collections, Hunter Library, Western Carolina Univ., Cullowhee, NC.
3. Horace Kephart, *Our Southern Highlanders: A Narrative of Adventure in the Southern Appalachians and a Study of Life among the Mountaineers* (1922; reprint ed., Knoxville: Univ. of Tennessee Press, 1976): 15-16, 29.
4. Horace Kephart, Bryson City, NC, to Albert Britt, Editor, *Outing* magazine, New York, August 26, 1912, Kephart collection, MSS 80-24, Western Carolina Univ.
5. Harold Farwell Jr. and J. Karl Nicholas, eds., *Smoky Mountain Voices: A Lexicon of Southern Appalachian Speech Based on the Research of Horace Kephart* (Lexington: Univ. Press of Kentucky, 1993).
6. Michael Montgomery and Joseph S. Hall, *Dictionary of Smoky Mountain English* (Knoxville: Univ. of Tennessee Press, 2004), xxv. The *Dictionary* acknowledges Hall's long career dating from 1937 and notes that "His systematic gathering of data on Appalachian speech was the first by a linguist and marked the beginning of the most extensive collection on southern mountain language in existence" (xv).
7. Kephart, *Our Southern Highlanders*, 350.
8. Horace Kephart, Bryson City, NC, to Albert Britt, Editor, *Outing*, New York, Aug. 23, 1919, Kephart collection, MSS 80-24, Western Carolina Univ.

9. North Carolina, Supreme Court, *North Carolina Reports*, Volume 183, Spring Term 1922, "State v. J. E. Burnett," filed February 1922, appeal from July term 1921; Kephart collection, Journal 3, MSS 80-24, pages 951.39–951.52, features newspaper clippings concerning the death of Hol Rose and trial of Babe Burnett.
10. Kephart collection, MSS 80-24, Western Carolina Univ., Journal 3, 951.53,"W.W. Thomason Is Subject of Two Chapters in New Edition of Book on Mountain People," clipping cited as Hugo (Okla.) *Daily News*, Jan. 28, 1923.
11. Horace Kephart, "The Mountain Moonshiner. II—Ways that are Dark," *Forest and Stream* 67 (September 22, 1906): 448, and Kephart, *Our Southern Highlanders*, 126-27.
12. Kephart, *Our Southern Highlanders*, 187–88.
13. Kephart, *Our Southern Highlanders*, 468.
14. Horace Kephart, *Trips in the Smokies 1929* (Bryson City, NC: The Bryson City Drug Co. / The Rexall Store, 1929), and Horace Kephart, *Trips in the Smokies 1930* (Bryson City, NC: The Bryson City Drug Co. / The Rexall Store, 1930).
15. For more on *Stark Love* and Kephart's involvement, see "Hollywood in the Hills: The Making of 'Stark Love,'" *Appalachian Journal* 18, no. 2 (Winter 1991): 170–220; and, J. W. Williamson, *Hillbillyland: What the Movies Did to the Mountains and What the Mountains Did to the Movies* (Chapel Hill and London: Univ. of North Carolina Press, 1995), 190–207.
16. Horace Kephart, "Roving with Kephart: Is Man-Hunting 'The Greatest Sport in the World?,'" *All Outdoors* 8, no. 5 (February 1921): 170.
17. Horace Kephart, "Afoot and Awing in the Great Smokies," *Field and Stream* 33, no. 9 (January 1929): 75.
18. Short for Oconaluftee, referring to the Eastern Band of Cherokees. Variant spellings of the name appear in the literature.
19. For this installment, Kephart notes that "Personal names in this chapter are invented. If I happen to use any that are real in the Sugarlands it is accidental. Names of localities are genuine throughout.—*The Author*."
20. In the revised edition of *Our Southern Highlanders*, the Rose family is identified as "A Family of Pioneers in the Twentieth Century."
21. A handwritten asterisk has this handwritten note on the page: "I warned him that search and seizure without a warrant was illegal—a violation of the Constitution of the U.S. He answered: 'I am ordered to do it; and I will obey orders.'"
22. Cicero, "The hours, the days, the months and the years go by." https://www.loebclassics.com/view/marcus_tullius_cicero-de_senectute/1923/pb_LCL154.81.xml paragraph 69.
23. Kephart neglected to include east Tennessee in his list of states containing part of Southern Appalachia.

6. FICTION

1. Gary Carden, *Outlander* (Sylva, NC: Gary Carden, 2012), 74.
2. Carden, *Outlander*, 75.
3. Carden, 74.
4. Robert Morgan, *At the Edge of the Orchard Country* (Middletown, CN: Wesleyan Univ. Press, 1987). BiblioBoard e-book.
5. Morgan, 10.
6. Morgan, 10.
7. Ron Rash, *Serena* (New York: Ecco, 2008).

8. George Ellison, "A Bear Hunter for the Ages," *Smoky Mountain News*, last modified 2017, http://smokymountainnews.com/news/item/12597-a-bear-hunter-for-the-ages.
9. Ralph Waldo Emerson, *Essays and Lectures* (New York: Library of America, 1983), 56, 55.
10. George Ellison, introduction to *Our Southern Highlanders*, by Horace Kephart (Knoxville: Univ. of Tennessee Press, 2002), xiii.
11. Horace Kephart, *Camping and Woodcraft* (Gatlinburg, TN: Great Smoky Mountains Association, 2011), 12.
12. Kephart, *Camping and Woodcraft*, 15.
13. George Ellison and Janet McCue, introduction to *Camping and Woodcraft*, by Horace Kephart (Gatlinburg, TN: Great Smoky Mountains Association, 2011), xxii–xxiii.
14. Louis D. Rubin Jr., *The Literary South* (Baton Rouge: Louisiana State Univ. Press, 1979), 74.
15. Ellison, introduction to *Our Southern Highlanders*, xlii.
16. Rubin, *The Literary South*, 76.
17. Williamson, F. Phillips, foreword to *American Sporting Books Series*, by M. L. Biscotti (Madison, OH: Sunrise Publishing Company, 1994), xi.
18. M. L. Biscotti, *American Sporting Books Series*, 11.
19. F. A. Behymer, "The Man Who Has Lived Two Lives," *St. Louis Post-Dispatch*, October 31, 1926.
20. *The Kentucky Encyclopedia*, edited by John E. Kleber (Lexington: Univ. Press of Kentucky, 1992), 361. Google books.
21. *Tennessee Encyclopedia*, s.v. "Emma Bell Miles," last modified 2018, https://tennessee encyclopedia.net/entries/emma-bell-miles/.
22. Richard Samuel West, *Satire on Stone: The Political Cartoons of Joseph Keppler* (Urbana: Univ. of Illinois Press, 1988), 4-9, 12.
23. West, *Satire on Stone*, 63-64, 71.
24. West, *Satire on Stone*, 324.
25. Dan Backer, "A Popular Medium," *Puck*, last accessed February 1, 2018, http://xroads .virginia.edu/~ma96/puck/part3.html.
26. *Field and Stream*, December 1909. Google books.
27. Horace Kephart, "The Girl with the Turquoise Eyes." *Field and Stream* (March 1918): 910–14.
28. Jim Merritt, "Looking Back: The War Years, the Jazz Age, and the Great Depression 1915–1940," *Field and Stream*, March 1995, 74. Google books.
29. Horace Kephart, "The Trail of a Bullet." Flynn's 6, no. 1 (April 18, 1925): 1–32; "The Trail of a Bullet." [Part 2.] Flynn's 6, no. 2 (April 25, 1925): 213–40.
30. George Ellison, introduction to *Smoky Mountain Magic*, by Horace Kephart (Gatlinburg, TN: Great Smoky Mountains Association, 2009), xxxi.
31. Kevin Brownlow and Karl Brown, "Hollywood in the Hills: The Making of 'Stark Love,'" *Appalachian Journal* 18, no. 2 (1991): 216.
32. Ellison, introduction to *Smoky Mountain Magic*, xxxv.
33. Ginseng.
34. The phrase "stretch hemp" refers to a hanging as the rope used was often fashioned from hemp.
35. Line drawings in story by Hy S. Watson. Henry (Hy) S. Watson (1868–1933), editor (1918–1924) and illustrator for *Field and Stream* (The American Museum of Fly Fishing, https://www.amff.org/portfolio/field-stream/
36. "Maud Muller" is a poem written by John Greenleaf Whittier.
37. Harold Farwell Jr. and J. Karl Nicholas (eds.) in their book *Smoky Mountain Voices: A Lexicon of Southern Appalachian Speech Based on the Research of Horace Kephart* (Lexington: Univ. Press of Kentucky, 1993) define "sulter" as "to swelter" (p. 162).

38. Unpublished MS.
39. Blurred—perhaps "affairs."
40. Leonard uses Tim instead of Tom in the letter.
41. Photocopy cut off; assume "added."
42. "The novel I'm" difficult to decipher.

7. THE CHEROKEES

1. Horace Kephart, *Our Southern Highlanders: A Narrative of Adventure in the Southern Appalachians and a Study of Life among the Mountaineers* (1913, reprint ed., Knoxville: Univ. of Tennessee Press, 2002), 30.
2. Many Eastern Band citizens dislike the term "reservation" for its suggestion that the federal government assigned land to the Eastern Band. They note that tribal leaders purchased the Qualla Boundary and other tribally owned property.
3. John R. Finger, *Cherokee Americans: The Eastern Band of Cherokees in the Twentieth Century* (Lincoln: Univ. of Nebraska Press, 1991), 1–16.
4. Significant works on early nineteenth-century Cherokee history and removal include William G. McLoughlin, *Cherokees and Missionaries, 1789–1839* (New Haven: Yale Univ. Press, 1984); William G. McLoughlin, *Cherokee Renascence in the New Republic* (Princeton: Princeton Univ. Press, 1986); Jill Norgren, *The Cherokee Cases: The Confrontation of Law and Politics* (New York: McGraw-Hill, 1996); Theda Perdue, *Cherokee Women: Gender and Culture Change, 1700–1835* (Lincoln: Univ. of Nebraska Press, 1998); Theda Perdue and Michael D. Green, *The Cherokee Nation and the Trail of Tears* (New York: Viking, 2007).
5. John R. Finger, *The Eastern Band of Cherokees, 1819–1900* (Knoxville: Univ. of Tennessee Press, 1984), 10–19.
6. Finger, *Eastern Band of Cherokees*, 20–28; Barbara Duncan and Brett Riggs, *Cherokee Heritage Trails Guidebook* (Chapel Hill: Univ. of North Carolina Press, 2003), 208; Abraham Eustis to Winfield Scott, July 3, 1838, Robert Anderson to C. H. Larned, September 16, 1838, C. H. Larned to Winfield Scott, October 3, 1838, correspondence pertaining to Cherokee removal, National Archives microfilm, M1475.
7. Finger, *Eastern Band of Cherokees*, 29.
8. Tyler B. Howe, "'The ancient customs of their fathers': Cherokee Generational Townhouse Politics of Mid-19th Century Western North Carolina," *Journal of Cherokee Studies* 29 (2011), 3–13.
9. Finger, *Eastern Band of Cherokees*, 44–45, 62–63, 69–70.
10. Finger, *Eastern Band of Cherokees*, 102–106.
11. Finger, *Cherokee Americans*, 78–79, 98–104.
12. Photo albums, Horace Kephart collection, Western Carolina Univ., Cullowhee, NC; Horace Kephart Journal 3, Horace Kephart digital collection, Western Carolina Univ., www.wcu.edu/library/DigitalCollections/Kephart.
13. Kephart, *Our Southern Highlanders*, xx–xxii.
14. Kephart, *Our Southern Highlanders*, 25, 69, 208.
15. Horace Kephart, "The Last of the Eastern Wilderness," *World's Work* (April 1926), 617; Horace Kephart to Zebulon Weaver, in U.S. Congress, House, *National Parks in Southern Appalachian Mountains. Hearings Before the Committee on the Public Lands*, 68th Cong., 2d sess., on H. R. 11980, "A Bill to Provide for the Securing of Lands in the Southern

Appalachian Mountains for Perpetual Preservation as a National Park (Washington: Government Printing Office, 1925), 23-26.

16. Finger, *Cherokee Americans*, 32; Andrew Denson, *Monuments to Absence: Cherokee Removal and the Contest over Southern Memory* (Chapel Hill: Univ. of North Carolina Press, 2017), 59–62.
17. Horace Kephart, "The Indian Blowgun," *Boys' Life* (1928), 35–36.
18. Horace Kephart, *The Cherokees of the Smoky Mountains: A Little Band That Has Stood Against the White Tide for Three Hundred Years* (Ithaca, NY: Atkinson Press, 1936), 3.
19. Kephart, *Cherokees of the Smoky Mountains*, 6.
20. Kephart, *Cherokees of the Smoky Mountains*, 6–7.
21. Kephart, *Cherokees of the Smoky Mountains*, 8.
22. Kephart, *Cherokees of the Smoky Mountains*, 25.
23. Kephart, *Cherokees of the Smoky Mountains*, 30.
24. Kephart, *Cherokees of the Smoky Mountains*, 31–32.
25. James Mooney, *History, Myths, and Sacred Formulas of the Cherokees* (1891, 1900; repr., Asheville, NC: Bright Mountain Books, 1992), 130–31, 157–59.
26. Kephart, *Cherokees of the Smoky Mountains*, 32–34.
27. Duane H. King, "The Origin of the Eastern Cherokees as a Social and Political Entity," in *The Cherokee Indian Nation: A Troubled History*, edited by Duane H. King (Knoxville: Univ. of Tennessee Press, 1979), 164–80; William Martin Jurgelski, "New Light on the Tsali Affair," in *Light on the Path: The Anthropology and History of the Southeastern Indians*, edited by Thomas J. Pluckhahn and Robbie Ethridge (Tuscaloosa: Univ. of Alabama Press, 2006), 133–64.
28. Kephart, *Our Southern Highlanders*, 16.
29. "Great Smoky Mountains National Park: The Rooftop of Eastern America," *Tennessee Wildlife* (1939), 8.
30. *Knoxville News Sentinel*, February 26, 1937; Denson, *Monuments to Absence*, 69–71.
31. Finger, *Cherokee Americans*, 114–17.

8. SCOUTING

1. George Ellison and Janet McCue, introduction to *Camping and Woodcraft*, by Horace Kephart (Gatlinburg, TN: Great Smoky Mountains Association, 2011).
2. Robert H. MacDonald, *Sons of the Empire: The Frontier and the Boy Scout Movement, 1890–1918* (Toronto: Univ. of Toronto Press, 1993), 12.
3. Benjamin René Jordan, *Modern Manhood and the Boy Scouts of America: Citizenship, Race, and the Environment, 1910–1930* (Chapel Hill: Univ. of North Carolina Press, 2016), 9.
4. MacDonald, *Sons*, 13.
5. Jordan, *Modern*, 21.
6. MacDonald, *Sons*, 13.
7. Jordan, *Modern*, 21.
8. Jordan, *Modern*, 10.
9. "Baden-Powell," *Scouts: Creating a Better World*, accessed September 9, 2017, https://www.scout.org/node/52292/introduction.
10. Jordan, *Modern*, 17.
11. Jordan, *Modern*, 40.
12. Benton MacKaye, "An Appalachian Trail: A Project in Regional Planning," *Appalachian*

Trail Conservancy, accessed September 9, 2017, https://www.appalachiantrail.org/docs/default-document-library/2011/04/16/An%20Appalachian%20Trail-A%20Project%20in%20Regional%20Planning.pdf, 1.

13. MacKaye, "An Appalachian Trail," 1.
14. MacKaye, "An Appalachian Trail," 9.
15. MacKaye, "An Appalachian Trail," 9.
16. MacKaye, "An Appalachian Trail," 9.
17. Corry Kanzenberg, "The Boy Scouts of America and Literature for Youth: 1910–1935," *Bridges and Trails: News from the National Scouting Museum* no. 1, (2012): 1,4-5, 8, https://filestore.scouting.org/filestore/alumni/pdf/BT_2012issue1.pdf, 1.
18. *Boy Scouts of America: The Official Handbook for Boys* (Garden City, NY: Doubleday, Page, 1911), Project Gutenberg, 2012, http://www.gutenberg.org/files/29558/29558-h/29558-h.htm.
19. Kanzenberg, "The Boy Scouts," 1.
20. Kanzenberg, "The Boy Scouts," 1.
21. Kanzenberg, "The Boy Scouts," 4.
22. Kanzenberg, "The Boy Scouts," 5.
23. See Jason Brady's bibliography of Kephart's collection of books in Hunter Library's Special Collections at Western Carolina University in the appendix.
24. H. W. Gibson, *Camping for Boys* (New York: Association Press, 1913), 5–6.
25. Gibson, *Camping for Boys,* 9.
26. Kathrene G. Pinkerton, *Woodcraft for Women* (New York: Outing, 1916); *Scouting for Girls: Official Handbook of the Girl Scouts* (New York: The Girl Scouts, Inc., 1920).
27. Pinkerton, *Woodcraft*, 95-96.
28. *Scouting for Girls*, 313.
29. Horace Kephart, "How to Cook in the Open," *Boys' Life*, May 1914, 26.
30. Horace Kephart, "How to Cook in the Open," *Boys' Life*, April 1914, 24.
31. Kephart, "How," May 1914, 26–27.
32. "Horace Kephart's Camping Articles," *Boys' Life*, April 1923, 29.
33. Horace Kephart, "Hiking Rations—What to Take," *Boys' Life*, May 1923, 5, 41.
34. Horace Kephart, "Hiking Rations—How to Cook 'Em," *Boys' Life*, June 1923, 30–31.
35. Franklin K. Mathiews, ed., *The Boy Scouts Own Book* (New York: D. Appleton, 1924), 183–184.
36. Horace Kephart, "The Indian Blowgun," *Boys' Life*, August 1928, 35.
37. Kephart, "The Indian Blowgun," 48.
38. Horace Kephart, "Mountaineering in the Appalachians," (unpublished manuscript, March 10, 1928), 4.
39. Kephart, "Mountaineering," 5.
40. Kephart often exaggerated his "hermit" experience on Hazel Creek and at times left an impression that he lived alone for three years from 1904 to 1907. Rather, he often lived with the Barnett family or was taking care of his sick father in Dayton, Ohio. For more information, see the introduction by Ellison and McCue to chapter one.
41. MS is torn on the right side. Brackets suggest best guess for letters/words missing.

9. PARK AND TRAIL

1. Daniel S. Pierce, *The Great Smokies: From Natural Habitat to National Park* (Knoxville: Univ. of Tennessee Press, 2000), 37–42. For other works dealing with the Great Smoky

Mountains National Park, see Margaret Lynn Brown, *The Wild East: A Biography of the Great Smoky Mountains* (Gainesville: Univ. Press of Florida, 2001); C. Brendan Martin, *Tourism in the Mountain South: A Double-Edged Sword* (Knoxville: Univ. of Tennessee Press, 2007); Richard D. Starnes, *Creating the Land of the Sky: Tourism and Society in Western North Carolina* (Tuscaloosa: Univ. of Alabama Press, 2005).

2. Pierce, *Great Smokies*, 48–49, 52–53, 62–63, 67–70.
3. Song sheet, undated, Great Smoky Mountains Conservation Association scrapbooks, Great Smoky Mountains National Park Library (Gatlinburg, TN).
4. Pierce, *Great Smokies*, 45–55.
5. Pierce, *Great Smokies*, 75–88, 90–94, 109–110, 124–29, 147–53.
6. Horace Kephart, "Then and Now," *National Sportsman*, April 1931; Arthur Perkins to Horace Kephart, January 22, 1930; Horace Kephart to Arthur Perkins, February 21, 1930; Michael Frome, *Strangers in High Places: The Story of the Great Smoky Mountains* (Garden City, NY: Doubleday, 1966), 326–328.
7. Horace Kephart, "Afoot and Awing in the Great Smokies," *Field and Stream*, January 1929, 26.
8. George Ellison, introduction to Horace Kephart, *Our Southern Highlanders: A Narrative of Adventure in the Southern Appalachians and a Study of Life among the Mountaineers* (1913; reprint ed., Knoxville: Univ. of Tennessee Press, 2002), xliv.
9. "A National Park in the Great Smokies," North Carolina Park Commission, 1925, Great Smoky Mountains National Park Library, 12; *Asheville Times*, July 19, 1925.
10. "A National Park for the Great Smokies," 10.
11. Pierce, *Great Smokies*, 58–60.
12. Kephart, "Afoot and Awing," 26.
13. Kephart, "Afoot and Awing," 26.
14. "A National Park in the Great Smokies," 4.
15. "A National Park in the Great Smokies," 2.
16. Kephart, "Afoot and Awing," 26.
17. "A National Park in the Great Smokies," 12.
18. Kephart, *Our Southern Highlanders*, 13–14.
19. C. Brendan Martin, "To Keep the Spirit of Mountain Culture Alive: Tourism and Historical Memory in the Southern Highlands," in *Where These Memories Grow: History, Memory, and Southern Identity*, edited by W. Fitzhugh Brundage (Chapel Hill: Univ. of North Carolina Press, 2000), 256.
20. "Taming 'Old Smoky' for a National Park," *New York Times Magazine*, March 25, 1928.
21. "Guide to the Great Smoky Mountains National Park," 1933, Great Smoky Mountains National Park Library, 112, 114.
22. Martin, "To Keep the Spirit of Mountain Culture Alive," 256.
23. Martin, "To Keep the Spirit of Mountain Culture Alive," 256–57.
24. Pierce, *Great Smokies*, 155–58, 160–62, 165–66.
25. Kephart to Pauline Kephart, Sept. 12, 1928.
26. There are twenty photographs illustrating the article, and a note indicates "All photographs illustrating this article copyright by Thompson Brothers, Knoxville, Tennessee."
27. Kephart *Pronounced Ah-hah-*loo*-nah, Ah-tah-*gaw*-hee, Daw-*tsee*-yee, with accent as indicated by italics.

APPENDIX I. "INDEX TO DIARY"

1. Kephart's journals and photo album are part of the Horace Kephart collection in the Special Collections of Hunter Library, Western Carolina Univ., Cullowhee, NC. The "Index to Diary" is in Journal 1 on pages ix–x. A virtual recreation of the photo album is available on the Hunter Library Special Collections digital projects website.
2. Horace Kephart, Bryson City, NC, to Albert Britt, Editor, Outing Magazine, New York, August 26, 1912, Horace Kephart collection, MSS 80-24, Hunter Library Special Collections, Western Carolina Univ. The letter is reprinted in chapter five of this book.
3. United States, Department of Agriculture, *Message from the President of the United States Transmitting a Report of the Secretary of Agriculture in Relation to the Forests, Rivers and Mountains of the Southern Appalachian Region* (Washington, DC: Government Printing Office, 1902). Kephart claimed that "In that dustiest room of a great library where 'pub. docs.' are stored, I unearthed a government report on forestry that gave, at last, a clear idea of the lay of the land." See *Our Southern Highlanders*, 14.
4. An entry about Dillsboro, located on the rail line, comments "Could have outfitted here" and may acknowledge that the town offered stores that would have satisfied his needs for provisions.
5. Part of this line was marked out but appears to read "25 & 50" in order to incorporate the additional text.
6. *Jackson County Heritage North Carolina, Vol. II* (Cullowhee, NC: Jackson County Genealogical Society, 2000), 313–14, identifies the Turpin couple as David Wesley (1845–1909) and Mary Ann Messer Turpin (1843–1927).
7. Probably a reference to clearing weather conditions given previous references to rain.
8. The photo album contains a picture, p. 1, that is captioned "Visitors." The men have been identified primarily as members of the Robinson family who lived near Dillsboro, specifically Jeff, James W., Erastus, James Henry, and Joseph T. Robinson, as well as an unidentified individual.
9. Kephart Journal 1, p. 39, contains typed notes on "Seasonal changes" for his "Camp on Tuckaseegee," dated September–October 1904, and for "Medlin," from November 1904–January 1905. The September 22, 1904, entry for Tuckasegee mentions "First autumn wind (N.W.), cool and bracing" and indicated "Night cold. 50° at daylight; could see breath."
10. This might be an abbreviation for Nantahala Gorge.
11. This refers to a photo caption by Kephart in which, purportedly, the Turpin family adopted a child left in their custody.
12. For additional information see Richard D. Starnes, *Creating the Land of the Sky: Tourism and Society in Western North Carolina* (Tuscaloosa: Univ. of Alabama Press, 2005), 6-7, 83-84, 174-80.
13. Possibly Black Rock mountain in northern Jackson County, with an elevation of 6,100 feet and part of the prominent Plott Balsam Range. The photo album, p. 9, contains a picture with the caption "Candler, Jeff and Joe Robinson, and Jeff's stepson—(summit of Black Rock, Sep. 1, 1904)." This photograph may be associated with that expedition.
14. Unlike the rest of the index, the words "The Book. A devil's tattoo in my head" are written in pencil rather than in ink. "Devil's tattoo" refers to a tapping or drumming of fingers or feet denoting nervousness.
15. The High Falls of the Tuckasegee are in Jackson County, NC, south of Kephart's camp on Dicks Creek. The construction of Glenville Dam in 1940 restricted the flow of water over

the rock formation. See William S. Powell and Michael Hill, *The North Carolina Gazetteer: A Dictionary of Tar Heel Places and Their History*, 2nd ed. (Chapel Hill: Univ. of North Carolina Press, 2010), 532.

16. Journal 1, p. 39, has a comment on weather conditions for September 22, 1904, noting "Sourwood turning scarlet. Persimmon leaves falling."
17. Harold F. Farwell Jr. and J. Karl Nicholas, eds., *Smoky Mountain Voices: A Lexicon of Southern Appalachian Speech Based on the Research of Horace Kephart* (Lexington: Univ. Press of Kentucky, 1993), 94, identifies Indian turnip as a jack-in-the pulpit.
18. Farwell and Nicholas, *Smoky Mountain Voices*, 45, defines a "corncracker" as a small corn mill with limited output for meal.
19. In Journal 1, p. 330, Kephart comments that "Stella Turpin carried two gallons of buttermilk four or five miles to hotel at Dillsboro, sold it for 20¢, and walked back, keeping up this trade all summer, every other day."
20. Whittier is a town on the border of Swain and Jackson Counties in North Carolina.
21. Kephart notes in Journal 1, p. 39, "Oct. 15. First frost. (Killing frost at Falls of Tuckaseegee, Sep. 15.) Usually frost at night from this on. Had been a drowth for two months; many springs gone dry."
22. "Milk-sickness" is an affliction caused by drinking milk, or its by-products, from cows that have eaten certain poisonous roots. See Farwell and Nicholas, *Smoky Mountain Voices*, 111.
23. The Snowbird Mountains are located along the border of Cherokee and Graham Counties in North Carolina.
24. Journal 3, p. 951.38, contains Kephart's "original notes of interviews with Harkins and Candler at Dillsboro, N.C., summer of 1904." Herschel Harkins provided Kephart with information on moonshining activities, also referred to as blockading. See *Our Southern* Highlanders, 173–79.
25. A picture in the photo album, p. 10, has the caption "Addio! Sunday, Oct. 30, 1904." An entry in Journal 1, p. 39, elaborates on the weather the day Kephart broke camp on Dicks Creek with the poetic notation "Oct. 30. A perfect Indian summer day, effect intensified by characteristic hazy atmosphere of mts. Air just cool enough to invigorate. Bright sunlight and sharply cut shadows in foreground; mts. not half a mile away enveloped in blue haze; farther peaks blending with a faultless turquoise sky."
26. Probably a reference to the steep grade of the rail line at Nantahala Gorge.
27. A notation in Journal 1, p. 39, concerning seasonal changes at Medlin on November 13, 1904, reads "Five inches snow fell during night. 27° at 7 a.m.; 29° at noon. Sun enters hollow 9 a.m., leaves 3 p.m." Children and adults going barefoot in snow also appears in *Our Southern Highlanders*, 291–92.
28. A butteris is a cutting instrument used for paring the hoofs of horses and mules.
29. Kephart discusses ginseng, including its importance to the local economy, in *Our Southern Highlanders*, 39–41.
30. This entry may be in parenthesis as laurel is often called ivy and rhododendron referred to as laurel in Southern Appalachia. See Farwell and Nicholas, *Smoky Mountain Voices*, 95.
31. Kephart's *Forest and Stream* article "Eyes That Shine in the Dark," published September 2, 1905, was dated August 5 from Medlin. Kephart commented: "About six years ago I wrote to you, in jest, a little comment on the old hunter's saying that there are only two large animals whose eyes will not shine by reflected light, namely man and hog. I write now in earnest to report the case of a man whose eyes do 'shine in the dark' like a cat's. He is a Carolina mountaineer and neighbor of mine, Walter Proctor by name. His eyes are gray, the irises

small, and the pupils more sensitive, I think than normal. . . . When sitting in a dark room I have seen his eyes flare as a lamp approached, precisely as the eyes of a deer or a cat will shine under such circumstances."

32. Historian Dan Pierce notes that Hazel Creek in the late 1800s and early 1900s experienced periods of economic boom and bust spurred by the arrival of the railroad in the area and the subsequent activities of logging companies and mining interests. Kephart witnessed life on Hazel Creek during an economic downside between periods of relative prosperity. See Daniel S. Pierce, *Hazel Creek: The Life and Death of an Iconic Mountain Community* (Gatlinburg, TN: Great Smoky Mountains Association, 2017), 41–52.
33. This may refer to marking trees to indicate the direction of a path. The article "Kephart Tells of Search in Smokies," *Asheville Times*, September 22, 1929, invokes the practice.
34. The numbered sections 22, 27, 29, and 30 of the index are listed on the bottom right of page 1 after a mark showing a distinction, rather than being part of the overall sequence. Entry 40 marks the beginning of page 2 of the index.
35. This might refer to one of two mountains in Swain County, NC.
36. Likely the settlement of Bushnell, located along the railroad and often mentioned in Kephart's writings.
37. Hyde is featured in *Our Southern Highlanders* in the chapter "A Bear Hunt in the Smokies."
38. In Journal 1, p. 81, Kephart states, "I first saw the gulf of Godforsaken one January evening from the bleak summit of Siler's Bald." The locale is described in greater detail in *Our Southern Highlanders*, 214, during a 1919 venture as "a weird and forbidding land. Vast labyrinths of rhododendron covered those profound and dismal depths, impenetrable, sunless in winter, dead but for the murky evergreen of shrubs and spruces. The place was unearthly in its dreariness and desolation."
39. The phrase "Sheriff Collecting Taxes" is used in the album, p. 15, though the picture is missing. It is also used in *Our Southern Highlanders* as a photo caption, opposite p. 40, as "At the Post-Office. (Sheriff Collecting Taxes)."
40. An eastern towhee bird. See Farwell and Nicholas, *Smoky Mountain Voices*, 97.
41. A species of North American bird.
42. In *Our Southern Highlanders*, 72, Kephart comments that, "On April 19, 1900, a blizzard from the northwest struck the Smokies. In twenty minutes everything was frozen. At Siler's Meadow seventeen cattle climbed upon each other for warmth and froze to death in a solid hecatomb. A herdsman who was out at the time, and narrowly escaped a similar fate, assured me that 'that was the beatenest snowstorm ever I seen.'"
43. Bill Cope is featured in *Our Southern Highlanders* in the chapter "A Bear Hunt in the Smokies."
44. Jack Coburn was an early friend of Kephart on Hazel Creek. See Pierce, *Hazel Creek*, 41–42.
45. Silers Bald is a mountain in the Great Smoky Mountains bordering Swain County, NC, and Sevier County, TN.
46. Probably a reference to Granville Calhoun, a friend of Kephart on Hazel Creek. See, Pierce, *Hazel* Creek, 42.
47. For details on the operations of the W. M. Ritter Company and the Taylor & Crate Lumber Company on Hazel Creek, see Pierce, *Hazel Creek*, 41–44, 55–67.
48. Possibly Horse Cove in Swain County, NC.
49. Perhaps a reference to the regional place names, and their origins, that captured Kephart's attention. This was an enduring interest as seen in the article "Kephart Writes of Odd Names in Smoky Mountains," *Asheville Times*, March 2, 1930.

50. A community in east Tennessee.
51. Spence Field is a mountain "bald," or highland meadow, on the North Carolina-Tennessee border in the Great Smoky Mountains.
52. A medicinal mixture containing rhubarb and opium used for intestinal problems. See *The New American Encyclopedic Dictionary* (New York: J.A. Hill & Company, 1906), 866.
53. This may refer to Balsam Gap, located on the border of Haywood and Jackson Counties, NC, and reputedly the highest standard-gauge rail point east of the Mississippi River.

APPENDIX 2. HORACE KEPHART'S LIBRARY

1. H. C. Wilburn to Leonard Kephart, 24 April 1936, Hiram Wilburn Papers, GRSM 13406, GSMNP Archives.
2. H. C. Wilburn to I. K. Stearns, 12 June 1936, Hiram Wilburn Papers, GRSM 13406, GSMNP Archives.

Selected Bibliography

Alley, Felix E. *Random Thoughts and the Musings of a Mountaineer.* Salisbury, NC: Rowan Printing Company, 1941. See chapter twenty-one, "The History of the Carolina Mountaineers Is a History of Progress," 455–71.

Behymer, F. A. "Horace Kephart, Driven from Library by Broken Health, Reborn in Woods." *St. Louis Post-Dispatch,* October 31, 1926; reprinted in the *Asheville Citizen,* December 12, 1926.

Bowers, John Christopher. "The Writings of Horace Kephart." MA thesis, Western Carolina University, Cullowhee, NC, 1996.

Bridges, Anne, Russell Clement, and Ken Wise. *Terra Incognita: An Annotated Bibliography of the Great Smoky Mountains, 1544–1934.* Knoxville: University of Tennessee Press, 2014. See chapter eight, "Horace Kephart," 205–21.

Brown, Karl. "Hollywood in the Hills: The Making of 'Stark Love.'" *Appalachian Journal* 18, no. 2 (Winter 1991): 170–220. An introduction by Kevin Brownlow (pp. 171–73) accompanies Brown's account of the filming of the motion picture *Stark Love* in the 1920s (pp. 174–220) and includes his meeting with Kephart.

Carden, Gary. "An Outlander Comes to the Hills: Despite Flaws, Kephart's Writing Opened the Eyes of the World to WNC." Review of *Our Southern Highlanders. Smoky Mountain News* 2, no. 2 (June 12–18, 2002): 26, 28.

———. *Outlander: A Play about the Creation of a National Park.* Afterword by George Ellison. Sylva, NC: Gary Carden, 2012.

Casada, Jim. "Horace Kephart: The Man and the Myths." *Smoky Mountain Living* 4, no. 3, (2004): 100, 104-106.

———. "Introduction" to *Camping and Woodcraft: A Handbook for Vacation Campers and for Travelers in the Wilderness,* by Horace Kephart, vii–xxxiii. Two volumes in one. A facsimile edition. Knoxville: University of Tennessee Press, 1988.

———. "Writers of the Purple Prose." *Wildlife in North Carolina* 52, no. 1 (January 1988): 16–21.

Duncan, Dayton, and Ken Burns. *The National Parks: America's Best Idea.* Video recording. "Going Home" [1920–1933], episode 4. Boston: PBS, 2009.

Ellison, George. "Introduction" to *Our Southern Highlanders: A Narrative of Adventure in the Southern Appalachians and a Study of Life among the Mountaineers,* by Horace Kephart, ix–xlviii. Knoxville: University of Tennessee Press, 1976, 1984.

———. "A Quest for Wilderness." In *Wildlife in North Carolina,* edited by Jim Dean and Lawrence S. Earley, 91–99. Chapel Hill: University of North Carolina Press, 1987.

Ellison, George, and Janet McCue. *Back of Beyond: A Horace Kephart Biography.* Great Smoky Mountains Association, 2019.

Ellison, George, and Janet McCue. "Introduction" to *Camping and Woodcraft,* by Horace Kephart, vii–lxxv. Two volumes in one. Gatlinburg, TN: Great Smoky Mountains Association, 2011.

Farwell, Harold F., Jr., and J. Karl Nicholas, eds. *Smoky Mountain Voices: A Lexicon of Southern Appalachian Speech Based on the Research of Horace Kephart.* Lexington: University Press of Kentucky, 1993.

Finger, John. "Introduction" to *The Cherokees of the Smoky Mountains,* by Horace Kephart. [s.l.: s.n.], 1936; reprint, Gatlinburg, TN: Great Smoky Mountains Association, 2010 ed.

Frome, Michael. *Strangers in High Places: The Story of the Great Smoky Mountains.* First edition. Garden City, NY: Doubleday, 1966; revised ed., Knoxville: University of Tennessee Press, 1980; expanded ed., Knoxville: University of Tennessee Press, 1994. See chapter twelve, "Horace Kephart," 145–60.

"Horace Kephart" and "Horace and Laura Mack Kephart & Family" manuscript collections. Special Collections, Hunter Library, Western Carolina University, Cullowhee, NC. The resources include Kephart's research journals, correspondence, publications, photographs, maps, and memorabilia.

"Horace Kephart" collection. Mountain Heritage Center, Western Carolina University, Cullowhee, NC. The collection contains artifacts related to Kephart and his family.

Horace Kephart Foundation. *An American Legend: Horace Kephart, His Life and Legacy.* Written, compiled, and directed by Libby Kephart Hargrave; produced by Libby Kephart Hargrave. Bryson City, NC: Horace Kephart Foundation, 2017. DVD documentary.

"Horace Kephart: Revealing an Enigma" and "Great Smoky Mountains—A Park for America." Online resources, available through Hunter Library, Western Carolina University, Cullowhee, NC. These online exhibits, assembled as a collaboration of research partners, collectively feature materials such as Kephart's journals, photographs, maps, and related publications.

Kephart, Horace. *Smoky Mountain Magic.* Introduction by George Ellison and foreword by Libby Kephart Hargrave. Gatlinburg, TN: Great Smoky Mountains Association, 2009.

Marshall, Ian. *Story Line: Exploring the Literature of the Appalachian Trail.* Charlottesville: University Press of Virginia, 1998. See chapter four, "Horace Kephart's 'Man's Game' and the Community of Our Southern Highlanders," 70–87.

Maxwell, Martin W. "Horace Kephart: An Introduction to His Life and Work." MA thesis, Wake Forest University, Winston-Salem, NC, 1982.

Miller, Clarence E. "Horace Kephart, A Personal Glimpse." *Missouri Historical Society Bulletin,* 15, no. 4 (July 1959): 304–10.

White, John. *Lost Masterpiece: Karl Brown's "Stark Love."* [s.l.]: Poppie Productions, 2014.

Williamson, J. W. *Hillbillyland: What the Movies Did to the Mountains and What the Mountains Did to the Movies* (Chapel Hill and London: University of North Carolina Press, 1995), 190–207, describes Kephart's contribution to filming of *Stark Love.*

OTHER SUGGESTED RESOURCES

Gore, Daniel. *Ways That Are Dark: A Musical Companion to Horace Kephart's Our Southern Highlanders.* Spokane, WA: Elephant Rock Records, 1997.

Gray, Sam. *Hazel Creek: Patterns of Life on an Appalachian Watershed.* [s.l.: TVA, Division of Land and Forest Resources, ca. 1984].

McDade, Arthur, ed. *Old Smoky Mountain Days: Selected Writings of Horace Kephart, Joseph S. Hall and Harvey Broome.* Seymour, TN: Panther Press, 1996.

Oliver, Duane. *Along the River: People and Places.* [s.l.]: Duane Oliver, 1998.

———. *Hazel Creek From Then Til Now*. [Maryville, TN.]: Duane Oliver, 1989.
Pierce, Daniel S. *Hazel Creek: The Life and Death of an Iconic Mountain Community* (Gatlinburg, TN: Great Smoky Mountains Association, 2017.
Rash, Ron. *Serena: A Novel.* New York: Ecco, 2008.

Index

Page numbers in *italics* refer to illustrations.